Excessive Appetites:
A Psychological View of Addictions

SECOND EDITION

Excessive Appetites:
A Psychological View of Addictions

SECOND EDITION

Jim Orford

School of Psychology
The University of Birmingham, UK

Northern Birmingham Mental Health NHS Trust

JOHN WILEY & SONS, LTD

Chichester · New York · Weinheim · Brisbane · Singapore · Toronto

Other Wiley Editorial Offices

John Wiley & Sons, Inc., 605 Third Avenue,
New York, NY 10158-0012, USA

WILEY-VCH Verlag GmbH, Pappelallee 3,
D-69469 Weinheim, Germany

Jacaranda Wiley Ltd, 33 Park Road, Milton,
Queensland 4064, Australia

John Wiley & Sons (Asia) Pte Ltd, 2 Clementi Loop #02-01,
Jin Xing Distripark, Singapore 129809

John Wiley & Sons (Canada) Ltd, 22 Worcester Road,
Rexdale, Ontario M9W 1L1, Canada

Library of Congress Cataloging-in-Publication Data

Orford, Jim.
    Excessive appetites : a psychological view of addictions / Jim Orford.—2nd ed.
        p. cm.
    Includes bibliographical references and index.
    ISBN 0-471-49947-1 (cloth)—ISBN 0-471-98231-8 (pbk.)
    1. Substance abuse. 2. Gambling. 3. Psychosexual disorders. I. Title.
    RC564.O76 2001
    616.86—dc21   00-068508

British Library Cataloguing in Publication Data

A catalogue record for this book is available from the British Library

ISBN 0-471-49947-1 (cased)
ISBN 0-471-98231-8 (paper)

Typeset in 10/12pt Monotype Times by Originator, Great Yarmouth
Printed and bound in Great Britain by Biddles Ltd, Guildford and King's Lynn
This book is printed on acid-free paper responsibly manufactured from sustainable forestry, in which at least two trees are planted for each one used for paper production.

To Judith, Tim, Paul and Will
Family of a partially recovered workaholic

Contents

About the Author

Jim Orford trained in clinical psychology at the Maudsley Hospital, Institute of Psychiatry, London, and later obtained his PhD at the Addiction Research Unit at the Institute. His career has involved substantial commitments to the development of services for people with alcohol problems in Exeter, and the training of clinical psychologists in Exeter and later in Birmingham. Apart from a special interest in the addictions, and particularly their impact on the family, about which he has researched and written extensively, his main field of interest is community psychology. He is co-editor of the *Journal of Community and Applied Social Psychology*, and in 1992 Wiley published his *Community Psychology: Theory and Practice*. He now heads the Alcohol, Drugs and Addiction Research Group at the University of Birmingham.

Preface

Some 15 years have passed since I wrote the Preface to the First Edition of this book. Since then 'the addictions' have continued to flourish—not only in the form of very troublesome states of being that affect very large numbers of people, but also as a clinical and academic field of study and practice. While millions of people have become addicted in the last 15 years, and been hurt in the process, more and more research has been carried out and yet more has been written on the subject. Although the phenomenon of addiction appears to be universal and timeless, it is surprising what a difference 15 years can make to the appearance of the field. At the time of writing the first edition of *Excessive Appetites*, cocaine, for example, merited only limited attention, but within only a few years cocaine, and then crack cocaine, would constitute possibly the most worrying addiction of all, at least in some parts of the West. Binge eating disorder, to give another example, had not yet made its appearance as a term in the professional literature on eating disorders. When it came to constructing a psychological model of the addictions, learning based upon the relief of withdrawal symptoms was probably still the leading idea 15 years ago. Since then withdrawal relief has become less prominent, and positive incentive explanations more so. Cognitive science has started to provide some of the leading ideas in the field.

The core ideas around which this book is written have, nevertheless, remained the same. An addiction, or an 'excessive appetite' to be more precise, is the same whether its object is alcohol, gambling, heroin, tobacco, eating or sex. It is best thought of as an over-attachment to a drug, object or activity, and the process of overcoming it is largely a naturally occurring one. In that sense the Second Edition is in essence no different from the First. To do justice to some of the developments that have taken place in the meantime, however, it has been necessary to substantially rewrite the book. When I embarked on preparing a second edition I naively assumed that this would be a comparatively easy task. I was quite wrong. If references are a rough guide to the extent of rewriting, then the following figures may be of some interest. Of 640 works referenced in the First Edition 280 have survived to appear in the Second. In the process 590 new references have been added.

One thought that has haunted me in preparing this edition is that the basic idea of excessive appetites is now well accepted. If it needed to be articulated in the mid-1980s, this is no longer needed now. How rewarding it would be if that were the case! Although there has been a slow movement in the direction of accepting the reality of addiction to activities other than the taking of drugs, the field remains focused on 'substances' and there have been some moves in the *opposite* direction. The ideas pendulum, forever swinging between the psychobiological and the psychosocial, has generally been moving towards the former over the last 15 years. For example, in reviewing what had been written about addiction in that period, I was struck by how much had been written about brain functioning and addiction, and how little, in comparison with what I had read 15 or more years earlier, had been written about the deviance-amplifying effects of social reactions to behaviour. At the time of writing this later Preface, an important report by the Police Foundation in the UK has just recommended reclassifying (downwards) the seriousness of certain categories of drug, such as cannabis and ecstasy, on the grounds that the current heavy response of the law to possession of such drugs makes the matter worse rather than better. This recognition by the police of the deviance-amplifying effects of the law has not been reflected in what I have been reading of the academic literature on addictions.

How excessive appetites develop, change and might be prevented or treated remain lively and controversial issues, as does the more fundamental question of what an addiction really is. This is the central question which, perhaps surprisingly, remains something of a puzzle even now, despite all the activity—personal, media, professional, academic—that has been devoted to it. It is that central mystery that has intrigued me throughout my career and which is the reason for this book.

In the earlier Preface I stated that the ideas contained in this book had been germinating for a long time and had been nourished by people and influences too numerous to mention. That general statement has continued to be true. I mentioned a small number of individual people who had been particularly influential in my early career, in particular Griffith Edwards who headed the Addiction Research Unit at the Institute of Psychiatry, London, where I worked for 10 years in the 1960s and 1970s. He later developed the National Addiction Centre at the Institute, and became editor-in-chief of *Addiction* (formerly the *British Journal of Addiction*) which under his editorship has become the recognised leading journal in the field (website http://www.tandf.co.uk). I have continued to be lucky enough, as time has gone on, to work alongside colleagues who have been greatly supportive in our work in the addictions field. This includes my close friends and colleagues Richard Velleman and Alex Copello, and many other colleagues at the Department of Psychology at the University of Exeter, the School of Psychology at the University of Birmingham—especially my colleagues in the Alcohol, Drugs and Addiction Research Group—and in NHS Trusts in Exeter and North Birmingham, and collaborators in the Alcohol, Drugs and the Family Research Interest Group in the UK, and in the United Kingdom Alcohol Treatment Trial Research Group. My horizons have been broadened by having had the opportunity to work closely with my friend Guillermina Natera and her colleagues at the Institute of Psychiatry in Mexico City, and having enjoyed collaborating with the Living With Alcohol Programme of Northern Territory Health, Australia.

I am glad to be able to acknowledge permissions to use extracts from published works as follows: Academic Press (extracts from Janis and Mann, 1968); Carfax and *Addiction* (Bryant *et al.*, 1991; Lindström, 1991; Miller, 1996; Orford, 2001; Rounsaville *et al.*, 1993; Stockwell *et al.*, 1993; Veale, 1987; and a modified form of my paper on hypersexuality which appears here as Chapter 6); the British Psychological Society (Beebe, 1994); Elsevier Science (Gold and Heffner, 1998); International Universities Press (Goodman, 1993); the *Journal of Studies on Alcohol* (Jessor and Jessor, 1975; and Project MATCH Research Group, 1997a); Oxford University Press (Warburton, 1988); Kluwer Academic/Plenum Press (Robins *et al.*, 1977); Rand McNally and Company (Janis and Mann, 1968).

Finally my sincere thanks to several secretarial colleagues who have typed parts of drafts, but especially to Pat Evans who has laboured long and hard to produce the last several drafts and the final manuscript.

Jim Orford
Birmingham, June 2000

CHAPTER ONE

Changing the Shape of the Field

Intemperance—N. *intemperance*, want of moderation, immoderation, unrestraint, abandon; excess, excessiveness, luxury. *Redundance;* too much. *Superfluity;* wastefulness, extravagance, profligacy, waste, consumer society. *Prodigality;* want of self-control, indiscipline, incontinence. *Laxity;* indulgence, self-indulgence. *Habit;* drug habit. *Drug-taking;* high living, dissipation, licentiousness, debauchery. *Sensualism;* overeating. *Gluttony;* intoxication, hang-over. *Drunkenness.*

(*Roget's Thesaurus*, Kirkpatrick, Penguin Edition, 1998, p. 645)

We need a theoretical model of how addictions arise, what they are, and of how they decline. None of these requirements for a model of addictions can be fully met by the major ways of understanding addictions which are dominant today.

(Brown, 1997, p. 16)

The development of desires and inclinations—appetites—is basic to life. This book is about how some appetites can get out of hand and become excessive. There exists a range of objects and activities which are particularly risky for humans, who are liable to develop such strong attachments to them that they then find their ability to moderate their behaviour significantly diminished.

At one time people who indulged in consumption of a drug or engaged in some other form of activity to the point of social or physical damage, and continued with such behaviour despite contrary statement of intent, and despite recommendations from others, were said to be suffering from a form of mania, such as dipsomania, narcotomania, kleptomania or pyromania (Stekel, 1924). The people so afflicted were in the grip of 'morbid appetites' or were suffering from 'diseases of the will'. Although such language is now largely outdated, the phenomena to which it referred have continued unabated, and an adequate understanding of them is of the utmost importance both to public health and to theoretical psychology.

'Addiction' is an apt, commonly understood word to use with respect to excessive appetitive behaviours, but it has the important disadvantage that it has come to be overly identified with drugs that have an effect on the central nervous system. More than that, it has become identified with a narrow range of such drugs, particularly those that have been outside the law in the West in the late 20th century, and especially with heroin. Not only has this distorted the provision of services for people who might be in need of help in overcoming an excessive appetite, but in my view it has very seriously biased our understanding. This restricted focus on a particular part of the phenomenon which we should be endeavouring to understand continues to lead us astray, although, as I shall attempt to demonstrate, there are some healthy signs that researchers and theorisers in the field are searching for a more comprehensive account. Meanwhile, the field is still frequently confined to 'drug addiction' or 'substance abuse' in a way that is unhelpful for the development of a complete theory.

An aim of the present book is to contribute to changing the shape of the addiction field. Placing drugs, or 'substances', in the centre of the picture has led us—or misled us, I would argue—to view some of the properties that these drugs have in common as core elements of addiction. There has thus grown up a concept of addiction that gives privileged place to short-term pharmacological effects on the brain from ingesting substances, and the longer term adaptations that the nervous system may make to the regular presence of brain-acting drugs—neuroadaptation as manifested by tolerance and withdrawal effects. Although, as we shall see, there has been some softening on the question of whether the latter 'symptoms' are essential for a diagnosis of addiction, they remain important in most expert definitions of 'drug dependence'. Whilst the shape of the field was dominated by drugs, and particularly by those such as heroin and cocaine which have caused the powerful countries of the world so much trouble in the late 20th century, other forms of excessive appetite have been marginalised.

The present thesis is that drugs such as heroin and cocaine are special cases of a much more general and fundamental phenomenon. Placing other biological appetites, notably eating and sex, as well as non-biological activities, such as gambling, at centre stage gives us a completely different perspective. Although the commonplace term 'addiction' remains as apt as before, for scientists preferring a more exact term, 'excessive appetite' defines the field rather than 'drug dependence'. It is not to 'substances' that we are at risk of becoming addicted, but rather to 'objects and activities' of which drugs are a special example. This new perspective allows different comparisons to be made, new concepts to be privileged and arguably a more comprehensive and satisfactory model to be developed of how people's appetites can become out of control.

The remainder of this book is divided into three parts. In Part I, five forms of excessive appetite are introduced in turn. My purpose is to show that each of these forms of behaviour can lead to excess which is highly distressing for those concerned, including close family and friends who are affected by it. It is also an aim of these early chapters to illustrate the many points of similarity in terms of the phenomenology, problems of definition, and social policy issues. Although my sources are admittedly second- or third-hand, I have also attempted in places to introduce historical and anthropological perspectives because they can aid comparisons. For example, whilst modern tobacco smoking may appear very different from injecting heroin, it may be easier to see a

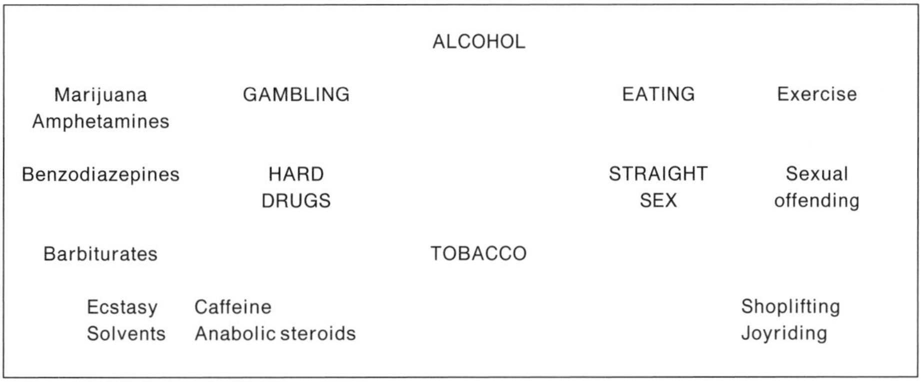

		ALCOHOL			
Marijuana Amphetamines	GAMBLING			EATING	Exercise
Benzodiazepines	HARD DRUGS			STRAIGHT SEX	Sexual offending
Barbiturates		TOBACCO			
Ecstasy Solvents	Caffeine Anabolic steroids				Shoplifting Joyriding

Figure 1.1 Excessive appetites: the shape of the field.

comparison with 19th-century opium taking in England, or with 20th-century coca use in the Andes.

The five excesses which together make up Part I are drinking, gambling, drug taking, eating and exercise, and sex (Figure 1.1). These are the core addictions. In each case the evidence is compelling that the activity is so potentially addictive that it can get sufficiently out of hand that it spoils the lives of many people. The inclusion of alcohol needs little defence. Although it might be said to be an 'artificial' appetite, since life does not depend on it, the scale of its consumption almost everywhere in the world is so colossal that it is hard to imagine human civilisation without it. Furthermore, the fact that it is highly dangerous on account of its propensity to addict is hardly controversial. Hence the numbers of people who enjoy alcohol are in the billions, and the numbers whose lives are spoiled by it are in the hundreds of millions. It is bound to be at the centre of any model of addiction.

If there is one form of excess that is crucial to the argument of this book, it is excessive gambling. This is because, like alcohol, the penetration of gambling into human social life is deep and long-standing. At the same time, again like alcohol, its potential for excess has been long recognised and is not in dispute. What is strange is why it has been consigned to a peripheral position in the addiction field in modern times. It offers the biggest challenge to the conventional wisdom on the subject, and arguably the greatest opportunity for development of a comprehensive understanding of addiction. It is not simply that we might reluctantly allow it a place on the edge of our gaze, but rather that it needs to be restored to a proper, central position in order to correct the eccentricity of previous thinking that has come about as a result of attending far too closely to a limited class of addictive activities. This is a suitable place to acknowledge that the present author is by no means alone in suggesting that we change the structure of the field. Nor is it any surprise that notable examples of psychologists who have been promoting the same or similar ideas are those who have had particular interest in excessive gambling (e.g. Dickerson, 1990; Griffiths, 1996; Brown, 1997). If thinking about addiction is going to change, the study of excessive gambling is likely to be one of the richest sources of new ideas.

Although part of the argument of this book is that drugs have occupied too dominant a position in our field, they clearly merit a prominent place. What to include in the relevant chapter (Chapter Four), however, was not totally clear. Since alcohol has been given its own chapter, then tobacco consumption, arguably the single activity associated with more excess than any other, might also have merited a chapter to itself. To include caffeine, kava, qat and anabolic steroids, but not to mention barbiturates or hallucinogens, may also seem out of order. But my purpose in Part I is to illustrate the diversity of appetitive activities that can be associated with excess, as well as to raise questions about the definition and nature of addiction. Some of the drug types that I have included in Chapter Four challenge existing views about addiction. It is interesting, and hopefully constructive, to ask whether we can be addicted to caffeine or cannabis, kava or qat. Indeed, it turns out that forms of drug taking with potential for excess, particularly when historical and geographical dimensions are added to the picture, are so varied—some 'hard' some 'soft', some illicit and some prescribed, some ancient and some modern, some natural and others synthetic, some stimulating and some calming—that a study of drug taking in all its variety raises in itself all the same questions of definition, psychological theory and social policy, which are posed by considering all the excessive appetites collectively.

Some may question the inclusion of eating as an activity to which people can become addicted. Since it is a necessity, surely it is something upon which everybody is dependent? Furthermore, at present the scientific and professional worlds of 'drug addiction' and 'eating disorders' are utterly separate. In fact, when preparing the First Edition of this book in the early 1980s I was uncertain about including eating in a book on addiction, and I was not sure that I had made the right decision to do so. By the late 1990s, however, I was in no doubt. The parallels between what is now called bulimia and binge eating disorder and other forms of excessive appetitive behaviour are many. The continued separation of the addiction and eating-disorders fields has probably got much to do with their history (associated with anorexia and obesity in the case of eating), and different populations (adolescent women being a particular focus for eating). If these arbitrary and superficial differences can be put aside, it can be seen that there are many opportunities for mutual borrowing of ideas that are helpful in the construction of a more comprehensive view of addiction. Many over-eaters remark on the addiction-like nature of their behaviour, and the idea that forms of over-eating such as bingeing can be thought of as an appetite that has become excessive is even easier to accept. As I hope will become clear in Parts II and III, there are many points of theory about excessive appetites where a consideration of excessive eating is particularly helpful. They include the concept of behavioural 'restraint', the 'abstinence violation effect', appetite-specific attentional effects, and the equivalence of theoretically distinct treatments.

One of the most challenging ideas for students of addiction brought up in the scientific and professional world of the late 20th century is that of 'sex addiction'. In fact, the evidence is overwhelming that ordinary, 'straight' sex does, for many people, get so out of hand that it becomes difficult to control despite its excessiveness. The inclusion of Chapter Six on sex addiction or 'hypersexuality' was never in doubt. Problems, for individuals and for societies, of restraining an appetite which always threatens to get out of control, is perhaps clearest of all in the case of sex. In China, excessive sexuality ('womanizing') was long considered one of the four major 'vices' or 'disasters', along with gambling, drinking and smoking opium (Singer, 1974). The interesting question for us is how it is that the Chinese recognised sex as one of the main human appetites that could become disastrously excessive, while lately in the West we have viewed it as outwith the boundaries of the addiction field. This may partly be because it is now unfashionable to speak of excessive or immoderate sexual behaviour, and the inclusion of sex as a potential addiction may appear to be to reintroduce a moralistic element into the discourse about addiction, which modern expert theories have been at great pains to eradicate. Another reason why excessive sexual behaviour may appear a strange companion to such excesses as excessive drinking, gambling and drug taking, may be that our understanding of the latter has been over-influenced by the presentation of these problems in clinical settings, whereas excessive sexuality, although undoubtedly a fact, comes to the attention of therapists comparatively rarely. It is the very fact that excessive sex is different in these respects, not sharing in some of the biases of the conventional addiction field, that makes its inclusion one of the best aids to the development of a truly comprehensive psychological view of excessive appetites.

Why stop with these five—or six if tobacco is counted separately? There are three reasons. First, they represent the clearest and best documented examples of the phenomenon of addiction: they are all activities which ordinarily are unexceptional and unproblematic, but which cause many people great conflict because they have developed such strong attachments to them. Second, they are all extremely common. These are not rare species. So common are they that it is probably no exaggeration to suppose that only a minority of people are lucky enough to go through life untouched by one of these core excessive appetites, either because of developing such an appetite themselves or through experiencing the impact of addiction in a close family member. The costs of this core group of excesses—in terms of human distress, morbidity and mortality, and economic costs—are enormous, ranking with health priorities such as cancer, heart disease, HIV and AIDS. That the addictions do not receive comparable attention can be attributed to the prevailing attitude towards them of tolerant acceptance: addiction has long been with us, the benefits to commerce and government revenue are huge, and we have numerous, well-tuned ways of failing to recognise the scale of the problem.

The third reason for concentrating on the core five or six excessive appetites lies in the danger of trivialising the debate about addiction if the concept is extended too far. For example, those who are most sceptical about the whole concept of 'addiction' are prone to ask rhetorical questions of the form, 'I like playing tennis and writing books on psychology; does that mean that I am addicted to tennis and book writing?' (Eysenck, 1997, p. 168). Those who are much more sympathetic to the concept of addiction may still dilute it by suggesting a resemblance between what I am calling the core addictions and such things as parachuting, crosswords, gum chewing, nail biting or having cornflakes for breakfast (Stepney, 1996). Others have suggested that it is possible to be addicted to work (Haberman, 1969), power (Kielholz, 1973) and love (Peele and Brodsky, 1975). Although people can potentially become excessively attached to any activity, and there is no easy dividing line to be drawn between those activities to which people often get so attached and those that rarely cause addiction, it threatens to diminish the importance of the topic by too readily extending the concept in these ways. It is possible to conceive of lives whose quality is diminished by an excessive attachment to work or to playing a particular sport, and it may be instructive to consider the ways in which such 'addictions' differ from the core five or six, and to ask ourselves why they are so much less common. But nothing should be allowed to detract from the seriousness of the main forms of excessive appetitive behaviour which adversely affect the quality of people's lives to such an extent and on such a scale.

We must, nevertheless, acknowledge that the boundary around the core of our subject is a fuzzy one. As Figure 1.1 suggests, there exists a number of activities, which, although they are less clear or less well-documented exemplars of excessive appetitive behaviour, may sometimes give rise to a state sufficiently similar that the term 'addiction' or 'excessive appetite' may be appropriate and helpful. Whether these should have been included in the present book has been a somewhat arbitrary decision. Most of the drugs shown in Figure 1.1 which have a comparatively strong case (marijuana, amphetamines, etc.) or a weaker case (ecstasy, caffeine, etc.) have received some attention (in Chapter Four) and the same is true for exercise (included in Chapter Five). Each of these fitted easily into their respective chapters, and each was thought to raise constructive questions about the definition and nature of excessive appetite.

Of those other, non-core addictions which might well have been included in the present book but which have been excluded because they found no convenient place in the chapter structure, the possibility of addiction to certain forms of crime, and to the Internet, deserve mention. The possibility that the repetitive committing of certain forms of crime might, for some people, be helpfully seen as addictions has been considered at length in a book edited by Hodge *et al.* (1997). In the present writer's opinion, the best case is made out for some instances of car theft or 'joy riding' (Kilpatrick, 1997). Many young men, stealing cars on a very regular basis, do describe a pattern of behaviour remarkably like problematic, youthful drug taking. Similarly, McGuire (1997) describes the small number of cases of apparently 'irrational' (i.e. not motivated by material gain) or addictive 'shoplifting'. The latter is perhaps the modern equivalent of what was once referred to as 'kleptomania'. Perhaps because of the concern it arouses, and the amount of attention it has received, there is probably more evidence for the value of conceiving of many sexual offenders as addicted to their crimes (McGregor and Howells, 1997).

Of great interest to those of us who wish to understand addiction is the possibility that some people might become so attached to using the Internet that it becomes to some degree out of their control, bringing their behaviour into conflict with other needs and activities, hence on balance spoiling rather than enhancing their quality of life. This idea has been convincingly proposed by Young (1998) in her book, *Caught in the Net*. In that book she presents a great deal of case material, and a description of her own methods of counselling for excessive Internet users, which she claims to have been highly popular and effective with the large numbers of people who have contacted her for help. Griffiths (1999), in the UK, has also argued that the Internet can for some people be addictive. He argues that this is one example of a new phenomenon of 'technological addictions' which also include television addiction, computer addiction, and video- and computer-game addiction. Shaffer (1996) has argued, like Young and Griffiths, that new technologies such as the Internet have the capacity to powerfully shift subjective experience, which in his view makes them potentially addictive. There have been reports in the press of the setting up of mutual help websites with names such as *netaholics anonymous*, and *webaholics anonymous* (*El País*, 13 July 1997).

Only the novelty of 'Internet addiction', and the consequent comparative lack of information about it to date, has prevented me from considering it at any length in the current Second Edition of this book. If evidence continues to accumulate about it, then it will undoubtedly present a tremendous challenge to prevailing views of addiction, and thereby another invaluable aid to understanding what addiction is really all about. At the same time, the spectre of Internet addiction may present us, at the beginning of the 21st century, with a warning of where technological advance, combined with the human potential of becoming excessively attached to activities, may take us in the future. It has often been said that societies are at their most vulnerable to addiction when exposed to new objects or activities to which they are unaccustomed. Alcohol for indigenous people in Australia and North America is one example, and heroin and cocaine in the inner cities of industrialised countries in the 1980s and 1990s are others. Will the Internet and other technological advances bring with them similar 'epidemics'?

PART I

The Excessive Appetites

CHAPTER TWO

Excessive Drinking

Drunkenness is an enticing, bewitching sin, which is very hardly left by those that are addicted to it. Neither the word nor rod of God prevaileth with men to leave this sin, but they go on sinning against light, sinning against the counsels and reproofs, and tears of friends, against the checks of their own Consciences, though the Lord afflict them in their bodies, estates, good names, yet stil they persevere in this sin.

(Stockton, *Warning to Drunkards*, 1682, p. 95, cited by Warner, 1994, p. 687)

Booze: Even though 'booze' has a time-honored place in the common lexicon of slang, the word carries an inescapable array of negative associations. Such terms as 'booze merchants' or 'booze barons' are sometimes used to describe people in the beverage alcohol industry. The phrases are not considered to be laudatory.

(Report of a joint working group on terminology prepared by the US Center for Substance Abuse Prevention, and the International Center for Alcohol Policies, an organisation funded by the drinks industry, 1998, p. 17)

In any outline of the forms of appetite that can become so excessive that they can spoil people's lives, alcohol is sure to occupy a central position. It is a relatively uncontroversial and seemingly timeless example of the principle that some of us can lose control over a form of activity which, for most people, serves as a pleasurable and moderate indulgence. It forces upon our attention the major questions that this book must attempt to answer: How does addiction arise? What is its nature? How do people rid themselves of it? Before embarking on the search for answers to such questions, we need to lay out a picture of the phenomena with which we are dealing, starting in this chapter with excessive drinking.

I shall begin by quoting from one or two of the many autobiographical accounts written by excessive drinkers in order to illustrate the point that individual people can and do describe experiencing intense personal suffering which they attribute to their own excessive drinking behaviour. In her book, *I'll Cry Tomorrow*, the US actress Lilian Roth (1978) described 16 years of existence in 'a nightmare world' of virtually continuous overdrinking and intoxication which culminated in her conviction that she was being driven insane. The final scenes depicted in her book are ones of degradation, of self-imposed solitary confinement and of a serious risk of death from alcohol poisoning, suicide or accident. Earlier in her book, however, there are significant descriptions of her behaviour which raise key issues about the very nature of the phenomenon of losing control over consumption. These are the very questions with which we are centrally concerned here and to which this book will return repeatedly. For example:

> Although beer by day and liquor by night satisfied me while I [had been] busy . . . , now my nerves demanded more. I switched from a morning beer to a jigger of liquor first thing after I awoke. It seemed a good formula. I improved upon it by pouring two ounces of bourbon into my breakfast orange juice so [my husband] was none the wiser.
>
> (Roth, 1978, p. 113)

Later on she described escalation to a new level of excess, and dated this from an occasion when a shopping expedition turned into a drinking session and a bartender advised her to carry drink with her in future:

> I realised that I could never go out of the house again without liquor. Orange juice and bourbon in the morning was not enough. The physical demand was growing. I would need liquor more often—not because I wanted it, but because my nerves required it. Soon I was slipping down doorways, vanishing into ladies' rooms, anywhere I could gain privacy, to take a swift drink ... The two-ounce bottles graduated to six-ounce, and then to a pint, and in the last years of my marriage ... wherever I went, I carried a fifth of liquor in my bag.
>
> (Roth, 1978, pp. 113–114)

Quite apart from the overall theme of her account, which is the attribution of her problems to a growing addiction to alcohol, two features are particularly noteworthy and are typical of many such accounts. First, there is the use of the word 'demand'. She does not 'want' to behave in this way but something alien to her own wishes demands it. In her case the demand is ascribed to her 'nerves' and then later to a 'physical' need. The second feature is the growing secrecy of her behaviour, and her involvement in deceit. Both features indicate conflict, first within herself and second between herself and other people. An adequate psychological understanding of excessive appetitive behaviour must account for both these types of conflict—intrapsychic and interpersonal.

Well-known British excessive drinkers of recent times include the England international footballer Tony Adams, and the comedian Peter Cook. Adams' autobiography (1998) is a positive read, since it documents the maintenance of his highly successful footballing career despite the increasing encroachment of his heavy drinking and drunkenness which affected his ability to give of his best as a player, contributed to a broken marriage and produced a salutary period of imprisonment for drunken driving. The following extract describes his self-administered detoxification:

> For so long I had done my best to avoid the conclusion, but I could no longer. I was, I am, an alcoholic. I was at that point they call the rock bottom. I was sick and tired of being sick and tired. I just wanted to stop drinking. I had asked many times to do that, but at that time I felt I was asking from the bottom of my heart. And I felt I was beaten. My soul was screaming out for help ... Then I got into a T-shirt and shorts and crawled into bed. There, curled up in the foetal position, I sweated, and sweated, and sweated. All night the water poured out of every pore of my body ... Over the next 36 hours or so, I alternated between hot sweats and cold shivers, getting up only for small portions of nourishment: cereal, toast, soup, scrambled eggs, the things that comfort you as a sick child. Dehydrated, I drank jugs of water. And I wept as I had never wept before, the pain of a dozen drinking years that I had somehow mixed with being a professional footballer oozing out. At times my body demanded a drink but I ignored it, though I'm not sure how.
>
> (Adams, 1998, pp. 21–22)

Thompson's (1997) biography of Peter Cook, on the other hand, has no happy ending. Indeed, a review of the book in *The Guardian Weekly* of 7 September 1997 states, '... if you want to maintain a happy memory of Cook as one of the most gifted comedians who ever lived, don't read much of the last 200 pages' (Lezard, 1997). Peter Cook died at the age of 57 from a gastrointestinal haemorrhage resulting from severe liver damage. It seems he had been drinking excessively for years. Interviewed shortly after his death, his ex-wife spoke of events that had occurred 18 years earlier:

> These days it would be easier to get help, but then it was all a huge secret, which made it more of a strain. In the end I could cope with the other women but not with the bottle. I lost that battle because Peter didn't want to win it. He made it clear that he wanted to drink and nothing would stop him, even though he knew it would kill him—it was a vicious circle.
>
> (Thompson, 1997, p. 367, in part from *Sunday Express*,
> 15 January 1995)

Fellow comedian John Cleese believed that:

> Peter almost took the choice that he would rather live a shorter time and drink. That was the great sadness, because his close friends ... made some feeble attempts to say something. He responded not in an unfriendly way but with slightly humorous defiance.
>
> (Thompson, 1997, p. 444, from *The New Yorker*, 23 January 1995)

A BIT OF HISTORY

Adams uses the term 'alcoholic' about himself and many would apply it to Cook. Modern medical use of the term 'alcoholism' to refer to a disease-like entity is often attributed to the psychiatrist E. M. Jellinek and to his book, *The Disease Concept of Alcoholism*, published in 1960. The medical concept of 'alcoholism' is in fact a hundred or more years older than that, as Jellinek himself was at pains to point out, and the notion of excessive drinking as an individual trait involving an interference with freedom of choice to take or leave drink as the individual desires is older still. According to Warner (1994) the elements of an individual, disease-like conception of habitual drunkenness existed in Britain as early as the beginning of the 17th century, well ahead of the Enlightenment and bourgeois individualism which others (e.g. Levine, 1978, see below) have identified as the period when individual models of alcohol addiction arose for the first time. On the contrary, Warner argued, it would be quite wrong to assume that earlier generations were blind to addiction because of the mindset of pre-industrial society. In fact, it was clergymen and other moralists who seemed to have been most observant in England in Stuart times, and in the following century those who wrote tracts and pamphlets during the decades of the 'gin epidemic' of the 1720s to 1740s. Warner's examination of 17th century sermons, previously ignored by historians of drink, revealed a common vocabulary of compulsion and addiction. The earliest she unearthed was attributed to John Downame who wrote of some of his parishioners:

> ... they who addict themselues to this vice, doe finde it so sweete and pleasing to the flesh, that they are loth to part with it, and by long custome they turne delight into necessitie, and bring vpon themselues such an vnsatiable thirst, that they will as willingly leaue to liue, as leaue their excessiue drinking; and howsoeuer the manifold mischiefes into which they plunge themselues, serue as so manie forcible arguments to disswade them from this vice, yet against all rules of reason, they hold fast their conclusion, that come what come may, they will not leaue their drunkennes.
>
> (Downame, 1609, p. 101, cited by Warner, 1994, p. 687)

Already in this early description there appear the essential ingredients of a plain, straightforward statement of what constitutes addiction. Indeed, it has hardly been bettered since as a working definition. Here we have recognition that, by long usage, an activity that was originally pleasurable has become a 'necessity'; that a strong craving is part of the experience; and that despite the many harms that it has brought, neither the exercise of reason nor encouragement from others have been sufficient to bring about control. As we shall see many times, late-20th-century experts have brought muddle and confusion to this plain account, attempting to import new-fangled ideas from the theories in which they have been schooled. As we consider, later, some of the ways in which psychologists and others have tried to understand addiction, we would do well to return to remind ourselves of the insightful observations of the Reverend Downame.

Later in the same century, another clergyman proclaimed that habitual drunkenness was a disease so 'epidemical', that, 'all the Physicians in England know not how to set a stop to it' (Bury, 1677, cited by Warner, 1994, p. 688). Warner concluded her important paper by asking the difficult question: Whether the locus of social control over behaviours such as drinking was, in the early modern period about which she was writing, external or internal? She argued that clergy and others promoted family and internal controls in that period, since the chaos of those times, with an exploding population, much internal migration and a wholly inadequate constabulary, made reliance on external social control impossible.

Unlike Warner (1994), Levine (1978), on the other hand, writing with particular reference to the United States, had argued for the emergence of the idea of individual habitual excess or addiction only towards the end of the 18th and the beginning of the 19th centuries. Prior to that time, he concluded, drunken excess was well recognised as something that many colonials indulged in sometimes and which some indulged in often, but which was viewed as the result of free individual choice and not as something that constituted a problem in itself. Unlike Lilian Roth's and Tony Adams' understanding of their excessive drinking, habitual drunkards were so because they liked it and chose to be that way. This preaddiction view was based, Levine pointed out, on the philosophical premise that it is impossible to differentiate between Desire and Will. As he so rightly said, this distinction is the kernel of the concept of 'addiction', and is much in evidence in Roth's, Adams' and other modernday accounts of excessive drinking.

This is not to say that drunkenness was not viewed by some as either extremely troublesome or very sinful. Indeed, the early to middle 18th century in England offers a notorious example of alcoholic excess on a large scale. Economic and legislative factors seem, according to Coffey's (1966) account, to have been the major influences. French imports of wines and spirits were prohibited towards the end of the previous century and English brewers learnt to distil gin, which had been introduced from the Low Countries, from English grain. Total consumption of gin in England rose from half a million gallons in 1685 to 11 million in 1750. Controlling legislation was attempted in 1729 and 1736, but the first attempt was too weak to be effective and the second law, too repressive, was flouted. Effective legislation came in 1751 through limitations on the issue of retail licences and the introduction of stiff penalties for unlicensed retailing. Consumption dropped to under two million gallons within a decade and to around one million by 1790.

Much of the poverty and lawlessness of the period was, and has been since, attributed to drinking, particularly by the London poor. Amongst other ill effects, a staggeringly high infant-mortality rate (75 per cent before age 5 according to one historian) was blamed upon a combination of maternal excessive drinking and the practice of dosing babies with gin either to quieten them or as a deliberate act of murder. Hogarth's print, *Gin Lane*, depicting drunkenness, pawning, child neglect, starvation, emaciation, suicide and a thriving trade of pawnbrokers and undertakers, may have been one of the influences for reform. By contrast, his print, *Beer Street*, is a portrait of restraint and prosperity. Despite Warner's (1994) evidence, it is not clear that there was any generally accepted concept of 'addiction' or 'dependence' at this time in England. Those who gave evidence to the 1834 Select Committee's *Inquiry into Drunkenness* (1968), were still taking a largely moral view, particularly of drunkenness and the, '... misery and immorality of the lower orders amongst the working classes ...' (from the evidence given by J. R. Farre, Esq.), which was assumed to be the *result* of excessive drinking rather than its cause.

The change in thinking that he believed occurred shortly thereafter, Levine (1978) attributed to a total change in the philosophical climate of the times, associated with the emancipation of the new middle class for whom self-control and self-restraint became cherished values that signalled and helped retain their position in society. Deviant excess was now an abnormality, which in an otherwise respectable person could only be ascribed to a sort of sickness, a disease of the will. Whether this reading of history is right or wrong, it was Levine's view that writings on drunkenness with a modern 'addiction' ring to them began to appear only at the end of the 19th century. Certainly the evidence given to the 1872 Select Committee on *Habitual Drunkards* (1968) strikes a very different note to that given to the Committee of 1834. The inclusion of the word 'habitual' in the title is itself an immediate indication of the recognition that individuals can acquire a special propensity to excess: we are now dealing not just with instances of drunkenness, but with people, unlike others, who are in the habit of getting drunk regularly. There was even recognition by some who gave evidence of the variety of forms of excessive drinking which Jellinek (1960) was to note many years later. For example, a Mr Mould anticipated Jellinek's distinction between gamma (loss of control) and delta (inability to abstain) types:

> I should divide habitual drunkards into two classes; those who drink impulsively, and not continuously, and who are of the most violent and dangerous characters, and require immediate control and restraint; and those who continuously drink and get into a kind of soddened and muddled state.

Thomas Trotter in Britain and Benjamin Rush in the United States are names particularly associated with the new way of thinking (Jellinek, 1960; Levine, 1978). The latter especially, better known now for his works on mental illness, is remembered as a forerunner of presentday medical specialists on the subject. According to the then editor of the *Quarterly Journal of Studies on Alcohol (QJSA)*, Rush was responsible for the earliest US publication of any scientific note on the subject of 'inebriety'. Despite being first published, in all probability, in 1785, in many ways it bears remarkable similarities to many modern publications on the subject. It bore the title: *An Enquiry into the Effect of Spirituous Liquors Upon the Human Body and Their Influence upon the Happiness of Society*, and was reprinted by the editor of the *QJSA* in 1943.

The 19th century was a century of temperance societies and workers in the USA (the movement there has been described by numerous writers, including Jellinek, 1960 and Levine, 1978), in Britain and Ireland (again numerous sources, but see especially Longmate, 1968, Shiman, 1988 and Greenaway, 1998). Part of Levine's argument was that the emerging medical view of habitual excessive drinking as 'addiction' and the temperance aim of reducing habitual drunkenness went hand in hand; but that the temperance movement, in the United States at least, became preoccupied with the political goal of total prohibition at the end of the century (the same was true in England also); and that the alliance of medicine and temperance only resurfaced in a new form with Alcoholics Anonymous (AA) and a renewed medical interest in the 1930s and 1940s. This is clearly to cut a very long story short. What is persuasive, however, is Levine's point that temperance (religious, nonscientific) and medical (supposedly scientific) approaches were by no means as antithetical as might be supposed. We shall see later that these two currents have been inextricably interwoven in recent times also.

One of the hallmarks of 19th-century temperance which finds its modern equivalent in certain aspects of AA procedure and in professionally directed group therapy for 'alcoholics' was the public announcement or confession and the taking of an abstinence pledge. One of the first such confessions recorded was made by James Chalmers of New Jersey who in 1795 made the following sworn and witnessed statement.

> Whereas, the subscriber, through the pernicious habit of drinking, has greatly hurt himself in purse and person, and rendered himself odious to all his acquaintances and finds that there is no possibility of breaking off from the said practice but through the impossibility to find liquor, he therefore begs and prays that no person will sell him for money, or on trust, any sort of spirituous liquors.
>
> (Cherrington, 1920, cited by Levine, 1978, pp. 153–154)

The loss of freedom or willpower where drink is concerned is clearly expressed in this statement and the confessor appeals to externally imposed restraint to help him overcome his lack of internal self-control.

The role of pledge taking is nowhere better illustrated than in accounts of Father Mathew's campaign in Ireland. A whole chapter in Longmate's book, *The Water Drinkers* (1968), about the temperance movement in Britain, is devoted to this one man's influence on Irish drunkenness in the 1830s and 1840s. During his public tours of the country it is estimated that he administered two million pledges to nearly a quarter of the population (O'Connor, 1978). Longmate, who was well aware of the possibilities of exaggeration in the accounts of this campaign, declared:

> The transformation of Ireland during the Father Mathew years was by any test remarkable ... By the end of 1841 it was claimed that there were at least five million on the teetotal roll in a population of eight million. Brewers and distilleries went out of business and publicans deserted their trade.
>
> (Longmate, 1968, p. 114)

For a variety of reasons, however, the effects of this campaign appear to have been shortlived in Ireland. Father Mathew was a charismatic leader who left little organisation behind him, his movement was not linked directly to the Catholic Church, and, furthermore, Ireland was shortly to be preoccupied with the stress of the potato famine. By comparison, Father Cullen, the founder of the Pioneer Total Abstinence Association, was far better organised and established, and the association he founded lived on in Ireland as a significant influence (O'Connor, 1978). Pledge taking, in one form or another, has played a role in giving up excessive drinking in many parts of the world at many times. For example, in parts of Mexico, up to the present day, it is common for men, often strongly encouraged by their wives, to take a religious oath, in the presence of the local priest, foreswearing alcohol for a fixed period of time, such as 6 or 12 months (Orford, 1992c).

In her history of temperance in Victorian England, Shiman (1988) stated: 'By the time Queen Victoria passed away, drunkenness was no longer treated with the good-hearted tolerance of former times' (p. 244). This macro-level change in attitude was soon followed, not by the national prohibition which some had hoped for, but by an elaborate licensing system which might be seen as a form of control on a national scale. It was also associated with a great deal of activity at the level of community. As Shiman noted, by late Victorian times there was scarcely a town in Lancashire or the West Riding of Yorkshire that was without its own Temperance Hall which often served as a centre for a flourishing teetotal group. Teetotal local councillors were proud of drink-free public libraries, parks and civic receptions. Many areas declared themselves prohibition areas, containing no alcohol-sales outlets, and the idea that all communities should have the option of declaring local prohibition was prominent on the national political agenda of the time.

Industrialisation, urbanisation and the desire of working people to better themselves through education, work and respectability seem, according to the historians (e.g. Shiman, 1988), to have been among the factors that created the climate for this response on a community or societal level. In Britain, in the middle to late 20th century, alcohol problems have largely been seen in individual terms, and control at the community level has been missing. There may be interesting parallels to be drawn, however, between industrial communities in Victorian England and some present-day indigenous groups around the world (e.g. some Australian aboriginal and indigenous Latin American communities) which, in the face of a variety of threats to their existence, including widespread excessive drinking, are opting for a form of local alcohol prohibition (Fleming *et al.*, 1991; Eber, 1995).

Greenaway (1998) has nicely described how the social history of the public house in Britain during the last hundred years has mirrored the gradual shift over this period in our conceptualisation of the whole alcohol question. One hundred years ago the drink question, and more specifically the nature of the public house, were, he concluded, moral issues. In the late Victorian period there were a number of moves made to eliminate the vested interest of the publican in increasing sales, either by outright nationalisation or by local monopoly control by the municipality or a single non-profit-making company. Greenaway cited notable proposals by Joseph Chamberlain, a radical mayor of Birmingham (who was very impressed by the monopoly company that had been set up in Gothenburg in Sweden, and which he visited in 1876) who sought, as in his other undertakings, to combine the advantages of profit, efficiency and the public good; and that of the cocoa manufacturer and philanthropist, Joseph Rowntree, and his research associate, Arthur Sherwell, whose proposal was outlined in their influential study, *The Temperance Problem and Social Reform* (1899).

The whole temperance question was quickly transformed by the outbreak of war in 1914. In 1915 a Central Control Board (liquour traffic) was set up which imposed restrictions on strengths of beverages and hours of sale, throughout the country, in order to combat drunkenness among troops and absenteeism among shipyard and munitions workers, which were felt to be adversely affecting the war effort. In addition, the Board carried out a number of experiments directed at improving public houses themselves. The scheme in Carlisle, a town that experienced a large influx of construction navvies and munitions workers during the war, was one of the largest and most thoroughgoing, and one of the few to survive into the inter-war period. The Board took over the management of almost all sections of the Trade, closed many backstreet pubs and set about reshaping the character of the others.

After the war the Board was swept away and, according to Greenaway, '... with it the idea of proactive, state "alcohol policy"' (p. 177). The Trade and temperance reached an accommodation in the form of the Licensing Act of 1921 which retained, of the war-time regulations, only high taxation and shorter national opening hours. Since then home secretaries, Greenaway states, have had little interest in drink issues, temperance faded away, the Carlisle scheme became an historical oddity, and the nature of public houses has steadily changed from the cramped, overcrowded and unhygienic pubs of the 1920s to the leisure-oriented, comfortable places of the late 20th century, providing food and a range of alcoholic and soft drinks for both sexes and all ages at less restricted times. It is interesting to note that those early attempts to reform the British public house never spoke with a consistent voice on the question of whether the object was to provide an austere, uncomfortable but controlled environment with the aim of reducing consumption, or to civilise drinking by providing greater comfort and a range of other facilities. These different temperance and reforming views regarding drink were, as we shall see in Chapter 6, parallel to those that pertained in debates about sexuality and vice generally (Mort, 1987). As Greenaway pointed out, these controversies about the improved public house, '... represent an interesting example of the debate between prohibitionist and harm-minimization models of alcohol control' (p. 180).

MODERN CONCERN ABOUT EXCESSIVE DRINKING

Of present-day concern about excessive drinking there can be little doubt. The concept of a disease-like entity and the terms 'alcoholism', 'alcohol dependence' or 'problem drinking', to describe it, have by now achieved widespread acceptance by members of the professions and the lay public, well beyond the USA where AA originated. Among those who know most, at first hand, about excessive drinking are close family members who are concerned about a relative's excess, and who are themselves adversely affected by it. These 'concerned and affected others' include parents, partners and children, and in some cultures uncles, aunts, nephews, nieces and cousins (Orford *et al.*, 1998a, 1999a).

An account by one such is that written by Caitlin, the Irish wife of the Welsh poet Dylan Thomas (Thomas and Tremlett, 1986). Attracted at first to the exciting social life that Dylan led in London pubs, when they later moved away from London and settled to have a family Caitlin described feeling increasingly neglected and abandoned. Hers is a moving book which speaks of the pain and distress that relatives can suffer, and of the deep conflicts and confusion which they can experience about ways of coping. She thought of leaving Dylan but never felt that she could. Instead, she joined him in his drinking every evening in the local pub, explaining that she would have felt even more abandoned if she had let him go alone.

There have been a number of studies of family members' attempts to 'cope' with another's drinking (e.g. Orford *et al.*, 1998b). In her research with young, married, Finnish couples, Holmila (1991) asked about the ways in which partners attempted to control each other's drinking in the course of everyday family life. Finding a great deal more control of husbands' drinking by wives than vice versa, she concluded:

> This activity can be seen as caring work. Paying attention to another person's behaviour and attempting to direct it certainly is work. Time and energy are demanded as are planning and reflection. It is work also in the sense that the wider society expects it, and strong ideological forces bind women into this task. This work is performed in all kinds of families, not just in the alcoholic family.
>
> (Holmila, 1991, p. 3)

Finland, where there has been a strong history of attempts to control people's drinking, also provides a good example of collaboration between family and State. Jarvinen (1991) described the 'customer surveillance system' that operated in Helsinki liquor stores in the 1940s and 1950s. Under this system everyone was required to purchase alcohol from one particular liquor store and all purchases were registered. Inspectors could carry out interrogations if it was thought that purchases were excessive, and might call on people at home, interview neighbours and obtain relevant information from police or social authorities. Alcohol 'purchase cards' could be suspended for a period up to 1 year. Under this system female customers, according to Jarvinen, were of great importance, not so much as excessive drinkers themselves, but as procurers of alcohol for their husbands or as accomplices in controlling their husbands' excess. The following case is illustrative:

> Mrs B, a 28-year-old Helsinki factory worker, was interrogated in a liquor store in 1951. She had bought 58 bottles of Schnapps over the last 3 months. After a house call the inspector wrote: 'Mrs B is a tip-top woman, sweet and good-looking. Her husband, a house-painter, drinks too much, but he does his work well. In collaboration with this wife it should be possible to reduce Mr B's drinking. On any account, Mr B is not to be informed of our agreement concerning his wife's liquor purchases'.
>
> (Jarvinen, 1991, pp. 3–4)

If, as recent evidence suggests (see below), in the region of two to three million adults in the UK are 'alcohol dependent' at any one time, it is likely that the number of 'concerned and affected others' might run to 4–6 million or more. Spouses and children are those likely to be most affected. For example, even allowing for the fact that a relatively high proportion of alcohol problems occur in young adults aged 16–24, the number of excessive drinkers who are parents with children or adolescents in their care must be at least several hundreds of thousands in the UK, and it follows that children, currently living with parents who are excessive drinkers, must exist in very large numbers indeed, probably in excess of 1 million in Britain (Velleman and Orford, 1999). In the USA, one widely quoted estimate puts the number of children currently under the age of 18 and living with at least one parent with a drinking problem at 6.5 million (Russell *et al.*, 1985).

The large mass of family members affected by excessive drinking, unlike Caitlin, have not written autobiographies, and their experiences go largely unrecorded. From research carried out in south-west England and in Mexico City—two contrasting sociocultural groups—we have suggested that there are several core aspects of the experience of close relatives of people whose drinking is excessive. This core experience, which may be near-universal—transcending culture, socioeconomic circumstances, and the particular relationship of the relative to the person whose drinking they are affected by (whether son or daughter, husband or wife, father or mother, or other)—consists of: finding the excessive drinker unpleasant to live with (because of verbal or physical aggression, mood swings, lying and poor communication generally); being concerned about his or her health or work or education or performance; experiencing financial difficulties as a result of excessive drinking; being aware of harmful effects on the family or home as a whole; feeling anxious and worried, or helpless and despairing, or low and depressed; and oneself experiencing poor general health or specific physical symptoms which the relative attributes at least in part to the stress of living with the effects of excessive drinking (Orford *et al.*, 1998a).

There has now been a great deal of research on the experiences of children, brought up by one or more parent who drank excessively. Still one of the most comprehensive studies was Matejcek's (1981a, b) investigation of 200 4–15-year-old children from intact families in which the father had been registered at one of Prague's anti-alcoholic counselling centres in the mid-1970s, compared with a matched sample of control children. Teachers and parents were interviewed and the children independently tested. That was just one of many studies that have now been conducted, and which show conclusively that children and adolescents, while living at home with an excessively drinking parent, are significantly more likely to experience problems of maladjustment of all the major types with which child psychologists are familiar: emotional problems, conduct difficulties, and school and learning difficulties (West and Prinz, 1987; Velleman and Orford, 1999).

As always, young people's behaviour is of particular concern, including their own levels of drinking. In Britain in the second half of the 1990s, part of that concern focused upon 'alcopops'. As Sutherland and Willner (1998), introducing the report of their survey of over 5000 11–16-year-olds from six schools in different locations around England, put it:

These sweet-tasting alcoholic drinks, which first arrived in the United Kingdom in 1995, have generated a moral uproar, fuelled by suggestions in the popular media that young adolescents are being 'seduced' into drinking these potent but pleasant-tasting drinks and that the extent of their consumption has reached epidemic proportions.

(Sutherland and Willner, 1998, p. 1200)

Sutherland and Willner expressed concern at the rate of regular drinking (at least once a week for at least 3 months) which was estimated at 30 per cent of 11-year-olds rising to 83 per cent at age 16. About half the drinkers preferred alcopops to other types of alcoholic drink, more so for girls, and more so at the younger ages. Use of alcopops was considered further worrying because it was significantly associated with a greater frequency of drunkenness, with tobacco smoking, and to a lesser extent with other drug use. Comparison with the results of earlier surveys suggested that drinking among English teenagers might have risen considerably, and because alcohol was by far the most commonly consumed drug, Sutherland and Willner raised the question whether alcohol could be viewed as a 'gatekeeper' drug, leading on to the use of tobacco and illicit drugs. Following their study of 14–18-year-olds in north-west England, Parker *et al.* (1998) also noted the large quantities of alcohol regularly being consumed by many teenagers, but concluded that the danger of alcopops had been exaggerated.

Peter Cook is just one of millions whose premature death has been attributed to excessive drinking. The relationship between alcohol and morbidity and mortality has been much studied. Anderson *et al.*'s (1993) review of research relating individual alcohol consumption to risk for a variety of physical illnesses found evidence for a relationship between level of alcohol consumption and risks of liver cirrhosis, cancer of the oropharynx, larynx, oesophagus, rectum (beer only), liver and breast, and high blood pressure and stroke, with an increased risk of cardiac arrhythmia, cardiomyopathy and sudden coronary death also being associated with heavy drinking (they also found some support for the possibility that drinking might actually *protect* against the risk of coronary heart disease, but this was achieved only at very moderate levels of consumption, of less than 10 g of alcohol a day, which is slightly over 1 standard British 'unit' of alcohol).

Among individual studies that have considered the contribution of heavy drinking to mortality are Rossow and Amundsen's (1997) study of deaths over the following 40-year period, amongst 40 000 Norwegian men conscripted to the armed services in the early 1930s, and Marshall *et al.*'s (1994) 20-year follow-up of 90 men treated as part of our treatment-versus-advice study of the late 1960s (Edwards *et al.*, 1977a). Of the Norwegian cohort, over 1000 had subsequently been registered as receiving treatment for excessive drinking, and they were found to have 3.3 times the general mortality rate, four out of ten of this group dying before the age of 60. Of Marshall *et al.*'s London-treated sample, 44 had died and death certificates were obtained for 43. Compared with population norms, the mortality rate for the group as a whole was 3.6 times expected. Thirty-two of the deaths occurred before age 65, and excess mortality was particularly high between the ages of 45 and 54. The commonest causes of death were diseases of the circulatory system (coronary thrombosis 6, cardiac failure 3, cerebrovascular accident 3, pulmonary embolism 1), neoplasms (carcinoma of the bronchus 11 and of the rectum 1), injury and poisoning (6), diseases of the respiratory system (5) and diseases of the digestive system (4). On only 4 of the 43 death certificates was 'chronic alcoholism' mentioned and on three others alcohol was mentioned in the context of alcohol poisoning in conjunction with some other drug.

There have now been a number of studies in which general hospital patients have been screened for drinking problems (e.g. Lloyd *et al.*, 1986). Our own study, which involved bedside screening, using a computer-administered questionnaire, of over 500 in-patients admitted to one of six medical wards of a district general hospital in south-west England concluded that 43 per cent of men and 18 per cent of women patients 35 years of age or younger were 'risk drinkers'. To qualify as risk drinkers patients had either to report drinking more than the recommended maximum safe quantity per week for their sex (21 standard units for men and 14 for women) or to achieve more than a minimal score on a simple, weighted combination of questions about binge drinking, drink-related harm, contemplating changing drinking, and a much-used four-question screening questionnaire known as CAGE (felt should Cut down, anyone Annoyed you by suggesting you cut down or stop, felt Guilty, early morning Eye-opener drink) (Orford *et al.*, 1992).

Waller *et al.* (1998) reported the results of a survey of all general hospital accident and emergency departments in England. Nurses replying to the survey on average estimated 19 per cent of A&E attendances to be alcohol related, and doctors' average estimate was 16 per cent. Assaults were thought by both nurses and doctors to be the most difficult to cope with. Other alcohol-related problems that they were required to deal with were: alcohol withdrawal symptoms, self-injury, alcohol poisoning, road-traffic accidents (motor-vehicle drivers, motor cyclists, cyclists, pedestrians), accidents in the home and accidents in the workplace.

Ill-health-related costs are only a part of the economic costs attributable to excessive drinking. Reviewing studies that had tried to estimate the total financial cost of alcohol excess to countries including England and Wales, the USA, and Australia, Godfrey (1997) concluded that such costs may be equivalent in total to between 2 and 5 per cent of the gross national products of the respective countries, although the larger part of this may be attributable to occasional excessive drinking by people who are not regular very heavy drinkers. Within these totals, lost productivity is likely to form a large part, as a result of effects of excessive drinking on availability or supply of labour (because of premature deaths, unemployment, sickness absence and absenteeism) and productivity itself (because of inefficiency, reduced uptake of training, lack of promotion/skill enhancement and restricted occupational choice). Godfrey and Hardman (1994) estimated the costs for England and Wales associated with the drinking of those consuming over 50 units of alcohol a week. The results, shown in Table 2.1, show a total estimated cost of nearly £3 billion in 1992. Even this is clearly a conservative estimate since it included only costs associated with the drinking of heavy drinkers; nor does it include crime, other than drink-driving and drunkenness offences, nor lost productivity as a result of impaired work performance. The Association of Chief Police Officers (1998, cited by Alcohol Concern, 1999) has estimated that the annual cost of policing alcohol-related incidents, alone, is approximately £6 billion.

Excessive drinking is widely accused of being highly 'costly' to nations around the globe, including those undergoing rapid change and development. Russia is just the latest where attention has been called to the malignant role of heavy drinking in national decline. Sidorov (1995), for example, claimed that the average prevalence of 'alcoholism' was 200–250 per thousand adults, with an estimated 10 per cent of workers in the nuclear-energy industry, for example—one of the lower risk groups in fact—suffering from alcoholism. The high proportion of marital separations and divorces attributed to excessive drinking has been of particular concern in Russia (Stack and Bankowski, 1994) and in the former USSR as a whole (Sysenko, 1982).

Until the later decades of the 20th century, people in many parts of the less industrialised world had access to alcohol only in the form of beverages produced at home or on a very local basis, and in some parts of the world people were totally unexposed to alcohol. The way in which such exposure has increased dramatically in all 'developing' parts of the world in the later years of the century—as a result of the growth of cash economies, the commercialisation of alcohol beverage production and the globalisation of the drinks trade—has been noted by many (e.g. Curry, 1993; Kunitz and Levy, 1994; Liu and Cheng, 1998; Room, 1998).

Liu and Cheng (1998) noted that in traditional agrarian society the use of alcohol was, '... for the most part integrative, conflict-reducing, and reinforcing of community identity ...' (p. 168). An example is provided by Hagaman (1980) who reported on her observations of beer and its use among a small group of people in Northern Ghana whom she referred to as the LoBir. Not only was beer among these people a necessary and sacred accompaniment to almost all rituals and ceremonial occasions, but it also served as a vital source of cohesion in an otherwise rather dispersed and loosely organised group of people. The main drinking setting was the home, and the main drinking time the afternoon. Beer was essential to social exchange of all kinds. In an otherwise impoverished diet, beer also had an important nutritional function, and in an area inhabited by all kinds of parasites it was relatively safe to drink. Hedlund and Lundahl (1984) also considered the way in which beer drinking and beer brewing in central Africa (e.g. in rural Zambia) traditionally functioned:

> ... as a mode of integrating the community, of confirming authority and social relations, of maintaining individual reciprocal relations, and of redistributing surpluses from wealthy households, which thus obtain a reputation for generosity and concomitant social prestige.
>
> (Hedlund and Lundahl, 1984, p. 62)

Such patterns are changing fast. From another continent, Kunitz and Levy (1994) reported their observations on returning to study drinking amongst Navajo indians in North America 25 years after their first study there. They argued that Navajo alcohol use was learned in the 19th century by observing Anglo-American frontiersmen, and that alcohol was consumed both at home in controlled

Table 2.1 Costs of alcohol misuse: England and Wales 1992 (reproduced by permission from Godfrey and Hardman, 1994)

	£m
1. The social cost to industry	
(a) Sickness absence	1059.20
(b) Housework services	71.15
(c) Unemployment	244.08
(d) Premature deaths	956.39
	2330.82
2. Social costs to the National Health Service	
(a) In-patient costs—direct alcohol diagnosis	40.80
(b) In-patient costs—other alcohol-related diagnosis	120.17
(c) General practice costs	3.06
	164.03
3. Society's response to alcohol-related problems	
(a) Expenditure by national alcohol bodies	0.48
(b) Research	0.88
	1.36
4. Social cost of material damage—road-traffic accidents (damage)	152.25
5. Social cost of criminal activities	
(a) Police involvement in traffic offences (excluding road-traffic accidents)	7.17
(b) Police involvement in road-traffic offences (including judiciary and insurance administration)	21.26
(c) Drink-related court cases	26.56
	54.99
Total (excluding unemployment and premature death)	*1502.98*
Total (including unemployment and premature death)	*2703.46*

settings by men and women and at large gatherings where young men in particular might get quite drunk; but, because until the 1930s alcohol was difficult to obtain as a result of isolation and lack of cash to buy alcohol, the effects of alcohol use were originally not highly disruptive. Later, however, cash compensation for Government destruction of the Navajo livestock economy, experience of Navajos outside the reservation during the Second World War and improved communications with the outside world meant that alcohol became much more available and accessible to virtually everyone. New patterns of drinking, in which access was not limited and use not constrained by pre-existing norms of obligation, had devastating effects. They concluded that, 'Virtually all Navajo men have drinking histories that by the most commonly used criteria would class them as alcohol abusers ...' (p. 237).

Kunitz and Levy (1994) made the interesting additional observation that, '... the findings of this study ... lead us to conclude that we are not dealing with a single disease process so much as with the undesirable consequences of excessive alcohol consumption' (p. 238), and that alcohol use and misuse amongst the Navajo is, '... an inextricably social and cultural phenomenon' (p. 234). They noted that prevention and treatment programmes with indigenous people, initiated in the

1960s, were inappropriately, as it now seemed, based on the idea that alcohol abuse was best thought of as a disease, or at least as a problem characterising individuals.

Liu and Cheng (1998) provided an interesting example of the introduction of drinking to a small, isolated society previously quite unacquainted with alcohol. They carried out a household survey of indigenous Yami people on Orchid Island, an offshore island of Taiwan. Alcohol was introduced to the Yami by the Han Chinese who started to import cheap rice wine to the island in the 1970s. In addition, since the 1980s, many young Yami people had temporarily migrated to Taiwan whilst maintaining contact with their island of origin. Although the rate of alcohol 'abuse' and alcohol 'dependence' that they found amongst the Yami was less than that reported in other surveys amongst other Taiwanese indigenous groups from the main island of Taiwan, the lifetime rate of alcohol abuse among Yami men was found to be 20 per cent, and the 1-year prevalence 10 per cent, both figures being very significantly higher among the unmarried, those without religious belief and particularly among those who had spent several years on the main island.

Reviewing the evidence from a number of countries, particularly in West Africa and the Western Pacific, Curry (1993) concluded: that production and consumption of beer, wine and spirits was increasing in virtually every developing region of the world; that beer was an item of growing importance in consumption patterns in developing countries; that rapid growth of consumption in developing countries was generally followed by an increase in alcohol-related problems that imposed severe strains on scarce economic and social resources; and that alcoholic-beverage industries developed at a rapid pace in countries with no industrial tradition, encouraged by the transfer of capital and technology from brewers in developed countries; that traditional checks on drinking (e.g. the taboo on women drinking, restriction of young men's drinking by their elders, unavailability of beer on a daily basis) were being weakened, encouraged by the break-up of family structure and traditional lifestyles; that on the whole governments had not noticed this and had not acted to create new controls; that excessive alcohol consumption played a role in causing or at least compounding plights such as drought, inflation or economic decline, AIDS, uncontrolled population increase, family breakdown, crime, malnutrition and ill-health; and, all in all, that alcohol was acting as a significant factor constraining development in the Third World.

In the UK, as almost everywhere, the late 20th century has seen the general loosening of state controls on alcohol consumption tempered by concerns expressed in a range of expert reports. Among the latter have been reports from the Royal Colleges of Physicians (1987), General Practitioners (1986) and Psychiatrists (1986), proposals for a National Alcohol Strategy for England produced by the national organisation, Alcohol Concern (1999), and *Tackling Alcohol Together*, produced by the Society for the Study of Addiction (1999). The conclusion that excessive drinking represents a preventable cause of numerous physical, psychological and social problems, and that it is therefore a matter of the utmost importance for public health, is powerfully stated in the World Health Organisation (WHO) report, *Alcohol Policy and the Public Good* (Edwards *et al.*, 1994, 1995):

On a world scale drinking results in diverse suffering and costs of enormous proportion which have an impact on the health and welfare of men and women; children and adults; the poor and the rich; those who do the drinking and those who suffer from the drinker's behaviour, in nearly every country of the globe. Alcohol is a highly significant public health issue ...

(Edwards *et al.*, 1995, p. 174)

The report advocated a multi-faceted public-health approach targeting not just the drinking of the minority of excessive drinkers, but rather the drinking of society at large:

... policy must be willing to take the totality of the drinking population as defining the scope for public health action. Society's drinking problems will, on the large scale, be dealt with effectively through understanding and influencing the total and dynamic system which comprises society's drinking ... A policy mix which makes use of taxation and control of physical access, which supports drink driving counter-measures, and which invests broadly in treatment and particularly in primary care is, on all the research evidence, likely to achieve success in reducing the level of problems.

(Edwards *et al.*, 1995, pp. 175, 178)

Sulkunen (1997) has pointed out that the foregoing approach to alcohol control may be seen as contrary to the value placed in modern democratic society on the right to pursue one's own lifestyle as a private matter and not something that should be regulated by public rules. In the name of the 'public good', however, Edwards *et al.*'s report advocated that, '... moderate drinkers should sacrifice some of their pleasure and comfort to show solidarity with those more at risk' (Sulkunen, 1997, p. 1118).

This appeal to the public good may be seen, on the other hand, as a corrective to the responsibility that has been placed in modern times solely on individuals to control their own consumption and any harm related to it. Room (1997) has argued that this burden on individuals is a peculiarly modern phenomenon resulting from the commercialisation and globalisation of the manufacture and supply of alcoholic drinks which were formerly local matters and highly controlled by local customs, or were the subject of temperance or prohibitionist movements.

Whether those concerned professionally with alcohol and public health should 'collaborate' with the drinks industry is a matter that has led to heated exchange. Wallack, a professor of public health in the University of California, has strongly argued the view that, 'The alcohol industry is not your friend?', to give the subtitle of his *British Journal of Addiction* editorial (1992). A representative of the alcohol industry, in reply, argued for 'dialogue'—a word preferred to 'collaboration' (Mitchell, 1995). The importance of language in this debate is pointed up by the report of a joint working group on terminology (1998) prepared by the Center for Substance Abuse Prevention in the USA (part of the US Department of Health and Human Services) and the International Center for Alcohol Policies, an organisation funded by the US drinks industry and based in Washington DC. The report makes fascinating reading. A large part of this report was devoted to an annotated list of terms. Among the entries were the following:

> *Drug pusher and Legal drug pusher:* These are inflammatory and, most people would agree, inappropriately insulting terms when used to describe individuals who produce, sell, serve, or offer alcohol for legal consumption (p. 17). *Use:* Although a word of only three letters and one syllable, 'use' speaks volumes in terms of its associations with the culture of illegal drugs. Those who see alcohol as properly categorised with 'other' drugs—their legal status notwithstanding—find 'use' to be an appropriate term in reference to alcohol consumption (p. 23).

COUNTING AND DEFINING EXCESSIVE DRINKING

A major consequence of viewing drinking excess as a disease-like property of individuals—whether in Britain, Russia or amongst the Navajo of North America—is that the matter becomes suitable for investigation by the methods of epidemiology. It becomes a question of recognising 'cases' and of counting heads. It becomes reasonable to ask how many people 'suffer' from it, and it becomes important to know the answer in order to plan preventive and treatment services. The ways in which epidemiologists have gone about this task of estimating the numbers of excessive drinkers in a community are most instructive if we wish to understand what they have meant by 'alcohol dependence' or a 'drinking problem'.

Surveys have been of two quite distinct types. One is the reporting-agency survey which relies for its estimates of prevalence upon the likelihood of people with drinking problems being known to one or more of a number of agencies in a particular area. An early example was Edwards *et al.*'s (1973) survey of agencies in the Camberwell area of South London. Some years later Weisner and Schmidt (1995) reported on a similar comprehensive study including agency-based surveys carried out in one Northern Californian county in the USA. The locations covered in such surveys include many of those shown in Table 2.2, which lists the various institutions, agencies and organisations, both statutory and voluntary, formal and informal, whose personnel, either knowingly or unknowingly, are likely to meet individuals with drinking problems or members of their families. Almost all these agents are to be found in every locality in the UK. The list is a large one, although probably not comprehensive; it reflects the fact that forms of alcohol-related harm include the medical, social and legal, and affect all ages including the very young and the elderly. The list covers a formidable array of personnel who should have some familiarity with, and some understanding of, the nature of drinking problems in order to respond appropriately to those among their clients, patients, customers or members whose problems are thought to be at least partly related to their consumption of alcohol.

Prevalence figures arising from agency surveys (e.g. Edwards *et al.*, 1973 produced a 1-year prevalence figure of 4.7 'alcoholics' per 1000 adults) represent what might be termed the known or 'labelled' prevalence and are clearly unsatisfactory to the epidemiologist if a 'true' picture of actual prevalence is required. They do, however, give some indication of the extent to which the problem is visible. The second type of survey is the more familiar household survey, in the course of which a sample of the population is asked a series of pertinent questions. Such surveys are more germane in the present context, not just because they may produce a more 'accurate' prevalence estimate, but because in the course of such research the investigators must operationalise what they mean by 'alcohol dependence' or a 'drinking problem'. This provides us with invaluable insights into the nature of the concepts being employed.

One of the most comprehensive general-population surveys carried out in Britain was that conducted by the Office of Population Censuses and Surveys (OPCS) in 1993 (Meltzer *et al.*, 1994, 1995). The sample consisted of 10 000 adults aged 16–64 years living in private households. In this sample 30 per cent of men and 15 per cent of women reported usually drinking more than the maximum 'recommended sensible level' of 21 units a week for men and 14 for women; 8 per cent of men and 2 per cent of women drank 'very heavily' (more than 50 units for men and 35 for women). Informants were classified as 'alcohol dependent' if they responded positively to 3 or more of the 12 statements shown in Table 2.3. By this criterion 75 per 1000 men and 21 per 1000 women were considered to have been 'dependent' on alcohol in the year prior to the survey. The highest prevalence was among young men aged 20–24 years where the estimated rate was 176 per thousand.

The definition of 'dependence', based on any 3 of a collection of 12 statements, is of course arbitrary. Although there is rough agreement about some of the indicators of dependence, the sets of items preferred by different investigators vary from one to another. An alternative set of questions, currently popular in the UK, is the 10 items constituting the Leeds Dependence Questionnaire (LDQ) (Raistrick *et al.*, 1994). These are also shown in Table 2.3. A comparison with the 12 statements of the OPCS reveals the rather different set of assumptions about what constitutes dependence, the LDQ being based more upon preoccupation with drinking and loss of control, the OPCS questions more on withdrawal effects.

Is it sensible, though, to think of 'dependence' as just one thing and to attempt to define and count it using just one set of questions? Based on his extensive travels for the WHO, and thus less hampered than most by a stereotype of the form excessive drinking might appear to take in his own culture, Jellinek (1960) was able to describe the different forms that excessive drinking took in different parts of the world. His book is therefore still one of the best sources of description of the variety of drinking phenomena with which a psychological account of excessive drinking must deal. He attempted to make sense of the diversity he found by describing five species of 'alcoholism' denoted by the first five letters of the Greek alphabet. He reserved the word 'disease' for the gamma (loss of control, more common in spirit-drinking countries such as the USA) and delta (inability to abstain, more common in wine-drinking countries such as France) types, for only here did he believe there was a 'physiopathological process' involving adaptation of cell metabolism, the acquisition of tissue tolerance and the experience of withdrawal symptoms. People who experienced one of the other three varieties (alpha—psychological dependence; beta—regular heavy drinking producing

Table 2.2 Community agencies in a position to detect and respond to excessive drinking (adapted from Orford, 1987, table 1.5)

General practitioners	Health visitors	General hospital staff
Practice nurses	District nurses	Services for children or adolescents, and their families
Psychiatric hospital staff and community mental health staff	Social services	Services for older adults
Local authority housing departments	Probation services	Magistrates courts
Prison	Police	Lawyers
Clergy and voluntary organisations (including citizens' advice, Samaritans, marriage guidance, women's aid)	Services for single, homeless people, and casual users of night shelter, reception centre, and cheap commercial hostel accommodation	The workplace (including employers, personnel officers, industrial medical officers, company nurses and colleagues)
Teachers	Licenced premises, especially public houses	Family and friends.

physical damage; epsilon—bout drinking) were 'alcoholics' but not suffering from disease.

Although Jellinek's classification system has not stood the test of time, the distinction between 'alcohol addiction', roughly corresponding to Jellinek's gamma and delta types, and other varieties of 'problem drinking', is quite frequently made. For instance, Wilkins (1974) drew this dividing line in an early survey of excessive drinkers in general medical practice. In his own group practice, with a list of approximately 12 000 patients, he recorded, over a period of 12 months, 46 'alcohol addicts' and 41 further patients with 'serious drinking problems' not amounting to 'alcohol addiction'. In contrast, a landmark expert report from the WHO (Edwards *et al.*, 1977b) found such a distinction impossible to make. In that report neither term, 'alcoholism' nor 'alcoholics', was recommended. In place of Jellinek's five central varieties of 'alcoholic' appeared 'the alcohol dependence syndrome', a variable entity compounded of varying amounts of abnormal physiological response to alcohol, abnormal drinking behaviour and abnormal subjective experience of drinking. This term, 'alcohol dependence syndrome', with its two-edged implication that excessive drinking can amount to an abnormal entity but one that is highly variable in its manifestations, was then adopted by such bodies as the British Department of Health (DHSS, 1981) and was used by the Royal College of Psychiatrists (1979) in preference to the term 'alcoholism' which was considered too imprecise for modern usage. The new term and the model of excessive drinking to which it refers have been major features of the academic and professional literature ever since.

A lot of effort has gone in to trying to establish, via the statistical procedure of factor analysis, whether a single underlying factor is sufficient to account for the variations between people in terms of the various supposed signs and symptoms of

Table 2.3 Two alternative sets of questions that have been used to measure alcohol 'dependence'

OPCS Survey Questions (Meltzer *et al.*, 1995)	Leeds Dependence Questionnaire items (Raistrick *et al.*, 1994)
Once I started drinking, it was difficult for me to stop before I became completely drunk	Do you find yourself thinking about when you will next be able to have another drink?
I sometimes kept on drinking after I had promised myself not to	Is drinking more important than anything else you might do during the day?
I deliberately tried to cut down or stop drinking, but I was unable to do so	Do you feel your need for drink is too strong to control?
Sometimes I needed a drink so badly that I could not think of anything else	Do you plan your days around getting and taking a drink?
I have skipped a number of regular meals while drinking	Do you drink in a particular way in order to increase the effect it gives you?
I have often had an alcoholic drink the first thing when I got up	Do you drink morning, afternoon and evening?
I have had a strong drink in the morning to get over the previous night's drinking	Do you feel you have to carry on drinking once you have started?
I have woken up the next day not being able to remember some of the things I had done while drinking	Is getting the effect you want more important than the particular drink or drug you use?
My hands shook a lot in the morning after drinking	Do you want to take more drink when the effect starts to wear off?
I need more alcohol than I used to, to get the same effect as before	Do you find it difficult to cope with life without drink?
Sometimes I have woken up during the night or early morning sweating all over because of drinking	
I have stayed drunk for several days at a time	

the 'alcohol dependence syndrome'. Much of this work was reviewed by Skinner (1990). The results are complicated and somewhat inconclusive, partly because the interpretation of a factor analysis includes a large measure of subjectivity and there is no agreed criterion for the existence of a single factor. The precise results depend to some extent upon the sample: clinical samples tending to show all signs and symptoms loading on a single factor, with individual elements of the supposed syndrome being much less highly correlated in community samples. Skinner himself was attracted to a hierarchical model consisting of a single, broad, general factor plus a number of more specific factors. He cited earlier work by Wanberg and Horn (1983) who found 17 first-order factors tapping specific areas (e.g. drinking to manage mood, withdrawal, guilt or worry about drinking), six second-order factors (e.g. obsessive-sustained drinking, anxious concern about drinking) and a third-order general factor representing involvement with alcohol in a broad sense. In Skinner's own research, evidence was found for a model that included a general factor dominated by alcohol-dependence symptoms, as well as three specific factors (frequency of heavy drinking, maximum quantity consumed, and health/legal problems) (Skinner, 1990).

Using data from a national household survey of over 3000 people in the USA, Hasin *et al.* (1994) tested the so-called 'bi-axial' concept of excessive drinking which pictures alcohol dependence as constituting one axis, and alcohol-related problems constituting a second dimension. The results suggested to Hasin *et al.* that there was little support for the bi-axial view and that a single factor better described the results. Although it was possible to see two factors in the data, corresponding to dependence (withdrawal avoidance, narrowing of drinking repertoire, and salience of drinking, having highest loadings) and alcohol-related problems (social problems, and home problems, having the highest loadings), these two factors were themselves highly correlated (0.73) and the first unrotated factor accounted for much more variance than any of the following factors. Confirmatory factor analysis supported a single factor. All the criteria included had high loadings on this factor, with the possible exception of 'narrowing of drinking repertoire'. Salience of drinking had a particularly high loading ('at times, needed a drink so badly, couldn't think of anything else but alcohol'; 'alcohol interfered with activities/hobbies'), but was considerably less frequent in the sample as a whole than social problems ('heated argument while drinking'; 'fights while drinking'; 'felt drinking had a harmful effect on friendships and social life'), impaired control ('once started drinking, difficult to stop before completely intoxicated'; 'kept on drinking after I promised myself not to'; 'deliberately tried to cut down or quit, unable to do so'; 'felt drinking was not completely under control') and health problems.

One of the most serious criticisms of these attempts to establish agreed, universally applicable, scientifically reliable and valid, criteria for diagnosis is the problem of social and cultural relativism. As Room *et al.* (1996) pointed out, using these definitions and their associated measures internationally, as is intended, may be particularly hazardous, '... when the resulting measures are to be used to compare rates or trends across cultures and societies, while the operational criteria are based on material drawn from a narrow cultural range' (p. 201). As a result of their studies in nine contrasting cultures, involving attempts to translate and back-translate interview instruments based on the WHO International Classification of Diseases (ICD) criteria, plus interviews and focus groups with key informants in different countries, questionnaires completed by local clinicians, and trials of diagnostic instruments with actual cases in alcohol and drug treatment agencies, Room *et al.* found a number of difficulties in the way of achieving cross-cultural comparability.

These difficulties existed at a number of different levels. At the level of individual interview questions, a major finding was that in several locations (e.g. Bangalore, South India; Ibadan, South Western Nigeria; and Seoul, South Korea), the idea that individuals could describe and report upon emotional states, in the detached way expected of interviewees in countries from which the instruments originally derived, was often a foreign one. Words and phrases such as, 'feel emotionally', 'feel', 'anxiety' and 'emotion' were difficult to translate. Similarly, concepts such as

drinking 'causing' trouble, presumed a style of self-consciousness and causal attribution which was unrecognisable in some cultures. At the level of individual
criteria there were further linguistic difficulties. In some instances a culture
simply lacked a means of exactly translating a concept such as 'tolerance' or
'irresistible urge'. In other cases the criterion was difficult to understand in
certain cultural situations. The idea of spending an increased amount of time
seeking or using alcohol made little sense to informants in Santander, Northern
Spain, or Ibadan in Nigeria, since alcohol was so easily available. Nor did it make
sense in Bangalore since time was not viewed as a scarce or expendable
commodity. The notion of neglecting alternative pleasures caused trouble, for
example, in Jebel, Western Rumania where it was remarked by one informant
that 'almost all pleasures are related to alcohol consumption' (p. 213). At the
level of diagnoses there was substantial variation from one site to another in the
threshold for identifying and defining dependence. Particularly illuminating
examples were found in Bangalore in India, where only a minority of men
drank at all and almost no women drank. In this setting, where there was much
disapproval of drinking, it was clear that the threshold of positive responses to
certain questions had been set so low that inappropriate diagnoses of dependence
were made. For example:

> A Bangalore drinker who consumed the equivalent of two European bottles
> of beer (a total of 700 ml) once every 2 months, and had never drunk more
> than this, nevertheless qualified for three criteria of dependence: he reported
> that drinking has less effect on him than it used to; his family and friends
> objected to his drinking, but he continued to drink, and when he had had
> tuberculosis his doctor had advised him to stop (he had indeed stopped for a
> few months but then started again); and he had wanted to stop or cut down
> drinking but could not.
>
> (Room *et al.*, 1996, pp. 215–217)

Room *et al.* rather cautiously concluded that, 'The goal and promise of a valid and
useful cross-cultural epidemiology of alcohol and drug conditions remains before
us, in no way invalidated by the results of ... [this] ... study. But the results do
highlight the challenges inherent in this endeavour' (p. 217). One of the commentators on Room *et al.*'s paper, however, was less cautious:

> ... it would be hard not to conclude that so far the efforts to develop
> universally valid instruments for the diagnosis and measurement of sub-
> stance use disorders have failed, and that the observed cultural variety in
> the meanings and interpretations of alcohol and drug use promises little
> success in the present circumstances.
>
> (Partanen, 1996, p. 225)

Similarly, Skinner (1990) wrote:

> Given the preliminary nature of much of the empirical research, one must
> seriously question the 'premature' adoption of this concept [dependence] in

official classifications. ... presently, we must contend with a fairly high level
of construct slippage and measurement noise in the system. I view the
dependence syndrome concept as a stepping-stone that should be used,
improved upon, and then possibly discarded. We may have already
passed the half-life of this concept.

(Skinner, 1990, pp. 46–60)

Others have raised what is perhaps a far more fundamental issue. Partanen (1996)
put it thus:

The irony of the situation is that these matters are primarily dealt with in a
health perspective—internationally WHO is the main actor. Yet in many a
developing country alcohol- and drug-related problems are essentially problems caused by poverty and coping with them is hampered by corruption. In
the most extreme cases—and the history of colonialism knows many—these
problems are a consequence of the total breakdown of society. In yet other
countries such as Japan, and presumably also Korea, heavy male drinking
and its consequences are essentially related to the patterns of work life and
the relationships between genders. Such examples suggest that the very logic
of substance use disorders in particular cultures derives from the socioeconomic and cultural matrix of the whole society.

(Partanen, 1966, p. 226)

These thoughtful comments pose many of the dilemmas with which this book
attempts to deal. If harmful consequences are central to the concept of alcohol
'dependence', can 'problem drinking' be defined absolutely and independently of a
person's social environment, his or her responsibilities and obligations and the
ways family and others respond? Are there cultures which promote drinking for
reasons, and with a style, that are abnormal by the standards of others? Is
someone who drinks heavily and regularly, but who is unconcerned, more or
less 'dependent' than someone who drinks less, and less often, but who is more
concerned? How can one distinguish between being unable to stop and not wanting
to stop? These and other questions are relevant not only to excessive drinking but
also to excessive behaviour of the kinds considered in the following four chapters.

   They should not, however, stand in the way of our recognising the facts of
excessive alcohol drinking. These include the distress at being unable to control
their drinking of which Lilian Roth and Tony Adams wrote and of which countless
others have complained; the distress of Peter Cook's friends and family, and
countless others, at seeing people they care about apparently spoiling their lives;
the needs to which Father Mathew and the temperance campaigners were responding when they used their influence to reduce or prohibit consumption; the preoccupation of governments past and present with the task of restraining excess;
and the flourishing of self-help and professional forms of 'treatment' for alcohol
'dependence'. There may be disagreement about how best to construe excessive
drinking, and about its causes and solutions, but of its existence there can be no
doubt.

CHAPTER THREE

Excessive Gambling

By the effects of the lottery, even under its present restrictions, idleness, dissipation, and poverty are increased, the most sacred and confidential trusts are betrayed, domestic comfort is destroyed, madness often created, crimes, subjecting the perpetrators of them to the punishment of death are inflicted and even suicide itself is produced.

(House of Commons Select Committee, 1808, cited by Miers, 1996, p. 354)

Gamble, gamble, gamble your life away ... you might as well have put the money down the drain ... you've got to face the truth that you're having a love affair, and it's with a machine whose lights flash, takes your money and kills your soul.

(A 'fruit machine addict', aged 20, cited by Griffiths, 1993a)

Like alcohol, gambling deserves a central place in our picture of the addictions. Like alcohol, it seems always to have been with us as a popular form of activity which can easily get out of hand and become excessive and difficult to control. Unlike alcohol, though, its position within most late 20th-century models of addiction has been at best peripheral. This state of affairs, strange from the perspective of the model to be developed in this book, undoubtedly has much to do with the dominance in expert thinking of heroin, cocaine and other drugs that are illegal in our times. This restricted focus on drugs, and what is more an even narrower focus on certain classes of drug, has arguably led us astray in developing a comprehensive understanding of addiction. Understanding excessive gambling has a particularly important part to play in helping us develop a fuller and less biased account.

The idea that the appetite for gambling could become excessive is no more a modern invention than is the notion of alcoholic excess. As Lindner (1950) put it, 'The fact that [it] ... could assume a pathological form characterized by symptoms related to the various addictions ... seems always to have been common knowledge among common folk everywhere' (cited by Herman, 1976). An article by Clemens France in the *American Journal of Psychology* for 1902 chronicled the many nations from ancient to modern which have been accused of fostering widespread gambling of a harmful kind. Since Roman emperors and their wives have been charged with all manner of behavioural excesses, it is not surprising to find that several emperors, including Augustus, Caligula, Claudius and Nero, were cited as having been 'addicted' to gambling. Even Domitian, who so effectively demonstrated his concern over excessive drinking by having half the vineyards in the Empire destroyed (Glatt, 1958), is described as 'an inveterate gambler'. Under Constantine, '... every inhabitant of that city [Rome], down to the populace, was addicted to gambling' (Steinmetz, cited by France, 1902, p. 366). Many societies, according to France, had found it necessary to have legal controls on gambling behaviour. In the England of Henry VIII legislation was passed prohibiting common people from playing cards except at Christmas (France, 1902, p. 368), and Italy of the early 16th century was one of a number of countries which, from time to time, legislated for total prohibition of gambling but failed to suppress it.

Many of the descriptions of gambling which France unearthed from an earlier period are remarkably similar to current accounts of 'compulsive gambling'. Amongst his historical witnesses were the Englishman, Cotton (1674), whose description of gaming as, '... an enchanting witchery ... an itching disease ...', is well known, and the Frenchman, Barbeyrac. In the latter's three-volume work, *Traite du Jeu*, published in 1737, Jean Barbeyrac had this to say:

> I do not know if there is any other passion which allows less of repose and which one has so much difficulty in reducing. ... the passion of gambling gives no time for breathing; it is an enemy which gives neither quarter nor truce; it is a persecutor, furious and indefatigable. The more one plays the more one wishes to play; ... it seems that gambling had acquired the right to occupy all [the gambler's] thoughts. ...

The idea that *it* takes over, becomes a preoccupation, and that the wish to reduce or leave off altogether is opposed by a stronger force that leaves the will powerless, is as clear here as in Lilian Roth's and Tony Adams' modern-day accounts of addiction to alcohol.

The Russian novelist Dostoevsky is often referred to as the most famous of all 'compulsive gamblers'. There have been a number of case studies of the writer, mostly by psychoanalysts; one of the best known being that by Squires published in the *Psychoanalytic Review* in 1937. He drew on about 50 sources, including Dostoevsky's own letters and his second wife's diary. From the latter's account of the year in which they married, Squires concluded that Dostoevsky was, 'Powerless in the clutches of his terrific gambling mania, which blunted his sense of moral responsibility as effectively as extreme alcohol addiction could' (p. 372). Stripped of the glamour that surrounds the life of a world-renowned artist struggling with his temperament and his appetites, Dostoevsky's life story contains moments that compare with the experiences of the most obscure man or woman who has struggled with an excessive appetite for gambling.

In his short novel, *The Gambler*, which he intended partly as, '... a firsthand and most detailed portrayal of roulette gambling ...' (Minihan, 1967, pp. 314–315), the hero, Aleksey Ivanovitch, describes the intense attraction of the sights and sounds of the gambling hall:

With what trembling, with what faintness of heart I hear the croupier's cry ... With what greed I look at the gambling table along which are strewn louis d'or, friedrichs d'or, and thalers, at the little columns of gold when they are scattered from the croupier's shovel into piles glowing like fire, or columns of silver a yard high lying stacked round the wheel. Even while approaching the gambling hall, two rooms away, as soon as I begin to hear the clinking of money being poured out, I almost go into convulsions.

(cited by Minihan, 1967, p. 319)

His relationship with his second wife Anna seems to have contained episodes the recounting of which would be thoroughly in place at a meeting of Gamblers Anonymous (GA) or of GamAnon (for family members of 'compulsive gamblers'). They were constantly in financial difficulties and Fyodor Dostoevsky was for ever trying to relieve them by further gambling. His gambling was interspersed with protestations of regret and requests for forgiveness and more money with which to make good former losses. On one occasion Fyodor and Anna travelled to Baden–Baden so that Dostoevsky could gamble. They stayed about a month, Anna spending the days waiting in their hotel room. The infuriating inconsistency in the behaviour of someone whose appetite is excessive is well portrayed in a passage in Minihan's biography which relates to a period just after the birth of Fyodor and Anna's first daughter. The confinement had been expensive:

Dostoevsky went a third time ... He lost, pawned his ring and begged his wife to send him the last hundred francs: '... Don't consider my request for a hundred francs mad. I'm not mad. And also don't consider it depraved; I won't act meanly, won't deceive, won't go to gamble ...' On the same evening he wrote a second letter; he had lost the money received from pawning his ring ...

(Minihan, 1967, p. 332)

Another historical witness to the capacity of gambling to become excessive was Lady Florence Bell, who described the results of her investigations of the lives of working people in Middlesbrough, England, in the late 19th century:

... we know that the individual is generally the worse for gambling; that it tends to debase character, and to lessen the sense of responsibility. But these and other phrases of the kind are not very much good when addressed to men or women full of the excitement of the fray ... the lookers-on try in vain to stem the tide, see one tragedy after another that no power, no persuasion seems able to prevent, and feel well nigh hopeless as to the possibility of arresting this great disintegrating process. Many ways have been tried by the well-meaning, but the forces arrayed against them are overwhelming. It is a terribly unequal fight that is being waged.

(Bell, 1907, pp. 260, 266)

The view that gambling is itself undignified and appealing to the irrational and irresponsible parts of human mentality still survives (Cornish, 1978; Herman, 1976). It offers 'something for nothing', involves 'unnecessary risk', offers gain at the expense of others' loss and is contrary to the principle of reward for effort. Such a view was well represented in the report of the Royal Commission on Betting, Lotteries and Gaming in 1951, and in publications of the Churches' Council on Gambling in the UK in the 1960s (e.g. 1960–1968).

COMPULSIVE GAMBLING

Although 'excessive' and 'immoderate' were adjectives often employed to qualify the term 'gambling', and hence the possibility of moderate use was acknowledged by implication, moderate and immoderate forms of gambling were not often clearly separated in the minds of writers on the subject. The idea that people can be more or less clearly separated into one group or another, or at least that we may talk and write as if they were, is a relatively recent invention. Stekel (1924) recognized gambling as one of the 'manias'—others, for example, being dipsomania, narcomania and nymphomania—and psychoanalytic writers have recognised for some time that gambling, like sexual and other types of appetitive behaviour, could take on a compulsive form (e.g. Bergler, 1958). The creation of 'compulsive gambling' as an entity, and the possibility of 'treatment' for it, are quite new, however.

Accounts by psychiatrists and others of cases they had treated for 'compulsive gambling' started to appear in the 1960s (e.g. Barker and Miller, 1968; Goorney, 1968). The case histories given by Barker and Miller illustrate the harm that can be associated with gambling For example:

> He had gambled in 'betting shops' for more than 2 years and had lost over £1,200. Initially he ascribed his gambling mainly to boredom, but he had recently gambled to repay his debts, which exceeded £100. His usual practice was to spend all his salary (£15 to £30 per week) in a betting shop on Saturdays. He invariably reinvested his winnings on horses and returned home with nothing so that his wife and children went without food, clothes and fuel ... Matters came to a head when he put his own money and the complete pay packet of a sick friend (who had asked him to collect his pay) on one horse and lost £40. This resulted in 18 months probation. His gambling had been causing serious marital difficulties and was affecting the health of his wife and his eldest son. He was referred for treatment by his doctor.
>
> (Barker and Miller, 1968, pp. 288–289)

A number of major books on the subject, and surveys of Gamblers Anonymous— which is closely modelled on Alcoholics Anonymous—appeared in the 1980s. In his classic work, *The Chase*, based on the qualitative analysis of material from lengthy interviews with 50 'compulsive gamblers' in the USA, mostly but not all members of GA, Lesieur (1984) referred to the ways in which a compulsive gambler often developed an 'exploitative' relationship with his work (a limitation of this otherwise excellent study is that all the participants appear to have been men). A plant supervisor, for example, was able to take time out of work because of the comparatively unsupervised nature of his own occupation:

> I was spending more time on my gambling than I was at my job. Spend the day reading the newspapers and sneak out to the track, the afternoon or something like this. Especially when I got on salary work. I had a company car and took it to the track. That is when the hell started. The lying, cheating … and all the things that a compulsive gambler does. Taking time off from work, conniving (lying to your boss, telling him you are going to be somewhere and you are not, go to the race track instead, and stuff like that). I mean you are not paying attention to your job.
>
> (Lesieur, 1984, p. 91)

On the basis of his interviews Lesieur described how compulsive gamblers might work part-time, overtime, sometimes two jobs at once, in order to gamble or pay gambling debts; would often borrow from close friends at work, get advances in pay, steal money and items for ready cash, and in other ways exploit fellow employees, the boss, customers and business associates; would often leave jobs so they would not have to pay debts; and would commonly be simultaneously holding loans from a number of different sources, not uncommonly six or more sources at one time.

A later survey of over 400 members of GA from around the then Federal Republic of Germany also found a large proportion (55 per cent) reporting having obtained money for gambling through illegal means (Meyer and Fabian, 1992). Compared with those not reporting such activity, those who had committed offences reported gambling significantly more often and for longer, with higher stakes and larger losses. Statistical analysis of the data supported the hypothesis that 'pathological gambling' could lead to delinquent behaviour. Most offences were non-violent offences against property, such as theft, embezzlement, fraud, forgery of documents, tax evasion or manipulation of gambling machines, but a minority also admitted to robbery or blackmail.

Ladouceur *et al.*'s (1994) Canadian study of GA members is another that paints a picture of how serious the adverse impacts of excessive gambling can be upon finances, work and crime. Over half of the participants in this survey had been spending more than $1000 a month on gambling, and 83 per cent had had to borrow money during the past year in order to gamble. Some 62 per cent had borrowed money from relatives or friends, and 20 per cent from 'loan sharks'. Both lateness and absence from work were very frequent, and in addition more than half reported that they had often been irritable at work and frequently had difficulties in concentrating as a result of the pervasive nature of thoughts about gambling. Over a third had stolen money from their employers in order to gamble, nearly half of them more than once. A third had already lost jobs because of gambling problems and others had nearly done so. Altogether, two-thirds reported having engaged in illegal acts of one kind or another in order to finance their gambling, including falsifying documents or forging signatures, embezzlement, signing cheques without sufficient funds, filing false income-tax returns or neglecting to pay income tax, making false statements to insurance companies, non-violent theft, violent theft, shoplifting and fencing stolen goods.

Although excessive gambling, more than is the case for most excessive appetites, is most often depicted as an excess which causes harm for others, it is also acknowledged in the literature that excessive gambling may not be good for the gambler's mental health either. In a study of over 200 members of GA in the USA (Lorenz and Yaffee, 1984) reports of psychological and stress-related physical conditions experienced during the worst period of gambling were common. Most commonly reported were: depression (46 per cent); knotted stomach, loose bowels, constipation or colitis (42 per cent); insomnia (35 per cent); feeling faint, dizzy, clammy or sweaty hands, or perspiring heavily (31 per cent); and headaches or migraines (29 per cent). The authors of that report described a 'syndrome' in which some medical and emotional problems were associated with a desperate need for money, and feelings of guilt and depression. In their later survey of 60 members of GA in French-speaking Canada Ladouceur *et al.* (1994) reported that more than two-thirds of respondents indicated experiencing depressive moods, insomnia, headaches or stomach aches, at least once a week, attributed to gambling. Dickerson (1990), in a review of the psychology of gambling as a compulsion, referred to the high rate of depressive disorders among 'pathological gamblers' treated in hospital, and to the high rate (about 20 per cent) of a history of attempted suicide in such groups.

It is effects on family relationships, however, that are most often highlighted in descriptions of excessive gambling. In their book, *When Luck Runs Out*, Custer and Milt (1985) devoted a chapter to compulsive gambling in the family, stating:

> ... compulsive gambling ... spreads out and affects every person with whom the compulsive gambler is closely involved—his wife, his children, his siblings and parents, his other relatives, his friends and business associates ...
> It is the nature of emotional disorders that when one member of the family is afflicted, the effects are felt by all the others There are few, however, in which the impact is felt with such severity as in the case of compulsive gambling.
>
> (Custer and Milt, 1985, pp. 122–123)

Lesieur (1984) referred again to the way in which a compulsive gambler 'exploits' his family financially. This takes a variety of forms including using entertainment money, funds from part-time jobs and overtime money; borrowing from parents or in-laws; lying to his spouse about true extent of earnings; referring to 'bills' or 'deductions' from wages which in reality did not exist; 'borrowing' from family resources such as savings and life insurance; selling or pawning his own or family members' possessions; hiding loans; and finally when all else fails using money that is required by the family for essentials. As one respondent put it:

Sold my tools, sold my car, sold my camera, sold my wrist watch. Sold personal things, antiques that I brought from Europe. I sold them for gambling. A stamp collection. Yes, I sold everything.

(Lesieur, 1984, p. 69)

And as one wife stated:

I didn't have any idea that he took out these loans. And he made agreements that they were confidential loans. Some of them would just not call the house, how could you suspect?

(Lesieur, 1984, p. 71)

For several wives, in contrast, there were repeated threatening calls and harassment from creditors at home.

A total of 81 per cent of Lorenz and Yaffee's (1984) GA members reported hiding their gambling from their spouses. In a parallel survey of over 200 wives of compulsive gamblers (all members of GamAnon) Lorenz and Yaffee (1988) explored the feelings experienced and stress-related conditions suffered by these wives during the worst of their husbands' gambling. Most commonly reported were: feelings of anger and/or resentment (74 per cent); depression (47 per cent); feeling isolated from the gambler, lonely or alone (44 per cent); feeling guilty and responsible for causing or contributing to the gambling (30 per cent); feeling confused (27 per cent); and suffering chronic or severe headaches (41 per cent); irritable bowels, constipation, diarrhoea (37 per cent); feeling faint, dizzy, having cold, clammy hands, excessive perspiring (27 per cent); and hypertension, shortness of breath, rapid breathing or other breathing irregularities (23 per cent). A total of 66 per cent reported an unsatisfactory sexual relationship at that time, a figure that fell to 29 per cent after gambling ceased. Almost all (86 per cent) had contemplated leaving the gambling spouse and 29 per cent had separated from him.

The topic of excessive 'fruit-machine' playing among young people requires special mention. Griffiths has done much to raise awareness about this phenomenon in the UK. In his 1990 paper he reported the results of informal discussions and observations conducted between himself and a group of eight 'self-confessed addicted adolescent fruit-machine gamblers' at their local amusement arcade. The group had been contacted via the author's brother, also described as a 'fruit-machine addict'. The average age of the group was 19 years but all of the group reported beginning fruit-machine playing by the age of 11. Five of the group claimed that they were addicted at the age of 13 and all acknowledged being addicted to machines by the age of 15. A number of serious problems had been experienced:

By far the major problem, which was apparent in all eight cases, was the constant need to play and spend all their own (and others' borrowed) money at every available opportunity. (For example, one participant had actually spent all his money given as Christmas presents before midday on December 25th at a local arcade). This had left them all in debt at some time in their adolescent lives and had forced two of them to seek help from Gamblers

Anonymous. All of the group wishes they could stop gambling, and the assertion that 'fruit machines should be banned' because they are 'deadly' and 'life-destroyers' was re-iterated a number of times during the course of the discussion.

(Griffiths, 1990, p. 123)

Elsewhere Griffiths (1993a) has reported the results of a questionnaire survey of 19 'former adolescent fruit-machine addicts' contacted through the organisation Parents of Young Gamblers, a self-help group set up in the 1980s for parents concerned about the excessive gambling of their adolescent children. Fifteen were men and four women, and the average age was 19 years. In the case of one 18-year-old man who took part in this small survey, participation led to regular contact over a 6-month period between Griffiths and both the young man and his mother, resulting in a very valuable case study (Griffiths, 1993b). According to Griffiths, David (not his real name) was brought up in a seaside town with a younger sister by loving and understanding parents in a secure and stable background. Up to the age of 14 he had good reports from school and was a member of a county swimming team. His mother described him as loving, lively, good at school work and sports, and someone whom she could be proud of. The first sign that anything was wrong were phone calls from David's swimming club wanting to know why he had started to turn up late or failed to turn up altogether for swimming practice, and from his school informing his mother that David's work was going downhill and that he did not seem to be trying. The School asked if he might be on drugs. Later, according to his mother:

His change in lifestyle became obvious. He'd come in after school and leave the house. I'd plead with him to stay but it didn't seem to make any difference. He would just go. He seemed to have completely lost his respect for us. It was difficult to know what to do. We couldn't physically keep him at home, lock him in his room. . . . I began to find money missing from my purse. . . .

(Griffiths, 1993b, p. 390)

From David's own account:

As for obtaining money, I did this in any way possible no matter who I might hurt or what I may destroy. If I wasn't actually gambling I was spending the rest of my time working out clever little schemes to obtain money to feed my habit. These two activities literally took up all my time . . . When my financial resources ran out I would simply depend on somebody else's, no matter who or how close to me this person was . . . I sold a great deal of my possessions to subsidise my 'fruit-machine' addiction . . . This led me to selling my motorbike after owning it for just three months. The four hundred pounds that I received for the bike lasted just a day. . . . During four years of compulsive gambling I think I missed about six or seven days of playing fruit machines . . . I ate, slept and breathed gambling machines . . . All I can remember is living in a trance for four years . . . As if I had been drunk the whole time. ... I lost a great deal of childhood with my parents and only sister which I can never replace. I still get very depressed when I think of the amounts I stole from family and close friends which are totally unrepayable.

(Griffiths, 1993b, pp. 35, 36, 41)

DOES GAMBLING ADDICTION EXIST?

Custer and Milt (1985) defined 'compulsive gambling' as:

> ... an addictive illness in which the subject is driven by an overwhelming uncontrollable impulse to gamble. The impulse progresses in intensity and urgency, consuming more and more of the individual's time, energy and emotional and material resources. Ultimately, it invades, undermines and often destroys everything that is meaningful in his life.

(Custer and Milt, 1985, p. 22)

This special entity or syndrome idea of excessive appetitive behaviour has come in for much the same kind of criticism when applied to gambling as it has when applied to the drinking of alcohol. Indeed, just because gambling is not a pharmacological agent, anything resembling a disease concept of excessive gambling may lack the plausibility which the disease concept of 'alcoholism' possesses. Herman (1976), for example, clearly regarded the GA tendency to define all problems as stemming from 'compulsive gambling' as an over-simplification which was functional for its members rather than being an accurate statement of cause and effect. As he said, 'This kind of single cause theory may not satisfy the moralist, but it may be just the ticket for the relatively uncomplicated rehabilitation of the member' (p. 101). He stated his view that there were no dividing lines between moderate gamblers, heavy gamblers, problem gamblers, addicted gamblers, compulsive gamblers or pathological gamblers, and that creating a separate category of 'compulsive gambler' served no useful purpose. Indeed it, '... generates a set of new problems that would not otherwise exist' (p. 103).

There have, nonetheless, been a number of attempts to define problematic gambling precisely and to operationalise it in the form of specific criteria. Leading amongst these attempts have been various revisions of the American Psychiatric Association's (1980, 1994) *Diagnostic and Statistical Manual* (DSM). As has been the case with both alcohol and drug dependence, the nature of these criteria and the changes that they have undergone in successive revisions in a short space of time reflect the arbitrariness involved in trying to pin excessive gambling down to a condition that can be diagnosed. The third edition (DSM-III) conceived of 'pathological gambling' as a disorder of 'impulse control' (along with klepto-mania, pyromania and 'explosive disorders') whose essential features were described as a, '... failure to resist an impulse, drive or temptation to perform some act ... an increasing sense of tension before committing the act ... [and] ... an experience of either pleasure, gratification or release at the time of committing the act' (American Psychiatric Association, 1980, p. 291, cited by Knapp and Lech, 1987, p. 22). Although 'compulsive gambling' was the lay term, and the one used by GA, it had been felt—quite misleadingly in my view—to be a misnomer since unlike true compulsions gambling was often pleasurable but difficult to resist (Lesieur and Rosenthal, 1991). There were two criteria for pathological gambling in DSM-III, both of which had to be satisfied. First, the individual needed to be, 'chronically and progressively unable to resist impulses to gambling'. Second, gambling had to, 'compromise, disrupt or damage family, personal and vocational pursuits', as indicated by at least three of seven possible harms (Knapp and Lech, 1987).

An important change occurred in the listed criteria between 1980 when DSM-III was published and 1987 when the revised version (DSM-III-R) appeared. The revised criteria had been specifically modelled on alcohol and drug dependence. Hence, whilst harm remained in the form of three items about social, educational, occupational, leisure, financial and legal difficulties, 'pathological gambling' was now considered to be a form of 'dependence' (although it still had the uncertain status of a 'disorder of impulse control not elsewhere classified') and the criterion of impulsiveness was replaced by six items to do with preoccupation, gambling more than intended, the need to increase the size or frequency of bets, restlessness or irritability if unable to gamble, chasing losses and repeated efforts to cut down or stop (Lesieur and Rosenthal, 1991). At least four of the total of nine criteria were required to be satisfied for a diagnosis of pathological gambling. As Lesieur and Rosenthal noted, all criteria, with the exception of 'chasing losses', had their counterpart in the diagnostic criteria for alcohol, heroin, cocaine or other forms of drug dependence. The criteria for 'pathological gambling' according to the 4th ed. of DSM are shown in Table 3.1. Five now had to be met for a diagnosis. A number of the former items had been reworded. One new item had been introduced, item (5), concerning gambling to escape from problems or to relieve unpleasant feeling states, which is particularly interesting because it goes beyond describing an excessive form of behaviour, and specifies a motive for the behaviour.

As Dickerson (1990) has pointed out, this attempt at 'medicalising' excessive gambling has led to serious conceptual problems. Although he believed that the inclusion of 'pathological gambling' in the DSM system had been a crucial factor leading to the development of treatment services and research, he detected, and he is certainly not alone, major difficulties in the attempt to create an objective, diagnostic category. He preferred a broader concept of 'excessive' or 'problematic' gambling, defined as gambling that is frequent, at times uncontrolled, and has resulted in harmful effects. Elsewhere he described such gambling as, 'costly, all engrossing, addictive-like' (Dickerson, 1989, p. 157).

Others have drawn attention to the same kind of definitional problem which Room *et al.* (1996) and others have found in applying criteria for alcohol dependence and misuse. McConaghy (1991), for example, described the case of a 65-year-old woman who sought help and was successfully treated for a gambling problem although she did not satisfy DSM-III-R criteria. She believed her gambling had been excessive for 15 years and had become a 'real problem' in the previous 18 months. She had 'become fascinated' by slot machines which she

Table 3.1 DSM-IV criteria for 'pathological gambling' (*Diagnostic and Statistical Manual of Mental Disorders, American Psychiatric Association, 1994, p. 618*)

A. Persistent and recurrent maladaptive gambling behaviour as indicated by five (or more) of the following:
   (1) Is preoccupied with gambling (e.g. preoccupied with reliving past gambling experiences, handicapping or planning the next venture, or thinking of ways to get the money with which to gamble)
   (2) Needs to gamble with increasing amounts of money in order to achieve the desired excitement
   (3) Has repeated unsuccessful efforts to control, cut back or stop gambling
   (4) Is restless or irritable when attempting to cut down or stop gambling
   (5) Gambles as a way of escaping from problems or of relieving a dysphoric mood (e.g. feelings of helplessness, guilt, anxiety, depression)
   (6) After losing money gambling, often returns another day to get even ('chasing' one's losses)
   (7) Lies to family members, therapists or others to conceal the extent of involvement with gambling
   (8) Has committed illegal acts such as forgery, fraud, theft or embezzlement to finance gambling
   (9) Has jeopardised or lost a significant relationship, job, or educational or career opportunity because of gambling
   (10) Relies on others to provide money to relieve a desperate financial situation caused by gambling

B. The gambling behaviour is not better accounted for by a Manic Episode

had played at a club in her late 30s but had only more recently had the opportunity to play regularly once her children had left home. The amount of her losses had gradually increased, until recently when she had been playing machines six days a week, often taking $100 at a time and staying all afternoon, losing about $2000 a year and $600 in the previous month. She still had sufficient money for household expenses but would have preferred to spend the money helping her children financially and giving her grandchildren gifts and she frequently felt guilty about this. Her husband was now retired, and as he was playing bowls for several hours several times a week he was not complaining about her gambling. At follow-up a month after treatment she described a 'huge improvement'. She had been playing machines no more than once a week, taking $30 at a time and only staying an hour and a half.

Becoña (1993) is another who found the DSM criteria too restrictive in practice. His solution was to employ three categories associated with a decreasingly severe threshold for definition. Four or more symptoms on the DSM-III-R list resulted in a diagnosis of 'pathological gambling' in accordance with others' usage. Two or three of these symptoms were sufficient for 'problem gambling'. Finally, if a person had one or no symptoms on this list but spent more than 25 per cent of personal income or dedicated 2 or more hours a day to gambling, he or she was considered an excessive 'social gambler'. It hardly needs to be pointed out that there is a large measure of arbitrariness about these definitions.

Behind the conceptual gymnastics of those who have tinkered with DSM and other definitions lurks the question whether an activity such as gambling, not in itself the ingestion of a substance, can be truly addictive. Not everyone is convinced. Walker (1989), for example, considered the issue to be unresolved and stated that, '. . . until gambling can be shown to have the properties of a psychological addiction, the effort to generalise theories of addiction to include gambling are likely to remain futile' (p. 198). He acknowledged that for some people gambling becomes a problem in their lives, that for some people gambling is associated with actions that are detrimental to family, friends and society, and that some have difficulty controlling their gambling. He suggested that this may fall short of the full criteria for psychological dependence; for example, gambling may be motivated largely by the desire to win money rather than by the pleasure intrinsic to the activity itself, and the main problem for problem gamblers may simply be losing too much money. This seems to the present author to confuse the What and the Why of addiction. Addiction should be defined in terms of the strength of a person's attachment to the activity as indicated by such criteria as: frequency, regularity and quantity; preoccupation with and priority given to the activity; the subjective feeling of being dependent or addicted; financial, social and legal harm caused by the activity; and difficulty in reducing or giving up despite activity-related harm. The origins of and motives for the behaviour, which in any case are likely to be complex, are another matter.

Griffiths (1996) is one who is clear that 'behavioural addictions' really exist. Cases of 'gambling addiction' that he had encountered in the course of his research (e.g. the young man described in Griffiths, 1993b) satisfied his criteria for addiction. The criteria that he favoured were those put forward by Brown (1993) as being common to a range of drug and non-drug addictions. These criteria are: that the activity has become the most important in the person's life, dominating thinking, feelings and behaviour (salience); reports of a pleasurable change in mood as a consequence of engaging in the activity (euphoria); evidence that increasing amounts of the activity are required to achieve former effects (tolerance); and unpleasant feeling states and/or physical effects when the activity is discontinued or suddenly reduced (withdrawal symptoms); conflict between the addict and those around him/her, or intrapsychic conflict, about the activity (conflict); and a tendency for the activity to be quickly reinstated after even a long period of abstinence or control (relapse).

It should be noted here that Brown (1993), in stating his common criteria for addiction, sought the same advantages accruing to DSM-III-R and DSM-IV, in appealing to such drug-like 'symptoms' as tolerance and withdrawal. It is as if gambling has been admitted as a potential addiction by arguing that it mimics addictive drugs. In this respect, the findings of Wray and Dickerson (1981) are often cited. They reported that 30–50 per cent of a sample of GA members described disturbances of mood or behaviour on ceasing to bet. The most commonly reported symptoms were irritability, restlessness, depressed mood, poor concentration and obsessional thoughts. Wray and Dickerson likened these to withdrawal symptoms reported by excessive drinkers, but Walker (1989) described such symptoms as mild and psychological when compared with drug withdrawal symptoms which were frequently physiological and typically more severe.

Lesieur (1984), himself a sociologist, described some years ago the tensions between the sociological and medical views of pathological gambling. For one thing, contrary to the medical view, social scientists are likely to think of excessive gambling as lying on a continuum, and to view as artificial any dividing line between a category such as 'pathological gambling' and other forms of gambling. Another difference is the relative emphasis that social science is likely to place on social as opposed to individual causes of problems such as excessive gambling. Third, and perhaps the most interesting, is the issue of determinism versus voluntarism. Contrary to such deterministic views as the psychoanalytic idea that excessive gambling is produced by an unconscious 'need to lose' (Bergler, 1958), social scientists were likely to make the opposite assumption that most people are free to choose how to behave. Having carried out the detailed interview studies of 'compulsive gamblers' which resulted in his book, *The Chase*, which was to become a classic in the field, Lesieur was clearly in a personal and scientific quandary over what position to adopt himself. He resolved his dilemma, as the present author would argue anyone with a close knowledge of excessive appetitive behaviour must do, by acknowledging the complexity of the phenomena he was interested in and refusing to countenance either of the extreme and oversimplified views, the medical or the sociological. He argued that the category 'compulsive gambler' does serve a useful purpose so long as it is recognised that it is a 'typification' rather than an absolute category. On the question of determinism versus voluntarism he came to the interesting conclusion that an adequate model of compulsive gambling implies, 'a limited voluntarism (or soft determinism if you prefer). People feel compelled yet still have choices ...' (p. 246). Such a position begs many questions, however, and the present book will return to examine this idea in greater detail in Part II.

It is partly the implication of reduced responsibility for behaviour which lies behind criticisms of the concept of 'compulsive gambler', as it does behind criticisms of any designation implying that excessive appetitive behaviour is the result of a condition over which a person has only limited control. In the case of gambling this debate was nicely illustrated by a leading article which appeared in *The British Medical Journal (BMJ)* for 13 April 1968 which followed a report in *The Times* of 2 April describing how a 'compulsive gambler' had been referred to a medical specialist and treated by the use of brain surgery. The *BMJ* leader objected to the involvement of psychiatry in such cases: 'The gambler enjoys every bit of his "compulsion" ... He may say "I cannot stop", but what he means is that he does not want to stop—the attractions are too great'. These statements go right to the heart of the dilemma presented by the phenomena of excessive appetitive behaviour. How is it possible to posit a 'disease of the will' when the object of a person's so-called compulsion is an activity which constitutes for most people a source of enjoyment? The leader went on to press the distinction between true compulsions and excess behaviours like gambling and drinking:

> ... the rituals of the compulsive [i.e. the true compulsive] are uncontrollable because they arise outside consciousness. The gambler's behaviour is a source of pleasure ... the compulsive's is a burden which makes him

anxious and depressed ... the excessive gambler lacks a sense of responsibility or of duty to society, but again this does not make him a psychiatric casualty. Every man in the street can imagine himself in his place ...

The distinction between true compulsions and excessive behaviours is the same distinction which convinced other psychiatrists (e.g. Moran, 1975) that the expression 'pathological' was preferable in the case of gambling, although it did not necessarily convince them that excessive gambling was outside the realm of psychiatry or the other helping professions. Nor did it so convince a number of readers of the *BMJ* who wrote protesting about the leader (e.g. Carstairs, 1968; Gunn, 1968).

These and other clinicians who have been asked for help by people in distress over their own or a family member's gambling are left in no doubt that it is an over-simplification to state that all gamblers enjoy their gambling and could control their behaviour if they wished. They are as impressed by the accounts which some people give of the difficulty of controlling an activity which has become greatly excessive and damaging as have others been by the accounts of those who wish to control their drinking, drug taking, smoking, eating or exercising, but find they cannot. Words such as 'addiction' or 'dependence', or terms such as 'compulsive gambling', seem to serve the purpose of 'explaining' or at least of describing such apparent paradoxes.

ESTIMATING THE PREVALENCE OF EXCESSIVE GAMBLING

National surveys of adults have been carried out in Australia (Dickerson *et al.*, 1996; Productivity Commission, 1999), New Zealand (Abbott and Volberg, 1996), the USA (Gambling Impact and Behavior Study, 1999) and most recently in Britain (Sproston *et al.*, 2000). In addition, separate surveys have been carried out in many of the states in the USA (Volberg, 1996) and in most of the provinces of Canada (Ladouceur, 1996). The estimated recent prevalence, among adults, of what is usually called 'pathological gambling' in these surveys is remarkably similar, lying in almost all cases between 1 and 2 per cent. There is some variation in the way in which these figures are calculated, but they generally refer to recent period-prevalence (sometimes referring to the period of 6 months prior to the survey, sometimes 12 months) and are based upon answers to a standard, 20-item questionnaire known as the South Oaks Gambling Screen (SOGS) developed by Lesieur and Blume (1987). The items include questions about going back another day to win back money lost, gambling more than intended, being criticised by others over gambling, feeling guilty about gambling, having difficulty stopping gambling, and losing time from work because of it. No less than half the items, however, refer to borrowing money to gamble from various sources (household money, spouse, other relatives or in-laws, credit cards, etc.). In a number of surveys this questionnaire has been administered over the telephone.

In much the same way that DSM definitions of alcohol and drug 'dependence' have been found to be too restrictive, omitting many people with problems relating to their alcohol or drug use (hence the need to add a category of 'alcohol abuse' and 'drug abuse'—see Chapter Four), so have criteria for 'pathological gambling' been found to be too narrow. This has led most survey researchers to adopt two levels of definition: (1) pathological gambling and (2) problem gambling not amounting to pathological gambling. Like all such definitions, the cut-off points are arbitrary. Recent researchers have, however, at least adopted consistent definitions which have been operationalised in terms of SOGS. Five or more affirmative answers out of the 20 possible has generally been taken as an indication of 'probable pathological gambling', and three or four affirmative as an indication of 'problem gambling'. Using these criteria, most surveys in other countries have found a percentage of adults varying between 1.5 and 5 per cent who are classified as 'problem gamblers' in addition to the 1–2 per cent classified as 'pathological gamblers'. For example, Abbott and Volberg's (1996) New Zealand survey, which is one of the best, found a 6-month period-prevalence of 1.2 per cent for pathological gambling plus 2.1 per cent for problem gambling. The Gambling Impact and Behaviour Study (1999) in the USA estimated 2.5 per cent of adults to be 'pathological' or 'problem' gamblers, and the latest Australian survey found 2.3 per cent to have 'significant gambling problems' (Productivity Commission, 1999).

Several surveys have been reported from different regions of Spain (Becoña, 1996). One such was from Seville in the Andalucia region (Legarda *et al.*, 1992), and another was carried out in the seven largest urban centres in the Galicia region (Becoña, 1993). Both employed face-to-face interviews with representative samples of adults in their own homes, the Seville study using a translation of the SOGS questionnaire and the Galicia study using questions based upon the revised version of DSM-III. The estimates from Seville were 1.7 per cent of the population as probable pathological gamblers plus 5.2 per cent problem gamblers. The Galicia estimates were 1.7 per cent pathological gamblers plus 1.6 per cent problem gamblers.

It is interesting to note, however, that only a minority of those identified in such surveys say they feel personally that they have ever had problems with gambling. This was true, for example, of only 4 of the 28 problem gamblers and 5 of the 14 probable pathological gamblers, identified by Volberg and Steadman (1988) in their telephone survey of 1000 representatives of the adult population of New York State, USA.

The sex ratios found in the US and Spanish surveys are of particular interest. These surveys have consistently found that between 30–35 per cent of excessive gamblers are women, a considerably higher percentage than those found amongst treated samples (Volberg and Steadman, 1988, cited a figure of 7 per cent and Legarda *et al.*, 1992, 13 per cent). It is also out of line with the popular stereotype of excessive gamblers as almost entirely male. Similarly, again inconsistent with findings from treatment samples and popular stereotypes, most of these surveys have found the highest rates of excessive gambling among younger adults, aged under 30 or 35.

Hraba and Lee's (1996) results of a random household telephone survey of 1000 adults in the state of Iowa, USA is relevant here. Overall, men reported more gambling than women, but this was due to the greater 'scope' of their gambling rather than to differences in gambling frequency or quantity. A higher percentage of women than men reported any recent bingo gambling (38 versus 22 per cent), and very slightly more women than men reported recent casino gambling (28 versus 25 per cent). Men, on the other hand, more frequently reported betting on games in public (40 versus 19 per cent), sporting events in which people participated themselves (25 versus 9 per cent), other sporting events (40 versus 24 per cent) and betting on the stock market (35 versus 19 per cent). The most frequently reported form of gambling for both sexes was a lottery (75 per cent of men and 73 per cent of women). Although their measure of problem gambling makes it difficult to compare with other studies, they did report that there was no difference in average problem-gambling scores between the sexes.

Duvarci *et al.* (1997) reported the use of SOGS and questions based on DSM criteria in a small sample in Turkey, another country that has experienced considerable liberalisation of laws governing lotteries and casino gambling in the 1980s and 1990s. Several DSM and SOGS items were found to be poor discriminators of high- and low-scoring sub-groups, mostly for cultural reasons. For example, 'not repaid loans' is not itself considered an offence in Turkey where a person's family will usually take responsibility for repaying debts. Similarly, 'borrowing money from spouse' was not discriminating because, according to Duvarci *et al.*, it would be usual for Turkish men to take charge of a wife's income if she had any. Other comments made by these authors are probably relevant elsewhere and not just in Turkey. 'Escaping from problems' or 'relieving dysphoric mood' were mostly not considered causes of gambling. The DSM criterion of escalating amounts of money bet was found to be discriminating, but for most this was attributed to 'chasing losses' rather than to increasing the amount bet in order to 'achieve the desired effect'.

The methodology employed in these surveys has been criticised more generally by Dickerson and Hinchy (1988) on a number of grounds. They argued that techniques such as the SOGS questionnaire may produce false positives, hence over-estimating the prevalence of excessive gambling, by including people who do not gamble very frequently, or who take part in forms of gambling that carry less risk of compulsion (they cited, controversially, lotteries in this regard), or whose gambling problems are no longer current. They also argued that involvement in gambling should be viewed as lying on a continuum of increasing commitment which would suggest a number of different estimates depending upon the level of excess rather than simply one or two estimates of the numbers of people who can be labelled as 'pathological' or 'problem' gamblers.

Consistent with this philosophy, they arrived at a number of estimates of the prevalence of excessive gambling in the Australian Capital Territory based upon a two-stage procedure. At the first stage use was made of two population surveys, one to establish the percentage of the total population engaging in off-course race betting once a week or more, the second to establish a similar figure for poker-machine playing, these thought to be the two commonest forms of betting in the Capital Territory that would give rise to risk of excess. At the second stage more detailed interviews were carried out with two samples of gamblers, one members of the general public who had just placed a bet in an off-course agency, and the other a random sample of poker-machine players attending a social club. Taking into account both the percentage of the population gambling regularly, and the percentages of interviewed gamblers who gave indications of excessive gambling, Dickerson and Hinchy estimated that between 0.25 and 1.73 per cent of the population of the Capital Territory were likely to be excessive gamblers depending upon the strictness of the criterion adopted. They preferred the lower estimate and strictest criterion, which required that a person be betting once or more a week, responded affirmatively to either or both of two questions about losses (losing more than can afford six or more times; losing more than planned on four or five of the last five sessions) and answering affirmatively to three of the following four questions: usually or always chase losses; betting causing debts; want to stop or cut back; have tried stopping.

Lesieur (1994) took up some of these points about survey methods. He agreed that a two-stage method, consisting of screening followed by more detailed interviewing, was the preferred method. He was critical of the use of instruments which had not been so well validated as SOGS; but rather than surveys having over-reported the prevalence of excessive gambling, Lesieur believed it more likely that there has been an under-estimate of prevalence because of more frequent gamblers being unavailable for screening or interview, missing hospital and prison populations and the presence of individual under-reporting and denial.

One of the first surveys of young people and gambling in Britain was Moran's (1987) survey of the head teachers of 30 secondary schools in four London boroughs. Problems related to pupils' behaviour were associated with reported fruit-machine gambling, and the latter was considerably higher in schools which had a greater number of machines and more amusement arcades in their localities. He concluded, as others have done, that the Trade Code of Practice excluding children from access to fruit machines, was evidently not effective. Head teachers' reports suggested that consequences for some children could be very disturbing. One head was quoted as saying:

> Once the habit is established, there is a serious interference with school work and truancy often occurs. This leads to a situation in which the children even resort to extortion, in order to continue to play on the machines. This has led to violence in the playground. Often, the most serious effects are on the home. Parents are distraught because money is stolen from the family and from friends. Ultimately, domestic relationships are eroded because all sense of trust is lost, as a consequence of the incessant stealing and lying.
>
> (Moran, 1987, p. 12)

Griffiths (1990) and Fisher and Griffiths (1995) reviewed several surveys of young people and gambling that had taken place since Moran's (1987) survey of head teachers. Because machine gambling has been legally available to children of any age in the UK, and because this form of gambling appears to have particularly great addiction potential, British surveys have focused upon this form of gambling unlike those in the USA. Particularly large surveys were carried out in the UK by the National Housing and Town Planning Council (1988) and by the Spectrum Children's Trust (1988) (both cited by Griffiths, 1990). The former involved nearly 10 000 school children aged 13–16 from 17 different schools in six different local education authorities, and the latter involved nearly 2500 aged 11–16 from one county in south-west England. These and other surveys suggested, according to Fisher and Griffiths (1995), that at least 65 per cent of adolescents played fruit machines at some point during adolescence, that around 35 per cent had played fruit machines in the last month, and that between 5–10 per cent were regular machine players, playing at least once a week. Fisher's own survey (1995, cited by Fisher and Griffiths, 1995) of nearly 1000 adolescents residing in one seaside town (where the accessibility of amusement arcades to young people was particularly great) suggested that 7 per cent fell into the 'probable pathological gambling' category. Harmful consequences included truancy, stealing, trouble with parents and/or teachers, borrowing money, using lunch money, irritability and poor school work. For example, the National Housing and Town Planning Council Survey (1988) reported 17 per cent of children financing gambling by using lunch money, 7 per cent by stealing, and 6 per cent truanting. The Spectrum Children's Trust Survey (1988) reported 4 per cent stealing, 4 per cent truanting and 2 per cent doing both in order to play fruit machines (Griffiths, 1990).

Although gambling machines were not widely available in public in the same way in the USA at that time, research reported by Jacobs (1989) suggested that large numbers of legally under-age young people who lived within easy access of casinos were gaining access to gambling and that slot-machine playing was the most popular form of gambling. Contrary to the view that excessive gambling was largely an adult problem, surveys of high-school youth in the USA and Canada carried out in the 1980s, and reviewed by Jacobs (1989), suggested that teenagers might be particularly vulnerable. Summarising the results from five such surveys from the USA (involving a total of over 2500 students) and one from Canada (involving over 1500 students), Jacobs found a median 9 per cent of students for whom gambling was reported to have harmed family relationships, 9 per cent reporting that they had committed illegal acts to obtain gambling money or to pay gambling debts, 5 per cent who would like to stop gambling but who could not or who believed gambling was out of control and 5 per cent who met GA or DSM-III criteria for 'compulsive' or 'pathological' gambling. If percentages are based upon only those who had any experience of gambling (roughly half the total number) then they obviously appear greater still (e.g. a median 20 per cent of all those who had gambled at all in the previous 12 months said they would like to stop but could not or believed their gambling was out of control). Dealing in drugs, working for a bookmaker, selling sports cards and shoplifting, were among the more frequent illegal means used by high-school students for obtaining money to gamble or to pay gambling debts. Since the large majority of high-school students represented in these surveys were under 18 years of age, the gambling activities reported by them would themselves have been illegal. Jacobs concluded that as many as 7 million juveniles might have been gambling for money with or without adult awareness or approval in the USA at that time, and that more than 1 million of them were probably experiencing serious gambling-related problems.

More than a third reported their first experience with gambling for money before 11 years of age, and three-quarters or more before they were 15. Since the evidence suggested that legal controls on juvenile gambling were widely flouted, and, furthermore, that parents were nearly always aware of their children gambling and in many cases appeared to condone or encourage it, Jacobs asked how this state of affairs could be accounted for. Perhaps parents believed that legal sanctions would be effective in discouraging any really serious gambling amongst teenagers. Perhaps under-age gambling was simply dismissed as being harmless amusement. Perhaps there was a hesitancy amongst adults to face up to their role in fostering child and teenage gambling. Or perhaps the situation simply reflected delayed awareness on the part of parents and others that teenage gambling was becoming a problem.

In a survey of just over 1000 young people of average age 17 years, drawn from six schools, plus volunteers from first-year students at four campuses at one university, all in the western suburbs of Melbourne, Australia, Moore and Ohtsuka (1997) concluded that gambling problems were at a *low* level, given the high access that young Australians had to different forms of gambling, and the positive social norms regarding gambling that were prevalent. On the other hand, results they provide in their paper might equally be taken the other way. A total of 29 per cent reported often trying to win back money lost in gambling; 14 per cent to having gambled more than was meant at times; 8 per cent to sometimes trying to keep the amount gambled secret from family and friends; 5 per cent wanting to cut down the level of gambling but finding it difficult to do so; 4.5 per cent having on occasions taken time off school or work to gamble; and 3 per cent endorsing the item, 'to some extent, I have a gambling problem'. Boys were significantly more likely than girls to report playing cards for money, betting on pool games, and horses or dogs, on sports, betting at casino gaming tables and playing poker machines at sports clubs. Girls, on the other hand, were more likely than boys to play bingo or to buy lottery tickets. Buying lottery tickets was overall the most frequently reported form.

SOCIAL POLICY ISSUES AND GAMBLING

Whatever the rights and wrongs on the issue of whether excessive gambling constitutes any sort of entity or condition, and if so what such an entity should be called, and how prevalent it is, it remains a fact that the availability of opportunities for gambling represents for society the same sort of behavioural control problem which alcohol presents. The control of gambling activities is as perennial a concern for national governments as has been the control of alcohol consumption. The difficulty of getting legislation right is well illustrated for gambling in recent British history by the permissive Betting and Gaming Act of 1960 and the quickly following and relatively restrictive Betting, Gaming and Lotteries Act of 1964 and Gaming Act of 1968. There is a parallel here with the reversals of the Acts of 1729, 1736 and 1751 which were aimed at the control of the sale of alcohol (see Chapter Two).

The last years of the 20th century were ones of decreasing restriction. Fisher and Griffiths (1995) stated, 'The last decade has witnessed an unprecedented deregulation of gambling in numerous jurisdictions throughout the world' (p. 239). The support of governments combined with advances in electronic machine technology have resulted in a boom in the gaming-machine industry with machines displacing traditional table games in casinos as well as proliferating in places such as amusement arcades, cafes, airports, bars, restaurants and corner shops. This story is repeated around Europe. In Spain gambling by any means was legalised only as recently as 1977 and slot-machine gambling was legalised in 1981. Becoña *et al.* (1995) reported that there had been nearly half a million such machines installed in leisure centres, casinos, bingo halls and almost every bar and restaurant in the country. In the last few years increasingly strict legislation had emerged, as a result, they believed, of the growing social outcry in the face of gambling-related problems. In 1989, only 8 years after the initial Royal Decree legalising slot machines, a further decree restricted the number of machines in bars, cafes, hotels and similar establishments, and increased taxation. Only 3 years after the second Royal Decree, a parliamentary report was proposing greater control on under-age use of slot machines, smaller prizes, research into the connection between gambling and crime, and more support for people with gambling-related problems.

Germany is another country where a rapid growth in opportunities for gambling, especially on machines, has led to attempts at restrictive legislation. Meyer (1992) reported a seven- to eight-fold increase in amusement arcades offering machine gambling in Western Germany between 1974 and 1989. The Gambling Decree, regulating the operation of gambling machines, permitted no more than 10 machines in amusement arcades and two in pubs and restricted the stake per game to no more than 0.30 DM, the running time per game to 15 seconds, and the maximum winnings per game to 3 DM. These regulations were designed to protect the gambler from an 'excessive exploitation of the gambling urge' (cited by Fabian, 1995), but were successfully circumvented by the gaming industry by, for example, designing 'special' games allowing the playing of a series of games in quick succession with doubling of stakes from game to game, and dividing arcades into mini-gambling halls so that practically any number of machines could be installed (Meyer, 1992; Fabian, 1995). Following public debate about the dangers of 'pathological gambling', the German Bunderstag called for measures that would lessen the incentive for gamblers on slot machines. These were in the form of voluntary self-restricting 'agreements' by the industry. They included limitations on 'special' games, the introduction of a compulsory break of 3 minutes after 1 hour of uninterrupted gambling, prevention of simultaneous gambling on more than two machines, and a requirement for notices to be placed on the front of slot machines about the dangers of frequent gambling and about the possibilities of treatment. These measures were, however, described as 'only cosmetic' by Meyer (1992), and 'probably negligible in effect' according to Fabian (1995).

The report of the latest Australian survey (Productivity Commission, 1999) begins:

> But even by Australian standards, the recent proliferation of gambling opportunities and the growth in the gambling industries have been remarkable. Liberalisation of access to innovative poker machines and casinos has led this expansion, fuelled in part by the revenue needs of state and territory governments.
>
> (Productivity Commission, 1999, p. xv)

The report concluded that the prevalence of problem gambling was directly related to the accessibility of gambling, particularly gaming machines. Similarly, the Gambling Impact and Behavior Study (1999), particularly concerned with the growth of casino gambling in the USA, found that the availability of a casino within 50 miles of people's homes was associated with approximately double the prevalence of problem and pathological gambling. From Canada, Room *et al.* (1999) reported the results of surveys carried out in the Niagara Falls area before and after the opening of a new casino, and compared results with those from similar surveys carried out elsewhere in Ontario Province. They concluded that the opening of the casino had resulted in more gambling by local residents and a increase in reported gambling problems. The latter were largely manifest in people's private and family lives, and public support for the casino was strong.

Disagreement and conflict at the level of public policy has also been evident in Britain. The Royal Commission on Betting, Lotteries and Gaming (1949–1951) made the following recommendation about 'fruit machines':

> The particular danger we see in this type of machine is that, since it does not require the intervention of an attendant in order to give the prize, it is capable of a rapidity of turnover which would render the element of gambling, even within the strict limits which we have set, no longer trivial. We, therefore, recommend the provision of machines of this type should be illegal.
> (Royal Commission on Betting, Lotteries and Gaming, 1949–1951, para. 433, cited by Moran, 1987, p. 12)

This recommendation was not accepted, however, and the Betting and Gaming Act (1960) and the Gaming Act (1968) legalised gaming machines with the comparatively permissive regulations controlling them which have been in operation ever since. Machines available at the time were thought not to present any serious problems compared with uncontrolled commercial gaming casinos. As the Royal Commission on Gambling (1976–1978) pointed out:

> The original conception of amusements with prizes was that the player would be concerned less with the prospect of a win than with the pastime itself, to which the chance of winning a small prize would add little more than an agreeable fillip.
> (Royal Commission on Gambling, para. 23.1, *Final Report* 1978, cited by Moran, 1987, p. 23)

In the mid-1980s, however, the Home Office responded to increasing public concern by undertaking:

> ... a preliminary investigation into the prevalence and character of amusement machine playing by young people under sixteen with a view to establishing the existence or otherwise of a significant social problem requiring legislation ... [which concluded] ... the scale of the problem does not appear to warrant legislation. Very few young people are at risk of becoming

dependent upon amusement machines and no evidence is found of any association between the playing of machines and delinquency.
(Graham, 1988, pp. i, iii, cited by Fisher, 1991, pp. 218–219)

This report, and its conclusions, were roundly criticised by Fisher (1991) and Griffiths (1991) for failing to review the existing literature comprehensively, showing a disproportionately critical attitude to that research that *had* concluded that a problem existed and for carrying out its own research which devoted very few questions to fruit-machine use and which did not take even elementary steps to ensure participants of confidentiality.

A number of authors have commented upon the way in which governments have encouraged and profited from the recent growth in gambling. For example, Becoña *et al.* (1995) could be writing of governments in a number of countries when they wrote that permissive legislation was justified by the Spanish government on grounds that it provided entertainment to millions of tourists, a boost to government revenue and a discouragement to Spaniards gambling their money abroad. Shaffer *et al.* (1994) suggested that young people in the USA were encouraged to gamble by the explicit endorsements of government and church, through advertising and product promotions, and the absence of warnings from public-health officials. They pointed out that in Massachusetts, where they were carrying out their work, for the first time this century high-school students had lived their entire lives with legalised gambling, and this gambling was state endorsed, state provided and state marketed. Gambling had become 'normalised'.

In the USA McMillen (1996) observed a shift since the 1970s from a predominant focus on the, '... dysfunctional and immoral aspects of gambling ...' (p. 8) towards a greater emphasis on, '... economic and legal-administrative factors associated with the smooth operation of a newly legal industry' (p. 8). This was reflected, for example, in the writings of Eadington (e.g. Eadington and Cornelius, 1991, cited by McMillen, 1996) on casino policy in North America, built, as McMillen saw it, on a stand in favour of commercialisation, a laissez-faire approach to casino development and a limited conception of the role of the State in controlling people's opportunities to gamble or in coercing them to forms of lifestyle behaviour thought to be healthy or moral. McMillen's (1996) analysis led him to the view that the days in which gambling was seen, unlike other leisure activities, in moral or ethical terms, and an assumption that the State had a responsibility to intervene to restrict gambling in the interests of the common good, had given way in recent times to a much greater emphasis on gambling as an acceptable leisure activity, to which people have a right, contributing positively to the leisure and tourist industries, and increasingly under the commercial control of transnational companies. As he put it, '... traditional gambling cultures are being colonised by global gambling culture ...' (p. 23).

Dombrink (1996), too, commented on the remarkable increase in the scale of legal gambling in the USA in the 1980s (a growth rate in double figures each year during that decade), the diversification of gambling activities during the same time and the way in which gambling had avoided both much moral censure and being the object of much public-health concern. Dombrink considered this to require explanation, in view of the ambivalence with which gambling had been viewed in the USA historically, and in view of the moral 'backlash' of the 1980s in the USA which led to various moral 'wars' on other 'vices' such as abortion, prostitution, pornography, homosexuality and drugs. State lotteries in particular, starting with New Hampshire in 1964, had spread virtually throughout the USA, and much, careful public-relations work on the part of legal gambling operators had contributed to a view of gambling as a comparatively harmless, leisure activity which, in the process, made a very positive contribution to State funds (the idea of State-operated gambling being more acceptable than the State offering drug clinics or brothels).

The perennial debate over the pros and cons of gambling is further illustrated by bingo and the lottery in the UK. Of the forms of gambling available in Britain in recent times, bingo is the one most commonly perceived to be associated with women (McMillen, 1996 expressed surprise that gambling had been so little considered by feminist researchers and writers). In fact, Dixey's (1996) analysis of bingo suggested that it has been associated both with gender and with social class, perhaps more strongly with the latter. For many working-class women, from the 1960s onwards, bingo halls provided a safe and congenial place to socialise. Indeed, so ordinary a feature of life did going to bingo become, that 42 per cent of women surveyed by Dixey and Lean (cited by Dixey, 1996) in the early 1980s, when asked whether bingo was regarded as a form of gambling, said that it was not. According to Dixey, the commercialisation of bingo, part of a long-term trend from Victorian times onwards towards the commercialisation of working-class leisure, came about as a result of a loophole in the 1960 Betting and Gaming Act. The Gaming Act of 1968, which established the Gaming Board and reintroduced a number of restrictions, recognised that bingo had become a very popular game, especially among housewives, and that provided players were not exposed to the temptations of 'hard gaming', it was appropriate to take, '... a benevolent view of bingo provided it remained a neighbourly form of gaming played for modest stakes ...' (Gaming Board report, 1969, cited by Dixey, 1996, p. 138).

Comments on recent British experience of the inauguration of the National Lottery, have been provided by Miers (1996) and by Creigh-Tyte (1997). In the 16th and 17th centuries, State lotteries were used to raise funds for London's water supply, to pay the salaries of civil servants and to finance the colonisation of America. Later, lotteries were used to fund public works including the establishment of the British Museum and many North American universities. Despite this role of public lotteries in funding good works in earlier times, a Select Committee report in 1808 was highly critical of them, and they were abolished in Britain in 1826, remaining illegal until the 1930s. Although charitable lotteries were legal from the 1930s onwards, these remained small scale and by the early 1990s Britain was virtually alone among Western countries in having no national State lottery. The 1978 Royal Commission on Gambling recommended one, but it was not until the National Lottery Act of 1993 that it became a reality. Tickets for the first weekly lotto game were sold in November 1994, with the first National Lottery scratchcard introduced in March 1995. A second, mid-week, lotto draw was introduced in February 1997. Exceeding all expectations, National Lottery sales reached totals of £5.4 and £4.7 billion in 1995–1996 and 1996–1997 respectively. According to survey research published by the Office of the National Lottery (OFLOT, 1996, cited by Creigh-Tyte, 1997) almost two-thirds of the adult population had played the lottery within the last week, around 30 million Britains were regular players, and the number of outlets selling tickets exceeded 24 000. Concern has been expressed about the large size of individual jackpots and 'rollovers', the likelihood that the lottery operates like a regressive tax, with poorer people spending a much higher proportion of their income (LeGrand, 1995) and the difficulty of preventing young people from betting on the lottery under the minimum permitted age of 16 (Fisher and Balding, 1996, cited by Creigh-Tyte, 1997).

The official, British government view is that, provided certain controls are exercised (the minimum age; no door-to-door or street sales; no games that involve interactive play), then the lottery represents a harmless, even 'tasteful', form of leisure pursuit providing very suitable means of raising money for national good causes which otherwise might have a lower priority call on public funds. The vision was that the National Lottery should be:

> ... amongst the best in the world, capturing the imagination of the nation with a series of fun and simple, high quality games. The Lottery should be seen as a tasteful and acceptable way to win money, whilst generating money for the National Lottery Distribution Fund (NLDF). It must be run in a fair and trustworthy manner that is beyond reproach.
>
> (OFLOT, 1994, cited by Miers, 1996, p. 344)

Indeed, Miers detected an intention to promote the lottery as hardly constituting gambling at all. The following is telling:

> The National Lottery will be of a different nature from the kind of gambling which is legislated for by the Home Office under existing gambling laws. It is intended to be addressed to a different market and not to be thought of as gambling in the same way. In that respect, the fact that it is absolutely a matter of chance, and there is no skill involved in the decision which the individual player takes, is a critical one.
>
> (National Heritage Committee, 1993, cited by Miers, 1996, pp. 366–367)

Not only does the above quote display a staggering misunderstanding of the nature of gambling, but it completely fails to address the likely differences in impact of the now twice-weekly lotto game and scratchcards. Since the latter involve much shorter odds and allow repeated play, it might be likened to a paper gaming machine, and the operator might be accused of, '... eliding the distinction between soft and hard gaming ...' (Miers, 1996, p. 346).

A further, and potentially even more harmful, effect of the introduction of the National Lottery, noted by both Miers and by Creigh-Tyte, is the likely 'ratchet-ting-up' effect on gambling generally in the UK. Miers predicted further liberal-isation of all forms of gambling, not only on the ground of unfair competition, but also because the Government would become increasingly dependent upon lottery funds, which experience in other countries suggests tend to decline after a period of initial enthusiasm, leading to pressure to introduce more stimulating games and in other ways to remove restriction. In the wake of the National Lottery, football-pools promoters in Britain, for example, had already succeeded in liberalising the rules under which they had operated for many years: reducing the minimum allowable age to 16, permitting newsagents to collect the stakes as well as to distribute pools coupons, to introduce jackpots and to allow rollovers.

The National Lottery and its after-effects represent just the latest in a long history, going back to the Crusades when King Richard I forbade gambling among soldiers below the rank of Knight (McMillen, 1996) and earlier, of society struggling, in the case of gambling, with the same kind of dilemma that is presented by all appetites that can cross the boundary between moderation and excess. Society's problem is how to arrive at a balanced response which helps to minimise the dangers of immoderate use while at the same time detracting as little as possible from the enjoyment associated with the moderate use by the majority of citizens. The problem for us is how to explain how an activity such as gambling can give rise to the serious excess to which so many historians, biographers and researchers have been ample witness.

CHAPTER FOUR

Excessive Drug Taking

While the marijuana habit leads to physical wreckage and to mental decay, its effects upon character and morality are even more devastating. The victim frequently undergoes such degeneracy that he will lie and steal without scruple; he becomes utterly untrustworthy and often drifts into the underworld where, with his degenerate companions, he commits high crimes and misdemeanours.

> (International Narcotic Education Association, USA, 1936, cited by Edwards, 1968)

Addiction to cocaine is rapid and overwhelming, rendering the user power-less over the choice to abstain or moderate ...

> (Miller *et al.*, 1989, p. 390, cited by Ditton and Hammersley, 1996, p. 10)

... anyone who says coke is addictive is talking bullshit. It's a very greedy sort of drug, that's all ...

> (A participant in Ditton and Hammersley's research, 1996, p. 58)

In the popular imagination of the second half of the 20th century, 'drugs' are not in the same category as drink and gambling, and certainly not of the same kind as eating, exercise and sex, all of which, certainly the last three, are acceptable in moderation, although they carry the risk of excess for a minority. In fact, even a cursory examination of the literature demonstrates the variety of forms of drug and drug taking in the present day, the variety of forms of use of the same drug at different historical periods, and differences in attitudes, reactions and attempts to control drug taking at different times and in different places. Many of the same questions about the nature of excessive behaviour, of definitions of 'dependence' and of the appropriateness of different forms of control and treatment, which were raised in the cases of drinking and gambling, arise again with drug taking. The study of drugs, in addition to the drug 'alcohol' which has been given a chapter to itself, is vital in order to establish a psychological theory which does justice to the full range of excessive appetitive behaviours. The topic is a vast one and this chapter will focus on three classes of drug which represent the diversity of the field and raise particular questions for us: the opiates, tobacco, and stimulants, particularly cocaine. Reference will also be made, however, to a number of other types of drug, including cannabis, benzodiazepines and anabolic steroids, which present particular challenges for a view of excessive appetites.

THE OPIATES

Whatever arguments there may be about the real nature of 'addiction', there can be no disputing troublesome opiate taking as a social fact; something described by many who believe they have experienced it themselves and the existence of which is acknowledged by countless others. The story starts with opium.

As has been the case with most troublesome drugs, opium was formerly used with approval as a medicine. It had been used in the relief of pain, to induce sleep and calm, and to control such common symptoms as cough and diarrhoea, and had been so used for hundreds of years. Laudanum, a mixture of opium and alcohol, was introduced by the English physician Thomas Sydenham late in the 17th century, and it was to laudanum that one of the most celebrated self-confessed drug takers of all time, Thomas de Quincey, became 'enslaved'. His, *The Confessions of an English Opium Eater*, first published in the *London Magazine* in 1821, is thought to have been of much influence in the slow development of awareness during the 19th century that opium taking might be extremely difficult to leave off. He first used opium, on the recommendation of a friend, to relieve unpleasant facial pain which had lasted for several weeks. In his confessions he sung the praises of opium not only for its ability to relieve his pain but also for the positive enjoyment which the drug brought him; so much so in fact that some have accused him since of being responsible for initiating many others into opiate use. It appears from his confessions that de Quincey took laudanum only occasionally, recreationally, and for pleasure, for a period of nearly 10 years. For much of this time he confined his use to one or two occasions a week, and used it to enhance the pleasure of solitary walks around London or visits to the opera.

At this stage he extolled opium's advantages over alcohol. Alcohol's enjoyment was 'gross and mortal', opium's 'luxuries' were 'divine'; the pleasure from alcohol intoxication, quickly declining, was a 'flickering flame' compared with the 'steady and equable glow' from opium; wine 'disorders the mental faculties, ... robs a man of his self-possession, ... unsettles the judgement ...'; opium, on the other hand, 'communicates serenity and equipose to all the faculties ...' (pp. 213, 383).

Only later, after these years of intermittent and moderate use, did de Quincey become, '... a regular and confirmed opium-eater' (p. 398). Following a recurrence of stomach pain which he had had as a youth, he started to take opium daily and increased his dose eventually to 8000 drops of laudanum a day. It was only then that he became aware of the 'addicting' properties of the mixture which he had formerly seen in such a favourable light. He wrote of, '... the morbid growth upon the opium-eater of his peculiar habit' (p. 417), and of, '... the accursed chain which fettered me' (p. 211). The conflict which he described puts his experience on a par with that of Lilian Roth, Dostoevsky and others who have struggled to control excessive appetites.

Enormous changes have taken place in society's reactions to opiate use since the early 19th century and it is of the utmost importance to appreciate that the social context surrounding it is utterly different for a modern street addict than it was for de Quincey partaking of his laudanum. De Quincey lived at a time when opium taking was tolerated and quite unrestricted, a state of affairs diametrically opposite to that which exists now. Great detail was added to our knowledge of opium use and reactions to it in the 19th century by the historical research of Berridge. She commented that, prior to the Pharmacy Act of 1868:

> Imported opium, mostly Turkish in origin, could be bought almost any-
> where—not just from chemists, druggists, or pharmacists, but in village
> shops, from grocers, general stores, and corner shops in the back streets
> of the growing industrial cities.
>
> (Berridge, 1977, p. 78)

Increasing concern was expressed about working-class opium use in particular, and use by women was as much cause for concern as use by men. Even those who were not prepared to accept that regular opium use was widespread among adults were concerned about the dosing of infants with opium-containing preparations such as Godfrey's Cordial, Daffy's Elixir, Dalby's Carminative and other 'children's draughts' (Berridge, 1978).

Of particular relevance to the theme of this book is Berridge's (1979) attempt to trace the development of concepts of 'addiction' in the 19th and early 20th centuries. She pointed out that although the early part of the 19th century was characterized by increasing concern about the consumption of opium and the harm it might be causing, there was a general lack of medical conceptualisations, and certainly very little formal use of the notion of 'addiction'. Although de Quincey's confessions, and particularly the comments which they contained on opium eating by Manchester cotton workers, were important in bringing the subject to public attention, they were not much discussed in medical circles until late in the 19th century when the concept of 'addiction' was developing. Early medical involvement in fact was prompted much more by concern about infant mortality, about the open sale and availability of poisons and about the question of whether opium taking shortened life. De Quincey, incidentally, who declared his habit, was refused life insurance on the latter grounds by 14 companies in succession.

This stage in the development of medical thinking gradually gave way to the emergence of a concept of 'addiction' that was given great impetus by the increasing use of the hypodermic, allowing for the accurate and rapid administration of a narcotic, in the later part of the century, and awareness of the existence of 'morphinism', particularly amongst doctors themselves. Morphine, the active ingredient of opium, had been isolated in 1803 and became available in pure form towards the end of the century (Kurland, 1978). Nevertheless, as Berridge noted, the new concept of addiction was a hybrid theory incorporating both medical and moral ideas. For one thing, it had close links with both temperance and anti-opium agitation. Hence the new addiction view incorporated much of the moral perspective of the temperance movement and in many ways the new approach was harsher, combining as it did moral and medical condemnation. The two were linked in the concept of 'inebriety'. According to Kerr, then President of the Society for the Study of Inebriety, there was a disease of inebriety allied to insanity and characterized by an overpowering impulse or craving for the oblivion associated with 'narcotism'. The disease took various forms depending upon the drug employed: alcoholomania, opiomania, morphinomania, chloralo-mania and chlorodynomania (Kerr, 1889, cited by Berridge, 1979, p. 76). Whether later, 20th century, concepts of 'addiction' and 'dependence' have succeeded in unravelling the moral and medical strands is a debatable question. As we shall see in later chapters there are many who believe that they have not.

British medical opinion was influenced, too, by the campaign against Britain's involvement in supplying opium to China, which provides a fascinating 19th-century example of the dynamics of national and international control of a substance that readily gives rise to excess. Opium smoking in China, as opposed to opium eating or opium drinking which were the customs in India and elsewhere, spread to such an extent as a result of the East India Company's operations that in 1729 the Imperial Court in Peking banned the importation of opium except under licence for medical use. Penalties for dealing in the drug were to include the wearing of a large wooden collar, known as a cangue, and the receipt of up to a hundred strokes of the bamboo. Just as in the West 200 years later, however, this edict did not prevent continued trading and the entry into China of large quantities of opium from British India, mainly through Canton. By the 1830s a member of the Imperial Court, Hsü Nai-Chi, who had lived in Canton, was recommending legalisation on familiar pragmatic grounds:

> The law as it stood, Hsü argued, had demonstrably failed. It was no good saying that this was because it was unenforceable. As the ban had failed to prevent the drug from entering the country, it could not be said to do any good; but demonstrably it did immense harm, breeding crime, banditry, extortion and blackmail.
>
> (Inglis, 1976, p. 111)

Lin, the newly appointed Commissioner for Canton, however, favoured a twin-pronged attack, equally familiar to us now, of tightening of controls on illegal imports plus prevention, particularly directed at the young:

> To facilitate detection of opium-smoking among the young, who were most in need of protection, schoolmasters were to report any student who to their knowledge took the drug; and also to form the students into groups of five, each being responsible for the good behaviour of the other four ... Members of the public who in their own interest admitted their addiction would be helped to give up the drug.
>
> (Inglis, 1976, p. 117)

Heroin was first synthesized in 1874 and interestingly, in view of the present-day use of methadone in the treatment of heroin users, it was itself used for a while in the treatment of 'morphinism'. Indeed, for a few years heroin was welcomed as a useful medication for a wide range of conditions. However, the medical use of heroin naturally gave rise to cases of 'heroinism' much as morphine had resulted in cases of 'morphinism' before it.

The history of Western reaction to heroin in the 20th century illustrates a number of points. It shows the intense concern of lawmakers with the control of a drug believed to be highly dangerous, but also illustrates how divergent may be the responses in different countries. The USA has led the rest of the world in a harsh approach (Brecher, 1972; Musto, 1991; Humphreys and Rappaport, 1993). The first local statutes regulating the formerly unrestricted use of opiates in the United States were passed in San Francisco in 1875 and New York in 1904, but the real turning point, according to most later writers, was the Harrison Narcotic Act of 1914. The Act required the registering and taxing of all producers, importers and sellers of opiates, but was not intended as a prohibition law and was not to apply to a, '... physician ... in the course of his professional practice ...'. The latter, however, was interpreted by law-enforcement agents to mean the treatment of disease, and 'addiction' did not qualify as such. There had in fact been a number of clinics, more than 40 in number and mainly private, set up for the treatment and legal dispensing of opiates to 'addicts'. These had come under criticism for their lack of treatment orientation and what was seen as their maintenance of 'morbid appetites'. Many doctors were prosecuted under the new Act, all the clinics had closed within 10 years of the Act being passed, and hence the Act became a de facto Act of prohibition.

How society should respond to the continued, and in recent years increasing, supply of substances with addiction potential is, as one director of an Australian drug treatment service put it, 'a never ending story' (Wodak, 1990). In the same year that he was writing in the Australian journal, *Drug and Alcohol Review*, Prime Minister Thatcher was telling The World Ministerial Summit to Reduce the Demand for Drugs and to Combat the Cocaine Threat which she convened in London, 'I can assure you that our Government will never legalise illicit drugs'. During the Conference, *The Times*, in an editorial entitled, Drugs and Realism (10 April 1990), stated, in contrast, 'Few observers ... are in doubt that somehow, the next decade will see at least part of this international business [the drugs trade] brought within legal control' (News and Views, 1990). The matter is in fact a thoroughly complicated one. The range of drugs under consideration is wide, including substances as different as heroin, cocaine and cannabis, and the availability of these and other drugs in different strengths is an ever-changing pattern (Farrell and Strang, 1990). Whether that strengthens or weakens the case for legalisation is not clear. The point for present purposes is the fact of the controversy itself. Substances that are highly pleasurable to take, create difficulties, and these difficulties are played out at the level of mental conflict for individuals who become addicted, families who are affected by addiction, and citizens and policy makers who must decide how to maximise the public good and minimise harm. It is as difficult for societies to know how to cope with the phenomenon of addiction as it is for individuals who are personally affected by it.

The contrasting ways in which problems of excessive illicit drug use can be managed is well illustrated by what was happening in the Netherlands and the USA, two countries where very different attitudes prevailed. The contrast between the Dutch and US approaches was nicely brought out in the July 1994 issue of *Addiction* which carried a report of an interview with a drug user attending a drug-treatment facility in Utrecht at the time of a conference on the theme of 'harm reduction' that was being held in the Netherlands and which had brought in a number of international experts. 'Jan', the drug user, explained that he was on prescribed methadone, but was still regularly using other drugs intravenously and was still involved in crime. He described the kind of ambivalence about continuing or giving up drug use which is such a hallmark of excessive appetites of all kinds. He stated that he wanted to stop using drugs and reorient his life but had tried to detoxify a number of times without success, and hence was not now very hopeful. He was critical of the policy of US methadone programmes when it was explained to him that they would not be so tolerant towards continued, illicit drug use and a deviant lifestyle (Ball and van der Wijngaart, 1994).

Particularly interesting were the two appraisals of the interview, one US (Ball) the other Dutch (van der Wijngaart), with which the article ended, and a number of invited commentaries that followed. The predominant view from the USA was that Jan was stuck and unmotivated and that the high level of tolerance showed by the Dutch treatment facility might be encouraging this. For example:

> Low threshold programs were originally intended to provide easy entry into the formal treatment system ... it has emerged that many, perhaps most, patients become stuck at the low threshold level, where they receive services which improve their quality of life but do not have to make the major behavioural changes required by more rehabilitative regimes ... experienced addicts (e.g. Jan) ... are likely to get trapped at the low threshold.
>
> (Reuter, 1994, p. 807)

This line was supported by a commentary from Germany which went so far as to say:

> Could it be that the therapist [in the Dutch programme] supports the client's opinion that drug taking and stealing is a normal facet of social behaviour ... Self-help abstinence groups use the term co-dependence for people in the environment of addicts who pretend to help them, but in reality support the maintenance of addicted behaviour ...
>
> (Bühringer, 1994, p. 811–812)

The Dutch view that their approach maintained contact with users with continued opportunities for education and change was supported by a commentary from Australia:

> ... the Dutch appear to have been far more successful in attracting and retaining a large proportion of persons dependent on heroin in methadone treatment ... [An] important aspect of harm reduction is the emphasis on

trying to prevent patients from irreparably damaging their health, social or
legal status in the knowledge that sooner or later many drug users find their
own way of stopping successfully.

(Wodak, 1994, p. 803–804)

Because, even now, the proportion of people who use illicit drugs excessively is a
small minority of the population, and because of the illicit and therefore partly
clandestine nature of the activity, producing sound estimates of the size of the
problem is extremely difficult. On the basis of the available evidence, however,
Hartnoll (1994) estimated that there were between one half and 1 million people
in Europe who were 'dependent' and/or 'problematic' opiate users at the beginning
of the 1990s. This corresponds to a rate of between 150 and 300 per 100 000 of the
population. His estimate for the USA was about twice that rate. These overall
figures mask large geographical variations. In Europe rates appeared to be much
higher in some countries than in others (high in Italy, Spain and Switzerland and
lowest in Finland, Ireland and Sweden) with higher rates in major cities than
elsewhere: a particularly high rate was reported for Glasgow, for example, and
in the USA estimates for New York City were 6–10 times higher than the national
average. According to Hartnoll problematic opiate use in both continents was
more common in areas of lower socioeconomic status and social marginalisation.
Marked gradients of drug problems according to the wealth or poverty of areas in
the city had been found, for example, in Barcelona and Dublin. In all studies of
problematic opiate use males had outnumbered females by a ratio varying from
2 : 1 to 4 : 1.

The national UK household survey referred to in Chapter Two (Meltzer *et al.*,
1994) found 2.2 per cent of 16 to 64-year-olds (2.9 per cent of men, 1.5 per cent of
women) to have been 'dependent' on drugs other than alcohol and tobacco within
the last year, and a reporting agency study in three inner-London areas estimated
rates of 'problem' drug use among 15 to 49-year-olds to be 3.1, 3.3 and 3.6 per
cent (Hickman *et al.*, 1999). The latter study used what is known as the 'capture–
recapture' method of estimating prevalence by obtaining information from two
separate sources and calculating the likely prevalence from the two numbers
found and the degree of overlap (e.g. if two sources, such as specialist-
treatment-agency records and police-arrest records, each report a large number
of 'cases' but have only a small proportion in common, then the true prevalence
is likely to be comparatively large). Figures produced by these British studies are
for all 'drugs' and only a proportion relate to opiates. In one of the inner-London
areas (with an overall estimated prevalence of 3.1 per cent), the figure for opiates
alone was calculated at 1.3 per cent.

Because social and cultural influences are so powerful in the case of nearly all
excessive appetite behaviours, and particularly so in the case of drug use, the
picture is a constantly and rapidly changing one. There are changes in the social
groups most involved in problem drug use, the types of drugs being used and the
methods of administering them. The recent history of illicit drug use in western
Europe illustrates the influence of rapidly changing markets and fashions, and the
effects that the passage of a few years, or a few hundred miles, can have upon the
opportunities and risks to which people are exposed. This is clear for Britain in the

contrast between the heroin epidemic of the early to mid-1980s, which involved mainly heroin injecting, and poly-drug, more usually oral, use in the early 1990s, with evidence of a resurgence of heroin taking in the late 1990s, this time more often involving smoking ('chasing') (Parker *et al.*, 1998).

Spain provides a particularly good example of the spread of different drug habits within one country. Probably influenced by the greater availability of brown heroin, from Iraq and Pakistan, more appropriate for smoking than injecting, Spain, like Britain and a few other European countries, experienced in the 1980s and 1990s a rapid increase in the habit of taking heroin by a form of smoking or inhaling known as 'chasing the dragon' or 'Chinesing', which originated in Hong Kong and spread in the 1960s, 1970s and 1980s to a number of south and south-east Asian countries, but not to countries elsewhere in the world (Strang *et al.*, 1997). What is particularly interesting, however, is the spread of this habit across Spain during the 1980s and 1990s from its origins in the Canary Islands and the south-west of peninsula Spain to Cataluña in the north-east. De la Fuente *et al.* (1997) reported the results of a survey of 900 regular heroin users, half recruited from treatment centres and half street users not recruited via treatment, a third recruited in each of three cities, Seville in the south-west, Madrid in the centre of the country and Barcelona in the north-east. The route of administration of heroin depended far more upon which city a person lived in than upon individual factors, and it varied significantly by date of first heroin use. In Seville, smoking was already, with injecting, one of the two most popular first routes of administration of the drug, even for those who started taking heroin in 1980 or earlier. By the early 1990s, smoking had taken over as the first route of administration for almost all new users. At the other extreme of the country, smoking, virtually unheard of as a first route of administration in 1980 or earlier, was still a minority preference in the early 1990s, sniffing and injecting still being more popular. The greatest increase in smoking had occurred in Madrid where it was the least popular first route for administration in 1980 or earlier, but by far the most popular by the early 1990s.

Another illustration of how quickly and dramatically the scene can change is provided by a study of the drugs associated with drug-related deaths in Edinburgh and Glasgow in 1991 and 1992 (Hammersley *et al.*, 1995). A four-fold increase in such deaths occurred in Glasgow between 1991 and 1992, without any comparable increase occurring in neighbouring Edinburgh. It appeared on analysis that most of the extra deaths occurring in 1992 in Glasgow could be attributed to an increased use of dangerous combinations of heroin, tranquillisers (often injected) and alcohol.

But rapid changes in opiate consumption habits were certainly not confined to western Europe. Just one example comes from Wu *et al.*'s (1996) description of the drug scene in a remote, rural area in Asia. They interviewed around 1500 young men (aged 18 to 29), over 400 of whom were drug users, in one county in Yunnan Province, in south-west China, bordering on Myanmar. They reported that between the 1950s and 1979, when China's opening-up to the West made it easier for traffickers to smuggle heroin over the border from Myanmar, China had been very successful in controlling opium use. Since then, the use of both opium and heroin had increased dramatically. The numbers of documented drug users known to the county police department had increased from 3000 opium users in 1982 to 6500 in 1994, and from 56 heroin users in 1986 to 1855 in 1994. Reconstructing the drug histories of their interviewees, Wu *et al.* were able to confirm the rapid rise in the rate of the taking up of opium or heroin use by young men in the county in the late 1980s.

TOBACCO

Along with the opiates, alcohol and cannabis, tobacco must be rated as one of the most ubiquitous and socially significant of all drugs. Yet until recently attitudes towards tobacco could scarcely have provided a bigger contrast to attitudes towards the opiates. As van Lancker (1977) put it, '... smokers almost all over the world can now enjoy their habit with the tacit approval of their government, vigorous encouragement of the tobacco industry, absolution of their church, and the resigned silence of their physicians'. Indeed, acceptance has been so great, the licit involvement of governments and commerce so strong, and until very recently the dangers of the drug so ignored, that tobacco was scarcely recognised as a 'drug' at all. Jaffe (1977) cited Brill, a pioneer of the psychoanalytic movement, who believed that, 'most of the fanatical opponents of tobacco that I have known were all bad neurotics', and a German pharmacologist, who believed smoking to be:

> ... an enjoyment which man is free to renounce and when he indulges in it he experiences its benevolent effects on his spiritual life ... [unlike wine] ... it adjusts the working condition of the mind and the disposition of many mentally active persons to a kind of serenity or 'quietism' during which the activity of thought is in no way disturbed ...
>
> (Lewin, 1924, cited by Jaffe, 1977, p. 207)

Of particular interest is Jaffe's quotation from Sir Humphrey Rolleston whose report on opiates in the 1920s was to be of great importance in laying the foundations for the comparatively permissive British approach to heroin prescribing in the 1960s. On tobacco, he is quoted as saying:

> This question turns on the meaning attached to the word 'addiction' ... That smoking produces a craving for more when an attempt is made to give it up ... is undoubted, but it can seldom be accurately described as overpowering, and the effects of its withdrawal, though there may be definite restlessness and instability, cannot be compared with the physical distress caused by withdrawal in morphine addicts. To regard tobacco as a drug of addiction is all very well in a humorous sense, but it is hardly accurate.
>
> (Rolleston, 1926, quoted by Jaffe, 1977, pp. 207–208)

Russell (1971) was one of the first to argue that cigarette smoking was a 'dependence disorder'. He pointed out that most people who smoked went on to become regular smokers. We should not be surprised that this is the case, he wrote, since the absorption of nicotine through the lungs during smoking is about as rapid and efficient as an intravenous 'fix' of morphine or heroin (p. 3). There was many a smoker who would, '... reach for a cigarette first thing on waking, will seldom go more than an hour without a cigarette, and, should his supply run out, will go to great lengths to obtain more' (p. 4). In this way the heavy smoker maintains a certain level of nicotine more or less continuously throughout the waking day.

As we should by now expect, however, efforts to define tobacco 'dependence' demonstrate all the problems of attempting to make a definable disorder out of a problem of excessive habitual behaviour. The problem is almost exactly parallel to problems incurred in trying to define 'alcoholism', 'compulsive gambling', 'compulsive eating', 'exercise dependence' or 'hypersexuality'. At one time the World Health Organisation (WHO) wished to distinguish between 'addiction' and 'habituation', defining the former as:

> A state of periodic or chronic intoxication, detrimental to the individual and society, produced by the repeated administration of a drug; its characteristics are a compulsion to take the drug and to increase the dose, with the development of psychic and sometimes physical dependence on the effects of the drug, so that the development of compulsion to continue the administration of the drug becomes an important motive in the addict's existence.
>
> (WHO, 1964)

'Habituation', on the other hand, was defined as:

> A condition resulting from the repeated consumption of a drug. Its characteristics include: a desire (but not a compulsion) to continue taking the drug for the sense of improved well-being which it engenders; little or no tendency to increase the dose; some degree of psychic dependence on the effect of the drug, but absence of physical dependence and hence of an abstinence syndrome; detrimental effects, if any, primarily on the individual.
>
> (WHO, 1964)

Quite apart from the evident difficulties in deciding whether a desire is sufficiently strong to be rated as a compulsion, and whether society is or is not harmed, the difference hinged upon the questions of the development of tolerance (and hence the likelihood of increasing the dose) and the presence of a syndrome of effects upon withdrawal or abstinence.

Later, finding the distinction unworkable, WHO recommended dropping both terms, substituting the single concept of 'dependence', arguing that each drug produced its own brand of 'dependence' (dependence of nicotine type, dependence of morphine type, etc.), and that increased tolerance and an abstinence syndrome would be more or less a feature of the picture in different cases and with different drugs. The 'alcohol dependence syndrome', discussed in Chapter Two, was a development of that thinking.

Whatever the ins and outs of such wrangles over definitions, the evidence that many people are 'addicted' to tobacco smoking, in the lay sense of that word, is overwhelming. There is still no better evidence for this than the results of the study

Table 4.1   Percentage of dissonant smokers (McKennell and Thomas, 1967)

	Adolescents (%)	Adults (%)
Dissonant		
Wish and tried—highly dissonant	38	30
Wish but not tried—dissonant	11	15
Consonant		
No wish but tried in the past—consonant	22	22
Neither wish nor tried—highly consonant	29	33

of adults' and adolescents' smoking habits and attitudes, carried out for the British Government Social Survey by McKennell and Thomas (1967) in the 1960s (Table 4.1). In the Summer of 1964 they interviewed a representative national sample of 854 16–20-year-olds and 984 adults over 20.

Their report was particularly noteworthy for the introduction of the concept of 'dissonant smoking', a simple and straightforward concept which may go some way towards clearing a great deal of the confusion that surrounds such terms as 'addiction' and 'dependence'. A 'dissonant' smoker is simply someone who would like to behave otherwise than he or she does: someone who smokes but would prefer not or who smokes more than an amount considered ideal. As McKennell and Thomas wrote, 'One of the most remarkable findings that emerges from social surveys of smokers' habits and attitudes is the very large number who either express a wish to give up smoking or else have tried to do so' (p. 96). Dissonance was operationally defined by them in terms of just two questions: 'Would you like to give up smoking if you could do so easily?' and 'Have you ever tried to give up smoking altogether?'. Table 4.1 shows the percentages of respondents defined by them as dissonant or consonant in their smoking on the basis of the answers. They commented: 'Dissonant smokers appear to be people who are trapped by the smoking habit, somewhat against their will. The majority of them have in fact tried several times to give up smoking ...' (p. 90). They presented a great deal of evidence on the development of smoking, particularly during the teenage years, and they pointed out how the majority of respondents who had smoked at all reported escalating to regular and often 'addicted' or 'dissonant' smoking within an average of 2–3 years.

If addiction is judged solely by the criterion of difficulty in leaving off a behaviour despite wishing to do so, then tobacco may be judged to be not simply addictive, but probably the most addictive of all substances. Some 20 years later Jarvis (1987) estimated that around 70 per cent of smokers said they would like to stop—a dramatic figure when it is considered how many millions of people must therefore be regularly indulging in a costly and risky habit which is not in accordance with what they would choose to do if free to make a choice. Data from a study of 250 16–35-year-olds (Orford and Velleman, 1990) are shown in Table 4.2. Compared with alcohol, cannabis, other illicit drugs and prescribed psychoactive medications such as benzodiazepines, tobacco stood out as being the

Table 4.2   Five classes of psychoactive drug by 'ever used', 'still using' and 'ever a problem' (244 16–35 year-olds, Orford and Velleman, 1990)

	% ever used	% still using	% use ever considered a problem
Alcohol	99	96	12
Tobacco	71	56	27
Prescribed	50	9	13
Cannabis	47	25	5
Other illicit	33	9	7

class of drug that was most often considered by these young adults to be a problem, and at the same time the class of substance, besides alcohol, for which consumption had most often *not* been given up.

The years since the McKennell and Thomas survey illustrate, yet again, how rapidly things can change in this field. At the same time these changes bring into sharp relief the central question concerning the nature of addiction itself. In the UK from the early 1970s to the early 1980s, for example, the number of smokers fell dramatically. In 1973, 60 per cent of adult males and 42 per cent of adult females were smokers, and by 1984 these figures had fallen to 40 per cent and 32 per cent respectively (Jarvis, 1987). But the majority of smokers still did not stop, and new smokers continued to be recruited in huge numbers. Most of these new recruits to smoking were children and young teenagers. Jarvis (1991) reported surveys of school pupils showing around 10 per cent of 11-year-olds to be smokers and nearly 40 per cent of 16-year-olds, with girls now actually taking up smoking slightly more often than boys (a reversal of the pattern maintained throughout the first half of the 20th century). A further trend had been the opening up of increasing differentials by occupation and social class. By the early 1990s the prevalence of smoking among British doctors was down to around 10 per cent compared with about 35 per cent for the population as a whole. Jarvis (1991), using data from the 1986 General Household Survey, showed that the prevalence of smoking varied from a high of 56 per cent for men and 43 per cent for women with manual occupations living in rented accommodation to a low of 32 per cent for men and 23 per cent for women with non-manual occupations living in owner-occupied accommodation.

In the late 1980s, as the real price of cigarettes was allowed to fall in Britain (reversing the trend of the previous several years), overall consumption started to rise again (Townsend, 1993). There was now little doubt or controversy over the fact that smoking was a major course of morbidity and mortality from some of the major diseases causing death in a country such as Britain, particularly premature deaths in middle age—lung cancer, ischaemic heart disease, and chronic-obstructive-airways disease. In fact, Britain has particularly high mortality rates for all the major smoking diseases, and it has been estimated that smoking accounts for over a third of all deaths in middle age in Britain and 18 per cent of all deaths (Townsend, 1993). So colossal is the scale of this particular appetitive behaviour and the sickness and death to which it contributes that Townsend estimated that if smoking prevalence could have been reduced by half, to 20 per cent, by the year 2000, around 19 000 premature deaths per year would have been avoided in the UK by that year, and that this figure would rise to around 50 000 from the year 2017. Assuming that the average person dying prematurely from smoking loses 12.5 years of life, she also calculated that nearly an extra 100 000 years of life would have been saved by the year 2000 and over half a million by the year 2017. The calculations that appeared in her important paper were based on careful estimates of the reductions in the numbers of smokers and cigarettes consumed which would have resulted from the various elements of a total-prevention package aimed at halving the number of smokers by the year 2000. The package she recommended consisted of: a ban on tobacco advertising and promotion, a sustained health-education campaign, GPs advising 95 per cent of their smoking patients to stop, a ban on smoking in public places, restrictions on smoking in the workplace, and, most effective of all, an annual increase in the real price of cigarettes of 5.25 per cent per year making a gross increase in price of 63 per cent by the year 2000.

The trend for girls and young women to start smoking in larger numbers than had previously been the case was already apparent in Britain by 1964 when McKennell and Thomas carried out their survey. They noted in their report, 'The pattern of female smoking had in fact been transformed over the past 20 years so as to resemble that which has long been established amongst males' (p. 14). Graham (1996) analysed the evidence on women's smoking in countries of the European Community in the second half of the 20th century. The evidence she reviewed suggested that in northern countries of the EC, such as Denmark, the Netherlands, the UK and Ireland, women's cigarette consumption tended to rise and then fall over the period between 1950 and 1990, at a time when men's consumption was steadily declining. Women of higher socioeconomic status were turning away from smoking at a faster rate, and in some countries, such as the Netherlands, age effects were very clear, with younger women much more often being smokers and showing a much clearer rise and fall in consumption over the period, while consumption and decline in consumption showed no such age effects for men. In southern countries of the EC, on the other hand, the earlier and longer term trend away from the use of naturally cured, dark tobacco, to flue-cured, bland tobacco in the form of commercially produced cigarettes, was still occurring in the years immediately after the Second World War. In countries such as Greece and Portugal, men's consumption was still on an upward trajectory in the post-war period, and in some southern countries, such as Italy and Spain, women's smoking was still increasing in the early 1990s. In the latter countries there was evidence of greater prevalence of smoking amongst *higher* socioeconomic status groups of women, although there was now some evidence, for example from Italy, that women of higher socioeconomic status might be giving up smoking in larger numbers.

Another change in recent times has been the diversification of markets for the sale of tobacco products, in the direction of the 'developing' world. It has been estimated that, while cigarette consumption is decreasing in developed countries by about 1 per cent annually, in developing countries by the 1990s it was increasing at around 3 per cent per year (Stebbins, 1994). Araya and Laranjeira (1991) concluded that, 'In many poor countries the epidemic of smoking-related diseases and deaths is posing a problem rivalled only by infectious disease and malnutrition' (p. 254). By 1990 WHO was estimating that smoking was responsible for 2.7 million deaths per year worldwide (almost 5 per cent of all deaths) and that tobacco's toll was projected to increase five-fold to 12 million a year by the middle of the 21st century, with most of the increase occurring in less developed countries (Stebbins, 1994).

Those who come from developing countries often find it difficult to reconcile the cost and vehemence of anti-drugs campaigns with which developed countries expect developing countries to cooperate, while at the same time the export of tobacco products to developing countries is encouraged in the name of free trade (Araya and Laranjeira, 1991). For instance, '... more Colombians die today from diseases caused by tobacco products exported to their country by American tobacco companies than do Americans from Colombian cocaine' (Colombian Cocaine and US Tobacco, 1988, cited by Stebbins, 1994, p. 113). Whether it is alcohol, tobacco, opium or cocaine that is in question, conflict over trade in the substances and objects that are liable to be consumed excessively are an almost universal aspect of the total picture. In the case of tobacco in developing countries, this enormous and increasing trade appears to be facilitated by a number of factors, which include pressures upon developing countries, often poor and in debt to richer countries, to open up their markets to free trade, and the arrangement whereby transnational cigarette companies avoid some of the criticism they would face on ethical grounds, by selling products through 'licencing agreements' wherein 'local' brands are marketed through the offices of a local company. Mexico is a good example. In that country it has been a priority of recent years to reform the economy and attract foreign investment. Inflation had been cut, hundreds of state-owned companies had been privatised, and the door has been opened to foreign goods and investment. No cigarettes were imported, but they were made by two Mexican companies, one a subsidiary of Philip Morris, the other holding a licence agreement with R. J. Reynolds, these then being two of the world's six largest tobacco companies, both based in the USA (Stebbins, 1994).

It is of little surprise, therefore, that the tobacco industry has come in for increasing attack. This represents a change, both in general attitudes and in the positions adopted by individual experts. Lando, a distinguished epidemiologist working in a school of public health in the USA, explained:

... although I remain strongly committed to smoking cessation, I am also increasingly committed to a more general attack upon tobacco and tobacco promotion. I have found myself politically radicalized during my last 10 years in this field. ... We must begin to confront the tobacco industry and its allies much more aggressively. I believe that we have both a special obligation and an opportunity to do so given our credibility as 'experts' and our knowledge of the horrendous health burden imposed by tobacco. Our work will have limited effect so long as the industry is allowed actively to solicit new recruits to replace those who quit or who die from smoking. It is time to stop blaming the victim—the individual smoker.

(Lando, 1991, pp. 650–651)

The rapid development of nicotine-replacement therapies (NRTs) has been one of the other important developments in the last quarter of the 20th century. The ingenuity that has been shown in devising ways of delivery nicotine to the human nervous system, in ways other than puffing at a lighted tobacco cigarette, illustrates, perhaps better than almost any other phenomenon, the power of addiction. The range of new nicotine-delivery systems now includes nicotine chewing gum (the first on the scene), nicotine skin patches, nasal nicotine spray, nicotine puffers, and nicotine lozenges (Russell, 1991). Of these, gum, skin patch and nasal spray have proved the most popular.

AMPHETAMINES AND COCAINE

The amphetamines constitute a further major drug category which raises salient questions about the psychological nature of excessive drug use. They have been in medical use for over 30 years for many conditions, particularly for depression and for weight control—yet a further example of the substitution of one appetitive behaviour for another (Swinson and Eaves, 1978). Reactions to them have followed the familiar pattern of medical enthusiasm followed by growing awareness of their dangers, followed, in the case of the amphetamines, by the introduction of legal and voluntary controls on prescriptions and availability in many countries. In Japan, for example, amphetamines had been freely available without prescription, and by 1954 it was estimated that 2 per cent of the total population was 'addicted', following which the problem was brought under control with the help of legal restrictions and the spread of information about their dangers. Sweden was just one of many other countries that legislated to restrict the availability of stimulants in the 1960s, in this case only two years after their prescribing had been legalised (Swinson and Eaves, 1978).

There is an argument that drug treatment services and research, and media attention, have been over-focused on heroin and other opiates, and more recently upon cocaine, and have neglected use of the amphetamines which may be more widespread and possibly more dangerous (Klee, 1992). Klee's research in the north-west of England suggested that there exists a wide range of amphetamine-using patterns, from occasional 'pill popping', through 'bingeing', to regular daily use, and that large numbers of young people were injecting amphetamines and sharing injecting equipment. Compared with heroin, amphetamine was comparatively inexpensive and maintaining a regular drug-using habit might be less of a problem. Amphetamine users had comparatively little contact with drug treatment services. Further dangers lie in the combinations of drugs that are used by amphetamine takers. It was commonly reported in Klee's research that amphetamines were used with other drugs including heroin to enhance the effect, cannabis to 'mellow' the effect, tranquillisers or barbiturates to help cope with the 'crash' that is often reported to follow the heavy use of amphetamines, and alcohol. Amphetamines were often reported to have been used with alcohol in order to delay intoxication from the latter.

The position of amphetamines as a class of drug that is used quite widely and apparently without many adverse consequences for many users, but which has considerable potential for being used excessively, is illustrated by two studies from Sydney, Australia. The first was a study of over 500 16–21-year-olds interviewed in public places such as drinking venues, markets, shopping centres and dance parties. All were people who had used at least one illicit drug (other than marijuana) in the previous 3 months. After marijuana, which had been used by 93 per cent in the previous 3 months, amphetamines were the drugs most commonly used (by 61 per cent) followed by hallucinogens (40 per cent), ecstasy (36 per cent) and sedatives (31 per cent), with inhalants, cocaine and heroin used less frequently (20, 20 and 15 per cent respectively). A minority of the sample reported that they had received treatment for a drug problem (11 per cent) or had been arrested for using or possessing drugs (14 per cent) and the majority (79 per cent) did not consider any of their drug use to be a problem. Drug use that was considered by young people to have been a problem was more likely to involve heroin, sedative, inhalant or cocaine use, while amphetamines were rarely associated with heavy or what was considered problematic use (Spooner *et al.*, 1993).

The second study, in contrast, concentrated on amphetamine users, recruiting participants via advertisements in local and specialist youth newspapers, peer referral, street contacts, contacts through user groups, and via treatment and health centres and key informants (only 13 per cent came via these latter agency contacts). Its conclusions were less sanguine. The median age of the 231 participants was 24 years and on average they had been using amphetamines for 7 years. The frequency of use varied greatly from daily (9 per cent) to less than monthly (29 per cent). Although snorting or swallowing were the most common methods of administration of the drug, just over two-thirds had injected amphetamines at some time and about half had reported that they usually injected. One-third were judged to be dependent on amphetamines. Hallucinations, episodes of aggression and violence, and panic attacks were reported by 46, 43 and 9 per cent respectively. Altogether a third, including those recruited from treatment sources, had received some form of treatment for a drug or alcohol problem, and one in four were currently receiving drug treatment. A total of 41 percent believed that they had needed treatment for an amphetamine-related problem at some time (Hall and Hando, 1994).

Cocaine, classed like the amphetamines as a stimulant, is of particular interest because it occurs naturally in the leaves of the coca plant and was introduced to Europe at about the same time as tobacco. This was yet another drug that met with medical enthusiasm in the 19th century, on the part of Freud among others, and was tried as a cure for both opiate and alcohol excess. It too emerged as a recreational drug amongst young adults in the 1960s (Schecter, 1978).

Chronic oral use of cocaine occurs in the form of coca-leaf chewing in South America, particularly in Peru. The problems such use poses for definitions of 'dependence', 'abuse' and excess are quite similar to those posed by 19th-century English opium-eating. According to Negrete's (1980) review, South American cocachewing was so widespread that it was, '... among the larger if not the most extensive narcotic problem in the world' (p. 285). 'Cocaism', he wrote,. was culturally accepted and there was considerable controversy over the use of coca and its effects. It seems that its use was 'utilitarian' as opposed to 'hedonistic'. Ostensibly it was used to help concentrate at work, to withstand the climate and harsh life often lived at high altitude. Coca leaves were still given in some places as part of wages. There was little evidence of obvious dependence: 'Coca chewing is a case of orderly moderate and social use of narcotics. It cannot be equated with the usually individualistic, anarchic and more symptomatic problem of cocaine abuse' (p. 286). The social and cultural setting, the user's motivation and other character-istics, the dose, and the route of administration of the drug were, if Negrete was right, as different from illicit cocaine-injecting in urban USA as fenland opium-eating in England was from the later junkie subculture.

The drug cocaine is surrounded by mystery and controversy. It has come into the public light in a big way since the first edition of this book was written, and of all the drugs under consideration here it is one that tests models of addiction particularly severely. Up until at least the 1960s it was used only by a compara-tively small number of people who were sufficiently well off to afford it, and whose lives were sufficiently unconventional to fit with its glamorous and elitist image (Bieleman *et al.*, 1993; Pickering and Stimson, 1994). Part of its image was also that of a drug that was comparatively harmless and which did not give rise to addiction because, unlike heroin and alcohol, its cessation was not associated with very apparent withdrawal symptoms (Bieleman *et al.*, 1993). As we shall see in Chapter Eleven, that conclusion that cocaine could not become addictive rested upon an over-simple, one-factor, theory of addiction that centred on neuroadapta-tion giving rise to tolerance and withdrawal symptoms.

Whatever the answer to questions about the nature of addiction itself, there is no doubting the fact that the image of cocaine has changed in the last 20 or so years. In 1975 Waldorf and his colleagues interviewed and observed a group of people who used cocaine intra-nasally and who had been doing so on average for 3 years. The group was made up of two extended families and others related to them through marriage or friendship. Half were men and half were women. Ages ranged from 16 to 51 although the median age was 26 years. Most had experi-mented with hallucinogens and a variety of other illicit drugs in the late 1960s and early 1970s. They considered cocaine a luxury drug to be shared with close friends. Four were daily users but most were casual users, and most did not believe cocaine to be addictive although they expressed respect for its potential for being abused. Very few negative effects were reported and these were minor: nose irritations, short-term fatigue following long nights of cocaine use, and in the case of the few daily users, occasional restlessness, irritability and edginess, and some disrup-tion in personal relationships. No one was 'addicted' or felt in danger of becoming so (Murphy *et al.*, 1989).

It is important to bear in mind that the majority of this group were from middle-class backgrounds, and for the most part the group, '... was comprised of grown-up members of the 1960s flower children era' (p. 430). When their cocaine use was first studied in the mid-1970s the 'epidemic' of cocaine use in the USA in the 1980s had not yet occurred. Similar, but probably somewhat less severe, epidemics occurred at around the same time in a number of other countries including Canada and Australia (Pickering and Stimson, 1994), Spain, Italy and Holland (Bieleman *et al.*, 1993). Not only did the prevalence of use of cocaine increase greatly in subsequent years, but the ways in which it was used, the means by which it was made available, and the social groups by whom it was used greatly diversified. Once again this illustrates the rapidly changing nature of appetite behaviour, especially drug use, with which a sound theory of addiction must deal. In addition to snorting cocaine, which is what the group studied by Murphy *et al.* in the mid 1970s had been doing, the injecting of a solution of cocaine became more widespread as did the smoking of cocaine and its purer form, free-base or 'crack' cocaine—so called because of the popping sound made by the crystals of crack cocaine breaking up when it is smoked. Crack cocaine in particular appeared to spread largely to economically deprived groups in cities in the USA, and it acquired an image as an extremely powerful and destructive drug, very different from cocaine's former reputation.

Despite the negative image of crack cocaine and the alarm associated with the use of cocaine in the USA in the 1980s, cocaine appeared to remain a drug that can be used in very different ways and with differing effects. Moosburger *et al.* (1990) contacted 50 current cocaine users in Sydney, Australia, using the 'snowball' or chain-referral technique. Nearly half of this group were occasional users who had never bought cocaine themselves, although eight of this group were ex-heavy users. At the other extreme were 11 regular users who were buying significant quantities of cocaine every week. Nearly all used snorting as the method of administration but four preferred injecting, three in combination with heroin and 30 per cent had tried free-base cocaine but none regularly. A total of 82 per cent considered cocaine to be psychologically addictive and 86 per cent thought it could lead to personality changes. Only 12 per cent, however, said their own cocaine use was not under control. A larger percentage (22 per cent) thought their tobacco use to be a problem, and quite high proportions were currently using other drugs (e.g. 40 per cent were smoking marijuana at least five times a week, 65 per cent using amphetamines, 36 per cent hallucinogens and 10 per cent heroin).

A number of authors have suggested typologies of cocaine and crack users. Bieleman *et al.* (1993), on the basis of a collaborative study carried out in Barcelona, Rotterdam and Turin, suggested four types: the leisure type, the instrumental type, the cocainist type and the poly-drug type. Power *et al.* (1995), on the basis of interviews with both clients of drug agencies and those not in contact with treatment services, in 10 different locations in England and Wales, identified three main groups: recreational users, 'salient' users and poly-drug users. The first group were divided further into 'occasional' and 'erratic' users. The poly-drug users, who were likely to be primarily opiate users, could be divided into those who used cocaine as a treat to supplement their opiate use ('supplementers') and those who had been converted to cocaine or crack as their main drug of use ('converters'). Waldorf *et al.* (1991), reporting on a study of 'heavy' cocaine users (spending a minimum average of around $200US a week on cocaine for at least 6 months) studied between 1985 and 1987, referred to: 'coke hogs' (i.e. excessive users), binge users, ceremonial users and 'nippers' (using small amounts but regularly). There is clearly a large measure of overlap between these topologies. All three groups of researchers recognised that cocaine use varies along a number of dimensions: whether it is used regularly or only on special occasions; whether its use is merely a part of other social activities such as partying, alcohol and cannabis use, or sexual activity, or whether it is the central focus of activity when it is taken; whether users feel that its use is well under control or is compulsive or addictive; whether or not it is associated with opiate use; whether users consume the drug intra-nasally and are very much against injecting, at one extreme, or prefer injecting at the other; and finally whether its use is felt to be unproblematic or associated with significant problems such as paranoia, negative effects on relationships with partners, family, friends or work colleagues, and financial, work or sexual problems (Waldorf *et al.*, 1991).

Even Murphy *et al.*'s (1989) group from the flower-children era had a varied outcome. Of the 27 members of the group interviewed in 1975, 21 were interviewed again in 1986. Some of the others had moved away and were uncontactable, but two of the original respondents had died, one of lung cancer but the other of gunshot wounds during a heroin-smuggling operation. Of the 21 interviewed, seven had continued to use cocaine moderately throughout the full 11 years that had intervened. Another group of seven were also using smallish amounts on special occasions by 1986, but had gone through a period of heavier use in the meantime. For the most part, however, they had been able to keep their use under financial, physical and social control even when using quite large amounts (2–3 gm per week for several months). All had been able to sustain their careers and family lives. Five were now abstinent from cocaine having passed through a period of heavy use, and it was this group who reported the most cocaine-related problems: 'Many eventually experienced physical problems because of their use and yet, despite at least one frightening episode ... continued using. They also experienced substantial guilt over money spent, drugs they had stolen and relationships that had been strained' (p. 433). One of the women members of the group, who had been one of the heaviest users in 1975, was said to be struggling with both alcohol and cocaine problems in 1986. Two others had become abstinent without ever having passed through a period of heavy use. Although Murphy *et al.* admitted that they might have been more sanguine in their original conclusions had they known in 1975 that several of the group would experience problems associated with their cocaine use, they nevertheless concluded:

> At least within our sample of long-term cocaine users, the tendency for use to escalate to abuse was neither inexorable nor inevitable. Most never came to use cocaine daily or regularly in heavy amounts, despite their routine ingestion of it and occasional 'binges', and despite both constant availability and the absence of abstinence norms in their social network ... If our subjects are any guide, then, moderate long-term use of cocaine need not entail wrecking one's life or significant social dysfunction.
>
> (Murphy *et al.*, 1989, p. 435)

After interviewing 133 people recruited in a number of Scottish towns, by snowballing or public advertising, who had used cocaine at least once in the last 3 years, Ditton and Hammersley (1996) came to much the same conclusions. Their participants were asked in detail about their cocaine use during three periods: during their first year of use, during their 'heaviest period' of use if one could be identified and during the 3 months prior to interview. Most were neither simply experimenters with cocaine nor unhappy with out-of-control use of cocaine. Like all activities that can become excessive, the Scottish cocaine users reported both positive and negative effects, with the balance in that sample towards the former (see Chapter Twelve for more detail). Although most were using considerably less by the time of the interview, and in some cases had stopped altogether, 79 per cent could identify a heavy period of cocaine use which on average had lasted just over 9 months. Some had used cocaine quite intensively during this period: 30 reported using cocaine daily for example. Using Bieleman *et al.*'s (1993) typology, 23 per cent were classified as having been 'cocainists' at some time and 34 per cent as poly-drug users. Of the remainder, 23 per cent were classified as leisure types, 17 per cent instrumental types, and 4 per cent were unclassifiable. Cocainists and poly-drug users used larger quantities during their heaviest periods of use, and were more likely to be men.

Ditton and Hammersley were particularly interested in the question of whether cocaine can be said to be 'addictive' or 'dependence' forming. One-third of their sample thought that cocaine, 'creates psychological dependence', but this view varied markedly by type: from 50 per cent amongst poly-drug cocaine users to 13 per cent among leisure types. Several participants were quoted as saying that cocaine was not addictive when compared with some other drugs such as nicotine or heroin:

> Cocaine has never got hold of me, because I've had an opiate addiction before, when I was young, I had a serious downer addiction then, and cocaine is nothing compared to an opiate addiction ... it just doesn't get a grip of you like that ... I mean it can fit in with your life style, where heroin can't ...
>
> (Ditton and Hammersley, 1996, p. 53)

Ditton and Hammersley's conclusion on this question was that cocaine, at least as used by their Scottish participants, '... is not addictive in the normal sense of the word' (p. 69). They appeared to offer this conclusion on the grounds that, while cocaine can, '... lead to protracted bouts of heavy or excessive use ...' (p. 70), '... most people who use frequently and heavily later managed to change this without assistance' (p. 120). The comparisons that they and their participants made are instructive here. They stated:

> In its addictiveness, cocaine is more like alcohol than like tobacco: most users have no problems, some have problems for a while which they sort out, and a few have life-long problems.
>
> (Ditton and Hammersley, 1996, p. 120)

Rather than saying that cocaine, *like alcohol*, has a high capacity for excess and addiction, they choose to compare it with tobacco, and some of their participants compared it with heroin. This is perhaps no surprise since the baseline against which they compared their results was a climate of scaremongering about cocaine, and particularly crack cocaine, and the reductionist assumption that a drug like cocaine is per se 'addictive'—'... psycho-pharmacological witch-hunting ...' (p. 114) as they called it.

They acknowledged that their sample may have missed out on some of those particularly dependent on cocaine. They further acknowledged that frequent use of larger quantities of cocaine is more likely to cause problems, including even 'addiction', and they predicted that the consumption of cocaine would probably become increasingly widespread. Even if no more than 10 per cent of users have problems—as with alcohol—this is cause for concern, they acknowledged. Some of their own participants spoke of the reality of troublesome, excessive cocaine use. For example:

> ... in the first year, I only did it twice, then the year after, went mad for it: every night for three months. I spent about a grand (£1,000) a week, ludicrous when you think about it. Every night until about 6 in the morning. I even used to go out and score at 2 in the morning ... and that would be the third time that night. That's the way cocaine gets you. That's why it's a complete waste of time ...
>
> (Ditton and Hammersley, 1996, p. 31)

CANNABIS DEPENDENCE: FACT OR FICTION?

Of the many other drugs which could be considered for what they might tell us about the nature of addiction, mention should be made of cannabis because of its long history and widespread current use, and because of the controversy which surrounds its use in present-day Britain, and the question of its 'dependence' liability' (Farrell, 1999). The model of excessive appetitive behaviour to be developed here (see Part II) might lead us to expect that excessive cannabis use would exist even if its probability among consumers is low and its personal and social consequences slight compared with those associated with excessive heroin or cocaine use. If large numbers of people take a drug that has positive psychological effects of the kinds attributed to cannabis, then it would be very surprising if at least some people did not take it very regularly and find it difficult to give it up when they tried to do so.

In their comprehensive review of the health and psychological consequences of cannabis use carried out for the Australian National Taskforce on Cannabis, Hall *et al.* (1994) considered carefully the question of whether there was a cannabis 'dependence syndrome'. Their answer was in the affirmative, the best evidence on prevalence that they found being the Epidemiological Catchment Area (ECA) study of 20 000 people in five areas across the USA (Anthony and Helzer, 1991, cited by Hall *et al.*, 1994) which produced a prevalence figure of 4.4 per cent for cannabis 'abuse' or 'dependence' combined, and a replication of that study with 1500 adults in Christchurch, New Zealand (Wells *et al.*, 1992, cited by Hall *et al.*, 1994) which produced a figure of 4.7 per cent. In the ECA study the prevalence figure was the highest of all drugs other than tobacco and alcohol (compared with 1.7 per cent for stimulants, 1.2 per cent for sedatives, 0.7 per cent for opioids). Hall *et al.* suggested that the risk must not be exaggerated, however, and that in terms of the risk to users, cannabis is more like alcohol than nicotine or opioids which produce a much higher ratio of dependence to use. It is noteworthy that, again, a comparison is made with alcohol, not to suggest the *high* level of risk but rather to suggest how comparatively safe the drug is!

Hall *et al.* argued that the recognition of cannabis dependence had been delayed for a number of reasons. One was a previous over-emphasis on withdrawal and tolerance as necessary criteria for dependence. A more liberal definition of dependence based on the concept of the alcohol-dependence syndrome, with greater emphasis on continued use in the face of adverse effects, had made it more possible to recognise cannabis dependence. Furthermore, up to that time it had been rare for people to present themselves in a treatment setting complaining of their difficulty in giving up cannabis. That had recently changed in Australia, as well as in the USA and Sweden, however.

Research carried out by Stephens and his colleagues in Washington State, USA is illustrative of the more recent trend for cannabis users to express concern and seek advice. In 1985 they carried out a telephone survey of users who were, 'concerned about their marijuana use', and logged 225 calls with such users in a 2-week period. A total of 90 per cent of those callers were already in treatment, but 2 years later they advertised through the media the availability of treatment for people who wanted help quitting marijuana use, and received 382 applications in less than 2 months (Stephens and Roffman, 1993). The average age of this group at the time of responding to the announcement was 32 years. They had started using marijuana on average at age 16 and the average member of the group had reached daily or near daily use by age 20. As a group they were very regular users. They had taken marijuana on average on 70 of the previous 90 days, over 90 per cent used it more than once on a typical day, and nearly 50 per cent used it four or more times a day. The average person had tried stopping or reducing use seven times previously (Stephens *et al.*, 1993). Moderate to high proportions reported adverse consequences from using marijuana in the previous 90 days: inability to stop using (93 per cent), feeling bad about using (87 per cent), procrastinating (86 per cent), loss of self-confidence (76 per cent), memory loss (67 per cent), withdrawal symptoms (51 per cent), family members complaining (47 per cent) and financial difficulty (41 per cent). A total of 80 per cent of the sample reported neither dependence on, nor difficulty giving up, any drug other than cannabis in the previous 90 days, and nearly 40 per cent reported never experiencing difficulty with any other drug.

In terms of reasons for wanting to stop taking cannabis, self-control emerged as the predominant motive (e.g. 'To show myself I can quit'), followed by health concerns, with direct social pressure from others having less influence (Stephens *et al.*, 1993). Although intrinsic, personal motives thus appear to be the most important, the conflict about marijuana use felt by the people who responded to these adverts probably derived from a complex mixture of personal and social sources (Stephens and Roffman, 1993). Not only had these individuals aged by an average of around 15 years since they first took cannabis, but also the climate of opinion regarding many social issues including drug use had changed in the country in which they were living during the intervening decade or two:

> Now in their 30s and 40s, many of the people who find themselves unable to
> stop smoking marijuana are faced with threats of urine screening on the job,

fears of modelling inappropriate behaviour for their children, seeing fewer of their friends continuing to use marijuana, and being aware that there is now far less acceptance of illicit drug use, marijuana included.

(Stephens and Roffman, 1993, p. 205)

Two non-treatment studies from New Zealand and Australia also suggest the existence of a minority of marijuana users who experience some conflict over their use and whose use might be said to be 'excessive'. In a telephone survey of New Zealanders aged between 15 and 45 years, Black and Casswell (1992) compared the rates of problems attributed to alcohol and marijuana use. Of the more than 5000 people surveyed 43 per cent had tried marijuana at some time in their lives and 17 per cent within the last 12 months. Of the whole sample, 26 per cent reported that alcohol had had some harmful effect within the last 12 months (eight specific problems were asked about). The comparable figure for marijuana was 7 per cent, but of course many fewer people were at risk of marijuana-related problems since fewer had used the drug at all during the period in question. The rate of problems was much higher (55 per cent) amongst the 800 or so respondents who had used both alcohol and marijuana in the last 12 months, but this group were much heavier users of alcohol than most of the sample. Focusing upon the 3 per cent of the total sample who were the heaviest marijuana users (more than 10 times in the last 30 days) produced very similar figures for problems attributed to alcohol and problems attributed to marijuana (65 per cent). The problems most frequently endorsed were: 'your financial position' (43 per cent affected by alcohol use, 42 per cent affected by marijuana use), 'your energy and vitality' (40 per cent alcohol, 41 per cent marijuana) and 'your health' (21 per cent alcohol, 25 per cent marijuana).

Reilly *et al.* (1998) interviewed 268 long-term, regular cannabis users (using at least three times a week for at least 10 years) living on a particular part of the northern coast of New South Wales, Australia—an area of relative social disadvantage, with a substantial traveller and transient population and a reputation for cannabis cultivation and use. Members of the sample, recruited by a snowballing technique, with all the advantages and disadvantages of that method, were aged on average 36 years, and had been using cannabis on average for 19 years. A total of 60 per cent used cannabis daily, a third used it throughout the day, and half reported that they had occasional cannabis 'binges', often at 'harvest time'. Three-quarters were members of family groups in which at least some others used cannabis, and of those currently in a relationship, three-quarters of their partners also used.

There were both positive and negative things to be said about using cannabis, although almost three-quarters believed that benefits outweighed risks, and most of the remainder felt that there was an even balance, leaving only 7 per cent who thought that cannabis had done them more harm than good. Among the many positive effects mentioned, by far the most common was relaxation or relief of tension: almost half said it was calming, slowed them down or helped them sleep. Almost all reported some negative aspects, however, such as illegality (29 per cent), high cost (14 per cent) and the social stigma of being a cannabis user (11 per cent). Substantial minorities reported a variety of negative effects including: paranoia or depression (21 per cent), feeling tired, unmotivated or being low in energy (21 per cent) and being forgetful and less able to concentrate (11 per cent). Nearly one in five were concerned about the effects on their lungs or respiratory system. Most had used other illicit drugs at some time in their lives (e.g. 75 per cent amphetamines and 71 per cent cocaine), and 30 per cent were considered 'at risk' because of their drinking on the basis of their answers to a standard screening questionnaire. Reilly *et al.* were also concerned that smoking cannabis before or during work was common, and that 90 per cent said they drove a vehicle at least occasionally shortly after using cannabis.

As with alcohol, the formidable problems of defining dependence and the tortuous attempts of the WHO and the American Psychiatric Association (APA) to reach agreement on a set of criteria for diagnosing dependence remain features of this field (e.g. Waldorf *et al.*, 1991). Both WHO's *Inter-national Classification of Diseases* (ICD) and APA's *Diagnostic and Statistical Manual* (DSM) have undergone regular revision over the years, and although the different versions of these two schemes show much overlap they are by no means identical. Rounsaville *et al.* (1993) reported the results of a field trial of the use of three separate sets of criteria (the revised third version of DSM, the fourth version of DSM and the tenth version of ICD—see Table 4.3) applied to the results of interviewing over 500 people in the USA. Most were in treatment for alcohol and/or other drug problems, but just over 100 were general psychiatric patients, and a similar number were recruited from the general population. Positive diagnoses were more likely to be assigned using DSM-IV than ICD-10 criteria (e.g. 60 per cent of the sample were diagnosed as 'alcohol dependent' according to DSM and 52 per cent according to ICD). Of the six classes of drug considered, marijuana gave most difficulty, 24 per cent being diagnosed as dependent on marijuana according to DSM criteria, but only 12 per cent according to ICD. These differences may be due in large part to the fact that differences between the two sets of criteria include mention in DSM but not in ICD of current legal or interpersonal problems, and recurrent use in situations in which use is physically hazardous.

BENZODIAZEPINE 'DEPENDENCE'

The medical prescribing of drugs such as the benzodiazepines (BZPs) or 'minor tranquillisers', which bears perhaps closer resemblance to middle-class opium taking in the 19th century than to deviant or illicit excessive drug use, poses a different kind of challenge to concepts of addiction or dependence. For a long time BZPs were thought to be of relatively low 'dependence potential'. Lader (e.g. 1981) was one of the first to draw attention to the possibility of 'dependence' on BZPs. There had already been many reports of tension, trembling, dizziness, insomnia, anxiety and even fits and psychoses upon discontinuing therapeutic use abruptly, and he reported similar experiences for 20 patients known to him who complained of difficulty stopping BZP use and who underwent withdrawal in hospital. About half of this group had escalated the dose to several times the usual and he attributed the 'symptoms' they experienced on cessation to 'withdrawal' on the

Table 4.3   Criteria for 'substance use disorders' according to DSM-III-R, DSM-IV and ICD-10 (reproduced by permission from Rounsaville *et al.*, 1993)

DSM-III-R dependence (three items required)
 (1) substance often taken in larger amounts or over a longer period than the person intended
 (2) persistent desire or one or more unsuccessful efforts to cut down or control substance use
 (3) a great deal of time spent in activities necessary to get the substance, taking the substance or recovering from its effects
 (4) frequent intoxication or withdrawal symptoms when expected to fulfil major role obligations at work, school or home
 (5) important social, occupational or recreational activities given up or reduced because of substance use
 (6) continued substance use despite knowledge of having a persistent or recurrent social, psychological or physical problem that is caused or exacerbated by the use of substance
 (7) marked tolerance
 (8) characteristic withdrawal symptoms
 (9) substance often taken to relieve or avoid withdrawal symptoms

DSM-III-R abuse (one item required)
 (1) continued use despite knowledge of having a persistent or recurrent social, occupational, psychological or physical problem that is caused or exacerbated by use of the psychoactive substance
 (2) recurrent use in situations in which use is physically hazardous

DSM-IV dependence (three items required)
 (1) tolerance
 (2) the characteristic withdrawal syndrome for the substance
 (3) the same substance is often taken to relieve or avoid withdrawal symptoms
 (4) the substance is often taken in larger amounts or over a longer period of time than intended
 (5) any unsuccessful effort or persistent desire to cut down or control substance use
 (6) a great deal of time is spent in activities necessary to obtain the substance, take the substance or recover from its effects
 (7) recurrent substance use resulting in inability to fulfil major role obligations at work, school or home
 (8) recurrent substance use in situations in which it is physically hazardous
 (9) important social, occupational or recreational activities given up or reduced because of substance use
(10) recurrent substance-related legal or interpersonal problems
(11) continued substance use despite knowledge of a persistent or recurrent problem(s) caused or exacerbated by the use of the substance

DSM-IV abuse (one item required)
 (1) recurrent substance use resulting in inability to fulfil major role obligations at work, school or home
 (2) recurrent substance-related legal or interpersonal problems
 (3) important social, occupational or recreational activities given up or reduced because of substance use
 (4) recurrent substance use in situations in which it is physically hazardous

ICD-10 dependence (three items required)
 (1) a strong desire or sense of compulsion to use a substance or substances
 (2) evidence of impaired capacity to control the use of a substance or substances (this may relate to difficulties in avoiding initial use, difficulties in terminating use or problems about controlling levels of use)
 (3) a withdrawal state or use of the substance to relieve or avoid withdrawal symptoms, and subjective awareness of the effectiveness of such behavior

ICD-10 dependence (three items required) (cont.)
(4) evidence of tolerance to the effects of the substance
(5) progressive neglect of alternative pleasures, behaviors or interests in favor of substance use
(6) persisting with substance use despite clear evidence of harmful consequences

ICD-10 harmful use (one item required)
(1) clear evidence that the use of a substance or substances was responsible for causing actual psychological or physical harm to the user

---

grounds that they were often untypical of the kind of anxiety for which the drug was probably prescribed in the first place, and that they subsided over a period of 2–4 weeks. Note here that Lader's concept of 'dependence' relied heavily upon medical evidence of 'withdrawal symptoms' and took little account of the psychological complexities introduced by those who have pondered the nature of 'addiction' in the context of such appetitive behaviours as drinking, gambling, tobacco or cannabis use.

One of the central issues that has preoccupied the individuals and committees who have deliberated on these matters is whether 'physical' or 'physiological' dependence, or neuroadaptation, of which increased tolerance to a drug and withdrawal symptoms are the prime indications, should be considered *essential* for a diagnosis of dependence. DSM, for example, appears to have vacillated on this question. In its first and second versions, the term dependence referred to both psychological and physical dependence, but in the third version signs of tolerance or withdrawal were considered necessary. Because of the fallibility of tolerance and withdrawal in the assessment of physical dependence, however, the revised version of DSM-III, and the subsequent DSM-IV, reverted to the previous position (Widiger and Smith, 1994). Others have argued that to have no essential criteria makes for an unsatisfactory 'shopping list' approach to diagnosis in which any combination of a certain number of items (say three) from a longer list (say ten) constitutes grounds for a diagnosis (Skinner, 1990).

Maletzky and Klotter (1976) reported a fascinating and detailed look at the attribution of 'dependence' on BZPs on the part of medical practitioners and patients at around that time. Of the 50 patients of a military psychiatric clinic who were participants in their study, half had increased the dose of diazepam used, many without asking their doctors, and most had not subsequently returned to the original level. There was considerable evidence of 'dissonance', to use the term that McKennell and Thomas employed in the context of smoking. A total of 24 patients had attempted to stop, all but 2 unsuccessfully, and 30 rated themselves as 'dependent' to some degree (14 'slightly', 8 'moderately', 4 'greatly' and 4 'severely'). Of those who had attempted to stop, 79 per cent experienced, '... withdrawal symptoms of moderate to extreme severity ...' (p. 106). The most common symptoms were anxiety, agitation, insomnia and tremor, and almost all complained of some symptoms not present before taking the drug.

The most intriguing part of their study, however, concerned the effect upon the attribution process of knowing whether the drug described was a minor tranquilliser or not. When a panel of general practitioners, general surgeons, internists and orthopaedic surgeons judged the degree of patients' 'addiction' from their replies to the standard interview which had elicited this information, without knowing the name of the drug involved, 31 were rated as having some degree of 'addiction' (20 at least 'moderately' so, and 9 of these 'greatly' or 'severely'). When the panel was asked to rerate the degree of 'addiction' having been told that the drug concerned was diazepam, only 14 were rated as showing any 'addiction' (only 5 'moderate' and none 'great' or 'severe'). Maletzky and Klotter added, 'Often physicians commented, with relief, that, "it was only Valium", thus could not be dangerous' (p. 111). This, '... overacceptance of diazepam's safety ... may be falsely based upon a narrow concept of addiction: [that] unless withdrawal symptoms mimic those of heroin or alcohol, a drug cannot be addicting ...' (pp. 96–97).

BZPs are further interesting because on their own they illustrate the great variety of ways in which substances can be used moderately or excessively. For one thing some are more often used to control anxiety and are often termed anxiolytics, whilst others are more often used to help with sleep and are often termed hypnotics (Hayward *et al.*, 1989). Some people use BZPs sporadically, as a 'standby', others regularly. Of the latter, some admit to using BZPs as a 'lifeline', without which they would be 'unable to cope' (Hayward *et al.*, 1989; McMurray, 1989).

Others have distinguished between appropriate *use* of BZPs as prescribed, which may be regular and may lead to 'dependence', and *misuse*, which is associated with active drug-seeking behaviour and use of other drugs (Bond *et al.*, 1994; Ross *et al.*, 1997). Until quite recently the former was thought to greatly predominate. Murphy and Tyrer (1988) contrasted the 'avoidance of discomfort by continued use' and 'the induction of pleasure by the drug', referring to these as, 'the two halves of psychological dependence ...' (p. 159). Although it was always difficult to know whether the discomfort that was being avoided was a reinstatement of the anxiety or sleeplessness for which BZPs had been prescribed in the first place, or to a new set of withdrawal symptoms, most use of BZPs was thought to be of the stable, non-misusing, discomfort-avoidance type. Indeed, since the number of prescriptions for BZPs in Britain in 1990 was still 16.5 million (a decrease of around 30 per cent since the peak of BZP prescribing in 1979) (News and Notes, 1992), it seems likely that this remains the predominating form of use.

CAFFEINE, ECSTASY, KAVA, QAT AND ANABOLIC STEROIDS: FURTHER CHALLENGES TO CONCEPTS OF ADDICTION

Caffeine presents another interesting case of a widely used drug, the potential for dependence and excess of which is controversial. It has been described as the most widely used psychoactive drug in the world, with the UK being a particularly high consuming country because of the large quantities of tea and coffee that are drunk (nearly 450 mg daily per capita, compared with just over 200 mg in the USA) (Gilbert, 1984, cited by Griffiths and Woodson, 1988). The fact that so many people take caffeine-containing beverages so regularly might be thought to be, in itself, an indication of the dependence-producing potential of this drug. Allbutt and Dixon, British pharmacologists writing in the late 19th century, certainly thought so. About the excessive coffee drinker they wrote:

> The sufferer is tremulous and loses his self-command; he is subject to fits of agitation and depression. He has a haggard appearance ... As with other such agents, a renewed dose of the poison gives temporary relief, but at the cost of future misery.
>
> (Allbutt and Dixon, cited in Peele, 1977, p. 105)

The evidence for caffeine 'abuse' or 'dependence', summarised by Hughes *et al.*, (1992), is, however, conflicting. On the one hand, laboratory studies have clearly shown the existence of withdrawal symptoms on the cessation of caffeine intake (Griffiths *et al.*, 1990; Hughes *et al.*, 1991). These experiments have involved the substitution of decaffeinated coffee for caffeinated coffee, and, in one experiment that Griffiths and six of his colleagues from the John Hopkins University School of Medicine in the USA performed on themselves, the double-blind substitution of placebo capsules for caffeine capsules (Griffiths *et al.*, 1990). Although not all participants experienced such symptoms, the commonest were headache, fatigue and drowsiness. Some have argued that these are never more than mild, while others have claimed they are often debilitating. The same experiments have shown that some people deprived of caffeine and experiencing withdrawal symptoms were then more likely to choose caffeinated coffee in preference to decaffeinated than were others who were not experiencing such symptoms (Hughes *et al.*, 1992).

On the other hand, caffeine appears to have only weak stimulant effects on mood, compared for example with amphetamine or cocaine, and Hughes *et al.* (1992) could find no convincing evidence that people feel their intake of caffeine to be out of control, nor that they become preoccupied with caffeine use to the point of neglecting other roles or activities, nor that people continue to take caffeine despite knowing that they have health problems that are aggravated by it, nor that people try to stop taking it and have difficulty doing so. Although there have been references in the literature to 'caffeinism' (Greden, 1981, cited by Hughes *et al.*, 1992), the overall conclusion of Hughes *et al.*'s review was that there was insufficient evidence to include caffeine abuse or dependence in new, updated versions of DSM or ICD. Hughes *et al.* (1992) were aware of the implications of recommending either inclusion or exclusion. On the one hand, exclusion might lead to accusations of inconsistency in handling different drug groups, and even a political cowardice, while inclusion would antagonise coffee manufacturers and perhaps the general public and some clinicians who might feel that the inclusion of caffeine abuse or dependence trivialised other more damaging substance-use disorders as well as unnecessarily enlarging medical diagnostic territory.

Part of the difficulty of understanding addictive behaviour, but also part of its endless fascination, is the rapidly changing drug-taking 'scene', with the appearance of new drugs on the market, the rise and fall of new fashions, and the associated flurry of media and legislative attention to new, real or imaginary, drug-related problems (Davies and Ditton, 1990). When the first edition of this book appeared in 1985, ecstasy was about to be made illegal in the USA, and was beginning to appear in night clubs in Ibiza heralding its widespread use as part of the rave dance youth culture of the late 1980s and 1990s in Britain (McDermott, 1993). In the 1990s it became, along with marijuana, amphetamines, LSD and amyl nitrite, one of the most widely used recreational drugs in countries such as Britain (Parker *et al.*, 1998). Based on reports of 100 ecstasy users in Sydney, Australia, Solowij *et al.* (1992) concluded:

> Ecstasy is an appealing drug to recreational drug users in that it provides an 'added bonus'. That is for those seeking primarily stimulant effects it also induces the positive mood, euphoric and intimacy effects; for those seeking an enlightened experience or perhaps emotional therapy and insight it pro-vides feelings of intimacy and closeness to others plus the stimulant-like alertness, talkativeness and energy. Further, it is a drug experience in which one feels that one can remain in control of one's thoughts and actions rather than the drug being in control.
>
> (Solowij *et al.*, 1992, pp. 1169–70)

If pleasure is the basis of addiction, as will be argued later, ecstasy should have a high addiction-creating potential. The conclusions of the small number of investi-gators who have so far considered ecstasy vary, however, regarding its potential for creating long-term dependence. Solowij *et al.* (1992) stated, '... evidence for the existence of "chronic" MDMA [methylenedioxymethamphetamine ...] users has yet to surface ...' (p. 1171), and Beck and Rosenbaum (1994) wrote, '... our overall assessment is that ecstasy has minimal abuse potential ...' (p. 127). This failure of ecstasy to produce the numbers of addicted individuals that might be expected, and its lack of popularity with established opiate and amphetamine users, is attributed by researchers such as Solowij *et al.* and Beck and Rosenbaum to other psychopharmacological properties of the drug which make it less attractive in the long term. Of the 100 users in Australia surveyed by post by Solowij *et al.*, and 100 users in the USA interviewed by Beck and Rosenbaum, many reported that pleasurable effects diminished with frequent use, and that unpleasant side-effects tended to increase when users tried to recapture their earlier experiences with the drug, either by repeating use of the same dose or by increasing the number of tablets taken, or by experimenting with other routes of administration such as snorting, injecting or taking the drug as a suppository. It is true to say, nevertheless, that experience of ecstasy use on a large scale is still sufficiently new that opinions about its potential for excess might well change as has been the case with many other drugs. Of Solowij *et al.*'s 100 informants, 47 believed that it was possible to become 'addicted' to ecstasy, 22 claimed they knew of someone who had been dependent on ecstasy and two people reported that they had felt dependent themselves. Of Beck and Rosenbaum's 100 research partici-pants, 14 had taken ecstasy over 100 times, and they cited one man who had taken the drug regularly over a period of 11 years, and another for 5 years. It is also important to be aware of the fact that both these research samples consisted almost entirely of educationally quite privileged people who were using ecstasy in particular social and recreational settings. If the potential for excess is powerfully moderated by the setting and context in which drug use takes place (Zinberg,

1978), then many of the factors making for greatest vulnerability to excessive use may have been absent.

In fact, a more pessimistic picture is painted by McDermott (1993) who carried out research with 50 young ecstasy users in Liverpool between 1989 and 1991. Although all of this group described their experience of ecstasy as having been a positive one, and most were limiting their use to special occasions or an occasional night out, a number described problems such as increased drug use of other kinds, crime, and employment, psychiatric and relationship problems. McDermott reported that for many ecstasy had acted as a 'gateway drug', a low-threshold initiation into drug use that led rapidly to experimentation with, or regular use of, other drugs. It seemed to be a catalyst for an increase in drug use for almost all of the group. Most preferred to supplement ecstasy with amphetamine, or to extend its effects with LSD. Six eventually sought professional help for drug-related problems. Five unemployed members of the group reported engaging in acquisitive crime to fund their ecstasy use. All had previously engaged in criminal acts, but their need to find money to go out several nights a week and to take ecstasy increased the incidence of crime such as shoplifting, cheque fraud, theft from cars, and breaking and entering. Five claimed they had lost jobs as a consequence of the impact of ecstasy on their lifestyle. Four experienced psychiatric problems of varying severity, and several reported suffering problems in their relationships. More notorious, and of greater interest to the media, have been the extreme, adverse, but comparatively rare, acute reactions to ecstasy, some leading to fatality (Solowij *et al.*, 1992; Beck and Rosenbaum, 1994).

Many examples could be given to demonstrate how the potential of a substance to be used to excess may depend crucially upon the social context in which it is used. Kava provides an interesting example. It is widely consumed in certain islands in the South Pacific, in the form of a drink, and is described as producing a mild soporific or narcotic-like effect associated with muscle relaxation (Prescott, 1990). Because kava appeared not to be associated with the physical and social harms associated with alcohol use, it was deliberately introduced into an Australian Aboriginal community in that region (Northern Territory) as a substitute for alcohol, and its use quickly spread to a number of other communities in Arnhem Land (Prescott, 1990). In Prescott's opinion this, '... exemplifies a naive view of drug effects which gives little consideration to the social context in which the drug is used' (p. 326). He reported that in countries such as Vanuatu and Tonga kava not only serves as a personal intoxicant, but is also part of ceremonial life and cultural tradition, with strong incentives to drink kava at particular times of day, in the context of a ritualised kava circle, and also in the performance of social and information exchange. Initial reports of kava drinking in Australian Aboriginal communities, on the other hand, suggested that it was often used primarily for its psychotropic effects, was often drunk in very large quantities, over an extended period and sometimes in combination with alcohol. Reports were appearing of adverse effects on health, which had not been expected.

Qat (khat, qhat), a plant containing, among other substances, cathinone, a stimulant with effects similar to amphetamine, offers another example. Griffiths *et al.* (1997) reported a study of 207 Somalian refugees living in London, regarding their use, by chewing, of qat. A total of 78 per cent of the interviewees, three-quarters of whom were men, had ever used qat. The drug was generally used two or three times a week, usually in the evening and usually with other people. Over half thought that most people did not experience problems with qat, and 90 per cent would rather their children used it than alcohol (almost all were abstainers from alcohol). On the other hand, 23 per cent were using daily or had done so in the previous year, weekly expenditure on qat averaged £28 and most reported adverse effects in the form of trouble sleeping, loss of appetite and mood swings. Between a third and a half reported consequent feelings of anxiety, depression and irritability, mostly mild but sometimes moderate or severe. Almost two-thirds reported using more or much more now than 1 year ago, and three-quarters reported using more or much more than they had done in Somalia. There was general concern that this form of drug use, perhaps relatively unproblematic in the country of origin, and seen by many as an acceptable way of maintaining Somalian identity in a foreign culture, was less regulated in London than it had been in Somalia.

The use of anabolic steroids (AS) as performance enhancers has become a matter of great concern in the sports world because of the questionable ethics of, and the need to control, competitive sports people artificially enhancing the ratio of muscle to fat, and their ability to train harder and to recover more quickly between bouts of heavy exercise (Korkia and Stimson, 1993). For our purposes, however, the use of AS raises further questions about the nature of excess.

On the one hand, it has been said by some that AS produces no euphoria or 'rush' or other immediate, psychological effects of a pleasurable kind, and that they are being used instrumentally to enhance performance over a longer period of time rather than as an end in themselves (Korkia and Stimson, 1993). On the other hand, AS users also report that while they are on steroids they experience a number of psychological benefits, including feeling powerful, more satisfied with body image, confident, pleased with themselves and an increased sex drive (Brower *et al.*, 1991; Korkia and Stimson, 1993). Furthermore, there is other evidence that AS may be misused in ways that make the world of AS use less clearly distinguishable from the world of illicit drug use. There is evidence that AS use has extended from competitive sports people to include a wide range of people such as those who regularly undertake weight training in gymnasia, and that many users inject steroids, take more than one type, mix AS with other drugs and take AS in doses several times larger than is recommended for therapeutic use (Korkia and Stimson, 1993; Shapiro, 1991). There is an illicit market in AS and most users do not disclose their use to their GPs (Korkia and Stimson, 1993). This 'misuse' has given rise to concern about the health risks of AS use, including the risk of HIV transmission from unsafe injecting practices. There have also been reports of aggressive and impulsive behaviour or 'steroid rage' (Korkia and Stimson, 1993; Shapiro, 1991).

A further shortcoming of any of the official definitions of dependence is that none fully covers all those people whose use of drugs, such as AS, incurs problems of these kinds, and who might benefit from advice or treatment. Hence both DSM and ICD include an additional diagnostic category, termed 'abuse' in DSM and 'harmful use' in ICD. The problems here are greater still than those encountered in trying to define 'dependence'. The criteria by which abuse or harmful use are to be judged are more socially and culturally relative and difficult to gauge reliably.

Furthermore, they may seem to imply a moral judgement, hence risking forfeiting the gains made in trying to define dependence as a disorder free of moral judgement (Widiger and Smith, 1994). The term 'abuse' has come in for particular criticism as being unscientific, pejorative and vindictive (Babor, 1990). Rounsaville *et al.* (1993), in their study comparing DSM and ICD criteria for various kinds of drug use disorder, found very low levels of agreement between DSM abuse and ICD harmful use. Most DSM abuse cases were considered by ICD criteria to show neither harmful use nor dependence, while most ICD instances of harmful use were diagnosed according to DSM as suffering from dependence.

Whether AS have any capacity for producing addiction or dependence is a moot point. Brower *et al.* (1991) reported the results of asking 49 male weightlifters about their use of AAS (anabolic–androgenic steroids). They represented the 12 per cent of men who admitted taking steroids from amongst all those screened in four gymnasia in one area in the USA. During the time of the study only two women steroid users were found; hence the study concentrated on men. They were predominantly men in their 20s who were lifting weights mainly to improve physical appearance or physical condition, but also 'for personal enjoyment' and 'to increase self-esteem'. Four-fifths had injected AAS and were calculated to be exceeding therapeutic doses by 2 to 26-fold. When DSM-III-R criteria for dependence were assessed it was found that at least one of the nine supposed symptoms of dependence was reported by 94 per cent, and three or more symptoms, consistent with a diagnosis of dependence according to DSM, were reported by 57 per cent. For example, 51 per cent reported taking more of the substance than intended, and 40 per cent expending a lot of time on substance-related activity. The most frequently reported dependence symptom, however, was withdrawal symptoms, of which the most frequently reported were: a desire to take more AAS (52 per cent), fatigue (43 per cent), dissatisfaction with body image (42 per cent) and depressed mood (41 per cent). The most frequent pattern of use, described by Brower *et al.* as 'cycling', involved periods of use followed by periods of no use.

Contrary to the assumption that AAS produced no euphoria, between a third and a half of Brower *et al.*'s weightlifters reported feeling 'high' on AAS, but reports of euphoria did not correlate with dependence symptoms, and Brower *et al.* were inclined to the view that addiction to AAS was driven more by the negative reinforcement of trying to avoid bad feelings about one's body than by positive reinforcement. They were impressed by the fact that many of the men had 'felt not big enough' before taking steroids, and that many still felt not big enough, the latter correlating with dependence symptoms. They speculated that body-size dissatisfaction might represent a psychological vulnerability to AAS dependence. Lastly, they reported a high level of alcohol consumption among the weightlifters but a low level of tobacco use.

In conclusion of this chapter, then, it can be stated with some conviction that the varied forms taken by 'drug addiction' pose as much of a challenge in themselves to the developments of a psychological understanding of excessive appetitive behaviour, as does a consideration of the similarities and contrasts found between excessive alcohol use and excessive gambling. Our theorising must embrace de Quincey's experience of laudanum as well as the modern experiences of 'addicts' whether from the affluent suburbs or the deprived inner city, whether in high-status employment or on the streets.

Nor can our model of addiction be based on the one drug, heroin, which has tended to monopolise our thinking in the recent past. Many of the assumptions about addiction, based on experience with heroin, are found wanting in the face of evidence of the potential for excess carried by other substances. We thought we knew where we were with heroin. But experience with tobacco, cocaine and marijuana call into question the centrality of such elements as euphoria and withdrawal. Our understanding of the excessive appetites must also account for the housewife 'dependent' on BZPs and the weight trainer 'abusing' AS. It must account, too, for the young glue or petrol sniffer in Japan (Wada and Fukui, 1993), Britain (Gossop, 1993) and Aboriginal Australia (Brady, 1992).

If that seems like a demanding task, the following two chapters set us an even greater challenge—how to account for the fact that many people report losing control over the normal functions of eating and having sex, and perhaps over exercising too.

CHAPTER FIVE

Excessive Eating and Exercising

These patients crave food like an alcoholic addict craves drink. Over and over [one patient] ... spontaneously compared her compulsive eating jags to the behaviour of an alcoholic. She said she could no more eat one piece of food than an alcoholic can take one drink. On an eating spree she would go from drug store to restaurant 'like an alcoholic making his rounds.'

(Hamburger, 1951, p. 491)

Obligatory runners are individuals who know pain. They compromise their bodies by continuing to run when injured. They forfeit jobs, marriages, friends, and other pleasures because of their running regimen. They plan vacations around running and when they are not running they ruminate endlessly about time, distance, food, and the proper shoes ... They work toward a lower percentage of body fat so that they can run faster or farther. They retire early in the evening and may begin running well before dawn. They almost always run alone. There is nothing in their lives that can equal the experience of running.

(Yates, 1991, p. 29)

The purpose of these introductory chapters is to draw parallels while at the same time pointing to contrasts which have to be accommodated in any satisfactory psychological model of excessive appetitive behaviour. The diversity of appetites which can become excessive is the point. The point is underlined in the present chapter, where we turn to eating—unlike those considered so far, a biological necessity, at least in moderation. At present the scientific and professional worlds of 'drug addiction' and 'eating disorders' are quite separate. But, as I hope to show in this chapter, the parallels are close ones and the separation has therefore hindered rather than helped the development of a comprehensive view of addictions.

In the case of eating, it has often not been excess itself which has occasioned concern but, rather like tobacco smoking, bodily damage or the risk of it. In particular, it was overweight or 'obesity' which first gave rise to interest in over-eating as a possibly 'addictive behaviour'. It was assumed that people who were very overweight were so because they ate excessively. Indeed, most psychological theories of 'obesity' attempted to explain why some people eat more than others (Ley, 1980). Later, evidence began to accumulate that 'obese' or considerably overweight people often eat no more (and some studies found less) than people of normal weight (Ley, 1980; James, 1976). It was recognised that other factors in the equation, particularly exercise (James, 1976), were important to an understanding of weight control, and that there were patterns of out-of-control eating not necessarily associated with over-weight. An influential early study was that of Stunkard (1959, cited by Leon and Roth, 1977) who described a number of eating patterns of obese individuals which he considered to be fairly distinct. One of these was the 'night eating syndrome' characterised by excessive eating in the evening, insomnia and avoidance of eating altogether in the morning. A second pattern he described was that of 'binge eating' in which large quantities of food would be consumed in a short period of time, these periods being interspersed with longer periods of normal or restrained eating. A further pattern he described, which he called 'eating without satiation', where a person found it difficult to stop eating once intake had started, he felt might be related to central-nervous-system damage.

Particular attention quickly focused on the pattern which Stunkard called 'binge eating' and which in early accounts was variously referred to by others as 'compulsive eating', 'bulimia nervosa', 'bulimarexia', the 'dietary chaos syndrome' or simply the 'stuffing syndrome' (Wardle and Beinart, 1981). A number of authors described people who showed extreme preoccupation with food and weight, who episodically consumed enormous amounts of food in short periods of time in an 'orgiastic' manner (episodes varying in frequency from more than once a day to once every few weeks), and who experienced guilt, shame, depression and self-condemnation following 'binges'. The parallel with apparently 'compulsive' patterns of gambling or drinking is immediately striking.

Loro and Orleans (1981) made a special study of binge eating amongst 280 'obese' and overweight adults attending a dietary rehabilitation clinic in the USA and found the phenomenon much more common than had been supposed. Just over half the sample reported, 'consuming large or enormous quantities of food in short periods of time', at least once a week and only 20 per cent stated that this never happened. Binges usually lasted between 15 and 60 minutes, rarely lasting more than 4 hours, and the number of calories consumed was usually within the range 1000 to 10 000. Bingeing was more common amongst those who reported already being overweight in childhood or adolescence. The latter were more likely to have had some psychological treatment for weight loss, which led Loro and Orleans to suggest that those who manifested binge eating might require more intensive treatment. They did not consider the possibility that binge eating might at least partly be a *consequence* of treatment or at least a consequence of efforts at self-control which had failed (Wardle and Beinart, 1981). They did, however, raise the possibility later in their paper that adhering to an overly strict and unrealistic diet could itself lead to a pattern of oscillating between self-denial, rigid dieting and fasting at the one extreme, and binge eating at the other.

Wardle and Beinart (1981), reviewing what had then been written about this pattern of eating, showed that although it had been reported to occur amongst people who were very overweight, it occurred also among people of normal weight, and among those who were below normal weight including those who were anorexic. Bruch (1974) was one of the first to describe a pattern of alternating bingeing and starving. These 'thin fat people', as she called them, often had a history of overweight. This and later reports described frequent self-induced vomiting and purging as well as fasting by people with this pattern, plus the sense of despair, shame and experience of preoccupation with eating or resisting eating, felt by the 'victims' of this 'condition'. Patients with anorexia nervosa had been noted sometimes to have periods of overweight in their previous or subsequent histories, and those who used vomiting and purging as well as dieting as ways of keeping weight down were recognised as a subtype within the category of anorexia (Wardle and Beinart, 1981). Nor, it seemed, were those experiences of uncontrolled binges, preceded and followed by stringent attempts at self-control and the use of deliberate weight-control methods including fasting and self-induced vomiting, limited to clinical populations. Wardle (1980) found that a group of women medical students reported an average of nearly five eating binges per month, and men two.

The recognition that apparently 'addictive' forms of eating were not confined to the overweight and that many 'obese' people might in fact eat quite normally were amongst the factors that produced a shift in attention from the variable overweight versus normal weight to a new variable, *restrained versus unrestrained eating*. It was pointed out that many people diet or 'watch their weight' closely, and that these vigilant or 'restrained' eaters differ from unrestrained eaters in theoretically predictable ways. For example, Herman and Polivy (1975), using their Restraint Questionnaire, which has been much used in research since, found that unrestrained eaters ate significantly less when made anxious, whilst restrained eaters tended to eat *more*. Coates (1977) summarised research by Herman, Polivy and others showing that while unrestrained eaters tend to eat less after a milk-shake 'preload', restrained eaters tend to eat *more*. Polivy (1976) found that restrained participants, after a preload which they perceived to be of high calorie content, ate more of a standard meal than did those who thought the preload to be of low calorie content, while unrestrained subjects did the reverse.

What is clear is that there are many individuals who experience an appetite for food which they or others judge to be excessive and which leads to self-initiated attempts at behavioural control or to recommendations for restraint from others. Early modern examples include Morganstern's (1977) case of an extremely overweight 24-year-old graduate student whom he called Miss C:

> In addition to eating three regular meals a day, the client reported that she ate candy and 'junk' all day long, completely unable to control herself despite countless attempts at dieting and medically prescribed appetite suppressants. Miss C also stated that she had been in some sort of psychotherapy for six, nearly continuous, years. This previous treatment had included two instances of hospitalization of very short duration and contact with five separate therapists whose techniques, reportedly, ran the gamut from psychoanalysis to desensitization ... A preliminary analysis of Miss C's eating habits revealed an enormous consumption of five principal types of

food: candy, cookies, doughnuts, ice cream, and pizza. Base-rate data for three weeks indicated that the client ate close to 200 pieces of candy and dozens of cookies and doughnuts per week. In addition, she indulged in pizza and ice cream at least once a day, and often as many as three times in the same day.

(Morganstern, 1977, p. 106)

Hamburger (1951) also referred to cases where excessive eating had apparently led individuals to steal food or money to buy food, to hide and hoard food, and to lie about their eating activities. Such accounts make it clear that there are closer parallels with the more readily acknowledged 'addictions' than might at first be supposed. Those who were writing from a psychoanalytical viewpoint—such as Fenichel (1945), Bruch (1974), and Wise and Wise (1979)—recognised an 'addictive' or 'neurotic' need for food. Bruch quoted 'typical' expressions used by some of her clients: '"I get 'mad' in my stomach", or "I get this gnawing feeling and nothing can change it but a luscious meal", or "It is my mouth that wants it; I know that I have had enough"' (p. 127). The familiar 'addiction' elements of an appetitive drive alien or in opposition to the conscious will or real self is found here as in accounts of excessive drinking, gambling or drug taking, and the drive in this case is felt to be located in the stomach or the mouth, anywhere in fact but in the seat of reason or will.

A patient described by Wijesinghe (1977) illustrated the, by then increasingly recognised, complaint of periodic excessive eating without marked overweight. The patient was a 37-year-old woman referred with a 6-year history of compulsive eating which had become progressively worse in the previous 2 years:

> It had started after her husband had left her, but even before that when she was depressed or frustrated she used to find solace in eating biscuits or chocolates .... There was a regular pattern of 'binges' two or three times a week. At the beginning of an episode she would have sensations which she described as 'feverish excitement' which would compel her to go to the nearest baker's shop and buy large quantities of sweet, starchy foods— cakes, biscuits, chocolates—and either drive out in her car to some secluded place or take the food home. She would then set about consuming this food in a voracious manner 'making a pig of myself' as she put it. This would continue for an hour or two, by which time she would feel 'bloated, tired and sick'. This would usually be followed by loss of appetite for a day or two, whilst she would feel extremely guilty. The abstinence from food after a compulsive eating episode kept her weight within bounds. Nevertheless it seriously disrupted her work ... and also her social life.

(Wijesinghe, 1977, p. 86)

It was the expression 'bulimia nervosa' that caught on as the term to signify that some, at least, of these forms of excessive eating might amount to a kind of disease entity. Crichton (1996) tells us that bulimia is an ancient Greek word, used by Aristotle among others, literally translated as 'ravenous hunger', probably the hunger (*limos*) needed to eat an ox, bull or cow (*bous*).

There has been some controversy over whether bulimia is a genuinely new disorder, unknown before the mid-1970s. Consistent with the view that it is, are a number of studies finding very different reported lifetime-prevalence rates of bulimia or binge eating among women in different age groups. For example, the New Zealand study of Bushnell *et al.* (1990, cited by Fairburn *et al.*, 1993) found a lifetime prevalence of bulimia of 4.3 per cent among 18–24-year-old women, 2.0 per cent among 25–44-year-olds and only 0.4 per cent among 45–60-year-olds. Similarly, the Norwegian study of Götestam and Agras (1995) found reported lifetime-prevalence rates of both bulimia and 'binge eating disorder' varying systematically with age group, from highs of 3.0 per cent for bulimia and 4.9 per cent for binge eating among 18–29-year-olds to lows of 0.6 per cent in each case for 50–59-year-olds. This supports the impressions of agencies specialising in the treatment of eating disorders whose business has increased dramatically since the mid-1970s. There is the view, however, that these forms of excessive eating are not new phenomena and that what has occurred is an increase in professional and public awareness, and changes in diagnostic and referral practices, greatly aided by the use of terms such as 'bulimia' and 'binge eating'. Fombonne (1996) is one author who considered the case for a real increase in the incidence and prevalence of bulimia to be unproven. He pointed out that there were no satisfactory studies of prevalence prior to 1980, that it is difficult to separate excessive eating from other forms of psychological difficulty such as depression and anxiety, which makes the interpretation of trends difficult and that there is plenty of evidence from earlier times that 'eating disturbances' such as dieting and body dissatisfaction were reported at high frequency among community samples of adolescent and young adult women (e.g. Dwyer *et al.*, 1969, 1970). Despite the increased publicity since then, it is probably still the case that most instances of excessive eating go unrecognised and untreated (Fairburn *et al.*, 1993). In that respect they are like most of the other forms of excessive appetitive behaviour considered in this book.

The core 'symptom' of 'bulimia nervosa' is bingeing. Until the 1980s most studies of this phenomenon had used self-report questionnaires which allowed for considerable latitude in defining a 'binge'. Since then, however, there have been a number of studies in which participants have been asked to keep daily diaries of food intake and eating habits, and other studies that have directly observed eating in a laboratory or hospital environment. A review of these studies (Walsh, 1993) confirmed that people diagnosed as suffering from bulimia were mostly women, and that they did often engage in discrete eating episodes during which they consumed great quantities of food containing large numbers of calories. What these studies also showed, however, was that the range of calorie intake during such 'binges' was wide, and that quantity of food consumed is not the only criterion by which people define an eating episode as a binge. Typical is a study by Rossiter and Agras (1990, cited by Walsh, 1993) of 32 women who kept a diary of all food consumed for 1 week. This group described 343 binges in total, with an average energy consumption of 1173 calories. Of these self-defined bingeing episodes, 17 per cent involved energy consumption greater than 2000 calories which corresponds to what is sometimes recommended as the average allowance for a whole day (Walsh, 1993). On the other hand, 28 per cent involved energy consumption lower than 500 calories, and the full range was from a low of 45 to a high of over 5000 calories.

Work by Walsh *et al.*, 1992 (cited by Walsh, 1993) provides an example of the observational studies. Their participants also had a high average consumption during binges but a wide range. They also confirmed that women with bulimia ate faster than control participants, consuming on average 81 calories a minute compared with controls' 38 a minute. Of additional interest was the observation that women with bulimia consumed on average fewer calories during non-binge meals compared with controls, a finding consistent with other reports that individuals with bulimia, when not bingeing, tend to restrict their calorie intake.

There is no evidence in these studies to support the often repeated depiction of binge eating being driven by 'carbohydrate craving'. Women with bulimia ate proportionately no more carbohydrate during binges than at other times. There was a tendency, however, towards consumption of dessert or snack foods, more characterised by sweetness than by high carbohydrate content. This may partly explain the relatively low calorie content of some self-defined binges. People define themselves as bingeing, not always on the basis of the amount consumed, but sometimes for failing to control the consumption of types of food that are thought to be inappropriate generally or inappropriate for the time of day or circumstances (Walsh, 1993).

Although most of the literature on excessive eating is not very specific about the types of food that are consumed excessively, there does exist a small specific literature on chocolate as the object of craving or addiction. Rozin *et al.* (1991) asked 250 university psychology students, and over 300 of their parents, about cravings for chocolate, and concluded that 14 per cent of the sons, 33 per cent of daughters, 14 per cent of fathers and 25 per cent of mothers showed 'substantial addiction' to chocolate based on their answers to questions about craving ('a strong desire, occurring at least a few times a month ... so strong that it will cause a person to go far out of his/her way to satisfy the craving'), withdrawal ('physical discomfort resulting from abstaining ... for a certain period of time'), lack of control ('difficulty in stopping the consumption') and tolerance ('individual doses (portions, levels) ... produce less of an effect than they used to').

Hetherington and MacDiarmid (1993) advertised for 'chocolate addicts' in their area of Scotland, and subsequently interviewed 50 people, mostly women, of ages ranging from 14 to 83. On average they were consuming 12 60-g bars of chocolate a week, which was calculated to be roughly four times the national average. Three-quarters considered their consumption of chocolate to be excessive, either because it contributed to overweight, because it was considered to be high in fat and of poor nutritional value and/or consumption was viewed as excessive compared with that of other people. Half stated that the consumption of chocolate interfered with their lives in some way. Two-thirds reported feeling irritable or deprived, angry or unhappy, when trying to cut down consumption, and a further 14 per cent had never tried to cut down. A total of 40 per cent said that they preferred to eat chocolate alone and in secret, and this sub-group were significantly more likely to be dissatisfied with their weight and shape, to hold more abnormal attitudes towards food and weight, and to score higher on indices of restraint and emotionally and externally controlled eating. The group as a whole reported feeling an improved positive mood during eating of chocolate, and a decreased positive mood again afterwards. The latter effect was particularly marked in the reports made by the sub-group of 'secret eaters'.

Participants in both the Rozin *et al.* (1991) and Hetherington and MacDiarmid (1993) studies attributed the addictiveness of chocolate to its sensory properties which made it a uniquely palatable, or 'moreish', food. Another finding common to the two studies was the menstrual cyclicity of chocolate craving reported by women participants, chocolate cravings being particularly associated with the pre-menstrual period.

Although bulimia is typically described as occurring in young women, this is not exclusively the case. Beck *et al.* (1996), for example, found among the records of a number of specialised hospital-treatment programmes a small number of people with an average age of onset of 60 years. Although this challenged the theory that excessive eating requires an adolescent onset, Beck *et al.* remarked that memories of childhood events persisted in these cases (e.g. in the form of memories of having been teased and criticised for excessive weight as an adolescent). Later in life bulimia had been precipitated by events such as bereavement or emigration, and was sometimes complicated by medical conditions that required or involved weight loss. The following is a case report concerning a woman who developed bulimia only after the age of 60:

> The patient, Mrs K, a 64-year old widow ... reported a 2-year history of bulimic episodes accompanied by self-induced vomiting and occasional laxative abuse. The frequence of bulimic episodes had gradually increased and, at presentation, they were occurring three of four times a day. In addition, she was attempting to adhere to a low calorie reducing diet ... She was intensely preoccupied with thoughts about her weight and shape, and was weighing herself up to six times a day ... Mrs K's weight of 57 kg was appropriate for her age and height ... [and] had been stable for many years ... The bulimic episodes were a source of considerable guilt and shame and had recently led to financial difficulties. The patient was a leading figure in the local slimming club and described ... a 40-year history of restrictive dieting ... She experienced her first bulimic episode at a wedding reception where, following an upsetting family disagreement, she lost control of her eating after which she induced vomiting ... Mrs K had been married for 40 years and had been widowed 2 years before the onset of bulimic episodes.
> (Coker, 1994, pp. 89–90)

Nor is loss of control over eating unknown amongst men. Tanofsky *et al.* (1997) made the point that, unlike bulimia or anorexia, men are well represented among those with 'binge eating disorder' (BED, see below). They reported a comparison of 21 men and 21 women with BED and found few differences in terms of the details of their eating disorder. The following is taken from an autobiographical account given by a man, trained and working as a clinical psychologist. Wilps (1990) described using eating for comfort as a child but dated his 'eating disorder' from a period of stress as a young adult coping with professional training, setting up home with a wife who was separated from her family and holding down a job as a new professional teacher, and a little later being frustrated in their efforts to have a child:

> I then began to diet in earnest ... Initially my food binges were rather benign, involving large 'peasant gourmet' dinners ... with my wife present ... By the time my graduate program was finished, our life as a couple had deteriorated severely ... The period of greatest symptom intensity ... lasted [seven years] and was characterized by increasing frequency of binges and corresponding increases in the disruption of my personal and professional life. My marriage dissolved during this time ... The effect of all this on my eating was to deeply cement bulimia as a part of my lifestyle ... my bingeing increased in frequency and became more clearly addictive in nature. I would experience waves of an aching, almost flu-like feeling in midafternoon during the week, and realize that I wanted to have a binge evening.
>
> (Wilps, 1990, pp. 16–20)

Finally a comparatively high rate of coexistence of excessive eating and excessive drinking or drug use has been pointed out by a number of authors. For example, Garfinkel *et al.* (1996) found a high rate of lifetime and current alcohol 'dependence' amongst those identified as meeting criteria for bulimia in their large sample of Canadian adults, with the rate being higher amongst those in the purging subtype (lifetime 53 versus 24 per cent non-purging type; currently 12 versus 2 per cent non-purging type). Lacey (1993) reported findings from 112 consecutive referrals of normal-weight bulimic women from two London boroughs. He reported a high rate of heavy alcohol use and of drug use, and the overlap between these 'self-damaging' behaviours led him to suggest the existence of a core group of 'multi-impulsive bulimics'. Each of the self-damaging behaviours was described as being associated with a similar sense of being out of control, and appeared usually to have a similar function in reducing or blocking unpleasant or distressing feelings. Crichton (1996) reported of the Roman Emperors Claudius and Vitellius, whom he claimed were probably the earliest well-documented historical figures who regularly binged and vomited, that they, '... were impulsive not only in their eating habits. Both drank heavily ... and both loved gambling' (p. 205).

DISAGREEMENTS OVER TERMS AND DEFINITIONS

All the signs of terminological confusion and conceptual acrobatics associated with attempts to define alcohol or drug 'dependence' or 'compulsive' or 'pathological' gambling are to be seen again in the scientific literature on bulimia and binge eating. The changes that had occurred in the last three versions of DSM (the American Psychiatric Association's *Diagnostic and Statistical Manual*) were well reviewed by Fairburn and Wilson (1993). The use of the term 'bulimia nervosa' dates from the work of Russell (1979, cited by Stunkard, 1993) who described 30 patients who were not markedly overweight but who had an excessive fear of becoming so, and who both vomited and purged themselves after bingeing. This

Table 5.1   Criteria for 'bulimia nervosa' according to DSM-IV (*Diagnostic and Statistical Manual of Mental Disorders*, American Psychiatric Association, 1994, pp. 549–550)

A. Recurrent episodes of binge eating. An episode of binge eating is characterized by both of the following:
   (1) eating, in a discrete period of time (e.g. within any 2-hour period), an amount of food that is definitely larger than most people would eat during a similar period of time in similar circumstances
   (2) a sense of lack of control over eating during the episode (e.g. a feeling that one cannot stop eating or control what or how much one is eating)

B. Recurrent inappropriate compensatory behavior in order to prevent weight gain, such as: self-induced vomiting; misuse of laxatives, diuretics or other medications; fasting; or excessive exercise

C. The binge eating and inappropriate compensatory behaviors both occur, on average, at least twice a week for 3 months

D. Self-evaluation is unduly influenced by body shape and weight

E. The disturbance does not occur exclusively during episodes of anorexia nervosa

   Purging type: during the current episode of bulimia nervosa, the person was regularly engaged in self-induced vomiting or the misuse of laxatives, diuretics or enemas
   Non-purging type: during the current episode of bulimia nervosa, the person has used other inappropriate compensatory behaviors, such as fasting or excessive exercise, but has not regularly engaged in self-induced vomiting or the misuse of laxatives, diuretics or enemas

---

combination of features is represented in the DSM-IV criteria for a diagnosis of bulimia which are shown in Table 5.1.

A number of difficulties have been found with these criteria, and the difficulties closely parallel those encountered in trying to set up more or less objective criteria for supposedly discrete conditions such as 'drug dependence' or 'pathological gambling'. One such problem is that core 'symptoms', such as binge eating in this case, themselves prove to be difficult to define closely. The second problem is that arbitrary rules have to be drawn up concerning, for example, the necessary frequency and duration of symptoms. A further difficulty is that social and cultural relativism cannot usually be eliminated, however hard the experts try (e.g. 'an amount of food which is definitely larger than most people would eat during a similar period of time in similar circumstances'). The greatest problem, however, is that of attempting to draw a line between people who have the disorder and the many others who may have many features in common but who are not thought to reach the laid-down criteria.

The definition of binge eating has undergone revision in the DSM system. Version III of 1980 and the revised version III of 1987 did not include the element of 'a sense of lack of control over eating during the episode' which is the criterion cited most often by binge eaters themselves (Telch *et al.*, 1998), and which by the time of drafting version IV was considered as important as the amount consumed. Versions III and III-R did include, however, a requirement that eating during a binge be 'rapid', an element which was later thought not to be essential and was dropped. Although the new definition may have been an improvement, it automatically excluded two other types of eating episode which some think should qualify as bingeing. The first occurs when a person eats a large amount of food in a short period of time without a sense of lack of control. The second occurs when a person does experience a lack of control and views the eating involved as excessive although the amount eaten is not abnormally large. These two instances have been referred to, respectively, as 'objective over-eating' and 'subjective bulimic episodes' to distinguish them from the 'objective bulimic episodes' that qualify as binge eating according as DSM-IV criteria (Fairburn and Wilson, 1993).

Among a sample of about 2000 female twins in Virginia, USA, aged on average 35 years, Sullivan *et al.* (1998) found that it was quite common to have ever binged (24 per cent), and not uncommon to have employed self-induced vomiting (5 per cent). Only 0.5 per cent, however, met DSM-IV criteria for bulimia, the 'bottle-neck' being the frequency of bingeing and vomiting required to meet the DSM thresholds—on average at least twice a week for 3 months. Sullivan *et al.* argued that there was no evidence to support the validity of this particular threshold. Using the criterion of risk to the co-twin of meeting the same definition of bingeing or vomiting, they suggested that one binge a week and two instances of vomiting a month might be more satisfactory. The arbitrariness involved is self-evident.

Similarly, Hay (1998) found that, of 3000 adults taking part in a health survey in South Australia, 3 per cent were currently regularly binge eating (once a week or more), but that strict dieting or fasting was less common (2.2 per cent of women, 0.7 per cent of men), and purging even less so (1.3 per cent of women, and no men). Using DSM-IV frequency criteria for binge eating would have led to the conclusion that only 0.3 per cent were suffering from bulimia. They also concluded that men might be more at risk for less serious eating disorders than had pre-viously been thought (e.g. current regular bingeing was almost as common among men as among women), and that it might also be more common than expected among middle-aged women.

Just as criteria for drug dependence have been found to exclude many people with serious problems of excessive drug use, concern was widely expressed that the criteria for bulimia exclude a whole range of 'eating disorders' which might best be thought of as constituting a spectrum of conditions. These conditions were variously described as, 'sub-clinical', 'sub-diagnostic', 'sub-threshold', 'sub-frequency' or 'atypical' (Shisslak *et al.*, 1995). Some of these might involve people meeting all the criteria for bulimia except that the frequency of their binges was less than twice a week or for a duration of less than 3 months. Others might be those engaging in inappropriate compensatory behaviour, such as vomiting, misuse of laxatives or excessive exercise, after eating relatively small amounts of food. Particularly common are thought to be instances in which people, usually young women of more or less normal weight but wanting to weigh less, are experiencing considerable distress and engaging in most of the problem-eating behaviours associated with bulimia, but failing to meet the criteria only because of the low frequency of the compensatory behaviours (Fairburn and Wilson, 1993; Shisslak *et al.*, 1995). This recognition led to a proposal for yet another diagnostic category, that of 'binge eating disorder' (Spitzer *et al.*, 1992, cited by Fairburn and Wilson, 1993). This required frequent binge eating (as for a diagnosis of bulimia) but did not require bulimia's criteria B, C and D (Table 5.1). In place of those criteria was substituted the requirement that binge eating episodes be associated with at least three of the following five characteristics: (1) eating much more rapidly than normal; (2) eating until feeling uncomfortably full; (3) eating large amounts of food when not feeling physically hungry; (4) eating alone because of being embarrassed by how much one is eating; (5) feeling disgusted with oneself, depressed or feeling very guilty after over-eating.

Not that the invention of 'binge eating disorder' overcomes the problem of definition. Brody *et al.* (1994) had two independent raters rate the presence or absence of binge-eating disorder, and individual criteria, from tapes of interviews with 20 people, 10 of whom were thought to have binge eating disorder. The *kappa* coefficient for agreement on the overall diagnosis was 0.70, and for individual diagnostic criteria it ranged from 0.39 ('eating large amounts of food throughout the day with no planned meal times') to 0.79 ('feeling disgusted with oneself, depressed or feeling very guilty after over-eating'). Brody *et al.* interpreted these figures as indicating that the diagnosis is at least as reliable as most DSM diagnoses, although the figure of 0.70 seems to the present author not to be particularly high, leaving considerable room for disagreement. Greeno *et al.* (1995) compared the results obtained with the Binge Eating Scale (BES), a questionnaire that has been widely used in research on the subject, with the Eating Disorder Examination (EDE), a standard clinical interview. They found that BES over-identified binge eating by the standard of the EDE interview, mainly because the binges referred to when completing the former were often either not large enough, not sufficiently out of control, or sufficiently frequent to qualify according to the latter. The best BES items, judged against the EDE as a standard, were those concerning preoccupation with food and eating, guilt after over-eating, difficulty controlling eating, and eating when not hungry.

Fairburn, Hay and colleagues argued that the existence of such a syndrome as 'binge eating disorder' had not properly been established, but that a catch-all category of 'eating disorders not otherwise specified (EDNOS)' should be included in the DSM manual instead (Fairburn and Wilson, 1993; Fairburn *et al.*, 1993). Hay *et al.* (1996) claimed to have found evidence in favour of this position in the results of a large study of young adult women screened for eating disorders in 19 general practices in urban and rural areas in Oxfordshire, England. After screening and interviewing a selected group of women, 248 with recurrent binge eating were studied further and the results subjected to a statistical cluster analysis in an effort to identify diagnostic groups. One group, with the most severe eating disorders, resembled the purging form of bulimia nervosa outlined in DSM-IV. A second, large group had a severe eating disorder with a high frequency of objective bulimic episodes, although most did not experience lack of control nor use self-induced vomiting or misuse laxatives or diuretics. They did, however, exhibit high levels of dietary restraint and extreme concern about shape or weight. A third group exhibited a high frequency of eating episodes in which they experienced lack of control, although the amounts consumed were usually not abnormally large. The fourth and largest group was a heterogeneous group with eating problems which were less severe. None of these groups according to Hay *et al.*, corresponded exactly to the purported 'binge eating disorder'. Once again we have an illustration of the improbability of being able to pin down excessive appetitive behaviour with a single, precise definition.

In a later paper reporting findings from the same group, but adding results from a 1-year follow-up, Hay and Fairburn (1998) concluded that bulimic eating disorders were best thought of as lying on a continuum which ranged from bulimia purging type—the most severe—through bulimia non-purging kind, to the least severe—binge-eating disorder. Garfinkel *et al.* (1996) came to a similar conclusion on the basis of their health survey of over 8000 adults in Ontario, Canada. Approximately 1 per cent had met criteria for bulimia (of whom 89 per cent were women), approximately one-quarter being of the purging type (i.e. using laxatives or vomiting as compensatory behaviours), the remainder being of non-purging type. In support of their conclusion that the purging type represented the more serious disorder, Garfinkel *et al.* cited the finding that the purging type had a higher rate of lifetime major depression (65 versus 24 per cent for the non-purging type) and of experiencing sexual abuse while growing up (53 versus 20 per cent). Hay and Fairburn (1998) found support for the same conclusions in the finding that those in the purging group were the most likely still to be experiencing an eating disorder 1 year later.

Like Walker (1989) in the case of pathological gambling, Wilson (1993) has questioned whether binge eating constitutes an 'addiction'. He recognised the apparent similarities between binge eating and psychoactive 'substance abuse'—a sense of lack of control, preoccupation, repeated attempts to stop, impairment of physical and/or social functioning, the fact that binge eating like a drug is often used to regulate emotions and to cope with stress, and that both may involve denial and secrecy—but argued that this did not make binge eating an addictive disorder. Unlike Walker, Wilson assumed that evidence of tolerance, and 'physical' dependence (e.g. on carbohydrate) are necessary before concluding that binge eating is an addiction. He admitted that these were 'traditional criteria', deriving from a disease model of addiction, but he failed to consider any alternative set of criteria.

THE FACT OF CONCERN OVER EXCESSIVE EATING

Quite apart from the identification of 'cases' who may or may not meet this or that arbitrary definition of a disorder, there can be no denying that concern about over-weight and over-eating is widespread in countries like Britain. In their survey in the London borough of Richmond, for example, Ashwell and Etchell (1974) had found that half of the women and a third of the men considered themselves to be over-weight. There was a strong but imperfect relationship between believing oneself to be overweight and Ashwell and Etchell's objective assessment of overweight arrived at by comparing actual weight with ideal weight for a person of 'medium frame' according to the Metropolitan Life Tables. Of women and men who were actually overweight by this index, 89 and 69 per cent, respectively, considered themselves to be overweight. Even of those considered objectively to be of 'suitable weight' (within 10 per cent either side of the ideal weight), 36 per cent of women and 17 per cent of men thought themselves to be overweight. This picture of widespread 'dissonance' regarding weight, even though overweight may not always be attributed to over-eating, is matched by a high level of interest in controlling eating and a high prevalence of attempts at dieting, particularly for women. For example, Ashwell and Etchell (1974) reported that two-fifths of their total sample (half of the women and a quarter of the men) had tried to lose weight at some time.

It is interesting to note the differences between the sexes which recur in studies of dieting. Unlike excessive consumption of alcohol, excessive gambling and some forms of disapproved of or excessive drug use, we are dealing here with a form of concern about behaviour which is decidedly more prevalent amongst women than men. There are various possible explanations for the difference—biological, psychological and sociological—but the fact of the difference in levels of concern remains and provides a striking contrast with some other forms of excessive appetitive behaviour. The sex difference, and the comparison with other forms of appetitive behaviour, are instructive also concerning the difference between 'objective' and 'subjective' indices. Although surveys in many countries have often shown a somewhat higher prevalence of 'objective' overweight and over-eating, or eating at times of stress, among women than men, it is 'subjective' *concern* about weight and eating which most clearly shows women well ahead of men (Dwyer *et al.*, 1970). There is substantial evidence that concern about perceived overweight, and interest in dieting as a means of reducing weight, are strongly sex-typed behaviours.

Certain groups of teenage girls continue to be amongst those with the highest levels of concern about weight and eating, and the most frequent reported use of control behaviours that are included in the standard lists of 'symptoms' of excessive eating disorder. Huon (1994), for example, reported the following among 15–18-year-old girls at three private schools in Sydney, Australia: 35 per cent 'very much preoccupied with weight'; 25 per cent 'mostly' or 'always' dieting; 11 per cent using purgatives to control weight, and 6 per cent vomiting; 33 per cent regularly over-eating to the point of discomfort or nausea; 26 per cent preoccupied with thoughts of how to avoid eating; 26 per cent being unable to control the urge to eat; 21 per cent experiencing loss of control if eating forbidden food. Overall Huon judged that 13 per cent fell into the 'severe binge eating' category and that a further 25 per cent might be thought to have a 'moderate eating problem'.

There can be little dispute, then, over the central point of the present chapter; that many people find it difficult to control their eating which they view as excessive. Nothing attests more clearly to this fact of serious concern about excessive eating and overweight than the recent history of remedies that have been attempted for excessive eating. These have included a number of quite radical treatments which have all been used at one time or another within the last few decades, principally in the treatment of 'obesity'. Amongst these are various forms of operation in which, by surgical means, a length of the intestine is bypassed. More than 30 such procedures have been described, the three in common usage being gastric bypass, gastric restriction and gastric banding (Thornley and Windsor, 1998). Although no well-designed trials with follow-up had been reported by the time Thornley and Windsor were writing, they concluded, as have others (e.g. Scopinaro *et al.*, 1996), that, if used correctly, the results of such surgery could be very positive in terms of weight loss and improved quality of life. In their opinion it remains, however, a 'blunt instrument', doing no more than enforcing a restricted calorie intake.

A further physical method, which nicely demonstrates both the 'dissonance' which some people feel about their eating and the conflict which their behaviour poses for them, consisted of fitting a 'dental splint' or 'jaw wiring' to prevent the person taking in other than liquid sustenance. Since some people were willing to put up with this restraint for several weeks or months at a time, and since it produced, not surprisingly, dramatic weight reductions, this method had a number of medical advocates at one time, but the long-term effects upon weight and quality of life were never established and the method was never widely used (James, 1976).

A range of medications have been prescribed to control excessive eating, as they have for all forms of excessive appetitive behaviour. The most popular in the case of excessive eating were the amphetamine-like stimulants used to suppress appetite—yet another example of the tendency to treat one form of excessive appetite with a procedure that puts the person at risk of developing another. There appeared to be general agreement that amphetamines were moderately effective in controlling appetite (Ley, 1980) although their long-term efficacy was doubtful (James, 1976). The use of agents such as fenfluramine with lower 'potential for drug abuse' than some others such as methamphetamine and amphetamine was recommended in the late 1970s, but in practice the prescribing of all appetite-suppressant drugs became less popular as recognition grew of the possibilities for excessive drug use (Thornley and Windsor, 1998). Dexfenfluramine was a comparative newcomer, given approval as an appetite suppressant in the USA only in the mid-1990s and hailed in the media as a possible 'miracle drug' (*Time Magazine*, 1996, cited by Thornley and Windsor, 1998), only to be withdrawn a few years later because of complications (Carek and Dickerson, 1999). Many have been scathing about drug treatments which have been fashionable and often lucrative to the manufacturers and suppliers, and have continued to be popular with physicians long after the theoretical rationale for their use has been repudiated and, in the case of the amphetamines, long after the possible dangers had been exposed. The worst abuse, according to Bruch (1974), was the fashion for 'treating' over-weight with 'rainbow pills', which consisted of various combinations of drugs offered in different colours, to be used at different times of day (p. 317). A small qualitative study which sought to find out why women continued to seek appetite-suppressant medication despite these negative expert views of their usefulness, suggested that they gave women a perception of control and confidence to continue with attempts at weight loss despite frustration at failed dietary regimes (Volume and Farris, 1998).

Starvation routines of one kind or another have also been used to try to bring about rapid decreases in weight and to 'break the habit' of over-eating. Short-term fasting, of a few days only, appears to be ineffective but there have been a number of published accounts of prolonged starvation, up to 100 days or more, in hospital. Such regimes, not surprisingly, had dramatic short-term effects upon weight, but the long-term effects were not so clear. There are also risks, with prolonged starvation, of adverse psychological reactions and several deaths were reported. Hence, compromises between short- and long-term fasting regimes were used including inpatient fasting for 1–2 weeks followed by 1–2 days of fast each week as an out-patient, or protein-supplemented out-patient fasting (James, 1976). These therapeutic experiments are revealing about the nature of eating as a possible 'addiction'. Excessive drinkers and gamblers, and those whose drug use or sexuality is excessive, have also been willing to undergo regimes involving total abstinence from the difficult-to-control behaviour.

Varieties of other methods have been used in the treatment of overweight, including acupuncture and hypnosis, but the most popular forms of treatment have consisted of dietary advice. About 100 years ago, when the Congress of Internal Medicine in the USA was discussing the pros and cons of various diets, those such as the Harvey–Banting diet of high protein content, Epstein's diet which was high in fat content, and the Dencel–Oertel Cure which involved fluid restriction and systematic exercise, had already become extremely popular (Bruch, 1974). In her time Bruch found numerous, varying diets continuing to be offered, all in her view fraudulently put over in a way that quite erroneously suggested that their use would be easy. Many were based either on 'counting calories' to reduce energy intake, or upon reducing carbohydrate intake, but others had included those involving protein only with vitamin supplements, amino acids and minerals with varied small quantities of carbohydrates, high egg diets, high grapefruit diets, chicken-only diets and many others (Bruch, 1974; James, 1976). Thornley and Windsor (1998) concluded, as have most reviewers, that diets have not been successful in maintaining long-term weight reduction.

The 1960s and 1970s saw a veritable explosion of techniques of 'behaviour modification' aimed at the control of over-eating. It is not surprising to find, for a start, that aversion techniques were applied to eating as they have been to virtually all forms of appetitive behaviour which can get out of control. Leon (1976) and Ley (1980) each reviewed the range of aversion and other behaviour modification methods of that period. Aversive stimuli included electric shock, foul-smelling substances (such as butyric acid, acetimide and pure skunk oil), cigarette smoke and pictures of the person who wished to reduce weight clothed in scanty underwear or swimwear. The connection between eating-related and aversive stimuli could be made in imagination, as in the procedure known as 'covert sensitization', and other imaginal procedures were used such as 'coverant control', whereby negative thoughts about eating were immediately followed by positive thoughts about being slim, followed by some 'high probability behaviour' such as answering the door or opening a magazine. Clients were rewarded with tokens or social approval by the therapist, by repayment in instalments of deposits put down at the beginning of treatment or by 'self-reward' of various kinds. The 1970s and early 1980s were a period when developments in behavioural treatments took the form of varieties of 'self-control' procedure. These techniques usually involved close 'self-monitoring' of food intake and weight; they aimed to modify eating style (e.g. by encouraging eating only at meals laid in one place, pausing between bites, chewing food well and leaving some food at the end of a meal); and involved controlling the environment in such a way as to reduce temptation (e.g. by avoiding exposure to unsuitably tempting foods, shopping after eating rather than before and asking other members of the family to prepare their own late-night snacks; Stuart, 1967).

The list of contents in *Behavioural Treatments of Obesity*, edited by Foreyt and published in 1977, illustrates the variety of behavioural approaches being used at that time. They included, 'massed electrical aversion treatment', 'aversion-relief therapy', 'self-managed aversion therapy', 'assisted covert sensitization', 'coverant control and breath-holding', 'self-management application of the Premack principle', 'social reinforcement', 'successive contracts', 'contingency contracting', 'bibliotherapy', 'self-directed program', and 'self-reward, self-punishment, and self-monitoring'. More recently, with a shift of focus from obesity towards 'bulimia' and other forms of excessive eating, or 'eating distress', and with the 'cognitive revolution' in behavioural treatment, 'cognitive behaviour therapy' (CBT) has taken over as probably the most popular treatment (see Chapter Thirteen).

The appeal of self-help and commercially run weight-reduction groups is further testimony, if any more were required, to the fact of widespread 'dissonance' over eating behaviour. When Ashwell (1978) was writing in the 1970s, Weight Watchers which started in the United States in 1961 and in Britain in 1967, was the largest of these groups with over 800 weekly classes in the United Kingdom and a million members all told. TOPS (Take Off Pounds Sensibly) could claim 345 000 members, in over 12 000 chapters throughout the world, with chapters delighting in names such as Taperettes, Shrinking Violets, Pound Pushers and Tummy Tuckers. Silhouette Slimming Clubs and Slimming Magazine Slimming Clubs were other British variants. US varieties included Over-eaters Anonymous, Diet Kitchen and Diet Workshop. In expert circles, dieting has acquired a bad name, partly because of restraint theory which suggests that dieting may induce bingeing and 'eating disorders' (see Chapter Eleven). So much so that some believe the anti-dieting message has gone too far. In Brownell and Wadden's (1992) view, for example, 'the public good' will not be served if individuals come to believe that: (a) diets do not work, (b) dieting is more dangerous than staying heavy and (c) excess weight is a trivial risk factor (p. 508, cited by Howard and Porzelius, 1999, p. 40).

It seems undeniable, then, that many people who try to control their eating are battling against an appetite of considerable strength. Millions of people feel that their eating is excessive, would like to be able to control it better than they do, but find great difficulty in so doing. As a result, people join, in their hundreds of thousands, organisations devoted to helping their members control their eating behaviour, and an enormous amount of clinical service and research time and effort has been devoted to devising ways of helping people achieve this aim. Hence the evidence for including over-eating as one of the core excessive appetites, or as an 'addiction' in the popular meaning of that term, is overwhelming.

EXCESSIVE EXERCISE

Can exercise, as some have suggested, also become excessive to the point of addiction? Attempting an answer faces us, yet again, with confusions, misunderstandings and inconsistencies in defining addiction. Griffiths (1997) provided the following case description:

> Joanna (not her real name) is 25 years old ... and although she did not identify herself as an addict she realised that she had a problem surrounding exercise ... Jiu-jitsu is the most important activity in Joanna's life above everything else. Even when not actually engaged in the activity she will be thinking about the next training session or competition. She estimates that she spends approximately six hours a day (and sometimes more) involved in training (e.g. weight training, jogging, general exercise, etc.) ... Joanna claims she gets highly agitated and irritable if she is unable to exercise. When her arm was bandaged up because of an arm injury she went for three hour jogs instead. She claims she also gets headaches and feels nauseous if she goes for more than a day without training or has to miss a scheduled session ... Joanna's relationship with her long term partner has finished as a result of her exercise ... She claims she has become 'a bit of a loner' with few friends as a result of her excessive exercising. Added to this her degree suffered because of the lack of time and concentration ... Joanna can only go a few days of no exercise before her day to day living becomes absolutely unbearable ... She has continually tried to stop and/or cut down but claims she cannot ... She is well aware that exercise has taken over her life but feels powerless to stop it.
>
> (Griffiths, 1997, pp. 163–165)

A number of terms have been used to describe the phenomenon of excessive exercising. They include: running addiction, obligatory running, running anorexia, compulsive athleticism, athlete's neurosis, morbid exercising, compulsive exercising, fitness fanaticism, zealous exercising, excessive exercising, exercise dependence (Farrar, 1992; Cockerill, 1996; Veale, 1987). Yates (1991), who has written one of the most extensive and interesting works on the subject and who has championed the expression 'obligatory running', defined those who experience it as: 'Individuals who will not or can not moderate their running in spite of clear contraindications such as a stress fracture or threatened divorce' (p. 28). Among the cases of obligatory running that Yates identified, in the course of a study of long-distance runners, is the following:

> Max is a 33-year-old divorced man ... He runs 40 miles each week. He has had a number of minor injuries such as stone bruises and a hamstring pull. Once he bruised his kneecap so badly he could not walk; he was told to stay off it for a week. After three days, he was back running ... It would take having his leg in a cast for him not to run, but then he would 'probably walk it' ... His greatest fear is that he would be injured so that he could never run again; if this were the case, he would want to kill himself. He runs regardless

of the weather or of how he may be feeling and he always runs alone ... He would like to run 60 miles a week. Through running, he has become more controlled and he has a greater degree of control over his life ... Although Max would like to be married again, he worries that it might interfere with his running. He has a girlfriend, but he is angry because she questions the value of his running and thinks that he uses it to avoid issues ... He would really like to find a woman to support him for a year so that he could spend all his time training.

(Yates, 1991, pp. 32, 34)

In Yates' (1991) view, 'obligatory running' qualifies as a disorder when inflexible adherence to the activity interferes with social or occupational functioning and other more productive or desirable behaviour. For Cockerill (1996) what distinguishes people who are dependent on exercising from those who are highly committed to exercising, but not dependent on it, is that the former 'organise their life round their exercise ...', whilst the latter, 'organise their exercise round their lives ...' (p. 5).

Although many writers are not convinced (e.g. Cox, 1999), attempts have been made, as might be expected, to create a diagnostic category. Table 5.2 shows Veale's (1987) list of diagnostic criteria for 'exercise dependence'. Note, again, how an effort has been made to incorporate this form of dependence on an activity into the model of drug or substance dependence, by using parallel language, and particularly by including increased tolerance and withdrawal symptoms as criteria. As we find time and again in writings on excessive appetites, those writing about excessive exercising are highly prone to question the existence of an 'addiction' by judging the phenomenon of excessive appetitive

Table 5.2 Veale's proposed diagnostic criteria for 'exercise dependence' (reproduced by permission from Veale, 1987, table 1)

(a) Narrowing of repertoire leading to a stereotyped pattern of exercise with a regular once-or-more daily schedule
(b) Salience with the individual giving increasing priority over other activities to maintaining the pattern of exercise
(c) Increased tolerance to the amount of exercise performed over the years
(d) Withdrawal symptoms related to a disorder of mood following the cessation of the exercise schedule
(e) Relief or avoidance of withdrawal symptoms by further exercise
(f) Subjective awareness of a compulsion to exercise
(g) Reinstatement of exercise after abstinence

Associated features
(h) *Either* the individual continues to exercise despite a serious physical disorder known to be caused, aggravated or prolonged by exercise and is advised as such by a health professional—*or* the individual has arguments or difficulties with his partner, family, friends or occupation
(i) Self-inflicted loss of weight by dieting as a means towards improving performance

---

behaviour against an inappropriate standard. Cockerill (1996), for example, argued against the use of the word 'addiction' in relation to what he called 'exercise dependence', on the grounds that:

> ... long periods of relatively intensive exercise require considerable mental and physical effort, whereas gambling, fruit machine playing and drug and alcohol addiction invariably do not require a similar degree of effort to become involved. In addition, exercise is more readily available than other potentially addictive behaviours, yet the effort required for it to become obligatory is great.
>
> (Cockerill, 1996, p. 6)

Not only does this argument involve the introduction of an unnecessary, additional criterion for defining addiction (i.e. 'effort'), but it is also the case that the wide range of other forms of addiction involve a great diversity of degrees of effort. Similarly, Yates (1991) attempted to draw a distinction between 'addiction' and 'compulsion':

> To call the activity disorders addictions would seem to be an oversimplification. A true addiction is ego syntonic, i.e. these persons enjoy drug use, they don't want to stop, and they are not concerned enough (by society's standards) about losing self control ... Compulsions on the other hand, are for the most part ego dystonic, i.e., these people do not enjoy what they are doing, although they may think that it is something they should do. They feel driven or compelled to continue the activity; they can't stop, even though they may want to stop, because they are mightily afraid of losing self control ... For [the obligatory runner] the sport is a deadly serious endeavor and he has no choice but to drive himself forward. There is more pain than pleasure, more compulsion than addiction, in the runner who struggles over the hill on the 21st mile of the marathon or winces as he pounds the pavement on a twisted leg.
>
> (Yates, 1991, pp. 58, 59)

This attempt, to distinguish an addiction from non-addiction on the grounds of enjoyment or pleasure or whether the activity is 'ego syntonic', which is based on a fundamental misunderstanding about the nature of excessive appetitive behaviour, is very commonly encountered. Yet Yates was aware that the distinction does not work in the case of excessive exercising, and that 'obligatory runners' are ambivalent about their activity, and experience a mixture of pleasure and pain:

> Yet these runners may claim that they run because of the sheer pleasure of running. However, obligatory runners who have been injured and can no longer run describe a different scenario. Some weeks or months post injury, they portray their running as having been strenuous and exhausting—a chore in which they forced themselves to engage for reasons that they did not completely understand. When obligatory runners are interviewed in

depth, and when they establish an affectual tie with the examiner, they tend to temper the glowing picture of the sport with a different theme.

(Yates, 1991, p. 59)

Another misleading idea is that, if exercise can sometimes amount to an addiction, it is, unlike most others considered in the present book, a 'positive addiction', since exercise is a highly approved and health-giving activity (Glasser, 1976). This idea is also liable to miss one of the central points about addiction. Although excessive appetites are immoderate forms of behaviour which are positive in moderation, it is their *excessiveness* which is distressing.

A relationship between excessive exercising and forms of excessive eating, such as binge eating and bulimia, creates further definitional and conceptual problems. Brewerton *et al.* (1995), for example, studied the medical records of 110 women who met the criteria for bulimia (71), anorexia (18) or both (21). A total of 31 (28 per cent) were found to be also experiencing 'compulsive exercising' as defined by exercising to control weight at least once a day and exercising for at least 60 minutes each day. Slightly fewer of those with bulimia than those with anorexia were thought to be exercising compulsively.

Most writers on the subject point out that many people who appear to exercise excessively are very concerned about body shape and weight, and may often be highly concerned with dieting or restraining their eating in some way. Indeed, the many points of similarity and overlap between excessive exercising and the 'eating disorders' prompted Yates (1991) to propose an inclusive category of 'activity disorder' to embrace disorders of exercising and eating. Whether people were more inclined to exercise or to restrain their eating might have more to do, Yates believed, with factors such as age and sex, with middle-aged men being more inclined to the former and young women more towards the latter. Veale wished to make a distinction between exercise dependence which was secondary to an eating disorder ('secondary exercise dependence') and 'primary exercise dependence' where the exercise was an end in itself with restrained eating being used to improve performance.

The idea of excessive exercising is particularly challenging to the view of addiction to be developed in the present book. Cox (1999) is one who has mounted a particularly powerful challenge on the basis of in-depth interviews she carried out with 10 people who responded to advertisements for those who considered themselves 'hooked' on exercising and who scored above the mid-point on an exercise-dependence questionnaire (Ogden *et al.*, 1997, cited by Cox, 1999). They described some costs associated with their exercising, including bad feelings if they found themselves unable to exercise:

Denise—if I don't train I'm niggly (irritable) and I'm miserable and I feel guilty and horrible and my day just falls to bits.

Gill—I do still get the same feelings of distress if I can't go because the exercise is such a major part of my life ... I get very very depressed ... I get to the point you know depression to the point where I can weep ...

berate myself for not going ... the lack of discipline to get me there and I perceive myself as being a very lazy person.

(Cox, 1999, p. 68)

But for the most part they described exercising as a health-giving and positive influence in their lives, associated with feelings of personal control, a sense of time structure and achievement of a desired body shape. Cox concluded:

... [it has been argued] that exercise dependence should be defined and used as a diagnostic category. If this occurs then people may begin to construct themselves and their exercise in this way and present with the 'problem' of exercise addiction (interestingly none of the people in this study saw their exercising as a 'problem'). As this happens medics will start to diagnose it and clinical psychologists, amongst others, will invent ways of 'treating' and 'curing' it. In light of what has emerged in this study, to view this as a pathology set within the individuals, with their behaviour as the symptoms, is clearly too simplistic.

(Cox, 1999, p. 74)

Nevertheless, it seems from what has been written on the topic, including descriptions of individuals such as Joanna and Max (see above), that exercising does have some potential for becoming excessive. As we shall see in Part II this is not altogether surprising in the light of the model to be developed here. Before concluding this introduction to a variety of excessive appetites, however, we need to consider a final one, sex addiction, which presents us with an equal if not even greater challenge.

CHAPTER SIX

Excessive Sexuality

... [Sexual desire is increased] to such an extent that it permeates all his thoughts and feelings allowing of no other aims in life, tumultuously, and in a rut-like fashion demanding gratification without granting the possibility of moral and righteous counter-presentations, and resolving itself into an impulsive insatiable succession of sexual enjoyment ... This pathological sexuality is a dreadful scourge for its victim, for he is in constant danger of violating the laws of the state and of morality, of losing his honour, his freedom, and even his life.

(Krafft-Ebbing, 1886/1965, pp. 46–7)

... [men who] have an insatiable appetite for women and seem irresistibly attractive to them ... there is something compulsive about their sexuality, unmerciless insistence that won't be denied or delayed ... they are strongly drawn to women, one would have to say addictively so. They require constant sexual companionship, whether in the form of wives, girlfriends or casual partners. Deprived of such companionship, they suffer from depression and anxiety ... For the pursuit and conquest of women is the central activity around which these men's lives are organised ...

(Trachtenberg, 1988, pp. 38, 71, 94)

Theoretical debate about addiction has been particularly informed by a consideration of the excessive use of substances, and particularly certain drugs that have been illegal in the late 20th century. It has been the argument of these opening chapters that this narrow focus has constrained our understanding and prevented the emergence of a complete theory of the 'manias', as excessive appetites would have been termed a hundred years ago. The debate must be widened, to include at least excessive gambling behaviour and excessive eating and exercise. The purpose of the last of these scene-setting chapters is to contribute further to the widening of discussion about the nature of excessive appetitive behaviour by considering a further example, namely sexual behaviour which is excessive.

It is important to make clear from the outset that this discussion is not concerned with sexual problems of a 'dysfunctional' kind such as difficulties in attaining erection or orgasm, nor forms of sexual behaviour which themselves are against the law, nor with minority sexual preferences. As with excessive alcohol use and excessive gambling, for example, the focus is upon a type of behaviour which in moderation is considered in our culture to be ordinary but which has become immoderate or excessive. This topic rarely receives serious scientific attention, and theorists see little need to account for it. This is partly because such behaviour rarely presents itself in a clinical setting, and partly perhaps because it is unfashionable to speak of excessive or immoderate sexual behaviour, and to suggest the existence of 'sex addiction' may appear to be in danger of introducing a moralistic element.

Neither feature is confined to sexual behaviour, however. A resistance to seeking help on account of an appetite that has become excessive is a feature of all types of such behaviour and there are good psychological reasons for this, as later chapters will attempt to make clear. The question is rather whether sexual behaviour can become the object of an appetite that is experienced by the individuals concerned to be, and observed by others to be, excessive? The tentative answer on the basis of the evidence to be adduced in this chapter is yes, and hence the psychological model to be presented later in the book must embrace these experiences and observations. Nor is excessive sexual behaviour peculiar among the excessive appetites because it is unfashionable or unpalatable to some to suggest its existence. Precisely the same attitudes have been held at one time or another about each of the appetites we are considering here, and there are parallels between excessive sexuality and, for example, excessive exercising or excessive cannabis use in the present day.

In the case of excessive sexuality it is more than usually difficult to sort out truth from fiction among professional, quasi-professional and lay contributions to the 'literature' on the subject. For example, the rulers of ancient Rome are cited frequently as instances of excessive sexual behaviour, as they are of instances of excessive appetitive behaviour of other kinds. In their book, *Nymphomania: A Study of the Oversexed Woman* (1965), Ellis and Sagarin (both men) discussed Tiberius's wife Julia, Justinian's wife Theodora and Claudius's wife Messalina (whose name is occasionally used to describe excessive sexuality in women—the Messalina complex) as possible 'cases' of 'nymphomania'.

Groneman (1994) reviewed the history of nymphomania as a diagnosis up to the 20th century. From 2nd-century Greece, where Galen believed it particularly occurred among young widows whose loss of sexual fulfilment could drive them to madness, up until the 17th century when cases were reported in Italy, France, Spain, Portugal, Germany and England, nymphomania was more likely to be termed *furor uterinus* or uterine fury. Krafft-Ebbing, in his notorious Victorian collection of sexual monstrosities and expressions of repressive sexual prejudice, *Psychopathia Sexualis* (1965, 1st ed. 1886), wrote of what he called 'hyperaesthesia' in which sexual desire was abnormally increased. Among the cases he cited was a married man of 53, a caretaker, who had nauseated his wife by being, 'insatiable in his marital relations'. Among other misdemeanours was his seduction of his sister-in-law and of a 16-year-old girl who was his ward:

His excuse was hypersexuality. He acknowledged the wrongfulness of his actions, but said he could not help himself ... There was no disturbance of his mental faculties, but the ethical elements were utterly wanting.

(Krafft-Ebbing, 1886/1965, p. 48)

This one quotation alone illustrates two general and related features of excessive appetitive behaviour. One is the function of the construction placed upon behaviour: in this case the construction 'hypersexuality' or something similar serves to explain if not excuse the behaviour. Second is the attribution of immorality or lack of 'ethical elements', particularly if the offered 'excuse' of a condition that renders behaviour difficult to control is not accepted. These features have an important role to play in a social psychology of excessive appetites and they will be discussed further in later chapters.

In a much later section of his influential work, Krafft-Ebbing cited case reports of 'nymphomania' and 'satyriasis' (the female and male variants, respectively), although the distinction between these and 'hyperaesthesia' was not made clear. Most of these cited reports had been previously published elsewhere. Indeed, the rumour-like spread of information about the wildest extremes of behavioural excess is abundantly obvious here and elsewhere in the literature; the same 'cases' are to be found repeatedly as evidence of the existence of certain 'conditions'.

In Krafft-Ebbing's time, hypersexuality was much more likely to be associated with women. By this time the view had taken hold that women were by nature less interested in sex, and although satyriasis, the male equivalent, was recognised, it was believed by doctors to occur far less frequently and to be less serious. As Krafft-Ebbing (1886/1965, p. 87) put it, 'predominating sexual desire in woman arouses a suspicion of its pathological significance' (cited by Groneman, p. 352).

Up until the 20th century most medical explanations were firmly biological and recommended treatments were physical. Renaissance doctors, for example, working within the model of humoral medicine, treated furor uterinus with bleeding, purging, emetics and herbal medicines. One French doctor of the 18th century stated that too much pleasure and high living, rich sauces, and spiced meat made the 'blood too abundant' and thus indulgent women were much more likely to succumb to nymphomania. One popular theory throughout the 19th century was that there existed a relationship between an enlarged or inflamed cerebellum and excessive sexual appetite. In the latter part of the 19th century the growth of gynaecology shifted the anatomical focus downwards, and surgical removal of the ovaries, and sometimes the clitoris and/or the labia, were used in the treatment of excessive sexual desire, although these treatments were always controversial among gynaecologists. Groneman found a number of medical reports in which doctors claimed that women patients had begged to be operated on, or their daughters to be operated on, because excessive sexuality had become unbearable. She found only the following, single account, from a woman, in her own words, calling herself a nymphomaniac:

She recounted her attempts to exercise her will against the overpowering nature of the desire: 'When I felt tempted, I would kneel and honestly pray to be kept from doing wrong, and then get up and do it [masturbate]; not because I wanted to, but because my life could not go on until the excitement was quieted' . . . She struggled with the feelings, 'At times I felt tempted to seek the company of men to gratify my passion, but was too modest' . . . She is 'treated' by having her clitoris removed, 'but it grew again . . . I tormented doctors to operate again . . . They did . . . [Even] while I was praying my body was so contorted with the disease that I could not get away from it even while seeking God's help'.

(Mills, 1885, pp. 535–537, cited by Groneman, 1994, pp. 357–358)

A very wide variety of terms have been employed at one time or another to describe excessive heterosexual behaviour. Sometimes subtle distinctions are drawn between the conditions to which they are supposed to refer, but mostly they are used synonymously. The list includes: the Casanova type, compulsive promiscuity, compulsive sexuality, Don Juanism or the Don Juan syndrome or complex, Don Juanitaism, erotomania, hyperaesthesia, hypereroticism, hyperlibido, hypersensuality, hypersexuality, idiopathic sexual precocity, libertinism, the Messalina complex, nymphomania, oversexuality, pansexual promiscuity, pathologic multipartnerism, pathologic promiscuity, satyriasis, sexual hyperversion and urethromania. This list is certainly not exhaustive.

Not very long ago, in the 1930s, 'nymphomaniacs' were referred to by doctors as women, '. . . who exceed the bounds of decent behaviour', as, 'morally insane,' driven by 'some moral poison' to carry out a 'disgraceful sacrifice of feminine honour' (cited by Levitt, 1973). Although the language had been moderated somewhat by the 1960s and 1970s, books and articles in respectable journals such as *Medical Aspects of Human Sexuality*, and *Sexology*, were still regularly testifying to the fact that individuals do sometimes complain of an inability to control their own excessive sexual appetite. Morse (1963) provided a 'case history' typical of many:

'I developed these tremendous urges', she explained . . . 'I couldn't think about anything but sex. It was on my mind constantly . . . my desires were just too strong for me . . . I thought maybe I should see a psychiatrist . . . I was . . . all set to be a good wife [but] I would go out and find a man. Any man . . . There was one magical cure for depression, something a lot better than tranquillisers. Sex.'

(Morse, 1963, pp. 40–42)

Despite Morse's statement that the histories he provided were, '. . . real histories of real individuals' (p. 12), it is difficult to know how reliable are the quotations he provided. Nevertheless, this story has the ingredients of the subjective experience of uncontrollable desire, behaviour felt to be inappropriately excessive by the individual concerned given her life circumstances, the use of behaviour to control unpleasant affects and guilt about behaviour—all frequent ingredients of excessive appetitive behaviour of other kinds. Other similar descriptions of excessive heterosexuality, in males as well as females, were provided by authors including Levitt (1973), Lewis (1971) and Radin (1972). In one of the more thoughtful articles on the subject of female excessive sexuality, Levitt (1973) described a person suffering from 'nymphomania' (a term he recommended abandoning) as, '. . . an emotionally disordered woman whose major symptom is an abnormally high frequency of sexual behaviour involving multiple persons, apparently without regard to their personal characteristrics, or to other aspects of reality' (p. 14). Radin (1972) described Don Juanism in the male as, '. . . a driving need to have sexual relations with a great number of women' (p. 4).

Another source of clinical material on excessive sexuality at that time was the writings of clinicians concerned with marriage and the family (e.g. Eisenstein, 1956; Dicks, 1967). Eisenstein listed 'hypersexuality' as one of six types of sexual problem affecting marriage, although he believed it was not a clinical entity in itself but rather a manifestation of neurosis. Sex became in such instances 'an addiction'. In his book *Marital Tensions*, Dicks wrote of the 'compulsive promiscuity pattern' of adultery. Eisenstein and Dicks agreed that such behaviour patterns were rarely described to clinicians unless the behaviour was known and objected to by the marital partner who insisted on help being sought. Students of 'alcohol dependence', 'compulsive gambling', 'drug addiction' and over-eating would probably agree that these conditions are also unlikely to come to clinicians' attentions unless they occasion harm, or the perceived risk of it, either to the individual or to others.

A further source of clinical material came from reports of the therapeutic use of antiandrogenic drugs such as cyproterone acetate for sex offenders or would-be offenders (e.g. Cooper *et al.*, 1972; Laschet, 1973). Although most people treated with such drugs had displayed unlawful minority sexual behaviour such as pedophilia or exhibitionism, over half of the series of 120 patients reported by Laschet (1973) were non-delinquent and 17 were described as suffering 'hypersexuality' with or without excessive masturbation. Other 'anaphrodisiacs' included benperidol, a 'major tranquilliser', and oestrogen. Other treatments for excessive heterosexual behaviour in that period included castration, used in cases of 'hypersexual delinquency' in some countries (Cooper *et al.*, 1972), and the occasional use of aversion and other behavioural therapies for 'compulsive masturbation' (Hodgson and Rachman, 1976), and even for infatuation and adultery with a next-door neighbour (Barker and Miller, 1968).

In case it should be thought that the medical treatment of excessive sexuality in women is a thing of the past, the following case of 'female hypersexuality' comes from the *American Journal of Psychiatry* for 1988:

> Ms A, a 40-year-old single woman, started having sexual intercourse at 12 years of age. Experiencing orgasm from the first, she soon developed a preference for multiple orgasms, with successive sexual partners, but usually supplemented their efforts by masturbating. This behaviour continued throughout her adolescence. At age 20 she sought psychiatric help, because her sexual behaviour conflicted with her religious beliefs and her relationships with men seemed meaningless. During the next 10 years she had individual psychotherapy, behavior therapy, and courses of antidepressants, neuroleptics, and benzodiazepines with little effect. At age 31 she sexually assaulted a man. Frightened by this, she gave up psychiatric

treatment and sexual relations. She masturbated six to eight times daily and avoided male company, but violent erotic dreams disturbed her sleep. Little changed during the next nine years; she lived alone, had the same job, and had a few female friends from her church. Ms A then sought help again, because changes at work had involved contact with young boys and she feared that she might sexually assault them. Her previous medical, psychiatric, and family histories were unremarkable, and the results of a physical examination, including a gynaecological examination, were normal. The patient's need for reduction in libido and her hypersexuality without evident cause led to a trial of the antiandrogen agent cyproterone acetate. ... Within a few days she stopped masturbating, the erotic dreams ceased, and males did not evoke sexually aggressive feelings.

(Mellor *et al.*, 1988, p. 1037)

SEXUAL ADDICTION?

There have not been the same intellectual tussles over the exact definition of hypersexuality as there have been over some other forms of addiction or dependence, but there have been some efforts to define excessive sexuality as an addiction. One of the first modern attempts to do so was Carnes' (1983) *Out of the Shadows: Understanding Sexual Addiction*. In that book a number of 'cases' were cited, although the extent to which these cases are real or synthesised from a number of accounts was not made clear. Carnes did make a strong case for sexual addiction, on the basis of his experience of hearing about excessive sexuality in the course of his work running a family centre for 'chemically dependent families'. His stress was on the 'unmanageability' of excessive sexual behaviour, which he contrasted with sexual behaviour which, although it might be regretted or put an individual at risk in some way, did not interfere with the rest of the person's life, and which was in that sense 'manageable'.

One of the fullest treatments of this subject is Goodman's (1998) *Sexual Addiction: An Integrated Approach*. It is rare to find such a lengthy and serious academic treatment of excessive sexuality. The book starts and ends with five clinical vignettes (disguised illustrative examples, not case reports) which well illustrate the kinds of problem the book is dealing with and the kind of treatment the author uses. Of the five, one was a woman, and between them they covered excessive numbers of partners (unpaid), excessive paid sex, and excessive masturbation and use of pornography. One also involved the problem of indecent exposure which illustrates a point Goodman makes that excessive ordinary sex and sex offending (or 'paraphilias' as he called them) often co-occur. Three had, or had had in the past, other addictions including alcohol, other drugs and binge eating, again demonstrating one of Goodman's points, namely that sexual and other forms of addiction co-occur much more frequently than they would by chance alone.

The first part of his book was spent on terminology, trying to square the idea of sexual addiction with definitions of addiction, and defending sexual addiction against some common arguments against the concept. Goodman concluded that it had features of both a compulsive and an impulse disorder, but that neither were adequate, and that the cases he described fitted perfectly happily within the class of 'addiction', defined as:

> ... a condition in which a behaviour that can function both to produce pleasure and to provide escape from internal discomfort is employed in a pattern characterized by 1) recurrent failure to control the sexual behavior, and 2) continuation of the sexual behavior despite significant harmful consequences.
>
> (Goodman, 1998, p. 18)

This, again, provides an example of an unnecessarily elaborate definition betraying the author's own views on why excessive sexuality occurs in individual cases. The idea that sexual behaviour, which could become excessive, functions *both* to give pleasure *and* to provide escape from discomfort, although there may be much truth in it, is surplus to requirements. Recurrent failure to control, and continuation despite harm, constitute the core of the definition. More detailed diagnostic criteria, suggested by Goodman, are shown in Table 6.1.

Another who has written at length on the subject, in a more popular form, is Trachtenberg (1988). He interviewed at some length 50 men whom he believed suffered, like himself, from 'the Casanova complex'. These were men:

> ... who have a repeated history of one-night stands, aborted love affairs or broken marriages; who continually end their romantic relationships; who are chronically polygamous or unfaithful ... For these men, women and sex serve the same function as drugs or alcohol, providing a high that is at once exhilarating and numbing.
>
> (Trachtenberg, 1988, pp. 18, 181)

Among famous Casanovas, Trachtenberg listed Lord Byron, Gary Hart (once US presidential hopeful), Frank Sinatra, Ernest Hemingway and John F. Kennedy. The prototype, is, of course, Jacques Casenove de Seingelt whose 18th-century Memoirs provide ample evidence of the 'single-minded intensity' with which he pursued women. Trachtenberg is another, however, who could not resist imposing on the basic, simple, idea that sexual appetite can become strong and out of control his own idiosyncratic views about the nature of addiction:

> By 'addiction' I do not mean the physical necessity that binds a junkie to heroin or a smoker to nicotine. I use the word to connote a psychic state that often predates the addict's first encounter with his drug and that remains unchanged throughout the career of his substance abuse. It is characterized not only by feelings of worthlessness, the conviction that one deserves nothing more than the destiny of a drunk or junkie, but by a blurred and tenuous sense of self—a fundamental uncertainty about one's own existence.
>
> (Trachtenberg, 1988, p. 28)

Table 6.1 Criteria for 'sexual addiction' according to Goodman (reproduced by permission from Goodman, 1998, pp. 233–234)

A maladaptive pattern of sexual behavior, leading to clinically significant impairment or distress, as manifested by three (or more) of the following, occurring at any time in the same 12-month period:

(1) tolerance as defined by either of the following:

    (a) a need for markedly increased amount or intensity of the sexual behavior to achieve the desired effect

    (b) markedly diminished effect with continued involvement in the sexual behavior at the same level of intensity

(2) withdrawal, as manifested by either of the following:

    (a) characteristic psychophysiological withdrawal syndrome of physiologically described changes and/or psychologically described changes upon discontinuation of the sexual behavior

    (b) the same (or a closely related) sexual behavior is engaged in to relieve or avoid withdrawal symptoms

(3) the sexual behavior is often engaged in over a longer period, in greater quantity or at a higher level of intensity than was intended

(4) there is a persistent desire or unsuccessful efforts to cut down or control the sexual behavior

(5) a great deal of time is spent in activities necessary to prepare for the sexual behavior, to engage in the behavior or to recover from its effects

(6) important social, occupational or recreational activities are given up or reduced because of the sexual behavior

(7) the sexual behavior continues despite knowledge of having a persistent or recurrent physical or psychological problem that is likely to have been caused or exacerbated by the behavior

Trachtenberg touched on a familiar theme when he posed the rhetorical question whether he was not simply describing normal male behaviour. He answered his own question by claiming that although the Casanova figure has been envied by men, he is nevertheless an anomaly in Western culture, distinguished from most men by the unceasing nature of his sexual behaviour. Among the cases he described is the following:

> Sam, forty-three, is a middle-level executive in the San Francisco office of a national insurance company. He has the air of someone who is used to more power than his position carries, and he often tells women that he is a senior officer in his firm. His first marriage ended when his wife discovered that he was being unfaithful to her ... After four years of renewed bachelorhood, during which he had brief sexual encounters with dozens of different women, Sam remarried. He describes Elaine, his second wife, as 'a wonderful person, my confidante, my best friend. She takes care of the house. She takes care of the kids. She does everything that the good American wife is supposed to do' ... Sam needs, or feels he needs, more than this, and he has

been pursuing sex outside his marriage since shortly after the wedding. For the first few years, he favored the anonymous, one-night encounters he was familiar with from earlier on. He went to bars or clubs three nights a week, connected with someone and then had sex with her at her apartment or, occasionally, in a parked car. After a while the physical and emotional costs of this regime caught up with him: 'I began to feel that it was all sort of hollow and sordid. It wasn't just that I wanted intercourse. I wanted conversation, warmth, understanding, and you don't get that in a one-night stand. Also, I was starting to worry about bringing something back home—at that time it was herpes, before the whole AIDS thing started'. At present Sam dates two women who work in his office. He sees each of them at least once a week and sometimes over the weekends, telling his wife that he has to travel for business. Neither mistress knows about the other, and one doesn't even know that he is married. In addition there are four other women whom he meets every few weeks for an evening of casual sex.

(Trachtenberg, 1988, pp. 165, 166)

Trachtenberg argued that Casanovas, like Sam, consistently endanger what they know to be in their best interest. All in his experience had sacrificed at least one marriage or important relationship, and many had compromised careers. Most were indulging in regular, unsafe sex, hence risking HIV infection. About half of the men he interviewed claimed that their womanising was not a problem, but others had sought help with their compulsive sexuality. Some had entered psychoanalysis or other therapy, and a few had consulted with ministers, priests or rabbis.

Shortly after the present author published an article on 'hypersexuality' (Orford, 1978, on which the present chapter is partly based), a report on the article appeared in the press in the USA (*Los Angeles Times*, 10 December 1978), and a number of people wrote to me offering their personal experiences. The following is an extract from one of these:

My name is ... I'm a recovering sexaholic. That's like an alcoholic who can't control and enjoy his drinking, only it has to do with lust instead of booze. I didn't get that way overnight; it took a lot of practice. Let me tell you my story. It all started innocently enough: From age nine on, picture-fantasies, impressing into my formative sexual experience patterns that would shape my destiny. And becoming a young husband and father never changed that basic programming. Sex complicated things. The next stage was affairs—and lightning never struck me dead. So I began to pursue it. And 'real' picture-women had to be pursued, notwithstanding huge hunks of will power, piety and self-denial. Then it began pursuing *me*, and by age 33 I was scoring 'connections' on the streets. I had no way of knowing that the whole process was creating a deadly false reality and short-circuiting my ability to have normal relationships with anyone. I tried everything to stay stopped. Churches. Prayer. Prayer and fasting. The ministry. Leaving the ministry. Three psychiatrists, group therapy, chemotherapy, and finally, exorcism. Marriage itself had been two grand attempts to force it out of my life. But progression of the disease was relentless. And then the miracle came. One night I found myself in an Alcoholics Anonymous meeting. People as desperate over alcohol as I was over lust, living free of their obsession. Here was a program of recovery that was *working* for them. And has been for me ever since.

The whole idea of 'sexaholism', 'uncontrolled promiscuity', 'sex addiction' or 'hypersexuality' as something that warrants a special name of this kind, has been much criticised and the arguments are remarkably reminiscent of those that have been used to challenge concepts such as 'alcohol dependence', 'compulsive gambling' or 'exercise addiction'. Criticisms of the concept of 'hypersexuality' fall under a number of related headings, and most of them apply equally whatever terms are employed to describe the supposedly abnormal sexual behaviour. One of the strongest arguments is that it is impossible to separate normal and abnormal sexual behaviour in other than an arbitrary way, and that there is no evidence of a separate sub-population of people whose behaviour is excessive and qualitatively different from that of others (Lewis, 1971; Levitt, 1973). The following quotation from Kinsey *et al.* (1948) is a good summary of this particular criticism:

> Even the scientific discussions of sex show little understanding of the range of variation in human behaviour ... such designations as ... excessively active, over-developed, over-sexed, hypersexual, or sexually over-active, and the attempts to recognise such states as nymphomania and satyriasis as discrete entities, can, in any objective analysis, refer to nothing more than a position on a curve which is continuous ... Such a continuous and widely spread series raises a question as to whether the terms 'normal' and 'abnormal' belong in a scientific vocabulary.
>
> (Kinsey *et al.*, 1948, p. 199)

The continuum is artificially split into abnormal and normal parts by the fact of a very small number of people complaining of excessive sexuality who have come the way of clinicians over the years. The special problems of this small minority have created a biased and generalised view (Lewis, 1971). This bias was displayed, for example, by Auerback (1968):

> Habitually promiscuous persons ... come from disturbed homes where there were inconsistencies in training and discipline ... Often [promiscuous] women have never accepted their femininity and they may have a large degree of unconscious homosexual colouring in their personality ... they are often neurotic and immature, using sex in a manner comparable to a child who masturbates ... Frigidity is common in the nymphomaniac ...
>
> (Auerback, 1968, pp. 39, 44)

Such 'explanations', attributing excessive behaviour to underlying deficiencies of personality or character, are of course common in certain types of clinical account, and in the context of excessive sexual behaviour they illustrate again the very different perspectives taken by those who approach the subject from acquaintance with a small number of individuals who have sought help and those, such as epidemiologists, who approach it from a study of normal populations.

Kafka (1997) provides an illustration of the danger of arbitrariness in relation to excessive sexuality, much as we have found previously in attempts to define alcohol or drug 'dependence' or an eating 'disorder'. Kafka argued that Kinsey *et al.*'s (1948) concept of 'total sexual outlet' (TSO) had been neglected, and that there existing survey evidence suggested that a TSO of seven or more times a week for at least 6 months might serve as a good threshold for defining 'hypersexual desire'. He admitted, though, that some surveys suggested that this frequency of sexual outlet was quite common in some social groups (e.g. in what Kinsey *et al.* termed the occupational 'underworld'). Among 100 men seeking treatment for what he called 'paraphilia-related disorders' (especially compulsive masturbation, protracted promiscuity, and dependence on pornography) Kafka found an average reported TSO of 8.2 per week.

As an aside here, it may be noted that Kafka (1997), like Carnes (1983) and Goodman (1993, 1998), ran into difficulty in seperating the kinds of 'excessive but ordinary' sexual behaviour with which this chapter is principally concerned (and which Kafka calls 'paraphilia-related disorders') from the committing of sexual offences (or 'paraphilias' as Kafka and Goodman call them). Both Kafka (1997) and Goodman (1998) believed that the two categories overlap, and the view of Carnes (1983) was that both should be included in a total concept of sexual addiction which he conceived of as consisting of three levels: excessive heterosexual behaviour, including excessive masturbation and use of pornography constituted level 1; offending behaviour including exhibitionism, voyeurism, indecent 'phone calls' and 'taking indecent liberties' constituted level 2; and the most serious of sexual offences, including child molestation, incest and rape, made up level 3.

Gold and Heffner (1998) concluded their review of the literature in the area of sex addiction with the statement that it had, '... reached a point in its conceptual development that is likely to rapidly culminate in stagnation. The literature on this topic consists largely of theory and conjecture based almost entirely on clinical observation rather than on research findings' (p. 379). Several of the conjectures about sexual addiction touched on in their review illustrate, in a way that is now very familiar to us, the tendency to include in a definition of addiction some unnecessary elements that go far beyond a straightforward description of behaviour being excessive and difficult to control. For example, some (e.g. Levine and Troiden, 1988, cited by Gold and Heffner, 1998; and the latter themselves in places) seem to view the idea of sexual addiction as having greater legitimacy if it can be shown that reported sex addicts have other clinical symptoms or levels of psychological symptoms that underlie their sexual behaviour and which set them apart from non-addicts. Another view (e.g. Fischer, 1995, cited by Gold and Heffner, 1998) appears to assume that labelling certain behaviours as addiction is tantamount to saying that it, '... can never be fully overcome ...' (Fischer, p. 5). Yet another common, confused and confusing, assumption, encouraged by DSM-IV rules (American Psychiatric Association's *Diagnostic and Statistical Manual*), is that addictive behaviour must, by definition, be pleasurable, since otherwise it would qualify as a proper 'compulsion', and hence would warrant a different kind of diagnosis. Since sex addicts, like other kinds of addicts, often say that their behaviour is now unsatisfying or even aversive (whatever it may have been in the past), then, so it is argued, the behaviour cannot truly be thought of as indicating addiction.

Other unnecessary notions are those which propose underlying motives opposite to those which are supposed to underlie 'normal' behaviour (e.g. people who indulge in a great deal of heterosexual behaviour really hate the opposite sex, or are really homosexual, or really find such behaviour very unsatisfying; people who gamble excessively really have a wish to lose, not to win). Such ideas support the division into normal and abnormal types but are clearly extremely difficult to prove or disprove. For example, there was a popular idea that 'nymphomaniacs' are unable to achieve orgasm, but this has been rejected by many writers on the subject, even on the basis of their knowledge of highly unrepresentative clinical samples (e.g. Ellis and Sagarin, 1965, p. 25).

As with 'alcohol dependence', however, the commonest concept underpinning the notion of abnormal hypersexuality is that of 'uncontrol' or 'loss of control'. Numerous writers have criticised the loose application of such terms in this context as others have for alcohol dependence. For example:

> Words like 'uncontrolled' when they are used as trait names, have an all-or-nothing flavour. They sound like dichotomies; the person is either uncontrolled on every occasion or controlled on every occasion. But certainly it is possible that an individual who has good self-control may become uncontrollable on a few special occasions. Or a person who is generally poorly controlled may nonetheless clamp down on his impulses occasionally. Once we allow that control—uncontrol is a continuum rather than a dichotomy, theory is again beset by the aggravating need to establish cut off points.
>
> (Levitt, 1973, p. 16)

It is hardly surprising that precise definitions of terms have been even less forthcoming than in the cases of excessive drinking, gambling, drug taking, eating and exercising. Particular writers may have a clear idea of the concept but can convey it only in the most indefinite terms. For example, Ellis and Sagarin (1965) considered the chief characteristics of 'nymphomania' to be lack of control, continuous need, compulsivity and self-contempt (pp. 26–27). As Levitt (1973) pointed out, 'The key words that have repeatedly appeared in definitions of nymphomania are unusually relative and ambiguous' (p. 15). Under these circumstances it is not surprising to find that the experts are at pains to define 'true' or 'real' cases. For example, to Auerback (1968) the 'real nymphomaniac' was not just someone with an unusually large number of sexual contacts and partners, but was also someone, '... with no positive feelings emotionally' (p. 210). Terminology can become quite confusing. Ellis and Sagarin (1965), despite making a serious and lengthy attempt to be clear thinking on the subject, created confusion by referring to the rarity of 'true' or 'endogenous' 'nymphomania' which Ellis claimed not to have seen, '... in my many years of clinical practice' (p.29). They distinguished 'true nymphomania' from 'compulsive promiscuity' and in the remainder of their book appear to have been referring to the latter whilst using the former term. Elsewhere they referred to 'controlled promiscuity' and 'genuine nymphomania' among other terms, without clear exposition of the differences.

One familiar strategy for survival in such a conceptual jungle is to divide people up into types. This appears to deal with the frequent criticism that a single concept of 'hypersexuality' ignores the evident heterogeneity of people so defined, but such attempts are as open to criticism on grounds of arbitrary labelling and imprecision of definitions as is the single global concept. Lewis (1971), for example, described no less than nine types, including 'the frigid nymph', 'the promiscuous teenager', 'the sexual compensator' and 'the latent lesbian'. Oliven (1974) distinguished 'sociocultural deviance' from 'pathologic promiscuity' in women, and among males drew a subtle distinction between the emotional distance of the Don Juan, motivated purely by the incentive of sexual conquest, and the Casanova who wreaked still greater havoc by his repeated entanglements that were both sexual *and* affectionate (pp. 423–425).

A further, major shortcoming of a concept such as 'hypersexuality' or 'sex addiction' which implies a pathological or illness-like entity is that it relegates differences in social habits and customs, and reactions to deviance, to a position of relative unimportance. This is particular folly when discussing sexual behaviour, and understandably concepts such as 'hypersexuality' and 'nymphomania' have been frequently criticised on these grounds. Criticisms include the charge that calling any form of sexual behaviour 'addiction' can only be based on a socially relative judgement and may be dangerously stigmatising (Gold and Heffner, 1998):

> The diagnosis of sexual addiction or compulsion rests on culturally induced perceptions of what constitutes sexual impulse control ... The invention of sexual addiction and sexual compulsion as 'diseases' threatens the civil liberties of sexually variant peoples.
>
> (Levine and Troiden, 1988, pp. 351, 361, cited by Gold and Heffner, 1998, p. 368)

Even within a relatively homogeneous culture there are sub-cultural and individual differences in what counts as 'normal' sexual behaviour. For example, Kinsey *et al.* (1948) were at pains to point out that differences between high-frequency and low-frequency sexual behaviour found among US males were of unusually large magnitude as judged by biological standards, and that discussions of what is right and proper in sexual behaviour are bound to be biased by the position of the discussants on this dimension (pp. 198–199). On the basis of his British survey, Eysenck (1971) argued for the importance of the *reaction* of different personality types to their own sexual behaviour. A person, high on the extraversion scale of his inventory, typically described relatively 'promiscuous' behaviour but was not dissatisfied. Eysenck described such a person as 'a happy philanderer'. In contrast, the high neuroticism scorer reported relatively much guilt and low satisfaction. Iwawaki and Eysenck's (1978) study comparing the sexual attitudes of British and Japanese students showed that overlying great individual variation in sexual behaviour and attitudes there have been, and perhaps still are, large differences in the formal and informal rules governing sexual behaviour to be found in different social and cultural groups.

In Marshall and Suggs (1971) even more divergent cultural attitudes were described, varying from the highly permissive (by our standards) sexual culture of Mangaia in the South Pacific, to the highly repressive sexual atmosphere of the west coast of Ireland. Marshall's (1971) observations in Mangaia, the most southerly of the Cook Islands, led him to believe not only that adults assisted youths in early sexual behaviour and that there was great freedom and encourage-ment for premarital sexual intercourse, but also that the system of beliefs that upheld this pattern of conduct was in many respects quite contrary to our own. There was the belief, for example, that avoidance of continuous or regular inter-course with the same partner prevented pregnancy. By contrast, Messenger (1971) described Inis Beag, as he called the island off the west coast of Ireland which he studied, as '... one of the most sexually naive of the world's societies' (pp. 14–15). He observed that discussion of matters even slightly sexual was avoided, that boys and girls, and to a large extent men and women, were separated in their social lives, that nudity was abhorred, and that there was even an absence of a 'dirty joke' tradition on the island. Normal, informal, social control, in which the fear of embarrassment played a major part, was aided by 'clerical social control' in the form of the repressive activities of the local priests and the occasional visit to the island of week-long missions conducted by Redemptorist priests who had commonly taken 'controlling one's passions' as their theme (abstaining from intox-icating drink being another favourite). Clearly, what counted as 'hyper' or 'excessive' sexuality was not the same in two such divergent cultures as Inis Beag and Mangaia.

A most persistent criticism that notions such as 'hypersexuality' ignore social relativism concerns the 'double standard'. As Golden (1968) put it: 'Perhaps the most apparent influence on our attitudes about human promiscuity relates to gender differences. People tend to view women as being 'promiscuous' and do not attach the same label to men' (p. 48). Many writers on the subject (e.g. Ellis and Sagarin, 1965) have commented on the apparent greater clinical incidence of 'nymphomania' than of male variants (satyriasis, Don Juanism, etc.), despite evidence from surveys that males indulge in a greater amount of pre- and extra-marital sexual behaviour with a larger number of partners. Thus, the social reaction is different, and the individual herself as a recipient of society's attitude reflects this in her own reaction to her own behaviour:

> ... when a male in our society is highly promiscuous, nothing is done about it. In fact, his peers usually look up to him, they envy him: when a female behaves in a similar fashion, she is scorned, and if young, often taken in hand by the authorities. Every effort is made to have her *condemn* herself ...
>
> (Ellis and Sagarin, 1965, p. 177, their emphasis)

The above statement may, arguably, be less true in 2000 in the UK than it was in 1965 in the USA, which itself would be some indication of the importance of social norms. Many who have considered the matter carefully are of the opinion that the problems resulting from excessive heterosexuality are the result of personal or social *reactions* to behaviour that appears to break current local norms rather than the result of anything intrinsic to the behaviour itself. As Golden (1968) put it, 'it doesn't make so much difference what one does as how one feels about it' (p. 53). Kinsey *et al.*'s (1948) view was that:

> Most of the complications which are observable in sexual histories are the result of society's reactions when it obtained knowledge of an individual's behaviour, or the individual's fear of how society would react if he were discovered.
>
> (Kinsey *et al.*, 1948, p. 202)

The great importance of both individual and wider societal reactions to appetitive behaviour has arisen with each of the excesses considered here, and this will be one of the main themes of Chapter Twelve. Suffice it to say at this point that the choice of the word 'excessive' to describe the forms of behaviour of interest in this book was made for the very purpose of underlining the relativity of reaction to behaviour.

SOME FAMOUS CASES

Notwithstanding the argument about social and cultural relativism, it is difficult to deny that some individuals have expressed distress and concern over their difficulty in controlling heterosexual behaviour that has become, in their terms, excessive. One outstanding work of undoubted relevance to the theme of this chapter is the anonymous 11-volume autobiographical sexual history, *My Secret Life*, written by a Victorian who called himself merely Walter (Anonymous, 1966). We are fortunate in having two published and quite extensive analyses of *My Secret Life* and it is upon these that the following discussion is based. The first consists of two lengthy chapters in a book on sexuality and pornography in mid-Victorian England written by Stephen Marcus (1966) and based on material in the archives of the Institute for Sex Research (The Kinsey Institute) at Bloomington, Indiana. The second analysis, itself in two volumes, is by two psychologists, Eberhard and Phyllis Kronhausen (1967), and which quotes extensively from Walter's original. The two analyses take contrasting views of Walter's sex life and a comparison of them reveals many of the uncertainties and contradictions over the definition of excess in the area of sexual behaviour, and hence about the nature of excessive habitual behaviour in general.

Marcus and the Kronhausens agreed, first of all, that the work is probably authentic; that despite the seemingly incredible number of sexual partners whom Walter claims to have had, and the way the work concentrates exclusively upon matters sexual from the beginning of the first volume to the end of the last, the 11 volumes do largely represent the carefully recorded facts of the sexual life history of one man. Indeed, the Kronhausens were inclined to think that My Secret Life's preoccupation with sex makes the work more credible; they argued that Walter developed an almost scientific interest in the subject. Certainly he reported developing the habit of recording his sexual behaviour in minute detail as soon as possible, usually within a day or two of the relevant events taking place; the work contains a questionnaire which he 'administered' orally and discreetly to as many of his partners as he was able; and one volume contains three essays which he hoped might impart useful knowledge to the young on matters, '... which owing to a false morality is a subject put aside as improper' (Marcus, 1966, p. 165). Marcus believed the writing of this work, basically factual though it might be, served psychopathological needs in the writer. Even the Kronhausens, who took the more liberal, sympathetic, view, conceded that, '... the scabrous terms and frankly pornographic manner of expression are the least genuine ...', and were perhaps, '... thrown in for the author's own retrospective benefit or ... for the benefit of a prospective readership which demanded this kind of presentation' (Kronhausen and Kronhausen, 1967, p. 326).

My Secret Life certainly portrays a man who was, to use the Kronhausens' preferred term, 'sexually active'. Despite, or perhaps because of, a childhood and adolescence characterised by the sort of ambivalence towards sex which we have come to associate with Victorian England—a mixture of dire warnings against masturbation from his uncle and intensely exciting partial sexual experiences with servants—and despite a lengthy, though unhappy, marriage, he acquired a large appetite for heterosexual variety which he pursued vigorously. His partners were legion and ranged from the high class to the low, from the courtesan to the 'park doxie', from the lengthy affair to the most casual of commercial arrangements, from the mature to the quite immature. In later life he seems to have acquired particular 'taste' (a metaphor, no doubt ugly to some, which makes the appetitive nature of much sexual behaviour quite explicit) for very young virgins— a taste perhaps shared by many of his contemporaries (Pearson, 1972).

The two analyses took contrasting views. To Stephen Marcus, *My Secret Life*, '... revealed to us the workings and broodings of a mind that had for an entire life-time been possessed by a single subject of interest' (pp. 86–87). He referred to Walter's 'compulsive promiscuity', his 'compulsive need for variety, for having many different women all the time' (pp. 172–173), and his, 'obsessional state, his hypersexuality ...' (p. 176). 'The need for variety ...', he wrote, '... is itself monotonous ...' (p. 181). The author could not be thought of, he suggested, as an ordinary or normal person; his appetite was, '... strong, unreflecting, unconscious and unmanageable' (p. 178), it turned women into 'commodities', 'objects', and its outcome was frequently 'brutal and disgusting' (pp. 157, 160).

The Kronhausens were less blunt and straightforward. They admitted that, 'compulsive sexuality' is '... exemplified by the author of *My Secret Life*' (p. x) although they disclaimed the use of the term themselves by attributing its use to Marcus. Later they wrote:

> The only thing about Walter's sexuality which we do consider pathological or neurotic, and here we agree with Prof. Marcus, lay in its obsessive-compulsive nature, which drove him literally from one sexual experience to another, with little time or interest for anything else, and which makes everything about him seem so grotesquely overdone and out of proportion.
>
> (Kronhausen and Kronhausen, 1967, p. xix)

They noted that early on in his life Walter, '... gave up a job in the War Ministry and assured promotion in order to devote himself more fully to his erotic interests'

(p. 4). They agreed with Marcus, too, that Walter's behaviour with women was usually, '... clearly unromantic and unequivocally self-motivated ... never anything like the kind of attitude that one, rightly or wrongly, describes as "love" in sexual relations' (p. 126). Although Walter had on the whole, '... emancipated himself from the prevailing scruples and conventions of his time' (p. 183) and, '... felt little need to change and modify his style of life' (p. xxi), nevertheless he was by no means free of guilt and conflict. For instance:

> Yet, many a time, after such pleasure, I have been *disgusted with myself* for my weakness and have tried to atone for it—without the object of my solicitations ever having been aware of the reasons for my ultra-kindness.
> (Kronhausen and Kronhausen, 1967, p. 183, their emphasis)

At one period, conflict was particularly evident. Walter had a relatively long-term liaison with one particular partner at this time (indeed, Marcus believed Walter made her his second wife, although the Kronhausens thought Marcus was mistaken) and aspired to be faithful to her:

> ... Yet, such is my sensuous temperament ... that no matter how much I struggle against it, I find it impossible to be faithful to her ... I have wept over this weakness, I have punished myself by self-imposed fines, giving heavily to charities, thus disposing of the money which I would have paid for other women [a strategy later recommended by some behaviour therapists!] More than that—I have masturbated to avoid having a woman whose beauty has tempted my lust ... I have made love at home with fury and repetition so that no strength should be left... Always useless; the desire for change seemed invincible ... My life is almost unbearable from unsatisfied lust ... It is constantly on me, depresses me, and urges me to yield.
> (Kronhausen and Kronhausen, 1967, p. 184)

Further relevant historical case material was provided by Stone (1979) in his book, *The Family, Sex and Marriage in England 1500–1800*. Stone described in some detail the sexual exploits of two diarists, Pepys and Boswell, who experienced dissonance on account of their own sexual behaviour. According to Stone, Pepys had some physical contact with no fewer than 50-odd women in the last 9 years before his young wife's death. He was restrained by fear of venereal disease and of pregnancy, and unlike Walter was not so absorbed in his pursuit of sexual pleasure that he allowed this to interfere with his work in the Navy Office.

This was the period of the Restoration when the monarch, Charles II, set a standard of sexual permissiveness in his court which others followed. Nevertheless, Pepys was perhaps too close to the Puritan period of anti-hedonistic restraint to be free of a guilty conscience. Stone stated:

> Finally, he was constantly torn between his nagging puritanical conscience and his irrepressible sensuality and love of pleasure. Forever making good resolutions, and forever breaking them, he lacked a strong moral centre to hold him together. Meticulous to a degree in his business affairs at the Navy

Office, his private life was something of a mess, simply because he pursued women as a form of relief from the tensions in the office ... Pepys was a naturally prudent and cautious man, at the mercy of a growing sexual obsession ... He recorded what he regarded as his failings as an aid to his reformation and at the New Year he would make futile good resolutions to be more chaste in the future. Pepys was a man at war with himself, and as such was an epitome of his time and his class.

(Stone, 1979, pp. 344, 349, 350)

A hundred years later, when James Boswell was writing his diaries and letters, sexual permissiveness had become more the norm. The Puritan period was well gone, and the Victorian age was yet to come. Nevertheless, Boswell, brought up by a Calvinist mother, was not free of sexual guilt. He was, '... blessed or burdened with an overwhelmingly powerful sexual drive ...' (p. 352) which, as with Walter, caused him to pursue women irrespective of social class or marital status. In his 20s, before his marriage, he had numerous mistresses and liaisons and had sexual relations with well over 60 different prostitutes in many countries in Europe as well as in England and his native Scotland. He suffered from at least ten outbreaks of gonorrhoea before his marriage and seven after, and certainly appears to have obtained no lasting benefit from remedies such as Leake's Genuine Pills, The Specific, Lisbon Diet Drink, Doctor Solander's Vegetable Juice or Doctor Keyser's Pills, advertised in fashionable newspapers of the time.

Nevertheless he was continually worried about the rights and wrongs of his sexual behaviour and on one occasion tried to increase his self-control by writing, '... a discourse against fornication along the hellfire and brimstone lines of his early education by his mother' (p. 353). Later he confided in his new friend Dr Johnson whom he greatly admired and who gave him stern advice on the subject. He drew up an Inviolable Plan of moral reform and regeneration and was able to report that he had been chaste for almost a year. After his marriage to Margaret Montgomerie he wrote no diary for 3 years until he went on a trip to London which revived his old temptations and made him resolve, '... never again to come to London without bringing my wife along with me' (p. 363). He failed to keep that resolution, was soon back to his old ways and after only a few years of marriage was thrown into moral indecision:

... I told her I must have a concubine. She said I might go to whom I pleased ... but I was not clear, for though our Saviour did not prohibit concubinage, yet the strain of the New Testament seems to be against it, and the Church has understood it so. My passion, or appetite rather, was so strong that I was inclined to a laxity of interpretation, and as the Christian religion was not express upon the subject, thought that I might be like a patriarch; or rather I thought that I might enjoy some of my former female acquaintances in London ... the patriarchs, and even the Old Testament men who went to harlots, were devout. I considered indulgence with women to be like any other indulgence of nature. I was unsettled.

(Stone, 1979, p. 365)

The remaining years of his marriage were characterised by the kind of conflict and vascillation that have been described in connection with other forms of excessive appetite. He was, 'Always confessing to his long-suffering wife, always repenting, always relapsing ...' (p. 367). Glimpses of his wife's reactions are almost as interesting as Stone's account of Boswell's behaviour itself. She was forgiving of his dalliance with prostitutes: on one occasion, when Boswell returned home and confessed, he wrote, 'She was good humoured and gave me excellent beef-soup, which lubricated me and made me feel well' (p. 370). She was less forgiving, however, of his affection for other women, and was cooler in her reaction if she thought that Boswell had been sober at the time of an infidelity.

It is clear from Stone's account that Boswell could equally well have figured in the chapter on excessive drinking. Within 3 years of his marriage, there is talk of frequent all-night drinking bouts, of decreasing control over drinking and increasing wildness associated with drinking. At one point Boswell returned home after drinking and smashed up all the dining-room chairs, throwing them at his wife. Stone recorded that at this time, '... a new vice of all-night gambling at cards was growing steadily upon him' (p. 366). A few months later, he was, '... plunged into an endless round of alcoholic excess, all-night card-playing and promiscuous whoring' (p. 366). A few years later he was confessing, 'I am really in a state of constant, or at least daily, excess just now' (p. 371).

After his wife's death, and the death of Dr Johnson which also deeply affected him, he became, according to Stone, '... a habitual drunken lecher, a familiar figure staggering through the less reputable streets of London ... A man plagued by inherited manic depression, an evident failure as a husband, a father and a lawyer, driven by a lust for female flesh that he was unable to control, constantly more inebriated than was seemly ...' (p. 373).

Stone was impressed by the way Boswell was racked by guilt on the subject, particularly over his infidelity to his wife, the way that he tried unsuccessfully to think the problem through rationally, the way in which he was solemn in discussion on the topic and the way in which he constantly sought advice: 'No one seems to have been particularly shocked by his indiscretions and infidelities, or by the grossness of his appetite. Dr Johnson advised chastity, General Paoli and Temple marriage, and Rousseau a mystical view of sexual passion which would exclude his brutish couplings' (p. 378).

There is, then, sufficient evidence to conclude that excessive heterosexuality exists as a social fact. There is testimony to the fact that some people have sought specialist help because they wished to restrain their sexual behaviour (heterosexual behaviour with adult partners) but were unable to do so. Others have confessed to such dissonance to a professional confidant even though they did not seek help directly for that complaint; and Pepys, Boswell and Walter are at least three who have written at length of their own excess and at least occasional feelings of discomfort about it. Although there is a great deal of evidence of this kind, it is admittedly in the form of extended clinical and autobiographical anecdote rather than hard scientific evidence. There are two reasons, however, why this evidence should be taken seriously in any debate about the nature of excessive behaviour.

First, the phenomenon of the excessive heterosexual should be expected from what we know of drinking, drug taking, gambling, eating and exercising. The majority engage in each of these rewarding or potentially rewarding activities in moderation or not at all, while a minority show very heavy, frequent or immoderate indulgence and run the risk of incurring various 'costs' (loss of time, loss of money, social rule-breaking, bodily damage, impairment of performance, etc.). As heterosexual behaviour must be rated one of the most rewarding of activities widely available, it would be most surprising if there were no excessive or 'compulsive' heterosexuals. As already mentioned in Chapter One, in China, according to Singer (1974), 'womanising' was long considered one of the four major 'vices' or 'disasters', along with gambling, drinking and smoking opium.

Society has interfered formally in the control of heterosexual behaviour much as it has with drinking, gambling and drug taking, and there are examples of the law's involvement in relatively recent British social history. For example, in 18th-century Scotland, Trevelyan (1967) tells us, where the law and social conduct was ruled by the Kirk Session and the Presbytery:

> The adulterer or fornicator of either sex was exposed on the stool of repentance in church, to the merriment of the junior half of the congregation, to the grave reprobation of the more respectable, and to the unblushing denunciations of the minister, renewed sometimes for six, ten or 20 Sabbaths on end.
>
> (Trevelyan, 1967, p. 455)

A century earlier in England, under church law, the 'libertine' had been required to stand publicly in a white sheet for adultery or fornication, and under Puritan lay law an act was passed in 1650 punishing adultery with death (p. 246). Much later, in Victorian times, Government in Britain involved itself in the control of sexual behaviour, or at least the control of the behaviour of two groups of the urban poor—prostitutes and the lower orders of the armed service, with the passing of the Contagious Diseases Acts of 1864, 1866 and 1869 (Mort, 1987). As so often seems to have been the case with legislation designed to regulate the appetites, it took several attempts to get legislation anywhere near right, and even then the Acts remained highly contentious and were repealed in the 1880s.

The second reason for wanting to take what anecdotal evidence exists seriously is that the phenomenology described in Walter's autobiography and in other accounts is remarkably parallel to accounts of the experience of some excessive drinkers, drug addicts, gamblers and over-eaters. Each contains reference to the experience of having an 'uncontrollable' desire, or to being 'driven' to activity. Preoccupation with the object of these desires and with the act of consuming or partaking of it is another recurrent theme. The behaviour itself is felt inappropriate and in excess of what the individual or other people or both would consider normal. Of most significance, the experience of conflict and the attendant ambivalence and guilt are described. Attempts at self-control, through a variety of tactics, are usually described as well. These and others are features common to the experience of excessive appetitive behaviour whether the object be the consuming of alcoholic drinks, the placing of bets or heterosexual activity with an adult partner.

Finally, any easy dismissal of the idea of sex addiction or hypersexuality must deal with the existence of 12-step-model mutual-help groups. Goodman (1998) mentioned four organisations of this kind in his book. These are Sex Addicts Anonymous, Sex and Love Addicts Anonymous (SLAA), Sexaholics Anonymous (SA), and Sexual Compulsives Anonymous. Among other things Goodman tells us about those groups is that in SLAA, sexual sobriety is defined as not indulging in, '... any sexual or emotional act which, once engaged in, leads to loss of control over rate, frequency or duration of its recurrence, resulting in worsening self-destructive consequences' (p. 265), while in SA sobriety is defined more strictly as no sexual activity other than with a spouse. In fact, the rise of such mutual-help groups is probably nothing but a return to one of the preoccupations of the Oxford Group Movement, the forerunner of Alcoholics Anonymous and of modern 'concept houses' such as Synanon and Phoenix Houses for the reform of 'drug addicts' (Russell, 1932; and see Chapter Fourteen here).

It is clear also from the various criticisms of the concept of 'sex addiction', 'hypersexuality' or 'nymphomania', which have appeared in the literature, that the phenomenon of dissonant heterosexuality poses conceptual dilemmas and problems of definition remarkably similar to those faced by students of excessive drinking, drug taking, gambling, eating and exercise. The debate between Marcus and the Kronhausens over Walter's case exemplifies this. Criticisms of reifying the condition as a 'mania' or an 'ism', and of underpinning such concepts by invoking such indefinite 'symptoms' as loss of control and craving, exactly parallel criticisms which have been made of disease concepts of 'alcoholism' and 'compulsive gambling'. Control is a central psychological concept for the understanding of excessive behaviour, but the field of 'alcohol dependence' studies, for one, has been bedevilled by an all-or-nothing concept of control and uncontrol in precisely the same way as have discussions of excessive sexuality.

Debate over definitions in this area is intriguingly reminiscent of debates on the same subject when drug taking, drinking, gambling, eating or exercising are under discussion. In none of these areas is there agreement about the precise points on the continuum at which normal behaviour, heavy use, problem behaviour, excessive behaviour, 'mania' or 'ism' are to be distinguished one from another. When reading of the supposed characteristics of the 'real nymphomaniac', we are haunted by memories of attempts to define the 'real alcoholic' or the 'real compulsive gambler'. Was Walter pathological, a 'real hypersexual', or was he merely extremely sexually active and emancipated for his time? Was he a suitable case for treatment, or for censure and punishment when his behaviour contravened the law?

With this chapter, Part I is concluded. Five appetites—more if different groups of drugs are counted separately or if exercise is added as a distinct form—which can become excessive to the point of attracting the world 'addictive', have been presented. They constitute the core phenomena with which a model of addiction must deal if it can have any claims to be comprehensive. It is now the task of Part II to present a model which makes such claims.

PART II

How Excess Develops

CHAPTER SEVEN

Taking Up Appetitive Behaviour

It just grew, all of us, right around the same age. One started and then their pals started and then another lot started and it just ended up most of us were more or less using.

(Donna, quoted by Taylor, 1993, p. 37)

I've had it drummed into me ever since I was little how bad it is and what it does to people. [Who by?] My mum and dad. Watch documentaries on it. I've seen how it's affected friends. I've seen people get into debt. I think if you're the kind of person that can enjoy yourself you don't need it. I don't think anyone needs it ... I'd be too scared ... I feel very strongly ... I've never been tempted and I don't think I ever will be ...

(Ellen, cited by Parker *et al.*, 1998, p. 100)

The task of the rest of this book is to attempt to develop a psychological view of the origins, nature and resolution of the range of excessive appetitive behaviours introduced in Part I. This chapter is concerned with origins. To review exhaustively theories and empirical research on the causes of excessive alcohol use, other forms of drug use, gambling, eating and exercise, and sexual behaviour would be a task way beyond the scope of this chapter or the abilities of this writer. Rather, the purpose has been to examine selectively some of the major contending theories and some of the research which seems to be the most outstanding, and to use this work to build a unified perspective on the taking up of the types of excessive behaviour with which this book is concerned.

PERSONALITY AND SOCIAL INFLUENCE IN ADOLESCENCE AND YOUNG ADULTHOOD

There are many possible starting points for this exercise and I have chosen to commence with the work of R. and S. Jessor and their colleagues, from the University of Colorado, for a number of reasons. Although their original study was carried out some years ago, it is an outstanding example of a certain kind of research which has been very popular in the study of alcohol, tobacco and other drugs. These are studies of drug-using behaviour among young people, usually school or university students, usually resident in the USA, and less often in Canada, Britain, Scandinavia or elsewhere. These studies, the Jessors' among them, as well as being motivated by the special concern which many feel for deviance occurring in the young, are concerned with teasing out the antecedents of individual differences in behaviour: Why do some young people use or abuse a drug while others do not? Although the authors of most of these pieces of research have few pretensions that their studies have direct relevance for an understanding of excessive behaviour later in life, it is a not unreasonable assumption that the origins of excess lie in adolescence at a time when most people adopt the relevant behaviours for the first time. This is an assumption to which this chapter will return to examine more critically later. Another reason for starting with the Jessors' study, beside the fact that it has now become a classic, is that their original samples have since been followed up into young adulthood (R. Jessor *et al.*, 1991). At the same time, it must be noted that the lines of research on which this chapter will concentrate do tend to focus on 'substances'. Sex gets a look in, but eating hardly figures at all—a symptom of the artificial fragmentation of the addiction field. The balance is restored, however, in the following chapter.

The Jessors' original study, summarized in their book, *Problem Behaviour and Psycho-Social Development* (1977), and in several papers (e.g. Jessor *et al.*, 1973), was unusually comprehensive in at least three major respects. First, they recruited participants at three different ages at school (13, 14 and 15 years) and college at age 19. Second, and of the utmost importance, they followed people longitudinally for 3 years asking questions about the development of behaviour and attitudes yearly, collecting data from participants on a total of four occasions. Third, and of particular relevance to our present purpose, they did not confine their enquiry, as many researchers have done, to a single form of potentially excessive behaviour, but rather asked about a number. Some of those, namely alcohol use, marijuana use and sexual behaviour, are forms of behaviour with which this book is particularly concerned, while others, such as 'general deviant behaviour' (behaviours including lying, cheating, stealing, aggression and vandalism), and 'activist protest' or political activism, are of less concern to us. As an aside here, the inclusion of political activism as an object of study in research on adolescent problems or deviant behaviour gives pause for thought. If it is clear that this betrays the prejudices of US research fund-givers at that time, concerned about youthful deviance including protests against the Vietnam war, we should perhaps ask whether the same applies to the other behaviours in their list. The importance of reactions to behaviour, and the ways in which these may change radically from place to place and epoch to epoch, is a theme already introduced in the previous chapters, and is one to which we shall return in Chapter Twelve.

There can be no doubt that this study represents one of the most serious attempts of its kind to come to terms with the complexity of the determinants of early individual differences in the uptake of a number of potentially troublesome behaviours. Unlike many theorists of social behaviour, the Jessors were persuaded that these behaviours had multiple determinants and in particular that individual differences could be explained in terms of a number of facets of individual *personality* plus a number of different aspects of a person's *environment* as perceived by the individual. Their model, then, was a combinational one, based on the view that neither individual temperament nor a person's social context alone can be held accountable for excessive or 'deviant' behaviour, but that some combination of the two can. The Jessors employed multiple-regression analysis to explore the best combination of variables for the prediction of a particular criterion. The general results of this analysis of their complex data tended to support the Jessors' multi-variate view, certainly for high-school students. They stated, '... the final multiple regression equations for the ... different problem-behaviour criterion measures ... always *included at least one personality and one perceived environment variable*' (Jessor and Jessor, 1977, p. 140, their emphasis).

In the personality domain, results lent particular support to the hypothesis that general 'intolerance of deviance' would operate as an important personality control against indulgence in early drug use, sexual and other non-conforming behaviours. The measure of intolerance of deviance consisted of questions about 26 forms of behaviour (e.g. 'to take something of value from a store without paying for it', 'to cheat on an important exam') to be responded to on a 10-point scale running from 'not wrong' to 'very wrong'. Students who more often endorsed the view that such actions were wrong consistently tended to be those who reported relatively little involvement in 'deviant' behaviour. It was as if the holding of such views exerted a restraining influence upon certain kinds of behaviour, or at least upon reporting them.

Of all the variables examined by the Jessors, the one which was the most strongly and consistently correlated with criterion behaviour variables was a variable in the perceived environment domain which they called, 'friends models problem behaviour' (elsewhere termed 'social support for problem behaviour') concerned with the prevalence of models among friends for engaging in drinking, drug use or sexual behaviour (e.g. 'Do you have any close friends who drink fairly regularly?' 'About how many of your friends have tried marijuana?'). About the only failure of the friends-models variable was its failure to correlate with sexual behaviour among college students.

Many of the same variables which correlated significantly with behaviour at one point in time were also predictive of occurrence of these behaviours occurring for the *first* time within the subsequent 1–3 years. For example, those who became users of marijuana for the first time between the third and fourth years had a significantly higher number of 'friends models' for this behaviour at year 3 than did those who remained non-users at year 4. This was true for boys and for girls, while value on academic achievement, for example, was significant for girls only (those valuing academic achievement most being more likely to remain non-users). Similarly girls who valued academic achievement more highly were more likely to remain virgins at year 4 (again this did not hold for boys), girls with higher 'intolerance of deviance' were more likely to remain virgins (again no difference for boys), while a higher level of 'friends models' for this behaviour predicted transmission to non-virginity for both sexes.

In a series of published papers the Jessors also showed that it was not just a simple matter of personality and perceived-environment variables being correlated with the behaviours in question, or of their being able to predict the uptake of behaviours in the subsequent 1–3 years. In addition, there was evidence that those

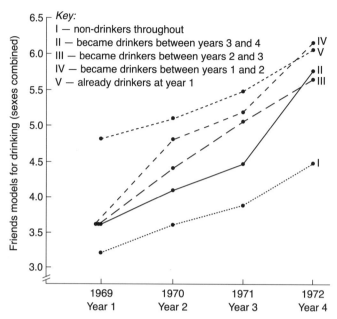

Figure 7.1   Development of friends models for drinking and time of onset of drinking in the Jessors' high-school study (reproduced by permission from Jessor and Jessor, 1975).

who adopted the new behaviours reported *changes* in personality or perception of the environment which were consistent with becoming a drinker or a drug user. For example, Jessor *et al.* (1973) showed that those who became marijuana users between one year and the next also showed significant changes, in comparison with those who remained non-users, in the direction of valuing independence more than achievement, reporting less compatibility between attitudes of parents and peer group, greater use of marijuana by friends, less endorsement of negative functions of marijuana, a greater involvement in general deviant behaviour, more sexual experience and a higher frequency of drunkenness.

Another way to illustrate their thesis about transition during adolescence is to depict graphically the way in which levels of certain variables changed over a period of years for those who already indulged in a particular behaviour at the beginning of the study, those who showed a transition during the course of the study, and those who did not indulge throughout the course of the study. An example is shown in Figure 7.1 which concerns the onset of drinking in the high-school study. A number of things are apparent from this graph. First, it is clear that changes in drinking status took place against a general background of increasing modelling of drinking by friends. Other things being equal, as these adolescents were getting older they were exposed to more examples of drinking by their friends. At the same time, they themselves were likely to be 'losing their innocence' since there was a similar trend occurring towards more tolerance of deviant behaviour. Nevertheless, the separation of those who were users at the beginning and those who remained non-users throughout is clear in Figure 7.1, even though both groups partook of the general trend. Between these two groups lie those who reported a change in behaviour at some point in the course of the study. Their friends models for drinking were closer to those of non-users at the beginning of the study but by the end of the study were closer to those of continuous users. In the meantime they had shown changes in friends models which were greater than average, and these changes sometimes took place in the year in which they reported becoming a drinker, sometimes they ante-dated this change and sometimes they occurred in the year following. The same pattern was found when intolerance of deviance was looked at in this way in place of friends models.

The Jessors' studies, which have been illustrated in some detail here, are informative on a number of points and set the scene for an acceptable model of the development and the recession of excessive appetitive behaviour. They inform us that the factors influencing development are multiple—no single-factor theory is likely to be adequate; that the origins of excess are likely to lie as much in social norms and group pressure as in character and attitudes; that the uptake of new behaviour does not occur in a psychological vacuum but as part of a constellation of changing beliefs, preferences and habits of thought, feeling and action; and that appetitive behaviour cannot be divorced from the demands, both biological and social, of the stage of the life-cycle at which a person finds him or herself.

Since that time, a number of researchers have continued to pursue the aim of teasing out statistically the process whereby some adolescents take up risky drug taking while others do not. As the Jessors' exemplary work illustrated, this is a highly demanding aim, but some good research has been done particularly in the USA where concern about youthful drug use has been strong. Evidence has accumulated in support of a multi-factor model of the initiation of drug use with both individual–personal and social-context factors being seen as important. In line with the development of thinking regarding the multi-factor origins of a variety of other health risks, writers on the taking up of drug use have also attempted to differentiate between vulnerability or risk factors on the one hand, and protective or resiliency factors on the other hand (see the comprehensive review by Hawkins *et al.*, 1992). Furthermore, there has been increasing recognition of the importance of the time dimension and the need for models that do justice to the complex ways in which people become involved in drug use, or do not as the case may be, and thereafter continue to use drugs or discontinue use, and in some cases become progressively more involved in drug taking. Since the testing of such models requires large sample sizes, ideally longitudinal research designs, good measures, and sophisticated statistics, it can be appreciated that this task taxes psychological research methods to their limits.

One such attempt to examine the time dimension was made by Duncan *et al.* (1995) using an overlapping age cohort design. A total of 345 11–15-year-olds and their families were recruited through newspaper advertisements, radio and television, and fliers distributed at schools in north-western USA. They were divided into five separate age cohorts (11, 12, 13, 14 and 15 years old at the first assessment) and they were assessed again at yearly intervals over a 4-year period. By means of this design it was possible to chart the development of alcohol, tobacco and marijuana use between the ages of 11 and 18. It was found that levels of use of the three different substances were highly correlated initially, and in addition those adolescents who increased their use of one substance more rapidly over time were also more likely to increase their use of the other two substances. This positive correlation between adolescent alcohol, tobacco and other drug consumption is a regular research finding (e.g. Blaze-Temple and Lo, 1992; Farrell *et al.*, 1992; Derzon and Lipsey, 1999; Parker *et al.*, 1998; Pedersen and Skrondal, 1999). Consistent with other findings reviewed by Hawkins *et al.* (1992), family cohesion was associated with reduced initial levels of substance use, and perceived peer encouragement for substance use had a significant positive association with initial level of use. Increases in peer encouragement, furthermore, continued to have a positive influence on increasing substance use over time. Sample size was not enough to explore sex differences fully, but it was found that young women tended to be higher in initial levels of substance use, and young men were more likely to significantly increase their use over time.

Complementing Jessor and Jessor's (1977) largely white, middle-class sample, Farrell *et al.* (1992) reported the results of a study of early-teenage public-school pupils, mostly African American, in one city in south-east USA. They asked about a number of possible risk factors for drug use, basing their choice upon Jessor and Jessor's problem-behaviour theory, Kandel's stage theory (see below), and peer-influence theory. Their study was cross-sectional, but the large numbers involved (over 2000) enabled them to divide the sample into two halves, developing a scale of the strongest set of predictors with the first half, and cross-validating it with the second half. Their final scale of risk factors included 11. Among those most strongly associated with drug use at this early age were three related to peer variables—friends approve drugs, friends use drugs, and felt pressure to use drugs. Two others were related to delinquency—history of trouble with the police, and high delinquent behaviour, demonstrating the early link between drug use and delinquency. Also included were history of tobacco and alcohol use. Marijuana use was 7.9 times as prevalent among those with a history of tobacco use than among those without, and was 6.7 times as prevalent among those with a history of alcohol use than among those without. The equivalent relative-risk figures for use of other drugs were 3.5 in the case of history of tobacco use and 3.3 for a history of alcohol use. Other factors that made up the set of risk factors were: being home alone after school; knowing adults who used drugs; low use of demanding activity as a coping strategy; and expectation of using drugs. Crum *et al.* (1998) later reported a longitudinal study of inner-city Chicago black children that spanned no less than 25 years from the early primary-school years until the participants were in their early 30s. Not only was alcohol 'abuse' or 'dependence' at the later age significantly predicted by a number of educational variables assessed during adolescence (less frequent working on homework with family, no family rules about school, dropping out of high school), even when those with an early age of abuse or dependence were excluded from the analysis, but it was also, just as significantly, predicted by teacher ratings of underachievement in the very first year of schooling (a relative risk of 1.6).

There have been many pieces of research showing that the risk factors for taking up tobacco smoking are as many and varied as are those that apply to other forms of drug use and potentially excessive appetitive behaviours, including both individual–personal and social factors. Just one was Byrne *et al.*'s (1993) analysis of over 6000 smoking questionnaires returned by 12–17-year-olds in schools chosen for diversity of socioeconomic status in Canberra, Adelaide and Launceston, in Australia. Discriminant-function analyses, to try to discriminate regular smokers from non-smokers, carried out for the boys and girls seperately (girls were more often regular smokers than boys after age 13), suggested the importance of a variety of types of factor, confirming previous work. Attitude factors were discriminating: low recognition of the smoking/health and fitness link, and for boys a low belief in the importance of physical condition. Personal factors were highly discriminating: low self-rated school performance, low self-esteem, 'neuroticism' and low conformity. But most discriminating were friends who smoked, and belief in peer pressure ('all the other kids do it', 'pressure from friends', 'kids who smoke are popular'). Additionally, 'mother smokes' was important for girls, and teachers smoking for boys.

Another was a survey of young British teenagers carried out by the Office of Population Censuses and Surveys (OPCS) (Goddard, 1990, 1992). A large sample of children at the beginning of their second year of secondary school (aged around 12 years) were interviewed, and re-interviewed 1 year and 2 years later. The most important risk factors, summarised by Goddard (1992), were: being a girl; having brothers or sisters who smoked; having parents who smoked (which was predictive only for teenagers without smoking siblings); living with a lone parent; having relatively less negative views about smoking; not intending to stay on in full-time education after 16; and predicting that they might be smokers in the future (surprisingly, whether friends smoked was not included in the study on the doubtful grounds that friends were likely to be a less important influence on smoking at such an early age). At this comparatively early stage of smoking careers, smoking behaviour was reported to be comparatively unstable: categorising young people as smokers, non-smokers or ex-smokers, as one might do in the case of adults, was thought to be inappropriate (e.g. 48 per cent of those who had tried smoking once by the time of the first interview apparently did not smoke again: Sutton, 1992). Others have concluded similarly that there is often a period of experimentation, of variable length, sometimes involving cessation of smoking followed by re-uptake later on, and not always progressing towards regular daily smoking (McNeill, 1991; Stanton *et al.*, 1996), and that predicting change of smoking status in the teenage years is very difficult (Engels *et al.*, 1999).

On the other hand, a substantial degree of continuity is also found in such studies. In the OPCS study 82 per cent of those smoking regularly at the first interview were still smoking at the second, and 89 per cent of regular smokers at the second interview were still smoking at the third (McNeill, 1992). In a study of 1000 adolescents born in 1 year in the early 1970s in Dunedin in New Zealand, surveyed when they were 15 and again at 18, Stanton *et al.* (1996) found that 88 per cent of 15-year-olds who were daily smokers were still daily smokers at age 18, and only 5 per cent had not smoked in the month before the assessment at 18 years of age. Derzon and Lipsey (1999), having analysed the results of 64 studies, concluded that early-teenage smoking, along with own and friends' use of substances, especially alcohol and marijuana, were the best predictors of later adolescent smoking.

Other work has extended this kind of enquiry beyond the teenage and college years. McGee and Newcomb (1992) reported the results of a prospective study of young people in the USA who first provided data in their early teens, and then at 4-yearly intervals, for a total of four occasions, until their early to mid-20s. At least 600 young people were involved at each stage. Using the multivariate statistical method known as structural equation modelling, they found, as had the Jessors, a strong general factor at each stage, combining extent of drug use, sexual involvement, criminal behaviour, social non-conformity and, at the first stage, low academic orientation. Social non-conformity was very significantly correlated with drug use at all four ages (the lowest correlation, 0.57, being at the fourth stage). The three elements making up social conformity were: low religiosity, low law abidance, and liberalism (as is the case with many such reports in academic psychology journals, the socio-political components of such measures pass without much comment). Particularly notable also were the very high correlations between degree of drug use and sexual involvement at stages 2 and 3 (questions about sexual involvement, which included number of sexual partners, pregnancy and venerial disease, were not asked at the youngest stage). By stage 4 the drugs–sexual involvement correlation, although still statistically significant, had fallen to a much lower level.

Also of particular interest, because of the controversy about the cause-and-effect relationship that exists between drug use and criminality (see Chapter Eleven), were the significant associations found between degree of drug use and extent of criminal behaviour at stages 2–4 (criminal behaviour was not asked about at the youngest age). Although questions about criminal behaviour included questions about acts ranging widely from minor fights to major acts of vandalism, and positive answers did not therefore imply criminal conviction or even necessarily behaviour that was against the law, these significant correlations do at least show that the positive association between drug use and delinquency is likely to exist at least as early as the mid-teens.

R. Jessor *et al.* (1991) themselves followed up their high school and college samples (see above) on two later occasions, in 1979 and again in 1981, by which time the former high-school students were in their mid-20s and the former college students in their late 20s. They were very successful in retaining 94 per cent of their samples over the intervening 6–9 years. They re-applied almost all the same questions that they had used earlier, but dropped one of the problem behaviours, namely sexual activity, since precocious sexual activity had been the factor of interest during adolescence and this was no longer of relevance in early adulthood. Newcomb (1993) criticised this later work of Jessor *et al* on the grounds that an opportunity had been lost for redefining problem behaviours relevant to young adulthood. Among the list of adulthood problem behaviours that he would like to have seen included was number of sexual partners, which would have been of interest from the perspective of excessive appetites. Neither Jessor *et al.*, nor Newcomb in his critique, make any mention of gambling or excessive eating or exercising. The problem behaviours of interest to Jessor *et al.*, like most of the literature reviewed in this chapter, remained highly focused on alcohol, tobacco, marijuana and other illicit drugs. The only exception was general deviant behaviour which included lying to cover up something the respondent did, writing bad cheques, starting fights and stealing.

It is interesting to note, first of all, the apparently high rate of problem drinking and of drug use. By the last wave of questioning, 27 per cent of former high-school men and 10 per cent of women met Jessor *et al.*'s criteria for problem drinking as did 20 per cent of former college men and 7 per cent of women. The criteria for problem drinking were broad: reporting having been drunk more than six times in the past 6 months or reporting three or more of eight negative consequences of drinking (criticism from friends, missing work or calling in sick, difficulties with spouse or partner, problems on the job, trouble with the police, accidents at home or at work, driving after drinking, and parents and siblings expressing concern over the person's drinking). A total of 40 per cent had used marijuana in the last 6 months, and percentages of 'heavier users' (used ten or more times in the previous month and usually used twice a week or more when available) varied from 4 per cent of former college women to 23 per cent of former high-school men. Percentages who had used cocaine at any time in the last 6 months were 21 per cent for both groups of women, 31 per cent for former college men and 34 per cent for former high-school men. Correlations between the various indices of drinking and drug use were, as we would expect from other research, positive and mostly substantial, which Jessor *et al.* reported as evidence to support their idea of a 'syndrome' of problem behaviour in young adulthood.

Again, as in adolescence, there was strong support for Jessor *et al.*'s problem-behaviour theory based on personality–environment interactionism. Each of the adulthood problem behaviours, and a multiple-problem-behaviour index created by summing the different problem behaviours, correlated significantly with variables in both the personality and perceived-social-environment domains. Friends models for drug use provided the strongest and most consistent correlate. Jessor *et al.* construed the correlates of adulthood problem behaviour as generally reflecting a tendency to unconventionality or non-conformity, both in personal attitudes and beliefs and in the support provided for problem behaviour in a person's social network.

Particularly interesting were the changes that occurred between adolescence and adulthood. These, Jessor *et al.* concluded, were generally in the direction of greater conformity, and often these changes were opposite in direction to those that had been seen to occur during the high-school or college years (e.g. attitudinal intolerance of deviance, which had been declining in the earlier years, showed a marked increase between adolescence and adulthood). In the former college sample, who appeared to have been exposed to a particularly high level of social support for drug use during the college years, friends models for drugs had decreased substantially by their late 20s. On the whole it was those who had showed evidence of being most unconventional in adolescence who changed most in the direction of conventionality, and those who showed the greatest change towards conventionality tended to be those who decreased problem behaviours. Thus there is general support in these results for the idea of 'maturing out' (Winick, 1962) of youthful excessive appetitive behaviour, associated with a change in lifestyle towards greater conformity, reflected in personal attitudes, social-network support and their own behaviour. Not all the results, however, were totally in keeping with this neat picture. Although friends models for drug use declined for the former college participants, change was in the opposite direction for the former high-school students; and friends models for drinking increased between adolescence and adulthood for both samples. Furthermore, although there was a general decline in drinking problems and in drug use, the decline was not always great, particularly for former high-school men. In the latter sub-sample, 34 per cent were designated problem drinkers and 33 per cent heavier marijuana users at the last point of questioning during adolescence, compared with 28 and 30 per cent respectively at the last point of questioning in young adulthood. For former college men, problem drinking and heavier marijuana use declined from 28 and 38 per cent to 15 and 14 per cent.

A further question asked by Jessor *et al.* was whether problem behaviour in young adulthood could be predicted from personal and social proneness in adolescence. The results were complicated but on the whole were supportive of the influence of both personality and perceived social environment on problem behaviour over the interval of 6–9 years. What was particularly striking about these results, however, was the substantial correlations between personality and the perceived environment both synchronously and across time, showing that these should not be thought of as two separate 'systems'. Correlations between adolescent personality and adulthood perceived environment were generally stronger than the reverse, suggesting that personal selection of the individual's later environment might be an important process.

ADDING COMPLEXITY:CRITERIA, STAGES, TRANSITIONS AND TRANSACTIONS

For our purposes, one of the possible limitations of most of these studies of individual differences in alcohol use, smoking, other drug use and sexual behaviour among adolescents and young adults is that they largely concern the development of normal or non-problematic behaviours, or at least they blur the distinction between the normal and the problematic. Sadava has consistently drawn attention to the difference between substance use and problematic consequences of use, and the importance of differentiating between them in research. In 1985 he reported a review of a number of published studies in which the average correlation between the two was only 0.37. His own study of employed adults, reported in the same article, produced an almost identical correlation of 0.38. He argued that problem-behaviour theory needed to be revised to consider drinking and drinking problems separately.

For all their strength, this constituted a weakness of the Jessor and Jessor (1977) and Jessor *et al.* (1991) studies (e.g. drinking and drinking problems were often combined in one index in their reports, and some forms of drug use, including marijuana use, were treated as problem behaviours per se without enquiring whether such use was thought to be associated with adverse consequences). The importance of making the distinction was illustrated by Sadava and Pak's (1993) report of a follow-up of Canadian students 1 year after they had left university. They used a sophisticated analysis in which drinking and drinking problems were examined separately, and drinking quantity/frequency was partialled out in some of the analyses of drinking problems. Using correlations, partial correlations, change scores and hierarchical multiple regression, they examined the importance of a number of predictors, assessed while students were still at university. As expected they found the pattern of predictors to be somewhat different for drinking and drinking consequences. When drinking was the criterion, social-network variables such as support/sanctions for drinking and for drunkenness, and social models for drinking, were most predictive, as was positive expectancy of using alcohol to cope with stresses and frustrations, with stress itself being comparatively less important. When adverse consequences was the criterion, perceived stress, life-change events and depression, and low satisfaction with general social support were comparatively more predictive, and social-network variables comparatively less so.

In an earlier study Sadava and Forsythe (1977) had examined separately the correlates of frequency of cannabis use, time as a user (in an attempt to measure continued involvement and commitment to using the drug), range of poly-drug use and adverse consequences of use. The separate study of these four criterion measures is supported by their finding that the average intercorrelation amongst these measures was a mere 0.23. Not surprisingly under these circumstances, correlations with personality and social-influence variables showed considerable variation from criterion to criterion. Sadava and Forsythe used an analytic technique known as canonical-correlation analysis in which independent 'canonical variates' are extracted, each variate being a composite of 'predictor' scores and criterion measures. In their analyses the first variate extracted appeared to reflect moderate use. The only 'predictor' with a substantial loading on this variate was social support for drug use, high tolerance for drug use loading moderately in addition. The second variate extracted, on the other hand, was interpreted as indicating 'abuse' (note the possible objections to the latter term, discussed in Chapter Twelve). A range of 'predictors' was related to this pattern. Social support for drug use loaded again but less highly than for moderate use, tolerance of general deviance now had a stronger loading, and there was a major contribution from initial and increasing expression of fear of the consequences of use. The latter, Sadava and Forsythe suggested, indicated, '... conflict within the individual in that the pattern of use represents both a means toward satisfaction of goals and coping needs, and a source of fear of consequences' (p. 236). Conflict has a major part to play in the model of excessive behaviour being developed here and is something to which we shall return in much more detail in Chapter Twelve.

It is clear, then, that the criterion problem is a highly complex one. Being a cannabis user is not the same as being an excessive opiate or poly-drug user, even though there is a large body of public opinion in countries such as the USA and Britain that would have it so. Being a recreational user of cocaine is not to be equated with being a 'coke hog'. Being sexually very active is not the same as being compulsive about sex or running into problems as a result of sexual behaviour. Nor is drinking at a greater than average frequency for the individual's age group necessarily the same as being a problem drinker. Becoming involved in gambling is not to be equated with persistent or problem gambling. The difficulty does not of course stop there. Having more problems connected with drinking than most other adolescents or young adults is not the same as having a problem sufficiently great to cause the individual to seek professional help. Nor can it be assumed that the former is a stage in a predictable process which will lead to the latter, and that those identified as having greater problems than their peers at an early age will be very likely to turn up in the ranks of the excessive alcohol users at a later age. In fact, the logic of the numbers involved is against this possibility. Population surveys of drinking practices (e.g. Meltzer *et al.*, 1995) show young males in their late teens and early 20s to be the group who report the highest frequency of drinking problems. It might be concluded that many young adults, in the natural course of events, become more restrained in their drinking as they get older rather than moving on to greater levels of excess. There is indeed much evidence, which will be examined more closely in Part III, that this conclusion is correct.

The question, then, is whether those predictors of individual differences in early appetitive behaviour are good for predicting later more excessive and problematic forms of the same behaviour. Robins *et al.*'s study (1977) of heroin use and addiction among US soldiers returning from the Vietnam war is an important and instructive one in this regard. Robins found that it was very difficult to predict, other than extremely weakly, 'addiction' to heroin after return to the USA on the basis of factors known prior to service in Vietnam such as demographic factors, parental behaviour (including broken homes, parents' arrests, drug use and drinking problems), own deviance and even own pre-service drug use. On the other hand, by 'decomposing' the process into the three stages shown in Figure 7.2—using heroin in Vietnam, continuing to use after Vietnam and becoming 'addicted' after Vietnam—it was possible to show that transition from one stage to the next could be predicted much more strongly, if still very imperfectly. At the first stage, pre-service drug use (especially use of amphetamines, barbiturates or narcotics) was the factor most predictive of being a user of heroin in Vietnam. A total of 28 per cent of those using in Vietnam continued to use heroin on return to the United States—stage 2. This was the most difficult stage to predict, although pre-service drug use was positively related as were demographic factors, in particular being black, coming from an inner-city area and being relatively young. Of those who continued to use heroin after Vietnam,

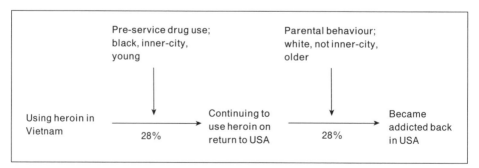

Figure 7.2 Predictors at different stages in a drug-using career: study of returning Vietnam veterans (adapted by permission from Robins *et al.*, 1977).

the proportion who became 'addicted' was again 28 per cent. Factors which predicted this last transition, from using upon return to the USA to becoming a heroin addict, were different from those that were predictive earlier. First, the most strongly predictive of this later transition was one with virtually no predictive power at earlier stages, namely 'parental behaviour'. Even more striking was the finding that the direction of prediction was reversed for the scale of demographic factors. Whereas it was the black, inner-city, young soldiers who were most likely to become users in Vietnam and to continue with use afterwards, it was the older, white post-Vietnam heroin user from outside inner-city areas who was at the greatest risk of becoming addicted.

As Kandel (1978) put it in her review of youth drug studies at the time:

> Whereas most studies compare youths within a total population on the basis of their use or non-use of a particular substance, [these] results ... suggest a different strategy, namely the decomposition of the panel sample into appropriate subsamples of individuals at a particular stage who are at risk for initiation into the next stage. Because each stage represents a cumulative pattern of use and contains fewer adolescents than the preceding stage in the sequence, comparisons of users and non-users must be made among members of the restricted group that has already used the drugs at the preceding stage. Unless this is done, the attributes identified as apparent characteristics of a particular class of drug users may actually reflect characteristics important for involvement in drugs at the preceding level.
>
> (Kandel, 1978, p. 15)

If Robins had not 'decomposed' her sample of Vietnam veterans in this way, several of her findings might not have emerged because no single variable was strongly predictive at each and all of the three stages. The kinds of transitions described by Robins are, of course, very different from some of those that the Jessors and others have studied. For one thing, her participants were unusual by virtue of having experienced, within a fairly short space of time, two quite different sets of circumstances, which apart from anything else involved living in two areas of the world geographically quite distant and poles apart with regard to availability of and attitudes towards the use of certain drugs. For another, while Vietnam veterans returning to the USA were moving from a culture of high to one of lower drug availability, the Jessors' high-school students were in a sense moving in the opposite direction. The Jessors', and other studies like theirs, were at least in part studies of the adoption of new behaviours in line with prevailing developmental trends. This is particularly true for such transitions as those from sexual inexperience to sexual experience and non-drinker to drinker, in which cases they were observing the rate of uptake of new behaviours which in the course of time were to be taken up by the large majority. In one sense at least, Robins was observing the downward arm of a developmental process, while the Jessors and others like them were examining the upward arm. This is illustrated by the fact that virtually none of Robins' participants took up heroin use in the USA who had not also been heroin users in Vietnam. In fact, the natural course of events was in the opposite direction, with over 70 per cent of users in Vietnam reporting giving up on return home. The question of why some people take up drug use can, under those circumstances, be turned around to ask why it is that some people did not follow the normal course of events, which was to give up heroin use on returning from overseas service.

Nevertheless, the idea of a stepwise transition from one status to another, with differing factors predicting different stages, has wide relevance for understanding excessive appetitive behaviour and Robins' sample was not as anomalous as it may appear. After all, when we move from examining transitions that are developmentally normal (e.g. from sexual inexperience to sexual experience) to those that represent increased involvement in activities that are non-normal or defined by many as deviant or excessive (e.g. using illicit drugs or becoming a regular, heavy gambler), then we are dealing, like Robins, with a diminishing sample at risk. The question is: Why do some people go on to greater levels of deviance or excess while many do not?

Similarly, although the geographic change makes Robins' sample unusual, there is nothing unusual about major changes in life circumstances, particularly in late adolescence and early adulthood. Moving from the single to married state, from adolescence to adulthood, from being a pupil in full-time education to being a worker, or becoming unemployed, each involves large changes in roles, self-concept and experience of pressures and constraints towards or against indulgence in behaviours of one sort or another, and it is probably at these points of change that the most dramatic transitions in behaviour occur. Vietnam veterans may constitute extreme examples of a very general phenomenon, namely change of behaviour in response to changes in life circumstances.

Research carried out since the important early studies of Robins, Kandel and others has continued to demonstrate the complexity of the developmental pathways involved.

Although their study was cross-sectional, McCusker *et al.*'s (1995a) study of 860 14–18-year-olds in north Wales is of particular interest. The authors analysed their results in terms of four groups of young people differing in their position regarding illegal drugs (cannabis, heroin, amphetamines, cocaine, ecstasy, magic mushrooms and LSD), in a creative attempt to discriminate between risk and protective factors, and also to try to determine which correlates of drug use might be antecedents, and which consequences, of drug use (a complication frequently referred to but often ignored—e.g. by Hawkins *et al.*, 1992, in their review). The four groups into which the sample was divided were: the *resistant* group, comprising those who reported they had never used any illegal drugs and who stated they would definitely refuse the chance to take any of these drugs; a *vulnerable* group representing those who, although they reported never yet using any illegal drugs, stated that they either would or might do so; an *experimental* group comprising those who had used at least one illegal drug but only once or twice; and the *repeated-user* group consisting of those who continued to use at least one illegal drug either sometimes or regularly. The proportions of the sample falling into those four groups were 63, 11, 14 and 12 per cent, respectively.

The vulnerable group were similar to the experimental and repeated-user groups, but significantly different from the resistant group in terms of a number of factors, leading McCusker *et al.* to posit them as risk factors. These included: lower levels of satisfaction with life at home and at school; more frequently having been in trouble with parents and teachers; and higher scores on a scale of hopelessness. The vulnerable group was also similar to the experimental-user group in endorsing significantly more positive effects expected from drug use and significantly less negative effects (although it is interesting that all four groups on average endorsed more negative than positive expected effects).

In distinction to the four above-mentioned risk factors, McCusker *et al.* also identified a number of factors in terms of which the vulnerable group were similar to the resistant group, but significantly different from the two drug-user groups. They concluded that such factors are protective. These included relatively more time spent on activities with family and relatively less time spent on activities with friends, and relatively more church attendance and relatively less attendance at discos or night clubs (although on average all groups spent more time in peer activities than family activities, and were more likely to attend discos or night clubs than church). There was also evidence that having two parents living at home, and having had previous school input on drugs education, might be acting as protective factors.

Finally, factors distinguishing the repeated-user group from the experimental-user group were: using an increased range of drugs; having a greater proportion of friends who also used illegal substances (a majority of both groups had some friends who used drugs, but the proportions reporting that *most* of their friends used drugs differed significantly—44 per cent of repeated users versus 11 per cent of experimental users); relatively more positive and fewer negative effects of drugs expected; and a smaller proportion choosing to respond in Welsh (all were offered Welsh or English, and overall about a quarter chose Welsh).

Hence this study produced a number of interesting findings that help unravel some of the many strands involved in some of the early taking up of an appetitive behaviour that may later become excessive. Many of the factors identified are likely to have complex and changing relationships with drug use as the Jessors and others have found (e.g. positive and negative expectancies of the effects of drugs appear to be associated with initial vulnerability, and expectancies are bound to change once people have actual experience of the effects). Similarly, engaging in peer-centred activities, becoming exposed to the possibility of drug use and knowing friends who are taking drugs are all likely to be related, and the cause-and-effect relationship between friends' use of drugs and the individual's own use of drugs is likely to be bi-directional.

In a study carried out in New York State, Wills *et al.* (1996) followed a group of over 1000 adolescents surveying them on three occasions, at annual intervals, when they were on average 12, 13 and 14 years of age. Like McCusker *et al.* (1995a) they had some success in separating out factors that might be influential in the process of starting to use substances, and those associated with becoming more involved in substance use. This they did by first carrying out a cluster analysis to identify different types of substance user, and second performing a discriminant-function analysis. The cluster analysis identified five groups: stable non-users (50 per cent of the sample) showed almost complete non-use of substances at all three times; minimal experimenters (26 per cent) who reported minimal use at all three times; late starters (14 per cent) who reported experimental use only at age 12 and 13 but increased use at age 14; an escalator-1 group (6 per cent) who showed more use than others at age 12 and increased use across the 3 years of the study; and an escalator-2 group (4 per cent) who increased to a higher level (by age 14 most were daily smokers, at least monthly users of marijuana and at least monthly users of alcohol, reporting having drunk at least three drinks per occasion at least twice in the last month).

The first discriminant function separated non-users, experimenters, late starters and escalators. This first function was most strongly associated with friends' smoking, with life stress, friends' beer drinking and 'hanging out' coping being moderately associated. The second discriminant function was smaller but potentially of importance since it separated the escalator-1 and escalator-2 groups. Of particular interest was the fact that the set of variables associated with the second function was rather different, including such variables as anger coping, and value discrepancy (value placed on independence minus the value placed on achievement).

Even the link between adolescent and early-adult substance use and friends' use, which emerges so strongly in so much research from the Jessors' (1977) onwards (Hawkins *et al.*, 1992; West *et al.*, 1999), has been shown to be much more complicated than might at first be supposed. One study confirming the crucial but complex role of friends in the taking up of alcohol consumption involved nearly 1000 16-year-olds followed up at intervals from birth in Christchurch, New Zealand (Fergusson *et al.*, 1995). Of this cohort 9.3 per cent were identified as 'abusive or hazardous' drinkers at age 16 on account of the frequency or quantity of their drinking or reports of associated problems. The most significant pathway to this type of risky drinking at age 16 was affiliation with friends who used substances (tobacco, alcohol and/or illicit drugs) at age 15. Although other background factors did not provide independent addition to the prediction of the criterion of risky drinking at age 16, there was evidence that some had played a part in earlier pathways towards affiliating with substance-using friends at age 15. These background variables included: a relatively disadvantaged family social position (less well-educated parents, lower occupational status, younger mother, Maori parentage, single-parent family); more changes of parent figures by age 12; evidence of conduct/oppositional behaviour according to maternal and teacher reports at age 8; and higher maternal and paternal alcohol consumption at age 11. Hence having substance-using friends was the common final pathway to risky drinking as a 16-year-old, but to attribute such drinking simply to the influence of friends would be to ignore a likely complex interaction of antecedent factors of social, family and personal kinds.

What is more, the formation and interactions among peer groups of adolescents are themselves complicated matters, and a correlation between the individual's own and his/her friends' behaviour is not necessarily indicative of the *influence* that friends have upon each other's behaviour, but might equally be attributable to a process of *choosing* friends who like and do the same things, as some of Jessor *et al.*'s (1991) findings, discussed earlier, suggest. Ennett and Bauman (1994) were able to examine this closely in a sample of nearly 1000 ninth-grade (average age 14 years) school pupils in North Carolina, USA, who were followed-up a year later when they were in the tenth grade. By asking participants to nominate their three best friends, and by linking the data from different pupils and across the 2 years, it was possible to categorise each as being either a 'clique member', a 'liaison' (not being a member of a clique but providing a link between cliques) or an 'isolate', and to map the movement between different social positions between ninth and tenth grade. The behaviour of particular interest was tobacco smoking, but the findings may equally well apply to other particular forms of appetitive behaviour. Although the results supported peer-group influence (ninth-grade non-smokers were significantly more likely to become tenth-grade smokers if they were members of, or linked to, cliques containing smokers in the ninth grade), the results suggested that self-peer correlations found in research on taking up appetitive behaviour are likely to be equally attributable to selection processes. Between the ninth and tenth grades, adolescents (whether initially clique members, liaisons or isolates) were significantly more likely to join cliques whose behaviour (containing smokers or not) corresponded to their own ninth-grade behaviour. This is among the most sophisticated research of a statistical nature that has been carried out on this topic, but it surely only begins to scratch the surface of a complex phenomenon. Just one further complexity revealed by Ennett and Bauman's study was that smoking was in fact significantly more common among social isolates (28 per cent versus 14 per cent of other adolescents at tenth grade).

In this chapter we have dipped into what has become a large body of research on the taking up of appetitive behaviours, especially the consumption of substances, in adolescence and early adult life. We have learnt that the early origins of such behaviours are multiple, involving some combination of individual–personal and micro-level social environmental factors, and that these influences combine in complex ways as people's lives develop over time. This is a salutary lesson to learn at the outset, since the addiction field, like many others in the social and health sciences, is littered with the remains of theories about origins which have turned out to be greatly over-simple or limited in scope.

Although the kind of research reviewed above has been a good place to start in a search for a satisfactory model of the excessive appetites, it leaves much out of account. It says little, for one thing, about the functions that appetitive consumption might be serving for people: what pleasures, what rewards might people be gaining from drinking, binge eating or taking drugs? This is the subject of the next chapter, which draws on different areas of research. Another major limitation of the studies reviewed in this chapter is their historical, geographical and cultural circumscription. The Jessors' study, with which this chapter started, was confined to largely white, middle-class samples in a single mid-western community in the USA, and most have been carried out in the English-speaking industralised Western world between the 1960s and 1990s. Although in one sense these restrictions serve an important research purpose, namely that of limiting undue heterogeneity of samples so that close attention may be paid to the personality and micro-level social influence variables already discussed, there is no doubt that these studies miss the wider social and cultural perspective, which will be the subject of Chapter Nine.

CHAPTER EIGHT

Personal Inclinations

Few writers appear to have recognised that pleasure is a main motivation for the use of drugs, for they are too busy seeking a deficit in the
individual ...

(Sargent, 1992, p. 74)

Opium leads the organism towards death in euphoric mood ... Do not
expect me to be a traitor. Of course opium remains unique and the euphoria
it induces superior to that of health. I owe it my perfect hours. It is a pity
that instead of perfecting curative techniques, medicine does not try to
render opium harmless ...

(Jean Cocteau, 1930/1991, *Opium: Diary of a Cure*, pp. 194–195)

Of course it is hard, the physical demands are enormous, the concentration
and commitment needed leave no place to hide, no reserves to harbour—but
in that giving of everything I find release into peace and a great joy.

(Cudahy, 1989, a long-distance runner, cited by Cockerill, 1996, p. 13)

To consider the personal functions that the risky appetites might serve, let us begin
by considering the premise that they are powerful 'mood modifiers'. In recent years
there have been considerable gains made in constructing more detailed models of
how appetitive behaviours may be used by people to change their emotions.
Generally there is support for the view that all the potentially excessive behaviours
considered in this book constitute powerful means of emotional regulation, and,
furthermore, despite appearing to be very different (one an 'illicit drug', another a
widely approved recreational substance, another a game-like activity, others
necessary sources of good health in moderation) they may have much in
common in their abilities to help people modify their feelings in desired directions.

THE TENSION-REDUCTION HYPOTHESIS

A major legacy of the clinical tradition in the study of appetitive behaviour is the
tension-reduction hypothesis. The reduction of tension is a motive to which people

frequently attribute appetitive behaviour, particularly if it is excessive. At least in the case of sedative–hypnotic and tranquillising drugs such as the benzodiazepines, there exists a pharmacological basis for the expectation that use of these drugs may be functional because they relieve the experience of tension or anxiety. In the case of most of the other appetitive behaviours with which we are concerned, tension reduction is controversial.

That statement is certainly true when the behaviour in question is the consumption of the major Western recreational drug substances, tobacco and alcohol. In the case of tobacco smoking, Nesbitt (1969) drew attention to the paradox created by the reports of many smokers that they feel more relaxed when smoking, despite the evidence that smoking actually *increases* arousal, as indicated by increases in blood pressure, heart rate, acetylcholine release, signs of arousal in electroencephalogram (EEG) recordings, and improved vigilance and reaction time performance. Schachter (1973) attempted to explain Nesbitt's paradox in two ways. First, a person might feel more 'relaxed' because any increase in arousal which occurred for any other reasons (e.g. because of tension within the social group of which the smoker was a part) would be experienced as relatively less arousing if arousal started from a relatively high level as a consequence of smoking (the law of initial values). Second, if arousal was attributed to smoking rather than to circumstances, a person might 'feel' less aroused than if an increase in tension could be attributed only to the circumstances in which the person found him or herself. On the face of it neither of these mechanisms would appear to account very satisfactorily for the experience of feeling more *relaxed*.

The findings themselves are in fact more complex than at first appears to be the case. Reviewing the evidence, Paxton (1980) found some evidence for 'de-arousal' effects of smoking. For example, some smokers had shown EEG changes that indicated a decrease in arousal, and one study had found clear evidence of skeletal-muscle relaxation in the form of depression of the patella reflex which could account for feelings of relaxation. Some experimental work with rats had suggested that both EEG and behavioural arousal was dependent upon dose, with an initial increase in arousal followed by a decrease with larger doses of nicotine. Dose-dependent effects are not at all uncommon with psychoactive drugs. The possibility of opposing effects of different dosages provides scope for a drug to be used in different ways, and indeed Paxton concluded his review by proposing that smokers might use tobacco to vary arousal levels in *either* direction.

Much the same thing had been proposed by others (e.g. by Matarazzo, 1973), namely that smoking might be a response to the need to maintain a 'steady state' of arousal, whether this requires an increase or a decrease in stimulation or stress. Incidentally, in this context he noted how frequently aggression had appeared in studies on smoking, both as a mood that often triggers smoking and as a trait that had been found to be more present among smokers than non-smokers. The essential point for present purposes is that the mood-modifying properties of a variety of appetitive activities should be taken seriously and that attention should not be limited to 'tension-reduction', unless we define tension broadly to include anger and possibly a whole range of felt emotions.

These observations on smoking are very significant because they lead directly to a crucial point that can be made about appetitive behaviour in general, namely that behaviour can serve many *different* functions for different people and, in addition, that it can serve different functions for a single individual. If tobacco smoking can be shown to produce opposite effects only when arousal of psycho-physiological kinds is being examined, how much greater must be the scope for smoking to result in various quite disparate kinds of desired effects when the whole panoply of social, psychological and physical outcomes is considered. The same can be said of alcohol and other drug use, eating, exercising, gambling and sexual activity. This being the case, we should hardly expect to be able to predict, par-ticularly over any great span of time (e.g. from adolescence to middle-age), who will and who will not gain such reward from appetitive behaviour that they are at risk of initiating, continuing or escalating the activity.

The recognition that there are important individual differences in accounts that smokers give of their motives for smoking, or the types of occasions on which they smoke, led a number of researchers to look for different types of smoking. One of the first such typologies was developed by Tomkins (1968) who concluded that there were four main types: positive affect (motivated by the arousal of positive feelings), negative affect (motivated by the reduction of negative feelings including tension and anxiety), addictive, and habitual smoking. The second of these, negative-affect smoking, comes closest to the idea of tension reduction. Among the five inner-need factors found by McKennell and Thomas (1967) the one coming closest to tension reduction was one which they labelled 'nervous irrita-tion': high scorers on this factor said they were likely to smoke, 'when irritable', 'when anxious or worried', 'when angry' and 'when nervous' (p. 63). Russell *et al.* (1974) found seven factors including a 'sedation' factor to which two items in particular contributed: 'I smoke more when I am worried about something' and 'I light up a cigarette when I feel angry about something'. These two items were among the most frequently endorsed both by participants in their main sample (a cross-section of staff of a London teaching hospital) and in their smoking-clinic sample. In fact, the first of these two items was the most frequently endorsed of all 34 items in their analysis in the case of the smoking-clinic sample, and was ranked second for the main sample (the most frequently endorsed item for the main sample being, 'after meals is the time I most enjoy smoking').

Since Russell *et al.*'s (1974) research on smoking motives, others have pursued this same line of research with broadly similar results. For example, Tate *et al,* (1994) gave a modified version of Russell *et al.*'s smoking-motives questionnaire to nearly 400 smokers who participated in either clinical trials of smoking cessation or laboratory smoking projects at the University of Michigan, USA, and they re-identified the same seven motives found by Russell *et al.* Oei *et al.* (1991) adminis-tered a 'Why do you smoke?' questionnaire to over 200 smokers, some of whom were seeking treatment for their smoking, in Brisbane, Australia producing four factors including one referred to as smoking as a 'crutch' or for tension reduction (when upset, when angry, to take mind off worries).

Whether smoking really does help many smokers in the way they describe—particularly controlling stress and maintaining alertness—or whether they just think it does, is another matter. West (1993) concluded that there was no clear scientific evidence to support the belief of many smokers that cigarettes enhanced their lives or helped them to cope better with life's demands. He conceded that this might be because such positive effects are difficult to detect, because many other factors are operating at the same time or because such effects are subject to tolerance, or are limited to people who are particularly stressed or under particularly adverse social circumstances. On the other hand, he argued, it might be the case that smoking has no positive effects upon performance or mood, but that smokers are persuaded of such effects by propaganda and popular culture, or that smoking may simply serve to provide relief from deficits in performance and mood produced by chronic smoking itself.

Parrott (1995, 1998) has consistently argued, on the basis of his own experiments and reviews of other research, that the apparently beneficial effects of smoking on mood are attributable to smoking restoring normal functioning in regular smokers whose mood is impaired, or is in danger of becoming so if they do not smoke again soon, as a result of time having passed since the last cigarette. He is therefore firmly in support of the 'deprivation-reversal' model for smoking and mood rather than the 'nicotine-resource' model favoured by Warburton (1988, cited by Parrott, 1995) and others. The latter supposes that smoking serves as a genuine 'tool' or resource for producing pleasurable mood states. The evidence for the deprivation-reversal model rests on findings that: anxiety/stress rises for smokers between cigarettes and declines on smoking; that regular smokers report no lesser feelings of anxiety/stress than non-smokers; that feelings of anxiety/stress rise to levels above normal if smokers are deprived of smoking; and that smokers report reduced stress levels once they have successfully given up smoking. The evidence suggests that the same picture holds for the supposedly beneficial effects of smoking on arousal and concentration (Parrott, 1998). The same phenomenon has been described by Rogers (1998) in the case of caffeine: reaction times were worse if coffee drinkers were given placebo rather than caffeine first thing in the morning after drinking regularly up until the previous night, but those who had abstained from caffeine for over a week performed significantly *better* with placebo than with caffeine on the same task.

Al-Adawi and Powell (1997) took advantage of Ramadhan as a natural experiment in smoking deprivation to test the similar hypothesis that regular smokers depriving themselves of smoking for a period of time—some participants in their experiment abstained each day during daylight hours while others abstained throughout Ramadhan—would show a deficit in general-motivational state. Each of their tests of general motivation (e.g. persisting at a difficult task) showed a decline in performance after 6 hours or more of not smoking and a restoration of normal functioning for those quitting for the day only, shortly after their first cigarette in the evening. Participants had, of course, fasted also during the day, but the first meal of the evening did not have the same effect. Al-Adawi and Powell (1997) interpreted the results of their smoking-deprivation study as providing some support for the theory that deprivation is associated with down-regulation in dopamine activity which is restored to normal with renewed smoking (see Chapter Eleven).

Although it may therefore be argued that self-accounts of reasons for and occasions of smoking, or indeed of any other appetitive behaviour, are misleading, it does appear that the reduction of tension or of other unpleasant effects is part of the reason given by many people for their smoking. Data from early surveys of drinking habits suggested that the same is true for alcohol consumption (e.g. Edwards *et al.*, 1972). As with smoking, however, the experimental evidence on the tension-reducing properties of alcohol is inconclusive (e.g. Cappell and Herman, 1972; Hodgson *et al.*, 1979a). That research suggests that effects depend at least on dose, on individual differences and on such factors as expectation. For example, small doses of alcohol appeared in at least one experiment to reduce anxiety for the college students who served as participants (Williams, 1966), while larger doses produced reports of increased anxiety.

Hodgson *et al.* (1979a) pointed out that there are learning mechanisms which may explain the development of a drinking habit on the basis of tension reduction, even if it is the case that drinking frequently fails to relieve tension or even increases it. First, each separate drink during a drinking occasion may be followed by a brief period of tension reduction, even though the cumulative effect of drinking heavily may be the opposite. Second, drinking may be reinforced by tension reduction only intermittently, a case of 'partial' reinforcement which is known to lead to behaviour which is relatively difficult to extinguish. On the basis of their clinical experience, Hodgson *et al.* preferred a third explanation, similar to part of Schachter's (1973) explanation of Nesbitt's smoking paradox, based on the notion of the relativity of reinforcement. Even if anxiety increases as a result of prolonged drinking, this may still be reinforcing if it is less distressing than the frustration, anxiety or withdrawal symptoms that the person *expected* to experience if he or she had not continued to drink. Hull (1981), too, pointed out how very complex is the question of whether alcohol reduces tension. Different studies suggested that alcohol might increase muscle relaxation even though it does not reduce self-reported anxiety; that, in addition to its other effects, the realization that the individual is consuming alcohol might itself increase tension (particularly for people who feel guilty about it); and that it may decrease heart rate, even when self-reported anxiety is unaffected.

ALTERNATIVES TO TENSION REDUCTION

Among attempts to construct alternative models of alcohol's reinforcing effects are those of Hull (1981), Steele and Josephs (1990), Sayette (1993) and Cooper *et al.* (1995). In place of the tension-reduction hypothesis Hull (1981) proposed a 'self-awareness' model. The proposal was that alcohol reduces the consumer's level of self-awareness, thereby decreasing sensitivity to information about present and past behaviour. If behaviour is, or has been, inappropriate and liable to self- and other-criticism, then a reduction in self-awareness may provide a source of psychological relief. Hull reviewed an impressive array of research which was consistent with this theory, although it is admittedly difficult to test and many of the results could be interpreted in other ways. Studies included one in which participants who had consumed alcohol made fewer self-focused statements than those who had consumed only tonic water and studies showing that those who had consumed alcohol performed less well on various tasks but at the same time were unaware of the inferior quality of their performance.

On the basis of their own programme of research and a review of that of others, Steele and Josephs (1990) concluded that the varied effects of alcohol could be explained in terms of the impairment of information processing that accompanies intoxication, including impairment of the ability to abstract and conceptualise, to encode large numbers of situational cues, to use several cues at the same time, to use active and systematic encoding strategies and to elaborate cognitively in a way that is needed to encode meaning from incoming information. As they put it:

> Alcohol makes us the captive of an impoverished version of reality ... It causes what we have called an *alcohol myopia*, a state of shortsightedness in which superficially understood, immediate aspects of experience have a disproportionate influence on behaviour and emotion, a state in which we can see the tree, albeit more dimly, but miss the forest altogether.
>
> (Steele and Josephs, 1990, p. 923)

They went on to conclude, from their reading of the evidence, that, although the effects of alcohol on mood and feelings can be traced to this short-sighted processing of information, the effects that are experienced depend on the individual's prior state and on the social context. In particular they believed effects depend upon the presence of inhibition conflict, intrapsychic conflict, the existence of salient worries and the availability of distracting activities. Taking inhibition conflict first, their idea was that impaired information processing places people's behaviour more under the control of immediate cues that may elicit 'impulsive' social behaviours (aggression, help-giving, gambling, self-disclosing, etc.) which might normally be restrained by information which is more difficult to process (awareness of the likelihood of retaliation for aggression, the time costs of giving help, anticipated losses from gambling, the dangers of self-disclosure, etc.). They presented evidence in support of their prediction that alcohol will only result in more of such behaviours if such conflicts already exist. In fact, Masserman and Yum (1946) and Conger (1951) had proposed such a theory years earlier.

As well as acting to block such inhibition conflicts, alcohol may be powerfully reinforcing by reducing intrapsychic conflicts. For example, Steele and Josephs (1990) cited a study by Banaji and Steele (1989) who asked participants to rate the personal importance of 35 trait dimensions as well as their 'real' and 'ideal' standing on each dimension, both before and after consuming alcohol or a placebo drink. They found that becoming intoxicated significantly inflated positive self-descriptions, but only on 'strong-conflict' traits (i.e. those that were rated as important and which gave large real–ideal discrepancies). Again their model supposed that these effects are a consequence of the poor information processing associated with alcohol intoxication. This effect might be thought of as a modified form of self-awareness effect, but in this case the effect is thought to be less direct and more variable (i.e. alcohol does not affect self-awareness directly and reliably, but affects it only under certain conditions and only as a consequence of poor information processing).

Their model also predicts that tension reduction may be an effect of alcohol, and may be powerfully reinforcing, but will occur only under certain conditions. For such an effect to occur, they argued, there needs to be both pre-existing salient worries or chronic stress and the opportunity to engage in activities that distract attention from those worries. Under these conditions alcohol was predicted by Steele and Josephs to have a powerful tension-reducing effect. Once again this effect is attributed to impoverished information processing associated with intoxication, which allows attention to be allocated away from salient worries and towards the distracting activity. For example, in one of the experiments carried out by Steele and colleagues participants' anxiety was assessed while they waited to give a difficult speech (about 'What I dislike most about my body and physical appearance'). Half were mildly intoxicated and half were sober. Of each group, half engaged in the distracting activity (they rated art slides) while the other half did nothing. The only group experiencing a reduction in anxiety during the waiting period were those who were intoxicated and engaged in distracting activity.

Each of these cognitive theories, and others like them (e.g. Sayette, 1993), falls short, however, of providing a general model of alcohol's effects. Hull (1981), for example, was aware that no single theory could totally account for the use and misuse of alcohol, and that his model was an over-simplification. Explanations of alcohol's effects have had to face up to the fact that these vary widely and are highly irregular, both between people and between different occasions for the same person (Steele and Josephs, 1990). Although self-awareness, for example, is sometimes found to be reduced after the consumption of alcohol, the effect has sometimes been found to be the reverse (e.g.Yankofsky *et al.*, 1986).

A more general cognitive model supposes that effects are strongly influenced by what a person expects of a drug like alcohol. Two illustrative studies, one from the Netherlands the other from Norway, examined the relationship between young people's drinking and their expectations, both positive and negative, of the effects of drinking on them. Wiers *et al.* (1997) studied a total of over 500 Dutch youngsters in three groups: 11–15-year-old school pupils, school pupils of 16 and older and university students. They asked their participants to estimate expected effects after a few drinks (low-dose expectancies). These fell, according to their analysis, into the three positive and two negative sets of expectancies shown in Table 8.1. They were also asked for their expectations of the effects of drinking after many drinks (high-dose expectancies), which were found to divide simply into positive and negative expectancies. Negative expectancies were correlated with lower levels of drinking for many of the groups. There were, in addition, some relationships between positive expectations and more drinking, and these were mostly low-dose expectancies (e.g. sexual-enhancement expectancies were correlated with drinking for the youngest groups of males and the two older groups of females; positive cognitive and motor-enhancement expectancies were correlated with drinking for the youngest and the oldest group of males). Only for the schoolboys aged 16 and over was there a correlation between positive high-dose expectancies and drinking, this being the group who reported drinking on average the greatest number of drinks per occasion, and the group characterised by the highest high-dose positive expectancies and lowest high-dose negative expectancies.

Aas *et al.* (1998) studied drinking and alcohol expectancies among 600–700 Norwegian teenagers who filled in questionnaires three times at 12-month

Table 8.1 Low-dose alcohol expectancies for secondary-school pupils and university students (reproduced by permission from Wiers *et al.*, 1997, figure 1)

Sexual enhancement (+)
  It is arousing to dance
  People talk about sex more easily
  People kiss more readily

Cognitive and motor enhancement (+)
  People get good ideas
  People can write poems more easily
  People can ride their bike fast
  People are good at pinball

Celebration/group acceptance (+)
  People find a dinner party festive
  People enjoy watching TV together
  One is more readily accepted by a group

Cognitive and motor impairement (−)
  People have difficulties expressing themselves
  People become bad at snooker
  People cannot think clearly

Inhibition/negative mood (−)
  People do not feel like making love
  People feel unattractive
  People feel insecure
  People become gloomy about the future
  A party becomes annoying

intervals. They were aged on average 13 years on the first occasion. Over the 3 years of the study, both drinking and positive expectations of the social effects of drinking (e.g. 'people become more friendly when they are drinking', 'parties are more fun with alcohol', 'people get into better moods when drinking') increased. Much as Jessor and Jessor (1977) had shown in an older age group in the USA, employing variables such as attitudes towards deviance and friends models for drinking, Aas *et al.* found drinking and expectancies marching hand in hand over the years of early adolescence (e.g. those who reported taking up drinking for the first time between time 2 and time 3 had showed an increase in social facilitation expectancies at time 3). Using structural equation modelling to test whether the data best fitted a model of expectancies leading to alcohol use, or vice versa, or both in reciprocal fashion, Aas *et al.* found greater support for the expectancy-leading-to-consumption model, but some evidence of the reverse especially at early stages of drinking.

Cooper *et al.*'s (1995) yet more general model of alcohol's effects on emotions supposes that alcohol has two main and distinct classes of effect and two corresponding sets of motives for drinking. One, which they referred to as the 'enhancement' motive for drinking refers to people's use of alcohol to increase positive emotions. The second, corresponding to the 'coping' motive for drinking, refers to use of alcohol to decrease negative emotions. The likelihood that these constitute distinct motivations for drinking is supported by the evidence, reviewed by Cooper *et al.*, that negative and positive mood and emotion form two distinct superordinate dimensions, with unique patterns of relationships to other variables (e.g. positive emotion covarying with positive life experience, frequency of social contacts, sociability and companionship, and negative emotion being related to stress and poor coping, health complaints and frequency of unpleasant events), which may correspond to two general motivational systems underlying behaviour and mood (the behavioural-inhibition system, and behavioural-activation system: Gray, 1972), perhaps underpinned by discrete neural pathways.

Data from their own study which involved two 2-hour interviews with members of community samples of approximately 1000 adolescents and 1000 adults, yielded support for Cooper *et al.*'s model. Most importantly, from their point of view, it suggested that both types of motivation were related to the extent of adolescents' and adults' alcohol use (a measure based upon a combination of quantity and frequency). Interestingly enough, drinking to enhance positive emotions was more strongly related to the extent of alcohol use than was drinking to cope with negative emotions, for both adolescents and adults. On the other hand, and as Cooper *et al.* predicted, drinking to cope with negative emotions had a direct relationship with drinking problems, independently of its effect upon the extent of alcohol use per se. This kind of direct effect upon drinking problems was absent in the case of drinking to enhance positive feelings. The basic model held up irrespective of age, sex and ethnicity.

Of particular interest from the present perspective was the existence of a significant, positive correlation in both the adult and adolescent samples, between the two supposedly distinct forms of motivation. Although this in no way invalidates the central point that alcohol use is probably motivated both by the desire to enhance positive feelings and the wish to reduce negative ones, it does suggest that many people who drink for one reason may also drink for the other. Indeed, Cooper *et al.* calculated that only 11 per cent of adult drinkers and 14 per cent of adolescents could be classified as coping drinkers, and 13 per cent of adults and 16 per cent of adolescents as enhancement drinkers (operationally defined as being above the median on one scale but below the median on the other), leaving the majority that could not clearly be classified as one or the other. Both adult and adolescent 'copers' were significantly more depressed, and adolescent 'copers' relied more heavily on maladaptive forms of emotional coping, held significantly stronger expectancies for tension reduction and reported significantly more drinking problems. In contrast, adult 'enhancers' reported higher levels of positive affect and stronger expectations for socio-emotional facilitation from alcohol and adolescent 'enhancers' reported higher levels of sensation seeking and drank significantly more.

No better way has been found of predicting the potential of a drug for being used excessively than to directly ask people who have been given the drug what subjective, emotional effects they experience, and whether they like them (Bigelow, 1991). The simplest of all measures is a 5-point forced-choice rating scale of liking for the drug. Slightly more sophisticated are visual analogue scales, sets of mood adjective rating scales or questionnaires, producing in each case a profile of self-reported, emotional effects on consuming a drug. For example, visual analogue scales (consisting of 100-mm lines on which people mark the degree to which a certain effect was experienced) for 'stimulated', 'aroused', 'active', 'awake', etc., contribute to a score for stimulation effect; whilst 'elation', 'happy', 'euphoria', 'confident', 'high', etc., contribute to a euphoria score (Foltin and Fischman, 1991). A much used set of mood scales is the Profile of Mood States (McNair *et al.*, 1971, cited by Foltin and Fischman, 1991) which yields scores for anxiety, depression, anger, fatigue, vigour, confusion, friendliness and elation. Other scores can be derived such as arousal (the sum of anxiety and vigour minus the sum of fatigue and confusion) and positive mood (elation minus depression).

The Addiction Research Center Inventory is a widely used true–false questionnaire with separate scales sensitive to the effects of various groups of drugs that are used excessively. Scales include the pentobarbital–chlorpromazine–alcohol group scale (PCAG) which measures sedative effects; the lysergic acid diethylamide (LSD) scale which measures hallucinogenic and somatic effects; the amphetamine (A) scale and the benzedrine scale (BG), both of which measure stimulant effects; and the morphine–benzedrine group scale (MBG) considered to be an indicator of euphoria (Evans *et al.*, 1991). Examples of MBG scale items are:

> Today I say things in the easiest possible way
> Things around me seem more pleasing than usual
> I have a pleasant feeling in my stomach
> I fear that I will lose the contentment that I have now
> I feel in complete harmony with the world and those about me
> I can completely appreciate what others are saying when I am in this mood.

Items in the PCAG scale include:

> My speech is slurred
> I am not as active as usual
> I have a feeling of just dragging along rather than coasting
> I feel sluggish
> My head feels heavy
> I feel like avoiding people although I usually do not feel this way.
> (Bigelow, 1991, p. 1618)

Where do the other non-drug forms of appetitive behaviour fit into the tension-reduction or mood-control scheme? In the case of gambling it has often been suggested that, far from being a purely instrumental, affectively bland, activity motivated largely by financial reward, it is in fact for many people an emotionally intense and complex experience. Many writers on the subject of gambling have reported the emphasis that gamblers often put upon the excitement associated with gambling, and have suggested that an increase in arousal may be one of the most important, perhaps the most important, reinforcer for gambling behaviour (e.g. Lesieur, 1984; Carroll and Huxley, 1994; Griffiths, 1995a). Most agree that gambling is like a 'drug' in this respect, and that emotional regulation may be much more important than financial gain for understanding gambling. For example, most of the 30 regular fruit-machine players (playing at least once a week) studied by Griffiths (1995c) reported feeling excitement during playing as opposed to before or after playing. In his report of interviews with 50 compulsive gamblers, Lesieur (1984) wrote:

> *All* compulsive gamblers (and many non-compulsive gamblers) talk of the action aspect of gambling. It is described in terms of 'getting my rocks off', 'adrenalin flowing', and most often compared to sexual excitement ... Each win is described in terms of being a 'high', and each loss is a 'downer' or 'depressing'. These are *emotional* rather than purely economic terms and states.
>
> (Lesieur, 1984, p. 44)

In fact, early psychophysiological studies conducted under laboratory conditions found no evidence for an increase in arousal with gambling, but since Anderson and Brown (1984, cited by Griffiths 1995c) raised the question of ecological validity and found that regular gamblers showed substantial increases in heart rate when gambling in a real casino, reliable increases in cardiovascular activity have been observed during fruit-machine playing (Carroll and Huxley, 1994; Griffiths, 1995c). It has also been suggested that depression may predispose to gambling and that gambling may act for some people as an effective 'anti-depressant', but Griffiths (1995c) found little evidence for this effect in his study of regular fruit-machine players. Carroll and Huxley (1994) reported that in their interviews with young fruit-machine gamblers it was relief of boredom that was constantly referred to, and Lesieur suggested that an important mechanism for mood regulation might be distraction since, once engaged in gambling, the gambler, '... becomes oblivious to his surroundings and concerned with the action itself' (Lesieur, 1984, p. 46).

Rather as Cooper *et al.* (1995) found for drinking, Lesieur and Rosenthal (1991) reported finding evidence for two primary motives for early involvement in gambling, 'action seeking' and 'escape seeking'. The fact that most of the literature has highlighted the former may be related to it being more common, according to Lesieur and Rosenthal, among male gamblers. They reported finding that more than half the women excessive gamblers interviewed by Lesieur (1988, cited by Lesieur and Rosenthal, 1991) stated that they initially viewed gambling as a means of escaping from problems in their home lives, in their pasts or in relationships. Those who gambled as an escape frequently described their gambling as an 'anaesthetic' which 'hypnotises' them, a phenomenon described by Jacobs (1988, cited by Lesieur and Rosenthal, 1991) as a dissociative state akin to a memory blackout, trance or out-of-body experience. Cocco *et al.* (1995) reported evidence indicating that there might also be important differences in emotional effects associated with different forms of gambling. They tested the hypothesis that poker-machine players might be gambling to *reduce* arousal associated with stress, while horse-race bettors might be gambling to *increase* arousal, finding some support at least for the former proposition.

The idea that an abnormal appetite for food might be the result of eating serving the function of anxiety reduction is an old one, and was termed by Kaplan and

Kaplan (1957) the 'psychosomatic concept of obesity' (note that they accepted, as did most authorities then, that obesity and excessive eating were so closely linked as to be almost one and the same thing). They assumed that emotional tensions, whether described as 'fear', 'loneliness' or 'feelings of unworthiness', for example, could be conditioned by association, in childhood, with feelings of hunger for food. Hence, a person might 'feel hungry' when tense. In addition, or alternatively, feeding might be associated with relaxation or tension relief, and hence food might acquire, to use the language of learning theory, extra reinforcing properties in addition to its value as a hunger-reducing reinforcer. In its supposed anxiety-reducing properties, Kaplan and Kaplan likened eating to, '... the excessive ingestion of alcohol, masturbation, compulsive behaviour, and interpersonal contact' (p. 190).

In fact, the experimental and survey evidence, reviewed by Leon and Roth (1977), and Ley (1980), gave mixed support to the hypothesis that eating reduces anxiety for the obese or 'latent obese' (restrained eaters). Leon and Roth, however, doubted the conclusiveness of these findings based as they were upon necessarily contrived laboratory situations. Under these circumstances, as in alcohol and gambling experiments, it was difficult to be certain that anxiety had been aroused which is at all comparable with the real-world tensions which some people describe as being relieved by eating, and also whether the eating behaviour observed (eating is usually under the guise of a 'taste test') was comparable with everyday eating.

With the shift of interest towards 'bulimia' and 'binge eating', more recent studies of eating and emotion have focused on the cycle of emotions associated with binges. Beebe (1994) reviewed a number of studies showing that individuals suffering from bulimia tend to experience predictable emotional changes across the binge–purge cycle. Typical findings were those of Hsu (1990) who asked 50 women, who were being evaluated at an eating-disorder clinic in Pittsburgh, USA, to choose up to four feelings from a list of fifteen which best described their moods at five points during an episode: before the binge, during the first part of the binge, when feeling full, during self-induced vomiting and after vomiting. The majority chose 'anxious/nervous/tense' to describe their feelings before a binge, and the same was true for 'frustrated' and 'depressed/unhappy'. The proportion picking 'anxious/nervous/tense' fell consistently across the remaining four stages of the binge–purge cycle (mood state at the end of the cycle was relatively dominated by feelings such as 'guilty', 'relieved', 'exhausted' and 'dirty'). 'Frustrated' was picked by far fewer women at all stages after the first, whereas 'depressed/unhappy' showed a complex profile with peaks before bingeing, when feeling full and after vomiting, and troughs during the first part of the binge and during vomiting.

The theory that forms of appetitive behaviour that have the potential for excess are often motivated by escape from self-awareness, which has been influential in the search for explanations of the excessive use of alcohol (see above), has also been found useful by those striving to understand the link between eating binges and mood change. Indeed, Heatherton and Baumeister (1991) reviewed evidence suggesting a high incidence of alcohol and/or drug abuse among women with bulimia and a high incidence of eating disorders among samples of drug users (see also Chapter Five). They described 'escape theory' as they called it, like Steele and Josephs (1990), in a way that highlights cognitive functioning:

> Central to escape theory is the notion of multiple levels of meaning, which are linked to multiple ways of being aware of oneself and one's activities ... In this view, low levels of meaning involve narrow, concrete, temporally limited awarenesss of movement and sensation in the immediate present. High levels of meaning invoke broader time spans and broader implications. High levels also involve comparison of events (and the self) against broad standards such as norms and expectations ... At the lowest levels, self is reduced to body, experience is reduced to sensation, and action is reduced to muscle movement ... Indeed, a shift to low levels of awareness may be a means of removing long-range concerns and lasting implications from worries, threats and pressures.
>
> (Heatherton and Baumeister, 1991, p. 88)

Although there is evidence consistent with the escape theory of binge eating (e.g. that binge eaters have high expectations for thinness, tend to have a negative view of themselves and have higher than average levels of emotional distress), such findings may have other explanations (including the possibility that they are a consequence rather than a cause of excess), and direct evidence for 'cognitive narrowing' during bingeing is absent (Heatherton and Baumeister, 1991; Beebe, 1994). Beebe concluded that escape theory is promising but needs to be combined with other ideas such as restraint theory (see Chapter Twelve).

In the case of exercise, it is well documented in the literature that regular runners report significantly less tension after running (Wormington *et al.*, 1992). It has been further suggested that exercise-induced tension reduction is most effective when the exercise itself is able to divert a person from anxiety-provoking thoughts. Wormington *et al.* themselves asked 21 endurance runners to complete the Profile of Mood States inventory before and after running. Post-running reported tension was significantly lower than pre-running. It is interesting to note that tension was reported to be particularly high prior to serious training and especially high prior to taking part in a competition. Although this in itself is hardly surprising, it is worth speculating whether there are analogous processes in the case of other forms of appetitive behaviour whereby anticipating engaging in the behaviour is itself responsible for producing an elevation in a negative-mood state which carrying out the behaviour can help reduce.

Cockerill (1996) wrote:

> Carmack and Martens (1979) ... found that those who are committed [to running] experience a euphoric, meditative state which they termed 'spinning free,' a condition which Bannister (1973), the world's first four-minute miler, referred to as, 'being one with the seashore'. Cudahy (1989), an ultra-distance runner has expressed a similar mental state while running with these words: 'There are changes in mental and physical states which are somehow related to the act of continuous movement allied to minimal rest

and sleep. For instance, time loses its exactitude, hours pass like moments, but a moment may expand and hang outside any time constraint'.

(Cockerill, 1996, p. 13)

Evidence for the inseparability of positive and negative reasons, as found by Cooper *et al.* (1995) in the case of alcohol, for indulging in behaviours that may become excessive, comes from a study by Slay *et al.* (1998) of over 300 adults taking part in an annual 4-mile road race in mid-west USA. Sub-groups of 'obligatory' and 'non-obligatory' runners were selected on the basis of scoring in the top and bottom quartiles of the distribution of scores on a 21-item Obligatory Running Questionnaire (e.g. 'When I miss a scheduled exercise session I may feel tense, irritable, or depressed'; 'If I feel I have over eaten, I will try to make up for it by increasing the amount I exercise'). The obligatory runners scored significantly more highly both on negative motives for running, such as escape (e.g. 'It allows me to get away from other people') and addiction (e.g. 'I feel anxious, irritable, depressed if I stop') and, unexpected by Slay *et al.*, positive motives, such as challenge (e.g. 'It provides one with a physical challenge'), health/fitness (e.g. 'It helps me stick to a healthier diet'), social (e.g. 'It allows me to meet new people') and well-being (e.g. 'It improves my general mood').

Heatherton and Baumeister's (1991) reference to self-awareness being reduced, at the lowest levels to body and sensation, suggests that alterations in the nature of attention or self-awareness might be one of the most powerful accompaniments of sexual behaviour also, and might therefore help us understand excessive forms of sexuality. Several of the clinical and autobiographical accounts referred to in Chapter Six (Samuel Pepys is a good example) suggested that excessive sexual behaviour might serve mood-modifying functions and those who have written more popular accounts of excessive sexuality have tended to write, as have many of those writing about compulsive gambling, about the stimulant-like qualities of hypersexuality. For example, of one of his interviewees whom he considered to be a case of the 'Casanova complex', Trachtenberg (1988) wrote:

For Saul, love is thrill-seeking—each of his relationships is a quest for a transcendent, peak experience ... that overcharged, superlative feeling that we're driving somewhere at ninety miles an hour.

(Trachtenberg, 1988, pp. 44, 55)

Escape or distraction have appeared as suggested functions of both drinking and gambling and are perhaps just as salient in the case of sexual behaviour since it both involves the focusing of attention in a direction which may be removed from the source of anxiety and, in addition, can involve intense cognitive activity in the form of fantasy. In so far as different forms of appetitive behaviour have these important psychological elements in common, it may not be so fanciful to think of them as partially equivalent and to speak, for example, of gambling or excessive eating as 'masturbation equivalents'. Is it possible, then, that one of the most significant functions of appetitive behaviour is to provide activity, the exact form of which is unimportant compared with its ability temporarily to distract attention from unpleasant emotion, in the same way that activity can temporarily reduce

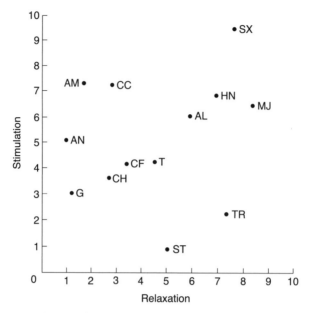

Figure 8.1   A comparative ranking of substances and activities in terms of pleasure-stimulation and pleasure-relaxation (reproduced from Warburton, 1988 by permission of Oxford University Press): AL—alcohol; AM—amphetamine; AN—amyl nitrite; CC—cocaine; CF—caffeine; CH—chocolate; G—glue; HN—heroin; MJ—marijuana; ST—sleeping tablets; SX—sex; T—tobacco; TR—tranquillisers.

physical pain, and that sexual behaviour is the prototypical behaviour in that respect?

Warburton (1988) asked people who had experience of a variety of drug and other appetitive activities, thought to be potentially addictive, to complete visual analogue scales indicating their stimulating and relaxing effects. The results, summarised in Figure 8.1, show that some of the most popular drugs, including alcohol, nicotine and marijuana, lie near to the diagonal axis of Warburton's figure, indicating, as should hardly surprise us, that they can have both relaxing and stimulant effects. Sex occupies a paramount position as the activity that can bring about both these effects, and in each case more strongly than almost all the other appetitive behaviours which were included.

It is clear, then, that most and probably all of the appetitive behaviours with which this book is concerned have in common the propensity either to alter mood in various complex ways or at least to offer the expectation that their consumption or use will change mood. These commonalities could partly explain some of the links between different excessive appetitive behaviours noted by P. Miller (1980). He pointed to findings: that dieters, unlike non-dieters, eat more after thinking they have consumed alcohol; that drinking increases smoking rate among smokers; that there is a tendency to increase weight on giving up smoking; that smoking often increases for excessive drinkers who give up drinking; and that alcohol use has been noted to increase for heroin 'addicts' who give up heroin. He might have added the tendency of doctors to prescribe drugs with 'dependence potential' to help people overcome drug 'addictions' and other kinds of excessive appetitive behaviour. The explanation put forward by Miller for these commonalities was that they are linked via a common difficulty in maintaining stability of arousal level. Brown (1997), too, has put what he calls 'management of hedonic tone' at the centre of his psychological model of the addictions. For him, it is a person's discovery of a means of controlling mood and emotion (collectively referred to as 'hedonic tone') in desired directions which lays the foundation for the development of addiction.

THE PERSONAL FUNCTIONS OF APPETITIVE BEHAVIOUR

Some time has been spent considering the possible mood-modifying or attention-modifying functions of appetitive behaviours. But although such theories have an important place in the catalogue of ideas about the causes of excess, they hardly exhaust the possibilities. Furthermore, much of the foregoing research and theorising about emotional and cognitive effects, recognising complexity though it does, is in danger of being charged with reductionism since it treats human actors as if they can be studied satisfactorily in the laboratory with little or no reference to the setting and social context within which appetitive activity normally takes place, and the meanings that users ascribe to the activity.

One of the commonest approaches to appetitive behaviour has been a general functionalist one. Sadava (1975) reviewed work on drugs within that tradition. Two main points emerged. First, it is very evident that the list of the functions of drugs reported by consumers or inferred by observers was a lengthy one and, second, the point was strongly made that the functions served by drug use are not universal but to a large extent vary with, and are a reflection of, the age, sex and socio-cultural position of the user. To illustrate these points, Sadava culled from the literature the following possible functions of opiate use in urban slums: to achieve detachment; to reduce threats to feelings of adequacy; to reduce drive states; to suppress pain and discomfort; to achieve a state of aloofness and isolation; to protect against depression, psychotic reaction or sadistic impulses; to forget personal problems; to cope with sexuality; to help control social anxiety; to allow the expression of dependency; to express rebellion or hostility against the dominant culture; to enhance peer status; to relieve a sense of boredom; to provide some sense of purpose in an otherwise purposeless life; to relieve frustration or anxiety; and to expiate guilt by self-punishing behaviour. Thus, even confining attention to one group of drugs within one broad socio-cultural setting, the range of suggested functions is very wide indeed.

The same was true of the list Sadava produced for opiate use by 'physician addicts', although some of the functions in this case were different from those proposed for urban-slum use. The list included: to relieve fatigue; to cope with marital problems; to relieve physical distress; to provide an alternative to excess alcohol use and to relieve alcohol hangovers; to relieve role strain inherent in their job; to relieve the conflict between the activity of their job and passivity; and to enhance fantasies of omnipotence.

By way of even greater contrast, stated reasons for opium use, mostly dissolved in water or smoked raw mixed with animal drug, in a largely desert region of Rajasthan in northern India included: for a reprieve from the worries and anxieties of drought during the dry season; the enhancement of fellow feelings among male members of the community who would often consume opium together in groups that combined different castes; to enhance the status of young men and to show their manhood; because no employment could be found; to mitigate various health problems including chronic cough, diarrhoea and various aches and pains (it was sometimes prescribed by local doctors); to overcome mental trauma; for its aphrodisiac qualities; and to calm children (Ganguly *et al.*, 1995).

To these differences in social context should be added the observation that the functions of drugs can be very different for men and women, even though they be of the same generation and social position. This emerged strongly, for example, in Cooperstock and Lennard's (1979) analysis of the stated functions of prescribed tranquilliser use. Like US physician opiate users, their Canadian men mainly described drug use to ease the stress and conflict of their work, while the more numerous women in their sample emphasised using drugs to help cope with the strains and role conflicts of being wives and mothers.

The differing motivations of people occupying different social positions is suggested by Buchanan's (1993) comparison of low-income (almost all black) and middle-income (mostly white) young teenagers recruited from five schools in the San Francisco Bay area in the USA. Qualitative analysis suggested three main themes providing a contrast between the two social groups. Those from low-income families were more likely to describe poor experiences of school and with the police. They were also more likely to express the view that one did not interfere in other people's choices about using drugs. For example:

Tiffany: Like if you try to tell 'em not to do it, then they'll, you know, blow everything out of proportion and start, 'Why are you tellin' me what to do? You're not my mother', you know.

Frank: If they want to throw it (their life) away on drugs, that's them. Some people don't like other people butting into their business. I just kinda keep it to myself. I figure if they want to do it, it's not my part to tell 'em not to.

(Buchanan, 1993, p. 638)

The third, and perhaps most interesting, theme contrasted the predominance of financial motivations for drug use expressed by the low-income youngsters and the fun motivation described by the middle-income group, as shown in Table 8.2.

Kaplan and Kaplan (1957) performed the same task of listing the various functions which it had been suggested might be served (in this case by over-eating). They included the reduction of anxiety, insecurity or indecision, a diversion from monotony, the relief of frustration or discouragement, the expression of hostility, self-indulgence, a way of rewarding oneself for some task accomplished, rebellion against authority and control, submission to authority, self-punishment and self-degradation, guilt-reduction, exhibitionism, to gain attention or care, to test love and affection, to justify failure, to sedate, to avoid

Table 8.2 Examples of accounts of motivations for drug use given by teenagers in contrasting social groups (adapted from Buchanan, 1993, table 5, page 635)

Low income	Middle income
Margaret: That's all they do, that's the main thing now, selling drugs. The boys around here, if they don't sell drugs, they call them stupid 'cause they don't know how to survive and stuff like that. They be tellin' 'em they can make—they can get 'em all kinds of fresh clothes and stuff like that, which they can, you know, if they start sellin'.	*Ellen:* Having fun. I mean, that should just be your motto having fun, and if drugs fall into that category, go for it. You know, I mean, just follow your intuition.
Jacqueline: Like my friend, he told me he sells dope, but what he does, he gives money to his mother so she can pay the rent, 'cause she doesn't have a job everyday. They just think of some way to help out.	*Matt:* You know, I can live without it, but it's kinda fun, you know. It's not totally okay, but sometimes it's fun. I don't smoke it alone. I just usually do it with my friends.

competition, to avoid maturity, to substitute for pregnancy, to protect against sexuality, and, among the poor, to diminish fear of starvation. The Kaplans suggested that the great range of functions listed, and those mentioned above by no means cover their list, indicated that any emotional conflict might be the cause of over-eating and that the psychological factors involved were non-specific.

Bruch (1974), too, was critical of what she called the 'thermodynamic approach' to excessive eating with its prescription of 'eat less and exercise more' (p. 29), because it ignored the many psychological functions to which eating could be put:

> Food may symbolically stand for an insatiable desire for unobtainable love, or as an expression of rage and hatred; it may substitute for sexual gratification or indicate ascetic denial; it may represent the wish to be a man and possess a penis, or the wish to be pregnant or fear of it. It may provide a sense of spurious power and thus lead to self-aggrandizement, or it may serve as a defence against adulthood and responsibility. Preoccupation with food may appear as helpless, dependent clinging to parents, or as hostile rejection of them.
>
> (Bruch, 1974, p. 44)

Bruch's ideas were derived from close knowledge of individuals who had sought help. Such data have advantages and disadvantages as bases for an explanation of excessive appetitive behaviour. On the one hand they suffer by being selectively based upon clinical cases. On the other hand, they provide a relatively rich source, often the only such source, of in-depth knowledge of individuals whose appetites have become excessive.

Also developed in a clinical setting was Slade's (1982, cited by Leung *et al.*, 1996) idea of 'setting conditions' for 'eating disorder', referred to by Leung *et al.* as being the most promising theory in the area. These conditions were hypothesised by Slade to involve a combination of 'general dissatisfaction with oneself and loss of control over one's life' and 'perfectionist tendencies'.

Button and his colleagues made a particular study of the self-esteem component of Slade's model. In one study it was shown that girls with low self-esteem at age 11–12 were at significantly greater risk of developing symptoms of 'eating disorders', as well as other psychological problems, 4 years later (Button *et al.*, 1996, cited by Button *et al.* 1997). In a later paper Button *et al.* (1997) reported the results of using a self-esteem interview with 31 15–16-year-old girls selected from a much larger number recruited from nine schools in a predominantly middle-class area in the south of England. Of these, 16 were chosen because of above-threshold scores on the Eating Attitudes Test (EAT) and 15 controls were chosen for low EAT scores. Of the larger group of over 600 girls from whom those interviewed were chosen 56 per cent said they felt too fat and the same percentage had at some time used one or other weight control strategy (45 per cent had dieted, 37 per cent had used strenuous exercise, 9 per cent had induced vomiting, and 3.5 per cent had used laxatives).

The self-esteem interview was designed to rate and explore self-esteem in five areas: general, school work, peer relationships, family relationships and physical appearance. The 16 high-EAT schoolgirls who were interviewed were rated lower than the 15 controls on all five aspects of self-esteem, and the differences were significant for general, family and physical. On further exploration, it was found that the most commonly invoked disliked characteristic of self, contributing to general low self-esteem, was external appearance. Reference was often made to specific body parts, mainly around the legs, bottom and thighs. In exploring contributions to low self-esteem specific to physical appearance a wide variety of body parts were again mentioned, but a higher percentage of high-EAT-scoring girls made general negative statements about their bodies, such as 'my features as a whole', 'flab in all the wrong places', 'pretty much everything'. Button *et al.* commented, 'The most striking feature was the spontaneity and frequency with which girls referred to their physical appearance when elaborating on their general dissatisfaction of themselves' (p. 45). They viewed their findings as support for the argument that weight control and eating disorders are an expression of problems with self-image and self-confidence.

Self-esteem is not well represented in research on taking up alcohol, tobacco or other drug use. The difference might be attributable to the more exclusive clinical focus in the eating disorders field compared with the much more mixed clinical and social orientations in the alcohol and drug fields. The difference might, on the other hand, be related to the general failure, referred to in Chapter Seven, to focus separately on different stages in the taking-up process. The initial taking-up of the behaviour has been of great interest in the drug field but of no interest in the eating field where only excessive or problematic eating is of concern. The two fields might simply be focusing upon different parts of the same process.

Detailed work on self-esteem, such as Button *et al.*'s, is certainly lacking in relation to drugs. Even relatively superficial surveys, however, suggest the range of motives for appetitive behaviour. The range of self-reported motives for smoking, for example, has been referred to earlier in this chapter. For example,

McKennell and Thomas (1967) found two social-motive factors which were combined in Russell *et al.*'s (1974) typology to form factor III (psychosocial smoking). One of these they termed simply 'social smoking', highest scorers being those who said they liked to smoke, 'in company', 'at a party', 'when talking' and who, 'get more pleasure out of smoking when in company than alone'. It is with the second of these two factors that we move further into the realm of more complex personal motivation. Highest scorers on this factor, the 'social confidence' factor, were those who said, for example, that they, 'felt happier with other smokers than with non-smokers', 'smoking helped them to feel more sure of themselves and gave them confidence with other people', that they, 'felt that by smoking they looked more relaxed to others and fitted in better in a group', and in the case of adolescents that, 'smoking helped them to feel more grown up'. McKennell and Thomas in fact found that adolescents scored particularly highly on this factor, but that this motive for smoking became less prominent in smokers' self-reports with increasing age. Bynner's (1969) study of teenage smoking suggested the great importance of a person's self-concept and the image of an activity such as smoking as a means of promoting or enhancing a desired self-image. Although the self-concept and its assessment are complex matters (e.g. is it more important what a person thinks of herself or what she thinks *others* think of her?; how many additional 'layers' of the self-concept should we distinguish?), the results of Bynner's study were in general fairly clear. On the whole, young people who smoked in the 1960s were seen by themselves and by their peers as more tough and precocious than non-smokers.

Leventhal *et al.*'s (1991) later perspective on adolescent smoking also highlighted adolescents' representations of self, of peers, and of self as viewed by peers. According to this view, social behaviours (of which smoking is only a part; manner of dress, music, use of other substances being related behaviours) are:

> ... a product of experiments in role playing, or attempts to project an image that will be validated (responded to) by the peer audience as credible and acceptable rather than rejected as foolish and out of step. When self-validation and reciprocity in role enactment is successfully achieved, a sense of mutuality is created, that is, a sense of shared feelings, likes and dislikes, and social values. Mutuality is the core of friendship and it frames or brings together social cues, responses and feelings to form new motivational structures.
>
> (Leventhal *et al.*, 1991, p. 585)

In the case of gambling, too, it has been recognized that there might be 'expressive' motives for participation in addition to those that are purely economic or 'instrumental' or mood modifying. Suggestions have varied widely. At one level, for example, it has been suggested that gambling enables people who are lower in status in a competitive society to compensate by 'achieving' in a world where very different skills and abilities operate. A number of observers of gambling (e.g. Herman, 1976 in the case of on-course horse-race betting in the USA and Newman, 1972 for East End London betting shops) similarly proposed that gambling was largely motivated by the opportunities it provided for exercising intelligent choice, the experience of control, the opportunity to discuss with others and to appear knowledgeable. Against the latter suggestion others pointed out that little discussion and interpersonal contact was to be observed in betting shops (Dickerson, 1974).

There seems little doubt though that the appetitive behaviours with which we are concerned can each serve a very considerable variety of functions. Nor can we omit sexual behaviour from this generalization. It too can clearly serve many human personality functions (Hardy, 1964). Gross (1978), for example, pointed out that sex for men could serve the needs for success (producing a high rate of orgasms in partners being merely the modern fashionable equivalent of achieving a large number of sexual conquests), of control and power (men are still much more likely to be expected to be the initiators of sexual activity, and are expected to be knowledgeable and not to have to seek advice), and for aggression and violence (Gross reviewed evidence that some degree of aggression on the part of males in the course of sexual activity is widespread and by no means confined to occasions of acknowledged rape). It follows, surely, that no theory of the causes of excessive appetitive behaviour could succeed that was based upon the assumption that such behaviour served one particular function, such as tension reduction, or escape from self-awareness, for each and every person whose behaviour became excessive. A psychology of excess must take into account the great diversity of purposes to which these behaviours can be put.

Among these purposes might be coping with the after-effects, even many years later, of adversities experienced in childhood. The intense focus of recent years on childhood sexual abuse and its possible long-term effects, including a number of forms of excessive appetitive behaviour, has given this idea a new impetus. In one study of women recruited from general practices in one English county (Welch *et al.*, 1997), for example, women with bulimia were significantly more likely to report having experienced sexual abuse in the year prior to the onset of bulimia (which occurred on average at age 15.5 years) than were control women at the same age (10 versus 2 per cent). The same was true of physical abuse (11 versus 2.5 per cent). Sexual and physical abuse were not the only adolescent events that distinguished the two groups, however. The general conclusion was that events which involved general disruption (a significant house move, a change in family structure) or which involved a threat to a person's sense of bodily integrity and safety (e.g. a significant episode of physical illness, pregnancy, sexual or physical abuse) were significantly more common among the women with bulimia.

From their experience and reading of the literature Root and Fallon (1989) described what they believed to be the functions of bingeing and purging behaviour among people with bulimia who had experienced physical or sexual abuse. The nine functions they described were: anaesthetising intense negative feelings such as rage, pain, fear and powerlessness associated with the experience of victimisation; purging, particularly vomiting, could be a symbolic attempt to cleanse oneself of a rape or sexual-assault experience; bulimia as an outlet for anger in a currently abusive relationship; bulimia as a justification that the person is worthless and deserves the abuse; bulimia as an attempt to establish psychological and physical space since bulimia is hidden and private; a desperate attempt to control the person's environment via her body; the body becoming an object of hatred by transferring intense rage towards the abuser to an intense hatred of one's own body; bulimia as a predictable experience in an otherwise unpredictable world; and bulimia as a way to cope with stress and to relieve tension.

Evidence has also been accumulating in support of a link between childhood physical or sexual abuse and excessive drinking or drug taking in adulthood, at least among women (Langeland and Hartgers, 1998). Much of the evidence comes from samples of women already identified on account either of known alcohol or drug problems or alternatively earlier child abuse. Boyd (1993) and Swift *et al.* (1996) are examples of studies of the former kind. Boyd found that a high propor-tion (61 per cent) of 105 crack cocaine using women in the USA (60 of whom were in treatment) had at some time experienced sexual abuse. Although the definition of sexual abuse was a broad one, and not confined to childhood sexual abuse, the average age at first abuse was recorded to be as early as 13.9 years. Swift *et al.*, studying 267 women in treatment for alcohol and/or other drug problems in Australian cities, reported that 72 per cent had experienced physical or sexual violence at some stage in their lives and that 37 and 21 per cent reported having been sexually abused and physically abused, respectively, under 16 years of age. An example of the second kind of study, starting with a sample of people with a known history of childhood sexual abuse, was reported by Roesler and Dafler (1993). Of 36 women and 8 men in their study who fulfilled criteria of childhood sexual abuse by reporting unwanted sexual contact before the age of 16 with someone at least 4 years older, two-thirds of the women and three-quarters of the men also fulfilled criteria for lifetime prevalence of substance abuse or dependence.

Avoiding some of the problems of using selected samples, Wilsnack *et al.* (1997) reported significant associations, in a national US sample of women, between reported childhood sexual abuse (CSA) and a number of indices of alcohol problems or dependence in the last 12 months and lifetime use of prescribed, illicit and over-the-counter drugs (e.g. 23 per cent of those reporting CSA, compared with 8 per cent of those not reporting it, had had one or more harmful consequences from their drinking in the previous 12 months, and the equivalent figures for lifetime use of illicit drugs were 13 and 5 per cent). The definition of CSA was comparatively broad, including any intrafamilial sexual activity before age 18 that was unwanted or involved a family member 5 or more years older, any extrafamilial sexual activity before age 18 which was unwanted, or before age 13 involving another person 5 or more years older. Others have produced negative results for childhood sexual abuse. Fleming *et al.* (1998), for example, found a strong association between reports of violence at home before age 16 and later alcohol problems as an adult among Australian women, but no association for CSA.

There now exists a very large literature on the childhood family antecedents of adulthood excessive drinking. The main focus of this work has been, not upon the facts of childhood abuse specifically, but rather upon the possible transmission of drinking problems from one generation to the next. Again many studies have started with selected samples of adults already known to have drinking problems, and those studies have generally reported very high rates of parental excessive drinking. More modest effects have generally been found with unselected, community samples, and more recent writings on the subject have stressed the resilience of young people growing up after facing the adversity of having had a parent with a drinking problem, as much as the risks that such offspring run as a result of their childhood experience (Velleman and Orford, 1999). This literature also supports Sadava's (1985) insistence that use and problematic use should be separated, since there appears in community studies to be little difference in the frequency or even quantity of alcohol consumed by those with and without parents with drinking problems. When attention is focused on *problematic* use, on the other hand, offspring of parents with drinking problems do appear to be at somewhat increased risk. In our study of 169 offspring of parents with drinking problems, aged between 16 and 35 years, we found the relative rate of current 'risky drinking' compared with similarly aged young adult controls to be 1.4 for men and 3.5 for women. A particularly crucial mediating variable in our study, as in several others, was the degree of childhood family discord, of which an important element was the existence of domestic violence, especially violence between parents (Velleman and Orford, 1999).

Even in the case of tobacco smoking, a number of studies have now shown that adolescents who experience early psychological difficulties or family discord are particularly at risk. For example, Fidler *et al.* (1992) found, amongst children with special educational needs in two areas in England and Scotland, that children with emotional and behavioural disorders were particularly at risk of smoking. Within a 7000–8000 strong cohort of 10–18-year-olds in the USA, Escobedo *et al.* (1998) found scores on a scale of depression and anxiety to be predictive of taking up smoking within the following 4 years. Of those in the higher scoring group, 18.5 per cent took up smoking during that time, compared with 6.9 per cent of those in the lower scoring group. It should be noted that depression-anxiety scores were also correlated with a number of other variables including low school performance and family poverty. In our own study of young adults with and without parents with drinking problems we found a significantly higher percentage of heavy smokers (smoking 20 cigarettes or more a day) among the former group (Orford and Velleman, 1990).

PSYCHOANALYTIC VIEWS

Despite all the evidence and clinical wisdom, of which the foregoing provides merely a taster, suggesting that excessive appetites might often serve deeper functions, a model which supposes that addictive behaviour serves personal functions for people who are particularly vulnerable on account of difficulty in dealing with strong emotions, linked to past events or circumstances in their lives, has not been to the forefront of professional and academic research and writing in recent times. Behavioural, cognitive, medical, epidemiological, social and 12-step models have been much more prominent. This is certainly true of the alcohol, tobacco and drug fields, has become so in gambling studies, but is less the case for excessive eating and for excessive sexuality. The greater prominence of psycho-dynamic ideas in the field of eating disorders may be due in no small part to these being more common among women, and among young women in particular, who are closer in age to events and circumstances of their childhoods.

Although psychoanalysts have not on the whole pressed any great claim to understand or to be able to treat excessive appetitive behaviour, there have been sporadic attempts to develop a psychoanalytic view. Bergler's theory of the origins of excessive gambling, for example, has been highly influential. He first put forward his view, that 'real' or neurotic gamblers had an unconscious wish to lose, in an article in the 1930s. There followed several further publications and popularisation in several magazines such as *Reader's Digest* in the 1940s, and the theory of the unconscious wish to lose was later adopted by Gamblers Anonymous. Bergler was impressed by the excessive gambler's almost fanatical belief in the possibility of success: '... his illogical, senseless certainty that he will win' (1958, p. 15). He was struck, as others with very different theoretical positions have been when considering this and other forms of excessive appetitive behaviour, by the selective nature of reminiscences, the dwelling on success and the relative forgetting of numerous failures. Bergler concluded that the motivation for 'real' or excessive gambling must be unconscious. The fanatical, and illogical, belief in success was like the child's feeling of omnipotence or megalomania. Growing up involved replacing these feelings with the 'reality principle' largely instilled by parental figures. Gambling offered the perfect rebellion against this principle, because in gambling chance rules, and the virtues of honesty, logic, reason and justice—all virtues that parents had taught—conferred no advantage. Hence, gambling revived old childhood fantasies of grandeur and, more important, '... it activates the *latent rebellion* against logic, intelligence, moderation, morality, and renunciation' (p. 18, his emphasis). It enabled the individual:

> ... to scoff ironically at all the rules of life he has learned from education and experience ... Since the child has learned these rules from his parents and their representatives ... his rebellion activates a profound unconscious feeling of guilt.
>
> (Bergler, 1958, p. 18)

It was this unconscious rebellion against parents that was responsible, in Bergler's view, for the neurotic wish to lose, because, like all acts or feelings of rebellion against parents, whether conscious or unconscious, it produced feelings of guilt and an unconscious tendency to self-punishment. Although Bergler seems to have been unaware that motivation can change greatly with the development of excess, his was a persuasive argument for one particular kind of expressive motivation for excessive appetitive behaviour. It is of interest that it is the 'wish to lose' part of Bergler's formulation that has been best remembered, although it is by no means the most prominent part of the theory expounded in his book, and it is probably the aspect of his ideas which fits least well with observations made by others about excessive gambling and other forms of excessive appetitive behaviour. On the other hand, his descriptive account of excessive gambling (e.g. the way in which it precludes other interests, and in particular the way in which it involves distorted thinking), plus his views on the possible function of excessive gambling as rebellion, are well described, and have parallels in others' descriptions of other forms of excessive behaviour.

In 1933, Rado had presented a psychoanalytic view of 'pharmacothymia' (drug addiction) remarkably similar in outline to parts of Bergler's (1958) view of 'compulsive gambling'. Like many others, his view was, '. . . not the toxic agent, but the impulse to use it, makes an addict of a given individual' (Shaffer and Burglass, 1981, p. 78). Drugs which could be classed as 'elatents', either allaying or preventing pain or producing euphoria, could magically restore that feeling of omnipotence associated with infantile narcissistic gratification which is forced to give way to 'the realistic regime of the ego' with increasing age. This 'elation' lasted, however, only a short while, with inevitable return to feelings of depression now exacerbated ('sharpened by contrast') and with the addition of a sense of guilt and increased fear of reality. As Rado put it, '. . . the ego has become more irritable and, because of the increased anxiety and bad conscience, weaker . . .' (p. 83). The cyclical state set up what Rado referred to as a 'pharmacothymic regime' standing in contrast to a 'realistic regime', i.e. '. . . this illness is a narcissistic disorder, a destruction through artificial means of the natural ego organization' (p. 83). Although couched in the psychoanalytic language of the time, Rado's understanding that the emotional changes associated with drug taking changed with continued use, producing 'diminishing returns', is not inconsistent with other theories, including the 'opponent process theory' (Solomon and Corbit, 1973), which was developed at a much later date and in a quite different psychological tradition (see Chapter Eleven).

The clinical emphasis on excessive sexuality in women, at least in the past, may also be partly responsible for the greater prominence of psychodynamic models in that field, but a more important factor is the intense interest that psychoanalysts and their successors have taken in normal and abnormal sexuality, coupled with the different focus of behavioural and cognitive psychology on sexual dysfunctions or illegal forms of sexual behaviour.

Goodman's (1998) book on sexual addiction was referred to at some length in Chapter Six. His view of sexual addiction, which he extended to a model of addiction generally, was firmly in this personal vulnerability/affect regulation/ psychoanalytic tradition, despite his insistence that it was theoretically integrative. He outlined a two-factor theory. The first, and most important, factor was an underlying 'addictive process' which is to do with character formation, and which leaves some people particularly vulnerable to dependence on external objects as a means of regulating their internal emotional state and sense of self. This is in line with the general run of psychoanalytic theorising which stresses the multiple personal functions that addictive behaviour serves, and in particular their role as, '. . . a splint for an individual's self-esteem or sense of self . . . or as an attempt to heal the self' (p. 196).

Each of the clinical vignettes included in Goodman's book was used to illustrate this point about the multiple personal functions that sexual addiction can serve. In *Harold's* case, for example, his addictive use of normal heterosexual behaviour was thought to serve the following inter-related functions: (1) to counter feelings of emptiness, deadness, anhedonia, dread and directionlessness; (2) to ward off separation anxiety and castration (mutilation) anxiety; (3) to defend against his own sadism and sexual aggressiveness; (4) to restore his sense of narcissistic equilibrium, to stabilise his sense of self and to ward off fragmentation anxiety; (5) to confirm his sense of specialness, the power of his attractiveness and his fantasy that he could violate 'the rules' without harmful consequences; (6) to find the limits of his omnipotence, to provoke the environment into providing the structure that he was not able to provide for himself; (7) to win the admiration of other men; (8) to bring on himself punishment and thereby to expiate his guilt; and (9) to call out for a strong and caring man who would save him from being destroyed by castrating, devouring women (p. 325). Although Goodman tried to reassure his readers that he was not resurrecting the old idea of a single type of addictive personality, as opposed to a range of vulnerable character types, nevertheless his emphasis was firmly on personality functioning and away from attraction to or desire for addictive substances or objects. This is clear when he wrote, '... our tendency to focus our attention on whether or not a particular behavior or substance is "addictive" is misguided. While behaviors and substances vary in the likelihood that they will be used addictively, "addictiveness" is more a property of individual persons than a property of behaviors or substances' (p. 19). References to character or personality disorder—narcissistic, neurotic or borderline—are never far away.

The second factor in Goodman's model is the choice of the addictive object, sex in the case of *Harold* and the other people about whom Goodman wrote in his book. He was clear that from the perspective of his model this second stage in the addictive process was much the less important. His emphasis on the first factor—the underlying personal, emotional vulnerability—marks off this type of model of addiction very clearly from the dominant view in addiction studies, namely that the substance or activity itself is everything. It is thus much easier for those who take a perspective like Goodman's to work across different addictions and to move away from the compartmentalisation of the excessive appetites field which has been such a feature of it. From his perspective it is not a case of cross-fertilisation across different addictions, since they are one and the same thing. Only the comparatively unimportant matter of choice of addictive object is different.

Others who have taken similar perspectives include Yates (1991) and Diaz and Fruhauf (1991). In his book on eating and exercise disorders, Yates (1991) reviewed a number of approaches including those of the object relations and self-psychology schools. Both viewed 'eating disorders' as being precipitated by strong and difficult-to-control emotions and assume a personal vulnerability—difficulty achieving autonomy or in developing self-regulatory functions—rooted in early failures of caretaking. Yates' view was that while such a model might fit some of the 'sickest patients' (p. 122), it was not applicable across the board since many people with eating disorders or obligatory running are otherwise quite well functioning.

Although Yates was not attracted to the emphasis on personal pathology and malignant parenting as a general model of compulsive eating or exercising, his experience led him to the view that preoccupation with diet and/or exercise was a major means by which obligatory runners and eating-disordered women main-tained a homeostasis, and that there were at least five different intrapsychic functions which the activity provided. This complex picture allows for a great deal of variation from one person to another and for one individual from time to time. The functions Yates listed were: self-regulation (dieting or exercise enabling a person to be soothed, energised, organised and/or to stabilise emotional state); self-definition (e.g. to prove that the individual is an effective athlete or can look like a fashion model); defence against receptive pleasure (defending against yielding and the impulse to rest or relax or be cared for); separation maintenance (using an activity as a means of separating or keeping distance from another person); and self-hurt (carrying dieting or exercising to such an extreme that the person experiences discomfort, outright pain and/or injury to the body). Note how this list of functions represents a mix of positive and negative.

A further, personal, element in Yates' model was the notion that the move from casual running or dieting to compulsive athleticism or eating disorder begins with an increase in self-dissatisfaction following a crisis of self-worth.

Diaz and Fruhauf's (1991) idea was that '... addictions can be understood as an excessive dependence on external structures (substances, situations, persons or even institutions) in order to maintain homeostatic functioning in situations that overtax internal regulatory mechanisms' (p. 97). The way in which their model was described made less explicit reference to hard-to-control emotions, speaking rather of 'self-regulation' generally, but it shared with models like Goodman's an emphasis on early vulnerability derived from childhood temperament and the quality of interactions with childhood caretakers. Diaz and Fruhauf acknowledged that their model might be seen as problematic on several counts:

> First, the approach suggests an exclusive focus on the addicted person (the host), leaving behind other major components, such as the psychoactive properties of different substances or the environmental characteristics that predict both frequency and severity of addictive behaviours. Second, because of the conceptual relation between self-regulation and the notion of free-will, there is a certain danger in returning to outdated (and proven useless) moralistic concepts that blame the victims. Finally, because self-regulatory deficits should be manifested with some consistency in addicted individuals across situations, self-regulation theory, as postulated, may come too close to the notion of an 'addictive personality'
>
> (Diaz and Fruhauf, 1991, p. 98)

Like Goodman, they claimed not to believe in an 'addictive personality', since self-regulatory deficits could co-exist with a wide range of different personalities. Theirs is perhaps better described as a personal-vulnerability model rather than one of personality per se.

THE LIMITATIONS OF PERSONAL EXPLANATIONS

Despite all the insights that there have been into the possible deep or dynamic personal factors that might play a part in the development of an excessive appetite, it is appropriate to retain a large measure of scepticism about the claims that are sometimes made about the importance of such factors, particularly when, as is so often the case, there seems to be an exclusive focus on the person. The sceptical view was well put some years ago by Cornish (1978) in his review of the gambling literature as it then existed:

> ... when behaviour is being discussed at the level of the individual a strong inclination exists to regard it as being determined by factors unique to that person and to be found by studying his personality and attitudes. The more intense a person's gambling involvement, the more likely it is to be ascribed to such 'internal' causes—on the assumption that 'external' or situational determinants are relatively constant for all gamblers. Similarly, since heavy participation is a minority behaviour, it is likely to be ascribed to pathological motives.
>
> (Cornish, 1978, p. 152)

'Simple person-centred forms of explanation ...' were popular, he argued, because a number of unwarranted assumptions were often made. One was that gamblers are similar to one another and different from non-gamblers. A second was that gamblers are engaged in a similar basic activity, hence ignoring the evident differences which exist between the various forms of gambling, as others had earlier ignored differences in eating or smoking patterns. Coupled with these assumptions was a third, of which Cornish was particularly critical, namely the assumption that explanations for the *initial* decision to gamble are closely related to those explaining *persistent* gambling. This lead to person-centred concepts stressing motives arising from maladjustments of personality and attitudes. What Cornish said about the tendency to privilege 'internal' causes related to personality or attitude applies with equal force to any form of appetitive behaviour. Much personality research has been post hoc, based upon examination of people whose appetitive behaviour has already come to notice as being excessive. This fact immediately gives rise to the most challenging question: Are we witnessing the causes of excess or its consequences?

It is hardly surprising then that ideas imported from personality theory in the hope that they might somehow provide the answer to one or other form of excessive behaviour have so often excited interest at first, but once tested have been found to be wanting. This particularly applies to concepts derived from relatively simple trait models of personality which scarcely do justice to some of the more complex and individual personality notions which have been put forward to explain appetitive behaviour. 'Sensation seeking' is one example that comes to mind in relation to gambling (Dickerson *et al.*, 1987; Coventry and Brown, 1993). But even the more thoughtful ideas, based on initial insightful observations, have often met with the same fate. A major personality theory of over-eating in the 1970s, *externality theory*, illustrates a number of the problems with research on personality and appetitive behaviour. Schachter (1971) proposed that while normal people eat largely in response to internal, hunger cues, overweight people eat more in response to external or situational stimuli. Schachter and others then carried out a series of intriguing experiments which tended to support this view. For example, preloading (i.e. feeding a person before an experiment) reduced the probability of eating in people of normal weight but not in those who were overweight;

palatability of food had more effect on the eating of the overweight; in the absence of food-related cues, the overweight were less affected by hours of food deprivation than those of normal weight; and eating in the obese was triggered by apparent time while in the lean it was triggered more by real time (the discrepancy being created by deliberately altering clocks or by studying participants who had travelled across time zones) (Ley, 1980).

To this point the externality theory was one linking the state of being overweight with one general aspect of responsiveness to specifically food-related cues or stimuli. It required the next step in order to qualify the theory as a personality theory, and with that step the implication becomes stronger that the tendency towards externality may have predated overweight and perhaps have been partially causative of it. This step was taken by Rodin (1978) who put forward the view that the obese were *generally* 'stimulus-bound' or especially reactive to salient external stimuli, not merely food-related ones. As is so often the case in an area short of strong theories, the idea of externality was hailed for some time as offering the key to understanding the often intractable problem of 'obesity', and the theory stimulated a great deal of research, but a consensus of opinion developed that the case for externality had been overstated (Ley, 1980).

For one thing, evidence suggested that external responsiveness, far from being peculiar to the very overweight, is to be found at all weight levels and might be most common among those who are slightly overweight or among 'restrained eaters' who may be of normal weight or below but who are deliberately moderating their eating in order to keep their weight down (Rodin, 1978; Ley, 1980). More seriously, there was confusion over whether externality was part of a special relationship between some people and the objects of their special interest or excessive behaviour (alcohol for excessive drinkers, gambling for compulsive gamblers, sexual stimuli for the hypersexual, etc.), or whether we were dealing with general external responsiveness as a personality characteristic which might confer some 'addiction proneness'. Tucker *et al.* (1979), who found some evidence for externality among 'alcoholics', raised the question of whether their finding had aetiological significance for alcohol 'dependence'. As they wisely pointed out:

> Though it may be that prior to developing a drinking problem, alcoholics respond differently than normal drinkers to internal and external stimuli related to beverage consumption, it is equally plausible that alcoholics' differential responsivity to these stimuli is a result of their having repeatedly engaged in excessive alcohol consumption. It seems reasonable to speculate after repeated episodes of excessive beverage consumption ... any control initially exerted by internal bodily cues over that consumption might diminish, whereas the external stimuli ... associated with that consumption might become more salient.
>
> (Tucker *et al.*, 1979, p. 150)

Although there is still to be found the occasional argument for an 'addiction-prone' personality, it became, and remains, the general consensus of opinion that no single personality type is prone to the excesses discussed in this book.

Repeatedly, individual personality-based theories of the origins of excessive behaviour turn out on close examination to have no more than limited value, and this should come as no surprise. The multiple-variable approach used to good effect by Jessor and Jessor (1977), Jessor *et al.* (1991), McGee and Newcomb (1992), and others; the importance of distinguishing problematic and non-problematic behaviour (Sadava, 1985); the longitudinal element which Robins *et al.* (1977) and others introduced and which showed how appetitive behaviour changes as part of a wider personal, developmental process, and how different personal and social factors are predictive at different stages in an 'appetitive career' (see Chapter Seven for each of these points); the huge number of different personal functions which appetitive behaviours can potentially serve; as well as the historical and cross-cultural perspectives introduced in the chapters in Part I and which show clearly how the psychological meaning and use of a drug or activity varies from time to time and place to place—all should alert us to the futility of the search for personality variables which could provide more than a very partial explanation of excessive forms of appetitive behaviour in general. Such theories may, however, be valid as explanations for the transition, or lack of it, from one stage of a developmental process to the next, for certain individuals in a certain socio-cultural position at one historical moment in time.

Although it is, therefore, important to retain a measure of scepticism about individual–personal explanations, and little credence can be given to any one particular such theory, it would be equally mistaken in the present author's view to dismiss such explanations totally as much of the literature on addictions now does. The currently dominant bio-cognitive-behavioural model of addiction is responsible, however, for an even more serious area of comparative neglect, namely that of the socio-cultural perspective. The following chapter attempts to restore the social context to its proper place.

CHAPTER NINE

The Social Context

Self-destructive addiction is merely the medium for desperate people to internalize their frustration, resistance, and powerlessness ... we can safely ignore the drug hysterias that periodically sweep through the United States. Instead we should focus our ethical concerns and political energies on the contradictions posed by the persistence of inner-city poverty in the midst of extraordinary opulence. In the same vein, we need to recognize and dismantle the class and ethnic-based apartheids that riddle the US landscape.

(Bourgois, 1995, p. 319)

Rachel: [Bulimia's] a metaphor for women's oppression ... no one group sets the image of women, but men are the ones who make decisions in this world, they control the media, they control the images of women ... Women exercise their power through exercising it on themselves more often. That's socially acceptable ... you're not allowed, you're conditioned not to express anger

(Brooks *et al.*, 1998, p. 198)

Yet she was also aware of how her limited options had shaped her life. 'I had not been educated as I wanted. I had earned my living by labor that occupied my hands, while my mind ambitiously dreamed of work that I would have to climb to. [In seven months in the hospital] I was not once troubled with nymphomania [because she was studying nursing]; but when I had to give it up and go away, crushed with disappointment, with weakness and poverty ... when I had to again spend my days in work that held no interest for me, the old morbid depression came back and with it the disease'.

(Mills, 1885, p. 536, cited by Groneman, 1994, pp. 357–357)

Research reviewed in Chapter Seven, from that of the Jessors (1977) onwards, took full account of relevant aspects of individuals' immediate social environments, such as their close friends' appetitive activities, but the focus of such work always remained the individual person. No serious attempt was made to assess the influence of the immediate or wider social or cultural milieu, or to develop an

explanation at the level of social group, class, gender or culture. Although ....
main focus of the present book remains firmly upon individuals—its aim being
to understand the conflict about their behaviour in which the likes of Peter Cook,
David, Jan, Miss C, Max and Sam (see Chapters Two to Six) found themselves—
this chapter attempts to create some semblance of balance by considering a number
of illustrations of the importance of social and cultural factors. Many examples
could be given, and those that follow have been selected to try and make the point.
They range from the ecological, which considers the immediate or micro-level
setting in which an appetitive behaviour such as gambling or drinking takes
place, to the more macro-level setting of the whole cultural group which sets
norms for behaviour or is exposed to new challenges to its normal ways.

ECOLOGY, SETTING AND AVAILABILITY

Studies into the different forms of appetitive behaviour have different strengths and
traditions and this constitutes one of the great benefits of considering a range of
appetitive behaviours side by side. Research on gambling has been helpful in
focusing attention on characteristics of the forms of gambling themselves, and
the settings in which gambling takes place, as factors that may put players at
risk for continued or excessive gambling. On the basis of the wide-ranging
evidence which he collected regarding the possible determinants of gambling,
Cornish (1978) concluded that a previous, almost total reliance upon person-
centred forms of explanation had resulted in neglect of the importance of situational determinants. His own view rested heavily upon the importance of availability and 'ecologic opportunity', as he termed it. He referred to numerous studies
showing the concentration of gambling outlets in working-class areas, for example,
plus the influence of the visibility and acceptability of opportunities for gambling
of different kinds. The free busing of customers to Nevada casinos, the attempt to
establish off-course betting facilities at cricket, golf and other sporting events, and
the placing of gambling machines in public houses were all commercial attempts
being made at the time he was writing (intensified still more since—see Chapter
Three) to increase the visibility and accessibility of opportunities for gambling.
There were, furthermore, structural characteristics which rendered different
gambling activities differentially attractive and some more prone to elicit excess
than others. Cornish did not use the term 'dependence potential', but he came close
to it when he stated that:

> ... forms of gambling which offer participants a variety of odds and/or
> stake-levels at which to make bets, and hence choose the rate at which
> their wins or losses multiply are likely to appeal to a greater variety of
> people ... When the opportunity to use longer-odds bets or higher stakes
> in order to multiply winnings or recoup losses rapidly is combined with a
> high event-frequency and short payout-interval, participants may be
> tempted to continue gambling longer than they might otherwise do.
>
> (Cornish, 1978, p. 168)

The range of odds and the range of the possible stakes—what Weinstein and Deitch (1974) called 'multiplier potential'—was just one of the structural variables which Cornish considered important. Others, which together make up structural 'profiles' of the different forms of gambling, include the interval elapsing between betting and paying out (the payout interval), the degree of active involvement of the bettor and the amount of skill involved, the probability of winning an individual bet, and average winnings per unit amount staked (the payment ratio). More recently, on the basis of their own and others' research with young gamblers, Fisher and Griffiths (1995) have described the following risky features of machine gambling:

> Slot machines are fast, aurally and visually stimulating and rewarding, require a low initial stake, provide frequent wins, require no pre-knowledge to commence play, and may be played alone ... structural characteristics of slot machines which are designed to induce the player to play and/or to continue playing are likely to play an important role. Such characteristics include frequent payout and event intervals, arousing near miss and symbol proportions, multiplier potential, better involvement and skill, exciting light and sound effects, and significant naming.
>
> (Fisher and Griffiths, 1995, pp. 240, 241)

Dickerson (1989) concluded that excessive gambling is associated with those forms that permit repeated and sometimes rapid cycles of stake, play and determination. Forms of gambling such as pools and lotteries, because they do not share these features, would rarely be associated with excess in his view. Interestingly, in this connection, Griffiths (1995b) has speculated about the addiction potential of scratchcard gambling. Not only is the accessibility of this form of gambling very high and the size of jackpots great (most gamblers appear to be more motivated by the size of a potential win than by its probability), but also knowledge of the result is immediate, payout may be made within a few seconds, and, most importantly in Griffiths' view, winnings can be re-gambled almost immediately. The acceptability of gambling and the widely held assumption that many forms of gambling are 'harmless', 'entertainment' or 'soft' are thought to be important. Most of the group of current, adolescent machine addicts described in Griffiths' 1990 paper had begun playing as children or young teenagers in non-arcade surroundings such as local cafés, chip shops or a leisure centre, because owners of these establishments had made no attempt to stop them playing. From a Spanish perspective, Becoña *et al.* (1995) considered the placing of machines in bars, and the association of gambling with drinking, as being of particular importance.

Drinking research has tended to focus on individual people's levels and patterns of consumption, and has neglected situational determinants of adverse drinking experiences (Mäkelä, 1996). Stockwell *et al.* (1993), on the other hand, focused precisely on drinking settings in their survey of over 1000 adults in Perth, Western Australia. A total of 8 per cent had experienced some form of acute alcohol-related harm in the previous 3 months, violent incidents being the most common. Their analysis, summarised in Figure 9.1, showed that licensed premises were settings

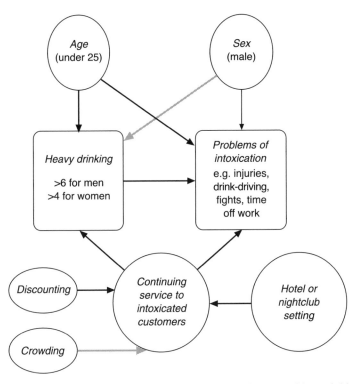

Figure 9.1 A path diagram illustrating the ways in which demographic variables, alcohol consumption and serving practices may determine the probability of alcohol-related harm occurring following drinking on licensed premises ($n = 321$). N.B. Links shown in lightface show associations significant at the 5 per cent level, those in boldface at the 1 per cent level (reproduced by permission from Stockwell *et al.*, 1993)

where harm was particularly likely to occur, and that bar staff continuing to serve customers who were obviously intoxicated was one of the correlates of harm.

A number of writers on drug use, from Zinberg onwards (e.g. Zinberg, 1978; Zinberg *et al.*, 1977), have argued that the use of drugs is regulated by informal social–ecological processes. Zinberg wrote of three factors influencing drug-using behaviour and experience: properties of the drug itself, the 'set'—the attitudes and personality of the individual drug user—and the social 'setting' in which drug use occurred. The drug and set factors had been over-emphasised in past research and thinking about drug use, and the social setting correspondingly neglected. Zinberg *et al.* studied illicit drug users whose consumption was controlled, stressing the importance of whom drugs were consumed with and the particular rituals and procedures followed in using them. Mugford (1991) took this line of thinking further by reviewing his own (Mugford and Cohen, 1989) and others' studies of cocaine users carried out during the 1980s. His conclusion was that studies in Australia, the Netherlands, Canada and the USA had all shown that cocaine was for most users well controlled, with the pleasures derived from its use exceeding any problems. This was achieved, 'By restricting use to special occasions and parties, by limiting purchase of the drug, by being part of a wider system of social ties based on family and work, and by having a knowledge of the dangers involved in use' (p. 250). Beck and Rosenbaum (1994), writing specifically about ecstasy, and Parker *et al.* (1998) writing of the 'normalisation' of drug use among British teenagers in the 1990s, also stressed the significance of becoming 'drug wise', the development of bodies of 'user folklore' and the learning of appropriate and inappropriate ways of consumption.

The so-called 'new wave' of excessive drug use that occurred in Britain in the 1980s led to a number of ethnographic or qualitative studies of drug use in which consumers were interviewed at some length and often quoted verbatim in the research reports. Notable among the British qualitative studies reported in the late 1980s or early 1990s were: Pearson's (1987) report of interviews held with heroin users in the north of England; Parker *et al.*'s (1988) programme of research about heroin use in the Wirral area of Merseyside, which included interviews with users both known and unknown to treatment agencies; and Taylor's (1993) study of women drug injectors in Glasgow, which involved over a year's participant observation of more than 50 women and in-depth interviews with 26 of them. To these can be added studies from Australia (e.g. Sargent, 1992; Crofts *et al.*, 1996) and the USA (e.g. Trotter *et al.*, 1995) which have also used ethnographic or qualitative methods.

What these first-hand accounts appear to demonstrate, apart from the complex mix of motivations for beginning to take drugs such as heroin, is the importance of the availability of the drug, particularly through friendship channels, and the ordinariness of the process of taking up use of the drug. People speak of a variety of benefits associated with early use of heroin, but they particularly speak of obtaining the drug from people they otherwise know and of learning to use the drug from such friends, and they often speak of starting to use as something than 'just happened' because it was available and widely used within their friendship networks:

> I started taking smack at school, 'cos everyone in the ... estate at that time was taking it and that was the only place you could buy pot and I sent one of me mates out from school one day to buy speed and he come back with smack and said this was all I could get and I said I don't want none of that, but in the end we ended up doing it because we was bored and we had nothing else to do. We was dabbling for about a year then ...
>
> (Dave, quoted by Parker *et al.*, 1988, p. 92)

Crofts *et al.*'s (1996) study of 300 young drug injectors in and around Melbourne, Australia, is a good illustration of the social nature of a form of appetitive behaviour which might seem to many to be particularly unsocial and abnormal. They used peer research workers, themselves young people with personal experience of injecting drug use, to contact current injectors from a variety of locations including their own social networks. Although this highly successful method of recruitment may have resulted in an unrepresentative sample—perhaps over-representing those who started to inject at a very early age, and perhaps over-estimating the social nature of early injecting drug use— it did result in a unique and valuable sample, widely dispersed across this one

Australian city. The average age of those recruited was 18.7 years and they had first injected at age 16.2 years on average. Nearly 90 per cent had injected within the year prior to being interviewed, mostly injecting amphetamines and/or heroin. Many had left home at an early age, and many reported severe domestic disturbances at home.

Nearly all of these young drug injectors could identify a significant other person who had initiated them into the practice of injecting. Only eight reported being self-taught, and only 12 per cent had injected themselves on the first occasion. Most were first injected by a friend or acquaintance, 10 per cent by partners or lovers (significantly more often the case for young women), 8 per cent by relatives, often brothers, and only 1 per cent by drug dealers. Almost half reported that their first injection was their own idea, and about a third that it was someone else's. The other person involved obtained the drug in 80 per cent of cases, although half paid for it at least in part. By the time of the interview, 47 per cent had initiated at least one other person into injecting, on average having initiated between one and two other people.

Trotter *et al.* (1995) described some results of a project that collected ongoing ethnographic data on drug-using social networks in one small south-west town in the USA. Although some people identified in the project appeared to be socially isolated in their drug use—13 per cent reported that none of the people they spent time with used drugs—the large majority appeared to be a member of one or other of four different network types. At the time of writing, Trotter *et al.* had data on 23 drug-using networks in this one small town. Five networks (type A) were the most closed, consisting of between five and ten mostly long-standing injectors of drugs, mainly heroin. Drug use was very secretive for members of these groups, most were married or in monogamous relationships and employed. Their social bonds were based on kinship and long-term friendship, but the primary purpose of the group was to pool resources for the acquisition of drugs and members socialised less than those in other types of network. Five networks (type B) were semi-closed and predominantly kinship groups. Members tended to have gone to school together and were often at 'raves' together. They were homogeneous in terms of socioeconomic status and ethnic identification. Drug use within these groups was almost a family tradition and there was much sharing of drug-using equipment.

Type C networks, of which there were eight, were described as semi-open, based largely on long-term friendships and often connections through work. These groups included both drug injectors and non-injectors, and multiple drugs were used. These groups were somewhat open to recruitment of new members, although this took time. Finally, five networks (type D) were the most open of the four types. The most common drug used was crack cocaine, and groups often included poly-drug users who were members of more than one group or who skipped from group to group. Crack dealers operated more openly than most of the other types of drug supplier, and profit was a major condition for establishing a relationship with a new recruit. Members were often young or new to the area, in transition between groups or had progressed to a stage of drug use that made them unattractive to members of the more closed groups.

As part of their programme of research in the Wirral, Parker *et al.* (1988) charted the epidemic-like rise in the prevalence of heroin use in that area of

Britain in the early to mid-1980s. Since this was a new phenomenon for the Wirral at that time, as it largely was for the whole of Britain, the taking up of this potentially excessive appetitive behaviour could be said to be an accident of history and geography. Within the area of the Wirral, the risk of becoming a young heroin user varied greatly depending on which of the 48 townships comprising the area a young person lived in. As had been the experience in cities in the USA earlier (e.g. Chein *et al.*, 1964), rates of drug use across the townships of the Wirral correlated with indices of social deprivation such as unemployment rate, local-authority housing, overcrowding, large families, single-parent households, proportion of unskilled workers and percentage of families having no access to a car (e.g. the ten townships with the highest rates of known opiate users had the higher concentrations of population and a mean unemployment rate of 20 per cent, while the nine townships with no known opiate users had an average unemployment rate of only 6 per cent).

Having documented the changes that had occurred in heroin and cocaine use in different cities in Spain in the 1980s and 1990s (see Chapter Four), Barrio *et al.* (1998) concluded:

> ... the most important factors explaining use of crack at the individual level are probably not personal characteristics of users themselves, but rather supra-individual factors that are ecological or cultural in nature and linked to the place of residence, such as the predominant routes of heroin use in the area, characteristics of the local drug market, and the influence of social networks in which the user is immersed.
>
> (Barrio *et al.*, 1998, p. 178)

It has become fashionable in writing about drug use to use the economic analogy of supply and demand. One of Parker *et al.*'s conclusions was that:

> ... the overriding factor in this situation has been the sudden influx and continuing constant supply of heroin at an 'affordable' price. To paraphrase an old saying, the water has to be there for the horse to be able to drink.
>
> (Parker *et al.*, 1988, p. 49)

Drug users, however, often prefer to see themselves as free agents in the matter, and personally responsible for any harm that may arise. For example:

> There's no one to blame for it. It's yourself. You're the one who decides to get into it, so it's on your plate. It was no one's fault. I just got into it. It was sheer, 'Oh that's nice like, I'll get into that like' ... If yer can say no, well fair enough, you're laughing aren't ya? If you can't say no, it's just hard shit. I'm not blaming anyone for my addiction, it's my own fault like. I accept that.
>
> (Eddie, quoted by Pearson, 1987, pp. 19, 20)

SOCIAL POSITION: UNEMPLOYMENT, CLASS AND GENDER

To what extent, though, is appetitive behaviour such as excessive drinking determined by an individual's social position including his/her employment opportunities? In fact, social variables such as unemployment and occupational status have been little studied in the alcohol field probably because of the dominance of the medical model, and in the UK at least the view has been that socioeconomic status is only important in determining the pattern of drinking and is practically unimportant otherwise, and that any factors in the experience of unemployment that might promote heavy drinking are likely to be cancelled out by the lower level of disposable income of the unemployed.

Ettner (1997) discussed the various links that might exist between unemployment and drinking. Losing a job may lead to lower consumption because of reduced income, but on the other hand might lead to higher consumption because of more leisure time being available. Losing a job might result in increased consumption in an effort to cope with the stress of job loss (recall that the evidence suggests that this is unlikely to be successful—see Chapter Eight), or the opposite as a result of relief from work-related stress. The relationship between job loss and drinking might be in quite the opposite direction, with excessive drinking leading to reduced productivity and a greater likelihood of becoming and remaining unemployed. It is perhaps not surprising, then, that results averaged across large groups of people tend to show small and inconsistent effects. In her analysis of her own data from a large, national US survey, Ettner (1997) found that not working, much of which was voluntary, tended to be associated with lower alcohol consumption and signs of alcohol dependence, but that involuntary unemployment tended to be associated with higher consumption, each of these effects being small.

Research has also been contradictory on whether unemployment in young people leads to increasing drinking. Plant *et al.* (1985, cited by Hammer, 1992) found no such effect in a 3-year follow-up of school leavers. In a national longitudinal study of 2000 Norwegian young people, aged 17–20 years at time 1 and followed up 2 and 4 years later, Hammer (1992) found that young men who experienced periods of unemployment in the 2-year time-2–time-3 interval were drinking more heavily than others at time 3. This effect was not found for women, and for men might have been due to selection into and out of employment. In a regression analysis controlling for time-2 alcohol consumption and a number of lifestyle variables (friends' drinking, income, visits to restaurants, etc.) no effect of having had unemployed periods was found. In fact, there was a significant reduction in drinking for those who were drinking most heavily prior to job loss, perhaps because of reduced income. Hammer did detect, on the other hand, a significant effect, among cannabis users, towards an increased frequency of cannabis consumption for those experiencing periods of unemployment. This might have been due, it is suggested, either to stress or the opportunity to buy and sell despite unemployment.

In a Dutch study of 1300 adults of all ages up to 69 years, followed up 9 years after they were first interviewed, Hajema and Knibbe (1998) examined the effects on drinking and heavy drinking (the frequency of drinking six or more glasses per occasion) of gaining or losing spouse, parental and employed roles. They found evidence for a number of effects for women: getting married led to reduced consumption and reduced heavy drinking; losing a spouse led to an increase in heavy drinking; and a change in parental role—either gaining or losing this role—led to reduced heavy drinking. For men, becoming a parent led to reduced heavy drinking especially in younger men aged between 16 and 24 years. They found no effects of changing employment status. Claussen (1999), on the other hand, found, among people unemployed for more than 12 weeks in one area in southern Norway in 1988, that remaining unemployed in the following 5 years was predictive of an alcohol 'disorder' in 1993, while having an alcohol disorder at the earlier time was not significantly predictive of remaining unemployed.

Two Swedish studies using a longitudinal design also suggest that employment factors may be much more important than has been supposed, and that they may be becoming more important. Unemployment was the variable of central interest to Janlert and Hammarström (1992). Their review of previous research suggested that the evidence for a link between unemployment and excessive alcohol use was tenuous, although a majority of studies revealed support for the suggestion that unemployment might increase alcohol consumption rather than decrease it. All pupils (over 1000) in the last year of compulsory schooling in one industrial town in northern Sweden, with a comparatively high rate of unemployment, completed a questionnaire in 1981 and 98 per cent (a remarkably successful response rate) did so again in 1986 when they were 21 years old. Experiencing unemployment during the intervening 5 years, and especially longer term unemployment (20 weeks or more), was positively correlated with alcohol consumption, for both men and women, at the beginning (1981) and at the end (1986) of the study period. For men, the correlation with alcohol consumption was stronger in 1986 than in 1981, and increasing consumption from 1981 to 1986 was also significantly correlated with unemployment. For women results were different suggesting that unemployment played a different role. Unlike young men's consumption which had increased in quantity six-fold in the 5 years that had intervened, women's average consumption had slightly decreased. The drop in consumption was actually greater for those who had experienced long-term unemployment, but this could largely be explained by the correlation between unemployment and motherhood.

Romelsjö and Lundberg (1996) used data from community surveys carried out in Stockholm County in 1970, 1984, 1990 and 1993, supplemented by data from national Swedish surveys carried out in the late 1960s and early 1980s, along with information on hospitalisations and rates of mortality with diagnoses of alcoholism, alcohol intoxication or alcohol psychosis from 1970 to the mid-1980s. In terms of consumption, men and women in occupational class I (non-manual occupations, medium and high levels) had the highest proportions of moderate or high alcohol consumers (more than 11 g of 100 per cent ethanol equivalent per day) in the earlier part of the period under study, but this trend had reversed by the early 1990s when those in occupational class III (manual workers) were most likely to be moderate or high consumers. The difference was significant when only high alcohol consumers were considered (more than 30 g per day for men and 20 g for women) (class I: men 3 per cent, women 2 per cent; class III: men 10 per cent, women 3 per cent).

What is particularly interesting is that hospitalisation and mortality social-class gradients, similar to those now found in rates of tobacco smoking in Britain (Jarvis, 1991) and very familiar to those who have studied morbidity and mortality because of physical ill-health generally (e.g. Townsend and Davidson, 1992), are clearly revealed by Romelsjö and Lundberg's results even in the earlier part of the study period when differences in consumption were, if anything, in the opposite direction. Even in the first half of the 1970s the age-adjusted standardised rate ratios (SRRs) for alcohol-related hospitalisations and mortality showed a marked and statistically significant gradient for men (for women the gradient existed only for hospitalizations and was less strong), with occupational class III showing the highest SRRs and class I the lowest in all cases. By the early 1980s (later figures are not provided by Romelsjö and Lundberg) most of these gradients had steepened still further, with manual workers showing hospitalisation and mortality SRRs several times those of medium- or high-level non-manual employees.

In fact, the highest SRRs in all cases were for those outside the workforce. The very high SRRs, ranging from 532 for alcohol-related hospitalisations for men outside the workforce to 1019 for alcohol-related mortality for the same group, indicate that both unemployed men and women in Stockholm County in the early 1980s were at 5–10 times the normal risk of being admitted to hospital or of dying with an alcohol-related diagnosis. SRRs had particularly increased for women outside the workforce between the early 1970s and early 1980s.

In Britain, Harrison and Gardiner (1999) examined records of deaths for 1988–1994 which explicitly mentioned alcohol as a cause (e.g. 'alcohol dependence syndrome', 'alcoholic cardiomyopathy', 'alcohol poisoning') and related these to occupational status. They found a clear 'social class gradient' for men, but particularly for men aged under 40 (men aged 25–39 in the unskilled manual occupational class were 10–20 times more likely to have been recorded as dying from alcohol-related causes than men in the professional group). They concluded that whereas earlier research had been equivocal on the relationship between class and alcohol-related mortality, sometimes finding *higher* status groups to be more at risk, from the 1980s negative gradients had become clearer. Their results for women, however, were less clear: younger women displayed the same kind of gradient, but for women of 40 or over the reverse was the case.

And what of an individual's membership of a gender class? In Chapter Five the point was made that 'eating disorders', although they exist and should not be neglected among men, are considerably more common among women, and that concern over excessive eating or weight is much more prevalent among females, particularly adolescents. Further evidence on this point will be presented in Chapter Twelve when discussing the way in which reactions to excess are socially relative. Meanwhile, let us hear from three of the women with 'bulimia' interviewed by Brooks (1998):

Annie: In the media it's always presented that you have to look a certain way ... that's what you're worth in our society.

Kim: We're supposed to retain our beautiful bodily shape ... Society expects women to look good.

Louise: The influence of the media on young people ... because you're not aware of it, um, there's nothing you can do ... it's so insidious ... we're constantly surrounded.

Gender issues were touched on in the above-mentioned studies of 1980s British heroin use. Female drug users were more likely than male users to have partners who also used drugs, and were more likely to have been influenced by their partners who might have introduced them to a drug, made drugs easily available, or acceptable, or may have acted as a role model (Parker *et al.*, 1988; Taylor, 1993, although Taylor and others have argued that this difference between the sexes may have been exaggerated in the past and may have been narrowing). Most of the women in Taylor's sample seemed not to blame their partners, however.

Women's position in the illicit drug scene was more of a focus for Sargent (1992) who interviewed a total of 88 women heroin users in London, Amsterdam and Sydney. Virtually equal numbers were interviewed in the three cities, each group averaging 27 or 28 years of age. The average length of time over which heroin had been taken was 8–9 years in each city, but whereas almost all injected heroin in London and Sydney, the largest proportion in Amsterdam used the 'chasing the dragon' route. Approximately two-thirds were interviewed in groups and one-third singly. In this and other respects Sargent's interesting study parts company with conventional survey research, and her theoretical approach to drug taking is a strongly feminist and anti-individualistic one. Her description of the results of her interviews contained much about women's position in drug scenes in relation to men, the fact that their initiation into drug use had often been by and with men, the idea that their dependence was as much social as dependence on the drug itself, and the often stated view that it was hard to come off heroin when in a relationship in the context of which the taking of heroin together had been important. For example:

> The most frequently occurring type of induction was the he-gives-and-she-uses pattern. 'He' is usually a powerful figure, often a pimp or a dealer (economically powerful), or he is the object of her love (emotionally powerful), or he provides protection (powerful support) ...
>
> (Sargent, 1992, p. 90)

Linda: ... Heroin sort of encompasses everything. It's friend, lover, entertainment—you don't need anything else ... I used to think it so romantic that he would fix me. I used to feel so close to him that I would trust him to stick this needle in my arm, and when we first used it felt so great together ...

> (Sargent, 1992, pp. 84, 92)

CULTURE

But the social and cultural nature of appetitive behaviour is best shown up by considering the matter at the level of whole socio-cultural groups. This is nowhere better illustrated than by the alcohol consumption and associated problems of indigenous or aboriginal people who have been exposed to domination by colonial immigrants and exposed to alcohol for the first time or to forms of alcoholic beverage with which they were not previously familiar. Aboriginal Australians provide one of the best examples (Kahn *et al.*, 1990). There has been much stereotyping and prejudice regarding Aboriginal drinking, but very few objective surveys. Fleming *et al.* (1991) reported the results of a survey of 1764 Aboriginal people living in the Northern Territory and Hall *et al.* (1993) the results of a random sample survey of 516 Aboriginal people living in the Kimberley area in the north of Western Australia. Both found high rates of abstention from drinking (59 per cent in Northern Territory and 48 per cent in Western Australia) with a significantly higher rate among women. Both surveys found the majority of drinkers to be consuming amounts considered harmful (more than 60 g of alcohol per day for men and 40 g for women). In addition, Hall *et al.* asked about a number of alcohol-related problems. For example, of drinkers, 55 per cent had thought that they should cut down on their drinking, 66 per cent reported experiencing amnesic episodes (blackouts), 49 per cent reported getting into fights, 41% reported an alcohol-related injury, and 79 and 30 per cent, respectively, had ever been incarcerated in a police lock-up or a regional prison.

The social patterning of drinking was displayed in the Northern Territory finding that the percentage of drinkers there varied systematically with the type of community in which people were living and the 'liquor status' of the community. The majority of those living in town camps in or close to urban centres were drinkers (74 per cent), compared with a third or less living in more remote cattle stations or outstations. Since 1979, communities in the Northern Territory could opt to become 'dry', and 34 per cent of Fleming *et al.*'s sample were living in communities that had done so. Only 28 per cent of this group were drinkers compared with 52 per cent of those living in communities with no restrictions. Their results suggest a strong sex effect here, with men being much less constrained by the lesser availability of alcohol than were women.

In reviewing these and other studies suggesting high rates of both abstention and problematic drinking among Aboriginal people in Australia, Kahn *et al.* (1990) reported that the most often cited causal factors for Aboriginal heavy drinking were those taken to be the psychological consequences of exploitation, socio-economic conditions, prejudice, discrimination and disruption of Aboriginal culture. These factors included loss of identity, particularly for males, loss of traditional lands bringing Aboriginal people to a state of being dependent fringe dwellers, loss of self-esteem, boredom, unemployment, lack of hope, feelings of rejection and/or inferiority. A large number of other factors have also been suggested, however, including: deliberate exploitation by Europeans using alcohol as a bribe for sex and entertainment, or for gain and manipulation because it induced poor judgement and ineffectiveness making Aborigines easy prey for exploitation; economic exploitation via 'grog-running' and taxation; observation of heavy binge-drinking habits of white farmers and miners; drinking as a symbol of equality, since Aboriginal people were denied unrestricted access to alcohol until quite recently (1971 in the Kimberley area of Western Australia—Hall *et al.*, 1993); traditional Aboriginal obligations to share resources and accept gifts; following traditional customs of sharing and consuming food as soon as it becomes available; and lack of opportunity to develop social controls over alcohol use in the limited time that Aboriginal people have been exposed to it. Many or all of these may be important factors, but whatever the case Khan *et al.* concluded that the relationship between Aboriginal alcohol use and social, psychological and health problems, '... cannot be examined outside the socio-historical context' (p. 358). Similarly Hall *et al.* concluded:

> ... a pernicious combination of poverty, welfare dependence, and the recent introduction of alcohol to a culture with little prior exposure to it, have produced drinking patterns in which average levels of consumption approach those reported in European clinical samples. As expected, this pattern of drinking has produced a high prevalence of alcohol-related problems.
>
> (Hall *et al.*, 1993, pp. 1097–1098)

The literature on drinking and related problems among North American Indians is larger but with many similarities (Brady, 1995). For example, Foulkes (1987), surveying alcohol use in one native American community in Alaska, reported 41 per cent of the population considering themselves to be excessive drinkers, 62 per cent regularly getting into fights when they drank and 67 per cent experiencing frequent blackouts. Most of the men in the community had been detained during the first 2 years of a programme, designed to reduce alcohol-related deaths in Alaskan communities, that involved the detention of people reported by relatives or friends as being out of control through drinking that endangered themselves or others. In discussion, Foulkes listed four factors that had appeared in the literature in an effort to explain heavy drinking among native Americans: being blocked for obtaining leadership positions in US society; response to the deterioration of a society under conquest; learning drinking behaviour from whites; and using intoxication to achieve Aboriginal goals. Foulkes added to this list the function of alcohol as a release for emotion among the traditional people where marital relationships in particular were emotionally restrained and where alcohol allowed greater expression of both affection and displeasure.

Besides these reports of the exposure to excessive drinking of indigenous groups, others have studied immigrant or minority groups or variation in ethnic identity within countries. For example, two British studies have focused on the drinking behaviour and attitudes of groups of young adults brought up in England but whose parents or grandparents had been brought up in a culture very different as far as drinking norms were concerned.

O'Connor's (1978) study involved interviews with over 700 18–21-year-olds plus separate interviews with most of their mothers and fathers. The sample was divided into those born of Irish parents, brought up and still living in Ireland; those born of English parents, born, brought up and still living in England; and a third sample of 18–21-year-olds born and brought up in England by parents who had themselves been born and reared in the Republic of Ireland (the Anglo-Irish group). O'Connor certainly produced evidence that an Irish upbringing exposed young people to abstinence norms, and that those young people born and brought up in England by Irish parents shared this early experience to some degree. The majority of Irish and Anglo-Irish young men and women in her sample had taken a pledge early in their teens not to drink until the age of 21. No member of the English sample had done so. More Anglo-Irish than English young people had parents who themselves had taken a pledge and who were now abstinent, although in both respects the Anglo-Irish group fell short of the Irish group. On the other hand, more Anglo-Irish fathers drank heavily than was the case in either the Irish or the English groups (rates of heavy drinking were uniformly low for all three groups of mothers). Despite their pledge-taking, Anglo-Irish youngsters reported starting to drink as often during their teens as did the English (e.g. over half the males before their 15th birthday) in comparison with a much lower figure for Irish youngsters (17 per cent of males drinking by age 15). Early drinking was hidden from parents most often for the Irish and least often for the English, and Irish youngsters reported hiding their current drinking from parents and feeling guilty and worried about their drinking more often than either of the other groups. Drinking at home occasionally with a meal was much more common an experience for the English. Anglo-Irish youngsters in particular were exposed to the conflicting influences of intolerance of drinking by their Irish parents, on the one hand, and permissiveness towards drinking on the part of their English friends.

The second study of English people with a strong family influence on their drinking, derived from a more abstinence-oriented culture, was our more recent study of African-Caribbean, Hindu, Sikh and South-Asian Muslim young adults brought up in the UK and now living in Birmingham or Leicester in the English Midlands (Purser *et al.*, 2000). Table 9.1 shows some of the results from that study. The South-Asian Muslim group (Pakistani and Bengali) drinkers, in particular, showed signs of being caught between the pro-drinking host culture, and the abstinence norms of their parents and the cultural group in Britain with which they identified more closely. While only a minority said they drank at all, most of those who did drink had abstaining parents. Most reported that their parents did not know about their own drinking, and most preferred that it should stay that way.

Two studies from different continents have examined individual differences in ethnic identity and drinking. Eide and Acuda (1996) surveyed 3000 secondary-school students from four provinces in Zimbabwe. Factor analysis of correlations between 14 items assessing cultural orientation suggested two oblique (correlated) factors, one an index of Zimbabwean orientation (listening to traditional music and black radio and reading non-English and Zimbabwean papers), the other an index of Western orientation (watching videos, television and films at the cinema, listening to funky and reggae music and Western radio). Whether or not the students had ever used alcohol was positively correlated with Western orientation and negatively with Zimbabwean, supporting the suggestion that Western cultural influences are among those that might explain the apparently growing alcohol problem in sub-Saharan Africa (see Chapter Two for a discussion of how drinking habits in 'developing' countries have been affected by commercialisation and globalisation of the drinks industry).

At the same time, Herd and Grube (1996) reported the results of a survey of around 2000 black people which was part of a larger national survey in the USA.

Table 9.1   Some results of a study of second-generation ethnic minority groups and drinking in the English West Midlands (Purser *et al.*, 2000)

	Black (%)	Indian Hindu (%)	Indian Sikh (%)	Pakistani (%)	Bengali (%)
Men					
Sometimes drink	87	34	71	15	24
Heavy drinking (>21 units/week)	34	4	24	4	5
Parents know about drinking[1]	72	61	72	25	17
Would rather parents didn't know[1]	7	15	6	25	39
Women					
Sometimes drink	80	22	25	8	15
Heavy drinking (>14 units/week)	18	3	5	2	4
Parents know about drinking[1]	73	31	17	10	11
Would rather parents didn't know[1]	11	42	57	100	67

[1] Drinkers only.

Their assessment of ethnic identity was broader than Eide and Acuda's, and covered social networks, participation in organisations, and attitudes to mixing with people of different races, as well as music and media preferences. Their factor analysis suggested four correlated factors. The results showed how complicated the issue of black ethnic identity drinking might be. Their hypothesis was that greater black identity would be correlated with less drinking and less heavy drinking, and that this relationship would be mediated by the greater religiosity and more moderate or abstemious drinking norms of those who had the greater black identity. This hypothesis was supported in the case of two of the identity factors: black socio-political awareness (importance of participation in black-equality organisations, of reading black newspapers and magazines, and black culture in everyday life) and involvement in black social networks (proportion of blacks in neighbourhood, at church, among friends, and in the neighbourhood when growing up). Results were exactly opposite to those predicted, however, in the case of the factor of exposure to black media (preference for listening to black radio stations, black music and watching black TV channels). The fourth factor, 'endogamy' (feeling less at ease with whites, thinking it better for blacks to marry only blacks, and reliance on relatives for help), produced a mixed result, showing a negative direct effect on drinking, but a positive indirect effect via its association with reduced religiosity. Herd and Grube concluded that in general their results supported previous studies suggesting that black communities often reinforce norms associated with abstaining and infrequent drinking and had exerted considerable social control to reduce heavy drinking and drunkenness. These norms, they suggested, stem from historical involvement of blacks in temperance campaigns and contemporary participation in the Protestant Church, also reflecting values associated with maintaining respectability, social betterment and upward mobility. At the same time, the complex associations with drinking behaviour that were found suggested to them that ethnic identity was multi-dimensional, and that undimensional scales for cultural identity used in many studies were insufficient.

In the case of eating, what has been of interest is the possibility that different ethnic groups, in countries such as the UK and the USA, might be more or less vulnerable to excessive eating because of their eating attitudes and behaviours. Although the picture that emerges from this research is not a clear one, results are sufficient to make it plain that ethnic differences do exist. For example, Akan and Grilo (1995) found that African American women students at one New England university had a significantly higher body mass index than Asian American or Caucasian students, but that the latter reported significantly higher levels of disordered eating and dieting behaviours and attitudes and greater body dissatisfaction than either of the other two groups. In a study of 846 11–18-year-olds from six London schools, Wardle and Marsland (1990) compared white, black and Asian teenagers. In terms of perceptions of their bodies, black boys were strikingly more satisfied with their size than white or Asian boys, and among the girls whites were most dissatisfied with their bodies and black girls the least. Controlling for actual body size (body-mass index) white girls more often than black or Asian girls described a range of body parts as 'too big'. Scores on a restrained eating and dieting scale were significantly lower for black girls and boys than for whites and Asians. On the other hand, Reiss (1996) found that African Caribbean women attending one of four family-planning clinics in North London had not only a significantly higher mean body mass index than white British women attending the same clinic, but also had significantly more disordered eating attitudes and a significantly higher level of abnormal eating behaviour. They were especially more likely than white women to answer affirmatively to the questions: If you over-eat do you feel very guilty? Do you feel a failure if you break your diet once? Would you say that food dominated your life?

Button *et al.* (1997) compared 130 white, 73 Asian and 22 black women who responded to a questionnaire delivered to patients of one general practice in Leicester, England. White women were the more frequent users of nearly all weight-control methods, and significantly so for self-induced vomiting, and black women the least frequent users. Previous work in the UK had suggested that Asian women would score most highly on the questionnaire assessing preoccupation and concern with eating and weight. Although they were the highest scoring of the three groups in Button *et al.*'s study, the differences were not significant, and the authors suggested that research should control for marital status (Asian women were more often married in their study), age, treatment seeking, country of birth and the proportions in the Asian group who were Muslim and Sikh.

There is a great deal more that could be said about the social context to developing an excessive appetite but perhaps enough has been said to ensure that as we continue to develop the excessive appetites view of addiction the social dimension will not be forgotten. Having now discussed at some length a number of the personal and social influences out of which people's attachments to appetitive substances and activities develop, and a number of the complex ways in which these factors combine and change over time, let us now turn to consider how it is that mild or moderate attachments may develop into strong ones. The social context will appear again, particularly in Chapter Twelve when considering social reactions to excess, and in Chapter Fourteen when examining the social dimension to the process of giving up excess. In Chapter Ten, however, our focus will again be upon the individual, as we try to understand how an ordinary appetite might escalate and become an excessive one.

CHAPTER TEN

Overcoming Restraint

Although winning money was the first thing that attracted me to playing
fruit machines, this was gradually converted to lights, sounds and excitement. I always received a great thrill from new machines with new ideas and
new lights and sounds.

(David, cited by Griffiths, 1993b, p. 393)

Never underestimate the strength of a habit.

(Reinert, 1968, pp. 37–38)

When you start the junk [heroin], and you think you are using it, you are not
conscious of the stage when it comes round and it is using you. You're just
no' conscious of that happening ...

(Rose, cited by Taylor, 1993, p. 47)

In our search for an explanation of how appetites that mostly give pleasure,
delight, joy or harmless entertainment can sometimes become so excessive that
they threaten to spoil our lives, let us begin by considering how appetitive behaviours are distributed in the population. One of the cornerstones of the new public
health approach to the prevention of excessive drinking that emerged in the late
1960s and 1970s was the now commonplace observation that alcohol consumption
by individuals within a population is distributed along a skewed frequency-
distribution curve of the kind shown in Figure 10.1. Once this important fact
was brought to attention there followed much controversy about the exact form
taken by the alcohol consumption frequency-distribution curve. Ledermann (1956)
proposed that mathematically the curve corresponded to a lognormal distribution,
although others (e.g. Skog, 1977; Hyman, 1979) pointed out that there existed a
whole family of lognormal curves (which differed in degree of dispersion around
the mean) and that there was even doubt whether the curves obtained took a
lognormal form at all. All that could safely be concluded was that such curves
are regularly found to be smooth, unimodal and markedly skewed towards the
higher consumption end of the distribution: the majority of people are found to
conform more or less to a relatively moderate norm (or, in certain sub-populations,
to an abstinence norm) with smaller and smaller proportions of people displaying
consumption in excess of this norm to a greater and greater degree.

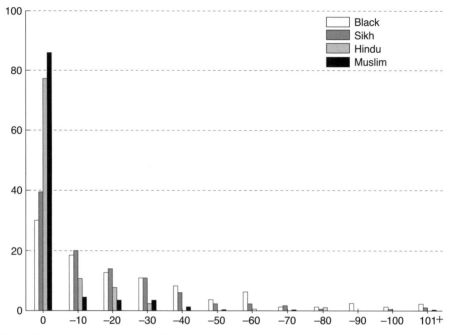

Figure 10.1   Skewed population frequency-distribution curves for alcohol consumption: data from Purser *et al.*'s (2000) study of the drinking of second-generation ethnic minority groups in the English Midlands. The figure shows percentages of men drinking different amounts of alcohol (standard units) in the previous 7 days.

There is good evidence that such a distribution is a feature of a number of the forms of appetitive behaviour with which this book is dealing. Although personal alcohol consumption provides the best documented example, data on frequency of sexual behaviour follow similar distribution curves. For example, the curves that can be drawn from data on total sexual outlet for US males produced by Kinsey *et al.* (1948, p. 200) in their classic survey of over 50 years ago show a peak at the low-frequency end of the range (with a mode at one or two outlets per week), with a long and continuous tail to the distributions showing ever decreasing proportions of people reporting increasing weekly frequencies up to 10–20 times a week. More recent British data illustrating the same phenomenon come from the National Survey of Sexual Attitudes and Lifestyles carried out in the early 1990s (Wellings *et al.*, 1994). In relation to the number of people's heterosexual partners (shown in Figure 10.2) Wellings et al commented on, 'One of the striking features of these data ... [is] the marked variability between individuals in the number of partners reported, and the extreme skewness of the distribution' (p. 94).

Similarly skewed is the distribution of frequency of eating binges among women in the general population according to Fairburn and Beglin's previously unpublished data, shown in Figure 10.3, obtained from patients in two general practices in Oxfordshire, England although here the norm is zero.

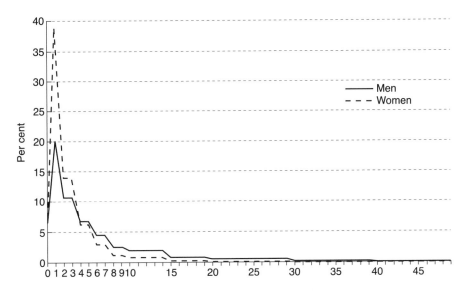

Figure 10.2 Number of lifetime sexual partners (data from the National Survey of Sexual Attitudes and Lifestyles, Wellings *et al.*, 1994, kindly provided by A. Copas).

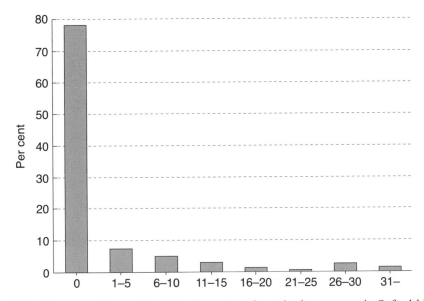

Figure 10.3 Frequency (3-month) of objective over-eating episodes—women in Oxfordshire, England (unpublished data kindly made available to the author by Fairburn and Beglin).

The same turns out to be the case for gambling activity in the general population as is demonstrated by data from the first British National Survey of the Lottery and other forms of gambling carried out in 8000 homes in Britain in 1999 (Sproston *et al.*, 2000). This is illustrated in Figure 10.4, which shows the

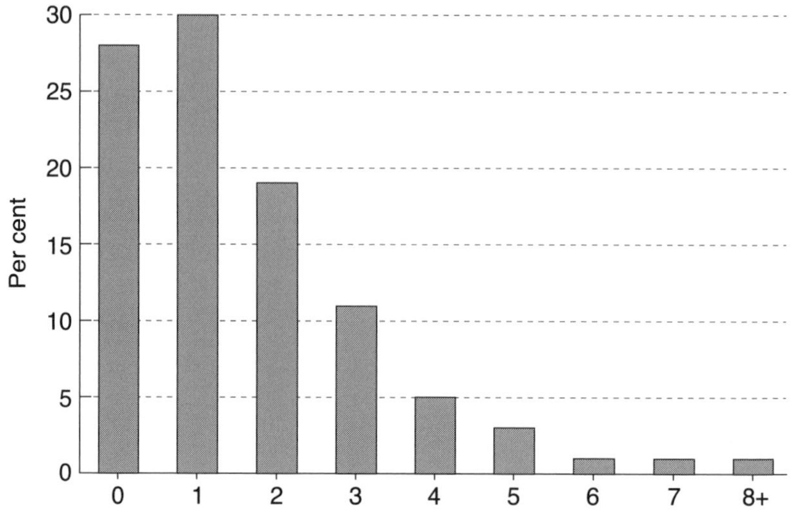

Figure 10.4   Number of gambling activities participated in within the last year (National Centre for Social Research, Sproston *et al.*, 2000).

distribution of number of different kinds of gambling activity (lottery, machines, horses, casino, etc.) taken part in during the year prior to the survey. From all that is known about the consumption of drugs such as marijuana or cocaine, to mention just two, it seems very likely that amount consumed in any given period of time, such as the last week or the last year, would be distributed in the population in the same way. Whether the peak of such a curve, representing the mode or norm, lies at or above the zero point, and how steeply the curve falls from the modal point, will vary with the nature of the activity and the particular population. Distribution of frequency of marijuana consumption in the last year among 18-year-old Britons in the late 1990s is likely to show a peak above zero and a relatively slow fall (Parker *et al.*, 1998), while the curve for their cocaine use or for marijuana consumption amongst their grandparents would have a zero mode and most likely a steep fall-off. What unites all such appetitive consumption curves, however, is their marked skewness, showing the existence of a long tail, representing minorities of people, distinguishable from the majority only quantitatively, who are involved in the activity to an extent far beyond the norm. Their appetitive behaviour is excessive, at least in the statistical one.

The existence of such distributions is fundamental to understanding the excessive appetites, and we must consider their meaning. The implications of these curves for prevention have been considered (e.g. in the case of alcohol), but they have been much less frequently considered as sources of possible theoretical insight into the nature of the processes determining excessive appetitive behaviour. There are, in fact, two general explanations for the generation of such distribution curves which are between them consistent with a great deal of the evidence discussed in the previous three chapters, and which may therefore help us explain excessive consumption.

DETERRENCE AND RESTRAINT

The first lies in the psychology of conformity. Here one of the most valuable sources of ideas is a paper written by Allport (1934) nearly 70 years ago. He noticed that certain behaviours, such as times of arrival for work or for a church service, and the speed of vehicles across intersections which carried 'Halt' or 'Slow' signs, followed skewed or reversed J-shaped frequency curves. He argued that this would always be the case when behaviour was subject to social control. Provided this control was effective to some degree, most people would more or less conform to the norm, rule, or law governing that behaviour, and decreasing proportions of people would deviate to an increasingly great extent. A mode at the zero point would indicate an abstinence, or non-indulgence norm, while a non-zero mode would indicate a moderation norm. The steepness of the curve would indicate the precision and/or effectiveness of the law or rule, or the strength of the informal social processes operating to restrain members of the community from behavioural excess. Allport referred to the skewed curve as the *conformity curve*, and he considered it to be the result of the imposition of conformity processes upon people's inclinations to do such things as stay in bed when they should be at work, or drive fast across junctions (these inclinations being themselves variable quantities). The position of an individual on the distribution was thus presumed to be the result of the opposing tendencies to conformity and indulgence.

In this important but now little remembered paper of Allport's we have one of the necessary basic components for an explanation of appetitive behaviour and its excessive forms. We have already met evidence, in Chapter Seven, that unconventionality and non-conformity were amongst the most significant predisposing 'person' variables for general deviance and appetitive behaviours, at least within the culture and times in which most of the research reviewed was carried out (Jessor *et al.*, 1991). The inverse relationship so often found between religiosity and drug and alcohol use and sexual behaviour (Hawkins *et al.*, 1992; Purser *et al.*, 2000) is further evidence. Although it must be presumed that Allport's assumptions, that conformity acts always to restrain and that biological influences act always in opposition to restraint, are too simple, the basic idea of forces in opposition is, I believe, essential to an understanding of excessive appetites. The perspective on excessive drinking, excessive gambling, drug taking and other similar forms of excess, to be developed in the remainder of this chapter and rest of the book, rests heavily upon the idea of opposing tendencies towards restraint versus appetitive inclination, the counter-balancing of incentive and disincentive, and the moral conflict between deviant excess and conforming moderation.

Many years later, Hyman (1979), trying to explain the positively skewed shape of the appetitive consumption distribution curve, pointed out that similar distributions are obtained for purchases of non-durable goods such as meat, clothing and fuel, for economic variables such as inheritances, bank deposits, total individual wealth, numbers of employed persons in industries and industrial profits, as well as for certain geographical variables such as numbers of inhabitants in towns, distances between cities of the same size and even the numbers and lengths of streams in river systems. Certain social variables such as numbers of surviving children and ages at first marriage are also distributed in a similar fashion. He put forward the hypothesis that the underlying theme of all such distributions is that of 'major' deterrences nipping the evolution of a phenomenon in the bud (though not entirely suppressing it) (p. 345). Just as there are a number of impediments to the further development of a river tributary (competition from other tributaries, insufficient rain, excessive evaporation, hard rockbeds, etc.) or the size of cities (competition from other cities, inability to generate exports, inability to provide a wide range of services, etc.), so the evolution of appetitive behaviour to higher levels of consumption might, he argued, be impeded by a variety of deterrences including (he was considering alcohol use) gastric distress, headaches and dizziness, a psychological make-up which makes intoxication seem unpleasant, family and friendship norms that proscribe heavy drinking, and competition from other activities for time and money. Although, as already stated, Allport's ideas focused solely upon conformity to rules or norms as the factor nipping deviance in the bud, the overall similarity between the two positions is striking. The idea basic to both is that of inclination restrained: in the one case by social conformity, in the other by deterring forces of various kinds, social and otherwise.

The idea of deterrence or control has a long history in criminology (e.g. Hirschi, 1969). Cornish (1978), for example, made use of such thinking in developing his own theory of gambling behaviour. Among the factors associated with non-gambling, which he cited, were frequent church-attendance, Protestant or sectarian beliefs, partner role-sharing, involvement in work-centred leisure activities such as studying at home, and involvement in political or community activities. These exercised inhibitory control over gambling not only because of the attitudes and social bonds antithetical to gambling which they implied, but also because they restricted 'freedom' to gamble on account of, '... activities, interests and social roles making prior calls upon a person's attention, time and income' (p. 158). One of the components of control theory was 'involvement': some people are just too engrossed in conventional activities to engage in delinquency. To Cornish it was a question of using time and money in ways incompatible with gambling. Certain ages and stages in life (e.g. in youth) might provide a temporary 'leisure vacuum', with fewer competing uses of resources. This is the simple but appealing idea that vulnerability to taking up and becoming more involved in risky appetitive behaviour has much to do with what else there is of a rewarding nature to occupy our time (Johanson *et al.*, 1996). Other constraining or regulatory factors are inherent in the activity rather than the person or his or her lifestyle. In the case of gambling, Cornish argued, controls are exercised over frequency of participation in certain forms of betting because access is limited (e.g. on-course betting), membership is required (e.g. gaming), play is supervised (e.g. bingo) or participation is necessarily spaced (e.g. pools betting). These obstacles in the way of greater participation may be placed by national or local statute but they operate at the individual level by entering into the attraction–deterrence equation which determines the behaviour of each individual.

This idea of inclining and restraining forces in opposition, inherent in general social learning theory (e.g. Bandura, 1977), has been employed by many theorists of drug consumption. Akers *et al.*'s (1979) explanation, for example, was one that built on both the notion of a balance between reinforcements and deterrences, and ideas about social conformity and control, drawing particularly on the 'differential association' theory of delinquency with its emphasis upon the norms and behaviours to be found in the social groups with which a person associates:

> Progression into more frequent or sustained use and into abuse is also determined by the extent to which a given pattern is sustained by the combination of the reinforcing effects of the substance with social reinforcement, exposure to models, definitions through associations with using peers, *and by the degree to which it is not deterred* through bad effects of the substance and/or the negative sanctions from peers, parents and the law.
>
> (Akers *et al.*, 1979, p. 639, emphasis added)

Others who explicitly applied the notion of deterrence or control to explaining variations in drug use include Staats (1978) who found support for the prediction that marijuana users were deterred from greater use by limitations of supply and access, and the need to keep use hidden from non-users. Staats was critical of the assumptions contained in alternative theories that drug use could only be explained by positing some strain propelling a person to use drugs, some function served by use, a deviant learning process, or the incorporation of societal reaction to use. Viewed from the control theory perspective:

> ... deviance is taken for granted; it is conformity which must be explained. The assumption is that without controls many would not remain conformists. Conformity is assured through controls and when they weaken, the probability of deviance increases.
>
> (Staats, 1978, p. 392)

Parker *et al.* (1998) are others who have written of young people's cost–benefit approach to making decisions about taking drugs:

> ... risk assessment is part of the cost–benefit calculation and it involves weighing up for each drug the likelihood of bad or frightening experiences, the health risks, and the impact of 'getting caught' by teachers, parents, employers or the police. These are weighted against the pleasure and enjoyment of particular drugs and their ability either to blank out stress and distress or most often help deliver cost effective, deserved 'time out' through relaxation and enjoyment from the grind of ordinary, everyday life.
>
> (Parker *et al.*, 1998, pp. 119–120)

The foregoing suggests that we should be looking for some kind of deterrent, restraint, control or conformity explanation for why it is that minorities of people indulge in appetitive behaviours to the extent that is so markedly deviant from the moderation or abstinent norms to which most of us adhere. This is a kind of pushing-down-of-natural-inclinations explanation. People in the extreme tail of the distribution curve are, according to this kind of view, those who have for whatever reasons not been restrained as the rest of us have. From the perspective of this kind of theory, the interesting question is not: Why do some people become excessive in their appetitive behaviour? But rather: Why are most people not excessive?

PRIMARY, POSITIVE-INCENTIVE LEARNING MECHANISMS

The second type of explanation for skewed frequency-distribution curves is very different, but is not incompatible with the restraint or control explanation. Here we are looking, not for an explanation in terms of dampening down appetitive inclinations, but rather in terms of how such inclinations might escalate or be amplified. We are looking for some kind of explanation that obeys what Aitchison and Brown (1966) called the *law of proportionate effect*, whereby the effect of any one influence upon behaviour is proportional to the cumulative effect of preceding influences. Whereas the influence of a large number of causes, acting independently or simultaneously, will tend to produce a normal (symmetrical and bell-shaped) distribution curve, the influence of a large number of factors operating according to the law of proportionate effect will produce a lognormal, or at least a markedly skewed, distribution. All the evidence is that appetitive behaviour of each of the kinds considered here is determined not by a single causative factor or even by a few factors but rather by a very large number of influences of biological, psychological and social kinds. Furthermore, because we are dealing here with human social behaviour which develops slowly within a social context, perhaps through a number of stages, these factors are not acting independently or at the same time.

To produce a skewed curve according to the law of proportionate effect we require a *developmental* theory, one that supposes that the chances of proceeding to the next 'stage', or of responding to the next positive influence inclining towards further 'consumption', are greater the more previous 'stages' have been passed through or the greater the number of previous influences that have been effective. Any theory which relies on an accumulation of influence would qualify. Aitchison and Brown (1966), in fact, built a machine which sorted grains of sand into a lognormal distribution by a clever arrangement of dividers which gave each grain a progressively greater probability of moving to the right depending upon the distance it had already been moved in that direction by previous dividers. It may not be too far fetched to suppose that those who experience the pull of an excessive appetite are in the grips of a similar kind of mechanism.

An obvious candidate for a developmental theory of addiction, which would satisfy the law of proportionate effect and provide a mechanism like Aitchison and Brown's, is some variety of learning theory, in particular operant learning theory. The basic tenet of operant theory is well known: behaviour is controlled by its consequences. Consequences which increase the frequency of the behaviour are termed reinforcers, and the behaviour which was instrumental in producing those consequences is said to be reinforced thereby. Thus habits develop.

The consequences of appetitive acts of the kind we are considering, and which might be instrumental in the development of habits, hence producing the kind of skewed curves shown earlier, may be quite basic. Since the first edition of this book was being written a consensus among experts appeared to be emerging suggesting that the personal rewards associated with appetitive behaviours, which have the potential of becoming excessive, might be related to certain definable processes occurring in the brain. A number of developments helped to bring about this apparent consensus. The first was the move away from a deficit-reduction, escape-avoidance, negative reinforcement model of addiction (see Chapter Eleven) towards one based upon the pleasure-seeking, approach, positive reinforcement significance of appetitive objects and activities. Central to the former was the development of tolerance to a drug, the experience of withdrawal symptoms when drug use stopped, and the negative reinforcement value of repeated drug use in order to avoid or escape from unpleasant withdrawal symptoms. Although deficit-reduction may still have an important part to play in a complete account of excessive appetitive behaviour, as we shall see in Chapter Eleven, there is now much greater agreement than there was that such mechanisms are probably secondary to ones based upon positive reinforcement or pleasure. This represents a complete about-turn in thinking about excessive appetites. When deficit models held centre stage the positive rewards obtained from drugs were considered marginal to the main issue. Indeed, the very word 'addiction' had, and perhaps continues to have, connotations of a pathological process occurring independently of any pleasure that an activity might bring, and outside of an individual's conscious control.

Another factor that has helped bring about this change has been the accumulation of research showing that many of the drugs which can give rise to excess in humans, bring about changes in certain definable neural systems in the brain. Attention has focused particularly upon the finding that a number of drugs increase neurotransmission in the mesolimbic dopamine system of the brain. This is especially true of amphetamine and cocaine but is also true for nicotine, morphine and alcohol. The crucial brain pathway for this transmission runs from a site known as the ventral tegmental area in the midbrain to the limbic areas associated with emotion, including the nucleus accumbens and the amygdala (Joseph *et al.*, 1996). Cocaine, which has been the subject of much research, appears to increase dopamine transmission by binding at the pre-synaptic membrane and hence preventing the recycling (or 're-uptake') of dopamine after the latter has played its part in neural transmission by binding at the post-synaptic membrane. Amphetamine, in addition, increases dopamine by releasing it in the terminal areas; nicotine acts by stimulating acetylcholine receptors on the dopamine cell bodies; and opiates act by inhibiting the action of GABAergic (gamma-aminobutyric acid) neurones which normally inhibit the cell bodies (Joseph *et al.*, 1996).

The idea that there might be a single, circumscribed system in the brain that is affected by most drugs that are used excessively, and that this mechanism might be the basis of drug reward is given strong encouragement by the development of ideas about brain mechanisms and appetite and reward more generally. Not only is the mesolimbic dopamine system affected by a number of different types of drug, but it is this same brain system that, as has been widely suggested, is involved in mediating reward and reinforcement of all kinds. Particularly intriguing have been animal studies of self-stimulation in which animals learn to press a lever resulting in the delivery of electrical stimulation, via implanted electrodes, to defined areas of the brain. Although areas that will elicit self-stimulation are to be found in all regions of the brain, electrodes placed in each part of the mesolimbic dopamine system support this kind of behaviour particularly easily and strongly (Kornetsky and Porrino, 1992; Joseph *et al.*, 1996). Dopamine neurotransmission has been found to play a role in both eating (e.g. dopamine antagonists reduce responding for food and food intake in animals) and sexual behaviour (e.g., dopamine agonists have been used in the treatment of erectile dysfunction in men, and the antagonist benperil has been used to control deviant sexual behaviour), and in both cases brain self-stimulation has been considered as a model (Cooper and Higgs, 1994; Levin, 1994).

Is there then, as Wise (e.g. 1994) has consistently argued, a basic brain system which mediates pleasure and reward, including that associated with brain stimulation, a variety of drugs which can be used excessively, food, and sex? This possibility of a single, fairly easily understood brain mechanism that could account for the capacity of a range of appetitive activities and substances to become excessive is very appealing. Is this why certain drugs and activities are potentially addictive? Because they each give rise to an excess of dopamine in the crucial brain area, and this is highly pleasurable and rewarding?

If only it were so simple! There are a number of potential complications. For one thing neuroscientists working in the drug area as well as those working on reward processes more generally have been setting their sights beyond the mesolimbic dopamine system (Terry, 1995). Although the consensus remains about the importance of dopaminergic transmission, most experts favour a more broadly based approach in which other forms of neural transmission, including serotonergic, opioidergic and noradrenergic, may also play vital roles in, for example, opiate, alcohol and even cocaine reward, with cholinergic transmission being additionally important in the case of nicotine (Ashton and Golding, 1989; Corrigall, 1991; Stolerman, 1991; Terenius and O'Brien, 1992; Gawin, 1991; Kranzler and Anton, 1994). Such systems might operate in parallel to the dopamine system, or in series with it as part of a chain reaction, or may act to modulate the dopaminergic system. In the case of food, and sex also, the picture is likely to be much more complicated than a simple dopamine-reward model would suggest, with the likely involvement of noradrenaline and serotonin in the case of sex (Levin, 1994) and opioid and benzodiazepine mechanisms in the case of food (Cooper and Higgs, 1994).

The complexities of brain and appetite go far beyond the question of which neurotransmitter systems might be involved in reward. For one thing the idea that there might be a 'reward system' in the brain that is activated by a variety of drugs implies a rather simple, unitary view of the reward or positive outcomes from drug consumption. As we saw in Chapter Eight, appetitive activities can do a variety of positive things for different people at different times, and often simultaneously for the same person. Those who have written about the rewarding functions of nicotine are probably those that have put most strongly the point that drugs can do a variety of rewarding things for people and that these effects are likely to involve a variety of different biological mediators. Ashton and Golding (1989), for example, referred to, 'intricately woven patterns of motivation' (p. 43), that are involved in the use of nicotine. Their view was that nicotine can simultaneously affect, 'all the major functional systems governing behavior' (p. 42), including those for reward, for goal-directed arousal, for learning and memory, for the control of pain, and for the relief of aversive states such as anxiety, frustration and aggression. To these Stolerman (1991) added the capacity of nicotine to aid task performance by increasing accuracy and sustained attention, and the role of nicotine in weight control, and O'Connor (1989) reviewed evidence suggesting that the sensory-motor pleasures associated with smoking, to which many smokers refer when asked why they smoke (e.g. Russell *et al.*, 1974), should be afforded a much more central place in our understanding of smoking. Pomerleau and Pomerleau (1989) referred to smokers learning to 'use' nicotine, 'to regulate or fine-tune the body's normal adaptive mechanisms' (p. 74), and listed a range of positive consequences of smoking, for which there is evidence in the literature, and the neurotransmission systems that they considered are associated with each.

The matter is more complicated still. In the foregoing discussion basic terms such as 'reward' and 'pleasure' have been used as if they were unproblematic. In fact, work on the brain, drugs and appetitive behaviour is throwing up an intriguing debate about the nature of reward or reinforcement, and whether these, whatever they are, can be equated with pleasure. Joseph *et al.* (1996) questioned the simple view that drugs and addiction have their main action by affecting a dopamine-reward system. They pointed out that many animal studies have shown that stressors and aversive stimuli of various kinds are also associated with increased dopamine release in the mesolimbic system, so it is not just rewarding stimuli that are so. They concluded that the activation of the mesolimbic dopamine system is central but that it is better to think of this as being associated with the increased *saliency* of stimuli, or stated another way, curiosity about them, whether those stimuli be rewarding or aversive, unconditioned or conditioned. In coming to this conclusion they drew particularly on work showing that amphetamine and nicotine disrupt 'latent inhibition' in animals. Latent inhibition is a phenomenon whereby repeated exposure to a neutral stimulus impairs its ability to subsequently enter into conditioned associations; in other words, stimuli become less salient as they become more familiar. This led them to the interesting suggestion that a major function of such drugs might be to bring about a kind of 'widening of the gates of consciousness' in which new associations with familiar stimuli are made more easily. This sounds contrary to the views of writers such as Steele and Josephs (1990, see Chapter Eight) whose conclusion was that drugs such as alcohol, at least, produced a *narrowed* perception of reality and poor information processing. The two ideas—of easier formation of associations with familiar stimuli and poor information processing on an abstract level—are not necessarily contradictory, however.

Joseph *et al.* (1996) also drew upon recent work on the phenomenon of sensitisation. This effect, opposite to the familiar and much longer recognised phenomenon of 'tolerance', refers generally to an *increase* in response to the same or weaker stimuli following presentation of a strong stimulus. In the context of drug use it refers to increased responsiveness to the drug following repeated drug administration (Stewart, 1992). Robinson and Berridge (1993) built a general incentive-sensitisation theory of addiction around this concept of behavioural sensitisation, otherwise known as behavioural facilitation or reverse tolerance. They also accepted the central involvement of the mesolimbic dopamine system, but concluded from their reading of the evidence that its function is not to give the experience of pleasure, nor to relieve the distress associated with drug withdrawal (the two main existing models of addiction, both of which they found wanting), but rather the attribution of incentive salience to the perception or mental representation of stimuli and actions. This makes the act of drug taking and stimuli associated with it highly salient, attractive and 'wanted'. An important aspect of this model is that 'wanting' is not to be equated with 'liking'. Indeed, with repeated drug taking the two are likely to become more and more dissociated. This is similar to the view of Joseph *et al.* (1996) who viewed it as simplistic to argue that dopamine release in the mesolimbic system can be equated with reward, or that drug taking in humans is only the seeking of reward. As they put it, 'drug addiction is probably not just hedonism run riot' (p. 61). It is important to point out that Robinson and Berridge's model is a developmental one since it requires repeated drug use for sensitisation to develop. They admitted that the memory of pleasure associated with drug use might play the more important part in the *initiation* of drug use. As an aside here it is worth noting that neuroscientists who have taken a particular interest in drug appetite are rather inclined to dismiss or minimise the importance of psychological or psychosocial factors, such as subjective experience or peer-group influence, relegating them to a role in the mere initiation of very early stages of a drug-using career before neuropsychological processes, the real causes of 'addiction', take hold.

Others who have questioned the nature of reward and pleasure include a number of contributors to the book entitled *Appetite*, edited by Legg and Booth (1994). Consistent with Robinson and Berridge's (1993) model, Legg (1994) concluded that brain self-stimulation acts by assigning incentive properties to environmental stimuli so that, for example, as in the early animal experiments on brain stimulation, a preference develops for the place where brain stimulation was received. Toates (1994), in outlining his incentive motivation theory of appetite, put most emphasis on the value of stimuli as incentives that both help to arouse motivation and form the targets of behaviour. Dopamine is important in this view but may be more important in preparatory than in consummatory behaviour. Wise (1994), whose general dopamine reward theory of appetitive behaviour has been prominent in the literature (it is usually referred to as the 'anhedonia' theory because the early experiments on which it was based concerned the blocking of reward by dopamine antagonists), has raised a number of fundamental issues. Like others, he was moving towards an emphasis on Pavlovian rather than Skinnerian ideas of reinforcement, placing more emphasis on conditioning and on incentive motivation than upon instrumental or operant conditioning (see below). Indeed, he suggested that the concept of 'psychomotor arousal' or 'psychomotor activation' might serve the field better now than the concept of 'reinforcement'. Like Robinson and Berridge (1993), Wise regretted associating reward with pleasure in the original exposition of his ideas, and was now of the view that reward (itself a complex idea subsuming several components) and subjective pleasure become dissociated, to the extent that searching for 'mental' causes of appetitive behaviour may actually hinder our understanding.

White (1996) went further in postulating three distinct forms of learning that are involved in drug use (see Chapter Eleven), each associated with distinct anatomical sites in the brain. He went beyond what many others have believed, not only by taking the focus away from the mesolimbic dopamine system, but also by assuming that different drugs have unique patterns of effect upon the three learning processes, rather than, as Wise and many others have assumed, that different drugs have a common brain action. White's interesting ideas remain somewhat speculative: Stewart (1996) referred to his analysis as, 'ambitious ... [and] ... difficult to sustain' (p. 956). Nevertheless, his paper was well received for the questions it raised and its departure from an oversimple and probably outdated notion of there being a 'single reward centre' in the brain to which we can attribute the potential of appetitive activities for becoming excessive (Fibiger, 1996).

An even more fundamental challenge to simple ideas of brain mechanisms and addiction, such as the dopamine–limbic system model, is the existence of non-substance or pure behavioural or activity addictions such as gambling. The latter is far less amenable to conceptualising in terms of neat ideas of brain reward mechanisms. There have been attempts to show that excessive gambling is associated with abnormalities of neurotransmission systems, as indicated, for instance, by endorphin or dopamine levels (e.g. Blaszczynski *et al.*, 1986; Bergh *et al.*, 1997) but the methodological problems involved in such research have not been solved and the results are not convincing. Nor should we expect them to be. If the action on the brain of a comparatively straightforward substance such as amphetamine or nicotine, given under controlled conditions, is found to be too complex to satisfy a simple brain action model, then the effects in the brain of a complex human activity such as gambling are hardly likely to conform to such a model either.

On the other hand, gambling does offer a perfect case for the application of operant and associative learning and conditioning models, more generally. Cornish (1978), for example, in his early, comprehensive review of the literature on gambling carried out for the British Home Office rested heavily on learning theory in his discussion of the determinants of continued participation once the initial decision to gamble had been taken. He reviewed evidence from experimental studies of simulated gambling showing that a favourable ratio of wins over losses leads to an increased frequency, or at least to the maintenance of the current rate, of gambling, the suggestion being that financial reward constitutes at least part of the reinforcement for gambling behaviour.

Although it may appear difficult for learning theory to account for continuing participation once gambling has started on the basis of financial reinforcement alone, when it is so apparent that commercial gambling is organized to make a profit for the promotors, and the gambler is likely to show an excess of losses over gains in the long term, learning theory is in fact ideally suited to explain this paradox, as well as the apparent paradox of all excessive appetitive behaviour— that the behaviour persists despite apparently producing for the person concerned more harm than good. There are three basic features of the process of operant learning which are known to all first-year psychology students, which between them probably go a long way towards explaining the insidious development of strongly habitual appetitive behaviour. One is the *partial* nature of much reinforcement: inconsistent reinforcement results in behaviour even more resistant to extinction than that produced by consistent reward.

Second, it is *probabilities* that are affected in learning. It is not a matter of one response taking the place completely of another, but rather of certain acts gradually becoming more probable. Third, there is the *gradient of reinforcement*, a phenomenon which serves to help explain such paradoxical behaviour as the consumption of substances which appear to produce harm or punishment in the long run. Behaviour may have both rewarding (immediate) and punishing (longer term) consequences, but it is the immediate consequences that are the most important in shaping habitual behaviour.

Thus, occasional, immediate financial reward would be expected to promote future gambling more than the later realisation of insufficient money for other purposes would restrain it. Indeed, the process of staking money or token chips or counters, and sometimes receiving concrete reward, seems to resemble operant experimental procedures used with animals to such an extent as to positively invite a learning analysis of gambling. This is particularly so since staking behaviour is not reinforced by a win on every occasion, and the particular schedules of reinforcement in operation are similar to VR schedules (variable ratio schedules: the probability of winning being dependent on the number of times a person stakes, the ratio of wins to number of times staked being made *variable* at least over the short run) which have proved capable of maintaining a high level of responding in animal experiments and rendering the behaviour in question relatively highly resistant to extinction. Cornish cited one example, the US 21-bell 3-wheel fruit machine set up to give a 94.45 per cent return on money inserted, which allowed players to make a win of some denomination on only 13.4 per cent of plays—'a very intermittent VR reinforcement schedule' (pp. 181–182). Lewis and Duncan's research (1958, cited by Cornish, 1978) certainly demonstrated that resistance to extinction of behaviour by participants who were trained to pull a lever on a modified 'fruit machine' was *inversely* proportional to the percentage of attempts resulting in reinforcement being given during the training period. As further support for the idea that intermittent-reinforcement schedules are at least partly responsible for inducing new behaviour early on which is then very hard to break off later, Cornish drew upon reports that excessive gamblers are likely to have experienced a particularly large early win or a streak of luck at the beginning of their gambling careers (Moran, 1970; Dickerson, 1974). The argument is that such experiences 'enrich' otherwise very intermittent early schedules of reinforcement. Sharpe and Tarrier (1993) suggested that gambling is reinforced through a combination of financial reward and increased autonomic arousal interpreted by gamblers as excitement. This arousal becomes associated with monetary reward, and thereby continued gambling is reinforced both through a partial reinforcement schedule of financial gain and a continuous reinforcement schedule of increased excitement.

CONDITIONED ASSOCIATIONS

The capacity for excess possessed by the appetitive activities considered here may be attributable in large part, not simply to unconditioned reinforcing actions in the brain or operant reinforcement of behaviour by its consequences, but to a multitude of conditioned associations with cues that precede or accompany the different phases of the appetitive activity and its aftermath. If an activity becomes at all regular or frequent, numerous opportunities arise for conditioning of formerly neutral cues. This is what others, such as Wise (1994) and White (1996), have termed incentive conditioning or incentive learning. Behaviour then comes to be as much under the control of antecedent or 'discriminative' stimuli which signal the likelihood of reinforcement following behaviour as under the control of the consequences of behaviour. Some of these discriminative stimuli are closely linked to the activity itself, such as the sound of a can being opened or the sight and feel of rolling a 'joint'. The graphic account of the characteristic 'stimuli' of the gambling casino provided by Dostoevsky in *The Gambler* (see Chapter Three) is a good case in point. A more modern example of the same thing—from David, the fruit-machine addict described by Griffiths (1993b)—is given at the beginning of this chapter. As well as the lights and sounds that he spoke of, other associated cues are to do with the setting in which activity often takes place, such as a particular time of the week or of the day, being with a particular group of friends or being in a particular place. Studies of 'relapse' suggest that the latter, which might be termed 'setting cues', constitute high-risk situations for people who are trying to moderate or abstain from appetitive activity (Glautier, 1994).

Conditioning by association also played an important role in Hardy's (1964) learned appetite theory of sexual motivation which was based upon the notion of an accumulation of positive affective sexual experiences:

> A new set of associations or meanings is formed. The activities which lead up to the initial erotic arousal now have a tendency to serve as cues leading to the arousal of sexual desire. Furthermore, as erotic experiences are repeated (a) the greater the association values of the cues to sexuality, and (b) the wider the range of cues to sexuality.
>
> (Hardy, 1964, p. 11)

Experimental studies with both animals and humans have repeatedly shown how activity-specific and setting cues, that in themselves have no intrinsic capacity to produce rewarding effects like those produced by an appetitive activity itself, can become conditioned stimuli through a process of classical, Pavlovian, conditioning, and hence acquire the capacity to motivate further appetitive activity (Glautier, 1994). For example, in an early demonstration of the phenomenon, Schuster and Woods (1968, cited by Kumar and Stolerman, 1977) showed that monkeys would respond more rapidly for saline plus the presentation of a red light than for saline alone, after being trained to bar-press for a morphine infusion accompanied by the red light. The red light was operating as a 'secondary reinforcer'. There are in fact two, or possibly three, different explanations for what is happening (O'Brien *et al.*,

1992; Glautier, 1994). Some responses that are elicited by formerly neutral cues in these experiments (i.e. conditioned responses) are drug-like in form whereas others are drug-opposite. For example, studies have shown that people's heart rates rise in response to cues associated with cigarette smoking, an effect that is like the initial effects of nicotine itself (Glautier, 1994). On the other hand, some studies have shown that stimuli repeatedly preceding opiate injections produce reductions in people's skin temperature, an effect that is opposite to the elevation in skin temperature usually produced by opiate injections themselves (O'Brien *et al.*, 1992).

In keeping with the dominant drive-reduction model of the time, earlier accounts of the role of cue conditioning stressed drug-opposite responses. By mimicking the usually aversive, psychobiological responses associated with withdrawal, formerly neutral stimuli, it was supposed, acquired the capacity to motivate further appetitive activity via drive-reduction or negative reinforcement. Wikler's (1973) model of conditioned opiate withdrawal is one of the best known. His theory was that relief of the distress occasioned by withdrawal constituted the main reinforcement for the consumption of narcotic drugs, and that withdrawal symptoms might become conditioned to aspects of situations specifically associated with the availability of these drugs. Hence, withdrawal distress, or something resembling it, might be experienced long after giving up and would act as a 'trigger' for further drug taking reinforced by relief of these 'symptoms'. His work with rats, made physically dependent and then withdrawn from morphine, suggested that 'symptoms' such as 'wet dog shakes' (shaking like a wet dog, a symptom observed to be associated with morphine withdrawal in rats) were experienced more frequently after withdrawal, in locations previously associated with morphine consumption. Glautier (1994) pointed out, however, that Wikler's model has sometimes been misunderstood. He did not, as some have supposed, suggest that neutral stimuli needed to be paired with the actual experience of withdrawal distress in order for drug-opposite responses to be conditioned. Wikler's model proposed that it was the association of neutral cues with drug taking itself, not withdrawal distress, that led to the conditioning of drug-opposing, homeostatic or 'adaptive' responses. In practice it has been very difficult to conduct experiments to discriminate between these two explanations.

The idea that what is conditioned is an adaptive or preparatory response, or an 'opponent process' (Solomon and Corbett, 1973; and see Chapter Eleven) has been particularly advanced by Siegel (1978, cited by O'Brien *et al.*, 1992; Siegel, 1986) who showed in a series of experiments on rats that morphine tolerance could be conditioned (e.g. animals showing tolerance to the pain-reducing effects of morphine following a history of morphine-taking showed much less tolerance if then tested for pain sensitivity in a novel setting). Experiments with other drugs, with animals and humans, support the idea that cue and setting factors need to be taken into account in understanding tolerance. Siegel (1986) viewed such conditioned tolerance effects as responses that were adaptive in the sense that they were anticipatory of the next administration of a drug. Indeed, he reviewed evidence suggesting that tolerance that was linked to a setting associated with previous administrations protected against fatal 'overdoses' which were much more likely to occur if the same quantity of drug was taken in a novel environment.

More recently, in line with the move towards positive-incentive models of appetitive motivation, greater emphasis has been placed upon drug-like conditioned effects. Rather than motivating further appetitive activity through the negative reinforcement mechanism of the relief of an aversive, withdrawal-like state, conditioned cues are thought to take on positive-incentive value, eliciting approach responses and signalling the probability of positive reinforcement. There have been clinical reports of 'needle freaks' who report euphoria from the mere act of self-injection even though no active drug is being injected (O'Brien *et al.*, 1992), but most positive-incentive conditioning is likely to be more subtle and more pervasive. White (1996) reviewed much evidence for conditioned cue preference, which refers to the preference shown by animals for approaching places in which drug administration has occurred. Much positive-incentive conditioning, in addition, is likely to be based upon what White called declarative learning, or learning about the relationships among cues and settings in the environment.

Work on conditioning is illustrated by O'Brien *et al.*'s (1992) studies of patients undergoing treatment for excessive cocaine use. In standard conditions in which the participants were exposed to both a neutral video-tape and neutral activity, and to a cocaine-related video-tape (showing buying and selling of cocaine and cocaine-administration rituals) and activity (involving handling drug paraphernalia and performing a simulated cocaine administration), former cocaine users showed decreased skin temperature, increased heart rate, and increases in skin conductance and ratings of the degree of subjective cocaine 'high', 'craving' or 'crash' when exposed to the cocaine-related materials (a minority of the participants were adamant 'non-responders' insisting that the cocaine stimuli triggered no craving, although physiological effects such as decreased skin temperature were sometimes present even in members of this group). As O'Brien *et al.* pointed out, these changes are both stimulant drug-like effects and signs of non-specific arousal. Teasdale (1973) had earlier argued that Wikler's theory of relapse was unnecessarily complicated. Because arousal is frequently a component of drug-withdrawal distress (studies of alcohol withdrawal in humans also show how difficult it is to discriminate between the symptoms of alcohol withdrawal and general anxiety), it is only necessary to hypothesise that *anxiety* becomes conditioned to drug-taking settings. This is important because it would follow that any situation giving rise to anxiety or tension could then provide the motivation for relapse.

Carter and Tiffany (1999) reported the results of a meta-analysis of 41 cue-reactivity studies: 10 of tobacco smokers, 18 of 'alcoholics', nine of heroin 'addicts' and four of cocaine 'addicts'. The findings were broadly in agreement with the positive-incentive, drug-like effects model, at least for smoking, drinking and cocaine. For heroin the results were less clear (e.g. skin temperature went down overall—a drug-opposite effect, and sweating went up, which neither model predicted). These authors struck several notes of caution. For one thing they found physiological effects to be small in comparison with effects of drug-relevant cues on self-reported craving, which were large. Furthermore, the effects on physiological indicators were consistently in the same direction irrespective of the particular drug involved: heart rate and sweat-gland activity increased and skin temperature decreased. This suggests that what may be happening when people were exposed to photographs, videos or other real-life or imagined images of the object of their excess, might not reflect conditioning at all, but rather the activation of a general positive-incentive state, or even just anxiety or frustration at not being able to consume the favourite drug depicted in the materials presented.

Powell (1995) reported an interesting experiment on responses to drug-related cues that bears on this issue. Eight people being prescribed the injectable opiate physeptone were observed (seven at home and one in hospital) preparing and administering an injection. Mood and possible withdrawal symptoms were assessed prior to preparing the injection, after preparation and after administering the injection. Powell found no hint of withdrawal-like or drug-opposite reactions in her study. In fact, the reverse pattern was apparent, with a general improvement in participants' mood and physical state as they prepared their equipment but before actually administering the drug. Powell concluded that the context, and in particular whether drug use was perceived to be available or not, might be crucial in determining the form of response to drug-related cues. If, as in most previous laboratory experiments, such cues were present but the taking of the drug was not perceived to be possible, then conditioned withdrawal effects might be more likely. On the other hand, if, as in her own study, drug taking was expected, then the cues might become conditioned stimuli for drug-positive effects instead. This confirms, if any confirmation were really needed, the importance of the setting in which activity occurs (Chapter Nine), and the need to temper laboratory findings with a large measure of 'real world' testing.

THE COGNITIVE ELEMENT

Although operant learning, based on the many and varied mood-modifying, social and other rewards from appetitive activity, plus conditioning to a wide variety of associated cues, may go a long way towards providing us with an explanation of the escalating or amplifying kind that would satisfy the law of proportionate effect, there is much more to it than that. At the very least, since the cognitive behavioural 'revolution' of the 1970s, even those whose model of human action is largely behavioural or neuropsychological are likely to acknowledge that the ways people think about what they are doing, or what they are about to do, are likely to be important contributors to the development of appetitive attachment.

This cognitive element takes a number of forms. One consists of the 'expectancies' that people hold regarding the effects that the taking of a substance is likely to have for them. This idea was introduced in Chapter Eight when looking at the expectancies of the effects of consuming alcohol held by young people (e.g. Wiers *et al.*, 1997; Aas *et al.*, 1998). Much evidence has accumulated that positive expectancies for alcohol are correlated with extent of drinking and with drinking problems (e.g. Stacy *et al.*, 1990; Sher, 1991). To give just one example of research that has been done on the subject, Cooper *et al.* (1992) found in a large, ethnically balanced sample of residents in Erie County, New York that expectancies for social pleasure, sexual enhancement, aggression and power, social expressiveness, and relaxation and tension reduction, as well as global positive effects, from alcohol, moderated the relationship between stress (the number of negative life events experienced in the last year) and the number of drinking problems reported. The group that stood out from the rest, by having a comparatively large number of drinking problems, was the group who had experienced several stressful life events *and* who held positive alcohol expectancies.

Although expectancies are likely to reflect, at least in part, people's prior experiences with alcohol, the argument is that, once acquired, such expectancies contribute to the increasing development of attachment to drinking. Indeed, so powerful may expectancies be that they may be responsible for a placebo effect, or for very different effects depending upon expectations associated with the setting in which a substance is consumed. Results of 'balanced placebo' experiments fairly uniformly showed that being told one is drinking alcohol is at least as powerful a factor as actually consuming the drug. For example, Vuchinich *et al.* (1979) found expectancy to be as important as receiving alcohol in producing laughter and mirth; Briddell *et al.* (1978) found the same for arousal to sexual stimuli; and Marlatt *et al.* (1973) found that being told one had received alcohol produced more continued drinking than actually having received alcohol.

These experimental findings were consistent with the thesis of MacAndrew and Edgerton (1970) who collected together anthropological material on drinking and behaviour associated with drinking ('drunken comportment' as they nicely termed it) in different cultural groups around the world. They argued that the social behaviour associated with drinking is so varied from culture to culture that the effects of alcohol must be mediated more strongly by social expectations than by pharmacological effects. If the meaning of alcohol to a particular group is such that aggressive behaviour is *expected* to follow its consumption, then consumption is more likely on occasions when aggressive behaviour is otherwise promoted, and aggression is the likely result. For other groups alcohol may have quite different meanings, be consumed in different settings and on different occasions, and produce different effects such as fun and laughter, or enhanced cooperation on joint ventures.

Expectancies start to be acquired early on. For one thing each of the forms of behaviour considered in this book has its own 'literature'. Sex (in the form of educative books, erotica and pornography) and eating (in the form of cookery books and dieting manuals) perhaps the largest. No one grows up without some knowledge of most of these behaviours and, with the exception of eating, early knowledge long predates the first experience of consumption. Few come to their first drug experience completely naïve, and the multi-faceted process of acquiring the sexual 'facts of life' is a lengthy one which starts early in life. Similarly, it has been demonstrated that children have already acquired definite expectations about alcohol's effects long before the teenage years (Jahoda and Cramond, 1972; Sher, 1991). Leventhal and Cleary (1980) argued similarly that the stage of preparation for smoking, and this might be a length stage, should be taken into account in considering the whole process of taking up smoking. As they put it, it is likely that 'smoking' begins well before a person tries the first cigarette, and that quite young children develop attitudes about smoking and have images of what smoking is like long before they try it for themselves.

Besides expectancies, another facet of the way people think about appetitive behaviour, which contributes to the strengthening of attachment, concerns the ways in which a person *attributes* physiological arousal to certain events and states (Schachter and Singer, 1962). It was Bruch's (1974) contention, for example, that eating could come to serve the many possible symbolic functions which she listed (see Chapter Eight) as a result of *mis*learning, usually starting in the family in the early years of life, leading to an inability of discriminate real 'hunger' from other signals of discomfort and from states of emotional tension. Eating for these 'wrong' reasons resulted in short-lived and unsatisfying eating 'cycles' in which eating afforded temporary relief from anxious or depressive feelings mistakenly experienced as the 'need to eat'. In this way '... the nutritional function can be misused in the service of complex emotional and interpersonal problems' (p. 50).

An early and highly influential sociological account of marijuana use was that of Becker (1963), who wrote of the importance of the meaning attributed by users to sensations experienced when using the drug. Becker concluded that the social group in which the drug was used was crucial in supplying the ideas out of which the novice user constructed his or her meaning of the marijuana experience and the pleasure it gave.

Similarly, Rook and Hammen (1977) criticised previous research on sexual behaviour for concentrating on sexual acts alone or upon the more biological components of sexual response. They attempted to provide a corrective by offering a cognitive perspective which in particular emphasised the way in which people appraise physiological responses and attribute them, or not, to sexual arousal. They argued that both physiological arousal and 'erotic labelling' were necessary for the subjective experience of sexual arousal. Because, particularly in the early phases of the sexual-response cycle, physiological responses are non-specific and in many ways resemble the types of response elicited at other times, wide latitude is possible in explaining arousal by attributing it to sexual feelings or by explaining it in some other way. Misattribution would therefore be expected to occur and Rook and Hammen cited experiments suggesting that it did. For example, men have been shown to give evidence of becoming more sexually aroused than control participants as a result of physical exercise followed by the viewing of an erotic film and, in one experiment, when being approached by an attractive woman on a fear-arousing suspension bridge! The argument is that both experiments provided a context (the film in one case, the attractive woman in the other) in which physiological responses aroused by other means (exercise in one case, fear in the other) could be attributed to sexual arousal. Along similar lines they suggested that drugs of many sorts might acquire their pharmacologically unjustified reputations as aphrodisiacs because they act like placebos which are not totally inert but which produce a range of non-specific physiological arousal cues which under the right circumstances people may readily attribute to sexual arousal.

Rook and Hammen further speculated about individual differences. People who have a relatively low threshold for sexual arousal, or who are sexually aroused by a wide range of stimuli, may find sexual arousal easily augmented once they perceive evidence that what they believe is sexual arousal has begun. The important point for present discussion is the suggestion that there may be processes at work which over time augment initial individual differences. Rook and Hammen's ideas are thus useful additions to the general theme of this and the following chapter, that excessive appetitive behaviour has a developmental aspect to it; that whatever its personal, social or biological origins, it can grow into something more powerful as a result of cognitive and other processes. Rook and Hammen pointed out that their perspective need in no way be specific to sexual behaviour; indeed, they had to draw upon research most of which lay outside that particular field of study.

The cognitive processes under discussion may operate outside or on the borders of consciousness. The cognitive revolution of the 1970s, however, was as much concerned with self-talk, self-statements and the use of self-instruction, which, like instructions from other people, occur overtly and are perceived consciously (e.g. Meichenbaum, 1977). Just as it can be shown that children can acquire the ability to perform certain complex tasks more quickly by talking to themselves (self-instructions) at appropriate points, so it may be the case that the human capacity for language contributes to the acquisition of excessive appetitive behaviour, quite apart from the role of language in social communication. The human being has the ability lacking in other animals, to tell herself that she is becoming sexually aroused, that he is looking forward to a forthcoming drink, that a particular horse in the next race is a good bet, or that it is time for a run. In the language of learning theory, this might be expressed by saying we have opportunities for 'rehearsal' of anticipated positive outcomes from behaviour, or for reinforcing ourselves in between times by covert thought processes involving imagination and fantasy. This may apply to all the appetites but has been especially highlighted in the case of gambling. Reference was made in Chapter Eight to Bergler's (1958) observations about 'compulsive gamblers': that they often showed an almost fanatical belief in the possibility of winning and that their recollections of past gambling were highly selective in favour of recalling successes and forgetting losses. Cornish (1978), Wagenaar (1988), and Griffiths (1994) are among those who have drawn attention to the variety of gamblers' cognitive biases which collectively offer a further powerful ingredient. These include various false beliefs (e.g. the illusion of control or belief in the importance of skill), cognitive biases (e.g. the well-known 'gambler's fallacy' whereby the gambler believes the probability of winning on a purely chance event, such as 'heads', increases the less it comes up, i.e. after a series of 'tails') and information-processing problems which may distort perception of probabilities and pay-offs.

One factor that has repeatedly been found to be associated with heavier involvement in gambling is the belief on the part of the gambler that he or she has some degree of control over the outcome through choice or skill. This factor is of particular interest since it is, at one and the same time, a feature of the gambler's attitude to the activity *and* something that can be influenced by the structure of the game itself. Young 'pathological' gamblers have been reported to differ from normal gamblers by having a greater belief in the role of skill in winning machine gambling, and in giving over-estimates of the amounts of money they are likely to win when they play (Carroll and Huxley, 1994; Griffiths, 1995a). Langner (1975, cited by Carroll and Huxley, 1994) carried out a number of experiments showing that if people can be given the 'illusion of control' when gambling (e.g. by being allowed to select a preferred number from a booklet of tickets rather than simply being handed a ticket) the perceived likelihood of winning is enhanced. Some people may be generally more inclined than others to believe they have control over events (have an 'internal locus of control'), but some forms of gambling have a number of devices built into them which are likely to encourage the illusion of control. In the case of gambling machines, these include 'buttons' for 'holding' and 'nudging' as well as signals to the player that a 'near miss' has occurred (e.g. two out of three correct symbols appearing on the pay line with the third appearing in the line just above or below) (Cornish, 1978; Carroll and Huxley, 1994; Griffiths, 1995b). The phenomenon of the illusion of control is closely linked to 'chasing losses' which Lesieur (1984) believed was at the core of the addictive potential of gambling. The fostering of the illusion of control and the many opportunities for staking again immediately or very shortly, and possibly increasing the stake at the same time, provided by forms of gambling such as horse-race betting or machine gambling, is a powerful combination.

We shall see in Chapter Fourteen how important talking, including talking to oneself or 'self-talk', may be in the process of giving up an excessive appetite. The hypothesis is that self-talk is equally important in the development of excess. As an appetitive activity becomes more habitual, and as its associations with cues of various kinds become stronger and more diverse, so, it may be presumed, behaviour is accompanied by increasingly frequent thoughts serving to bolster habitual behaviour at a new increased level. Such bolstering thoughts may take a variety of forms, including self-statements such as, 'Doing X is the only way I get to feel . . .', 'All men like me do X', 'If he's going to be like that then I'm entitled to X', 'If I didn't do X, then I'd probably do Y', 'X is one of the best things in life'. Such thoughts may be publicly stated, kept private or may scarcely be within awareness much of the time. Appetitive activities may become 'over-valued' in these ways, offering more in anticipation than in fact.

In summary, then, we can point to the existence of a compelling set of processes which, with moderate encouragement and not too many controls and restraints, can be capable of fashioning an excessive appetite out of modest beginnings. To this process, various schedules of positive or negative operant reinforcement, and an abundance of cues or discriminative stimuli acting as secondary reinforcers, along with a nexus of expectations, attributions and misattributions, fantasies and self-talk, all contribute. Thus, an inclination towards appetitive consumption can, under the right circumstances, grow into an attachment that finds a person well out along the tail of the consumption distribution curve, differing from his or her peers in terms of the frequency and quantity of activity, but more particularly in terms of the degree of his or her commitment to it.

CHAPTER 11

The Development of Strong Attachment

... from this date the reader is to consider me as a regular and confirmed opium-eater, of whom to ask whether on any particular day he had or had not taken opium would be to ask whether his lungs had performed respiration, or the heart fulfilled its functions.

> (Thomas de Quincey, *The Confessions of an English Opium Eater*, Collected Writings, vol. III, 1897, p. 400)

The addiction surfaces in the addict's inability to manage his or her life ... This unending struggle to manage two lives—'normal' and addictive—continues. The unmanageability takes its toll. Family and friendships are abbreviated and sacrificed. Hobbies are neglected. Finances are affected. Physical needs of other kinds are unattended. The addict's lifestyle becomes a consistent violation of his or her own values, compounding the same.

> (Carnes, 1983, pp. 12–13, writing about sexual addiction)

How can we understand the transition from appetitive behaviour, on the one hand, that constitutes acceptable, moderate indulgence and, on the other, highly troublesome and noticeable excess? Having considered in the previous chapter some of the psychological processes that can account for the development of an attachment to an appetite, we now need to explore the little understood transition from attachment to strong attachment, from a form of consumption that is manageable to one that is unmanageable.

The following quotation from Pearson's (1987) book illustrates the distinction, in this case in relation to heroin, between an activity over which one felt one had control, and one to which attachment is now sufficiently strong that control seems to have been diminished:

At first, it was just great. Me and my mates ... we didn't care about nothin', you know having a good time, having a toot and that. But then, it sort of turned round ... you just have a smoke, smoke the gear, and that's it like. There's nothin' else to bother about. I stopped going to football ... and I used to love football, you know, the match. I stopped going to concerts, going out like. That was it ...

> (Billy, 22 years, Manchester, cited by Pearson, 1987, p. 28)

Pearson was struck, as many have been who have witnessed at first or second hand the development of strong attachment to a potentially addictive behaviour, by the mostly gradual development of attachment:

> ... what these voices from the street seem to be saying to us is that the heroin experience is ... insidious ... edging itself into their lives by imperceptible degrees. Heroin's advance is not like some sudden cavalry charge; more like the slow trudge of a foot army. 'Junk wins by default' is how William Burroughs (1977, p. xv) described it thirty years ago.
>
> (Pearson, 1987, p. 63)

Also writing about heroin, Parker *et al.* (1988) provided some extended case studies that nicely illustrate the conflict that is created between an activity for which one has a liking, and awareness of the harm that it is causing. For example:

> I've spent, I don't like to think about it, y'know, hundreds and thousands of pounds, I've spent. It's a sin really but I can't handle it. I realise that it's not only an illness, I suppose, but it's quite selfish in a way. I've got this thing that I like, that I like to do, but maybe it's selfish, but on the other hand, I don't know. There's a conflict there and people get, well people like a drink or a smoke or whatever they do, they get off on whatever they do, but it's just damn not as expensive as the habit I've got, y'know ...
>
> (Allan, cited by Parker *et al.*, 1988, p. 85)

Pearson (1987) also noted the ambivalence that is present in so many accounts that people give of heroin's effects. The paradox of addiction is neatly summed up by one of his informants, Wayne, who said of heroin:

> Teks all yer worries away and then it becomes a bigger one itsen.
>
> (Cited by Pearson, 1987, p. 31)

Pearson (1987) and Parker *et al.* (1988) both described a process of social change that their participants saw as an integral part of the process of becoming more attached to heroin. The social aspects of this process involved a deterioration of previously established friendships and recreational patterns, a reduction in social options as non-working hours were increasingly used to 'score', more closely identifying with other drug users and finding it more difficult to see eye to eye with non-users, raising the necessary extra money for a drug habit by first depriving oneself of other things and later pawning and selling possessions, losing jobs, in some cases stealing from friends or other users, resorting to shoplifting, fraud or other crime, taking up drug dealing to support one's own habit or even to make profit, and in a minority of cases raising money by prostitution. The following is among the many quotations that could be given in support of this general picture of a series of vicious circles or a downward spiral involving decreasing options for raising money by legitimate means and decreasing contact with positive sources of life satisfaction that have no connection with drug use:

I haven't been out for a pint since … oh I don't know when. I've never known a smackhead go to pubs, never. It was … if you've got £15 to go out for the night, you're not going to spend it on ale. If someone says, 'Here y'are, are you coming out?' and you've got £15 you'd say 'No', go and buy three bags. I don't know anyone that'd rather go out than take it.

(Kevin, 21 years, Merseyside, cited by Pearson, 1987, p. 57)

BECOMING MORE DEEPLY COMMITTED

In the case of an injectable drug such as heroin, the transition to injecting from some other mode of administering the drug has been closely studied as a supposedly crucial step in the process of deepening attachment. For example, Griffiths *et al.* (1994) recruited a sample of over 400 heroin users in the London area, using heroin for a mean of 9 years (ranging from less than 1 year to 37 years), half presently in contact with a treatment agency and half not. They were interested in transitions between different routes of administration, and in particular in testing the commonly held assumption that inhaling heroin vapour (or 'chasing') would lead, and almost inevitably so, to the use of intravenous injection of heroin. They categorised people according to their main route of administration, defined as an exclusive or predominant route of administration that had lasted for 1 month or more. On this basis 54 per cent were classified as injectors and 44 per cent as chasers, the remainder having no predominant route.

The participants' reports in fact suggested fewer transitions than might have been expected. Of the injectors 46 per cent had never been chasers, and of the chasers 81 per cent had never been injectors (70 per cent had never injected at all). Of those that had made a transition, the largest number had started as chasers, or in a few cases smokers, and had later become injectors (this was the case for a total of 83 people or 37 per cent of those who were now injectors). Other patterns were reported, however, which did not correspond to this expected transition. A total of 13 individuals reported having made the opposite transition, from injecting to chasing, and 30 had made two transitions, 11 from chasing to injecting and back to chasing, and 19 from injecting to chasing and back to injecting. There appears to be some predictability, therefore, in the transitions that people make but there exist many deviations from the expected pattern. For those who had made a transition from chasing to injecting the mean time from first use of heroin to first heroin injection was 2.4 years. The time lag between first injection and transition to injection becoming the predominant route of administration was often short but this varied and the average was 1.2 years. A 'survival analysis' suggested that the probability of a chaser becoming an injector in any one year reached about 10 per cent after 4 years of chasing and remained at more or less that level thereafter. As a result the median survival time, by which it would be expected that 50 per cent of chasers had become injectors, was just over 8 years. Those who had remained stable chasers were less involved with the heroin-using sub-culture than were those who had made the transition to injecting; they had more social contact with non-users, and were much less likely to have friends who were heroin injectors. Stable injectors, who had made no transitions, were older, and started using heroin when younger, and had been using for longer than injectors who had started as chasers. Those who had moved from injecting to chasing were also older, more likely to be men and had used heroin for longer.

Pearson (1987), in his study of heroin use in the north of England, concluded that the decision to inject was determined by a variety of considerations including the greater cost-effectiveness of the injecting route and the availability of local knowledge and custom to support injecting within the drug-using sub-culture. It is important also not to lose sight of individual variation in the process of developing a strong attachment to an activity such as heroin use. Indeed, each of the previously cited researchers of 1980s British heroin use gave examples of people for whom heroin use opened up the possibility of social contact, others for whom fellow users provided much social support or communities that benefited by availing themselves of stolen goods at affordable prices. Nor should we accept uncritically the idea that the link between drug use, on the one hand, and a narrowing of social life or involvement in crime, on the other hand, is a one-way street.

For example, Hammersley *et al.* (1989) concluded, on the basis of interviews with nearly 150 drug users with criminal records, that although there was a relationship between involvement in taking opiates and crimes of theft and drug dealing, an 'economic dependency' model, whereby need for opiates simply determines the amount of crime committed, was too simple. The more complex model for which they found evidence allowed for several pathways to drug-related crime. One of these, corresponding to the economic dependency model, sees an escalation in drug use leading directly to theft. Another pathway sees theft, as part of a criminal career, preceding drug use but giving rise to it as a consequence of the availability of free money resulting from successful thieving. The third pathway sees drug use leading to drug dealing, thence to the availability of free money and from there to escalating drug use and theft as a consequence.

The same question can be asked about the known association between excessive alcohol or drug use and difficulties in marital and other relationships. Newcomb (1994) used data from two waves of his longitudinal study of young adults, who had attended schools in Los Angeles, to look for evidence that excessive alcohol or drug use led to relationship difficulties or vice versa. Over 400 people were asked questions on these topics at an average of 21.5 years of age and again 4 years later. Only included in the study were people who were in an intimate partnership relationship at the follow-up point. The majority of significant effects were in the direction of one or other form of drug use at the earlier time affecting negatively some aspect of the relationship at the later time. For example: for women, poly-drug use at time 1 predicted an increase in the number of divorces occurring during the next 4 years and cocaine use predicted a decrease in relationship cohesion; for men, high alcohol use predicted reduced relationship consensus and increased relationship trouble, and poly-drug use predicted increased relationship trouble. The results were in fact quite complex, however, and two significant predictions ran in the opposite direction: for women, support from partner predicted decreased later cocaine use; and for men, happiness with sex predicted less later hard-drug use.

A similar question was asked in relation to homelessness by Johnson *et al.* (1997). Is it the case that the relationship between excessive alcohol or drug use and homelessness is the end result of a process during which an individual's social and economic resources become depleted as a consequence of excessive use, or is it the case that excessive alcohol or drug use is a consequence of homelessness, perhaps as a means of adapting to life on the streets and coping with the stresses of homelessness generally? Johnson *et al.* cited Strauss (1946) who concluded, over 50 years previously, that both were probably operating amongst the homeless men he interviewed in Newhaven, Connecticut, with heavy alcohol use appearing to be a contributing cause of homelessness among approximately two-thirds, and heavy alcohol use a *consequence* of homelessness or related factors in the remaining third.

Johnson *et al.* interviewed over 300 people living in single-room occupancy hotels or attending shelters, soup kitchens or drop-in centres in the Chicago area. Although participants were interviewed only once, they were asked about ages at which they had first experienced homelessness and specific symptoms of alcohol or drug abuse, and the statistical technique known as proportional hazards regression was used to see which variables predicted these ages. The analysis suggested that excessive drug use was more strongly linked with homelessness than was excessive alcohol use. Although the relationship between excessive drug use and homelessness appeared to be reciprocal, with the occurrence of one of these putting people at increased risk for the other, evidence for homelessness predicting drug abuse was slightly stronger than evidence for drug abuse predicting homelessness (risk ratios of 3.36 and 2.44, respectively). Homelessness was a significant predictor of alcohol abuse (risk ratio of 1.65) but alcohol abuse did not appear as one of the significant predictors of homelessness. Johnson *et al.* concluded that the relationship between homelessness and substance abuse is a complex and varied one and that neither of the two simple causal hypotheses are sufficient alone to represent the dynamic relationship between the two.

Those who have written about compulsive gambling have also observed a process of deepening attachment to the activity. Both Lesieur (1984) and Custer and Milt (1985) placed 'chasing losses' in the centre of their explanations of what was happening, but also described, as an integral part of the process, vicious circles and spirals of diminishing social options, as others have described in the context of drug use. Lesieur (1984), whose book was called *The Chase*, described how 'doubling up' and other elements that encouraged continued play were built into many forms of gambling and into the informal culture of horse-race and other sports betting. Many gamblers to whom he had spoken had 'chased' on a short-term basis, confining chasing to single occasions. Gambling became compulsive, in his view, when individual occasions are linked by longer term chasing. This longer term chasing is motivated by financial and personal threat:

> The *financial threat* is typically a product of loans that have to be paid. Gamblers feel that the way to get the money is by more gambling, and this produces a spiral of more debts and gambling to relieve the debts. The *personal threat* is a product of potential embarrassment and losing of face if the gambling losses are ever made public. ... This fear of exposure

brings on a desire to eliminate the problem by gambling, and redeeming the tarnished self-image.

(Lesieur, 1984, p. 12)

The following quotation from Custer and Milt (1985) makes the same point that chasing has a number of motivations, and in addition makes the crucial point that the nature of the activity is changed in the process:

> ... a new and catastrophic element now dominates his betting style. Before all this happened—before the losing streak began—he was gambling to win. Now he is gambling to recoup. He is doing what gamblers call 'chasing'— the frenetic pursuit of lost money. The pursuit is fired by many fuels. There is the loss of the money itself and what that money could have bought for him. There is the loss of what the money symbolizes—importance, prestige, acceptance, recognition, friendship, power. There is the loss of self-esteem and of the feeling of invincibility ... There is also the loss of face with the other gamblers ... And there is just the plain sharp pain and chagrin of loss, the kind anyone feels when he loses or is robbed of something substantial. His obsessive gambling—his addiction—has now been in force for a number of years, but the motivating force has changed. Before, it was propelled by the euphoria of winning and the devouring desire to perpetuate it. Now it is propelled by the depression and anguish of losing and the overwhelming need to quell these feelings.

(Custer and Milt, 1985, p. 106)

We have confirmed that picture in research in the UK. Based on results of semi-structured interviews with 'problem gamblers' (Orford *et al.*, 1996), we concluded that, in addition to the primary positive experiences associated with their gambling (largely described in terms of arousal and excitement), there existed a powerful set of attachment-promoting 'secondary processes' which had the effect of adding a strong drive-reduction component to the primary, positive-incentive element (see Figure 11.1). The main component of this secondary acquired motivational cycle was a strong, negative feeling state associated with losing at gambling, associated with an increased desire to recoup losses by further gambling. Statements used by excessive gamblers in our sample to describe these strong negative feelings included: 'often talk to myself when I'd lost'; 'stupid'; 'feeling horrible about myself, guilty'; 'loss of more than a few pounds produces depression'; 'thinking what I could have bought with the money'; 'depressed, at the edge of despair, not sleeping, after a bad run'; 'feel sick, physically sick and disgusted with myself' (p. 53). It was the strength of these emotions that seemed to motivate the desire for further gambling, or 'chasing one's losses'.

Griffiths (1990) also confirmed the importance of the strong, changing emotions associated with excessive or regular gambling. He described anger, depression and generally low mood reported by adolescent excessive fruit-machine gamblers following playing, extreme lows or bouts of anger usually being experienced after a severe loss of money. In his study comparing 30 regular and 30 non-regular machine gamblers, Griffiths (1995c) asked about mood states before,

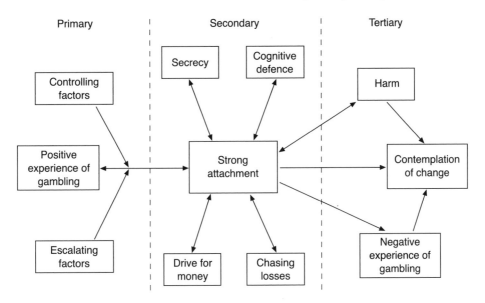

Figure 11.1 A model of strong attachment to gambling (reproduced from Orford *et al.*, 1996).

during and after playing fruit machines. Regular players were more likely than non-regular to describe feelings of being fed up or depressed at all stages. Particularly noticeable, however, was the significant increase in feelings of excitement, only *during* playing, for the regular gamblers compared with the non-regular; and feelings of bad mood or anger which were significantly greater for the regular than the non-regular players, only *after* playing.

Another component of the newly acquired drive state, that we identified as one of the consequences of the development of a strong attachment to gambling, was an increased drive to obtain money. Almost without exception problem gamblers described special attempts that they had made to obtain money in order to finance further gambling, including borrowing, stealing at home, obtaining loans and getting other people to pay off debts. The accounts were clear that these attempts to obtain money were the result of an attachment to gambling:

> It appears that a powerful secondary drive, to obtain money, had been created. What was also clear was that the development of this secondary drive to obtain money itself promoted further attachment to gambling since gambling, by its very nature, is seen as one way of obtaining money. Many of the ways problem gamblers used to obtain money resulted in increased debts, thus contributing further to the drive to obtain money (in this case to pay off debts), and to the value of gambling as a possible way of making money, and hence to a secondary cycle reinforcing the process of increasing attachment to gambling.
>
> (Orford *et al.*, 1996, pp. 52–53)

We identified what we thought was a further component of this secondary, acquired drive state associated with the strengthening attachment to gambling, namely 'secrecy'. A common theme in the accounts given by problem gamblers was the 'lying', 'deceiving', 'fooling' of girlfriends, wives and other significant people, that they found necessary in order to keep the latter in ignorance of the full extent of their gambling and associated harms such as debts. The important point, again, was the strength of emotions associated with secrecy and the attempts to maintain it:

> As with an increased drive to obtain money, and chasing one's losses, the need for secrecy seemed to give rise to a vicious cycle of artificially created, new motivation (to obtain money, to recoup losses, to keep behaviour secret), of strong, negative feelings (depression, anger, guilt, worry, desperation), and an increased inclination to gamble further (to recoup losses, to repay debts, to escape from bad feelings) as an habitual coping strategy.
> (Orford *et al.*, 1996, pp. 53–54)

It is important to be reminded, though, of the findings referred to above which suggested that the relationship between excessive appetitive behaviour and social harms such as crime, relationship difficulties and homelessness is unlikely to be simple, and sometimes the latter precedes the former (Hammersley *et al.*, 1989; Newcomb, 1994; Johnson *et al.*, 1997). Likewise, it must be supposed that financial difficulties and financial crime sometimes precede excessive gambling, however strong the evidence that the latter provokes the former.

In the case of excessive eating, although there is no direct parallel to work on routes of drug administration, there has been work on the developmental ordering of restrained eating, dieting and bingeing. Spurrell *et al.* (1997), for example, were interested in the development of the newly labelled 'binge eating disorder' (BED, see Chapter Five), and in particular the question whether, as has been reported for 'bulimia', dieting normally preceded, and therefore might be responsible for, bingeing. They asked 68 women and 19 men with BED, with ages ranging from 20 to 65, about the development of their excessive eating. Taking the sample as a whole there seemed to be support for the hypothesis that dieting preceded bingeing since the average age of first dieting was 17.6 years and the average age of first bingeing was 18.1 years. The variation was great, however, and the overall figures hid substantial differences in people's histories. In fact, a higher proportion of the sample (55 per cent) reported experiencing their first binges *before* first dieting rather than the other way round (45 per cent), and these two groups turned out to be very different in other ways. The former, binge-first group, had, on average, started to binge in their early teens and had first met BED criteria by their late teens. The latter, diet-first group, had, in contrast, first binged on average only in their mid-20s and had first met BED criteria in their early 30s. The binge-first group were also more likely to have had alcohol or drug problems and psychiatric diagnoses.

Stice *et al.* (1998) used the statistical technique of structural equation modelling (SEM), to test the related hypothesis that eating restraint leads to bulimic symptoms, among over 200 16–18-year-old female high-school students in one metropolitan area in south-west USA. There were two occasions of interviewing, with 9 months elapsing between time 1 and time 2. Half of the young women reported themselves to be free on both occasions of symptoms of bingeing, fasting and vomiting, or over-concern about size or body shape; slightly more than a quarter had such symptoms at one time of interviewing but not at the other; and rather less than a quarter reported symptoms on both occasions. Simple cross-lagged correlations suggested reciprocal influence, with both restrained eating at time 1 being correlated with symptoms at time 2 and symptoms at time 1 being correlated with restrained eating at time 2. When SEM was used to test whether one or other causal directional model provided better prediction than a reciprocal model, some evidence emerged for a model proposing that symptoms at time 1 were predictive of restrained eating at time 2, and not vice versa. These results were unique, according to Stice, in questioning the idea that restraint leads to symptoms.

Nevertheless, reviews of the literature (Howard and Porzelius, 1999; Guertin, 1999) conclude that there is not only substantial support for restraint theory (Herman and Polivy, 1975, 1980) with severe dieting being capable of inducing binge eating and usually preceding it, but that the evidence certainly exists that for many people the sequence of events is opposite, with bingeing preceding dieting.

In the case of tobacco smoking we can return to the results of McKennell and Thomas's (1967) classic study (see Chapter Four) to find support for a general progression theory, with motives for behaviour changing over time, in this case over a relatively short period of time during the teenage years. They found that the proportion of young people reporting ever having smoked went up sharply between approximately the 13th and 16th birthdays. Reports of first becoming a regular smoker (one cigarette a day or one ounce of tobacco a month or more) rose steeply between approximately the 15th and 18th birthdays. These changes corresponded with a changing pattern of reported motives and also with reported changes in the manner of smoking and its accompaniments. For example, 26 per cent reported inhaling tobacco smoke when first smoking, 60 per cent at the start of regular smoking and 89 per cent at the time of the survey. Similarly, 26 per cent reported having the occasional solitary smoke at the time of first becoming a smoker, 53 per cent when first becoming a regular smoker and 69 per cent currently. McKennell and Thomas concluded that it took on average 2–3 years from first smoking to become 'addicted'. Certainly there seems to be substantial support here for the view that for many people changes take place over a comparatively short period of time, such that behaviour which appears superficially to be the same as it was (smoking a cigarette) is, in many important respects, a quite different behaviour. It is carried out at different intervals following the previous smoke, in different social settings, with a different degree of self-consciousness and for different stated reasons.

THE EROSION OF DISCRIMINATION

One way of conceiving of the transition from a moderate to a strong appetitive attachment is to think of it as a process of generalisation or the erosion of normal *discrimination*. The constraints that are influential in curbing natural tendencies towards increased or excessive behaviour have their impact, we may suppose, through discrimination. For most people, training in appetitive conduct is a matter of discrimination. The rules to which socialising agents expect others to adhere are rules about settings and conditions under which consumption is appropriate. The variables in terms of which drinking, gambling, eating, exercise and heterosexuality may be defined as appropriate or inappropriate include time of day, company, day of the week, the meaning of the occasion (celebration, etc.), quantity consumed and so forth. Appropriateness may be defined in terms of quite complex combinations of such variables. For example, what is considered appropriate drinking at a Saturday-night party with certain people present (or not present) may be quite inappropriate with other combinations of day of the week, company and occasion. The overall rule guiding appetitive behaviour may be that it is acceptable 'in moderation', but this rule is likely to be made operational by a whole set of specific restraints inculcated by detailed discrimination training. The impelling sense of the wrongness of excessive behaviour is particularised by an impelling sense of the wrongness of behaving in a whole variety of very specific ways in a host of specific settings.

The majority of people at the moderate end of the consumption curve are discriminating; they know that there is a time and a place for gambling, drinking or taking drugs. When the circumstances are right for the development of a strong habit—when incentives are strong and disincentives relatively weak—then there will be a tendency for discrimination to be eroded and for behaviour to generalise to a range of additional stimuli or settings. The stronger the inclination to consume or approach under appropriate circumstances, the greater the tendency to do so under other circumstances also. Indeed, it is arguably the generalised inappropriateness of appetitive behaviour, or the failure to keep it within the confines of normal expectancy, that lead to it being branded as 'excessive' or as an 'ism'. It is, for example, the lack of discrimination in the sexual behaviour of Boswell (Stone, 1979) and other 'sex addicts' that draws comment, and the increasing regularity of his opium consumption, no longer tied to special occasions, that worried de Quincey. 'Moderate' or 'controlled' use, on the other hand, is characterised by rules of discrimination, usually promoted by the social groups or wider community of which a person is a member.

These rules are probably fairly general in kind and not dissimilar from one appetitive behaviour to another, even though some forms of behaviour are more widely acceptable than others. It seems, for example, that the ways in which some opiate and other drug users control their use, even in prohibitionist USA, are not dissimilar to the ways most drinkers control their alcohol use. This conclusion is based on the work of Zinberg *et al.* (1977, 1981) who studied controlled illicit drug use. They reported on interviews with 99 controlled users (96 being present or past controlled users of marijuana, 52 of psychedelics and 47 of opiates). They found controlled use to be characterised by maintenance of normal ties with non-drug consumers and with controlled consumers, the ability to discriminate between approved and disapproved ways of using the drug of choice, and rituals and procedures for drug use which kept its use within limits.

All subjects tend to maintain regular ties to social institutions, such as workplace, school, and family ... Controlled users maintain ordinary social relationships with nondrug users ... our subjects demonstrate an ability to keep drugs on hand for some time without using them, and to continue their leisure activities ... Rituals ... may include methods of procuring and administering the drug, selection of a particular social and physical setting for use, and special activities undertaken after the drug has been administered ... Virtually all ... required the assistance of other controlled users to construct appropriate rituals and social sanctions out of the folklore of practices of the diverse subculture of drug-takers.

(Zinberg, 1981, pp. 284–285, 290, 293)

Many of their controlled users had been using for periods of up to 10 years or more, and none of the groups selected for interview had shown a shift to less controlled use despite a variety of stresses and strains of normal living. The many rules that informants adopted were reminiscent of the rules and regulations surrounding normal alcohol use. In general, they served to define moderate use and to condemn compulsive use, to limit use to settings conducive to positive experience, to reinforce the notion that 'dependence' should be avoided, to assist in interpreting the 'high' and to support non-drug-related obligations and relationships. In terms of a cost–benefit type of social learning theory, the social groups and activities within which this controlled use was embedded constituted an important and valued part of life that made control desirable and excess potentially costly.

Reinert (1968) described the increasing preoccupation with the 'addicting' substance which occurred in his experience when a person had once had the kind of control that Zinberg and colleagues described and had then lost it. Reinert appreciated, in this writer's view correctly, the important role of widening cue linkage or cue reactivity:

Among many regular users of alcohol, a great variety of situations, modes, feelings and activities have become linked with alcohol in such a way that a greater or lesser feeling of discomfort is felt if alcohol is absent from the situation. This or that feeling, situation, party, event or hour of the day 'calls' for a drink ... The analogy to the smoker who cannot write a letter, think, make a decision, drive a car, play a hand of bridge, conduct an interview, converse or drink a cocktail without lighting up a cigarette seems remarkable ... The habit of ... daily life has extended its roots deeply into many aspects and facets of ... daily life. [There occurs a] complicated interwoven pattern of habits, of needs gratified, of pleasures derived and tensions released.

(Hochbaum, 1965, cited by Reinert, 1968, pp. 41–42, to show the similarities between the smoking habit and excessive drinking)

It is part of the anecdotal wisdom of Alcoholics Anonymous (AA) that any event (whether apparently unpleasant or pleasant) is an excuse for drinking for the 'alcoholic', and descriptions of other forms of excessive appetitive behaviour frequently stress the cure-all function which behaviour serves for the person whose appetite is excessive. The following example of one kind of female 'sexual promiscuity' is one instance:

> When she was depressed, the embrace of a new man gave her a lift. When she was happy, such an embrace constituted the perfect way of accenting and highlighting her happiness. When she was turned down for one job, sex soothed the injury. When she got another job, sex added to the celebration.
>
> (Morse, 1963, p. 43)

But is there not more to 'addiction' than the development of a strong attachment and a powerful habit based on the learning and cognitive processes discussed in the previous chapter and on generalisation and the secondary processes introduced in this chapter so far? At this point we need to take time to consider the long-held assumption that the core of addiction consists of changes in the central nervous system brought about by the heavy use of substances such as heroin and alcohol. That assumption represents a serious challenge to the whole thesis of this book: that addiction is best conceived of as appetitive behaviour that has become excessive as a result of a compelling combination of psychological processes, and that non-substance activities such as gambling can be just as addictive.

NEUROADAPTATION AND THE RELIEF OF WITHDRAWAL SYMPTOMS ARE NOT CENTRAL

The idea that 'dependence' can be, '... psychic and sometimes physical', was enshrined in earlier World Health Organisation (WHO) definitions of drug dependence (e.g. that of 1964), and, although more recent definitions have not stressed the separation of two types of dependence in that way, the view that 'addiction' is only a real driving force when it has a 'biological' basis is still widely held. The hallmarks of 'physical dependence' are generally taken to be two. The first is tolerance (i.e. a decrease in potency upon continued administration of a drug). The second is a withdrawal or abstinence syndrome (i.e. a definite, characteristic and time-limited set of symptoms) which appear when the drug disappears or is disappearing from the body, such as the restlessness, yawning, alternate feelings of hot and cold, 'cold turkey' skin, running nose, drowsiness, stomach cramps, vomiting and diarrhoea, perspiration and tremor which are classically associated with opiate withdrawal (Kurland, 1978).

The undisputed occurrence of these events in the case of some drugs nevertheless raises a host of questions concerning their links with appetitive behaviour. Do they occur in the case of other drugs? When they occur, how important are they in comparison with other factors in accounting for excessive drug use? How can they help, if at all, in accounting for non-drug forms of excessive behaviour? In the case of other drugs, it has not been at all easy to separate out the effects of a possible withdrawal syndrome from such confounding factors as the reasons for discontinuing drug use, the reasons for which drug use was started in the first place, the psychological effects of stopping and additional complicating factors such as nutritional deficiency brought about by inadequate diet during a period of drug use. If it can be established that a particular drug can produce such biological changes in the nervous system as a consequence of repeated use over a period of time, it cannot be supposed that we have thereby established the 'real' reason why that drug is sometimes used to excess. The question that does arise is how important this developmental process is in altering a person's motivation in comparison with the learning, cognitive, social and other developmental processes already outlined. A number of medical authorities have placed the development of an altered biological response to alcohol, for example, at centre stage when it comes to explaining excessive drinking. Jellinek (1960), for one, considered that only 'gamma' and 'delta' forms of 'alcoholism', characterised by tolerance and withdrawal symptoms, constituted *diseases*. Other forms, such as 'alpha alcoholism', characterised by psychological but not physical 'dependence', he considered were less central (see Chapter Two).

This element of biological change appeared still to have a central role in the later formulated 'alcohol dependence syndrome' (Edwards and Gross, 1976) which has been so influential in expert concepts of addiction ever since. The importance of biochemical changes in that formulation was shown by the use of the word 'core' which the authors used to qualify the word 'syndrome', and the listing of 'altered psychobiological state' (experience of withdrawal states, drinking for relief of withdrawal, tolerance) as one of three general signs of the syndrome. On the other hand, the word 'syndrome' was defined as, '... a number of phenomena tend[ing] to cluster with sufficient frequency to constitute a recognisable occurrence' (p. 1364), and it was stressed that some signs of 'alcohol dependence' might occur without others, and that it could be of variable degree. The deliberate looseness of the syndrome concept was emphasised. Most importantly, nowhere was it made clear whether 'altered psychobiological state' is a necessary condition, or whether the other two hallmarks of the syndrome, namely 'altered behavioural state' (culturally inappropriate drinking, heavy drinking, etc.) and 'altered subjective state' (heightened desire for drinking, preoccupation with drinking, etc.) might alone amount to a high level of 'dependence'. The implication is that 'dependence' is unlikely to reach its fullest extent without some element of altered neurochemical response to alcohol as a drug. Drinking for relief of withdrawal symptoms is a crucial element in such a formulation because it provides the necessary link between altered biological response to the drug and increased motivation for consumption. If the sequence of withdrawing, experiencing stressful withdrawal symptoms, taking a further dose and experiencing relief of withdrawal, is followed repeatedly, the motivation to consume the drug regularly will be much increased either because drug-seeking responses are strengthened (according to operant theory) or because expectancies for the relief of distress have been created (according to cognitive behavioural theory).

Attractive although that model was, it became clear that it had difficulty explaining a number of aspects of appetitive behaviour. For one thing, being a developmental model that requires a history of drug use prior to the development of tolerance and withdrawal symptoms, it was at its weakest when trying to explain the taking up of appetitive behaviour in the early stages of a drug-using career. Furthermore, studies of animals and accounts of humans with a history of regular drug use suggested that regular use is often maintained at levels below which withdrawal symptoms occur, and that 'relapse' or return to drug use can occur long after the cessation of withdrawal symptoms and/or in response to other stimuli and events (e.g. Pomerleau and Pomerleau, 1989; Jaffe, 1992). Furthermore, a deficit-reduction model based on the relief of withdrawal symptoms seemed less compelling as an explanation for the repeated use of cocaine which became the drug of greatest concern in the USA in the 1980s, but which does not give rise to the kind of gross withdrawal syndrome associated with heroin use (although, as we shall see later, Gawin, 1991 and others believed cocaine withdrawal had been under-estimated). If, as the present book argues, excessive eating, sexuality and gambling are as much excessive appetites as are different forms of drug addiction, then a deficit-reduction model is likely to be in even greater trouble as the leading explanation.

Jaffe (1992) carefully reviewed the arguments for and against this once widely held proposition that the development of a 'syndrome' of symptoms following withdrawal of a drug to which the nervous system had adapted (or the administration of a drug antagonistic to the drug of abuse), plus the further taking of the drug to avoid or relieve such symptoms, constituted the sine qua non of 'dependence' or 'addiction'. He reported the general move among WHO experts since the 1960s towards a more moderate position in which 'neuroadaptation' and relief of withdrawal, although still important, were no longer seen as central. The adoption of the term 'neuroadaptation' was meant to indicate the specialised and non-essential nature of the biological processes giving rise to tolerance and withdrawal, as opposed to the term 'physical dependence' which had often been taken to imply that addiction did not really exist unless these signs were present. Jaffe also documented the vacillations of the American Psychiatric Association and WHO, referred to in Part I of the present book, over whether tolerance and withdrawal were essential for a diagnosis.

Among the reasons that Jaffe gave for this move were the growing recognition of the importance of positive incentives for drug use and of brain reward and memory systems (see Chapter Ten), as well as animal and human research suggesting that strong motivation for the taking up or continuation of drug use can exist in the absence of withdrawal symptoms. More central to Jaffe's own understanding of the nature of addiction were: inclination to use, a cognitive assessment of the risks and benefits involved, the positive and negative consequences of using different drugs or not using drugs, and approach and avoidance learning based upon these experiences.

Even regular heroin users, it seems, are in some doubt about the centrality of the withdrawal syndrome. Once daily use of heroin had been established, according to Parker *et al.* (1988), the principal concern of the heroin users whom they spoke to was to obtain sufficient heroin to keep withdrawal symptoms at bay. Pearson (1987), on the other hand, found that a number of heroin addicts were of the view that the severity and importance of 'cold turkey' were exaggerated. For example:

> Coming off? It's nowt really, there's not much to it like. There's a few of us round here, who've all been on smack, got sick of it. And you get nowt over

there at the clinic, there's no methadone or what have you. So, you know, we just do it on us own like. It's bad for a few days, but ... Get stocked up with, you know, comics and magazines, chocolate and pop and that. Go to bed, and just sit it out. That's all there is to it.

(Ronnie, cited by Pearson, 1987, p. 154)

There was general agreement that the hardest part of overcoming excessive heroin use is not coming off but staying off, which supports the point that a model of addiction with neuroadaptation at its centre is always going to have difficulty explaining why there is a danger of relapse after the acute withdrawal phase has passed (Parker *et al.*, 1988; Pearson, 1987; Taylor, 1993).

A number of studies have focused on the supposed 'withdrawal symptoms' themselves, again adding to the complex picture. Among these are studies of alcohol, tobacco, cocaine and cannabis. Hawker and Orford (1998), for example, charted the symptoms reported by 70 excessive drinkers in the first few days after stopping drinking. Psychological symptoms such as agitation, irritability and depression predominated over physical symptoms such as tremor, sweating and dizziness, and the former remained at a high level for longer (declining on average after day 2 whereas physical symptoms declined from day 1). Furthermore, the stronger predictors of the severity of withdrawal were anxiety the day before stopping drinking and expectations of the severity of withdrawal, which provided a stronger prediction than the quantity and regularity of drinking that had preceded cessation. These latter findings were parallel to similar findings of Phillips *et al.* (1986) with heroin users stopping their drug use.

Tobacco smoking, as usual, constitutes an interesting example. In fact, it is one of the very best examples of behaviour involving the ingestion of a drug now agreed to have the potential for inducing altered biological response, but which it is recognised is used for a range of reasons. The existence of a withdrawal syndrome has only been recognised comparatively recently; only a proportion of regular smokers appear to experience noticeable withdrawal when they stop smoking; the evidence that severity of withdrawal is correlated with relapse is not convincing (West, 1991); and hence the importance of withdrawal for smoking addiction is far from clear (Jarvik and Hatsukami, 1989). One study which monitored the withdrawal symptoms of a large number of smokers over the first few days after stopping, and for a good follow-up period thereafter, was that reported by Gritz *et al.* (1991). The participants were over 500 daily smokers in the USA who either planned to stop smoking on the Great American Smokeout Day in November 1984 or who made a New Year's resolution to stop smoking on 1 January 1985. They were monitored at baseline and at 1-, 6- and 12-month follow-up, and a proportion were monitored in addition on days 1 and 2 following their target quit date and at 1 week follow-up. The large majority of those who stopped smoking reported at least one withdrawal symptom shortly after stopping: 87 per cent at day 1, 90 per cent at day 2 and 87.5 per cent at week 1. Severity was greatest at days 1 and 2, and the number of symptoms reported was greatest at week 1 follow-up. Severity and number of symptoms were still falling between month 1 and month 6, and substantial minorities were still reporting 'withdrawal symptoms' such as eating more than usual, restlessness, craving for cigarettes and impatience at 12-month follow-up. These same symptoms were among those most commonly reported in the acute phase in the first week after stopping. Of the symptoms monitored by Gritz *et al.* the most frequently reported were all psychological (in addition to those already cited they included: anxious/tense, irritable/angry, difficulty concentrating, excessive hunger, depressed, disorientated, loss of energy/fatigue). Physical or physiological symptoms assessed were all reported at a lower frequency (dizziness, stomach or bowel problems, headaches, sweating, insomnia, heart palpitations, tremors). With such a predominance of psychological 'symptoms' the question of specificity is inevitably raised: how many of such symptoms would be reported by non-smokers, or would have been reported by Gritz *et al.*'s abstinent smokers while they were still smoking?

Reference has already been made to the work of Russell *et al.* (1974), Tate *et al.* (1994) and others, who attempted to classify smokers according to self-reported motives (see Chapter Eight). Russell and his colleagues drew support for the importance of the pharmacological component of smoking 'dependence' from the results of their studies of motives. Two broad clusters of motives emerged, which Russell *et al.* labelled 'pharmacological' and 'non-pharmacological'. Motives indicating smoking for 'stimulation', 'addictive' smoking and 'automatic' smoking contributed to the first factor, and 'psychosocial' and 'indulgent' smoking contributed to the second. The three types of smoking motive which contributed most to the pharmacological dimension were those reported more frequently by clients of a smoking clinic than by members of the general population, and the same motives tended to be positively correlated with age, and had the stronger correlations with amount smoked. Russell *et al.* drew a most important conclusion, when they wrote:

> We suggest that it may prove more useful to classify smokers according to their position on the single dimension of pharmacological addiction to nicotine rather than in terms of their profile on the six types of smoking.
> (Russell *et al.*, 1974, p. 332)

The idea of progression from drug use motivated by social and other non-pharmacological rewards and incentives, to later use motivated in the end as much by relief or avoidance of withdrawal as by other reinforcements, was part of Russell *et al.*'s (1974) thinking as it has been in many models of excessive drug behaviour. Thus the proposal was that the drug nicotine takes a stronger and stronger hold, as smoking progresses, on individuals who initially smoked for reasons unrelated to the pharmacological properties of the drug.

As always, however, it is important to advocate caution in extrapolating in such a way from complex mathematical techniques. For a start, the amount of variance in the matrix of correlations amongst the six motive dimensions which was accounted for by the two higher order factors (pharmacological and non-pharmacological) was just one-quarter. Furthermore, there were some interesting details of the results which were not totally in keeping with the simple unidimensional conclusion reached by Russell *et al.* The items most strongly definitive of the pharmacological factor were not those contributing to the first-order 'addictive' component but were rather the following 'stimulation' and 'automatic' items (e.g. I smoke more when I am rushed and have lots to do; I find myself smoking without remembering lighting up). The so-called 'addictive' smoking items occupied a less clear position, contributing as a group almost as much to the non-pharmacological factor as to the pharmacological. The two items most definitive of the 'addictive' component were:

> When I have run out of cigarettes I find it almost unbearable until I can get some.

> I get a real gnawing hunger to smoke when I haven't smoked for a while.

In their later work, Tate *et al.* (1994) also produced two second-order factors (factor I and II) which they interpreted as representing pharmacological and non-pharmacological motives, respectively. Factor I, but not factor II, correlated significantly with smoking rate, years smoked, age and plasma-cotinine levels. Those research participants who were attending a clinic in an effort to give up their smoking had higher factor-I scores. Thus Tate *et al.* considered their results to provide further evidence in support of the separation of pharmacological and non-pharmacological motives for smoking and the increasing pharmacological role of nicotine as people's smoking careers develop.

As was the case with Russell *et al.*'s (1974) findings, however, a careful inspection of Tate *et al.*'s results shows a possibly less neat picture. First, the supposedly pharmacological factor I comprised not only addictive and automatic motives but also sedative and stimulation motives. These are psychological motives and to construe them as pharmacological is an over-simplification. As Tate *et al.* acknowledged, their results, based largely upon responses to a questionnaire, do not provide a direct test of the psychopharmacological effects of nicotine. In fact, correlations between sedative and stimulation motives reported in response to questionnaire items, and plasma-cotinine levels, were not significant, and the correlation between factor I as a whole and cotinine was modest (0.20). Furthermore, the total amount of variance accounted for by the two second-order factors was comparatively modest (28 and 18 per cent) suggesting that a simple separation of motives into these two neat clusters provides us with only a very approximate picture of the complexity of reasons for why people smoke. This is not to mention the assumption that automatic and addictive factors are linked to maintenance of nicotine levels and the avoidance or relief of nicotine withdrawal, an assumption which is questionable in the light of knowledge that non-drug forms of excessive behaviour such as addiction to gambling can be just as automatic and addictive.

Interesting results were also reported by Tiffany and Drobes (1991) who were in the process of developing a questionnaire on smoking 'urges'. From an initial pool of items they chose 32, eight intended to tap each of the following four supposed components: desire to smoke; anticipation of positive outcomes from smoking; anticipation of relief from nicotine withdrawal or from withdrawal-associated negative affect; and intention to smoke. The 32 items were given to 230 predominantly young (average age 21 years) daily cigarette smokers. Some were asked to abstain for 6 hours before completing the questionnaire, some for only 1 hour and some not at all. The results of administering the questionnaire were subjected to a factor analysis which suggested the existence of two factors. The first comprised several items from the desire to smoke, intention to smoke, and anticipation of positive outcomes categories, and seemed to reflect, '... a clear intention and desire to engage in smoking behavior that is anticipated as pleasant, enjoyable and satisfying' (p. 1471). The majority of items loading on the second factor came from the 'relief of withdrawal or negative affect' category, and the few positively loading items from the other categories suggested, '... a greater sense of exigency and imperative...' (p. 1471) ('all I want right now is a cigarette', 'my desire to smoke seems overpowering', 'nothing would be better than smoking a cigarette right now'). Although the second factor appeared to reflect relief of negative affect, its item content by no means suggests convincingly that it is withdrawal symptoms that might be relieved (the six highest loading items relate to anticipating being less irritable, and less depressed, less bored, less tired, being able to control things better and thinking more clearly). Furthermore, although scores on factor II increased with hours of abstinence, factor-I scores, which were higher at all abstinence intervals, also increased with abstinence interval, in fact comparatively more so between no abstinence and 1 hour's abstinence.

Cocaine presents another interesting challenge for the development of a satisfactory model of addiction. Bryant *et al.* (1991) interviewed nearly 300 people seeking treatment for excessive cocaine use, plus an additional 100 'cocaine dependent' people from the community, most of whom had not received any treatment. By careful interviewing it was determined whether each person met each of nine criteria for cocaine dependence, and the results were subjected to a modified form of factor analysis (latent-trait analysis) that allows for the skewed distribution of dichotomous variables and the inevitable covariation of some of the criteria (e.g. withdrawal and withdrawal avoidance). Paralleling the results of Tiffany and Drobes (1991) for tobacco, Bryant *et al.* found that a two-factor model fitted their data, with withdrawal and withdrawal avoidance forming a separate second factor. The correlation of their two factors was also high (0.62), however, and their preference was for a single-factor model. Using this model they plotted for each criterion its 'centrality' (i.e. its loading on the factor) and its 'severity' (i.e. a measure of the ordering of the criteria in terms of number of other criteria present or absent). The results are shown in Figure 11.2. Here it can be seen that withdrawal, and particularly withdrawal avoidance, are indicative of comparatively high severity (i.e. when they were present there was a probability that a comparatively large number of the other criteria would be present also). These criteria, however, were not particularly central to dependence as indexed by loadings on the single, general factor.

More central were the triad of: socially dysfunctional use (frequent intoxication or withdrawal symptoms when expected to fulfil major role obligations at work, school or home, or when substance use is physically hazardous); salience (important social, occupational or recreational activities given up or reduced because of substance use); and use despite problems (continued substance use despite knowledge of having a persistent or recurrent social, psychological or physical problem that is caused or exacerbated by the use of the substance).

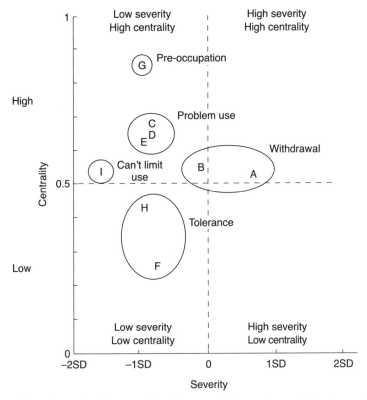

Figure 11.2   Plot of severity by centrality for cocaine-dependent criteria (reproduced by permission from Bryant *et al.*, 1991). *Key:* A—withdrawal avoidance; B—withdrawal; C—socially dysfunctional use; D—salience (work, family, friends); E—use despite problems; F—can't stop; G—preoccupation; H—tolerance; I—can't limit use.

Most central of all was preoccupation (a great deal of time spent in activities necessary to get the substance, taking the substance or recovering from the effects). Interestingly, criteria relating to what Widiger and Smith (1994) referred to as 'dyscontrol' were either low on severity ('can't limit use' [i.e. substance often taken in larger amounts or over a longer period than the person intended]) or low on centrality ('can't stop' [i.e. persistent desire or one or more unsuccessful efforts to cut down or control substance use]). Impaired control may be a key concept for understanding excessive attachment, but it is probably particularly difficult to assess.

According to Gawin (1991) cocaine addiction had forced a rethinking of the very nature of addiction because cessation is not associated with the gross physiological changes that often accompany heroin and alcohol withdrawal. Another point noted by Bryant *et al.* (1991) is that the transition to 'dependent' cocaine use is usually associated with a transition from occasional, single-episode use to a pattern involving high-dose bingeing. This is very unlike the regular daily-use pattern that is normal for 'dependent' tobacco smokers, many people who are dependent on heroin and some who are dependent on alcohol, and this is probably one of the reasons for the demise of the interesting idea of 'narrowing of the drinking/drug use repertoire' originally included as a central feature of the alcohol dependence syndrome. In Bryant *et al.*'s study withdrawal symptoms were counted as present in 52 per cent of the participants and withdrawal avoidance in 36 per cent, although Bryant *et al.* were not specific about the withdrawal symptoms involved. Gawin (1991) has argued, on the basis of human and animal research, that cocaine does produce a subtle, physiological, withdrawal syndrome. He distinguished this from the 'crash' of mood and energy that is known to occur within the first few days following abstinence. This 'crash', according to Gawin, consists of craving for cocaine, depression, agitation and anxiety, and in some people suspiciousness and paranoia, followed by mounting exhaustion and a craving for sleep (often assisted in practice by the self-administration of other drugs including marijuana, sedatives, opiates or alcohol). The crash is parallel to an alcohol hangover, and is not to be confused, in Gawin's view, with withdrawal, which may follow 1–10 weeks after abstinence. The essence of cocaine withdrawal, according to Gawin, is a protracted period of dysphoric mood, including decreased activation, anxiety, lack of motivation, boredom and marked diminished intensity of normal pleasurable experiences, which he has referred to as 'anhedonia', which lifts between 2 and 12 weeks. Because of the absence of gross physiological changes, precise and objective quantification of this cocaine-withdrawal syndrome is difficult and existing rating scales are not sufficiently sensitive.

Gawin speculated that this withdrawal state might be associated with a subsensitivity or down-regulation of brain reward regions affected by cocaine, as indexed by an increased threshold voltage required to elicit intracranial electrical self-stimulation of the brain in dopaminergic reward areas such as the nucleus accumbens. Al-Adawi and Powell (1997) interpreted the results of their smoking-deprivation study (see Chapter Eight) as providing some support for the theory that deprivation is associated with down-regulation in dopamine activity which is restored to normal with renewed smoking. Wise and Munn (1995) are others who have suggested that dopamine depletion and the attendant sub-sensitivity of the reward system, as shown by an increased threshold of electrical self-stimulation in rats after withdrawal from an intermittent high-dose amphetamine regime used in their experiment, might have more significance for explaining drug use than the classic withdrawal symptoms. Unlike the latter, which vary from drug class to drug class, and are much more pronounced in the case of some drugs than others, depression of the reward system might be a common denominator for all drugs with potential for addiction. This depression of the reward system might be thought of as a common 'opponent process' (see below) with a more obvious link to the habit-forming properties of drugs than the classic withdrawal symptoms (but note the danger of too simple a notion of 'reward' and 'brain reward system' as discussed in Chapter Ten).

Is there a marijuana-withdrawal syndrome? Animal studies, using tetrahydrocannabinol (THC, the active ingredient in marijuana), and experimental studies in which humans received relatively high doses of marijuana or THC, suggest that there might be (Wiesbeck *et al.*, 1996). Marijuana users have sometimes reported the possible existence of a withdrawal syndrome but it is difficult to know whether what they report is simply reflecting general levels of stress, coexisting mental-health problems or the consequences of intoxication or withdrawal from other substances. Wiesbeck *et al.* took advantage of interview material on drug taking from over 1000 people in the USA who were taking part in a genetic study of alcohol 'dependence'. Detailed questioning about marijuana use and withdrawal was confined to those who had used marijuana on 20 or more occasions in any one year. They were asked whether or not they had experienced any of seven marijuana withdrawal symptoms. Withdrawal was defined as occurring if a person reported two or more of these symptoms clustering together during at least one reported episode. This criterion included 16 per cent of those using 20 or more times in a single year. Only three of the seven symptoms asked about were reported by more than 50 per cent of even this minority of marijuana consumers. These were: nervous, tense, restless (94 per cent); sleep disturbance (76 per cent); appetite increase or decrease (63 per cent). The remaining four symptoms were all of a more physical nature and were reported by much smaller percentages (tremble, twitch; sweat, fever; diarrhoea, stomach problems; nausea, vomiting—all reported by 21 per cent or fewer). Even these low rates of withdrawal symptoms probably represent an over-estimate of the true picture since, because of the nature of the sample, the majority of those reporting marijuana withdrawal symptoms were also dependent on alcohol and some on other drugs also. A small group of 18 people reporting marijuana withdrawal in the absence of dependence on any other drug showed the same pattern of symptoms, however. Wiesbeck *et al.* concluded that the symptoms reported probably did represent a real marijuana withdrawal effect, but that the syndrome is comparatively mild.

Budney *et al.* (1999) reported on the withdrawal symptoms experienced by a very different group: 54 people seeking out-patient treatment for marijuana 'dependence', also in the USA. A total of 22 possible symptoms were asked about. During the most recent period of marijuana abstinence, 57 per cent of the participants had experienced six or more symptoms of at least 'moderate' severity, and 47 per cent four or more rated as 'severe'. Most of the symptoms rated as at least 'moderate' by 25 per cent or more were affective or behavioural (craving, irritability, depression, anger, nervousness, restlessness, sleep problems, strange dreams), reduction in appetite and headaches being the exceptions. Furthermore, this group of consumers was hardly typical, about a third having had problems with cocaine in the past, even more alcohol problems, and between a third and a half having had psychiatric problems. The extent of recent marijuana withdrawal symptoms correlated substantially with psychiatric severity.

Even in the case of an activity such as gambling, symptoms akin to drug withdrawal have been reported. Wray and Dickerson (1981) are often cited for their report that 30–50 per cent of a sample of Gamblers Anonymous (GA) members described disturbances of mood or behaviour on ceasing to bet. The most commonly reported symptoms were irritability, restlessness, depressed mood, poor concentration and obsessional thoughts. They likened these to withdrawal symptoms reported by excessive drinkers, although Walker (1989), who was sceptical about including excessive gambling as an addiction, described the symptoms reported by Wray and Dickerson as only mild and psychological when compared with drug withdrawal symptoms which he thought were often physiological and typically more severe. We asked 16 problem gamblers and 16 problem drinkers about their experiences of each of 28 possible withdrawal symptoms first thing in the morning during a period of heavy gambling or drinking (Orford *et al.*, 1996). A total of 14 were more psychological in content (e.g. anxiety or tension, agitation or restlessness, irritability, lack of energy, poor memory or concentration), and the other 14 were more physical (e.g. poor sleep, loss of appetite, muscle pains, aches or twitchings, nausea and retching, shakiness of hands). The gamblers reported virtually no physical symptoms, and the drinkers had more experience of each of such symptoms than did the gamblers, the difference being significant for each symptom with the exception of 'headaches'. Problem gamblers on average did report a few of the more psychological symptoms, although significantly fewer than the drinkers. The latter reported significantly more experience than the gamblers on anxiety or tension, irritability, lack of energy and poor memory or concentration. The gamblers had similar experience to the drinkers, however, in the case of feeling miserable or depressed, feeling as if you were going mad, smoking more.

We concluded that withdrawal symptoms, like those associated with some drugs, were not a feature of the experience of the problem gamblers who took part in that study, and that their 'compulsion' to gamble could not be attributed to a process similar to neuroadaptation and the relief of withdrawal symptoms by further gambling. At the same time, however, there was evidence that they were as strongly attached to their gambling activities (mostly betting on horse racing) as the drinkers were to their drinking. This evidence came from the administration of a new 24-item attachment questionnaire (AQ) designed to cover the following areas: strong desire; preoccupation; acting against judgement; loss of control; non-social activity; acquiring money for the activity by special means; feeling addicted or dependent; feeling depressed or guilty as a result; being criticised by others; and feeling the need to change. Parallel forms were developed for drinking and gambling. This was therefore an attempt to assess the degree of attachment to a drug or an activity without the presupposition, that lies behind questionnaires such as the severity of alcohol dependence questionnaire (SADQ, Stockwell *et al.*, 1983), the severity of opiate dependence questionnaire (SODQ, Sutherland *et al.*, 1986) and severity of amphetamine dependence questionnaire (SAmDQ, Churchill *et al.*, 1993), that neuroadaptation and withdrawal relief is at the heart of the matter. Average scores on the AQ were very similar for the drinkers and gamblers.

The conclusion that I come to on the basis of theoretical developments such as Jaffe's (1992) and the research on smoking, alcohol, cocaine, marijuana and gambling, reviewed above, is that withdrawal symptoms and their relief by further consumption or activity cannot be central to the process of strengthening and maintaining an excessive appetite, as was once supposed. For one thing, some appetites which can produce serious excess, of which gambling is the clearest example and cocaine perhaps another, do not lead to withdrawal symptoms of the kind associated with heroin and alcohol; and even in the latter cases the 'symptoms' experienced, including those that are central to understanding excess, are mostly psychological in nature or are much under the influence of psychological factors such as anxiety and expectations. A fully adequate model of strong appetitive attachment cannot be created out of neuroadaptation alone.

MEMORY AND ATTENTION SCHEMATA

A number of serious attempts to develop more complete models have been made, several of them featuring the concept of 'craving'. Although this notion has often been poorly defined and highly subjective it is immediately attractive as a candidate for helping to build a model that is not confined to pharmacological activities. An early example of such a model was Solomon and Corbit's (1973, 1974; Solomon, 1980) 'opponent process' theory of addiction which was part of their general theory of acquired motivation. The latter was based on the assumption that there exist brain mechanisms which function automatically to neutralise, '... all excursions from hedonic neutrality, whether those excursions be appetitive or aversive, pleasant or unpleasant' (Solomon and Corbit, 1973, p. 158). Affect-arousing stimulations, such as free-fall parachuting which produces terror in the novice, or opiate use which produces euphoria in the relatively new user, or love which gives rise to ecstasy in the newly attached, are followed, when the stimulation ceases, they theorised, by an 'opponent process' of opposite hedonic quality (relief, withdrawal, loneliness). With repeated stimulation of the same kind, the primary affective response (State A) diminishes in strength (less terror, euphoria or ecstasy—examples of adaptation), but the opponent process (State B) is strengthened (exhilaration, intense craving, and separation grief, respectively). It is this enhanced opponent process which was responsible, in Solomon and Corbit's view, for the development of 'addiction'. In cases where the A state is hedonically positive, the B or opponent state is aversive and increasingly so with repetition, and can be removed by reinstating the primary or A state:

> Because the B process is the opponent of A, the best way of getting rid of the B state is to use the substance which produces the A state. Thus behaviour involved in the use of the A-arousing substance will be strongly reinforced as an operant, because it produces A and it terminates B. The addictive cycle will lead to further strengthening of the B process. Therefore, amounts of the substance will have to be increased ...
>
> (Solomon and Corbit, 1973, p. 169)

As was mentioned earlier, down-regulation of brain reward systems has been suggested as one possible candidate for the B opponent process. If any such mechanism exists, we should expect not only 'addiction' to drugs which initially provides a hedonically very positive experience, but also 'addiction' to all activities which at first provide an intense positive affective experience of sudden and clearly marked onset. Gambling and sex are two examples, not mentioned by Solomon and Corbit, which clearly fit the bill. Theirs was a general theory of addictive behaviour, in no way limited to drugs, and is therefore of considerable interest to us here.

Leventhal and Cleary's (1980) model, which took advantage of the opponent process theory, but went beyond it, was specific to smoking. They reviewed work suggesting that heavy smokers, at least, were motivated to regulate or titrate the amount of nicotine in their bodies. They pointed out, however, that this model of smoking 'dependence' could not account for high relapse rates weeks or months after smoking had stopped, nor for the fact that altering nicotine levels experimentally (e.g. by reducing nicotine content in cigarettes or by providing nicotine chewing gum) did not result in the degree of alteration of smoking rate that should be expected, nor that smoking appeared to be responsive to changes in emotional states, environmental cues and stress. Leventhal and Cleary therefore went on to develop a 'multiple regulation model' which combined the nicotine factor and psychological elements. Their model goes some considerable way toward explaining both the strength and the complexity of the development of excessive appetitive behaviour, and, at the same time, can offer a partial explanation for excessive involvement in non-drug activities such as gambling.

They believed that emotional regulation was the key to smoking, which was stimulated by departures from emotional homeostasis. The reason that heavy smokers behaved in such a way as to regulate nicotine level was because certain emotional states had become conditioned to a drop in plasma-nicotine level. Hence, a drop in nicotine level stimulated 'craving', although other external stimuli could also generate this reaction. Leventhal and Cleary suggested two possible mechanisms to explain how an unpleasant feeling state ('craving') came to be linked to a fall in nicotine level. One, following the opponent-process theory, suggested that nicotine gives rise automatically to a secondary, negative response following the initial positive reaction, and that the former becomes stronger as the latter becomes weaker with increased experience of smoking.

Leventhal and Cleary's second possible mechanism for explaining how craving might become linked to a fall in nicotine level involved conditioning. If people used smoking to control their reactions to stress, then anxiety would reappear when smoking stops, and hence anxiety would be conditioned to a fall in nicotine level (note the similarity with Wikler's, 1973 and Teasdale's, 1973 conditioning theories of drug addiction, see Chapter Ten). Complexity was added to the model by assuming that several emotional processes might operate simultaneously; that changes in nicotine level generate a variety of bodily sensations that may themselves become conditioned to emotional states; that smoking itself can directly aid emotional control (e.g. by increasing alertness, by reducing feelings of social insecurity or by enhancing relaxation); and particularly that people will form a strong emotional memory of this complex action of smoking. It is this 'memory schema' that was responsible for provoking desire, or as they called it 'craving':

> What it does is provide a mechanism for integrating and sustaining the combination of external stimulus cues (social events, work, nothing to do, taste, etc.), internal stimulus cues (sensations from drops in plasma nicotine levels), and a variety of reactions including subjective emotional experience and expressive motor and autonomic reactions associated with the hedonic experience and with smoking. The elicitation of any of the components can provoke the remaining components of this memory schema. Hence it is the schema that makes possible the re-experiencing of craving when one sees someone else smoke and it is the schema through which nicotine loss stimulates craving because the sensory features of nicotine loss elicit the other affective components of the schema.
>
> (Leventhal and Cleary, 1980, p. 393)

A key point here, of importance for developing a *general* theory of excessive behaviour, is that the sensations generated by a drop in nicotine level were not themselves considered to constitute 'craving', but become 'craving' only after they were conditioned to environmentally stimulated negative feelings. Emotional regulation was the core of the model, not titration of nicotine level itself, even for heavy smokers. The use of nicotine across a broad range of life situations helped, Leventhal and Cleary suggested, to develop broad emotional smoking schemata which may be particularly difficult to break. This is the process of generalization of appetitive behaviour, or increasingly wide cue linkage, discussed earlier, which is probably of such crucial importance in the development of excess.

A later model of tobacco dependence based upon this idea of an integrated system or schema of elements that provide the motivating force for continued excessive appetitive behaviour, is Niaura *et al.*'s (1991) bioinformational model. This posits that information concerning drug use and its effects is represented as a 'propositional' neural network that encodes information about stimulus elements (settings and events that activate the network), response elements (including cognitions, physiological responses and drug-seeking behaviours) and meaning elements. Such networks develop through experience with drugs. 'Dependence', in this framework, is not defined by any single element, and can only be understood in terms of the extent and articulation of the network, the threshold for activation of part or all of it, the amount of automaticity and coherence among the response elements, and the dominance of the system in overriding other ongoing activities.

In their study referred to earlier, Tiffany and Drobes (1991) made much of the fact that their two smoking 'urges' questionnaire factors had a substantial positive correlation (0.66) suggesting that if the two factors do represent the operation of two systems, one associated with negative affect and withdrawal and the other with appetitive, positively reinforcing effects of tobacco, then it is more appropriate to see them as operating in an integrated way rather than as two independent systems. Tiffany's (1990) suggestion was that such behaviour represents skilled activity controlled largely by automatic processes organised in unitised memory structures in the form of action schemata. Urges and cravings are conceptualised as constellations of verbal, somatovisceral and behavioural responses supported by non-automatic cognitive processes. White's (1996) model, based on the idea of three parallel learning and memory processes (see Chapter Ten), is yet another in this apparently growing tradition of trying to account for excessive appetitive behaviour in terms of complex memory schemata based on past experience of the substance or activity. The three 'parallel processes' which he outlined were: conditioned incentive learning, whereby stimuli associated with drug use become conditioned and able to serve as incentives for future behaviour; what White called 'declarative learning', whereby learning takes place about the relationships among cues even when these are of no consequence; and habit learning, whereby stimulus–response associations are strengthened. In her commentary on White's paper, Stewart (1996) referred to these three systems as: affect, knowledge and habit, and in his commentary Drummond (1996) pointed out that over 200 years ago Rush (1785) referred to the principles of association, recollection and habit in understanding addiction. Nevertheless, such models represent a definite step forward in conceptualising addiction. For one thing they substitute more sophisticated ideas of notions such as craving and 'loss of control' in place of former conceptualisations, long recognised by careful observers to be over-simple (e.g. Keller, 1972; Hodgson *et al.*, 1979b; Heather and Robertson, 1983). Most importantly, for our purposes they have the great merit of being applicable beyond the domain of 'substances', within which the field has been unnecessarily confined in the past. At the same time, it must be noted that they clearly remain within the individualistic, even psychobiologically deterministic tradition of so much addiction theory, neglecting as they do the social and cultural context discussed in Chapter Nine.

It is admittedly difficult to test for the existence of such appetitive cognitive processes or schemata. One procedure, however, that has become popular for examining cognitive processing in the context of excessive eating in particular is the Stroop Test. This involves recording people's reaction times to naming the colours in which words are printed on pages consisting of rows and columns of words printed in different colours. The supposed value of the test is based upon the observation that reaction times are longer when the words themselves are semantically related to a topic that is particularly salient for the person concerned. Reaction times when colour-naming salient words can be compared with two kinds of control tasks: colour-naming neutral words (a comparatively easy task) and colour-naming colour words (e.g responding 'green' to the word 'brown' printed in the colour green—a comparatively difficult task). Although there is some dispute about whether the results are specific to people with 'eating disorders', as opposed to dieters in general (Long *et al.*, 1994), there have been consistent findings that people concerned about their eating show the expected effect of interference with colour-naming words related to eating, shape and weight, as revealed by comparatively long reaction times to such words, and that the effect disappears after successful treatment (Cooper and Fairburn, 1992).

McCusker *et al.* (1995b) extended this paradigm to study cognitive processing of smoking and alcohol-related words among excessive smokers and drinkers, respectively. Paralleling the results for excessive eaters, they found smokers, smoking at least 20 cigarettes a day, to be differentially slower than controls in colour-naming smoking-related words, and 'dependent drinkers' to be differentially slower than controls in colour-naming drinking-related words. In a third experiment, the dependent drinkers, despite their expected overall poorer performance than controls on a memory task, were comparatively better able than controls to memorise alcohol-related words out of a list of words they had just been shown which contained both alcohol-related and neutral nouns. Glautier and Spencer (1999), similarly, showed that heavier drinkers were more likely to spontaneously interpret ambiguous words, such as 'bar', 'pint', 'spirits', 'shot', in alcohol-related terms than were lighter drinkers (they were given 30 seconds to incorporate each word into a sentence). In a later series of experiments, McCusker and Gettings (1997) extended their work to gambling, showing again specific interference and memory bias effects for gambling-related words. Hence, there does appear to be considerable evidence that people whose appetitive behaviour is excessive show specific biases in cognitive processes such as attention and memory, specifically concerning materials that relate to the object of their excessive appetite.

McCusker *et al.* (1995b) interpreted their findings in terms of mental schemata that include propositions, rules and valenced expectancies about a drug or activity. Such schemata may be active or latent. Some elements may readily be brought into conscious awareness while others may remain pre-conscious and only accessed under certain conditions. Some elements may be difficult to verbalise at all. The salience and strength of a cognitive schema mediates attentional, perceptual and memory processes, and biases a person towards receiving information and stimuli pertinent to the schema in question, often in an automatic fashion. McCusker *et al.*'s understanding of schemata led them to be highly critical of any understanding of addictive behaviour based solely upon self-reported, conscious beliefs. Such verbalised outputs in their view represent merely the tip of an iceberg of cognitive structure and processes that may be controlling the behaviour in question.

In this chapter we have considered some of the psychological processes whereby people may become more deeply involved in an appetitive activity. This higher level of commitment or attachment may involve transitions to new ways of engaging in the behaviour such as injecting a drug or binge eating. The process is likely to involve the erosion of discriminations that ordinarily hold behaviour under a greater degree of restraint. Adding to the primary incentive mechanisms, discussed in the previous chapter, are now added a variety of secondary emotional cycles which amplify attachments still further by introducing new motivation of a drive-reduction kind. 'Chasing' is one such mechanism in the case of gambling, the increasing need for secrecy is another that applies across a number of the appetites, and neuroadaptation is another that applies to some of the drug appetites. The result is an increased attachment, best thought of as a 'strong appetite', which has at least three components: enhanced affective attachment to the object of the appetite, increased mental commitment and orientation towards the object, and increased regularity, volume or intensity of consumption or activity involving the object. The idea of appetite-specific attention and memory schemata captures at least the cognitive component of this concept.

But the foregoing is only part of the story. It leaves out of account a central element in addiction, namely conflict over behaviour. That is the central theme of the following chapter, with which we complete our account of the nature of excess. In the course of so doing, the social aspects of addiction, neglected in this and the previous chapter, are reintroduced.

CHAPTER TWELVE

Conflict and Its Consequences

The diary records a ceaseless battle between the id and the superego, between Pepys's powerful appetites and his nagging, puritanical, bourgeois conscience ...

(Stone, 1979, p. 350)

I feel I did much wrong. I wronged myself, and I have wronged my family. I still feel bad about that ... There has been forgiveness, but I have never forgiven myself. What I did was very wrong. I should never have done what I did. This failing is with me even today.

Even a dog is worth more respect than I am.
(Heroin addicts in Karachi, Pakistan, cited by Primrose and Orford, 1997, p. 401)

... [binge eaters] commonly engage in severe self-criticisms, self-condemnation, and self-punishment following a binge eating episode. Common themes of resentment and self-contempt over being overweight and having no self-control are combined with disgust, shame or guilt at having *failed* and 'blown the diet'.

(Loro and Orleans, 1981, p. 161)

EXCESS AS DEVIANCE

It will be the argument of this chapter that a fully comprehensive model of addiction must take into account the conflict that attends *excessive* appetitive behaviour. Much of what we think of as addiction consists of a person's reactions to having developed a strong and costly appetite, and of the ways he or she accommodates to the reactions of others. Such reactions and accommodations should be, in the present writer's view, at the very centre of a psychological understanding of excessive appetitive behaviour, although their importance is not fully acknowledged in most theorising about addiction.

We begin by looking at a perspective that takes a particularly strong line on the importance of social reaction to deviance. According to the perspective of deviancy theory, deviance is the breaking of rules, whether written or unwritten, and it can therefore only be understood by consideration both of the rules and of the behaviour which breaks them. This model therefore parts company with a disease view, and with most psychological perspectives in its major concern with the rules themselves, and with those that make them and enforce them. At its most succinct, the deviancy view is that, like beauty, '... deviance is in the eyes of the beholder' (Rubington and Weinberg, 1968, p.v).

Does this statement imply that there is nothing to deviance except the reaction to it, or that appetitive behaviour is only excessive if someone thinks it is excessive? Probably not. One of the more useful statements of the deviancy position for present purposes is the relatively early statement by Lemert (1951). He described his theory of 'sociopathic behaviour' as, '... one of social differentiation, deviation, and individuation ...'. By this he meant that social differences emerged between people, some appearing to become more deviant than others in certain ways, and that this process of differentiation had a variety of sources. He clearly recognised that in many instances a major source of social difference was some primary deviation which existed quite independently of social reaction and which could indeed be present at birth. Congenital blindness or physical handicap were examples. Even in such instances, however, he stressed the importance of societal reaction.

Very often the effect of the reaction might be an amplifying one. Indeed, the principle that reaction creates, or at least amplifies, original deviance became a central tenet of the deviance perspective in the 1960s (e.g. Wilkins, 1964). As Rubington and Weinberg put it, '... deviance becomes a matter of social definition. And this definition often produces the deviant acts' (1968, p. 4). Lemert's (1951) more general view, however, was that, while societal reaction always occurs, it is not always rejecting and segregating, and when it is, it has an effect which need not necessarily be an amplifying one. Thus, mutual-help groups, Alcoholics Anonymous (AA) and Gamblers Anonymous (GA) among them, are good examples of segregation which purports to be deviance *reducing*. Becoming a fully functioning member of one of these organisations demands not only attendance at an exclusive club, but also a vigorous mental segregation involving 'recognising', 'admitting' and declaring oneself to be 'different from other people'. The argument is that only by recognising oneself to be in a special class of 'alcoholic' or 'compulsive gambler', for example, can the member realise the impossibility of drinking or gambling like most other people, and only by this means can one obtain the motivation to give up one's deviance.

Despite this more moderate, general statement of the deviance position, it is the case that the greatest champions of the deviance perspective were particularly concerned with behaviour, the 'deviance' or 'problem' aspects of which could most readily be understood as almost pure social creations. Of appetitive behaviours considered here perhaps marijuana use is the clearest instance, where a strong argument can be made out for saying that virtually all the problematic aspects of the drug's use are the result of social reaction. It is with behaviour of this sort that deviancy theorists were most in their element and where the deviance model has strongest claims to have exclusive territorial rights. A firm deviancy view of illicit drug taking generally was taken, for example, by Young (1971) and by

Brecher (1972) and is a view to which many modern commentators on US and other approaches to drug control at least partly subscribe (e.g. Musto, 1991; Humphreys and Rappaport, 1993). When the notorious Harrison Narcotic Act of 1914 was passed in the USA, many medical commentators had been immediately aware of the 'deviance amplifying' effects of the Act upon opiate users. For example, an editorial in *American Medicine* for 1915 reported:

> Instead of improving conditions the laws recently passed have made the problem more complex. Honest medical men have found such hardships and dangers to themselves and their reputations in these laws ... that they have simply decided to have as little to do as possible with drug addicts or their needs ... The druggists are in the same position ... Abuses in the name of narcotic drugs are increasing ... A particular sinister sequence ... is the character of the places to which [addicts] are forced to go to get their drugs and the type of people with whom they are obliged to mix.
> (November 1915, pp. 799–800, cited by Brecher, 1972, p. 50)

As Wesson and Smith (1977) pointed out, in relation to the consumption of benzodiazepines, the term 'abuse', '... is likely to be applied to individuals living on the fringes of the dominant culture' (p. 55) rather than to those living within it who use similar amounts of a prescribed drug. The latter group's behaviour is more likely to be labelled 'misuse' or 'overuse'. If, as Wesson and Smith argued, use of the word 'abuse' involves a judgement of one person upon another, depending upon the age, social position and occupation of both, the quantities of drug taken, the reasons for which it is taken, whether it is taken orally or by injection and the source from which it is obtained, a parallel with other substances and activities is again readily apparent. Gambling, drinking, sexual behaviour and opiate use have more commonly been criticised discriminatively rather than wholesale, and have been judged on the basis of who is indulging in what form of the activity and why. One of the best examples is 19th-century concern with the motivations for opiate use. Quotations from the period show that discriminations were frequently made between medicinal use, or use as a pick-me-up by the under-privileged poor, on the one hand, and use as a 'stimulant' or a 'luxury' (hedonistic use) on the other. The former was frequently condoned, the latter was not (Berridge, 1979).

The same point that Wesson and Smith (1977) had made earlier about medically prescribed drugs, namely that a society's attitude to drug use is likely to depend upon who is using drugs and how, can be made in relation to stimulants:

> Cocaine, amphetamines and newer drugs such as MDMA [ecstasy] are perceived as social problems only under certain conditions ... Drugs are ... likely to appear to be a threat to society when they are used by socially deviant groups. When coca leaves were chewed by Indian labourers, cocaine used by mostly wealthy elites and amphetamines by Japanese pilots, or Swedish housewives, they were considered socially beneficial. It was only when they started to be taken in excess by a tiny minority of the population

that they were withdrawn from use as part of the fabric of everyday life.

(Pickering and Stimson, 1994, pp. 1388–1389)

Many of those who have written on the subject of heterosexual behaviour, including Kinsey *et al.* (1948), have frowned upon any idea of 'hypersexuality', taking the view that this is a 'condition' created entirely by social reaction (e.g. Gold and Heffner, 1998). Explicit deviancy and labelling-theory explanations of other kinds of excessive appetitive behaviour are relatively rare, but Sargent (1979) is one author who presented a power-relations theory of drinking and 'alcoholism', in this case in Australia. Her view was that 'alcoholism' is used by those of high status in society as a means of social control of those of low status:

An 'alcoholic' is a person who has been subjected to social control processes, which both discredit him and assign to him a particular role which may prove irreversible; 'alcoholic' is also a stigmatising label applied by the most powerful to the less powerful in order to justify exercising social control.

(Sargent, 1979, p. 92)

In the context in which she was writing, it was the indigenous people who were of lower status, and Sargent cited figures for rates of imprisonment as sentences for drunkenness in 1973 which certainly showed a sharp differential between towns with a high concentration of Aboriginal people (48 per cent receiving custodial sentences), other rural areas (13 per cent) and the major urban area, Sydney (1.4 per cent). She cited high rates of labelling Navajo Indians as 'alcoholics' by Anglo-US Americans, and the council provision of beer gardens in white former Rhodesia (studied by Wolcott, 1974) as further examples of the use of 'alcoholism' as a means of social control and repression.

Although a thoroughgoing deviancy view of excessive appetites such as Sargent's or Brecher's has rarely been taken and cannot in this writer's view provide a complete understanding, there have been a number of theoretical statements which make good use of a social reaction perspective. For instance, there have been few better attempts to construct a social view of the process of developing an excessive appetite than Bacon's (1973) description of, 'the process of addiction to alcohol'. He was concerned to explain the progression from 'impulsive' drinking towards 'compulsive' drinking. The former was, '... relatively careless, capricious, whimsical, perhaps spur-of-the-moment; nor did it occur on every or almost every occasion ...' (p. 4), while the latter was, '... more commanding, more frequent, more demanding, less individually and more automatically determined ...' (p. 4). The progression appeared to involve a, '... strengthening of the tendency to use alcohol for reasons other than merely those attached to the drinking custom' (p. 4). In addition, however, this progression was, he thought, aided by what he termed 'dissocialization'. An individual would show marked changes in terms of the groups to which he or she belonged, the movement being towards groups which tolerated more drinking and more drinking effects, and which in other respects were less demanding. This part of the process Bacon considered to be of vital importance on account of the behavioural control function of the groups of which a person is a member. Commentators on 1980s and 1990s heroin consumption in Britain noted the same social adaptations (e.g. Pearson, 1987; Taylor, 1993; and see Chapter Eleven).

In fact, Bacon was particularly at pains to correct what he saw as the undue emphasis usually placed upon the individual excessive user in the process. He pointed out that control processes are not learned by individuals alone, nor are they expected to be maintained without the collaboration of others. Losing control in his view was a phenomenon involving the actor and others. The 'symptoms' of 'alcoholism' were such because they were offensive or insulting to others. 'Alcoholism' could not in his view exist without the reactions of others, with the interaction revolving, '... around the individual's unusual and unacceptable use of alcohol ...' (p. 17). In particular, Bacon introduced the notion of 'disjunction in labelling'. The process of moving towards compulsive use was, he suggested, accompanied by increasing irritation, annoyance, distress and criticism from others, but particularly in the early stages this, often mild, negative social reaction was either not received at all by the drinker or could be lessened in its impact by misinterpretation or in other ways. Meanwhile, critics might be coming to label the excessive user as a problem drinker or 'alcoholic' to the point that others would speak of drinking as excessive even if the person had only had one drink or had not touched a drop for days. If this process proceeds to the point where the excessive drinker starts to be excluded from social groups, then the relationship between the drinker and, '... the carriers, signallers and enforcers of social control has been manifestly weakened' (p. 20). This is an example of the out-of-proportion response of which Lemert wrote, acting in a way that threatens to amplify excess.

Each of the forms of behaviour with which this book is concerned breaks social rules if it crosses certain, usually fairly indistinct, bounds between normality or moderation and excess or abuse. Social reaction is therefore a vitally important part of the necessary total account of excessive behaviour. Lemert's secondary deviance, created by social reaction, is undoubtedly a reality to some degree or other for anyone whose drinking, gambling, sexual behaviour, smoking, eating, exercising or drug taking becomes 'excessive' by their own definition or by the definition of any one person or group important to them, and Bacon's 'dissocialization' certainly becomes a reality for some. It must be said, however, that Lemert's distinction between primary and secondary deviance may be difficult to uphold. It suggests that primary deviance comes first, meets with social reaction, and that secondary deviance then ensues. Enough has been said already about the origins of different forms of appetitive behaviour to make it abundantly clear that pre-existing attitudes may affect behaviour very early, certainly before much of the learning process responsible for strong appetite has had a chance to occur. Ambivalence about drinking amongst Anglo-Irish youngsters or British Asians in London or Birmingham (Chapter Nine), is part of the social climate within which drinking behaviour develops, and is not just a reaction to the development of strong appetites on the part of a minority. The same can be said of the ambivalent attitudes to sex to which Boswell and Walter (Chapter Six) and generations since have been exposed during their upbringing, and of attitudes to gambling. Indeed, it might be said to be a chief characteristic of this whole range of appetitive behaviours that their use is attended by ambivalence. This is displayed by the concern that individuals and governments have shown in trying to draw distinctions between moderation and excess, by the need of legislators to create controls upon these behaviours, particularly upon behaviour of the young, and by the inconsistency that has been shown in the way these behaviours are defined and controlled from time to time and from place to place.

EXCESS AS COSTLY BEHAVIOUR

Important though social reaction is for a complete understanding of addiction, it is not the present view that addiction is socially constructed. The harms that follow the development of a strong appetite are real enough, and they impact upon individuals whose appetites have become excessive, as much as upon others who react to their behaviour.

Another way of viewing excessive behaviour is to see it, not as deviance, but as activity that incurs 'costs'. A constant theme of this book, and one that became a focus in Chapter Ten when trying to account for skewed population appetitive-behaviour distribution curves, is that excessive appetites cannot be understood without appreciating the importance of the balance struck between inclination and restraint, or, to put it another way, the balance between the positive and negative outcomes expected from behaviour at a particular stage of life. This view is that strong appetites can produce any of a whole range of effects some of which are harmful or may be perceived to be dangerous or potentially damaging. Some of these costs are physical, others are social. Some are immediately felt, others are anticipations. These negative effects may add to the pressures naturally restraining or disinclining a person from such behaviour.

Table 12.1 illustrates some of the costs or drawbacks that research has suggested are commonly associated with excessive alcohol, cocaine and cannabis use, gambling and eating. These pressures contrary to continued excessive behaviour or, to put it another way, pressures to conform to norms of moderation or abstinence, may be categorised in countless different ways. They might, for example, be listed under the three headings of *cost* (of resources spent in acquiring and consuming), *interference* (with other activities of the individual or of others) or *risk* (of future harm or discomfort). Alternatively they might be classified as *self*-generated pressures or pressures generated by significant *others*. The exact sources and extent of pressures felt by an individual towards the modification of appetitive behaviour will clearly depend upon social role, including whether the person has a family or not, what his or her occupation is, and upon the values and goals of the peer group. They will also depend, equally clearly, upon the particular form of appetitive behaviour involved. Some of the items shown in Table 12.1 may produce contrary pressures as a result of interference with other activities on account of a drug's pharmacological depressant effect. By contrast, pressure to modify smoking behaviour seems more likely to derive from the perception of risk of future bodily damage, and from awareness of continuing financial outlay. Heterosexual behaviour which is excessive may give rise to contrary pressure on account of social disapproval or the risk of it,

Table 12.1   Some of the costs or drawbacks of some forms of excessive appetitive behaviour.

Drinking (e.g. Orford *et al.* 1999b)	*Using marijuana* (e.g. Black and Casswell, 1992; Stephens *et al.*, 1993; Reilly *et al.*, 1998)	*Taking cocaine* (e.g. Murphy *et al.*, 1989; Ditton and Hammersley, 1996)	*Gambling* (e.g. Lorenz and Yaffee, 1984; Ladouceur *et al.*, 1994)	*Over-eating* (e.g. Fairburn and Wilson, 1993; Brody *et al.*, 1994)
Becoming argumentative	High cost	Physical effects (e.g. nose irritations)	Loss of money, debt	Feeling uncomfortably full
Hangovers	Illegality	Restlessness, insomnia	Borrowing and stealing	Putting on weight, danger of obesity
Affecting close relationships	Energy and vitality affected	Expense	Stress symptoms	Self-disgust, guilt feelings
Cost	Memory and concentration effects	Depression	Depressed moods	Solitary eating (and vomiting and purging)
Feel losing control	Concern about health	Disruption of personal relationships	Missing time from work or school	Feeling out of control

conscience and risk of physical infection. If sexual appetite is of the order that Walter claims his to have been (Chapter Six), then effort, financial loss and interference with other activities may also constitute important sources of disincentive.

Both the perceived benefits and the perceived drawbacks of appetitive behaviour are subject to individual differences of multiple origin and both are affected by developmental changes. Hence, the resultant is difficult to predict for any one person at any given time. The importance of the development of increasing strength of appetite lies in the way this balance is altered as a result. The final effect is highly uncertain, for, as inclination increases with appetite development, so too does the probability that increased 'costs' will operate as potential restraints upon further behaviour. A relatively strong investment in gambling, for example, carries greater risk of incurring financial 'costs', and an increased attachment to drinking, physical 'costs'.

There are at least two ways in which the operation of increased costs is variable: first their operation is highly relative; and second, as each comes into play, it may further alter the individual's circumstances and hence shift behavioural inclination in a direction and to a degree which it is difficult to anticipate. The first of these points should require little elaboration. People's circumstances are different, and so too are the cultural, social and family attitudes and values which govern their own reactions to behaviour and those of the people they mix with. Tolerance levels vary, and hence what counts as inappropriate behaviour is not a constant. What constituted excessive sexual behaviour on the west coast of Ireland in the 1960s is not the same as what would count as excessive in London in the 1990s, and what counts as excessive drinking is not the same among British Asian Muslims as amongst white Britons. Hence, what is felt as a cost of appetitive behaviour, and what leads to pressure for restraint will vary from place to place, from time to time and from person to person. This applies with greatest force to social costs generated by others, but as personal conscience is formed out of the milieu in which a person was socialized, it applies with almost as much force to many of the self-generated sources of restraint.

A brilliant illustration of the foregoing point is provided by Carstairs' (1954) anthropological account of the use of daru (a potent form of distilled alcohol) and bhang (an infusion of the leaves and stems of Indian hemp—cannabis) which he observed during a year spent in a large village in the state of Rajasthan in northern India. It was the contrast between the drug use and associated opinions of the two highest and most privileged caste groups, the ruling or warrior caste (the Rajputs) and the religious leaders (the Brahmins), which struck Carstairs most forcibly. As fighters, the Rajputs had the privilege of being allowed to eat meat and drink alcohol, and from Carstairs' account it appears they took full advantage of both, and their use of alcohol very frequently produced obvious intoxication associated with sexual and aggressive disinhibition. By contrast, the Brahmins unequivocally denounced the use of daru as being quite inimical to the religious life. Holy men insisted that a darulia (an 'alcoholic') was beyond salvation. Yet Carstairs witnessed time and again respectable Brahmins drunk on bhang, a state of intoxication which they believed not only to be no disgrace, but actually to enhance the spiritual life.

Carstairs made it his business to talk to as many villagers as possible about their views on daru and bhang. What struck him here was that while the Brahmins were unanimous in their negative views on daru, the Rajputs displayed towards this alcoholic beverage the same type of ambivalence with which we are familiar in large parts of the West. Many Rajputs were proud of drinking with discrimination. For example, 'My father used to drink a fixed quantity of daru from a small measure, every night. It was his niyam, his rule' (p. 226). Restraint, and the use of small measures, were stressed in discussion, particularly when emphasising religious values and observances. On the other hand, during evening hospitalities and in association with fighting, these restraints seemed easily forgotten. As one informant said, 'In time of war, when the drum beats, only opium and daru drive out fear' (p. 227). Age was probably a significant variable in the village of Carstairs' observations, as elsewhere. For example, 'Sahib, I am not interested in these things. These religious matters, usually one begins to be interested in them after the age of 50' (p. 228). In contrast to their emotive, but markedly ambivalent, attitude towards daru, the Rajputs held a phlegmatic and seemingly more objective view of bhang. For example, '... it's not a thing I like. It makes you very sleepy and turns your throat dry ...' (p. 228). The Brahmins too were matter of fact rather than lyrical about duru, but much more positive about bhang, seeing it as an aid to devotional acts, the practice of austerities of one kind or another and a general asceticism.

In a study that remains one of the best on drinking norms, McKirnan (1977, 1978) examined norms relating to the recognition of drinking problems in three contrasting areas in Montreal in Canada—a lower income area, a solidly middle-income area and an affluent suburban community. Respondents were asked to say how much they thought they themselves, a 'social drinker', a 'problem drinker' and an 'alcoholic', would be likely to drink (on average, maximum and minimum) in four different circumstances (lunchtime on a workday, in the evening with family, at a social event, while alone). Analysis revealed a significant main effect of type of community, anticipated alcohol consumption decreasing steadily from the low- to middle- to high-socioeconomic-status area. The more interesting results, however, concerned the range given by respondents between maximum and minimum consumption. Ranges were consistently greatest for the low-income area and least for the high-status community. The effect of these differences in range was to make the drinking norms for different categories of drinker much less distinct in the lowest income area. Whereas in the affluent suburban community respondents generally saw no overlap at all between their own drinking or the drinking of a typical social drinker and that of a problem drinker, there was more overlap in the middle income group and a great deal of overlap for the lowest status community (McKirnan, 1977). The implication was that tolerance of drinking considered deviant in some other communities would be highest in the lower income community, and labelling as 'problem drinker' or 'alcoholic' would not be made so readily there, at least on the basis of drinking quantity alone. McKirnan speculated that in such communities the *how* and *where* of drinking might be more important than how much.

The importance of social factors in the process of identifying and labelling deviance of the excessively appetitive type is nowhere better illustrated than in the literature on excessive eating. From Dwyer *et al.*'s (1970) classic paper entitled *The Social Psychology of Dieting* onwards the evidence has been abundantly clear that concern about weight and dieting behaviour are strongly associated with such variables as age, sex, social class and ethnicity, but particularly sex. Like all other investigators since then, Dwyer *et al.*, reviewing the evidence existing at that time, found women much more frequently than men showing concern about their weight and reporting dieting behaviour. For example, Dwyer *et al.* (1969) had found that 16 per cent of high-school senior girls and 19 per cent of the boys could be classified as overweight, but that over 80 per cent of the girls, in contrast with less than 20 per cent of the boys, expressed a wish to weigh less than they did, and 60 per cent of the girls but only 24 per cent of all boys had ever dieted. Almost all girls, other than the leanest, wished to weigh less than they did, while most boys at all weight levels wished to be heavier than they were. They cited studies showing that girls were more likely to know their weights accurately than were boys, and to weigh themselves more frequently. Similar findings are regularly reported up to the present time. For example, Wardle and Marsland's (1990) study of white, black and Asian teenagers in London schools (Chapter Nine) found the familiar marked sex differences, girls being significantly more likely to describe themselves as fat, more likely to judge parts of their bodies as 'too big', expressing more dissatisfaction with their bodies overall, and being more likely to say that they wanted to lose weight (57 per cent of the girls versus 23 per cent of the boys).

Another study of over 300 first-year psychology undergraduates at a university in South Australia found that women students were much less satisfied with their weight than were men, in the direction of wishing to be thinner, although objectively the women students were less heavy relative to their height. The majority of women (56 per cent) rated themselves as overweight to some degree, which was true of fewer men (27 per cent). On average, women wished to be 4 kg lighter than they actually were whereas men wished themselves to be 0.33 kg heavier. Women scored significantly more highly on the restrained eating scale that was used in the research. The correlation between actual weight and subjective overweight was significantly lower for women than for men (0.43 versus 0.69). For women, the greater the degree of subjective overweight the lower their self-esteem, whereas for men the opposite was the case (Tiggemann, 1994).

The second point, that the result of accumulating costs is difficult to anticipate, also requires relatively little elaboration. Increased costs may make for more effective restraint, but instead, or in addition, they may serve to *increase* the functional value of the appetitive behaviour. For instance, the increased nagging of a family member in response to eating that is seen as inappropriate or excessive may prove a source of restraint which is effective either temporarily or permanently. Alternatively, it may act to increase the over-eater's anxiety or level of frustration, or to strengthen cognitive tactics which bolster sentiments supporting current behaviour. Relatively extreme costs, such as marital breakdown, job loss or imprisonment, may act as brutal shocks which bring about self-restraint (or bring the gambler or drinker to his personal 'rock-bottom' to use an AA and GA expression), but alternatively may deprive the individual of the very social supports and resources which constituted the main sources of pre-existing restraint upon further excess.

Views of excessive behaviour as harmful or 'costly' social behaviour, or as deviance, are difficult to reconcile with a diagnostic view as enshrined in systems such as DSM (American Psychiatric Association's *Diagnostic and Statistical Manual*) or ICD (World Health Organisation's *International Classification of Diseases*). The former suppose that behaviour becomes of concern and leads to attempts at help-seeking and modification, the more it is seen to be creating harm, or the further it crosses the boundary between behaviour defined as normal and that thought to be excessive. The boundary is wide and unclearly marked and its position is highly socially and culturally relative. The latter, on the other hand, supposes that there are signs and symptoms, albeit often difficult to detect and clustering in different ways for different people, indicative of a diagnosable entity. The difficulty of applying the latter approach is obvious in the case of excessive sexuality (although Chapter Six made it clear that there have been many attempts to diagnose 'hypersexuality' or sex addiction), and perhaps in the case of excessive gambling and excessive exercising also, but all the chapters in Part I, without exception, illustrated the inconsistent and arbitrary ways in which supposed diagnosable entities have been defined.

The recognition of excess is not simply a matter of making a correct 'diagnosis'. What is 'excessive' is personally or socially defined and depends upon a person's age, sex, socioeconomic status, social network, responsibilities and a host of other factors. Equally relevant are characteristics of those such as family or general medical practitioner who know a person well enough to be in a position to add their own influential judgements as to whether behaviour is excessive or not. The more important question is not whether Jill is or is not suffering from bulimia or whether John is or is not an alcoholic, but whether they and others who have influence with them think their eating and drinking is excessive and should be controlled.

The importance of sex differences in eating concern and dieting gives us important insight into the nature of strong appetite more generally. The relationship between a young woman and her eating, if she perceives herself to be becoming heavy, who views herself as unattractive when overweight, who increasingly wishes to hide herself from social gaze, particularly that of men, and who is struggling unsuccessfully to modify her eating, is fundamentally different from the relationship between a young man and his eating where there is happy oblivion regarding the putting on of weight, and a perception of weight being associated with toughness, sporting ability and perhaps with a capacity for holding drink. The relationship between these two hypothetical people and their eating would be quite different even if pound for pound they had been eating equal amounts, and even if it was the case that they would experience an equal degree of struggle if they had equal motivation to reduce weight. It may reasonably be argued that strength of appetite or degree of 'dependence' is equal in these two cases. On the other hand, the psychology of someone who is subject to strong pressures towards reducing appetitive behaviour, but who finds these pressures met by equally strong inclination towards continued appetitive behaviour, is quite different from that of someone who does not experience such pressures.

My view has always been that contrary pressures deriving from awareness of the harmful consequences of drug use or other appetitive behaviour are not only important for an understanding of 'dependence', but are actually definitive of it. It is not just that 'addiction' is not apparent until a person wishes to give up drug use or until other people put pressure upon him or her to do so, but rather that the very notion of 'dependence' has no meaning until such circumstances pertain. Dependence can only be seen to exist to the degree that pressure is put upon the individual, or some incentive offered him or her, to reduce behaviour that has become excessive.

It is to underline this point that the adjective 'excessive' has been used throughout this book. It will be argued by some that 'excessive drinking', 'excessive gambling' and 'excessive heterosexual behaviour' are inadequate terms because they cannot be defined; they depend upon individual attitudes, social circumstances and cultural mores. This is exactly the point, however. It is just because definitions of what constitutes 'alcohol dependence', 'compulsive gambling', 'hypersexuality', drug 'abuse', 'over-eating' and 'obligatory running' are individually, socially and culturally relative that the word 'excessive' is so appropriate. The word offers no pretence that these things constitute entities that can be precisely defined and counted and compared across different social and cultural groups. As Cohen (1971) put it in his book, *Images of Deviance*, '... a problem can only be a problem to somebody. So, whenever we see terms such as deviance and social problems, we must ask: "Says who?"' (p. 17). Similarly, if we say that appetitive behaviour is excessive, we must ask: 'Exceeds whose definition of normal or moderate?'

APPETITIVE CONFLICT

The development of a strong appetite alters in a fundamental way the balance that has to be struck between inclination and restraint. What characterises a strong and troublesome appetite, as distinct from relatively trouble-free, restrained, moderate, or normal appetitive behaviour, is the upgrading of a state of balance into one of conflict. The difference is between behaviour which is mostly kept within moderate limits by a variety of discriminations and restraints, the influence of which may scarcely be consciously realised, and behaviour which gives rise to information that behaviour is 'in excess', is deviant, costly or should be brought under a greater degree of control. This 'information' may be conveyed by other people, by a mismatch between awareness of one's own behaviour and some idea about proper or ideal behaviour, or through bodily state or by some other means. At one end of the continuum lies unremarkable behaviour characterised by relatively little inclination and requiring little obvious restraint to keep it within bounds. At the other end lies behaviour that excites much emotion and arouses much comment, which seems to be characterised by a powerful drive, and which calls for relatively vigorous efforts at control. Either the person herself, or others or both are dissatisfied with the person's conduct. Either the person or others would like him to do less of it, or to do it less often or at different times, in different places or with different people, or else would like him to give it up altogether.

In fact, a number of early attempts were made to conceive of habitual appetitive behaviour in terms of balance or conflict. Although the general idea of a balance of incentives and disincentives has now been incorporated into mainstream addiction thinking, for example in the form of motivational interviewing and motivational enhancement (W. Miller and Rollnick, 1991; and Chapter Thirteen), this earlier theorising and some of its insights are not so well known in the field. This is despite the fact that one set of ideas (Heilizer, 1964) was put forward in the context of a discussion about alcohol, another (Astin, 1962) about 'bad habits' with special reference to drug addiction, and the third (Janis and Mann, 1968) about tobacco smoking. That these valuable contributions to theoretical discussion about excessive behaviour have been comparatively ignored can be partly attributed to the insulation of the specialist field of 'addiction' studies from the wider discipline of psychology, and partly to the general resistance there has been in the past to viewing an 'addiction' such as 'alcohol dependence' as an example of habitual behaviour.

Both Astin and Heilizer based their ideas on the model of approach-avoidance competition put forward by N. Miller (1944) and studied by him and others using laboratory animals trained to approach food and to avoid shock in the same place. Miller explained the experimental findings in terms of two gradients, one for the approach tendency (inclination towards appetitive indulgence in present terms) and the other for the avoidance tendency (restraint), with the strength of both tendencies increasing with nearness to the goal (the act of 'consumption'). Of particular interest in the present context was the suggestion that the degree of conflict was proportional to the height of the two gradients above the horizontal axis at the point of their intersection. This enabled a diagrammatic representation to be made of the contrast between a relatively low level 'normal' balance of motives which excited relatively little subjective distress and, on the other hand, a relatively intense conflict of two strong motives which was accompanied by marked ambivalence and distress.

Miller (1944) had assumed that the avoidance gradient was the steeper of the two (i.e. that restraint became *relatively* stronger the nearer the animal or person to the consumptive act). What was particularly intriguing about Astin's and Heilizer's theoretical contributions was their independent criticism of that assumption. They argued that when drinking behaviour, drug taking or 'bad habits' in general are involved, then the appetitive approach inclination may well become relatively *stronger* as the goal (the consumptive act) becomes closer. Interestingly, they reached this conclusion from different principles. Astin argued from the principle of *temporal contiguity* of behaviour and reinforcement. If the rewarding consequences of drug taking, for example, followed relatively soon upon consumption, while the punishing consequences were delayed (assuming a fairly immediate drug effect but delayed social harm), then the approach inclination would rise more steeply than the inclination to retreat from consumption as the goal was advanced upon. Heilizer's argument, more convincing to the present author, was that the relative steepness of appetitive and restraining inclinations (approach and avoidance motives) depended upon the relative importance of *internal and external cues*. As discussed in Chapter Ten, in the case of habitual appetitive behaviour, appetite may be strongly cued by external stimuli (the sights and sounds of people and places associated with gambling, for instance, or the sights and odours accompanying favourite foods) which become more and more prominent as the act of placing a bet or eating food is approached, while restraining cues may be largely internal cognitive representations of past and likely, but not totally certain, future events (e.g. what one's husband or wife will say, or what one will look like next week, or how much money one will have tomorrow), the force of which is likely to remain relatively constant as the act of consumption gets nearer. Hence, both authors, for different reasons, considered that the circumstances of the habitual drinker or drug taker might be that represented in Figure 12.1.

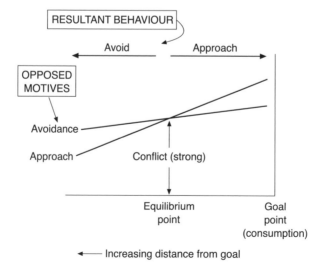

Figure 12.1   Avoidance-approach appetitive conflict: unstable equilibrium.

One consequence of viewing appetitive conflict in this way is that the dissonant smoker or drinker, attempting to refrain, experiencing avoidance-approach conflict, is in a state of 'unstable equilibrium' with the resultant of motives being such as to remove him, in one direction or another, further away from the point of intersection of gradients. Further *from* the goal than the intersection point, he should retreat still further from the goal, but between the intersection point and the goal he would be expected to experience an increasingly strong resultant inclination to smoke or drink. Behavioural self-control should be relatively easily exercised well away from the goal, but would be expected to be lost relatively easily if the drinker or smoker found herself, for whatever reason, beyond the danger point of no return.

These useful ideas provide one possible psychological explanation for the experience of 'loss of control'. The subjective experience of having an inclination so strong that self-control is severely diminished is a reality for people who experience strong and troublesome appetites, and whose personal accounts are full of references to the controlling influence of their desires and to the personal tactics and strategies which are adopted, some successfully some unsuccessfully, to try to reinstate self-control. One excessive gambler described giving his wife his week's wages for safe keeping and trying to ensure that he never went out with more than a pound in his pocket; another was driven to spend all day sitting in church to escape the temptation of betting. An excessive eater banned all cakes and other fattening food from her kitchen, and an excessive drinker gave up spirits and deliberately set out for the pub late in the evening to restrict his intake. One excessive heterosexual tore up his list of contacts, and another, like Walter (Chapter Six), masturbated before going out in an effort to reduce his inclination.

People who seek help on account of excessive gambling frequently describe a form of 'loss of control' in which they enter a betting office intent on placing one bet only before coming away, only to 'find themselves' still there several hours later having placed a series of bets and usually having lost a lot of money. Similarly, people who seek help on account of apparently compulsive over-eating often describe the struggle not to give in to the temptation of eating, say, a sweet biscuit, only to find that when the temptation is yielded to they 'lose control' and consume the whole packet and more. The chapters in Part I amply documented the demanding nature of the drives experienced by those whose appetite for drink, drugs, gambling, eating, exercise or sex is excessive. Astin's and Heilizer's idea of avoidance-approach conflict, with the approach gradient the steeper of the two, suggests that 'loss of control' is an expected consequence of the kind of unstable equilibrium which this kind of conflict produces. People with appetites of this sort are constantly trying to keep away from sources of temptation, but if they put themselves, or perhaps accidently find themselves, in the way of temptation (the equivalent of being 'near' to the 'goal' in the animal experiments) then inclination becomes relatively stronger and stronger and resolve becomes more and more difficult to maintain.

Thus, the element of conflict, introduced once appetitive behaviour becomes at all excessive by the standards to which the person concerned refers or is subject, changes the very nature of that behaviour in fundamental ways. Another feature which is likely to come into operation has been termed 'anticipatory anxiety'

(Rachman and Teasdale 1969). Pleasurable arousal at the prospect of appetitive indulgence is now a more mixed emotion, more likely to be described as tension or to be thought of as 'temptation'. For someone whose training has become 'obligatory' or who is conscious of fighting the urge to succumb to enter a betting shop or to buy an item of fattening food, the very prospect can produce a state of uncomfortable anxiety, even near panic. This, of course, produces a new dimension in the person's motivational state. One way of looking at it is to say that the anticipation of action makes acute the conflict that exists for the person over this particular kind of behaviour, and that indulgence is one way of temporarily resolving this aversive state.

In a sense, people experiencing avoidance-approach conflicts over gambling, drug taking or sexual behaviour are 'restrained' in the same way as a 'restrained eater' (see Chapter Five) and would be expected to indulge their appetites in compulsive binges similar in form to those of the 'binge eater'. In their discussion of binge eating, Wardle and Beinart (1981) put forward a very similar conflict view based on the idea of restrained eating. Some overweight individuals, under much social and medical pressure to reduce weight, plus diet-conscious people of moderate or even under-weight, were, they suggested, in an approach-avoidance conflict in relation to food. In their view this conflict led to 'externality'—eating largely being determined by external cues such as the smell, sight and taste of food, the sight of others eating and the passage of time. This proposed link between conflict and externality would lend support to Heilizer's particular model of avoidance-approach conflict and excessive appetitive behaviours which stressed the increasing importance of external cues associated with the appetitive object as the 'goal' or consummatory act was approached. Support for that model also comes from the more recent move towards highlighting associational learning and cue reactivity in the addictions generally (see Chapter Ten).

Wardle and Beinart (1981) suggested that an eating binge was a 'kind of capitulation' in the light of the belief that the decision to diet has already been broken. They pointed out that this is analogous to the response of an excessive drinker who attempts abstinence, but after one drink gives up and goes on a binge—the 'abstinence violation effect' (AVE). First put forward in the context of excessive alcohol use, the concept of AVE was later broadened out, in a way that made it much more compatible with the general view of excessive appetites being developed here, to include, '. . . any violation of a self-imposed rule governing consummatory behaviour' (Cummings *et al.*, 1980, p. 297). Cummings *et al.* described two components to the AVE: cognitive dissonance about the 'relapse' which was greater the longer the preceding period of abstinence and the greater the degree of private and public commitment to abstinence; and self-attributions of blame, personal weakness and failure which might provide the justification for and prediction of continuing excessive behaviour.

Grilo and Shiffman (1994) tested the prediction, derived from AVE theory, that people who had experienced stronger AVE following a lapse from self-control would be more likely to experience escalation. In the context of this study the prediction was that women who experienced feelings of guilt and self-blame, and a cognitive component involving self-attributions that were internal, global and uncontrollable, would go on to have a subsequent binge more quickly. They adopted the interesting strategy of conducting telephone interviews with women who regularly binged in order to obtain their accounts of bingeing as quickly as possible after binges had actually occurred. The 50 women who took part had been recruited via newspaper advertisements and were only included if they binged a minimum of once every 2 weeks but not more than once every 2 days. Telephone calls were scheduled at twice the reported binge frequency (e.g a woman who reported bingeing every 2 days was telephoned daily) in order to maximise the likelihood of contacting participants between discrete binge episodes and thus being able to focus on a single episode in the interview. Descriptions of two successive binges were obtained.

As predicted, latencies between one binge and the next were shorter when women had made internal and global attributions following the first binge, with less strong and less consistent results for uncontrollability and guilt feelings. Grilo and Shiffman ruled out the possibilities that significant results could be due to differences in severity of binges or to individual differences in general attributional style. They discussed several possibilities: that the attributional components of AVE might result in generalised feelings of helplessness and hopelessness which are associated with impairments in performance and coping; that comparing one's behaviour with a previous internal standard (e.g. being a perfect dieter) might also produce distress which might be coped with by further bingeing; or that a woman might attempt to cope mentally by redefining her self-image to fit the behaviour (e.g 'this just shows I am a powerless binger'). The last of these arguments is consistent with findings from smokers reported some years earlier by Eiser (1987) who found that the stable attribution 'I am hooked' was associated with lower levels of confidence in giving up smoking and hence with a lower level of intention to try to do so.

In the course of his study, mentioned in Chapter Eight, of 50 women who were being assessed for 'eating disorders' at a clinic in the USA, Hsu (1990) reported on statements that women reported making privately to themselves in the early part of an eating binge. Many of these correspond to the supposed components of AVE, and certainly Hsu took the view that they contributed to perpetuating the binge. One of the commonest types of statement was of the kind, 'Now that I've done it, I might as well go all the way'. The majority of women in the study reported making such self-statements early on in at least half of the binges they experienced. Other common themes were: bad feelings and self-condemnation (16 women reported saying things such as: I feel so bad, I feel awful, I feel guilty, I hate myself, you did it again, I'll never be a normal person, Once again I have not been strong enough, I deserve this); binge in order to vomit (12 women made self-statements such as: The fuller I feel it's easier to purge, Now I have to get rid of this, This is better than getting fat, I ate so much I have to get rid of this otherwise I will get fat); bewilderment over loss of control (11 made statements such as: Why can't I stop?, Why can't I control this?, Why am I doing this?, Why do I need this?, What's wrong with me?, I should have just taken a bite, I wonder when I'm going to stop); giving up (8 made statements such as: This is the last time, I will do good tomorrow, I won't eat anything tomorrow, I'll be stronger next time); and 5 admitted to wanting to binge because it was enjoyable (I might as well enjoy it, I really enjoy this, it tastes pretty good). Trachtenberg (1988) recognised the

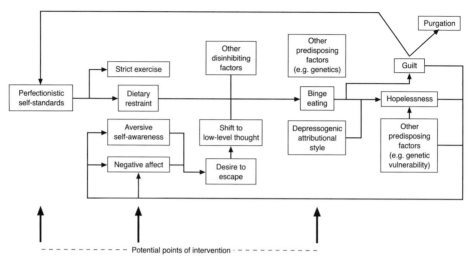

Figure 12.2   An integrative model of bulimia (reproduced from Beebe, 1994 by permission of the *British Journal of Clinical Psychology*, © The British Psychological Society).

importance of something very similar in the maintenance of excessive sexuality when he wrote: 'There is an element of resignation in the Casanova's surrender to the call of Eros, as though he were saying, "I know I shouldn't, but what the hell"' (p. 73).

Beebe (1994) provided a very helpful summary and appraisal of existing theories of the psychology of 'bulimia', finding support for a number of hypotheses, including the restraint hypothesis (individuals who consciously restrict their eating are more prone to binge, bingeing reflecting the loss of dietary control caused by interference with restraint), the escape hypothesis (thinking during a binge is 'narrowed' to reduce aversive self-awareness and negative affect produced by comparing the self against high standards—see Chapter Eight) and the hopelessness hypothesis (depression results from the perception of inability to control eating behaviour attributed to internal, stable and global causes). The restraint and escape hypotheses are most relevant to understanding events leading up to bingeing and purging, whereas the hopelessness hypothesis is most relevant to events following bingeing including during and after purging. Beebe found evidence for and against each of these theories alone and recommended an integration which is depicted in Figure 12.2, and was described by him in the following terms:

> In this model, bulimics hold themselves against high standards, potentially leading both to restrained eating and aversive self-awareness. Disinhibition may result from cognitive, pharmacological or emotional interference with the high-level thinking involved in dietary restraint. This emotional interference may be due to a motivated shift to low levels of thinking in response to aversive self-awaresss. As level of cognition is lowered, eating behaviour is disinhibited, leading to the binge. However, once higher-order thought resumes after the binge, bulimics may experience heightened

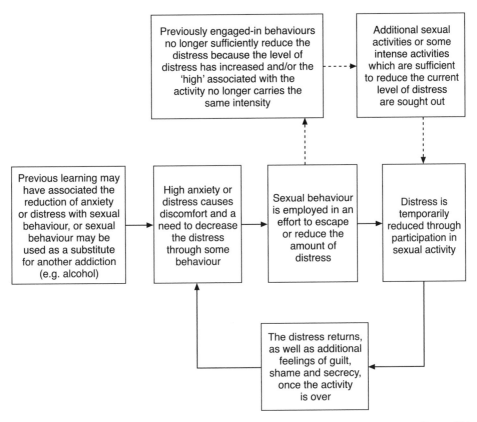

Figure 12.3 A cyclical model of sexual addiction (reproduced from Gold and Heffner, 1998 by permission of Elsevier Science).

> guilt and hopelessness, exacerbated by a pre-existing depressogenic attributional style. This hopelessness may maintain negative affect and aversive self-awareness, perpetuating and exacerbating bulimic symptoms.
> (Beebe, 1994, pp. 270–271)

Even such a comprehensive integration of psychological ideas about people's experiences leading up to, during and following an eating binge lacks a longer developmental perspective. The picture painted may represent a comparatively late-stage point in a descending 'spiral' (to use a word favoured by Beebe) that may have started in any one of a number of very different places. Stice *et al.* (1998) have questioned the often made assumption that bulimic symptoms are simply a *response* to negative emotional states. They suggested that there was likely to be a circular process or spiral in operation in which bingeing and purging, initially used to control negative emotions, might then contribute towards a more chronic state of negative affect. Gold and Heffner (1998) also offered the cyclical, and rather similar, model of sexual addiction, which is shown in Figure 12.3. They proposed that anxiety or other emotional distress is temporarily relieved through engaging in the addictive sexual behaviour; that addiction then causes more anxiety, shame and guilt, as the person concerned creates new difficulties or exacerbates old ones as a result of his or her behaviours, thus augmenting the need to reduce anxiety; this increased anxiety then fosters a further engagement in sexually addictive behaviours.

In the case of conflicted smokers, also, a cycle of events and associated feelings has been described which has obvious parallels in other forms of appetitive behaviour. Meyer *et al.* (1973) called this cycle 'postponement and plunge' because it consisted of repeated alternations between delaying smoking because of feeling out of control and shameful, followed by increasing tension and 'relapse' into smoking. Each phase, delay or renewed smoking, brought its own rewards (a feeling of pride and control in the delay phase, release and relief at the renewed smoking phase), but each led to a fresh building up of feelings (tension or guilt) that promoted the next phase. This cycle they viewed as a very brief abstinence–relapse cycle in which there was no serious intention to quit. Other smokers were true 'oscillators' showing longer periods of abstinence before return to smoking.

THE CONSEQUENCES OF DISSONANCE

It is, according to the view being developed here, the sense of conflict attending the development of strong appetitive behaviour which accounts for much of the behaviour seen by others as characteristic of those with an 'addiction', and which at an individual level is responsible for most secondary deviance. Many of these characteristic, secondarily deviant, features of behaviour, summarised in Figure 12.4, might well be termed the 'consequences of dissonance'. These include ambivalence, vacillation and inconsistency, all characteristics that make people with excessive appetites awkward to 'treat' and unreliable as 'patients'. Subject to opposing motives of great strength it is difficult to know one's own mind let alone to behave with any consistency. Different elements in the 'balance sheet', as Janis and Mann (1977) called it, may be relatively salient at different times, depending upon such things as time elapsed since last consumption, nearness to the appetitive 'goal' and the presence of different 'audiences'. Shortly after an episode of consumption, when the full force of the harmful consequences has been felt and while they are still freshly in mind, in the safety of a clinic or hospital and in the presence of the staunchest advocates of reform (e.g. 'therapist' and husband or wife), sources of restraint may be most salient and may come most readily to mind and be most easily verbalised. At contrasting times, and in quite other company, other elements of the balance sheet may be more salient. Oscillating between periods of abstinence and periods of excessive drinking becomes the pattern for many excessive drinkers who have reached a stage of undeniable conflict about drinking, as does oscillation between periods of smoking and giving up smoking for many dissonant tobacco users and between periods of dieting and bingeing for many over-eaters.

Although modern scientists and practitioners might prefer it to be otherwise, these dilemmas, consequences of the development of strong appetites, are in large part moral ones. Matters of morality, conscience and values weigh heavily for

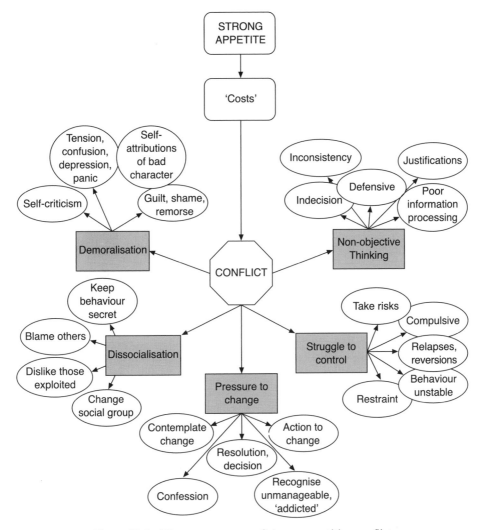

Figure 12.4 The consequences of strong appetitive conflict.

many people who seek help on account of the excessiveness of their appetites. Such moral 'costs', generated as a result of an awareness of mismatch between actual and ideal behaviour, are intertwined with the individual's awareness of more tangible physical and social harm, and with pressures put upon the individual by others who may be affected by the behaviour. It is a difficult task for the individual, or those who attempt to help him or her, to sort out which is which. Nevertheless, it is the case that, amongst the stated reasons for dissatisfaction, the need to restore 'self-respect', the desire to prove to oneself that one is in control of one's own behaviour or the need simply to do the right thing or to set a 'good example' for one's children, have a very important place.

Ambivalence is often associated with appetitive acts even in the early stages when such behaviour is first taken up. There is frequently a moral aspect, touching on notions of right and wrong conduct, even then. Moral dilemmas can arise in relation to each of the appetitive behaviours discussed, but are perhaps particularly evident in the case of sexual behaviour. Proscriptions on sexual behaviour in medieval Christianity (Bullough, 1977), and continuing through the centuries, taking a particularly powerful form in the 'purity movement' in late Victorian and early 20th-century Britain (Mort, 1987, 1998), have left a legacy of ambivalence and guilt surrounding sexual activities. The same may be said to differing degrees about indulgence in gambling, drinking, some other forms of drug taking and even of over-indulgence in eating. Myerson (1940) linked sexual behaviour and the use of alcohol in terms of the deep ambivalence which there is about each of them in Western thought, and in particular in terms of the conflict, which each gives rise to, between the opposing principles of hedonism and asceticism. Appetite, argued Myerson, was easy to understand, producing a, '... native pleasure which once experienced becomes consciously sought for' (p. 13), and in the case of the ingestion of food or the sexual act it is biologically functional. Asceticism, on the other hand, '... is a trend which, at least on the surface, runs counter to desire and satisfaction which is a denial of pleasure and its validity ... Pleasure in and of itself is stigmatised as unworthy except for the pleasure of renunciation and self-denial' (p. 13). The result was that each person brought up in a Western culture was, in the case of alcohol use and sex, bombarded by these two opposing sets of forces.

When the developmental processes outlined in Chapters Ten and Eleven have created a strong appetitive attachment, and behaviour has become more costly, and ambivalence has turned to distressing conflict, then moral issues are hard to avoid. The ethical elements in their appetitive conflicts are quite evident in accounts such as those of Tony Adams (Chapter Two), Dostoevsky (Chapter Three), Jan (Chapter Four), Miss C. (Chapter Five) and James Boswell (Chapter Six). Studies of the psychology of conscience and conflict and of the psychological effects of immoral actions point to some of the effects that are to be expected. These include self-criticism and remorse, a commitment to modify future behaviour, fear, guilt and shame, reparation, confession and reaction oriented towards external punishment (seeking out punishment or alternatively avoiding or escaping punishment by withdrawing from the vicinity of other people or hiding the consequences of one's acts) (Aronfreed, 1968; Klass, 1978).

An interesting set of findings concerns liking for the victim following an immoral action. The regular finding was that transgressions toward the victim resulted in increased *dislike* of that person, and this was particularly the case if the victim had few resources with which to retaliate. There are a number of possible explanations for that finding, one being that devaluation of a victim might arise from the feeling that the victim serves as an unpleasant reminder that one has broken a moral rule and hence is disliked.

These, then, are some of the further consequences we should expect from the development of strong and excessive appetite. In this light it comes as no surprise that studies of excessive drinkers and gamblers have found guilt, shame and secrecy to be 'symptoms' that are almost invariably present to some degree (Horn and Wanberg 1969; Orford *et al.*, 1996). Suicide is perhaps the ultimate response to chronic unresolved dissonance created by the rift between actual and ideal behaviour: the rate of suicide is known to be exceptionally high among excessive drinkers (e.g. Hawton, 1992; Vassilas and Morgan, 1997) and is believed to be similarly high among excessive gamblers (Dickerson, 1990).

Continued commitment to a form of behaviour which is harmful or troublesome calls for *dissonance reduction* in the interests of consistency. It is the central tenet of dissonance theory, which has been one of the most influential in attempting to explain the effects of attitude-discrepant behaviour, that the uncomfortable state of 'dissonance' arising from an awareness of behaviour being out of line with ideals, norms or expectations gives rise to motivation to reduce that state of discomfort. Thus, on theoretical grounds, if it is right to think of someone whose appetitive behaviour is excessive as essentially someone who faces a dilemma or conflict of a behavioural, conduct or even moral kind, we should expect such a person to experience discomfort and to be motivated to escape from it, much as people wish to escape from pain or anxiety. Indeed, this 'dissonance' should not be thought of as just theoretical, but as something very real, experienced as tension, depression, confusion or panic.

It is therefore only to be expected that people with an excessive appetite who continue to indulge that appetite will, as one dissonance-reducing tactic, attempt to justify the behaviour, either to themselves or to others. Such justification-promoting behaviour is probably to be seen as an integral part of excessive appetitive behaviour, even though it may appear quite transparent to the on-looker, and is yet another consequence of dissonance which makes its perpetrator yet more unpopular. The use of 'rationalisations' for behaviour is one way in which actions can be 'justified'. Davidson (1964), for example, asked continuing smokers for their reasons for continuing and called the replies that he received 'rationalisations'. These he classified as 'denials' (e.g. you can prove anything by statistics), 'demurring' (e.g. I have already cut down on my smoking), 'diversions' (e.g. polluted air is more dangerous), 'defiance' (e.g. I would rather enjoy life even if it is a bit shorter), 'gospels of moderation' (e.g. moderation is desirable in all things), 'doctrines of the lesser evil' (e.g. going without smoking makes me anxious, irritable, nervous and impossible to live with) and 'comments based on misinfor-mation' (e.g. there is no cancer in my family, so I don't have to worry). Boswell showed great inventiveness in rationalising his sexual excess when he appealed for support to the polygamy of the Old Testament patriarchs (Stone, 1979; see Chapter Six).

In the language of Janis and Mann's (1968, 1977) 'conflict theory of decision making'—another early model of appetitive conflict that has been influential in formulating a model of addiction as excessive appetite—the excessive drug taker, gambler or eater has begun to fall short of the ideals of 'vigilant information processing'. More will be said of this in Chapter Fourteen, when we consider the ways in which excessive appetites are successfully brought under control, but here we can usefully borrow from Janis and Mann's theory some ideas about the ways in which successful resolutions are avoided and how the conflict engendered by excessive behaviour and its consequences is perpetuated and in many cases worsened. Almost certainly, as we shall see in Chapter Thirteen, many people do in fact reduce their involvement in appetitive behaviour of one kind or another at various stages and at various levels of attachment. What concerns us here, however, is why many do *not*, despite mounting evidence, apparent at least to others, that the behaviour in question is harmful.

To the degree to which a strong affective–behavioural–cognitive attachment has formed to the behaviour, a significant 'loss' will be anticipated at the prospect of reducing one's involvement. The individual is in a sense 'committed' to appetitive behaviour which has become excessive. These were just the circumstances for decisional conflict according to Janis and Mann (1977). Emotions are involved: the ideas in play are 'hot cognitions' to use Abelson's (1963) vivid phrase. The stress associated with conflict is likely to produce in the, '... harassed decision maker ...', a '... further decline in cognitive functioning as a result of the anxiety generated by their awareness of the stressful situation' (Janis and Mann, p. 17). In plain language, it is difficult to think straight. Once again, then, we have a clear statement, this time from the perspective of the theory of decision-making, that conflict itself has consequences; that whatever led up to conflict, once conflict exists the psychological situation is no longer the same.

Besides 'vigilance' (scanning alternative solutions objectively) the main alternative styles of coping with decisional conflict according to Janis and Mann's model were 'hypervigilance', and 'defensive avoidance'. The first was likely, according to Janis and Mann, when conflict is severe but time to make a decision is short and the kind of scanning and weighing of alternatives that 'vigilance' involves are not possible. At its most extreme it resembles a kind of panic; thought processes are disrupted, memory span is reduced and thinking becomes simplistic. Although it was in the context of reactions to disaster warnings, or business decisions that have to be taken quickly, that 'hypervigilance' was most apparent to Janis and Mann, there are clear parallels with excessive appetitive behaviour. Excessive gamblers, for example, can reach a stage of near panic as a culmination of increasingly out-of-control gambling, mounting debts which are becoming quite beyond their capacity to cope with, and escalating social pressure and self-neglect. Cognitive functioning, in the sense of the ability for calm reflection and appraisal, is quite obviously impaired.

It is 'defensive avoidance', however, which has the clearest application to the decisional conflict faced by those with excessive appetites. As Lewin (1935) noted, there is a strong tendency for people to withdraw from making a decision at all if all the options that are open seem to involve major 'losses' or 'costs'. Cognitive-dissonance theorists have stressed that there is loss involved in all decisions, and that all decisions are followed by some dissonance, but decisions about excessive appetites are probably particularly good examples involving, as they do, either continued social and other losses from continued excessive behaviour, or the loss of a form of action that has served valued functions for the individual. Among tactics under the heading of 'defensive avoidance', Janis and Mann listed selective inattention to relevant informal or mass-media communications, distracting oneself, buck-passing and 'bolstering'. Signs of 'bolstering' included over-simplifying, distorting, evading, omitting major considerations, exaggerating favourable consequences, minimising unfavourable consequences, denying negative feelings about consequences, exaggerating the remoteness of any action required, minimising the social surveillance of new action ('no one will know if I don't live up to it') and minimising personal responsibility.

Their final tactic was recourse to alcohol or drugs! That Janis and Mann should recognise that excessive appetitive behaviour can provide a major alternative to dealing with decisional conflict, of which excessive appetites are themselves good examples, is an excellent illustration of the thesis being propounded here; namely, that excessive appetitive behaviour can take on additional dimensions as a result of the conflict it produces. Here is a prime example of such a process: further excessive behaviour (Janis and Mann could have added over-eating, gambling and excessive sexual behaviour as behaviours to which reluctant decision-makers have recourse) is itself one way of coping with the dilemma created by excessive behaviour. The 'vicious circle' is plain.

The universality of defensiveness in the face of an awareness of one's own excess was illustrated by interviews with active heroin 'addicts' in Karachi, Pakistan (Primrose and Orford, 1997). The wider context in which that study was carried out was an 'epidemic' of problem heroin use in a culture with strong values supporting, for example, family loyalty and responsibility and respect for elders. When participants' values were considered alongside their own drug-related behaviour, and their reactions transcribed and coded, one of the commonest forms of response was termed 'defensive'. This included what we called 'selective rationalisation' (e.g. 'I used to use it at home, because if I used it elsewhere, then the people of the neighbourhood would see what I was doing'), 'blame' (e.g. 'she bribed my friends to get me on to the drug'), 'perfection' (e.g. 'thank God I have never had to steal from my home to finance my habit'), 'denial' (e.g. 'I do not understand myself to be bad, because I only use a very little. If I become like *B*, left home, and stopped washing and changing my clothes, so obviously I will become bad'), 'attribution of good motives' (e.g. 'I tried to share the drugs that I have') and 'self-righteous' (e.g. 'before I got caught in this, I gave my children a good training').

These changes that accompany excessive appetites, and which have been attributed here to conflict and its consequences, have often been misconstrued in the past. The kind of mental face-saving or attempted justification which, it is being argued, follows from the conflict in which an excessive appetite places an individual, is not merely unpopular with other people but often gives rise to charges that the person concerned has not just a fault in behaviour but, more fundamentally, a fault in character. Nor is this just a layman's error. Indeed, psychiatric texts have often reflected considerable confusion about the link between forms of excessive appetitive behaviour such as alcohol and drug 'dependence', on the one hand, and aspects of character or personality, on the other. In some psychiatric systems of classification, these forms of behaviour were actually listed as 'personality disorders' and it has been known for psychometric tests of 'psychopathy' or 'personality disorder' to be validated against criterion groups which included 'drug addicts' and 'alcoholics' amongst the supposedly 'personality disordered' criterion group (P. Miller, 1980). This is probably because many of the consequences of dissonance outlined above are behaviours that might be seen, depending upon the perspective of the observer, as defects of *character*.

Attribution theory in social psychology provides a useful perspective here. Jones and Davis (1965) asked themselves how it was that an observer perceived a *disposition* in the person they were observing on the basis of the latter's behaviour: in short, how did they move, 'From acts to dispositions'—the title of Jones and Davis's classic contribution. Their theory was that of 'correspondent inferences'. Correspondence they defined as, '. . . the extent that the act and the underlying characteristic or attribute were similarly described by the inference' (p. 223). For example, if an individual is observed to be devious about his or her gambling or sexual behaviour, under what conditions will the inference be made that the individual is a devious *person*?

The answer Jones and Davis gave was that correspondent inferences would be made when the observer saw that the observed person had a reason for acting as he or she did (the intention), had knowledge that the act would produce the effect it did, and had the ability to bring the act and its effects about. In so far as appetitive behaviour is seen to be motivated by desire for pleasure or gain of some kind, and to the extent that the person is seen to have known what they were doing and to have had the ability to do it and to foresee the consequences, then the correspondent inference will be drawn. One variation on cognitive dissonance theory (Bem, 1967) in fact proposed that the individual herself draws inferences about her own behaviour in much the same way. This helps explain how it is that people with excessive appetites often wrongly draw the conclusion that their basic personalities or characters must be badly at fault to enable them to behave in a way so damaging to themselves and to others. It is not only other people who stand in judgement on the excessive drug taker, over-eater, excessive gambler or drinker, failing to understand the psychological processes involved: the man or woman involved is often his or her own sternest critic.

SUMMARY

The excessive appetites account of what addiction is and how it develops is now complete. Addiction, according to this perspective, is conceived of as a state of strong affective–cognitive–behavioural attachment to a particular activity. Drugs, or 'substances', constitute just one class of activities to which people can become strongly attached. Such strong attachments are costly, creating ambivalence for the person concerned, and bringing him or her into conflict with others. *Strong attachment* and *conflict* are the key terms.

The pathway from first involvement with activity to a state of conflict-creating strong attachment is often a long one, and the factors that are important along the way are many and varied. The different forms of excessive appetite, with their rather separate academic and professional literatures, have helped highlight different features of the development of strong appetite. Studies of teenage drug use, including tobacco, have focused our attention on the importance of friends' behaviour; research on gambling has suggested the importance of the structure of the activity itself and on people's cognitive beliefs about the activity; alcohol research has had particular strength in examining the possible mood-modifying functions of activities, including tension reduction and its alternatives; research on drugs, including amphetamines and cocaine, has encouraged us to look at possible brain reward systems; work on excessive eating has been particularly strong on the importance of restraint and its effects; and the literature on sexual addiction has helped us understand the role of conditioned associations as well as highlighting psychoanalytic views. At all points in the development of a strong appetite, social and cultural factors, often neglected in accounts of addiction, are of crucial importance. Such factors vary from the norms prevailing in one's social group, or the values in society associated with particular activities (e.g. the legal status of certain drugs, or values placed on certain body shapes), to unemployment and occupational status, or social or cultural deprivation and exploitation on a larger scale.

The conflictual attachment which is at the core of the present view of addiction is something that affects individual people and which places them at a distance from most of their contemporaries in terms of their level of engagement with and commitment to their particular activity. Strength of attachment develops over the years of a person's life, for some people deepening in the process. Control, restraints and discriminations are vital for keeping potentially excessive appetites constrained for most people most of the time. For some, on the other hand, they are eroded as part of an escalating or amplifying process which brings into play new sources of motivation. Thereby, many people find that an appetitive activity is no longer what it was, is no longer serving the same functions and is no longer as resistible. Many of those who find themselves in the grip of such a compelling process never consider having treatment for it (the subject of Chapter Thirteen), or otherwise making changes to halt or reduce the activity (Chapter Fourteen). The story of their excess stops here. For countless others, an understanding of their addiction is not complete without considering how excess is given up.

PART III

Overcoming Excess

CHAPTER THIRTEEN

The Place of Expert Help

[My mum] finally confronted me, and I did something which I'd never even thought of doing ... I told her everything—and that was the first massive step towards reaching the light at the end of the tunnel. Now that she knew everything I was able to talk to her ... enabling me to GIVE UP ... it was sheer will power ... with my family's backing to kick the [fruit machine] habit ....

(Respondent 11, male, aged 18, cited by Griffiths, 1993a, p. 40)

I give up, see I better give up drinking grog. I never get any tablet, anything, I just give up myself. I never drink. And today I never drink any beer or see them boys they drinking in my place and if they bite my arm for drink— nothing. They argue with ladies outside, that's why I give up today. This year early I give up the grog.

(A Torres Strait Islander, cited by Brady, 1995, p. 7)

In the previous chapter it was argued that excessive appetitive behaviour could not be properly understood without taking full account of conflict, ambivalence and dissonance over behaviour. Such behaviour cannot be comprehended unless cognisance is taken of the restraints and pressures which oppose it. Excessive appetitive behaviour is not just repetitive behaviour, but is repetitive behaviour which comes into conflict with other needs of the person or with those of other people in his or her life. The present chapter and the following one, which attempt to reach a psychological understanding of the processes that occur when people attempt to regain control over such behaviours, will pursue this line of argument by presenting a model based upon the resolution of conflicts. According to this way of understanding the problem, the task facing a person who has developed a strong and troublesome appetite is that of coping with the dissonance created between actual behaviour (e.g. gambling incurring heavy losses, sexual behaviour which runs counter to the person's moral standards, heavy drinking which threatens the stability of marriage) and sensible behaviour or right conduct (saving money, being monogamous, drinking socially and moderately). One set of options for the reduction of dissonance consists of actions and attitudes which will be construed by those who advocate change (family members, the person's medical practitioner, long-standing friends) as resistant or 'defensive'.

But another set of options consists of modifying appetitive behaviour to make it compatible with other needs, with other values or attitudes, or with the desires of other significant figures such as husband, wife and other family members. It is in fact the principal argument of Part III of this book that change, in the direction of moderation or abstinence, is a *natural consequence* of the development of strong appetite. To put it another way, it should be expected on theoretical grounds that adopting a new, reduced level of appetitive behaviour will be part of the natural history of strongly appetitive behaviour, following in some cases upon the development of distressing conflict as a result of the processes outlined in Chapters Ten to Twelve. A major problem in viewing change as a spontaneous, or naturally occurring process, is the qualification that it occurs as part of natural history in only a proportion of people whose appetitive behaviour develops to the strong and troublesome stage. Tony Adams successfully gave up his excessive drinking, but Peter Cook did not (Chapter Two).

EXPERT TREATMENT

Let us begin by considering the nature of some of the treatments that have been professionally prescribed for excessive appetitive behaviours. The most striking fact about these treatments is the great range and diversity of techniques which have been employed. It is not possible here to mention more than a proportion of them. Almost without exception they have been backed up by impressive rationales, and, although some have passed out of fashion, it is probably true to say that the majority still find favour somewhere. Table 13.1, for example, shows the list of treatments for excessive drinking compiled by Miller *et al.* (1995) in the course of their meta-analysis of treatment-evaluation studies. All that can be done here is to point out a number of facts regarding such impressive arrays of treatments.

Psychological treatments have been particularly diverse, and different forms of therapy have been in vogue for different types of behaviour at different times. Among behavioural therapies, aversion therapy, for example, has at some time or another been tried for almost all types of behavioural excess, but is no longer much practised. 'Rapid smoking', in which smokers were required to puff at a series of cigarettes much more rapidly than usual, appeared to hold great promise as a treatment for cigarette smokers at one time (Paxton, 1980), but then fell out of fashion, and 'self-control' procedures including 'self-monitoring', 'stimulus control', 'self-reward' and 'self-punishment' were fashionable in the 1970s when behaviour therapy for the treatment of excessive drinking, smoking and eating started to adopt a more human face and the idea caught on that people might 'be their own behaviour therapists' (the 'self-control' treatment movement— see Chapter Five). Other behavioural treatments used at that time or earlier included 'covert sensitisation' (a kind of aversion therapy in fantasy), video-tape confrontation for excessive drinking (being made to watch oneself intoxicated on video), and the use of 'deposit contracts' (depositing money at the outset of treatment which was returned in stages dependent upon appropriately moderate

Table 13.1 Treatments for excessive drinking which have been the subject of evaluation studies according to Miller *et al.*'s (1995) review.

Acupuncture	Community reinforcement	Metronidazole
Alcoholics Anonymous	approach	Milieu therapy
Antianxiety medication	Confrontational counselling	Motivational enhancement
Antidepressant medication	Covert sensitisation	Problem-solving training
Antipsychotic medication	Developmental counselling	Psychedelic medication
Aversion therapy, apneic	Disulfiram	Psychotherapy
Aversion therapy,	Educational lectures/films	Relapse prevention
electrical	Exercise	Relaxation training
Aversion therapy, nausea	Functional analysis	Self-help manual
BAC discrimination	General alcoholism	Self-monitoring
Behavioural contracting	counselling	Sensory deprivation
Behavioural self-control	Hypnosis	Social-skills training
training	Lithium	Systematic desensitisation
Brief intervention	Marital/family therapy,	Unspecified 'standard'
Calcium carbimide	behavioural	treatment
Client-centred therapy	Marital/family,	Videotape self-confrontation
Cognitive therapy	nonbehavioural	

Note: Miller *et al.* (1995) concluded that some forms of treatment, such as brief intervention and social-skills training, had received many more positive evaluations than others such as general alcoholism counselling and educational lectures/films.

or abstemious behaviour). Non-behavioural treatments have included just about the whole panoply of available techniques including individual non-directive psychotherapy, transactional analysis, hypnosis, marital therapy, family therapy and, perhaps most consistently popular of all, various kinds of group psychotherapy.

Behavioural treatments have continued to play a dominant role in the expert treatment of such excesses as smoking, eating and gambling. A large meta-analysis of treatments for tobacco smoking, for example, was carried out by Baillie *et al.* (1994). The results for all types of treatment were mixed, but overall they reported that simple advice and other brief interventions, nicotine gum, and various behavioural techniques (a mixed bag of rather poorly described interventions) each resulted in a higher proportion of smokers becoming abstinent than controls. Nicotine gum or patch combined with behavioural techniques has tended to produce better results than either alone (Cinciripini *et al.*, 1996, Richmond *et al.*, 1997).

More popular in the 1990s, to the point of becoming almost the number-one treatment of choice for most excessive appetitives in Britain and a number of other countries, has been 'cognitive-behaviour therapy' (CBT). CBT, as described by Thackwray *et al.* (1993) in the context of treatment for 'bulimia', focuses on:

> ... subjects' dysfunctional cognitive activity and binge–purge behavior ... with cognitive activity emphasized as a mediating factor between environmental antecedent events, behavior, and consequences. CBT incorporated both ... behavioral components ... and cognitive procedures focused on subject-specific dysfunctional beliefs and distorted cognitions. Specific CBT

procedures included cognitive restructuring, challenging dysfunctional beliefs, assertiveness, problem-solving skill building, and relaxation training. Self-monitoring data provided the basis for subject-specific examination of eating habits, cognitive distortions, and specific therapeutic suggestions. Modifications of cognitive distortions regarding food, weight, and body image were addressed in all cases. The therapist modeled challenging and clarifying of subjects' distorted thinking, and subjects were prompted to examine or reformulate their specific unrealistic rules and fears.

(Thackwray *et al.*, 1993, p. 641)

Two meta-analyses of the results of studies of the treatment of 'bulimia' have been reported, each reaching positive conclusions. Hartmann *et al.* (1992) analysed the results of 18 studies, mostly of cognitive and behavioural treatments, producing an average post-treatment effect size of 1.04 (i.e. the average difference in outcome between treatment and control groups was equivalent to just over one standard deviation in the distribution of outcome scores of controls). Effect sizes greater than 0.8 were described by Hartmann *et al.* as 'high'. Lewandowski *et al.*'s (1997) analysis was deliberately confined to studies that had taken a cognitive-behavioural approach to treatment. They found 26 such studies with mean post-treatment effect sizes of between 0.64 and 0.74 depending upon the exact outcome criterion. They described this as a 'large' effect, although Hartmann *et al.* (1992) would have rated this as only 'medium'. Unfortunately, these meta-analyses are limited by the absence of follow-up data. The requirements of the analysis prevented Hartmann *et al.* from including any such data, and Lewandowski *et al.* were able to include only a few such studies which produced between them a disappointing follow-up average effect size of 0.27. On the other hand, a particularly thorough follow-up study of treatment for 'bulimia-purging type' was reported from Germany by Fichter and Quadflieg (1997). As many as 94 per cent of the 196 women who entered 'broad spectrum behaviour therapy' were followed up 2 years later, and an impressive 96 per cent at a 6-year follow-up. The general pattern of results showed substantial improvement during treatment, a slight decline during the first 2 years of follow-up, with further improvement and stabilisation in the next 4 years. At the 6-year follow-up 21 per cent were considered still to be suffering from bulimia, a small number had shifted to other kinds of eating disorder, but 71 per cent were considered to show no major eating disorder by that time.

In the field of excessive gambling CBT has also become a leading treatment, taking over from aversion therapy which was popular in former years, although according to Blaszczynski and Silov's (1995) review there had been few methodologically strong studies of treatment for excessive gambling up to that time. The special value of the cognitive component in treatment for excessive gambling is based on the theory that cognitive distortions of one kind or another are an important element in maintaining problem gambling (see Chapter Ten) although greatest apparent treatment success had been produced in four studies using a multi-modal treatment approach which did not allow the value of the cognitive component to be isolated.

A further review of gambling treatment research was reported by López-Viets and Miller (1997). Their review covered psychodynamic, behavioural, cognitive,

cognitive-behavioural, multi-modal and pharmacological treatments, and Gamblers Anonymous (GA). They also found very few controlled studies in that field, but were able to report that the single case reports and small case series that had been reported had shown generally very encouraging results: it was not uncommon for two-thirds of problem gamblers to be abstinent or controlled at 6 or 12-months follow-up. The exceptional controlled studies were those reported by McConaghy *et al.* (1983, 1988) showing that imaginal desensitisation was better than aversion therapy but no better than imaginal relaxation (the significance of the latter finding will be taken up later), and the Spanish study reported by Echeburúa *et al.* (1994, cited by López-Viets and Miller, 1997) in which 64 excessive gamblers were randomly assigned to a waiting-list control or to one of three treatments including individual stimulus control with *in vivo* exposure and response prevention, and group cognitive restructuring treatment.

Sylvain *et al.* (1997) reported a small trial in which 29 excessive gamblers were randomly assigned to treatment or a waiting-list control group. The central element of treatment was the cognitive correction of erroneous perceptions about gambling, theoretically based upon the idea of cognitive distortions maintaining gambling, especially Langner's (1975) idea of the 'illusion of control'. Other elements of the treatment were problem-solving training, social-skills training and relapse prevention. Post-treatment results were significantly better for those in the treatment group. These good results were maintained at 6-months follow-up, although by that time no comparison with controls was possible.

One continuing feature of the expert-treatment picture is the important place occupied by drug treatments. Sometimes the rationale for medication has been the suppression of appetite; for example, the use of amphetamines as suppressants of the appetite for food (see Chapter Five) and antiandrogenic drugs to suppress sexual appetite (see Chapter Six). The 1990s saw a rise in popularity of certain pharmacological treatments for excessive drinking, including naltrexone, buspirone and acamprosate. The latter in particular, the precise action of which is unknown but which is thought to reduce craving by affecting several neurotransmitter systems including the GABA (gamma-aminobutyric acid) system (Pelc *et al.*, 1997), has become popular in countries where it is available. Schuckit (1996) reviewed the evidence for the efficacy of such treatments and concluded that clear, positive evidence was as yet lacking. He was particularly critical of the brief follow-up periods included in studies of acamprosate. Disulfiram (antabuse) has continued to hold a popular and unique place as a 'deterrent' drug which, when taken with alcohol, produces a highly noxious effect. Of particular interest is the fact that drugs with 'dependence potential' themselves, either known at the time or discovered later (e.g. morphine and heroin, see Chapter Four), have been widely used in an attempt to control strong drug-seeking behaviour. Tranquillisers and sedatives continue to be prescribed for people with excessive appetites, either to reduce anxiety or to combat symptoms of withdrawal from alcohol, tobacco or other drugs.

Drug treatments have sometimes been used quite explicitly as replacements for a drug used excessively. Best known is methadone (physeptone) pioneered by Dole and Nyswander (1965) as a treatment for heroin 'addiction' (Courtwright, 1997). The controversial rationale for its use is that, being a synthetic opiate, it relieves the craving set up by withdrawal of opiates, but, being a much longer acting agent, it requires to be taken less often and is less 'addictive'. Switching from illicit to medical supply should, at the same time, reduce the risks and harms associated with drug use. Finally, there is the intriguing fact that in the case of heroin and nicotine, at least, maintenance on prescribed doses of the drug itself has been used as a treatment. The prescribing of nicotine for smokers in the form of patch, spray or gum has become very popular (e.g. Russell, 1991 and see Chapter Four), part of the argument being that tar and other constituents of tobacco smoke are more harmful than nicotine itself. The argument for maintenance of heroin treatment is rather different; namely, that the harmful effects of regular heroin use lie more in the circumstances of its procurement and administration—involvement in criminal activity, use of unsterile apparatus, the risk of overdose—than in the fact of regular consumption itself.

THE SEARCH FOR BEST TREATMENTS HAS FAILED

The foregoing demonstrates two things. First, as we would predict from a consideration of the conflict that they are placed in as a result of the development of a strong appetite, people do often make changes in the direction of leaving off excess. As Schachter (1982) put it:

> It does appear that the generally accepted professional and public impression that nicotine addiction, heroin addiction, and obesity are almost hopelessly difficult conditions to correct is flatly wrong. People can and do cure themselves of smoking, obesity and heroin addiction. They do so in large numbers and for long periods of time, in many cases permanently.
>
> (Schachter, 1982, p. 442)

The second conclusion to be drawn about all the excessive appetites, as was concluded about excessive eating specifically in Chapter Five, is that the experts have been searching long and hard for the best treatment and in the process have been greatly creative in coming up with such diversity. This search has not been successful, however, and, as we shall see in this and the following chapter, the excessive appetites perspective would not lead us to expect that it would be.

The energetic search for successful treatments tells its own story. As Vaillant (1980) put it some years ago, each new treatment has its rationale and is pursued vigorously and optimistically by its initiators, but sooner or later turns out, when used routinely, to meet with much the same moderate level of success as did previous therapies. There is in fact a remarkable consistency in the conclusions reached by those who have reviewed studies of the effectiveness of treatment for different forms of excessive appetitive behaviour. When those receiving treatment have been randomly assigned to different forms of treatment, or when groups receiving different treatments have been carefully matched, the large majority of findings have been uniform (i.e. different treatments tend to produce very similar results). The difficulty experienced in demonstrating that any one treatment is superior to others, and the apparent uniformity in outcomes, should not be interpreted, as I hope to make clear later in this chapter, to mean that treatment never works. Nevertheless, it does have important implications for theory: it is what these conclusions may tell us about the nature of the processes underlying change which is of most interest here. Increased understanding of the change process may also add to our comprehension of the nature of excess itself.

Many reviewers have argued from the uniform treatment results that when treatments work they must be doing so because of the operation of 'non-specific' factors, or factors which are common to a variety of treatments despite their different theoretical bases and superficial appearances. Studies which particularly lend themselves to this type of interpretation include: those that compared a treatment having a strong theoretical rationale with one without such a rationale, the latter sometimes even contravening theoretically derived principles; those that have involved a comparison of treatments with contrasting theoretical rationales; and those that have found equal success with quite brief treatments or with simple advice or encouragement only.

An example of a study using a counter-theoretical treatment was one of a series of dieting experiments carried out by Ley *et al.*, (1974, cited by Ley, 1980). They used a 'willpower' control group who were recommended to carry out the opposite of the behavioural self-control procedures recommended to the main treatment-proper group. They were told, for instance, to shop only when hungry and to be sure to leave tempting foods around. No significant differences in weight loss were obtained. As Ley (1980) pointed out, all participants in that study received a lecture on weight control, and were monitoring their diet and their weight regularly. Similarly, a number of studies of treatment for smoking showed that conditions as supposedly different as support, contingent aversion therapy (aversive stimulation being delivered contingent upon smoking as dictated by theory) and non-contingent aversion (contrary to theory), had no differential effects on outcome (Carlin and Armstrong, 1968; Russell *et al.*, 1976). Similarly, Keutzer (1968) found that placebo capsules or tablets given under circumstances in which the, '... characteristics of the ... treatment setting and verbal communication of therapeutic intent [were] preserved', thus imparting an, 'illusion of authenticity', produced as much success in comparison with a no-treatment control group, as was produced by treatments such as 'coverant control' and 'negative practice' which were favoured at the time. Almost incidentally Keutzer added the very significant statement that common to all treatments was, as he put it, '... the collection of smoking data, the dispensation of resolution rearmamentation ... and discussion ...'. It is just these elements which, according to the view of treatment to be offered in this and the next chapter, are among the really effective ingredients of the change process.

Of particular note are studies appearing to show that treatments can be equally effective despite having totally different, and often quite contrasting theoretical bases. The most convincing such study is undoubtedly Project MATCH (1997a). This was the largest and most comprehensive study of the treatment of alcohol problems so far carried out. It involved more than 1700 clients with alcohol problems in the USA, nine treatment sites and 80 therapists. Clients were randomly assigned to the three treatments shown in Table 13.2: cognitive-behaviour therapy (CBT), motivational-enhancement therapy (MET) and 12-step

Table 13.2   Main results of project MATCH: per cent 'no drinking' or 'moderate drinking' following each of three types of treatment (adapted by permission from Project MATCH research group, 1997a)

	At 9 months follow-up		At 15 months follow-up	
	Aftercare	Out-patient	Aftercare	Out-patient
CBT	58.0	38.2	55.0	38.8
MET	49.2	37.8	50.8	44.4
TSF	53.4	46.3	53.9	44.9

CBT   Cognitive-behaviour therapy.
MET   Motivational-enhancement therapy.
TSF   12-step facilitation.

facilitation (TSF). The treatment period was of 12 weeks duration in each case but CBT and TSF involved planned weekly sessions for 12 weeks, and were thus more intensive than MET, which involved only four sessions during the 12-week period. There were two arms to the study, an aftercare arm ($N = 774$) and an out-patient arm ($N = 952$). Clients were followed up at 3-monthly intervals. The main follow-up points were at 9 months and 15 months after entry to treatment. As Table 13.2 shows, the three treatments, although very different in underlying philosophy, produced rather similar results. The only significant differences were in favour of TSF at 9 months follow-up in the out-patient arm, but by 15 months follow-up this difference had disappeared, although TSF was still in the lead if a strict abstinence-only criterion was adopted. The authors of the paper concluded that each of the three treatment types produced substantial changes but that there were no clinically significant differences in outcome between CBT, MET and TSF. This absence of a main treatment effect, found by many researchers in smaller studies, is itself remarkable, particularly as Project MATCH, for the first time, put into operation a standardised treatment based upon the principles of AA (TSF), compared it with familiar psychological interventions like CBT and MET, and found essentially no difference. Despite their radically different treatment philosophies, the end results were similar.

Complementing Project MATCH, Ouimette *et al.* (1997) reported the results of the treatment for 'substance abuse' of over 3000 men attending 15 centres for military veterans in the USA. This was not a randomised controlled trial but rather a naturalistic study of outcomes following programmes with contrasting theoretical orientations. Five were carefully chosen as 'pure' CBT-oriented, five pure 12-step, and five 'mixed'. Outcomes at 1-year follow-up were indistinguishable. Furthermore, in an important later paper from this research group, Finney *et al.* (1998) compared changes from before treatment with end of treatment for those being treated in the 12-step and CBT programmes. Whereas the former showed more change in terms of processes thought to be specific to 12-step treatment—such as attending 12-step meetings, reading 12-step materials and actually taking the steps recommended in the programme—in terms of processes assumed to be specific to CBT, and in terms of general processes, the groups did not differ in the ways that might have been expected (e.g. there was no difference in change in self-efficacy, positive outcome expectancies and positive reappraisal). In fact, 12-step clients experienced significantly more change in terms of processes such as stimulus control and counter-conditioning which are theoretically associated with CBT. Finney *et al.* concluded that, '... the proximal outcomes thought to be specific to cognitive-behavioural treatment are actually general proximal outcomes of both 12-step and cognitive-behavioral treatment' (p. 371). Thus these results support the view being developed here that processes of change are likely to be similar despite the trappings of treatment appearing to be very different.

Many others have noted, usually with some surprise, the similarity between the recommendations and practices of change methods that on the face of it would be expected to be distinctly different. McCrady (1994), for example, noted many similarities between AA and behaviour therapy in terms of: the emphasis on initial behaviour change (e.g. the AA slogan, 'bring the body and the mind will follow'), identifying and avoiding high-risk relapse situations, recognition that certain cognitions can be dysfunctional, and the advice to avoid negative affect (e.g. use of the AA acronym HALT, suggested that a recovering alcoholic should never get, 'too hungry, angry, lonely, or tired').

Treatments for excessive eating provide another example of the apparent similarity of outcomes of very different treatments. Agras (1993) provided a very good summary examining both treatment process and outcome associated with a number of forms of treatment for excessive eating. Two contrasting treatment types had been prominent in this field, namely CBT and interpersonal psychotherapy (IPT). Agras concluded that CBT and IPT, with very different theoretical bases, had produced more or less equivalent outcomes. This was particularly surprising since IPT appeared to take the focus of treatment off eating behaviour itself, something that would not be expected to be helpful from a behavioural perspective. The rationale for IPT, unlike that for CBT, is:

> ... based on an interpersonal view of the maintenance of [bulimia] ... [it] uses techniques derived from psychodynamically oriented therapies, but the focus is on the patient's current circumstances and relationships ... The initial four sessions were devoted almost exclusively to a detailed analysis of the interpersonal context in which the eating disorder ... had developed and been maintained. This led to the formulation of the patient's eating disorder in interpersonal terms ... No attention was paid to the patient's eating habits or attitudes to shape and weight, nor did the treatment contain any of the behavioral or cognitive procedures that characterized the other two approaches. There was no self-monitoring ...
>
> (Fairburn *et al.*, 1991, pp. 464–465)

Although cognitive and behavioural treatments for 'bulimia' predominated in Hartmann *et al.*'s (1992) review (see above) their analyses also included studies of three treatments that were explicitly psychodynamic and six others that made connections between symptoms of excessive eating and personal relationships (either with the therapist, with family or friends, or with 'inner objects').

Supporting Agras' (1993) conclusion, there was no correlation between average effect size and treatment orientation.

Support for this same position—that some of the most important elements in treatment for excessive appetitive behaviour may have their focus elsewhere than directly upon the appetitive behaviour itself—is provided by a study carried out in a very different tradition, reported by McConaghy *et al.* (1988). Their interest was in the treatment of excessive gambling using imaginal desensitisation (ID), a form of behaviour therapy in which a person visualises, in a relaxed state, situations leading to gambling, and then imagines *not* completing the gambling behaviour. Their previous research (McConaghy *et al.*, 1983) had suggested that this treatment was superior to traditional aversion therapy. In their 1988 paper they reported a further comparison of ID with imaginal relaxation (IR) in which visualisation, when relaxed, was of situations thought personally to be particularly relaxing, with no particular reference or relevance to gambling. Both ID and IR were given in 14 sessions over a period of 1 week's admission to a psychiatric unit, and all participants were followed up to 1 year. Although the numbers were small (ten in each group), the results appeared to show that both treatments met with considerable success, with very little to choose between them. ID appeared to be slightly ahead during treatment, but results for IR caught up and were slightly ahead by 1 year. McConaghy *et al.* concluded that IR was as good as ID, and that this supported what they called an 'organismic model' (i.e. that it was something about the organism that needed correcting and not the behaviour itself). This small and little-noticed study is potentially of the utmost importance for understanding the processes of change, since it suggests that successful treatment may not require any kind of focus upon the appetitive behaviour itself. Of course, it is impossible to know from the brief research report all that went on before and during the admission to hospital for a gambling problem. But the important point here is that the expert treatment provided specifically to correct excessive gambling—the element considered to be at the core of the process of change with treatment—in the case of IR made no reference to gambling at all.

Another possibility is that treatment focused on one appetite might be successful in reducing another even though the latter was not targeted. Two studies have been reported aimed at reducing smoking among excessive drinkers, a group known to include a large number of tobacco smokers. In one study over 200 excessive drinkers recruited via AA were assigned to one of three groups: behavioural group counselling plus exercise, behavioural group counselling plus nicotine gum, and a standard group programme plus attendance at four 12-step type Nicotine Anonymous (NA) group meetings (Martin *et al.*, 1997). In the other study, 12 in-patient alcohol-treatment facilities across three mid-west states of the USA were matched and then randomly assigned to a condition in which patients were offered four 10–15-minute readiness-to-change-model smoking-quit programme sessions or to a no-smoking-treatment control condition (Bobo *et al.*, 1998). Although there were some positive early results, in neither case were there any discernible effects on smoking at 12 months. What was particularly interesting in the Bobo *et al.* study, however, was the apparently favourable effect upon change in *drinking*. Both studies had been partly motivated by the wish to check whether attempts to get excessive drinkers to smoke less would interfere in a harmful way with their attempts to control drinking. Results on this score were reassuring in both cases. In fact, in the Bobo *et al.* study the alcohol-abstinence rate was significantly *greater* following the smoking programme, both at 6 months (51 versus 39 per cent) and at 12 months (43 versus 29 per cent) although, as the authors observed, this unanticipated result could have been due to the extra contacts involved (three of the four smoking sessions involved telephone contacts after discharge from hospital).

Equally intriguing are the results of those studies which have compared the effectiveness of treatments that differ markedly in intensity—and therefore usually in financial cost also. For example, in the excessive drinking treatment literature a number of early studies demonstrated that little difference resulted when long-term in-patient treatment was compared with short-term in-patient treatment (e.g. Willems *et al.*, 1973), when in-patient treatment was compared with out-patient treatment (Edwards and Guthrie, 1967), when long-term out-patient treatment was compared with short-term out-patient treatment (e.g. Armor *et al.*, 1978) or when relatively costly treatments were compared with relatively inexpensive therapies such as 'bibliotherapy'—the provision of books, pamphlets and instructional manuals (Miller and Taylor, 1980).

The effectiveness of brief interventions for excessive drinkers was reviewed by Bien *et al.* (1993) and by Babor (1994). The latter found 11 studies in which people had been randomly assigned to a brief treatment or a no-treatment control group. Nine of these produced positive results in favour of brief treatment. A World Health Organisation (WHO) study is probably the most impressive since it involved a total of 1559 heavy drinkers in eight separate countries (Australia, the UK, Norway, Mexico, Kenya, Russia, Zimbabwe and the USA) recruited from a variety of hospital settings, primary-care clinics, work sites and educational institutions (Babor *et al.*, 1994). General medical practices and general hospitals were well represented among studies reviewed by Babor as sites for recruiting excessive drinkers, and the UK and Scandinavian countries were very well represented. Most of the participants in these brief treatments were, according to Babor, 'problem drinkers', rather than 'alcoholics' or people with many dependence symptoms. In this regard Babor referred several times in his review to the notion of 'secondary prevention', but the distinctions between secondary prevention and treatment, and between alcohol dependence and harmful or problem drinking, are difficult to sustain, as Babor admitted.

In the treatment of excessive gamblers, too, Dickerson *et al.* (1990) reported the positive results of two variations of a brief treatment which used a self-help manual, adapted from Robertson and Heather's (1983) successful *Let's Drink to Your Health*, prepared for excessive drinkers. Gamblers were recruited by advertising publicly and were randomly assigned either to receive the manual through the post or in the course of an interview lasting between half an hour and 2 hours. The number of gambling sessions, and money spent on gambling per week, decreased for both groups, and these changes were maintained 6 months after initial contact, although money spent per gambling session had gone up again by 6-months follow-up, and reported effects on family, friends and work and finances were less favourable. There were no differences between the two groups but numbers in this study were small.

Particularly germane to the present argument are the results of those few studies that have examined the effects of simple advice or persuasion in comparison with 'treatment', controlling for the effect of expectation of future help. Bernstein (1970) reported the results of such a study of smoking. In comparison with 'treated' participants, those asked to quit on their own displayed as much change, but only if future aid was not expected. Bernstein stressed the need to inform participants that determination was the key to quitting and that no one else could help them in their attempt.

The present author and colleagues reported an essentially similar study of excessive drinkers (Orford and Edwards, 1977; Edwards *et al.*, 1977a). A total of 100 patients (all married men) were assessed and randomly assigned either to conventional hospital out-patient 'treatment' (with additional in-patient treatment for some) or to simple advice confined to a single session. Great care was taken to convey to participants in the advice group that the decision to change was theirs and that only they could take it and carry it through, and that for this reason no further help would be offered by the hospital. Our expectations were that standard treatment would be more effective overall, but that brief advice would work well for a proportion of people. We were surprised by the clarity of the results. At 12 months we could find no significant differences between outcome for the two groups although we looked at a range of outcome variables including those that were drink-focused and those that were non-drink focused.

Throughout the 1980s and most of the 1990s, one of the great hopes was that positive outcomes of treatment might be increased by judicious matching of people to treatments. It seemed entirely reasonable to suppose that one of the main reasons why it had been so difficult to prove that one treatment was overall better than another (i.e. treatment 'main' effects) was because the apparent similarity of treatments in terms of overall outcomes hides the fact that different treatments work in different ways and are therefore likely to benefit different people (i.e. client–treatment 'matching' effects). It was Glaser (1980), in particular, who proposed that the generally uniform findings in the treatment literature were due to a failure to appreciate, first, the differences, as opposed to the similarities between people, and, second, the failure to match treatment and person. As Glaser put it:

> If the population being treated is in fact heterogenous, but is dealt with as if it were homogeneous, those variables which are critical for successful client–treatment interaction for both forms of intervention will tend to be uniformly distributed in the differing conditions of the experiment, and the results in each condition will be the same for that reason.
>
> (Glaser, 1980, p. 180)

Matching research is a highly complicated undertaking involving potentially many combinations of client characteristics and treatment dimensions, as well as different outcome criteria: there is the possibility, not simply of client–treatment matches, but yet more complex client–treatment–outcome criterion matches (Miller and Cooney, 1994). Powerful research designs with large numbers of participants are necessary to tease out possible matching effects, and most of this research in the case of excessive appetites has been done in the alcohol-treatment field.

Despite some promising findings, the results of client–treatment matching research in the field of excessive drinking have been disappointing. Mattson *et al.* (1994) reviewed 30 such studies carried out over a period of 20 years, concluding that few generalisations about matching could be made. When hypotheses are stated in advance, as they should be if the results are to be convincing, most have been unsupported and in some cases even opposite to the prediction. For example, McKay *et al.* (1993) predicted that clients who were low in personal autonomy would be able to benefit more than others from the addition of 'conjoint' treatment (in which 'significant others', mainly spouses, were involved) to a skills-based programme of individual and group therapy. In fact, those low on autonomy had better results, in terms of family functioning, when assigned to the control group, and there was some evidence that those high in autonomy did better with conjoint treatment. After the event, McKay *et al.* speculated that this result might have arisen because people do better when their normal style is challenged by their treatment (e.g. as high autonomy might be by conjoint treatment). An alternative explanation is that a certain degree of personal autonomy is necessary in order to feel comfortable in, and hence to benefit from, treatment involving other people who may be critical of one's behaviour.

Some of the most ambitious studies, with designs strong enough to adequately test matching hypotheses, have produced mostly negative results. For example, matching was not well supported in the results of Babor *et al.*'s (1994) large, multi-country, WHO study of brief interventions. The most elaborate test of matching to date, however, was Project MATCH, referred to earlier. With its large number of participants, and hence good statistical power for detecting interaction effects, Project MATCH was in a stronger position than ever before to test matching hypotheses. On the basis of their search of the literature, these researchers set out to test 16 'primary' interaction effects that between them involved 10 different variables. For example, it was hypothesized that CBT would be superior for women and for clients with higher alcohol involvement; that TSF would be superior for men and for those with higher scores on a questionnaire assessing search for meaning in life; and that MET would be superior for those at earlier stages of change.

What is remarkable about the findings that have come out of that study so far is that, despite the care with which the matching hypotheses were formulated and the power of the statistical tests used to detect such matching effects, the results were almost as negative here as they were in testing for main treatment effects. Of the 16 matching hypotheses only one was clearly supported, and even this was only the case for the out-patient arm of the study. As predicted, CBT produced better results for clients with higher levels of psychiatric severity. The interaction effect was clearest at month 9 of follow-up but by 15 months the effect had disappeared. Nor was the effect precisely as predicted. It was predicted that CBT would be superior to TSF at high levels of psychiatric severity, but of equal effectiveness at lower levels. In fact, it was TSF that was superior to CBT at lower levels of severity, with the two treatments apparently of equal effectiveness at higher levels of severity.

In the second report from this study the results of testing 11 further client–treatment matching hypotheses were given (Project MATCH, 1997b). These were referred to as 'secondary' matching hypotheses since they were judged at the outset to have had less empirical support, or weaker theoretical justification, than the primary hypotheses. Again the results were somewhat disappointing. Only one of the 11 hypotheses was supported in the out-patient arm of the study, and only one of the 11—a different one—in the aftercare arm. The first predicted that clients with greater degrees of anger would have better outcomes when treated with MET since anger might be an important impediment to treatment, and MET was specifically designed to reduce resistance to treatment. The second, the alcohol-dependence hypothesis, predicted that clients with more severe alcohol dependence would do better with TSF which would provide a stronger message about the necessity for total abstinence, particularly important for those more severely dependent. A third hypothesis was supported in the out-patient arm, but in a direction opposite to that predicted. This was the social-functioning hypothesis which had proposed that clients functioning poorly socially would do better with CBT. In fact, relative to TSF and MET clients, those with *better* social functioning did comparatively well with CBT. As was the case with the primary hypotheses, others produced no significant results or results that were significant only during treatment or in the very early period of follow-up, or were inconsistent over time in a way that had not been predicted and which was difficult to interpret. Even those matches that received strongest support were not great in size, accounting for no more than 3–4 days of extra abstinence per month or two drinks fewer per drinking day for those in the top and bottom tenths of the distribution on the matching variable. The overall conclusion of the Project MATCH group regarding the general idea that matching clients to treatment would improve outcomes was negative:

> Matching effects of this magnitude and specificity, as presently understood, will likely have limited practical clinical significance. Despite the promise of earlier matching studies (Mattson *et al.*, 1994), the intuitively appealing notion that matching can appreciably enhance treatment effectiveness has been severely challenged.
>
> (Project MATCH, 1997b, p. 1690)

Despite the strength and sophistication of Project MATCH, it remains a possibility that the matching hypotheses studied were overly simplistic. It may be, for example, that the beneficial effects of giving particular people a particular treatment, or the harmful effects of giving others that treatment, are only apparent towards the extreme ends of a client-attribute continuum. It may be a case of capitalising on particular assets possessed by only a minority of people, or compensating for weaknesses that are again possessed by only a minority (Longabaugh *et al.*, 1994). Studies such as Project MATCH that are designed to be strong on internal validity may exclude those whose characteristics are comparatively extreme, thus reducing the prospects of finding matching effects and as a consequence reducing an important element of external validity. A further possibility, raised by the Project MATCH research group (1997b), is that matching effects may vary with the stage reached by a person in the change process. For example, those in the out-patient arm of their own study were mostly just beginning the process of stopping drinking (abstinence was the official goal for all clients in Project MATCH) while those in the aftercare arm had already completed a treatment programme involving abstinence. This could account, then, for one of the results of Project MATCH, which was on the face of it most disappointing, namely the failure to replicate any of the matching effects across the two arms of the study.

Although no studies of comparable scale have been reported for other forms of excess, authorities in related areas have also expressed some scepticism about the gains to be made from matching. Agras (1993), for example, on discovering from the research literature that treatments for excessive eating, as different in their theoretical rationales and methods as CBT and IPT, resulted in more or less equivalent overall outcomes (see above), was enthusiastic about the prospects of matching. Some 2 years later he had changed his mind as a result of research finding that IPT was unable to help those who had not responded positively to CBT (Agras *et al.*, 1995). He was being forced to the conclusion that, despite their apparent differences, CBT and IPT might be working through common, non-specific mechanisms after all. Their potentially important cross-over study had the weakness that IPT was only given following unsuccessful CBT. The study also lacked a follow-up.

Digiusto and Bird (1995) also concluded that different treatments for smoking might be so 'functionally equivalent' as to make matching unlikely. In their treatment trial for smoking they found support for only one out of 12 matching hypotheses, plus another result that was opposite to that predicted. Effects had vanished or become difficult to interpret by the 6-month follow-up. In their study of different ways of managing methadone-maintenance treatment for opiate addiction, Saxon *et al.* (1996) found a number of client–programme interaction effects, but no theory or hypotheses were offered by them to guide an interpretation of these effects, and the results were used *post hoc* to help explain programme main effects.

It is clear, then, that if there are client–treatment matches, they are hard to find and unlikely to be invariant across different populations and treatment settings. This is hardly surprising once we start to broaden out the picture and to put formal 'treatment' properly within the wider context of circumstances which aid personal change in behaviour. 'Treatment' has often been viewed narrowly as a neat package, as if it could be specified and applied in standard form by any competent therapist for many different clients in any setting (Athey and Coyne, 1979). There are a number of important respects in which this assumption is invalid in the case of psychological treatments. For one thing treatment techniques are rarely so well specified that they remain invariant: it is difficult to make certain that treatments are always given and 'taken' in the 'dosages' prescribed. Psychological treatments are usually complex and we can rarely be certain which components are 'taken' and have impact. Using a 'drug metaphor', as if such treatments can be prescribed like medication, may be wholly inappropriate (Shapiro *et al.*, 1994). We know that patients frequently ignore their doctors' instructions to take particular drugs, or to take drugs in the dosages and at the frequencies prescribed (Ley *et al.*, 1976). Psychological treatments are more complex still and research reports rarely provide the detail necessary to know what really happened from the helper's perspective, let alone that of the client.

One of the complexities which remains almost entirely unexplored to date is that there may be therapist main effects (i.e. some therapists may produce better outcomes than others overall) or therapist–client matching effects (some clients may do better with some therapists, other clients better with others), therapist–treatment matching effects (some therapists may produce better outcomes with one treatment, other therapists with another) or more complicated interactions still, involving different clients, different therapists, different treatments and different outcome criteria (Mattson *et al.*, 1994).

Neglect of the therapist variable, long recognised in psychotherapy research but remaining largely ignored in research on treatment for excessive appetites (Cartwright, 1981), is a further consequence of the assumption that treatment can be mechanically applied independently of personal qualities and preferences of the participants. It may be that some therapists are much more successful than others, independently of the type of programme or treatment techniques with which they are operating. Certainly some people are more interested in working with people with excessive appetites and specialising in this kind of work. Equally certainly there are many people in the helping professions who have relatively little experience of working with these groups of clients and who lack what Shaw et al (1978) called 'role security' in working with them. On account of the nature of excessive appetitive behaviour, including conflict and some of its undesirable consequences (see Chapter 12), attitudes of potential helpers undoubtedly vary from those that are unsympathetic and rejecting to those that are more accepting, optimistic and sympathetic (Cartwright, 1980). Such attitudes seem likely candidates for discriminating more successful from less successful therapists in working with those with excessive appetitive behaviour. Whether it is possible to identify other differentiating characteristics within a sample of helpers equally sympathetic and committed to working in this area remains an interesting question.

Majavits and Weiss (1994) reviewed the literature on the therapist factor, finding few consistent findings. Most promise was shown, not in terms of therapist characteristics, but in terms of measures of in-session interpersonal functioning. There was some consistency in the findings that when therapists displayed warmth, affirmation, understanding and *not* blaming or belittling, and when they and their clients satisfactorily established a good alliance, better results followed. Majavits and Weiss commented that, although it had been suggested that substance-abuse treatment might show especially great therapist variation because the clients are a difficult group to work with, in fact the careful selection and training of therapists and use of manuals to guide treatment may reduce therapist variation and the chances of finding therapist main or interaction effects.

McLellan *et al.* (1988) reported the results of an interesting natural experiment in which, because of the allocation schedule, clients of a methadone-maintenance programme were allocated virtually at random to one of four counsellors. Of the four, one produced significantly better results than others, but one significantly poorer. Investigation showed that these differences could be traced to the presence or absence of consistent and professional patient-management practices that were detectable in case notes. This may be a good example of extreme therapist differences which would have been erased in a well-designed treatment study involving treatment manuals, therapist training and close monitoring of treatment quality. Sanchez-Craig *et al.* (1991), after finding in their study that two therapists with 15 or more years of alcohol or drug counselling produced lower client drop-out rates and better outcome results than two inexperienced therapists who were new to the treatment of alcohol or drug problems, also recommended that research on therapist effects might be more promising than conventional research contrasting different treatments. McLellan *et al.* reviewed more than 50 studies of the effectiveness of three different types of drug-treatment counsellor: professional (holding a master's or higher degree), 'paraprofessional' (lower qualifications) and ex-addicts. They concluded that the results of this comparison were very clear: whatever differences there might be in outcomes produced by different therapists, they cannot be attributed to qualification levels or ex-addict status, since there were no differences in outcome between the three groups examined. This result is consistent with findings from research on the treatment of mental health problems more generally: 'paraprofessionals' produce outcomes equally as good overall as do 'professionals' (Durlak, 1979; Hattie *et al.*, 1984).

REVERSION AND RELAPSE

One of the principal reasons why the experts have been so much confounded in their understanding of the change process lies, according to the present view, in the ambivalence and conflict which are the hallmarks of an excessive appetite. Although one of the consequences of conflict, discussed in Chapter Twelve, is the contemplation of change as a natural occurrence, ambivalence about change and reversion to former excess are also naturally occurring consequences. It is part of clinical experience that it is relatively easy to help people make short-term changes in eating, gambling or drug-using behaviour. Maintaining cessation or reduction of behaviour is the problem. Many individuals who have struggled to control their own habitual behaviour testify to the same. To quote Hunt and Matarazzo (1973)—'As the late W. C. Fields observed about drinking, it is easy to stop. He had done it thousands of times!' (p. 111). Those who have examined treatment-research results report the same thing. For example, Litman (1976) concerning excessive drinking and Leventhal and Cleary (1980) for smoking noticed the high rates of success produced during or immediately after treatment in comparison with the relatively modest rates of success recorded at follow-up.

Hunt and his colleagues (e.g. Hunt and Matarazzo, 1973; Hunt and Bespalec, 1974) wrote a number of papers in the 1970s on the topic of relapse following treatment for drug problems, which are important for at least two reasons. First, Hunt noticed that there were certain aspects of the relapse process which were similar for smoking, drinking problems and heroin 'addiction'. Second, potentially important conclusions were drawn about the nature of the change process itself. Hunt's observation was that the 'relapse curves' following treatment for one or other of these problems, or the 'cumulative survival curves' as they should more correctly be termed (Litman *et al.*, 1979; Sutton, 1979), took similar negatively accelerated forms. These curves showed a rapid fall in the number of people surviving unrelapsed during the first few weeks after the termination of treatment, but levelled out around 3–6 months after treatment after which the curve reached an asymptote around 25 per cent, this being the proportion of treated individuals who appeared to have made a longer term change.

Hunt and his colleagues could well have included over-eating in their analysis even though 'relapse' may appear to be even harder to define in the case of excessive eating. Ley (1980) noted the high rates of relapse of the overweight after treatment and acknowledged that the maintenance of weight losses was a major problem for treatment. His review suggested that overall about one patient in five would maintain a substantial weight loss for a year or more after treatment, an estimate remarkably similar to Hunt and colleagues' estimate of the number of excessive drinkers, smokers and drug users who make changes that lasted for more than 3–6 months.

A number of criticisms have been made of Hunt's analysis and sometimes of the very concept of 'relapse'. Litman *et al.* (1979) and Sutton (1979) also criticised Hunt and his colleagues for placing too much emphasis on the shape of such curves when drawing conclusions about the process of relapse. Litman *et al.* pointed out that very similar negatively accelerated curves of this kind can be generated even when the ways in which the probability of survival changes in the months after treatment are very different. Sutton also pointed out that such curves are due to the operation of two very general processes, namely the progressive selection of individuals as time proceeds—once an individual has 'relapsed' then he or she does not enter into the calculations for later months which are thus based upon an increasingly selected sub-population—as well as the changing probability of survival with time. Since it is impossible to know how relatively important each of these processes is in any particular set of data, he argued that few conclusions about relapse processes can be drawn. Furthermore, Hunt's analysis assumed that group data were sufficiently meaningful to be interpreted, and contained the assumption that relapse is a single discrete event which marks a clear transition from a pre-relapse state to a post-relapse state. Litman *et al.*'s (1979) re-analysis of data from our treatment-versus-advice study (Orford *et al.*, 1976) showed how variable was the course of events for many individuals over a year's follow-up period with many individuals showing a relatively erratic course.

The whole notion of 'relapse' was later critiqued by Miller (1996) who saw a danger in construing this as a binary, quasi-medical, concept. Alcohol problems themselves consist of a number of only modestly correlated dimensions; there are many different ways of drawing 'relapse' curves as he showed, depending upon one's definition of a relapse (see Figure 13.1); the use of other drugs is usually ignored in considering relapse to alcohol use, as are reductions in parameters such as quantity, frequency and time using; and the connotations of failure and weakness inherent in the idea of relapse may lead to worse outcomes by a process of self-fulfilling prophecy. Garner and Woolley (1991) remarked, likewise, on the disadvantage of using an addiction/AA model in the eating-disorders field because of the dangers of dieting leading to restrained eating and hence to bingeing. Marlatt (1996), too, has acknowledged that the concept of

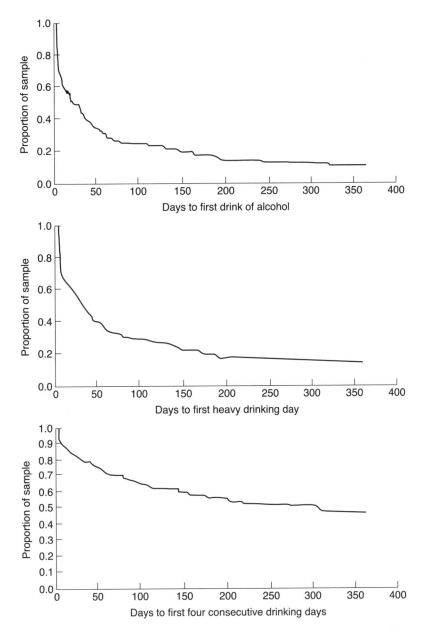

Figure 13.1   Three different relapse curves from one treatment study (reproduced by permission from W. R. Miller, 1996).

'relapse' derives from a limited, disease model, but has argued that such a concept was needed, like a Trojan Horse, for ideas about relapse prevention to be able to penetrate the field. It is interesting to note the use of the words 'abstinence' and 'abstinent' creeping into the literature on excessive eating and its treatment, referring, strangely, to abstinence from binge eating (e.g. Agras, 1993; Levine *et al.*, 1996).

Despite these valid criticisms, Hunt's analyses of the relapse process were valuable in pointing to the likely similarities in this respect between different forms of appetitive behaviour, and in generating valuable hypotheses about the change process. Criticisms that their 'relapse curves' were arbitrary and misleading overlooked the main features of Hunt and colleagues' analysis. Their observation was that the relapse curves descended rapidly at first 'as if' they would eventually reach zero, but in fact they tended to level out well above zero. Their interpretation of these relapse curves was that they represented two distinct processes, the first being a process of extinction or forgetting of the new learning that had taken place during treatment. This was responsible for the negatively accelerated form of the curve. They argued that because what was being dealt with was habitual behaviour, repeated in the past many times and thus 'over-learned', decay of what had been 'learnt' during treatment was often rapid and early relapse was frequent.

Hunt was concerned to account, in addition, for the fact that a substantial minority of formerly excessive drug users, drinkers and smokers seemed to arrive, nevertheless, at a favourable resolution of their problem which surmounted this decay process and lasted for at least several months and possibly permanently. Indeed, the longer-term follow-up studies (e.g. Thorley *et al.*, 1977; Edwards *et al.*, 1992; Collings and King, 1994) show that a sizeable minority of people who admit to appetitive problems or who seek help on account of them make changes which are very long-lasting, measured in terms of years rather than months. It is this second process which is most intriguing. The more interesting question is not why does 'relapse' occur in the majority of cases, for what we know about the nature of strongly appetitive behaviour would lead us to expect people to revert to former behaviour, but rather how do many individuals overcome the forces that lead most to revert, and manage to make dramatic changes in their behaviour? Hunt's guess about what was operating was:

> ... some kind of decision-making process or encoding, which isolates the response in question from the usual mechanisms of reinforcement and establishes the permanence of the behaviour outside the influence of rein-forcement.
>
> (Hunt and General, 1973, cited by Hunt and Bespalec, 1974, p. 87)

We shall return to consider Hunt's views on the change process in the following chapter when trying to construct an alternative, largely non-expert, model of change. Meanwhile it may be noted that the high rate of reversion or 'relapse' is a fact of life in the treatment of excessive appetites and is a major difficulty with which treatment must contend. The difficulty of finding main or even matching effects may have a lot to do with it, since any immediate or short-term effects of treatment are likely to be 'washed out' over time as more and more people revert to previous behaviour. It is not at all uncommon in the research literature on treatment for excessive appetites to find that a particular treatment can be shown to be more effective than control at short follow-up intervals (up to 3 or perhaps 6 months) with differences from control being non-significant thereafter. This was true, for example, in Allsop *et al.*'s (1997) study of relapse prevention in the treatment of excessive drinking; Finney and Moos' (1996) analysis of the benefits of in-patient treatment for excessive drinking; Sanchez-Craig *et al.*'s (1996) study of the effects of brief motivational interviewing for community drinkers who wanted to stop or cut down; Cinciripini *et al.*'s (1996) study of adding nicotine patch to behaviour therapy for smokers; Curry *et al.*'s (1995) large-scale trial of the effect of adding telephone counselling to self-help booklet and computer feedback for smokers; and, more generally, treatments aimed at weight loss for people who are overweight (Garner and Wooley, 1991). It is not always the case, however, that differential treatment effects do not last. There is even sometimes evidence that differential effects might be 'delayed', appearing only at later follow-up intervals. This was the case, for example, in a trial of cognitive-behavioural coping-skills training for cocaine 'dependence'. Skills training showed no improvement on standard clinical management at 1 or 3 months follow-up, but was significantly better at 6 and 12 months, suggesting to the authors that there might be non-specific effects of treatment early on, with the extra effects of cognitive behavioural treatment being maintained for longer (Carroll *et al.*, 1994). A similar effect occurred in a study comparing CBT, behaviour therapy (BT), and a contact plus self-monitoring control for 'bulimia'. All three treatments resulted in gains, suggesting the operation of non-specific factors, but by 6 months follow-up those receiving the control treatment had relapsed at a higher rate (Thackwray *et al.*, 1993).

UNAIDED CHANGE

If all the research activity directed at finding particular treatments for people with excessive appetites has only produced such a muddled picture, might we not conclude that the fundamental assumptions that have guided this research are wrong?

Lindström (1991) neatly summarised four different perspectives on, or assumptions about, the nature of treatment for alcohol problems (he might equally have been referring to any one of the other appetites), in the form of what he termed four 'hypotheses' (see Table 13.3). Few would now support the technique hypothesis which supposes that there is one superior treatment yet to be discovered, although most research in the field has probably taken that view as its starting point. The matching hypothesis (see above) was strongly held at the time that Lindström was writing; indeed, he was commenting on an influential US Institute of Medicine (1990) report, *Broadening the Base of Treatment for Alcohol Problems*, which rested heavily on the matching hypothesis. As we have seen, support for it is not very strong. My perspective on the treatment of excessive appetites lies somewhere between the non-specific hypothesis and the natural healing hypothesis. The former is based on the belief that treatment is effective but that all credible treatments produce equivalent results because the active ingredients are common to a variety of different approaches. Much of the evidence so far brought forward in the present chapter would lead us to support

Table 13.3   Assumptions regarding the treatment of alcohol problems (reproduced by permission from Lindström, 1991, p. 847)

	Is treatment effective?	Do therapies vary in efficacy?	Is there a superior therapy?
The technique hypothesis	Yes	Yes	Yes
The matching hypothesis	Yes	Yes	No
The non-specific hypothesis	Yes	No	—
The natural healing hypothesis	No	—	—

the non-specific hypothesis. The natural healing hypothesis implies, on the other hand, that the apparent benefits of treatment are illusory since what is being observed when treatment appears to work is the operation of powerful natural-change processes. Lindström's attitude to treatment research was very close to the one adopted here when he wrote:

> Perhaps psychosocial treatment research has started at the wrong end. Instead of moving from the top downward in Table 1 [Table 13.3 here], it might be more profitable to move from the bottom up ... it is my recommendation that research on treatment for alcohol problems should adopt a diversified strategy, with its main focus reoriented from the effects of specific techniques to natural healing processes, common therapeutic elements and effects of client–treatment interaction.
>
> (Lindström, 1991, p. 848)

Let us then take Lindström's lead and consider the idea of natural healing, or the possibility that there may be a substantial rate of what would at one time have been called 'spontaneous remission' from excessive appetitive behaviour in the general non-clinical population. Eysenck and Beech (1971) were of the view that spontaneous remission rates for appetitive disorders such as 'alcoholism' or drug 'addiction' would be negligible or small in comparison with those for problems such as phobias, obsessions and anxiety states. Research carried out since that time has tended to prove them wrong.

More than 20 years ago Roizen *et al.* (1978) concluded from their review of the literature concerned with those with drinking problems who had either been refused treatment or had refused it themselves, and from the results of their own longitudinal study of a sample of 21–59-year-old men in San Francisco, interviewed twice with an interval of approximately 4 years between:

> ... the general trend of [our] figures is clear, and it supports ... much of the earlier literature: By most criteria, there was a substantial amount of spontaneous remission of drinking problems in a population in which the overall trend in drinking problems was stable or even increasing. This suggests that the conventional clinical picture of drinking problems as relatively stable and lasting phenomena may need changing. Instead we might picture a great

deal of episodic and situational flux in a relatively large fraction of the
population that ever drinks enough to risk drinking problems.

(Roizen *et al.*, 1978, p. 214)

Important additions were made to that early statement by Saunders and Kershaw
(1979) who interviewed former 'alcoholics' and 'problem drinkers' in Clydeside,
Scotland, and by Tuchfeld (1981) in Texas, USA, who placed advertisements
requesting interviews with people who had given up drinking problems without
formal treatment. Both confirmed that their informants had given up former excess
and found them well able to describe the change and the circumstances in their
lives that might have accounted for it. In Saunders and Kershaw's study, getting
married (more likely for those who had been under 30 at the time), changing job,
and having a physical illness (more common for those over 30 at the time) were the
three most common causes of giving up a drinking problem.

Tuchfeld was struck by the resistance of many to being labelled 'alcoholic' and
their negative attitudes towards institutional forms of intervention. Many were
adamant that they had helped themselves without the aid of others. Among
factors associated with the problem resolution, Tuchfeld, like Premack (1970) in
his analysis of the reasons for quitting smoking (see Chapter Fourteen), put
'humiliating events' first in the list. For example, he cited instances of a
pregnant woman drinking and feeling her baby quiver and concluding she could
be harming her unborn child; the person who stopped drinking when his father
died having concluded that his own drinking was one of the causes of his death;
and a third lying in hospital and coming to the realisation that drinking had been a
major cause of health and other problems. A second factor was the role played by
'negative role models' such as Skid Row drinkers who shocked people into considering change. Loved ones, particularly family, were stated to play a major role,
particularly when they were seen to have provided persistent support. Religion and
religious conversion were mentioned as critical factors by some, but although a few
cases seemed like, '... classic cases of sudden religious conversion', most reflected,
'... an incremental process of commitment'. Tuchfeld concluded that few, if any,
cases in his study could be truly characterised as 'spontaneous' in the sense that
they occurred without apparent external cause.

Probably the most thorough study of the resolution of alcohol problems without
treatment was carried out by Sobell *et al.* (1991). They improved on previous
studies by devoting great care to defining treatment and excluding anyone who
had received treatments specifically for an alcohol problem according to their
definition. For example, while even one session of professional counselling specifically for an alcohol problem was considered to be 'treatment', warnings or advice
from friends, relatives or ministers were not, nor was admission to a detoxification
programme with no related treatment or counselling, nor attendance at just one or
two AA meetings, nor doctors' warnings simply to stop or cut down unless these
were accompanied by advice or counselling. They also took great care to check
that the alcohol problem had been resolved for at least 3 full years, that a drinking
history was reconstructed in great detail, and, most importantly, that a group of
excessive drinkers was included who had also not received formal treatment, but
whose drinking problems were *not* resolved. Sobell *et al.* advertised for both

resolved and non-resolved groups in the media around the greater metropolitan Toronto area, eventually recruiting 120 in the resolved group, comparing these with 62 non-resolved. They found no difference in the numbers of stressful life events reported by the two groups for a year prior to resolution (resolved group) and a randomly chosen comparison year (non-resolved group), demonstrating the importance of including a control group in such research. Qualitative analysis of accounts given by those in the resolved group suggested the importance of cognitive evaluation or appraisal as reasons for resolution for more than half of the group, and social support from family and friends, particularly partners, in maintaining change in the first 12 months after the initial resolution.

In a later paper, Sobell *et al.* (1996) reported relevant results from two Canadian general-population surveys, one national, the other confined to Ontario province. Again taking care in the definitions of a past drinking problem and current resolution of it (at least 12 months resolution, although more than half the resolutions had been for 5 years or more), they found that as many as 4 per cent of adult Canadians (and more in Ontario) were former problem drinkers who had resolved these problems, 78 per cent in both surveys doing so without any formal treatment. The proportion who had received treatment was higher in the case of those who were now abstinent (between one-third and a half—AA being the predominant source of help) than for those now drinking moderately (less than 10 per cent).

If it is the case that many excessive drinkers change without the aid of expert help, there can be little doubting the ability of many dissonant smokers to do the same. Horn (1972) reported some results of a study of 2000 cigarette smokers in the USA interviewed first in 1966 and again in 1970. Of the men, 26 per cent had stopped successfully for a year or more, of the women 17 per cent. On this basis Horn estimated that 13 million adults must have become ex-smokers in the USA in that interval of time, of whom he guessed that 99 per cent had done so without any treatment or formal help:

> The level of change in smoking habits in the United States has been quite massive and I regard it as a change in health behaviour that is largely dependent on individual decision.
>
> (Horn, 1972, p. 61)

Schachter (1982) is another who stated his opinion that the apparent resistance of addictive-appetitive behaviours to long-term modification might give a quite false impression because people who cure themselves may not be those that go to therapists, and most of the treatment studies are based on single attempts, whereas people who achieve success may often do so after multiple attempts. In order to study the natural history of attempts at self-cure of smoking and over-weight, Schachter interviewed 161 people who represented substantial majorities of two selected populations, the staff of a university psychology department and those who worked in shops and businesses on a particular stretch of the main street of one small town. Between them, these two groups covered a good range of social groups. With regard to smoking, 64 per cent of those who reported attempting to quit had succeeded at the time of the interview. A total of 88 per cent of these had been non-smokers for a year or more, and the average time since giving up was 7 years. Comparing these reports to those of formal treatment, Schachter concluded that, '... those who attempted to quit were at least two to three times more successful than were those self-selected subjects who in other studies went for professional help' (p. 439). Nearly half of those who had been heavy smokers (smoking at least 17 and an average of 33 cigarettes a day) reported major difficulties on giving up, such as marked irritability, sleeplessness, cravings, fevers and cold sweats, and another quarter of this group reported minor difficulties of this kind. Although the very large majority of former light smokers (smoking 12 or fewer cigarettes a day and an average of 7) reported no such difficulties, they were no more successful at quitting than the heavy smokers had been.

A total of 46 people had at some time been 15 per cent or more overweight, and of these 40 had made an active attempt to lose weight. Of this number over 60 per cent had succeeded in losing substantial amounts of weight and were no longer fat. Among the men 67 per cent had lost an average of 17.5 kg and an average of 13 years had elapsed after beginning to reduce, and among women 58 per cent had lost an average of 13 kg an average of 8 years after starting. Even among the most overweight, ranging from 30 per cent to over 70 per cent overweight, more than 60 per cent were classified as 'cured'. Success rates seemed to be markedly in excess of those reported in the literature on therapeutic outcome. Although self-selection may be the most obvious explanation for the disparity—only the most difficult cases seek formal help—the fact that treatment-outcome evaluations are based on studies of single attempts to give up excessive appetites may be equally at fault. From such results, Schachter pointed out, '... nothing can or should be inferred about the probable success of a lifetime of effort to quit smoking or lose weight' (p. 443). Of his sample two had at some time sought help for smoking and 12 for overweight. Of this number six were categorised as 'cured', a much higher success rate than those reported in the treatment literature.

The first study of excessive eating to follow a large sample of participants during the transition from late adolescence to early adulthood was reported by Heatherton *et al.* (1997). Participants were 500 women first studied in the early 1980s when, aged on average 20 years, they were attending a prestigious college in the north-eastern part of the USA. Concern over eating appears to have been particularly intense at that time, particularly at colleges of that kind, and a large proportion of young women rated themselves as overweight (52 per cent), wished to lose weight (82 per cent) and often dieted (23 per cent), despite the fact that only a tiny number were objectively overweight by population standards (between 1 and 2 per cent). The main interest of Heatherton *et al.*'s study was the changes, largely without the aid of treatment, that had occurred over the subsequent 10-year period. The general trend for women, despite a slight overall average gain in weight, had been towards a reduction in dieting and in the holding of attitudes thought to predispose to restrained eating and bulimia. Proportions of women now believing themselves to be overweight, wishing to lose weight and often dieting had fallen to 29, 68 and 11 per cent, respectively. The proportion of women thought to have eating problems had dropped dramatically. At college no less than 40 per cent had been categorised as either 'problem dieters' or as suffering from an 'eating disorder'. This figure had fallen to 16 per cent 10 years later.

One of the most thorough studies of change unaided by expert help was Biernacki's (1986) qualitative analysis of interviews with 101 former heroin addicts all of whom had recovered 'naturally', without treatment. The study was exemplary in terms of attempts made to get a varied sample, to check that participants really had been addicted to heroin, really had given it up and really had done this without treatment. Recruiting such a large sample of untreated recovered addicts proved difficult. Biernacki discovered early on that, '... naturally recovered addicts are much less socially visible and more isolated from other ex-addicts than are those who had been in a treatment program' (p. 204), but the sample was surprisingly easy to locate once people were sought by advertising (e.g. in local and underground papers). Later, sampling became more selective, for example to achieve a balance of the sexes, social classes, ethnic groups, and a reasonable representation of those such as doctors and nurses who had easy access to drugs. The final sample was aged on average 34, had been addicted to heroin on average for 6 years and had last been addicted 6 years previously (range 2–26 years). Only 38 were without convictions, and only three had engaged in no illegal activities at all in supporting their addiction. Biernacki developed a theoretical framework for understanding the change process which consisted of four stages: resolving to stop; breaking away from addiction; staying abstinent; and becoming and being 'ordinary'. We shall return to his ideas on change in Chapter Fourteen.

There is much evidence, therefore, that people with excessive appetites can rid themselves of them without formal external assistance, or as some had termed it, 'spontaneously'. This term 'spontaneous remission' has turned out to be a misnomer of course. As Roizen *et al.* (1978) pointed out it is a term derived from medical practice to refer to changes that occur apparently spontaneously or without clinical intervention. Thus, the assumption is that conditions are involved which generally require treatment of some kind. It is implied that what goes on in treatment is substantial and important, and that what occurs elsewhere is of secondary importance. Hence, any positive changes that occur without treatment are deemed 'spontaneous' and by implication, therefore, surprising and of unfathomable origin. The view towards which the studies of treatment and unaided quitting lead, reverses these assumptions, as indeed does the whole model of excessive appetitive behaviour being developed here.

IS THERE A BROADER CONTEXT?

The impressive body of research on unaided change indicates the importance of factors that may assist giving up excess quite outside any formal treatment programme. Even those who have focused on expert treatment, however, have been forced to recognise the role of these 'extraneous' factors. According to the excessive appetites model, such factors are in fact much the more important.

Virtually all the research literature on the effectiveness of treatments for excessive appetite behaviours has been based upon studies carried out in clinical environments where treatments can be delivered within a sufficiently controlled research design for 'internal validity' to be assured (i.e. to be reasonably confident that results can be attributed to a difference, or lack of it, between treatments). Random assignment of participants to different treatment groups, which preferably should include a no-treatment or minimal-treatment condition, has often been considered the gold standard of good treatment research, although studies in which groups have been matched by other means are sometimes included in reviews (e.g. Finney and Monahan, 1996). Moos and his group in California, however, have favoured a more naturalistic approach to the evaluation of treatment effectiveness, arguing that highly controlled studies often fail to achieve good 'external validity' (i.e. ability to generalise the results to real-world circumstances beyond a tightly controlled study) by excluding many potential participants, not making provision for longer-term follow-up, and particularly by failing to give due attention to the wider context in which treatment occurs (Finney *et al.*, 1996; Humphreys *et al.*, 1997).

Expert treatment, the detailed examination of which has probably attracted an amount of research attention out of all proportion to its importance, is directed at people who are at the same time being influenced by a host of factors quite beyond the control of those responsible for treatment. Many of these factors, 'extraneous' when viewed from the treatment perspective, operate more intensively, for far longer and hence seem likely to be by far the more influential. A point that is easily missed about treatment studies, is that the amount of outcome variance which can be explained at all, even when variation in client characteristics is added to variation in treatment, is usually quite small (e.g. Costello's, 1980, important meta-analysis of studies of treatment for excessive drinking).

Humphreys, Moos and their colleagues have been particularly strong in promoting the view that treatment for excessive appetites such as excessive drinking should take account of variance in the wider social context. Cronkite and Moos (1978) reported that the proportion of outcome variance accounted for by treatment and person variables in their naturalistic study of excessive drinkers treated in a variety of different settings was only 18–27 per cent depending upon outcome criterion. Although it is rarely done, some advance on these figures could be made by assessing the extent and quality of clients' environmental resources in the period during and following treatment. Moos *et al.* (1990) found not only that being married and having a job conferred a favourable prognosis, thus confirming some of the results of the unaided change studies, but, furthermore, that when such resources existed the perceived quality of these environments had predictive significance. The lower the degree of marital conflict, and, for unmarried clients, the greater the degree of job commitment and peer cohesion at work, the better the outcome for the drinking problem. Our own study of 'treatment' versus 'advice' produced a very similar finding, namely that higher levels of marital cohesion predicted a better outcome (Orford *et al.*, 1976). Clients who did well tended to attribute their success to improvements in their marriage or job circumstances, rather than to the advice or treatment received (Orford and Edwards, 1977).

In their study of the 3- and 8-year outcome for detoxification unit or information-and-referral centre attenders, Humphreys *et al.* (1996, 1997) also found evidence to support the general position that social context is important.

Friendship and extended family resources at baseline were predictive of outcome at 3-year follow-up, and more so for those without work and/or partners. The quality of extended family relationships assessed at baseline was again predictive of outcome at 8 years. Their group's overall position has been:

> ... traditional input-program-outcome modes of ... treatment and program evaluation are inadequate. Therapeutic efforts must go beyond the patient to deal with the contexts in which the patient functions after treatment ... Similarly, evaluation research paradigms need to be expanded to include assessment of the multiple settings in which patients are located after treatment ...
>
> (Finney *et al.*, 1980)

Many other studies could be cited in support of the point that the social context is important in the treatment process. For example, in a study of nearly 4000 smokers in a large US treatment trial, being married was one of the predictors of initial smoking cessation, and having no other smokers in the home, and having a 'helper' attend treatment sessions (for men only) were predictive of change and maintenance of change at all stages (Nides *et al.*, 1995). In a UK study of nurse-administered brief smoking intervention for 750 general practice patients, having a non-smoking partner and spending less time with smokers were also predictive of change sustained for 12 months (Sanders *et al.*, 1993). In Project MATCH, which overall found support for few matching effects (see above), it was found that among those in the out-patient group, those who at the outset of treatment had relatively high 'social support for drinking' (comparatively many close family and friends who were also heavy drinkers) were more likely to do well if they had been treated with TSF. This matching effect was accounted for, in their data, by the greater attendance at AA of TSF clients. The latter were encouraged to attend AA, were more likely than other clients to do so, and as a result their social networks became more supportive of maintaining non-drinking (Longabaugh *et al.*, 1998).

The attention of the experts has in fact been turning increasingly towards finding ways of working with family members and friends of people with excessive appetites. One notable method, originally termed, simply, 'intervention' (Liepman, 1993) deliberately uses family pressure to coerce 'alcoholics' into treatment. As part of this method, and unbeknown to the drinker, family members concerned about someone else's drinking are encouraged to recruit a network of other family members and friends, and train to stage a confrontation with the excessive drinker during which attempts are made to reduce 'denial' and to obtain the drinker's agreement to enter treatment. The intended spirit in which this is done is one of care for the drinker combined with considerable firmness—a good example of 'tough love' in action. This is clearly potentially a very powerful method, and one that might carry some dangers. The evidence to date is that holding such confrontation sessions is an ambitious undertaking which often proves to be impossible, and hence success rates are low compared with other less dramatic methods of helping concerned family members (Miller and Meyers, 1998). Other ways of deliberately harnessing the concern of 'significant others' include 'behavioural marital therapy' (McCrady, 1990; O'Farrell *et al.*, 1998), which has been used to treat excessive drug use, especially cocaine use (Fals-Stewart *et al.*, 1996), as well as excessive drinking, the 'pressures to change' approach of Barber and Crisp (1995) in Australia, 'unilateral family therapy' (Thomas and Ager, 1993), the 'community reinforcement' approach (Sisson and Azrin, 1993), 'network support therapy' (Galanter, 1999), and ARISE (a relational intervention sequence for engagement, Garret *et al.*, 1998) in the USA, and 'co-operative counselling' (Yates, 1988) and 'social behaviour and network therapy' (SBNT: Copello *et al.*, 1999) in the UK. SBNT, for example, is based on the idea that people are best helped to give up an excessive appetite such as excessive drinking if they can be assisted in mobilising the support of at least one or two close family or friends who can work together, in the first few weeks with the help of a therapist, to encourage and support the 'focal person' in his or her efforts to break the attachment to the appetitive activity.

In the report of their comprehensive international study of AA, Mäkelä *et al.* (1996) described a number of alternatives to, or offshoots from, AA, several of which built particularly upon the social support that such a mutual-help organisation can provide. For example, *Vie Libre* in France, *Danshukai* in Japan, and abstainers clubs in Poland, all, according to Mäkelä *et al.*, see support from family members as an important resource for recovery, and allow support membership from family members and others who want to promote the goals of the movement. In Mexico '24-hour groups' first split off from AA in 1975, providing assistance at special centres 24-hours a day, based on a recognition of the socioeconomic realities of the country and the rather different needs of many excessive drinkers there compared with countries such as the USA.

McLellan *et al.* (1994, 1998) have been attempting to shift thinking about treatment for excessive drug users in the USA towards a greater emphasis upon social needs. In their 1994 paper they reported the 6-months follow-up of approximately 600 excessive substance users, roughly equally divided between those whose primary drug choice was alcohol, or opiates, or cocaine. All were patients of one or other of 22 services in the Philadelphia area. Both substance use and social adjustment, including employment, crime, family and social relationships, were assessed. Results were similar across the three drug groups and across the different types of programme offered. Severity of drug problems at admission accounted for the largest proportion of variance in outcomes, both for substance-use outcome (12 per cent) and for social adjustment outcome (18 per cent). In addition the quantity of non-drug-focused treatments (including medical, psychiatric, employment and family services) accounted for 11 per cent of social adjustment at follow-up (but only 2–5 per cent of substance use), while the quantity of drug-focused services was hardly related at all to either kind of outcome (less than 1 per cent of the variance in both cases). In their 1998 paper McLellan *et al.* reported having taken this line of thought one stage further by 'enhancing', in a quasi-experimental design study, the addiction treatment provided in eight out of twelve public treatment programmes in the Philadelphia area, the other four serving as controls. The enhancement of treatment did not consist of more drug or alcohol counselling, since their earlier study had suggested that providing more of this would not result in better outcomes. Enhancement came, rather, in the form of supplemental social services provided by specially trained and appointed clinical case managers who arranged for people to be offered a core set of support services to assist them in areas such as education, employment, housing, recreation and parenting problems. At 6-months follow-up enhanced treatment was associated with better outcomes of a variety of kinds, including substance use, social, medical and mental health outcomes.

Work such as that of McLellan and colleagues recognises the broader social context in which expert treatment takes place but it still conceives of treatment as focused on individual people. There are many hints in the published literature that the process of giving up an excessive appetite can be a yet more social enterprise than the rather constricted, dominant, Western notions of therapy might suppose. Take, for example, the fascinating account given by Groth-Marnat *et al.* (1996) of quitting smoking in a Fijian village. Like many other 'developing' countries Fiji had seen a dramatic increase in smoking and at the time the study was carried out a third of the villagers were smokers. Earnings were low and up to a quarter of a smoker's salary might be devoted to smoking, a common feature of tobacco smoking in developing countries. The decision to quit smoking was a collective village decision, and an informal follow-up 9 months later found smoking to be almost non-existent in the village by then, and a more formal follow-up at 21 months indicated that smoking rates were still extremely low. Factors thought to be important included: the role of a trusted, professional, health-promotion team who had visited the village to discuss possibilities for reducing smoking, but had come to no clear conclusion; the village decision to quit, announced just before the health-promotion team left; collection and destruction of all cigarettes; holding a village kava ceremony; the declaring of a tabu on smoking and engendering the expectation that there would be harmful spiritual/supernatural consequences for anyone who broke it; and the total lack of sales outlets in the village, cigarettes coming in from trips the villagers made to large villages or towns some distance away. Local decisions to prohibit alcohol sales in indigenous communities in Latin America and Australia are other instances of social action to help individuals give up excess (Eber, 1995; Fleming *et al.*, 1991).

The picture of the change process that emerges from the literature on expert treatment and unaided change is not one, therefore, that suggests we may best understand giving up excessive appetites from the standpoint of any one expert theoretical model such as the cognitive-behavioural, interpersonal or 12-step models. We know that there are often reversions after treatment, and the process appears to be a more natural one, and perhaps more social in nature, than the expert models would suppose. But if the experts have got it wrong, how can we better understand how some people give up excessive appetites. The following chapter looks for an answer.

CHAPTER FOURTEEN

Giving Up Excess

Coming off drugs, then, is a complex procedure. It is not simply a case of making a decision not to consume particular substances. It is a process of decision-making based on a whole series of push-and-pull factors; some encouraging the women to want to quit, others pulling them back. Most of all, coming off entails establishing a whole new way of life and a new set of friends and companions. It was these issues which created and sustained the difficulties the women encountered in their endeavours.

(Taylor, 1993, p. 147)

The thinking process went on a lot longer and deeper. I really think I was sick and tired of it, really weary of it. Enough is enough.

(Cited by Sobell *et al.*, 1993, p. 222)

Don't for a split second allow yourself to think: 'Isn't it a pity or a mean injustice that I can't take a drink like so-called normal people'. Don't allow yourself to either think or talk about any real or imagined pleasure you once did get from drinking. Don't permit yourself to think a drink or two would make some bad situation better, or at least easier to live with ... Catalogue and re-catalogue the positive enjoyments of sobriety ... Associate a drink as being the single cause of all the misery, shame and mortification you have ever known ...

(From *15 Points for an Alcoholic to Consider when Confronted with the Urge to Take a Drink*, Alcoholics Anonymous, undated)

Drug taking, drinking, gambling, eating and exercising, and sex, all have the capacity to beget both pleasure and pain, fulfilment and harm. Accordingly, most societies have been at least ambivalent towards these activities and have been at pains to control them and to instil conformity to moderate, discriminating indulgence in them. Each individual person is heir to that ambivalence and continually faces a set of choices about the extent of her appetitive activity, although the weight of formal and informal pressures for and against greater or lesser indulgence may be so constraining that most people may not be aware most of the time that they are 'choosing' at all. If, however, because of the circumstances that pertain at certain stages of a person's life, because of the functions that appetitive behaviour serves at those stages, and because of developmental processes of individual and social kinds, behaviour exceeds the limits of what is considered normal, sensible or harmless, then the need to make a rational choice may become more salient. Paradoxically, choice has then probably become more difficult.

In Chapter Twelve it was argued that much of the behaviour of a person who experiences an excessive appetite can be understood as being a reflection of intensified conflict. Such a person shares the general ambivalence that people feel towards appetitive behaviour but experiences it to a heightened extent as a result of his increased attachment to it and the increased harm that it is causing him. It is part of the natural history, the argument continued, that people with excessive appetites should at some stage become aware of the need for change, or should at least be coerced by others into considering it. We should expect change towards reduced involvement to occur as part of the natural course of events. In Chapter Thirteen, some work was then reviewed which supports that expectation. One way to read the research evidence is to conclude that a great deal of change takes place outside of formal treatment. The latter, although probably effective to a modest degree, constitutes only a small part of the picture and matching of client to treatment type may not help much. Understandably, in view of what we know of excessive appetites, rates of reversion to excessive behaviour are high immediately following treatment. Impressive, however, is the fact that a substantial minority of people do make drastic changes towards reduced appetitive behaviour either following expert treatment or without it. The purpose of the present chapter is to propose a way to understand these changes.

CHANGE AS A COMPLEX, NATURALLY OCCURRING PROCESS

Trying to understand how people moderate or give up excessive appetitive behaviour has excited a great deal of comment and research activity. Much of it testifies to the confusing complexity of the process. At the same time, much of it makes it clear why change might often occur quite naturally in the course of people's lives, without specialised, expert help. The following are examples of the work that has been done.

Pearson (1987) and Taylor (1993), for example, considered the change process in their studies of heroin users in the north of England and women drug injectors in Glasgow, respectively. Both described change as a complex, naturally occurring process. According to Pearson, this process always involved a degree of subtle external compulsion or a calculation of the balance between the benefits and costs of continued drug use and, according to Taylor, reasons for coming off included both external factors such as hassles of various kinds, childcare or concern about one's health, plus an internal commitment or 'readiness'. Both authors concluded that overcoming withdrawal is not such a great restraint to change and can be exaggerated, but that staying off and building a new life is what is most difficult. Pearson wrote of the need to replace the 'routine' of heroin, building new routines, motivations and friendships. Taylor wrote of the need to avoid drug-using friends, and to create a whole new way of life with a new set of friends, plus the need to cope with 'the mental side', being alone with bad thoughts including guilt about past behaviour, and a lack of self-confidence.

Bammer and Weekes (1994), who carried out a small study of 18 Australians changing from being dependent on heroin to non-dependent heroin use (they were careful about their criteria here), also described change as a complex process. Some of this group had received treatment and some not, and their length of heroin use varied considerably. Many different factors appeared to have been important in change including: reaching a 'rock bottom', a personal crisis, witnessing someone else's crisis such as an overdose, forming a new relationship, having children, relocation to Australia or inter-state, leaving a relationship with a drug user (this applied only to women), needing to avoid police involvement or jail, becoming sick of the addict life, developing a purpose in life, helping others, work, use of marijuana, and dealing with the scars of one's early life, or of the heroin 'using life'. Some of these factors operated to motivate change, some to maintain it, and others contributed to both. Treatment, in the form of methadone maintenance or a therapeutic community, had helped in a number of very varied ways.

Klingemann (1991) reported on the process of change as described by a Swiss sample of people, some of whom had been excessive users of heroin, others of alcohol. He described this as a study of 'autoremission' although most of the sample had had at least minimal treatment contact, and it was not always well established that full recovery had occured. Klingemann's paper focused on the first of what were believed to be three stages of the change process: motivation, action and maintenance. It is the variation in the circumstances of change that comes across most strongly from his paper. For some, motivation to change appeared to result from an accumulation of stressors, in some instances giving the impression that the person concerned had experienced a 'reaching rock bottom'. Particularly often mentioned were 'loss events' including health problems, financial problems, job difficulties, problems obtaining enough alcohol or heroin, and separation or divorce, as well as experiences in the category of 'mental distress' including feelings of helplessness and insecurity, family tensions, fear of trouble with the police or authorities, tension with friends and thoughts of suicide. In some cases there appeared to be a gradual accumulation of such negative experiences, but in others a sudden change (e.g. as a result of a frightening emergency admission to hospital). In still other instances the emphasis in people's accounts was more upon positive events, new identities and 'maturing out' of addiction.

A particularly careful attempt to construct, retrospectively, the events that might have given rise to the resolution of a drinking problem was reported by Tucker *et al.* (1994) who tried to improve still further on the earlier such study by Sobell *et al.* (1993). Employing strict criteria for what constituted an alcohol problem and its resolution, they compared 21 resolved, abstinent, former problem drinkers (an average of 6 years abstinent) with 18 non-resolved. They asked about events occurring in the 2 years prior to resolution, or to a matched target date for the non-resolved, and 1 year following that date. Most striking was the importance of negative health events which were more common among the resolved in the years prior to resolution (especially in the year immediately prior) and which were reduced in the year following. Such events were mentioned by a majority of resolved former problem drinkers as constituting an important reason for resolution (more so than any other factor) and as a maintenance factor. Interestingly, negative work and legal events were high 2 years prior to resolution but reduced in the year immediately prior to it, suggesting to Tucker *et al.* that successful change might require a convergence of both motivating and stabilising influences. The former problem drinkers themselves were divided on the question of whether immediately prior influences, longer term influences, or both, were important in resolving to abstain.

Edwards *et al.* (1992) reported the results of the qualitative analysis of pre-attempt, attempt and post-attempt themes connected with 22 successful and 26 unsuccessful attempts to give up excessive drinking reported by 49 men 10 years after entering treatment in London. Like others they were impressed by the many extraneous events and circumstances that appeared to influence the change process, and concluded that the extra-treatment environment had been neglected. They found support for the influence of negative stressful events, positive events and 'Damascus events' occurring prior to successful attempts. They found very little mention of the importance of treatment or Alcoholics Anonymous (AA), but did find confirmation of Vaillant's (1983) finding that the substitution of some other habitual or preoccupying activity was often valuable, and for processes they referred to as 'altruism' (e.g. generosity towards others such as wife and family, AA members, neighbours) and 'rewarding' (e.g. enjoyment of health, job, family life, material success).

Another 10-year treatment follow-up, in this case of 44 out of 50 women treated for bulimia, was reported by Collings and King (1994). They reported, with evident surprise, that the outcome for this group was very good, with 52 per cent apparently fully recovered and only 9 per cent still showing the full bulimia syndrome, and continued improvement having occurred between the 5-year and 10-year follow-ups. Although they concluded that treatment is necessary, individuals themselves thought that positive change was the result of personal maturity and using one's own resources especially those of family and friends.

The universal nature of the process of giving up excessive appetites is illustrated by accounts obtained by Brady (1993, 1995) from Australian Aboriginal people in Northern Territory and South Australia. A number of the accounts illustrate how people can give up excessive drinking without treatment. One was cited at the beginning of Chapter Thirteen. In her 1993 paper, Brady focused on 37 such accounts of change that had occurred without specialised treatment. Nearly half of these changes were attributed to a medical condition or a doctor's warning (e.g. 'hard talk. The doctor gave me hard talk', p. 403). A quarter cited family considerations; either responsibilities for care of children or elderly relatives, or because a spouse had left. A quarter referred to the importance of Christianity in the change process: three had converted to Christianity at the same time they gave up excessive drinking and another six mentioned the way in which religion legitimised becoming abstinent and offered a social network supporting change. Brady also noted how common it was for those who had given up drinking to look back ruefully on the ageing effects of alcohol on themselves, and to observe this in others who had not given up drinking. Perhaps it is a case of 'ageing out' of excessive drinking rather than 'maturing out' as Winick (1962) had it.

DECIDING AND RESOLVING

Many students of the change process, including a number of those whose ideas have been described above, have spoken of an early stage in the process involving a higher mental process that they call 'resolving', 'decision making', 'strategic' or the like (see Table 14.1). For example, in the results of their study of change without treatment, referred to in Chapter Thirteen, Sobell *et al.* (1992) were particularly struck by the weight their participants gave to cognitive evaluations of their drinking and its effects. The following is an example:

> A growing sense of despair about his drinking, didn't want to live that way, couldn't do things while drinking. Felt he 'had reached a state of mind that day and probably after that day where I was prepared to do something with an appropriate trigger'.
>
> (Sobell *et al.*, 1993, p. 222)

Sobell *et al.* suggested that this cognitive evaluation process is characterised by people, '... weighing the perceived costs and benefits of continuing to drink and deciding that the adverse consequences outweigh the benefits (i.e. the scale has tipped)' (p. 222).

If it is the case that the maintenance of excess has much to do with the ready automatic activation of schemata, as Tiffany (1990), McCusker *et al.* (1995b) and others have suggested (see Chapter Eleven), then it is reasonable to suppose that the use of non-automatic, 'higher', cognitive processes may be necessary in order to block the habit. A number of models of change have been offered up based on this idea that change requires the automatic (some would use one or other of the disputed words 'impulsive' or 'compulsive') nature of addiction to be over-ridden by a more conscious, self-controlling mechanism, and most of these have suggested that change occurs in a series of logical stages.

It is certainly tempting to construe such changes in the language of decision-making. It seems intuitively correct to speak of someone with a strong appetite as facing a difficult 'decision' and the model of addiction as conflict developed in Part

Table 14.1 Cognitive factors in the change process

Maturing out	Winick (1962)
Resolving	Biernacki (1986)
Appraisal of danger	Janis and Mann (1977)
Humiliation	Tuchfeld (1981)
Decision making	Armor *et al.* (1978)
Contemplation	DiClemente and Prochaska (1982)
Cognitive evaluation	Sobell *et al.* (1993)
Self-regulation	Miller and Brown (1991)

II lends itself to this construction. According to this view the individual faces a choice between behavioural options. The choice is a particularly difficult one, because good intentions are opposed by an attachment which may have grown to considerable strength. Like other major life choices and decisions, however, it is one for which the individual is responsible and it will be made personally. Equally, however, like most choices, it will be made with the help, encouragement and manipulation of the most influential other people in a person's life. It is interesting to note that this language comes readily to mind when speaking of the decision to quit smoking, but is less familiar in the context of 'alcohol dependence', 'drug addiction', 'compulsive gambling', 'bulimia', or sexual 'addictions' such as 'nymphomania'. The latter constructions on behaviour are themselves products of a process of medicalising behaviour, a process that inevitably shifts the emphasis away from personal responsibility for decision-making and towards the acceptance of the existence of a disease or illness condition which requires treatment.

That successful change in appetitive behaviour is associated with some kind of higher order mental process of this kind was also suggested by W. Hunt and his colleagues who investigated 'relapse' curves (see Chapter Thirteen). H. Hunt (1968, cited by W. Hunt and Matarazzo, 1973) wrote:

> People do become persuaded, do see themselves and others differently, do come to view the world in new ways, and so on. These ideas and insights may be thought of as verbal or symbolic responses, however covert, with consequences ... that affect overt behaviours over a broad range... in a unitary fashion... such that the change is hard to explain in terms of piecemeal, response-by-response alteration ... In effect a new strategy appears to have been adopted, with the specific elements of the new behaviour representing tactical implementation of the strategy, as determined opportunistically by the present situation and by previous learning.
>
> (Hunt and Matarazzo, 1973, p. 113)

Such formulations of change which rely heavily upon cognitive processes do a number of things which we should expect of an explanation of the change process. They serve to unite knowledge about the different kinds of excessive behaviour which might otherwise be held distinct: to view the giving up of excessive drinking in terms of 'treatment' and the giving up of excessive smoking in terms of 'decision-making' is less helpful. They also unite clinical work carried out largely by professionals working with patients and clients in clinics, surgeries and community centres, with work done by epidemiologists and social scientists in the community. Finally, and possibly of most significance, they unify our understanding of how excessive appetitive behaviour is taken up and given up in terms of one model of appetitite motivation. They suggest that the processes at work are in essence the same as those affecting the behaviour of the Jessors' students (see Chapter Seven) faced with choices about the extent of their involvement in a variety of appetitive acts.

This model of the change process speaks of the making of decisions on the basis of an appraisal of the 'balance' of accumulated 'losses', 'costs' or harm resulting from behaviour versus the 'gains', or benefits, of pleasurable outcomes of appetitive behaviour. Conflict between the desire to continue with the appetitive behaviour on the one hand, and other needs (to be a bread-winner, to be a family person, to enjoy life, to have a clear conscience, to have friends, to have self-respect, etc.), on the other hand, which cannot be resolved by the defence mechanisms which have served up to that time, provides the motivation for change.

Motivated by the unhealthy state of the appetitive behaviour 'balance sheet', and prompted by some crisis event, the individual becomes sensitised, so the model supposes, to the possibility of new solutions. Although some possible solutions to such behavioural dilemmas may be suggested by experts, such as mental health professionals or self-help groups, there seems no particular reason to suppose that these have any monopoly upon advice that may be useful under such circumstances. It is not so much that change may be 'spontaneous', or 'unaided', but rather that, sensitised to the need for change, an individual may receive advice or encouragement from any one or more than one of a variety of sources, or indeed may 'come to her senses' as a result of her own appraisal of the state of affairs (Orford, 1980). A very similar understanding of change in drinking problems was reached by Armor *et al.* (1978). They found, as have others, that successful change was not strongly related to the amount of treatment received, nor was it easily predictable on the basis of the kinds of social and psychological client variables which they examined:

> We suggest that [recovery] has to do with individual factors, among which individual decision making might be especially prominent. Decision making, in this sense, refers to what is probably a highly complex cognitive process involving at least three components: (1) experience of the 'costs' of alcoholism that outweigh short-run reasons for drinking; (2) a breakdown of psychological defenses (e.g. denial) enabling a recognition of the problem; and (3) a commitment to change.
>
> (Armor *et al.*, 1978, p. 138)

The model of appetitive behaviour change developed and elaborated by Janis and Mann (1968, 1977) was also one of decision-making. In the earliest of these works, a 5-stage decision process was posited through which it was suggested a heavy smoker might pass having decided to stop smoking after having been exposed to anti-smoking publicity. The five stages in their model were: positive appraisal of danger, positive appraisal of a particular recommendation (R) for change, selection of R as the best alternative, commitment to the decision to adopt R, and adherence to R despite challenge. This scheme placed considerable emphasis on the existence of a specific recommendation for new behaviour, and the individual's evaluation of it and subsequent commitment to it. Again there was no suggestion here that the source of the recommendation need be expert or professional, although it might come from a prestigious source such as a general medical practitioner or a well-publicised report such as the *Surgeon General's Report on Smoking and Lung Cancer*. In their book entitled *Decision-making: A Psychological Analysis of Conflict, Choice and Commitment* Janis and Mann (1977) extended their ideas on conflict and decision-making to excessive eating, drinking, and drug taking, and put such appetitive decisions into the wider context of health-related decisions and important life decisions in general. 'Recommendations' had now been broadened to include all relevant 'communications'—personal or mass media—and also significant 'events'. This recognition that a variety of everyday happenings might provide the stimulus for reconsidering behaviour makes it doubly clear that change is to be expected both with and without the intervention of experts.

One of the implications of adopting such a view is that chronic excess is to be seen not as the inevitable result of a progressive disease process, but rather as the end result of a succession of wrong or failed decisions. Hence, a dissonant smoker is someone who has not only developed a strong appetite for smoking, but is also someone who has not yet reacted to the dissonance involved by becoming an ex-smoker or by making a drastic reduction in consumption. This leads to one important conclusion, stated earlier but worth repeating, namely that the prediction of whose behaviour will ultimately become so excessive that they seek help on account of it cannot be expected at the outset of a career. The model is not one of the unfolding of a process which was latent from the beginning and which could be predicted on the basis of personal or social factors, but rather one of uncertain movements upwards and downwards, with the ever-present possibility of removing oneself from the group at risk by making a decision to drastically reduce or perhaps abstain from consumption or activity.

Janis and Mann (1977) acknowledged that the first of their stages in particular, the necessary initial reappraisal, might occur slowly and gradually over a very long period of time—the 'slow burn' type of chronic reappraisal as they called it. Furthermore, they concluded that by no means all decision-makers proceeded smoothly through all five stages in the approved sequence. A variety of reversions and feedback loops occurred. They commented that smokers and dieters in particular often seemed to go through stages 1 and 2 and then back to the start, repeatedly, in a series of 'short-circuited decision loops'. Janis and Mann seem here to have observed about the excessive appetites something akin to Hunt and Matarazzo's finding of high relapse rates for the 'addictions' after treatment, which the latter writers interpreted in terms of the extinction of new learning in the absence of firm decision-making.

Of the different ways of responding to public-health messages or warnings or other communications or events which forced a reappraisal, it was 'vigilance' which Janis and Mann (1977) considered mostly resulted in the best decisions. This involved searching for relevant information and objectively appraising alternatives before making a choice, and it occurred when an individual was aware of the risks involved in behaviour, was hopeful of finding a better solution and believed there was time to search for the best solution. They recommended the full completion of an actual 'balance sheet' (part of their hypothetical balance sheet for a conflicted smoker is shown in Table 14.2) as a pre-decisional exercise encouraging vigilance. In support of this procedure, they provided the following quotation from Benjamin Franklin, writing to the scientist Joseph Priestley in 1772:

> When those difficult cases occur, they are difficult, chiefly because while we
> have them under consideration, all the reasons pro and con are not present
> to the mind at the same time; but sometimes one set present themselves, and

Table 14.2 Hypothetical balance sheet for a smoker challenged by publicity about smoking and lung cancer (adapted by permission of Academic Press, Inc. from Janis and Mann, 1968)

Alternative courses of action	Anticipated utilitarian consequences		Anticipated approval or disapproval	
	For self	For significant others	From self	From significant others
1. Original policy (continue smoking about one pack per day) (judged unsatisfactory)	+ Provides daily pleasure; sometimes relieves emotional tension	Helps me to get along better with my family and fellow workers	I pride myself on not scaring easily	My statistician friend will be pleased I do not accept correlation as proving causation
	− Possiblity of lung cancer; respiratory illness more serious; costs money	Family would suffer if I had cancer	I would feel untrustworthy and weak; I'd feel guilty for having ignored medical evidence if I became ill	Would lose respect since I told friends I was going to change my habits; doctor and other friends will continue to disapprove
2. New recommended policy (stop smoking) (judged mixed)	+ Chances of cancer greatly reduced; respiratory illness less troublesome; money put to good use	Family will feel more secure; good influence on children's smoking	Feeling of satisfaction; acting on evidence shows one is mature, realistic and intelligent	Friends will see I am living up to my commitment; doctor and friends will strongly approve
	− Unpleasant craving; more irritable and angry; possibly anxiety symptoms and overweight	Increased irritation and tension could strain the marriage	Might lose my temper more often, which would make me feel like a heel	My statistician friend will think I am stupid
3. Alternative compromise policy (smoke about half a pack per day) (judged most satisfactory)	+ Same as No. 1 to a milder degree, risk of cancer greatly reduced	Same as No. 2 to a milder degree	Same as No. 2 to a milder degree	Same as No. 2 to a milder degree
	− Same as No. 2 to a milder degree; no overweight; slight risk of lung cancer	Same as No. 2 to a milder degree	Going only part way may show a lack of self-control	Doctor and some friends will not approve of this compromise

at other times another, the first being out of sight. Hence the various purposes or inclinations that alternatively prevail, and the uncertainty that perplexes us. To get over this, my way is to divide half a sheet of paper by a line into two columns; writing over the one Pro, and over the other Con. Then, during three or four days consideration, I put down under the different heads short hints of the different motives, that at different times occur to me, for or against the measure. When I have thus got them all together in one view, I endeavor to estimate their respective weights; and where I find two, one on each side, that seem equal, I strike them both out. If I find a reason pro equal to some two reasons con, I strike out the three ... and thus proceeding I find at length where the balance lies; and if, after a day or two of further consideration, nothing new that is of importance occurs on either side, I come to a determination accordingly. And, though the weight of reasons cannot be taken with the precision of algebraic quantities, yet when each is thus considered, separately and comparatively, and the whole lies before me, I think I can judge better, and am less liable to make a rash step, and in fact I have found great advantage from this kind of equation, in what may be called moral or prudential algebra.

(Benjamin Franklin, cited in Janis and Mann, 1977, p. 149)

Benjamin Franklin was right, I am sure, about the limitations of mathematics here. At one time it was thought that quantifying the elements involved in decisions might provide better predictions of, for example, seeking change (e.g. Mausner and Platt's, 1971, use of 'subjective expected utility' or SEU theory), but such attempts at precision failed, as Franklin could have told us they would. A more general limitation of the balance-sheet approach is that it assumes that all sources of motive, both for and against appetitive behaviour, can be made public and cast in the form of statements which suggest understandable, even reasonable, motives. This may not always be the case, particularly in that part of the balance sheet concerned with positive motives for continuing with excessive behaviour. Habit may be based very largely upon processes that operate automatically, beyond full awareness. Indeed, the main argument of much of Part II of the present book was that the disease-like quality of habitual excessive behaviour is due to circumstances which allow the flourishing of strong attachment-forming processes, which in some cases are more than a match for forces of restraint, although the latter may appear much the more reasonable and may be much more easily listed in the form of words.

STAGES AND PROCESSES

A further limitation of purely cognitive models of change is that they take little account of what follows the making of a decision or a resolution to change. The idea that giving up an excessive appetite is best thought of in terms of a number of different stages involving a number of different processes, some cognitive or 'experiential' and some behavioural or action-oriented, is now very widely held as a result of Prochaska and DiClemente's well-known stage model of change (e.g. DiClemente *et al.*, 1991; Prochaska *et al.*, 1992). Although their ideas were remarkably similar to those of a number of earlier writers especially those of Janis and Mann (1977), Prochaska and DiClemente carried out their own programme of research on smoking and other addictive behaviours and put their ideas together in a form that was straightforward and appealing to addiction practioners. Like Janis and Mann (1977), they stressed that they pictured change, not as a straightforward linear movement through stages, but rather as a spiral, with people often recycling through earlier stages, frequently taking two steps forward and one step back, and making positive changes over longer rather than shorter periods of time.

For a number of years four stages figured in the 'stages of change' model as described in various papers by Prochaska and DiClemente and their colleagues. These stages were: precontemplation, contemplation, action and maintenance. A 'decision-making' stage, between contemplation and action had figured in that group's provisional thinking but factor analyses of their data had suggested only the four stages. Later, this missing stage, now termed 'preparation', was reintroduced on the grounds that an alternative multivariate statistical technique, cluster analysis, suggested that some people were indeed at an immediate stage, having gone beyond merely thinking about changing and, now having done some planning about how and when to change, were prepared to act (Prochaska *et al.*, 1992). The preparation stage was distinguishable from contemplation which was a stage in which people could remain stuck for long periods, characterised by an awareness that a problem exists and some thinking about overcoming it, but without commitment to take action. In view of what Sobell *et al.* (1993) and so many others have said about cognitive evaluation, it is notable that the stages-of-change group considered an important aspect of the contemplation stage to be, '... the weighing of the pros and cons of the problem and solution to the problem. Contemplators appear to struggle with their positive evaluations of the addictive behavior and the amount of effort, energy and loss it will cost to overcome the problem' (Prochaska *et al.*, 1992, p. 1103)

Less well known than the stages element of their model of change are the *processes* of change, of which there were believed to be the 10 shown in Table 14.3. These were developed by studying what had been written about change according to various leading schools of psychotherapy: hence the claim that the model is 'transtheoretical'. Subsequent work by the group showed that the same processes were used by those attempting to change an addiction, whether with or without formal treatment. Hence their claim was that the model truly cuts across the somewhat artificial distinction between 'treatment' and self-change, and is neither technique-oriented nor problem-specific (Prochaska *et al.*, 1992).

Evidence that some of these processes are used more at certain stages, and other processes more at other stages, comes from several studies including one of smokers over a 2-year period (Prochaska *et al.*, 1991 cited by Prochaska *et al.*, 1992). Some of the more cognitive processes—self-re-evaluation, consciousness raising, and dramatic relief—demonstrated significant decreases as smokers moved through the action stage, into maintenance. Conversely, other processes, particularly the more behavioural ones—stimulus control and counter-conditioning—showed increases as smokers moved from contemplation to action.

Table 14.3   Ten processes of change, with sample questionnaire items (Prochaska *et al.*, 1991)

Processes	Sample item
Consciousness raising	I look for information related to smoking
Self-liberation	I tell myself I am able to quit smoking if I want to
Social liberation	I notice that public places have sections set aside for non-smokers
Self-reevaluation	My depending on cigarettes makes me feel disappointed in myself
Environmental reevaluation	I stop to think that smoking is polluting the environment
Counterconditioning	I do something else instead of smoking when I need to relax
Stimulus control	I remove things from my place of work that remind me of smoking
Reinforcement management	I am rewarded by others if I don't smoke
Dramatic relief	Warnings about health hazards of smoking move me emotionally
Helping relationships	I have someone who listens when I need to talk about my smoking

Rather under-played in their summary of relevant research was the finding that the three processes ranked as the most used across smoking, overweight and general psychological distress were: helping relationships, consciousness raising and self-liberation. This is an important clue that some of the key processes may be very general ones indeed. Another interesting point to note is that the only process among the 10 which hints that there might be factors in society, beyond the individual, that might need changing (social liberation) quietly gets dropped, without comment, when it comes to reporting how processes change over time. It is quite clear that what we are dealing with all the time here, as might be expected from a Western-dominated psychology and psychotherapy literature, are problems and solutions conceived of in almost entirely individualistic terms.

Subsequent work has tended to support the broad outlines of the stages-of-change model suggesting that it might be applicable to a range of excessive appetites (not just to smoking which gave rise to the model: e.g. excessive drinking—Snow *et al.*, 1994; and eating disorders—Blake *et al.*, 1997), to people in different countries, and equally to men and women. For example, Dijkstra *et al.* (1996) found that the way people's personal pros and cons of smoking change and the way their self-efficacy changes over the five stages of the smoking-change process were in general similar in Holland, despite the fact that there were more smokers and less widespread intention to quit smoking in Holland than in the USA where the original work was done. At early stages in the process, increasing affirmation of the arguments pro stopping smoking was the main discriminator of one stage from the previous stage, with increments in self-efficacy being more discriminating at later stages. It may be noted, as a potential conceptual weakness, that the pros and cons of continued smoking were considered comparable with the cons and pros of quitting and were not separately assessed in Dijkstra *et al.*'s or other studies. The arbitrariness of the division between precontemplation and preparation stages, and between preparation and action, is also evident. In fact Dijkstra *et al.* defined the preparation stage slightly differently to DiClemente *et al.* (1991)—the latter had included having made a 24-hour quit attempt in the last year in their definition of preparation, but Dijkstra *et al.* did not.

O'Connor *et al.* (1996) looked for sex differences in use of the 10 supposed processes of change (shown in Table 14.3) in the initial data from DiClemente *et al.*'s smoking-treatment study. Multivariate statistical analysis supported the idea that there were two process factors underlying the 10 identified individual processes, one factor being experiential (cognitive), the other behavioural. As expected, analysis showed there to be a main effect by stage with some support for the view that experiential processes would rise at early stages (although this was true of behavioural processes also), with an increase in behavioural processes being more important at the action stage when signs of the use of experiential processes in fact declined somewhat. The sex differences were small, inconsistent with previous literature, and only appeared at the contemplation stage. O'Connor *et al.* concluded that their analysis provided support for the main outlines of the stages-of-change process, and for this process being essentially the same for women and men.

There have been a number of criticisms of the stages-of-change model (e.g. Davidson, 1992; Sutton, 1996). Sutton (1996) reviewed the evidence and concluded that the model was weak on conceptual and empirical grounds. He pointed out that not only were the distinctions between the supposed stages often arbitrary (e.g. between contemplation and preparation, and between action and maintenance), but also the correlational evidence was not, as it should be, that adjacent stages were moderately positively correlated and non-adjacent stages less so. The evidence, rather, showed that correlations between non-adjacent stages (e.g. contemplation and maintenance) were sometimes almost as large as those between adjacent stages; and furthermore that the correlation between precontemplation and contemplation was substantial and negative. There was to date no evidence, according to Sutton, that individuals could be found who had moved through more than two of the supposed stages, even in Prochaska *et al.*'s (1991) follow-up study of smokers. The model was unable to predict *when* people would move from one stage to another. When it came to the supposed processes of change, Sutton could find evidence only in support of the rather general hypothesis that most processes would be at a low level during precontemplation, and that the more behavioural processes would tend to be used more frequently in the action and maintenance stages. More precise hypotheses about the timing of different processes had not been supported, and there was no evidence that the use of a process was predictive of moving on to the next stage (e.g. Is consciousness-raising at the contemplation stage predictive of moving on to preparation and action, or is it a *substitute* for action rather than a step towards it?). Sutton concluded:

> ... outside treatment and intervention settings, people do not move through the stages of change in an ordered fashion. Nor do they cycle through the stages in the way that the spiral representation of the model suggests. Motivation or intention to change may be more realistically thought of as

a continuum with no necessary assumption that people move along this continuum in one direction or through a sequence of discrete stages ... The stages of change model is not an accurate description of how people change. It should be thought of not as a descriptive model but as a *prescriptive model*—a model of *ideal* change.

(Sutton, 1996, pp. 203–204)

My own view is more positive (Orford, 1992a). Although, like so many detailed models in psychology before it, the stages-and-processes-of-change model does not stand up well to testing in fine detail, it has helped us move forward towards a more comprehensive model of change. In fact, although the stages aspect of their scheme is the better known, it is probably the processes aspect that is most helpful. It is not so much how processes relate to supposed stages which is useful, but rather the way information about processes assists us in explaining why it is that treatments with very different rationales, or indeed no treatment at all, may in essence allow the same fundamental things to take place. For instance, one relatively early study that is particularly interesting, because it involved both people who were attempting to give up smoking alone and those who had enrolled in one or other of two treatment programmes (aversion and behavioural management) was that by DiClemente and Prochaska (1982). There were some differences consistent with treatment rationale. For example, those in the behavioural-management group rated social management (getting other people involved in efforts to stop) as relatively more important than those in other groups, with the self-quitting group rating it least highly. On the other hand, most of the results support the view that the essential elements of change are not peculiar to 'treatment', let alone to any one particular form of treatment. Rated as most important, on average, by all three groups, were self-liberation (e.g. 'it was really a day-to-day commitment not to smoke and to stay away from cigarettes that helped me to quit smoking'), counter-conditioning (finding other ways to relax and deal with tension) and feedback (becoming aware of the reasons for smoking). Thus, feedback was rated highly by those enrolled in the two forms of treatment, although neither was designed particularly to produce insight. Similarly, finding alternatives to smoking was rated highly by the self-quitting group, although they were given no help in finding alternatives.

In particular, the commitment process of self-liberation was given the highest ratings overall and DiClemente and Prochaska (1982) expressed surprise that this process had received such little attention in writings on therapeutic change. They were particularly puzzled as to why aversion clients should rate self-liberation so highly. They were along the right lines, I believe, when they suggested that, '... the ordeal of undergoing unpleasant procedures either reflected or increased the personal commitment of the subjects' (p. 141).

But, fertile though the processes idea has been, it does not go nearly far enough in exploring the naturalness of addictive behaviour change. It remains too close to the preoccupations of those whose main interest is in expert treatment. What is more, its brand of individualism is largely cognitive–behavioural and the claim to be non-denominational or 'transtheoretical' is surely exaggerated (Orford, 1992a).

It leaves out, in particular, three vast domains of human experience that cannot be ignored: the social, the spiritual and the moral.

THE SOCIAL DIMENSION TO CHANGE

The social dimension is fundamental to the view of change offered in the present book. In fact, most models of health-relevant behaviour change take some account of it. This is true, for example, of Fishbein and Ajzen's (1975, cited by Sutton, 1989) 'theory of reasoned action'. This theory is considered applicable to health-related and other behaviours thought to be under volitional, decision-making, control. The intention to undertake a behaviour, such as giving up an appetitive activity, is presumed to be a function, not only of the person's beliefs that the behaviour will lead to certain outcomes and his or her evaluations of these outcomes (i.e. attitude towards the behaviour), but also the person's beliefs that specific individuals or groups think that he or she should or should not perform the behaviour, and the individual's motivation to comply with their wishes (what the theory calls 'subjective norm').

It is recognised, therefore, that, when it comes to making health decisions, the norms within the social groups of which one is part, and what significant other people think, matter. In the case of excessive appetites, which are mostly associated with serious social costs, this is likely to be even more the case. Although it has been argued earlier that a person experiencing an excessive appetite is often the one who is most critical of her own behaviour, and the one who exercises the firmest control, it is the case that excessive appetitive behaviour is out-of-control behaviour and thus constantly invites attempts at control.

A number of writers on the subject of change for excessive drinkers or 'substance abusers' have asked the question whether change, or at least entering treatment, is not very frequently associated with a large measure of coercion on the part of significant others (e.g. Wild *et al.*, 1998; Copello, 1999). In fact, direct coercion in the form of mandatory treatment is quite common. Court orders with a 'condition' of treatment attached, including programmes for repeat drink-driving offenders, and employee assistance programmes, which retain employees in employment while, and on condition that, they undergo treatment, are examples. Social pressures to change can be much less direct, however, and are probably much more common. For example, Wild *et al.* (1998) asked 300 clients entering 'substance abuse' (mainly of alcohol or cocaine) treatment in Toronto, Canada, whether they had felt coerced. Some were entering 'mandated' treatment, and not surprisingly they were more likely to have felt coerced. But a third of them reported no coercion, and a third of those registered as entering treatment as 'self-referrals' had felt coerced. In another study, Polcin and Weisner (1999) asked nearly 1000 clients of alcohol-treatment agencies whether an ultimatum had been given to them prior to entering treatment. A total of 40 per cent of the sample reported receiving such an ultimatum from at least one person, the most common source being family members (legal and health-care personnel being other common sources), ultimatums from more than one source being not uncommon.

Using a different method to approach the same question, Hasin (1994) asked members of a national US sample of over 1500 men, all of whom were current or past heavy drinkers, about pressures to enter treatment that they might have experienced from different sources within their social networks. A total of 7 per cent had ever gone to any help source about a problem related in any way to their drinking. Experience of treatment was strongly related to a score designed to reflect the total social pressure received. Each possible source of pressure was scored 1 if another person had, '... liked you to drink less or act differently when you drank' (p. 662), and 2 if they had broken up the relationship or threatened to on account of the person's excessive drinking. Hasin's analysis provides a fascinating glimpse of the extent and kinds of pressure that different people can bring to bear. Mothers, for example, were the source of a great deal of pressure, but very rarely to the extent that merited a score of 2 on the pressure scale. Spouses or partners, on the other hand, brought to bear lots of pressure, rated both 1 and 2. Work associates and other people exercised relatively little pressure, but when they did it often rated a 2.

Some time before most of the research reported here appeared, Bacon (1973) had arrived at a conclusion about the everyday, social nature of the change process for someone with a drinking problem which makes much sense in the light of what is now known. His position was:

> The recovery personnel of prime significance are the associates, the signifi-cant others. Perhaps medical or welfare or religious or law-enforcement personnel are essential at this or that stage, are necessary requirements for the treatment process even to begin, but the crucial persons for recovery are the daily life associates through time, not the specialists during formal 'treatment' periods ... The treatment methods crucial for recovery ... are those processes and structures and interrelationships and attitudes and behaviours of the person and of the relevant surrounding others which rebuild control ... recovery itself comprises the moulding of such changes into a pattern of life, life through time, life with meaningful others, life more satisfying to the person, to his associates, and to the community. It is that moulding through time, persons, and society which is the core of treatment.
>
> (Bacon, 1973, pp. 25–26)

This kind of 'social moulding' was prominent, also, in another outstanding con-tribution to the literature on processes of change, namely Biernacki's (1986) report after interviewing Californian heroin addicts who had given up heroin use without expert help (see Chapter Thirteen). He outlined a 4-stage model of change. The first stage of his model consisted, for most people, of a more or less rational, thought-out process of resolving to stop. The social dimension entered at the second stage—breaking away from addiction. This involved difficult tasks such as finding jobs and filling time, but a central idea was the need to break away from the addict world either geographically or symbolically (although Biernacki acknowledged that not all heroin users are equally part of an addict world that is distinct from the 'straight' world). The task of staying abstinent (the third stage) was mostly about craving and coping with craving, a phenomenon that Biernacki thought sometimes resembled heroin withdrawal and sometimes the immediate positive effects of the drug, neither model being wholly correct (see Chapter Ten). Arguably the most interesting section of Biernacki's book, however, was his description of the three types of social-identity transformation, one or other of which seemed always to be involved when an ex-addict reached the final stage of 'becoming ordinary':

> One course of recovery is an *emergent* one. The addicted person, by fortuitous circumstances or as a result of deliberation and intention, actively attempts to forge an identity (or a number of identities) that had not existed socially or subjectively before or that had existed only in the most rudimentary and socially unrealistic form. A second course, *identity reverting*, involves the reestablishment of an old identity that had not been spoiled by the addiction but had been held in abeyance during it. A third course of recovery entails the *extending of an identity* that existed during the addiction to replace the primacy of the addict identity.
>
> (Biernacki, 1986, p. 143)

A number of the Aboriginal Australian accounts of change without treatment, given by Brady (1995), also illustrate the need to remove oneself from, or actively resist, pressure from others who continue to use in a way that one considers excessive or dangerous to one's new identity. For example:

> I [used] to take a cup of tea with me when they had a party. They all used to laugh and say, 'you know, you're just pretending'. I even had people come to my house and look in me fridge. And yet there was beer there, but it wasn't mine, it was my husband's. So, they still didn't believe, you know. This day I said 'oh bugger it, I'm gonna give up drinking'. And I felt really crook, I thought 'oh well, this is the end of me' sort of thing you know. And people said 'oh, have one more can, you know, you'll feel better'. 'No', I said, 'if I'm gonna give it up I'll give it up'. Oh you'll only last two days. No, bin one year.
>
> (A woman from Katherine in the Northern Territory, Brady, 1995, p. 28)

The importance of making social changes so that the former excessive behaviour is now discouraged rather than encouraged received strong support from one of the clearest findings of Project MATCH, described in the previous chapter, namely the finding that 'social support for drinking' could be reduced, and hence the probability of a good outcome of treatment increased, by facilitating attendance at AA. AA, Gamblers Anonymous, Sexaholics Anonymous and other 12-step groups that aim to help members combat excessive appetites are undoubtedly complex organisations serving, like most mutual-help organisations, a variety of functions for their members (Orford, 1992b). The function of providing mutual social support is one that has long been recognised (e.g. Bales, 1945). Whatever the essence of the change process that is occurring, it must be acknowledged that, at least in the case of self-help groups, it takes place within a group or social context, and this is an aspect which has usually been considered by those who have studied such groups to be of vital significance (e.g. Bales, 1945; Robinson, 1979). It may be that what is important here is the support which other group members can provide. Consistent with the foregoing discussion, however, is a slightly different view, namely that the group provides a new set of attitudes and values, and it is to the group's ideology or 'will' that the novice must submit if he or she is to become a successful member. These two views of the social role of the mutual-help organisation are not as incompatible as they may at first seem. Janis and Rodin (1979) described 'social support' as a resource which combines friendship with demands for conformity. 'Support' does not come without strings, but imposes certain obligations upon those who are in receipt of it. As Tony Adams has said of his continued attendance at AA, 'I keep going to the meetings because I need to remain around like-thinking, right-thinking people' (Adams, 1998, postscript, p. 366).

In the report of their study of the functioning of AA in eight countries, Mäkelä *et al.* (1996) stressed repeatedly that AA should be clearly distinguished from expert, professional treatment: it was not, in their view, a treatment modality but a mutual-help movement (i.e. '... an association or aggregate of groups whose members meet on an egalitarian basis to counteract through mutual interaction a common affliction or problem in their lives': p. 13). Like others who have studied AA in Britain (Robinson, 1979), the USA (Hopson and Beaird-Spiller, 1994) or Denmark (Steffen, 1997), Mäkelä *et al.* placed emphasis, in trying to understand how AA works, on the use of speech and language in AA meetings. They characterised talk in meetings as being quite unlike ordinary conversations in which people generally reply to what has been said by the previous speaker. Talk in AA meetings, on the other hand, is in the form of turn taking governed by rules such as, Do not interrupt the person speaking, Speak about your own experiences, Do not speak about other people's private affairs, Do not openly confront or challenge previous turns of talk, Do not present psychological interpretation of the behaviour of other AA members (pp. 140–141).

Steffen's (1997) account of AA in Denmark, a country to which AA came comparatively late, also focused upon AA stories told at meetings, as lying at the core of the recovery process, linking the individual and the collective via rules of story telling and anecdotes, case stories and myths. In this way experience is shaped and members are socialised into the AA philosophy through 'co-action' of speaker and audience. Hopson and Beaird-Spiller (1994) also emphasised language. They put forward their view of how AA works on the basis of interviews with a number of excessive drinkers. Their perspective, not dissimilar to the more psychoanalytic view of sexual addiction taken by Goodman (1998), was that drinking is used in an attempt to manage intense and uncomfortable emotional states for which language is either inadequate or unavailable. Hence AA meetings could be understood as offering a series of lessons in utilising language to represent the self. Members practice the use of language to express their feelings and, at the same time, have the experience of 'hearing their story' in others who have spoken. Cognitive strategies, or 'self talk' using AA sayings or slogans, are also used to cope with feelings.

These few illustrations, then, show us some of the many ways in which other people are significant in the change process, whether by encouraging, coercing, supporting, helping resist pressure, training in new ways of talking about the self, or assisting in the development of a new identity that involves new possibilities and new obligations incompatible with excess.

THE SPIRITUAL DIMENSION TO CHANGE

The possibility that conventional, expert formulations of the change process may have omitted some of the more profound elements has been recognised from time to time by some of the more thoughtful commentators. For example, Drew (1990) observed, 'We have produced a psycho-bio-social model of drug dependence that excludes the essence of human existence—options, freedom to choose and the centrality of value systems' (p. 208). Miller (1990, 1998) has written of the neglect of the spiritual component in the theory and practice of addictive-behaviour change despite its clear presence in the philosophy of AA and other 12-step programmes, as well as its clear representation in psychology in the past. In the following passage, he makes a good case that a kind of spiritual vacuum, or loss of a sense of meaning in life, might be just as strong a metaphor as any other for understanding addiction:

> Prior interests and activities are progressively shunned as drug use becomes the central and dominant object of attention. Forsaking all else, seemingly oblivious to the detrimental consequences, the addict walks a narrow path in search of euphoria and oblivion, and is increasingly lost in drugs' embrace. In sum, drugs come to occupy the position of a higher power. In this sense, addiction is one of the clearest enduring models of idolatry—giving to something material that which is the rightful place of God. This is ... [one] meaning of *spiritus contra spiritum*: spirits (or, more generally, drugs of abuse) drive out spirituality.
>
> (Miller, 1998, p. 981)

We have already noted that religiosity appears to be protective against the development of excessive appetites (e.g. Jessor and Jessor, 1977; Jolly and Orford, 1983, and see Chapter Seven), and the suggestion now is that spirituality and religion might be equally, if not more important, in giving them up. As beliefs associated with major world religions constitute some of the most all-embracing sets of norms about social conduct and the self, amounting to comprehensive moral or ethical systems or 'attitudes to life', it should come as no surprise to find strong moral reform or spiritual-change elements in those programmes or organisations that appear to have had the greatest impact in the control of excessive appetites, nor to find that giving up excess is not infrequently accompanied by a reversal or change in religious sentiment or observance. In terms of consistency theory, spiritual change may be seen as a widespread logical change in a whole set of attitudes about right and wrong conduct. Such a sweeping change may sometimes be necessary to support a radical reversal of conduct in one particular area, such as sexual behaviour or the consumption of drugs.

Table 14.4 Selected 12-step movements in the USA (reprinted by permission from Mäkelä *et al.*, 1996, p. 217)

Date founded	Name	Number of groups	International
1951	Al-Anon Family Groups	32 000	+
1953	Narcotics Anonymous	22 000	+
1957	Alateen	4 100	−
1957	Gamblers Anonymous	1 200	+
1960	Overeaters Anonymous	10 000	+
1971	Emotions Anonymous	1 200	−
1976	Adult Children of Alcoholics	1 800	+
1976	Debtors Anonymous	400	−
1976	Augustine Fellowship Sex & Love Addicts Anonymous	1 000	+
1982	Survivors of Incest Anonymous	800	+
1982	Cocaine Anonymous	1 500	+
1985	Nicotine Anonymous	500	+
1986	Co-Dependents	3 500	+

The continued prominence and growth of mutual-help organisations, and particularly AA and other 12-step organisations, in the spectrum of modern forms of help for people with excessive appetites, strengthens the argument that the change process is not to be understood most readily by accepting the supposed rationales of modern physical or psychological treatments, or by taking too seriously their techniques, but rather by an appreciation of the factors that are common to a variety of forms, whether religious, medical, psychological or unaided. In organisational terms, AA is a quite remarkable phenomenon. Mäkelä (1991) described the diffusion of AA around the world between the mid-1960s and the 1980s, and Table 14.4, taken from Mäkelä *et al.*'s (1996) report of their study of AA in eight different countries, shows the growth of 12-step programmes in the USA for groups other than 'alcoholics', but in all cases based upon AA principles. All the major excessive appetites considered in this book are represented.

The unprecedented success of AA, in terms of survival and widespread diffusion, Mäkelä *et al.* attributed in part to the maintenance of a mutual-help philosophy and independence from professionals, plus an autonomous group, segmented cell, almost classically anarchic form of organisation. Despite the common literature, and informal links, groups were found to be autonomous and economically independent, decision-making was by consensus, and election to positions on a national body were for a very short term only. Hence the professionalisation of leadership was minimised and effective organisational power remained largely at the level of egalitarian face-to-face interaction. These positive features of AA have always made it difficult to carry out the kinds of controlled outcome evaluations that would satisfy the scientific community. Results from a number of studies, however, do suggest that attendance at AA is beneficial. There have been two published meta-analyses of studies of AA affiliation and outcome. The more recent (Tonigan *et al.*, 1996) analysed 74 studies, mostly of an AA focus in professional treatment or the inclusion of AA in formal treatment, rather than of AA itself. Although most of the studies reviewed were found to be methodologically weak, the analysis was, like the earlier review (Emrick *et al.*, 1993) positive overall in its conclusions regarding the effectiveness of AA. A number of individual studies reported in the second half of the 1990s have tended to support the effectiveness of AA, and there are signs that psychologists in the USA at least are taking AA much more seriously than previously (e.g. McCrady *et al.*, 1996).

In their study of what happened to several hundred people originally contacted at an alcohol-detoxification unit or information-and-referral centre, Humphreys *et al.* (1994, 1996, 1997) found evidence for the importance of attendance at AA. First, they reported that AA attendance was one of the best predictors of reduced alcohol consumption and associated problems 3 years later (Humphreys *et al.*, 1996). Within their stress-coping model, they also reported that the number of AA meetings attended, controlling for initial coping and for involvement in professional treatment, predicted the use of active forms of coping, both behavioural and cognitive, at 3-year follow-up, as well as an increase in friendship support (Humphreys *et al.*, 1994). They later reported an 8-year follow-up of 395 people from the same sample, finding that involvement in AA in the first 3 years was still predictive of a good outcome at 8 years (Humphreys *et al.*, 1997). The inclusion of a 12-step treatment condition in the large-scale Project MATCH (1997a, b) is a sure sign of the importance of this approach as perceived by experts in the USA. Not only did that study find that the 12-step facilitation treatment, based on AA principles and encouraging clients to attend AA, was equally as effective as two other expert forms of treatment (see Chapter Thirteen), but across all the treatment groups in that study, both AA involvement and religious/spiritual involvement were found to be modestly positively related to outcomes (Miller, 1998).

Miller and Kurtz (1994) mounted a strong defence of AA based on their reading of key items of AA literature. They characterised the AA model as undogmatic and flexible in comparison with an old moral–volitional model, an essentialist personality model, or a simple dispositional disease model. They also argued that AA was not a treatment, but rather a way of living and being, adopting a broad spiritual-bio-psycho-social model. They made the further point that it was not specific to alcohol, only the first of the 12 steps even naming alcohol. Emphasis, rather, was upon spiritual processes and upon character as lying at the root of the problem. 'Character', Miller and Kurtz pointed out, is not to be confused with 'personality'. The former concentrates on faults or defects, with clear moral connotations, such as selfishness, grandiosity, resentment, defiance, dishonesty and obsession with control. Nor does AA believe in coercion, they argued. It does believe, however, in the individual's responsibility for choosing to act to aid recovery. For example:

> As active alcoholics, we lost our ability to choose whether we would drink ...
> Yet we finally did make choices that brought about our recovery ... we chose
> to 'become willing', and no better choice did we ever make.
> (Wilson, 1967, p. 4, cited by Miller and Kurtz, p. 163)

The importance of a religious, or at least spiritual, element in the AA programme is apparent in two ways. First, this element is made quite explicit in the 12 steps which are to be followed by members and which constitute the core of the process. God, or 'a Higher Power', are mentioned in no less than six of the 12 steps, and although new members are instructed to interpret the expression 'Higher Power' in any way they like, religious or otherwise, the religious connotation is clear. Second, it is possible to trace the lineage of many modern self-help organisations, via AA, back to the Oxford Group Movement, a worldwide and still-functioning organisation, originally known as the First Century Christian Fellowship and later as Moral Re-Armament (Sagarin, 1969; Glaser, 1973; Kaufman and de Leon, 1978). The founder and guiding light of the Oxford Group Movement was Dr Frank Buchman who patterned the organisation upon his idea of what Christianity was like before the advent of the organized Church, and it was from this source that AA received its ideas of self-examination, acknowledgement of character defects, restitution for harm done to others and working with others. Among the key practices of the Oxford Group Movement was 'sharing', by which was meant the open confession of sins at large public meetings or smaller 'house parties'. A key practice, 'guidance', meant the acceptance of divine inspiration as the sole indication of action. People who accepted guidance were said to be under 'God control'.

In fact, whether AA is a religious organisation is a moot point. It seems that AA lives with much ambiguity on these issues, which may represent a strength in terms of appealing to a wide membership. AA literature asserts that the fellowship is spiritual rather than religious, and Mäkelä *et al.* (1996) cited results from surveys carried out in five of the countries they studied, showing how variable is the interpretation of the expression, A Power Greater Than Ourselves, that appears in AA's 12 steps. At one end of the spectrum, 56 per cent of members in Poland considered that it referred to the Christian God, while only 13 per cent felt this way in Sweden. Almost identical percentages in the two countries (58 and 59 per cent, respectively) took it to refer to the AA fellowship or the power of the group.

The principles of AA have been successfully adapted to the needs of those with other excessive appetites. Glaser (1973) traced the lineage of modern drug-free therapeutic communities (sometimes referred to as 'concept houses'), of which Synanon in California appears to have been the first, and other communities such as Daytop Village in New York and Phoenix Houses in New York and Britain were later examples. The link with AA was via the founder of Synanon, Charles Dederich, who was himself a graduate of AA. According to Glaser, '... it is clear that Synanon evolved out of Alcoholics Anonymous' (p. 6). It was Glaser's view that Synanon introduced some important innovations in translating the AA type of self-help approach into a form that might work with excessive drug takers:

> Alcoholics Anonymous espouses a God-centred theology, whilst Synanon espouses a secular ideology ... However the change is one of content. The form is the same. Whether secular or sacred, a form common to all of these organizations is an intensely-held, highly cherished belief system ... Before Dederich, the programs had Religion; now they have religion ... Incidentally, the essentially religious nature of these programs ... may

partly explain the opposition to them by the mental health professions, which are famously and fashionably irreligious.

(Glaser, 1973, pp. 9–10)

There have been a number of studies of Gamblers Anonymous (GA), once again suggesting that basic principles can be adapted to different circumstances. In his description of what he called the 'inspirational' group therapy of GA, Scodel (1964) noted a number of AA-like features including the spiritual nature of the programme and the way frequent mention was made of newly acquired religiosity incorporated into the person's pronouncement of a reformation of character. The '... renunciation of hedonism and the (avowed) internalization of new, austere values' (p. 117), was also a major theme which he noted in group meetings. Frequent mention of adulterous sexual behaviour was also made, as it was with great regularity at Oxford Group confessionals (Glaser, 1973). On the basis of his observational study of 100 AA and 70 GA meetings in California in 1989 and 1990 and a number of interviews with members, Browne (1991) concluded, on the other hand, that the two were very different despite the common 12-step idea. Most GA groups were smaller, but the main differences detected by Browne were the down-playing of the explicitly spiritual aspects (e.g. the word God had been removed from the 12 GA steps), a de-emphasising of the steps themselves and of 'working the steps' which is so important to AA, a far greater emphasis upon members' financial circumstances in GA (e.g. Step 3 required GA members to make a searching and fearless moral *and financial* inventory of themselves), but most particularly the GA conception of the central problem being excessive gambling:

> In GA the dominant position is that gambling is the problem. And although some hold the view that gambling is merely a symptom of the real problem it is not the dominant view. In AA, on the other hand, the dominant position is that although alcohol is important, it is not the major problem the alcoholic has. Alcohol, for AA, is an epiphenomenon; the real problem is the self-centred, self-loathing or self-praising.
>
> (Browne, 1991, p. 197)

AA, GA, other 12-step organisations, and drug rehabilitation programmes such as Synanon, all have their roots in the Christian religion. Mäkelä *et al.* (1996) noted that AA's type of spirituality may have constituted a difficulty for those professing some other religions, or who are offended by AA's flexible idea of a Higher Power (e.g. in Islamic societies, and among more traditional and fundamentalist Christians, and orthodox Jews). It may also have been a difficulty, they suggested, for 'offspring of the European Enlightenment', particularly those with Marxist, scientific or humanist perspectives. Religions other than Christianity also have much to say, however, about the potentially excessive nature of appetites. In Islam, 'strong drink ... and games of chance ...', are prohibited as a result of the successive Revelations of the Prophet Mohammed (Baasher, 1981). In Buddhist teaching, according to Groves and Farmer (1994), ideas of 'craving', 'attachment' and 'false refuge' are central concerns. Hence addiction can readily be viewed as a false refuge and a source of attachment which unwittingly leads to suffering, and the treatment of excessive alcohol and drug users has sometimes occurred in an explicitly Buddhist context (e.g. in Thailand heroin users have been offered detoxification treatment using herbal medicines and religious rites, and in Japan excessive drinkers have been given a week's intensive meditation with reflections on family and close friends). We should not be surprised to note that between 20 and 30 per cent of 'opiate abusers' were found to be abstinent 6 months after leaving treatment in a Thai temple (Groves and Farmer, 1994), since this roughly corresponds to the proportion of people who remain unrelapsed after expert treatments of various kinds for a number of excessive appetites (see Chapter Thirteen).

GIVING UP EXCESS AS MORAL REFORM

Is it too fanciful then to go one step further and conclude that giving up an excessive appetite is essentially a process of moral reform? Many people who have written thoughtfully on the subject have at least come close to believing that it might be so. For example, Heather (1994) offered 'limited endorsement' of the lay view that addiction was, in essence, a problem of 'weakness of will', addiction being characterised by repeated breaking of strong resolutions to desist from behaviour, '. . . in the face of a strong desire to carry out the behaviour and in the presence of complaints by the person carrying out the behaviour that it is out of his or her control' (p. 135). Although Heather appeared to be on the brink of acknowledging that change might therefore be seen as a moral issue—he refers to addictions as 'sins of commission' and goes so far as to suggest that attempts to overcome addictions might, from this point of view, look more like 'moral education' than like 'treatment'—he was wary of being thought to be recommending, '. . . a return to a moralistic account of addiction . . .', and expressed a fear of appearing, '. . . to become involved in moral judgements and being thought "unscientific" on that account . . .' (p. 138). Similarly Miller (1998), in his discussion of spirituality and addiction stated, 'It is possible, however, to separate a spiritual model of addiction from moralistic views' (p. 982). The distinctions that Heather and Miller are making seem to the present author to be not so clear-cut.

Nor have they appeared so clear to a number of other writers. Particularly stimulating among writings about the spiritual elements of the change process are the ideas of Sarbin and Nucci (1973) on what they called self-reconstitution processes. They described a number of major themes which they claimed existed in descriptions of most successful programmes of conduct reorganisation whether these be religiously, politically or therapeutically motivated. Essentially they saw three central processes in successful reconstitution: (a) symbolic death; (b) surrender; and (c) re-education (re-birth). What they described was a kind of conversion process that began when the previous social identity was acknowledged to be bankrupt. 'Hitting rock bottom', a state believed by AA to be necessary before change can occur, is perhaps one kind of symbolic death, while 'humiliation' is another. The individual 'surrendered' to the conduct-reorganisation programme, and in particular to a group or individual who provided a role model for the new self. The role model might be a group of other individuals, an '. . .

abstract referent in a transcendental or theological system' (p. 186), or an individual 'teacher' or 'guide' (sponsor, priest, therapist, shaman, doctor, etc.).

The Oxford Group Movement, forerunner of AA, attempted to inculcate in its members four absolute values: absolute honesty, absolute purity, absolute unselfishness and absolute love. Many passages in *Alcoholics Anonymous* the fellowship's 'Big Book' (2nd ed., 1955) suggest that the programme involved a wide-ranging moral reform. For example, 'Selfishness-self-centeredness! That, we think, is the root of our troubles ... the alcoholic is an extreme example of self-will run riot ...' (p. 62). 'Admitting' to another human being was 'a humbling experience' and very necessary. This might take the form of a religious confession or it might be done with a doctor, a psychologist or maybe a family member or friend (but not to someone who would be hurt by it), but it must be entirely honest.

The circumstances were therefore right for a profound attitude and behaviour change, likened by one observer of AA (Tiebout, 1944) to a conversion phenomenon. The shift might come about rapidly and dramatically, as in old-style religious conversion, but more typically took place over a longish period of time. Before conversion, 'alcoholics' had a tendency, Tiebout observed, to be tense and depressed, aggressive, oppressed with a sense of inferiority, while at the same time harbouring feelings of superiority, lonely and isolated, egocentric and self-centred, defiant and walled off from others. Defiance and, '... the projections which produce and maintain it ...' (p. 7), he considered to be particularly typical and important. In Freudian terms, the individual had a 'big ego' typical of infantile narcissism. Successful passage through the AA programme involved a process of 'ego reduction', and this process of being 'cut down to size' required humility and 'surrender' to the programme. Scodel (1964) also described such dispositional changes in individuals who claimed to have been helped by GA. He wrote of people's accounts of acquiring 'tranquillity', 'a sense of purpose in life', having undergone 'a moral transformation', having cast off previous 'restlessness and instability', in favour of a 'more trusting, less exploitative approach to the world'.

Nor should it be supposed that such change processes, suggestive of a 'moral passage out of deviance' (Gusfield, 1962) are confined to excessive drinking or drug taking, or to mutual-help organisations like AA. Although the language is different, the ideas about change expressed by the self-control behaviour theorists of the 1970s are not dissimilar. Premack (1970) was one of that era who discussed self-control in its broader meaning. He concluded that current behaviour theory was radically incomplete, and that people in the real world exercised control over their behaviour by mechanisms other than those which had been put into practice in the laboratory and the behaviour-therapy clinic. His particular contention was that the circumstances for self-control of smoking in the real world consisted of some combination of knowledge of the smoking–cancer link, which served merely as a catalyst for change, coupled with some sort of humiliating experience (realising that one was putting money into the pockets of cigarette manufacturers, or that one was encouraging one's children to smoke; see Koski-Jännes, 1998, for a further good example of humiliation involving a child, this time in the context of giving up excessive eating). Central to Premack's formulation, as to the one being developed here, were the concepts of conflict and decision. According to Premack, whatever the nature of a decision, 'Its prime operational consequence is self-instruction' (p. 116). Internal anti-smoking statements occurred, and the individual might be likened to two people, one the behavioural agent, the other the critic who offers the agent advice, 'Don't do that' or 'Do, do that'. With his emphasis upon humiliation, Premack's (1970) understanding of the self-control process was highly dependent upon the potentially behaviour-controlling functions of a set of beliefs about right and wrong conduct, or conscience.

From a later period, and a different appetite, Brooks *et al.* (1998) reported upon the accounts of their experiences provided by 10 women and one man who responded to advertisements about their research, and who satisfied diagnostic criteria for 'bulimia'. One of the predominant discourses identified in these accounts was referred to by Brooks *et al.* as 'bulimia as a personality trait'. By far the most common trait mentioned was lack of 'willpower', 'self-control' or 'self-discipline':

> *Naomi:* I'm a weak person, I'm lacking self-will, will-power, um, taking the easy way out is how I see myself. That's how I see bulimia too … If I'm not eating the perfect diet I think I lack self-control in eating.
>
> *Ray:* Beneath that I'm very childish and a little lacking in self-discipline.
>
> *Jess:* Certainly a sense of lack of control.
>
> *Lisa:* I couldn't stick to a diet, so therefore I judged myself as having no will-power … It was about not having control.
>
> (Brooks *et al.*, 1998, pp. 200–201)

The idea of a conflict between the flesh and the spirit, or the body and the soul, is captured in another main discourse—'bulimia as action one performs on oneself'. As Brooks et al observed:

> The construction has also been used extensively in Christian discourse; for example, St. Augustine wrote of two wills within him, 'one the servant of the flesh, the other of the spirit' … and described the body as the 'enemy'. The mental self or soul is identified with will and control, and the bodily self with appetites which must be controlled.
>
> (Brooks *et al.*, 1998, p. 197)

It was part of Sarbin and Nucci's (1973) thesis about conduct change that change attempts must employ a theme acceptable to their times. It seems likely from historical accounts that the mid-19th century, both in Britain and the USA, was an era that saw many dramatic changes in drinking behaviour at least, brought about by evangelical religious means. In particular, as we saw in Chapter Two, the taking of abstinence pledges appears to have played a major part. At about the same time that one of the most famous temperance reformers, Father Mathew of Cork, was active in Ireland (see Chapter Two), the Washington Temperance Society in the USA, which originated in 1840, was claiming between 150 000 and 250 000 pledged members. The Washingtonians held meetings which sound to have been not dissimilar to those of AA 100 years later, but by comparison with AA they adopted a much more actively proselytising stance: each new recruit was to go out and obtain new pledges (McPeek, 1972; Sagarin, 1969). Despite the seemingly very different style of temperance-wrought changes of the 1830s and 1840s in comparison with those brought about with the help of professional treatment in the 1980s and 1990s, there are intriguing hints that the basic change processes have not altered. Exaggerated claims of treatment effectiveness were being made then as now: the number of 'backsliders' was thought to be 'very small' (McPeek, 1972, p. 409). On the other hand, McPeek was able to cite a prohibitionist senator who, 50 years later, could view the Washingtonians' success with greater objectivity:

> In a few years 600,000 drunkards have been reformed, of whom, however, all but 150,000 returned to their cups. The moral of this movement is that we must save the boy if we would be sure of the man ... To be sure, 150,000 reformed men had adhered to their pledges and were saved; but what are 150,000 among so many?
>
> (McPeek, 1972, p. 411)

The senator put the follow-up success rate at around 25 per cent. One history of the temperance movement, entitled *Battling with the Demon*, which McPeek cited, estimated that around seven out of ten of those who received temperance medals from Father Mathew in his campaigns relapsed into their old habits. The similarity between these estimates of around 25–30 per cent who managed sustained change in drinking habits following exhortation and pledge-taking within a religious context, and the percentages of success estimated by Hunt and his colleagues (e.g. Hunt and Matarazzo, 1973, see Chapter Thirteen) and other observers of the modern treatment scene, is striking.

Later, at the end of the 19th century and in the early years of the 20th, morality was part of a dominant discourse regarding drinking, gambling and sex. Early psychologists of that time had no hesitation in using the language of will-power. The value of thought control for habit development or change was recognised by Emile Coué, William James and others, before the advent of either AA or modern behavioural self-regulation methods. A succinct statement of Coué's view—'Our actions spring not from our Will but from our Imagination'—appears on the title page of the 1960 reprinting of Coué's *Self-Mastery Through Conscious Auto-Suggestion* and Brooks' *The Practice of Auto-Suggestion by the Method of Emile Coué*, both originally published in 1922. Coué's central suggestion was that when people 'will' to do things, being conscious of applying *effort*, they are likely to fail: but when they are convinced that they will do something—what Coué called 'imagination', although Brooks thought this is a misleading word and preferred to call it 'thought' ('expectation' might do as well)—then the action is performed *without effort*. Coué's first two laws of action were, first, that when the will and the imagination are antagonistic, it is always the imagination which wins, without exception; and, second, that in the conflict between the will and the imagination, the force of the imagination is in, '... direct ratio to the square of the will', a proposal which he emphasised was, '... not rigorously exact ...'! His advocacy of what might now be termed 'self-talk' or 'self-instruction' is well known, especially his use of the statement: 'Every day, in every respect, I am getting better and better' (Coué and Brooks, 1960, p. 23).

Even earlier, William James' observations on the subject of habit should ring many bells for latter-day students of excessive appetitive behaviour, once due allowance is made for the style and language of the times in which he was writing. He made much of the fact that the development of habitual behaviour caused a diminution of conscious attention over action, and that habitual acts consisted of chains of behaviour, each event 'calling up' the next, '... without any alternative offering itself, and without any reference to the conscious will ...' (James, 1891, p. 114). In considering how habits might be changed, James was much impressed by a chapter on, 'The Moral Habits' by a Professor Bain. He took from this chapter the following maxims:

> ... in the acquisition of a new habit or the leaving off of an old one, we must take care to launch ourselves with as strong and decided initiative as possible. Accumulate all the possible circumstances which shall re-enforce the right motives; put yourself assiduously in conditions that encourage the new way; make engagements incompatible with the old; take a public pledge, if the case allows; in short, envelope your resolution with every aid you know ... *Never suffer an exception to occur till the new habit is securely rooted in your life.* Each lapse is like the letting fall of a ball of string which one is carefully winding up; a single slip undoes more than a great many turns will wind again ...
>
> (Professor Bain on Moral Habits, quoted by William James, 1891,
> pp. 122–123, his emphases)

He cited Bain as believing that moral habits could be distinguished from others by the, '... presence of two hostile powers ...'. The task in habit change was to regulate these so that one had, '... a series of uninterrupted successes, until repetition [had] fortified it to such a degree as to enable it to cope with the opposition, under any circumstances' (cited by James, 1891, p. 123). That James was concerned with the general question of moral improvement is illustrated by his final suggestion, concerning habits of the will, that we should:

> *Keep the faculty of effort alive in you by a little gratuitous exercise every day.* That is, be systematically ascetic or heroic in little unnecessary points, do every day or two something for no other reason than that you would rather not do it, so that when the hour of dire need draws nigh, it may find you not unnerved and untrained to stand the test. Asceticism of this sort is like the insurance which a man pays on his house and goods.
>
> (James, 1891, p. 126, his emphasis)

The Salvation Army, at its height at around the time William James was writing, is an organisation that has been active in the field of controlling appetitive behaviour. As outlined in General Booth's book, *In Darkest England, and the Way Out* (1890), its purpose was to rescue large numbers of the 'sinking classes' from a sea of misery and temptation to excess in which drunkenness, gambling, adultery and fornication figured large. Over 80 years later, a self re-appraisal, *In Darkest England Now* (Salvation Army, 1974), appeared largely in the form of questions posed by an unidentified interviewer with answers mostly by Salvation Army workers, officers and clients. The interviewer seemed preoccupied with the question whether change towards 'social work' or 'community work' in the intervening years was inconsistent with Booth's exhortation to, 'go for souls and go for the worst'. With monotonous uniformity, all respondents replied that the spiritual, mental, physical, economic and other aspects of men and women are interdependent, and that the Salvation Army is continuing to save souls by doing social work. The 'penitent form' at which people kneel, confess and are 'saved' is mentioned a number of times, and of it a Salvation Army Captain said:

> [It] is a good place at which to make public decisions ... But these life-changing decisions can take place in personal conversation, perhaps over coffee, or kneeling in a sitting room ... We should not be too rigid about this, or legislate as to where conversion has to take place. It can be in a home. But of course, this decision can be confirmed in front of all the congregation at the hall.
>
> (Salvation Army, 1974, p. 127)

It is no accident that Gusfield (1962) wrote of the need for a 'repentent role' as part of the process of 'moral passage' out of deviance, and that Sagarin (1969) referred to users of those self-help organisations which seek for their members to conform to the norms of society, as 'penitents'.

Half a century or more later, when behaviour therapy had been invented, aversion therapy was popular in the treatment of almost all the excessive appetites considered in this book. Treatment involved experiencing electric shocks or drug-induced nausea in association with stimuli depicting the appetitive object. The commitment to carrying out such a 'treatment' and the process of going through this routine repetitively could scarcely have been better arranged for enhancing a new-found attitude towards the at-one-time attractive appetitive object. Whatever the effectiveness of this procedure in conditioning an aversive response, it contained, like Boswell's discourse against fornication (Chapter Six), all the ingredients of experiments for inducing dissonance, and its major impact was almost certainly the bolstering of a negative set towards the object of one's appetite, which must already have been developing in order for the 'patient' to be willing to enter treatment in the first place. Perhaps because he was an ordained minister, John Gardner could appreciate the symbolic elements in the aversion therapy he received:

> The great boon, for me anyway, was the feeling of freshness which accompanied the treatment: the body was livelier, eyes clearer, and a new alertness took the place of the former mental lethargy. Even more than this were the spiritual benefits. To one who had lived and thought for much of his life in terms of sacramental symbolism, it was easy to see how the sudden, sharp expulsion of alcohol, and its attendant poisons, from the body, could be allied with the exorcism of that devil-desire to drink: and on each fresh

appointment with the trolley of drinks there was a decisive sense of waking to a new life ... I recall those hours of sickness, sweat and churning bowels with some pleasure. Uncomfortable? Yes, of course. But the removal of a malignant tissue is uncomfortable; the cutting away of a diseased organ is not pleasant; and, if it offers you the chance of living a full and useful life, the discomfort is as a tiny grain of sand.

(Gardner, 1964, p. 215)

There is obvious similarity between the making of a pledge, making a resolution and stating a commitment. Could this be at the heart of the change process, whether it took place at a 19th-century temperance meeting, at a Salvation Army penitent form, at an AA or GA meeting, the aversion-therapy laboratory, in a Thai temple, in the form of a modern phoned-in pledge on a national No Smoking day, or in the counselling room? Again we find that the behavioural self-control theorists of the 1970s were trying to grapple with this apparent diversity. In their important contribution Kanfer and Karoly (1972) defined self-control as that special case of change in which a person wishes to bring about a reduction in the occurrence of a 'high-probability' behaviour. Necessary for this process to occur was a degree of self-monitoring of behaviour, not necessarily in the technical sense of keeping a record of behaviour, but in the general sense of being aware of behaviour, thinking about it and evaluating it. Kanfer and Karoly suggested that chains or sequences of actions involving such behaviours might be run off smoothly, automatically and without self-monitoring until such time as, '... a choice point is reached, when an external event interrupts and refocusses one's attention, when one's activation level changes or when the expected consequences of behaviour are not forthcoming ...' (p. 429). Once such a point was reached behaviour became subject to attempts at self-control, and behaviour was then monitored or 'edited' by comparison with stated intentions, plans, predictions, promises or resolutions. These were often embodied in a kind of 'performance promise' or 'contract'. Viewing self-control as a process that involves the negotiation of a contract with oneself or with others is potentially very fruitful because it helps to tie together the diverse forms and places of change and the otherwise separate strands of 'spontaneous' or unaided self-control, therapy-induced control and control by important others. The knot that tied them together according to Kanfer and Karoly was the contract:

Basically, a contract is an agreement that describes particular behaviours that must be engaged in by the contractors, under specific conditions ... A contract provides one means of social monitoring that clearly incorporates the elements of discriminative and contingency control. Our lives are fraught with situations of a contractual nature, varying in specificity and controlling power for enforcement (for example, employer–employee, buyer–seller, teacher–pupil, parent–child, and, most relevant for the current argument, therapist–client).

(Kanfer and Karoly, 1972, pp. 430–431)

It seems likely that, in their essentials, modern forms of 'treatment' for excessive behaviour are not as dissimilar to the 19th-century ways of changing people's behaviour as modern practitioners would like to suppose. There are numerous instances to be found of treatments which, when described, are seen to incorporate powerful consciousness-raising, attitude-changing and moral-value-enhancing elements which seem much more likely to be the active treatment ingredients than the components or processes supposedly active according to the treatment's theoretical rationale. If the effective functions of most treatments are to focus attention on the excessive behaviour, to instil the belief and to provide many repetitions of the message that the behaviour needs to be controlled, to provide the opportunity for a commitment to be made or a contract to be entered into, to engender the expectation that they will be honoured, and to open the way for a moral passage out of excess, this would explain the rather similar outcomes following the whole range of apparently very varied treatments.

In our study of therapeutic hostels for men with drinking problems (Otto and Orford, 1978), to give just one example, we were struck by the way in which staff descriptions of the progress of individual residents seemed to reflect an idea of far-reaching changes in values and conduct. Stopping drinking and staying stopped was only a part of it, and a part to which relatively little reference was made. More frequently mentioned were categories of behaviour which we termed 'responsible involvement' (e.g. 'putting in a lot', 'playing his part', 'part of the house'), 'sense, insight and openness' (e.g. 'realistic', 'thoughtful', 'an appropriate attitude', 'forth-coming'), and 'sociability' (*not*, e.g., 'aggressive', 'bitter', 'cunning, manipulative, exploiting', 'attention-seeking, cock-of-the-walk').

If this thesis is correct, that modern expert treatments contain a thinly concealed and mostly unacknowledged moral element, it should come as no surprise to find that alliances which more clearly expose that element have often formed around reducing excessive appetites. For example, Mort (1987, 1998) has chronicled the making and breaking of alliances between medicine, the church, feminism, govern-ment and the law that have been seen in relation to the control of 'dangerous sexualities'—the title of his book—in Britain since 1830. An early alliance between medicine, the church and emerging feminism eventually broke up because of the difference of opinion as to whether prostitution should be made more hygienic or should be prohibited altogether. Hemming (1969), in his discussion of conflicts over sexual and other kinds of behaviour, pointed out how hygienic and moral values were still mixed together a century later. Even in the late 20th century agencies of relatively recent origin, rooted in a modern professional mental health perspective, and others of longer standing with origins in religious and moral reform, have coexisted side by side. This is nowhere more obvious than in the agencies that serve homeless excessive drinkers. Wiseman (1970) gave a vivid description of the range of facilities used by skid-row 'alcoholics' in a US west-coast city. Among these were the county jail, the state mental hospital, a welfare home for homeless men, and, among a variety of others, a Christian missionaries' work and residence centre for handicapped men. Despite the very different per-spectives on excessive drinking held by these various institutions, men passed rapidly from one to another, and despite the contrasting beliefs and ideologies of those who worked with them, to those that used them they were interchangeable to a large degree. As Cook put it in his book, *Vagrant Alcoholics*, 'missions and psychiatry coexist painlessly and effortlessly' (1975, p. 172).

SUMMARY

Are we now any closer to understanding how some people give up an excessive appetite? In one sense there is no special explanation for why and how people make such changes, and it has perhaps been a mistake to look for one in the expert literatures on psychological therapies. The principal argument here has been that change is a natural consequence of the deep ambivalence and conflict which goes hand in hand with the development of a strong attachment to an appetitive activity. Because such conflicts are mental, social and spiritual–moral ones, we should not be surprised that the change process involves all those elements as well as changes in behaviour. Most studies of how people change have concluded that some higher order mental process, which we might wish to call 'decision-making' or 'resolving', takes place. The analogy of a 'balance sheet' of rewards and costs, in the face of which such decisions or resolutions are made, is an apt one. At the same time there is increasing recognition of the social nature of the process. The role of family, friends and associates in coercing people into attempting to change, supporting them while they do so, monitoring their new behaviour, and helping develop and cement a new identity, has been too little emphasised in the past. That the process of change is in large part one of spiritual change and moral reform is the most difficult for modern experts to accept, but psychological therapies now in fashion are recent newcomers, and a longer view of appetitive-behaviour change in the 19th and 20th centuries, as well as the continued predominance of AA and other 12-step associations, testify to the importance of the spiritual–moral element.

CHAPTER FIFTEEN

Excessive Appetites: A Social–Behavioural–Cognitive–Moral Model

... neither one person, nor a number of persons, is warranted in saying to another human creature of ripe years that he shall not do with his life for his own benefit what he chooses to do with it ... No person ought to be punished simply for being drunk; but a soldier or a policeman should be punished for being drunk on duty. Whenever, in short, there is a definite damage, or a definite risk of damage, either to an individual or to the public, the case is taken out of the province of liberty and placed in that of morality or law.

(J. S. Mill, 1859/1974, pp. 142, 149)

Most theoretical explanations of addiction are provincial, attending only to the unique characteristics associated with specific objects (e.g. alcohol, heroin, cocaine, lottery) and a narrow pattern of behavior (e.g. alcoholism, heroin dependence, cocaine dependence, pathological gambling). As the opportunities to engage in potentially addicting activities (e.g. gambling) become more prevalent because of widespread access, a more cosmopolitan model of addiction will be necessary ...

(Shaffer, 1996, p. 462)

A SUMMARY OF THE MODEL

The argument of the preceding chapters may be summarised as follows.

1. There exists *a range of appetitive activities* which can become so excessive that they spoil the quality of people's lives, seriously affect and give rise to concern among family and friends, are costly to communities as well as to individuals and families, attract terms such as 'addiction', 'dependence' and 'disease', and provoke the setting up of mutual-help and expert-treatment systems. This range of activities certainly includes drinking alcohol, gambling in various forms, the taking of a variety of different kinds of substance including 'hard

drugs', 'softer' recreational drugs and prescribed medications, as well as eating in the form of 'bingeing', and 'straight' sex. A number of other activities are strong candidates for joining this core group, and they include certain forms of exercising (discussed in Chapter Five) and perhaps some forms of crime such as 'joyriding', and now certain ways of using the Internet (not discussed at any length here, but see Chapter One). The total set is not adequately denoted as 'drugs' or 'substances', but is more correctly spoken of as *appetitive activities which can become excessive*.

2.   The degree of a person's involvement in each of these appetitive activities has *multiple interacting determinants*. These include features of character or personality, but some of the strongest determinants are ecological, socioeconomic or cultural, including the availability of opportunities for activity and the normative influence of friends. This wide range of determinants includes those that operate to restrain activity, or which offer disincentives, as well as those which operate to promote activity, or which offer incentives. Furthermore, each of the major appetitive activities considered can serve *numerous personal functions* for different individuals, and even within the same person. These include forms of mood modification as well as the enabling of many different forms of self-expression and the enhancing of many different kinds of self-identity. Cross-cultural and historical perspectives are invaluable in pointing to the different meanings which can be attached to the same activity, and to the different routes which may be taken towards excess. Most theories of the origins of addiction fail to address these complexities. Nearly all theories that have been proposed are either far too limited in the factors that they take into account, or are much too limited in their scope.

3.   *A longitudinal perspective is vital* for understanding appetitive behaviour and excess. Changes in behaviour are the rule rather than the exception, and frequently occur as part of a developmentally normal change in a whole constellation of attitudes, experiences, values and activities. When the circumstances are right—incentives relatively great and restraints relatively weak— attachment to an appetitive activity escalates according to the law of proportionate effect. As a result, the distribution of any measure of extent of engagement in activity is not normal in shape, but is markedly skewed towards the 'heavy consumption' end, with minorities of people finding themselves in the tail of the distribution curve. Different personal functions may be served by the same activity at different stages for the same individual, and different personal and social factors may be predictive of different transitions from one life stage to another. This emphasis upon appetitive behaviour as a dynamic, changing process through time provides further grounds for mistrusting simple predispositional theories of excessive behaviour.

4.   Learning theory provides us with the mechanisms required to explain the development of a strong appetite. The combination of positive incentive, operant learning, based on mood modification and other positive rewards from activity, plus negative reinforcement, 'coping' functions of activity, in combination with the establishment of associations between multiple cues and the appetitive activity, plus the abundant opportunities that exist for the development of behaviour-enhancing expectancies, attributions, images and

fantasies, provides *a powerful set of processes for the development of a strong attachment*. Circumstances are favourable for the development of a strong appetite when the availability of the activity is high, inclination relatively strong and restraints relatively weak.

5. This developmental process of increasing attachment is manifest in the form of increasingly generalised activity and the erosion of the discriminations which maintain normally moderate activity. Activity becomes more widely cue-linked, serves a wider range of personal functions, is more likely to serve intrinsic, personal, non-social purposes, and may become automatic and functionally autonomous. Underlying the increased salience of, and preoccupation with, activity are increasingly dominant and easily triggered memory and attention schemata for the activity. The development of a strong appetite gives rise to new, acquired motivation for activity in the form of *secondary emotional cycles* which add an important drive-reduction element. Examples are: chasing losses (gambling); neuroadaptation (some drugs); and maintaining secrecy (most activities).

6. Strong attachment to appetitive behaviour runs an increased *risk of incurring costs* which may be physical or social, immediate or longer term, affecting the self or others. Costs are personally and socially relative, however, depending upon numerous factors including age, sex, values, social roles and circumstances. Excess is not an absolute, but is personally and socially defined. Reaction against, or criticism of, appetitive activity is necessary in order for it to be labelled 'addiction'. Ambivalence is likely to characterise appetitive behaviour at all levels. The development of increased attachment, plus the incurring of costs, may result in a more obvious, and personally disturbing, conflict of motives. *The consequences of conflict* are an essential ingredient of addiction. They may be thought of as a set of tertiary processes, and their effect can be to further amplify the addiction process. They include: demoralisation, poor information processing, compulsive behaviour and alterations of social role and social group.

7. There is convincing evidence that giving up excessive appetitive activity, unaided by expert treatment, is very common. It is also the case that different forms of appetitive activity show similar relapse curves indicating quite high rates of reversion to excess shortly after treatment or other change attempts. Besides these naturally occurring processes, modern forms of expert treatment play a modest part in excessive appetitive behaviour change. There exists a very wide range of treatment rationales and procedures but they produce a rather similar and modest result in the short term, and may be operating according to *a set of common, fundamental change processes*.

8. In terms of the excessive appetites model, *giving up addiction is seen as a natural consequence of the conflict* that follows from the accumulation of 'costs' consequent upon the development of a strong attachment to activity. There is general agreement that there are at least two elements—perhaps 'stages'—to the change process: the first cognitive, in the form of a decision or resolution to change, and the second an action or behavioural component. The set of common change processes, thought to underlie both expert-aided and unaided change, includes *social and spiritual–moral processes* which have

been neglected in previous formulations of the change process. Social reactions to excess, including the responses of concerned and affected others, are influential in the process of giving up an excessive appetite. In addition, mutual-help, therapeutic community and other change-supporting agencies often combine moral–religious and medical–disease ideas and have historical links with religiously based organisations, supporting the view that change in appetitive behaviour constitutes a kind of moral passage.

WHAT KIND OF MODEL IS THIS?

The main blocks out of which the excessive appetites model is built are shown in Figure 15.1. The central line of the model almost certainly betrays a strong influence of behavioural psychology, much tempered by social learning and cognitive behavioural elements. I have also tried to make it clear throughout the book that the influence of the social context is ever present, even though it may sometimes temporarily drop from view (e.g. when considering the importance of cognitive schemata). Similarly Figure 15.1 shows the continual relevance of questions of values and morality, social conformity and spirituality. Hence, if the model is to be characterised at all in this way, it might be thought of as *a social–behavioural–cognitive–moral model*.

Among the kinds of model which excessive appetites is *not*, are disease and biological models. Although it is argued that, under the right conditions, appetites can become so strong that they seem disease-like, there are too many ways in which an excessive appetite is unlike a physical disease for that analogy to be very useful. I hope it is very clear that this model would lead us to expect that the search for a simple genetic signature for 'alcoholism' or 'compulsive gambling' would be doomed to failure. This is not to deny the probable contribution of genetic determinants at many points in developing and giving up addictions—to totally discount such influence would be to fly in the face of all we know about the complex interaction of genes and environment in the determination of all human behaviour. But although biology comes into the picture in many places—in the psychopharmacological effects of drugs for example, in brain systems that may underlie reward, in secondary neuroadaptation processes, or the effects of strong appetitive attachments upon mental and physical ill-health—the present model is in essence a psychological one. The argument has been that the psychological processes described are, between them, quite sufficient to explain how attachments to appetitive activities can become so strong that control is eroded, voluntarism limited and resolutions to change repeatedly broken, despite the fact that quality of life is being severely damaged.

At the same time, the excessive appetites model is clear on one central point, and in this it is in agreement with disease models. Addiction does exist. It is a reality. There is something there that cannot be explained simply in terms of reactions to deviant behaviour or self-attributions about behaviour that serve to reduce censure. Some writers have vigorously attacked the concept of addiction. One of the most cogent of such arguments was marshalled by Davies (1992) in his book, *The Myth of Addiction*. There is a tendency, however, for a straw man to be set up

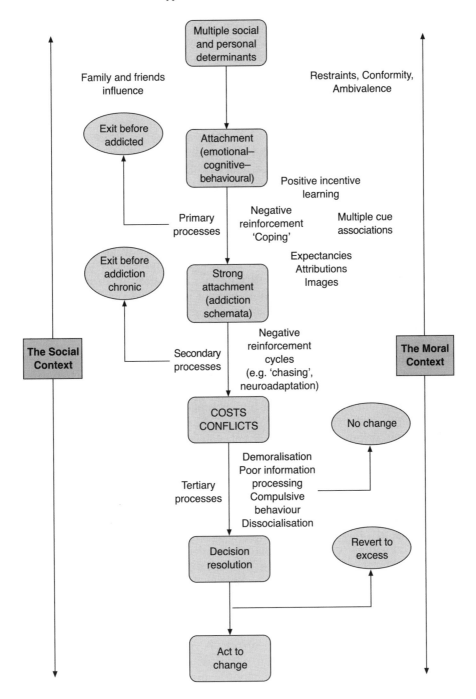

Figure 15.1   The excessive appetites model: a summary.

and knocked down in the course of his criticism. The word 'addiction' is taken to imply that control over appetitive behaviour is totally lost, and that the ability to modify behaviour in the light of external constraints (e.g. to smoke less if price rises) or to give up appetitive behaviour without treatment is inexplicable if addiction is said to exist. This may be true of an extreme 'disease' view of addiction, but it is certainly not true of most views of addiction including the present one.

The subtitle of Davies' 1992 book is *An Application of the Psychological Theory of Attribution to Illicit Drug Use*. There is no doubt that the attribution perspective has been badly neglected in the past and that Davies' book has done a lot to restore it to its proper place. The core idea put forward by Davies is that people are always making attributions about their behaviour, that there are a variety of possible attributions for appetitive behaviour of which being 'addicted' represents just one class, that attributions are functional in the sense that they are expressed in communicative language that varies with the demands of circumstances (e.g. contact with addiction-treatment services will make it more likely that 'addiction' discourse is used), and that no one attribution, explanation or form of discourse represents the single 'truth'. This is an important perspective and a vital corrective to the positivism of much addiction science. There is a tendency, however, for this view to be associated with a mild cynicism about any tendency to accept as the 'truth' things that people say about their own appetitive behaviour.

This is a distinctly different position from the one adopted in the present book. I believe there is a 'truth' to the experience of developing such a strong attachment to an appetitive substance or activity, that one's ability to modify that behaviour, in the face of mounting evidence that it is causing harm, is diminished. People are able to describe this experience to research interviewers and clinicians. It is an experience that is often distressing and bewildering to people, full of conflicts and contradictions, uncertainties and inconsistencies. It is certainly an over-simplification to say, either that excessive appetitive behaviour is free-choice behaviour, or that it is utterly compulsive and totally outside the realm of free will.

Where does the excessive appetites model stand on the important question of the loss of free will? Herrnstein and Prelec (1992, cited by Skog, 1994) listed four interpretations of addiction. The first is that of addiction as disease rather than choice, corresponding to the straw man referred to earlier. As Skog pointed out, modern addiction research has to a large extent discredited this model. The second is addiction as rational self-medication or the 'addict' as a rational consumer. Although it is a philosophical question to what extent behaviour is ever based on complete free will or rationality, the present argument is that appetitive careers may start rationally but often become markedly less so as people become strongly attached to the appetitive object. A process of increasing affective–behavioural–cognitive attachment to a particular form of behaviour produces an inclination sufficiently strong that behaviour is unresponsive to some of the normal restraints and controls. Behaviour is apparently self-defeating and often as mysterious to the individual as to those around her. Responsibility for action may truly be said to be somewhat diminished.

The excessive appetite view contains elements of Herrnstein and Prelec's interpretations 3 and 4. Number 3 is 'addiction as a primrose path', according to which people slip gradually into addiction not recognising that they are becoming hooked. This view captures elements of the all-important developmental component of the excessive appetite view. The fourth is 'addiction as divided self', which assumes that people harbour inconsistent preferences, either simultaneously or at successive stages. This may be another way of speaking of ambivalence and conflict which are central to the present idea of an excessive appetite.

Finally, a word about terminology. Throughout this book, the terms 'excessive appetite', 'strong attachment', and 'addiction' have been used almost interchangeably. I have distanced myself from the much used term 'dependence', and from individual terms such as 'alcoholism', 'compulsive gambling' or 'bulimia'. All the latter expressions, including 'dependence', are ambivalent on the question of whether addiction is a disease. They claim, or at least strongly imply, that addiction can be absolutely defined irrespective of history, culture, social position or moral values. The expressions 'excessive appetite' and 'strong attachment', on the other hand, deny such claims. They refer to circumstances in which people's activities have got them into serious conflict and trouble, but only because an appetite has grown to the point where it exceeds what is acceptable, or an attachment has become stronger to the point of significantly eroding freedom of choice.

An implication of that view is that we should reconsider the value of the attempts, exemplified by the World Health Organisation's *International Classification of Diseases* (ICD) and the American Psychiatric Association's *Diagnostic and Statistical Manual* (DSM), of trying to define certain disease-like conditions such as 'alcohol dependence', 'pathological gambling' or 'bulimia nervosa'. It is already evident that attempts to define these terms with any precision involve making arbitrary decisions, and almost always leave us wanting to make up for their deficiencies by creating additional categories such as 'alcohol abuse', 'problem gambling' or 'binge eating disorder'. But the excessive appetites model goes further in suggesting that any such attempt is bound to be spurious since the processes that give rise to strong appetitive attachment are normal ones and, although the distribution curves may be highly skewed, there is no point at which normality ends and abnormality begins. Furthermore, at the very core of addiction, according to this view, is not so much attachment *per se* but rather *conflict about attachment*. The restraints, controls and disincentives that create conflict out of attachment are personally, socially and culturally relative. No precise definition of addiction or dependence, however arbitrary, will serve all people, in all places, at all times.

How might this model be tested? Although as a comprehensive model its main function is not to generate testable hypotheses, there are points at which hypotheses can be formulated. For example, it would be predicted that the strength of attachment of excessive eaters to eating, or of excessive gamblers to gambling, as indexed by any valid method of accessing relevant appetite-specific cognitive schemata, would be equal in magnitude to the attachment of excessive tobacco smokers to smoking or excessive heroin users to heroin. In the field of treatment it would be predicted that, if credibility to clients can be equated, there would be no main treatment-outcome effects from comparing different forms of treatment, however distinct they might appear to be.

But the strictest test of whether this attempt to construct a comprehensive model has been successful is whether the excessive appetites model provides us with a better understanding of our own addictions, those of other people we care for, and those of people to whom we, in our professional roles, might be called upon to administer. Would it have helped Lilian, David, Jan, Joanna or Sam, whom we met in Part I (Chapters Two to Six, respectively)? Would it have provided the wives of Peter Cook, Dylan Thomas, Fyodor Dostoevsky and James Boswell with any greater insight into their husbands' behaviour? Would it have helped the Reverend Downame or Father Mathew? Would it have assisted those who tried to help Ms A., Mrs B. and Miss C. who appeared in Chapters Six, Two and Five, respectively? Would Thomas de Quincey and Samuel Pepys, I wonder, have appreciated this attempt at understanding?

References

Aas, H.M., Leigh, B.C., Anderssen, N. and Jakobsen, R. (1998). Two-year longitudinal study of alcohol expectancies and drinking among Norwegian adolescents, *Addiction*, **93**, 373–384.

Abbott, M.W. and Volberg, R.A. (1996). The New Zealand National Survey of Problem and Pathological Gambling, *Journal of Gambling Studies*, **12**, 143–159.

Abelson, R. (1963). Computer simulation of 'Hot' cognition, in *Computer Simulation of Personality* (eds S. Tomkins and S. Messick), Wiley, New York (cited by Janis and Mann, 1977).

Akan, G.E. and Grilo, C.M. (1995). Sociocultural influences on eating attitudes and behaviors, body image, and psychological functioning: a comparison of African-American, Asian-American, and Caucasian College Women, *International Journal of Eating Disorders*, **18**, 181–187.

Adams, T. (1998). *Addicted* (revised ed. 1999), CollinsWillow, London.

Agras, W.S. (1993). Short-term psychological treatments for binge eating, in *Binge Eating: Nature, Assessment and Treatment* (eds C.G. Fairburn and G.T. Wilson), Guilford Press, London, 270–286.

Agras, W.S., Telch, C.F., Arnow, B., Eldredge, K., Henderson, J. and Marnell, M. (1995). Does interpersonal therapy help patients with binge eating disorder who fail to respond to cognitive-behavioral therapy, *Journal of Consulting and Clinical Psychology*, **63**, 356–360.

Aitchison, J. and Brown, J. (1966). *The Lognormal Distribution*, Cambridge University Press, Cambridge.

Akers, R., Krohn, M., Lanza-Kaduch, L. and Radosvech, M. (1979). Social learning and deviant behavior: a specific test of a general theory, *American Sociological Review*, **44**, 636–655.

Al-Adawi, S. and Powell, J. (1997). The influence of smoking on reward responsiveness and cognitive functions: a natural experiment, *Addiction*, **92**, 1773–1782.

Alcoholics Anonymous (1955). *AA: The Story of How Many Men and Women Have Recovered from Alcoholism* (2nd ed.), AA, Stirling Area Services.

Alcoholics Anonymous (undated). 15 Points for an Alcoholic to Consider when Confronted with the Urge to Take a Drink.

Alcohol Concern (1999). *Joined Up Action on Alcohol: Proposals for a National Alcohol Strategy for England*, Alcohol Concern, London.

Allport, F. (1934). The J-curve hypothesis of conforming behaviour, *Journal of Social Psychology*, **5**, 141–181.

Allsop, S., Saunders, B., Phillips, M. and Carr, A. (1997). A trial of relapse prevention with severely dependent male problem drinkers, *Addiction*, **92**, 61–74.

American Psychiatric Association (1980). *Diagnostic and Statistical Manual of Mental Disorders* (3rd ed.), APA, Washington, DC.

American Psychiatric Association (1994). *Diagnostic and Statistical Manual of Mental Disorders* (4th ed.), APA, Washington, DC.

Anderson, G. and Brown, R.I.F. (1984). Real and laboratory gambling, sensation seeking and arousal, *British Journal of Psychology*, **75**, 401–410.

Anderson, P., Cremona, A., Paton, A., Tuner, C. and Wallace, P. (1993). The risk of alcohol, *Addiction*, **88**, 1493–1508.

Anonymous (1966). *My Secret Life*, Grove Press, New York.

Anthony, J.C. and Helzer, J.E. (1991). Syndromes of drug abuse and dependence, in *Psychiatric Disorders in America* (eds L.N. Robins and D.A. Regier), Free Press, Macmillan, New York.

Araya, R.I. and Laranjeira, R. (1991). Tobacco epidemic or bonanza? The global connection, *British Journal of Addiction*, **86**, 253–255.

Armor, D., Polich, J. and Stambul, H. (1978). *Alcoholism and Treatment*, Wiley, New York.

Aronfreed, J. (1968). *Conduct and Conscience: the Socialisation of Internalised Control over Behaviour*, Academic Press, New York.

Ashton, H. and Golding, J.F. (1989). Smoking: motivation and models, in *Smoking and Human Behaviour* (eds T. Ney and A. Gale), Wiley, Chichester.

Ashwell, M. (1978). Commercial weight loss groups, in *Recent Advances in Obesity Research II*, Proceedings of the Second International Congress on Obesity, October 1977, Washington, DC (ed. G. Bray), Newman, London.

Ashwell, M. and Etchell, L. (1974). Attitude of the individual to his own body weight, *British Journal of Preventive and Social Medicine*, **28**, 127–132.

Astin, A. (1962). 'Bad habits' and social deviation: a proposed revision in conflict theory, *Journal of Clinical Psychology*, **18**, 227–231.

Athey, G. and Coyne, L. (1979). Toward a rapprochement of empirical and clinical enquiry in evaluation of psychologically oriented alcoholism treatment, *Alcoholism: Clinical and Experimental Research*, **3**, 341–350.

Auerback, A. (1968). Satyriasis and nymphomania, *Medical Aspects of Human Sexuality*, **September**, 39–45.

Baasher, T. (1981). The use of drugs in the Islamic world, *British Journal of Addiction*, **76**, 233–243.

Babor, T.F. (1990). Social, scientific and medical issues in the definition of alcohol and drug dependence, in *The Nature of Drug Dependence* (eds G. Edwards and M. Lader), Oxford University Press, Oxford, 19–36.

Babor, T.F. (1994). Avoiding the horrid and beastly sin of drunkenness: does dissuasion make a difference? *Journal of Consulting and Clinical Psychology*, **62**, 1127–1140.

Babor, T.F., Grant, M., Acuda, W., Burns, R.H., Campillo, C., Del Boca, F.K., Hodgson, R., Ivanets, N.N., Lukomskya, M., Machona, M., Rollnick, S., Resnick, R., Saunders, J.B., Skutle, A., Connor, K., Ernsberg, G., Kranzler, H., Lauerman, R. and McRee, B. (1994). Comments on the WHO Report 'Brief Interventions for Alcohol Problems': a summary and some international comments, *Addiction*, **89**, 657–678.

Bacon, S. (1973). The process of addiction to alcohol: social aspects, *Quarterly Journal of Studies on Alcohol*, **34**, 1–27.

Baillie, A.J., Mattick, R.P., Hall, W. and Webster, P. (1994). Meta-analytic review of the efficacy of smoking cessation interventions, *Drug and Alcohol Review*, **13**, 157–170.

Bales, R. (1945). Social therapy for a social disorder—compulsive drinking, *Journal of Social Issues*, **1**, 14.

Ball, J.C. and van der Wijngaart, F.F. (1994). A Dutch addict's view of methadone maintenance—an American and a Dutch appraisal, *Addiction*, **89**, 799–802.

Bammer, G. and Weekes, S. (1994). Becoming an ex-user: insights into the process and implications for treatment and policy, *Drug and Alcohol Review*, **13**, 285–292.

Banaji, M.R. and Steele, C.M. (1989). The social cognition of alcohol use, *Social Cognition*, **7**, 137–151 (cited by Steele and Josephs, 1990).

Bandura, A. (1977). *Social Learning Theory*, Prentice-Hall, Englewood Cliffs, New Jersey.

Bannister, R.G. (1973). The meaning of athletic performance, in *Sports and Society* (eds J. Talamini and C.H. Page), Little, Brown, Boston (cited by Cockerill, 1996).

Barber, J.G. and Crisp, B.R. (1995). The 'pressures to change' approach to working with the partners of heavy drinkers, *Addiction*, **90**, 269–276.

Barbeyrac, J. (1737). *Traite du Jeu* (3 vols), Amsterdam (cited by France, 1902).

Barker, J. and Miller, M. (1968). Aversion therapy for compulsive gambling, *Journal of Nervous and Mental Disease*, **146**, 285–302.

Barrio, G., de la Fuente, L., Royuela, L., Díaz, A., Rodríguez-Artalejo, F. and Spanish Group for the Study on the Route of Administration of Drugs (1998). Cocaine use among heroin users in Spain: the diffusion of crack and cocaine smoking, *Journal of Epidemiology and Community Health*, **52**, 172–180.

Beck, D., Casper, R. and Andersen, A. (1996). Truly late onset of eating disorders: a study of 11 cases averaging 60 years of age at presentation, *International Journal of Eating Disorders*, **20**, 389–395.

Beck, J. and Rosenbaum, M. (1994). *Pursuit of Ecstasy: The MDMA Experience*, State University of New York Press, New York.

Becker, H. (1963). Becoming a marihuana user, in *Outsiders* (ed. H. Becker), Free Press, New York.

Becoña, E. (1993). The prevalence of pathological gambling in Galicia (Spain), *Journal of Gambling Studies*, **9**, 353–369.

Becoña, E. (1996). Prevalence surveys of problem and pathological gambling in Europe: the cases of Germany, Holland and Spain, *Journal of Gambling Studies*, **12**, 179–191.

Becoña, E., Labrador, F., Echeburúa, E., Ochoa, E. and Vallejo, M.A. (1995). Slot machine gambling in Spain: An important and new social problem, *Journal of Gambling Studies*, **11**, 265–286.

Beebe, D.W. (1994). Bulimia nervosa and depression: a theoretical and clinical appraisal in light of the binge–purge cycle, *British Journal of Clinical Psychology*, **33**, 259–276.

Bell, F. (1985, orig. 1907). *At the Works: A Study of a Manufacturing Town*, Virago, London.

Bem, D. (1967). Self-perception: an alternative interpretation of cognitive dissonance phenomena, *Psychological Review*, **74**, 183–200.

Bergh, C., Eklund, T., Sodersten, P. and Nordin, C. (1997). Altered dopamine function in pathological gambling, *Psychological Medicine*, **27**, 473–475.

Bergler, E. (1958). *The Psychology of Gambling*, Harrison, London.

Bernstein, D. (1970). The modification of smoking behavior: an evaluative review, in *Learning Mechanisms in Smoking* (ed. W. Hunt), Aldine, Chicago.

Berridge, V. (1977). Opium and the historical perspective, *The Lancet*, **9 July**, 78–80.

Berridge, V. (1978). Opium eating and the working class in the nineteenth century: the public and official reaction, *British Journal of Addiction*, **73**, 107–112.

Berridge, V. (1979). Morality and medical science: concepts of narcotic addiction in Britain, 1820–1926, *Annals of Science*, **36**, 67–85.

Bieleman, B., Díaz, A., Merlo, G. and Kaplan, C.D. (eds) (1993). *Lines Across Europe: Nature and Extent of Cocaine Use in Barcelona, Rotterdam and Turin*, Swetz Zeitlinger, Amsterdam.

Bien, T.H., Miller, W.R. and Tonigan, S. (1993). Brief intervention for alcohol problems: A review, *Addiction*, **88**, 315–336.

Biernacki, P. (1986). *Pathways from Heroin Addiction: Recovery without Treatment*, Temple University Press, Philadelphia.

Bigelow, G.E. (1991). Human drug abuse liability assessment: opioids and analgesics, *British Journal of Addiction*, **86**, 1615–1628.

Black, S. and Casswell. S. (1992). User reports of problems associated with alcohol and marijuana, *British Journal of Addiction*, **87**, 1275–1280.

Blaze-Temple, D. and Lo, S.K. (1992). Stages of drug use: a community survey of Perth teenagers, *British Journal of Addiction*, **87**, 215–225.

Blake, W., Turnbull, S. and Treasures, J. (1997). Stages and processes of change in eating disorders: implication for therapy, *Clinical Psychology and Psychotherapy*, **4**, 186–191.

Blaszczynski, A. and Silov, D. (1995). Cognitive and behavioral therapies for pathological gambling, *Journal of Gambling Studies*, **11**, 195–220.

Blaszczynski, A., Winter, S.W. and McConaghy, N. (1986). Plasma endorphin levels in pathological gambling, *Journal of Gambling Behavior*, **2**, 3–14.

Bobo, J.K., McIlvain, H.E., Lando, H.A. Walker, R.D. and Leed-Kelly, A. (1998). Effect of smoking cessation counseling on recovery from alcoholism: findings from a randomized community intervention trial, *Addiction*, **93**, 877–887.

Bond, A., Seijas, D., Dawling, S. and Lader, M. (1994). Systemic absorption and abuse liability of snorted flunitrazepam, *Addiction*, **89**, 821–830.

Booth, W. (1970, orig. 1890). *In Darkest England, and the Way Out*, Knight, London.

Bourgois, P. (1995). *In Search of Respect: Selling Crack in El Barrio*, Cambridge University Press, Cambridge.

Boyd, C.J. (1993). The antecedents of women's crack cocaine abuse: family substance abuse, sexual abuse, depression and illicit drug use, *Journal of Substance Abuse Treatment*, **10**, 433–438.

Brady, M. (1992). *Heavy Metal: The Social Meaning of Petrol Sniffing in Australia*, Aboriginal Studies Press, Canberra.

Brady, M. (1993). Giving away the grog: an ethnography of aboriginal drinkers who quit without help, *Drug and Alcohol Review*, **12**, 401–411.

Brady, M. (1995). Culture in treatment, culture as treatment. A critical appraisal of developments in addictions programs for indigenous North Americans and Australians, *Social Science and Medicine*, **41**, 1487–1498.

Brecher, E. and the Editors of *Consumer Reports* (1972). *Licit and Illicit Drugs: The Consumers Union Report on Narcotics, Stimulants, Depressants, Inhalants, Hallucinogens, and Marijuana—Including Caffeine, Nicotine and Alcohol*, Little, Brown and Co., Toronto.

Brewerton, T.D., Stellefson, E.J., Hibbs, N., Hodges, E.L. and Cochrane, E.C. (1995). Comparison of eating disorder patients with and without compulsive exercising, *International Journal of Eating Disorders*, **17**, 413–416.

Briddell, D., Rimm, D., Caddy, G., Krawitz, G., Sholis, D. and Wunderlin, R. (1978). Effects of alcohol and cognitive set on sexual arousal to deviant stimuli, *Journal of Abnormal Psychology*, **87**, 418–430.

British Medical Journal (1968). Compulsive gambler, Leading Article, **13 April**, 69.

Brody, M.L., Walsh, B.T. and Devlin, M.J. (1994). Binge eating disorder: reliability and validity of a new diagnostic category, *Journal of Consulting and Clinical Psychology*, **62**, 381–386.

Brooks, A., LeCouteur, A. and Hepworth, J. (1998). Accounts of experiences of bulimia: a discourse analytic study, *International Journal of Eating Disorders*, **24**, 193–205.

Brower, K.J., Blow, F.C., Young, J.P. and Hill, E.M. (1991). Symptoms and correlates of anabolic–androgenic steroid dependence, *British Journal of Addiction*, **86**, 759–768.

Browne, B.R. (1991). The selective adaptation of the alcoholics anonymous program by gamblers anonymous, *Journal of Gambling Studies*, **7**, 187–206.

Brown, R.I.F. (1993). Some contributions of the study of gambling to the study of other addictions, in *Gambling Behavior and Problem Gambling* (eds. W.R. Eadington and J. Cornelius), University of Nevada Press, Reno, Nevada, 341–372 (cited by Griffiths, 1996).

Brown, R.I.F. (1997). A theoretical model of the behavioural addictions—applied to offending, in *Addicted to Crime* (eds J.E. Hodge, M. McMurran and C.R. Hollin), Wiley, Chichester.

Brownell, K.D. and Wadden, T.A. (1992). Etiology and treatment of obesity: understanding a serious, prevalent, and refractory disorder, *Journal of Consulting and Clinical Psychology*, **60**, 505–517.

Bruch, H. (1974). *Eating Disorders: Obesity, Anorexia Nervosa, and the Person Within*, Routledge & Kegan Paul, London.

Bryant, K.J., Rounsaville, B.J. and Babor, T.F. (1991). Coherence of the dependence syndrome in cocaine users, *British Journal of Addiction*, **86**, 1299–1310.

Buchanan, D.R. (1993). Social status group differences in motivations for drug use, *The Journal of Drug Issues*, **23**, 631–644.

Budney, A.J., Novy, P.L. and Hughes, J.R. (1999). Marijuana withdrawal among adults seeking treatment for marijuana dependence, *Addiction*, **94**, 1311–1321.

Bühringer, G. (1994). Some questions about the harm reduction approach, *Addiction*, **89**, 811–812.

Bullough, V. (1977). Sex education in medieval christianity, *Journal of Sex Research*, **13**, 185–196.

Burroughs, W.S. (1977). *Junky*, Penguin (cited by Pearson, 1987).

Bushnell, J.A., Wells, J.E., Hornblow, A.R., Oakley-Browne, M.A. and Joyce, P. (1990). Prevalence of three bulimia syndromes in the general population, *Psychological Medicine*, **20**, 671–680 (cited by Fairburn *et al.*, 1993).

Button, E.J., Sonuga-Barke, E.J.S., Davies, J. and Thompson, M. (1996). A prospective study of self-esteem in the prediction of eating problems in adolescent schoolgirls: questionnaire findings, *British Journal of Clinical Psychology*, **35**, 193–203.

Button, E.J., Loan, P., Davies, J. and Sonuga-Barke, E.J.S. (1997). Self-esteem, eating problems, and psychological well-being in a cohort of schoolgirls aged 15–16: a questionnaire and interview study, *International Journal of Eating Disorders*, **21**, 39–47.

Bynner, J. (1969). *The Young Smoker*, HMSO, London.

Byrne, D.G., Byrne, A.E. and Reinhart, M.I. (1993). Psychosocial correlates of adolescent cigarette smoking: personality or environment, *Australian Journal of Psychology*, **45**, 87–95.

Cappell, H. and Herman, C. (1972). Alcohol and tension reduction: a review, *Quarterly Journal of Studies on Alcohol*, **33**, 33–64.

Carek, P.J. and Dickerson, L.M. (1999). Current concepts in the pharmacological management of obesity, *Drugs*, **57**, 883–904.

Carlin, A. and Armstrong, H. (1968). Aversive conditioning: learning or dissonance reduction? *Journal of Consulting and Clinical Psychology*, **32**, 674–678.

Carmack, M.A. and Martens, R. (1979). Measuring commitment to running: a survey of runners' attitudes and mental states, *Journal of Sport Psychology*, **1**, 25–42 (cited by Cockerill, 1996).

Carnes, P. (1983). *Out of the Shadows: Understanding Sexual Addiction*. CompCare, Minneapolis, Minnesota.

Carroll, D. and Huxley, J.A.A. (1994). Young people and fruit machine gambling, in *Appetite, Neural and Behavioural Bases* (eds C.R. Legg and D. Booth), Oxford University Press, Oxford, 285–304.

Carroll, K.M., Rounsaville, B.J., Nich, C., Gordon, L.T., Wirtz, P.W. and Gawin, F. (1994). One-year follow-up of psychotherapy and pharmacotherapy for cocaine dependence, *Archives of General Psychiatry*, **51**, 989–997.

Carstairs, S. (1954). Daru and bhang: cultural factors in the choice of intoxicant, *Quarterly Journal of Studies on Alcohol*, **15**, 220–237.

Carstairs, G. (1968). Compulsive gambler, Letter, *British Medical Journal*, **April**, 239.

Carter, B.L. and Tiffany, S.T. (1999). Meta-analysis of cue-reactivity in addiction research, *Addiction*, **94**, 327–340.

Cartwright, A. (1980). The attitudes of helping agents towards the alcoholic client, *British Journal of Addiction*, **75**, 413–431.

Cartwright, A. (1981). Are different therapeutic perspectives important in the treatment of alcoholism? *British Journal of Addiction*, **76**, 347–362.

Center for Substance Abuse Prevention/International Center for Alcohol Policies (1998). Joint Working Group on Terminology, CASP/ICAP, Washington.

Chein, I., Gerard, D., Lee, R. and Rosenfeld, E. (1964). *Narcotics, Delinquency and Social Policy: The Road to H*, Basic Books, New York.

Cherrington, E. (1920). *The Evolution of Prohibition in the USA*, American Issue Press, Westville, Ohio (cited by Levine, 1978).

Churchill, A.C., Burgess, P.M., Pead, J. and Gill, T. (1993). Measurement of the severity of amphetamine dependence, *Addiction*, **88**, 1335–1340.

Churches' Council on Gambling (1960–1968). *Annual Reports of the Churches' Council on Gambling*, CCG, London (cited by Cornish, 1978).

Cinciripini, P.M., Cinciripini, L.G., Wallfisch, A., Haque, W. and Van Vunakis, H. (1996). Behavior therapy and the transdermal nicotine patch: effects on cessation outcome, affect, and coping, *Journal of Consulting and Clinical Psychology*, **64**, 314–323.

Claussen, B. (1999). Alcohol disorders and re-employment in a 5-year follow-up of long-term unemployed, *Addiction*, **94**, 133–138.

Coates, T. (1977). Theory, research, and practice in treating obesity: are they really all the same? *Addictive Behaviors*, **2**, 95–103.

Cocco, N., Sharpe, L. and Blaszczynski, A.P. (1995). Differences in preferred level of arousal in two sub-groups of problem gamblers: a preliminary report, *Journal of Gambling Studies*, **11**, 221–229.

Cockerill, I.M. (1996). Exercise dependence and associated disorders: a review. Unpublished MS, University of Birmingham.

Cocteau, J. (1930/1991). *Diary of a Cure*, reprinted in *The Drug User Documents 1840–1960* (eds J. Stransbaugh and D. Blaise), Blast Books, New York and Dolphin-Moon Press, Baltimore.

Coffey, T. (1966). Beer Street: Gin Lane: some views of eighteenth century drinking, *Quarterly Journal of Studies on Alcohol*, **27**, 669–692.

Cohen, S. (ed.) (1971). *Images of Deviance*, Penguin, Harmondsworth, Middlesex.

Coker, S. (1994). Onset of bulimia nervosa in a 64-year-old woman, *International Journal of Eating Disorders*, **16**, 89–91.

Collings, S. and King, M. (1994). Ten-year follow-up of 50 patients with bulimia nervosa, *British Journal of Psychiatry*, **164**, 80–87.

Colombian Cocaine and US Tobacco (1988). *World Development Forum*, **15 June**, 6.

Conger, J. (1951). The effect of alcohol on conflict behavior in the albino rat, *Quarterly Journal of Studies on Alcohol*, **12**, 1–29.

Cook, T. (1975). *Vagrant Alcoholics*, Routledge & Kegan Paul, London.

Cooper, A., Ismail, A., Phanjoo, A. and Love, D. (1972). Antiandrogen therapy in deviant hypersexuality, *British Journal of Psychiatry*, **120**, 59–63.

Cooper, M.L., Russell, M., Skinner, J.B., Frone, M.R. and Mudar, P. (1992). Stress and alcohol use: moderating effects of gender, coping, and alcohol expectancies, *Journal of Abnormal Psychology*, **101**, 139–152.

Cooper, M.J. and Fairburn, C.G. (1992). Selective processing of eating, weight and shape related words in patients with eating disorders and dieters, *British Journal of Clinical Psychology*, **31**, 363–365.

Cooper, M.L., Frone, M.R., Russell, M. and Mudar, P. (1995). Drinking to regulate positive and negative emotions: a motivational model of alcohol use, *Journal of Personality and Social Psychology*, **69**, 990–1005.

Cooper, S.J. and Higgs, S. (1994). Neuropharmacology of appetite and taste preferences, in *Appetite, Neural and Behavioural Bases* (eds C.R. Legg and D. Booth), Oxford University Press, Oxford, 213–242.

Cooperstock, R. and Lennard, H. (1979). Some social meanings of tranquiliser use, *Sociology of Health and Illness*, **1**, 331–347.

Copello, A. (1999). Coercion in alcohol treatment: What can we learn from a review of the recent literature? Paper presented at the *Annual Conference of the New Directions in the Study of Alcohol Group, Manchester, May*.

Copello, A., Orford, J., Hodgson, R., Tober, G. and Barrett, C. (1999). Social behaviour and network therapy: basic principles and early experiences, *Addictive Behaviors* (in press).

Cornish, D. (1978). *Gambling: A Review of the Literature and its Implications for Policy and Research*, Home Office Research Study 42, HMSO, London.

Corrigall, W.A. (1991). Understanding brain mechanisms in nicotine reinforcement, *British Journal of Addiction*, **86**, 507–510.

Costello, R. (1980). Alcoholism treatment effectiveness: slicing the outcome variance pie, in *Alcoholism Treatment in Transition* (eds G. Edwards and M. Grant), Croom Helm, London.

Cotton (1674). *Compleat Gamester*, cited by Ashton, *History of Gambling in England* (cited by France, 1902).

Coué, E. and Brooks, C. (1960, orig. 1922). Self-mastery through conscious auto-suggestion, in *Self-Mastery through Conscious Auto-suggestion by Emile Coué, and The Practice of Auto-suggestion by the Method of Emile Coué* (ed. C. Brooks), Unwin, London.

Courtwright, D.T. (1997). The prepared mind: Marie Nyswander, methadone maintenance, and the metabolic theory of addiction, *Addiction*, **92**, 257–265.

Coventry, K.R. and Brown, R.I.F. (1993). Sensation seeking, gambling and gambling addictions, *Addiction*, **88**, 541–554.

Cox, R. (1999). A qualitative study of the meaning of exercise for people who could be labelled as 'addicted' to exercise—Can 'addiction' be applied to high frequency exercising? Unpublished Clinical Psychology Doctorate thesis, University of Birmingham.

Creigh-Tyte, S. (1997). Building a national lottery: reviewing British experience, *Journal of Gambling Studies*, **13**, 321–341.

Crichton, P. (1996). Were the Roman Emperors Claudius and Vitellius bulimic? *International Journal of Eating Disorders*, **19**, 203–207.

Crofts, N., Louie, R., Rosenthal, D. and Jolley, D. (1996). The first hit: circumstances surrounding initiation into injecting, *Addiction*, **91**, 1187–1196.

Cronkite, R. and Moos, R. (1978). Evaluating alcoholism treatment programs: an integrated approach, *Journal of Consulting and Clinical Psychology*, **46**, 1005–1019.

Crum, R.M., Ensminger, M.E., Ro, M.J. and McCord, J. (1998). The association of educational achievement and school dropout with risk of alcoholism: a twenty-five-year prospective study of inner-city children, *Journal of Studies on Alcohol*, **59**, 318–326.

Cudahy, M.S. (1989). *Wild Trails to Far Horizons*, Unwin Hyman (cited by Cockerill, 1996).

Cummings, C., Gordon, J. and Marlatt, G. (1980). Relapse: prevention and prediction, in *The Addictive Behaviors: Treatment of Alcoholism, Drug Abuse, Smoking and Obesity* (ed. W. Miller), Pergamon Press, Oxford.

Curry, R.L. (1993). Beverage alcohol as a constraint to development in the Third World, *The International Journal of the Addictions*, **28**, 1227–1242.

Curry, S.J., McBride, C., Grothaus, L.C., Louie, G. and Wagner, E.H. (1995). A randomized trial of self-help materials, personalized feedback, and telephone counselling with non-volunteer smokers, *Journal of Consulting and Clinical Psychology*, **63**, 1005–1014.

Custer, R. and Milt, H. (1985). *When Luck Runs Out; Help for Compulsive Gamblers and their Families*, Facts on File Publications, New York.

Davidson, H. (1964). Rationalizations for continued smoking, *New York State Journal of Medicine*, **15 December**, 2993–3001.

Davidson, R. (1992). Prochaska and DiClemente's model of change: a case study, *British Journal of Addiction*, **87**, 821–822.

Davies, J.B. (1992). *The Myth of Addiction, an Application of the Psychological Theory of Attribution to Illicit Drug Use*, Harwood Academic, Reading, UK.

Davies, J.B. and Ditton, J. (1990). The 1990's: decade of the stimulants? *British Journal of Addiction*, **85**, 811–813.

de la Fuente, L., Barrio, G., Royuela, L., Bravo, M.J. and The Spanish Group for the Study of the Route of Heroin Administration (1997). The transition from injecting to smoking heroin in three Spanish cities, *Addiction*, **92**, 1749–1763.

de Quincey, T. (1897, orig. 1822). *The Confessions of an English Opium Eater*, in *The Collected Writings of Thomas De Quincey, Vol. III* (ed. D. Masson), Black, London.

Derzon, J.H. and Lipsey, M.W. (1999). Predicting tobacco use to age 18: a synthesis of longitudinal research, *Addiction*, **94**, 995–1006.

DHSS (Department of Health and Social Security) (1981). *Prevention and Health: Drinking Sensibly*, HMSO, London.

Diaz, R.M. and Fruhauf, A.G. (1991). The origins and development of self-regulation: a developmental model on the risk for addictive behaviours, in *Self-control and the Addictive Behaviours* (eds N. Heather, W.R. Miller and J. Greeley), Maxwell MacMillan, Botany, NSW, Australia, 83–106.

Dickerson, M. (1974). The effect of betting shop experience on gambling behaviour, Unpublished Ph.D. thesis, University of Birmingham.

Dickerson, M. (1989). Gambling: a dependence without a drug, *International Review of Psychiatry*, **1**, 157–172.

Dickerson, M. (1990). Gambling: the psychology of a non-drug compulsion, *Drug and Alcohol Review*, **9**, 187–199.

Dickerson, M. and Hinchy, J. (1988). The prevalence of excessive and pathological gambling in Australia, *Journal of Gambling Behaviour*, **4**, 135–151.

Dickerson, M., Hinchy, J. and Fabre, J. (1987). Chasing, arousal and sensation seeking in off-course gamblers, *British Journal of Addiction*, **82**, 673–680.

Dickerson, M., Hinchy, J. and England, S.L. (1990). Minimal treatments and problem gamblers: a preliminary investigation, *Journal of Gambling Studies*, **6**, 87–102.

Dickerson, M., Baron, E., Hong, S.M. and Cottrell, D. (1996). Estimating the extent and degree of gambling related problems in the Australian population: a national survey, *Journal of Gambling Studies*, **12**, 161–177.

Dicks, H. (1967). *Marital Tensions: Clinical Studies Towards a Psychological Theory of Interaction*, Routledge & Kegan Paul, London.

DiClemente, C.C. and Prochaska, J.O. (1982). Self-change and therapy change of smoking behavior: a comparison of process of change in cessation and maintenance, *Addictive Behaviors*, **7**, 133–142.

DiClemente, C.C., Prochaska, J.O., Fairhurst, S.K., Velicer, W.F., Velasquez, M.M. and Rossi, J.S. (1991). The process of smoking cessation: an analysis of precontemplation, contemplation, and preparation stages of change, *Journal of Consulting and Clinical Psychology*, **59**, 295–304.

Digiusto, E. and Bird, K.D. (1995). Matching smokers to treatment: self-control versus social support, *Journal of Consulting and Clinical Psychology*, **63**, 290–295.

Dijkstra, A., De Vries, H. and Bakker, M. (1996). Pros and cons of quitting, self-efficacy, and the stages of change in smoking cessation, *Journal of Consulting and Clinical Psychology*, **64**, 758–763.

Ditton, J. and Hammersley, R. (1996). *A Very Greedy Drug: Cocaine in Context*, Harwood Academic, Reading, UK.

Dixey, R. (1996). Bingo in Britain: an analysis of gender and class, in *Gambling Cultures* (ed. J. McMillen), Routledge, London, 136–151.

Dole, V. and Nyswander, M. (1965). A medical treatment for diacetylmorphine (heroin) addiction, *Journal of the American Medical Association*, **193**, 646 (cited by Kurland, 1978).

Dombrink, J. (1996). Gambling and the legislation of vice: social movements, public health and public policy in the United States, in *Gambling Cultures* (ed. J. McMillen), Routledge, London.

Drew, L.R.H. (1990). Factors we don't want to face, *Drug and Alcohol Review*, **9**, 207–209.

Drummond, C. (1996). Human addicts and laboratory rats: two great armies marching in parallel, Comments on White, 1996, *Addiction*, **91**, 958–960.

Duncan, T.E., Tildesley, E., Duncan, S.C. and Hops, H. (1995). The consistency of family and peer influences on the development of substance use in adolescence, *Addiction*, **90**, 1647–1660.

Durlak, J. (1979). Comparative effectiveness of para-professional and professional helpers, *Psychological Bulletin*, **86**, 80–92.

Duvarci, I., Varan, A., Coskunol, H. and Ersoy, M.A. (1997). DSM-IV and the South Oaks Gambling Screen: diagnosing and assessing pathological gambling in Turkey, *Journal of Gambling Studies*, **13**, 193–205.

Dwyer, J., Feldman, J., Seltzer, C. and Mayer, J. (1969). Body image in adolescents: attitudes toward weight and perception of appearance, *Journal of Nutrition Education*, **1**, 14–19 (cited by Dwyer *et al.*, 1970).

Dwyer, J., Feldman, J. and Mayer, J. (1970). The social psychology of dieting, *Journal of Health and Social Behavior*, **11**, 269–287.

D'Zurilla, T. and Goldfried, M. (1971). Problem solving and behavior modification, *Journal of Abnormal Psychology*, **78**, 107–126.

Eadington, W.R. and Cornelius, J. (eds) (1991). *Gambling and Commercial Gaming. Essays in Business, Economics, Philosophy and Science*, Institute for the Study of Gambling and Commercial Gaming, University of Nevada, Reno.

Eber, E. (1995). *Women and Alcohol in a Highland Maya Town: Water of Hope, Water of Sorrow*, University of Texas Press, Austin.

Echeburúa, E., Báez, C. and Fernández-Montalvo, J. (1994). Efectividad diferencial de diversas modalidades terapéuticas en el tratamiento psicológico del juego patológico: un estudio experimental, *Análisis y Modificación de Conducta*, **20**, 617–643 (cited by López-Viets and Miller, 1997).

Edwards, G. (1968). The problem of cannabis dependence, *The Practitioner*, **200**, 226–233.

Edwards, G. and Guthrie, S. (1967). A controlled trial of in-patient and out-patient treatment of alcohol dependence, *Lancet*, **i**, 555–559.

Edwards, G. and Gross, M. (1976). Alcohol dependence: provisional description of a clinical syndrome, *British Medical Journal*, **i**, 1058–1061.

Edwards, G., Chandler, J. and Peto, J. (1972). Motivation for drinking among men in a London suburb, *Psychological Medicine*, **2**, 260–271.

Edwards, G., Hawker, A., Hensman, C., Peto, J. and Williamson, V. (1973). Alcoholics known or unknown to agencies: epidemiological studies in a London suburb, *British Journal of Psychiatry*, **123**, 169–183.

Edwards, G., Orford, J., Egert, S., Guthrie, S., Hawker, A., Hensman, C., Mitcheson, M., Oppenheimer, E. and Taylor, C. (1977a). Alcoholism: a controlled trial of 'treatment' and 'advice', *Journal of Studies on Alcohol*, **38**, 1004–1031.

Edwards, G., Gross, M., Keller, M., Moser, J., and Room, R. (eds) (1977b). *Alcohol-Related Disabilities*, World Health Organisation Offset Publication No. 32, WHO, Geneva.

Edwards, G., Oppenheimer, E. and Taylor, C. (1992). Hearing the noise in the system: exploration of textual analysis as a method for studying change in drinking behaviour, *British Journal of Addiction*, **87**, 73–81.

Edwards, G., Anderson, A., Babor, T.F., Casswell, S., Ferrence, R., Giesbrecht, N., Godfrey, C., Holder, H.D., Lemmens, P., Mäkelä, K., Midanik, L.T., Norström, T., Österberg, E., Romelsjö, A., Room, R., Simpura, J. and Skog, O. (1994). *Alcohol Policy and the Public Good*, Oxford University Press, Oxford.

Edwards, G., Anderson, A., Babor, T.F., Casswell, S., Ferrence, R., Giesbrecht, N., Godfrey, C., Holder, H.D., Lemmens, P., Mäkelä, K., Midanik, L.T., Norström, T., Österberg, E., Romelsjö, A., Room, R., Simpura, J. and Skog, O. (1995). *Alcohol Policy and the Public Good*, Oxford University Press, Oxford (summary and conclusions reprinted, *Addiction*, **90**, 173–181).

Eide, A.H. and Acuda, S.W. (1996). Cultural orientation and adolescents' alcohol use in Zimbabwe, *Addiction*, **91**, 807–814.

Eisenstein, V. (1956). Sexual problems in marriage, in *Neurotic Interaction in Marriage* (ed. V. Eisenstein), Tavistock, London.

Eiser, J.R. (1987). Attributions, beliefs and expectations. Paper presented at *Psychology and Addiction, Joint Annual Symposium of the Society for the Study of Addiction to Alcohol and other Drugs and the British Psychological Society, Cardiff, November*.

Ellis, A. and Sagarin, E. (1965). *Nymphomania: A Study of the Oversexed Woman*, Ortolan, London.

Emrick, C.D., Tonigan, J.S., Montgomery, H. and Little, L. (1993). Alcoholics Anonymous: What is currently known? in *Research on Alcoholics Anonymous: Opportunities and Alternatives* (eds B.S. McCrady and W.R. Miller), Rutgers Center of Alcohol Studies, New Brunswick, New Jersey, 41–76.

Engels, R.C.M.E., Knibbe, R.A. and Drop, M.J. (1999). Predictability of smoking in adolescence: between optimism and pessimism, *Addiction*, **94**, 115–124.

Ennett, S.T. and Bauman, K.E. (1994). The contribution of influence and selection to adolescent peer group homogeneity: the case of adolescent cigarette smoking, *Journal of Personality and Social Psychology*, **67**, 653–663.

Escobedo, L.G., Reddy, M. and Giovino, G.A. (1998). The relationship between depressive symptoms and cigarette smoking in US adolescents, *Addiction*, **93**, 433–440.

Ettner, S.L. (1997). Measuring the human cost of a weak economy: Does unemployment lead to alcohol abuse? *Social Science and Medicine*, **44**, 251–260.

Evans, S.M., Critchfield, T.S. and Griffiths, R.R. (1991). Abuse liability assessment of anxiolytics/hypnotics: rationale and laboratory lore, *British Journal of Addiction*, **86**, 1625–1632.

Eysenck, H. (1971). Personality and sexual adjustment, *British Journal of Psychiatry*, **118**, 593–608.

Eysenck, H.J. (rev. and exp. ed. 1997). *Rebel with a Cause: The Autobiography of Hans Eysenck*, Transaction, New Brunswick, New Jersey.

Eysenck, H. and Beech, R. (1971). Counterconditioning and related methods, in *Handbook of Psychotherapy and Behavior Change* (eds A. Bergin and S. Garfield), Wiley, New York.

Fabian, T. (1995). Pathological gambling: a comparison of gambling at German-style slot machines and 'classical' gambling, *Journal of Gambling Studies*, **11**, 249–263.

Fairburn, C.G., Hay, P.J. and Welch, S.L. (1993). Binge eating and bulimia nervosa: distribution and determinants, in *Binge Eating: Nature, Assessment and Treatment* (eds C.G. Fairburn and G.T. Wilson), Guilford, New York, 123–143.

Fairburn, C.G., Jones, R., Peveler, R.C., Carr, S.J., Solomon, R.A., O'Connor, M.E. and Burton, J. (1991). Three psychological treatments for bulimia nervosa, *Archives of General Psychiatry*, **48**, 463–469.

Fairburn, C.G. and Wilson, G.T. (1993). Binge eating: definition and classification, in *Binge Eating: Nature, Assessment and Treatment* (eds C.G. Fairburn and G.T. Wilson), Guilford, New York, 3–14.

Fals-Stewart, W., Birchler, G.R. and O'Farrell, T.J. (1996). Behavioral couples therapy for male substance-abusing patients: Effects on relationship adjustment and drug-using behavior, *Journal of Consulting and Clinical Psychology*, **64**, 959–972.

Farrar, J.E., (1992). Excessive exercise, in *Handbook of Differential Treatments for Addictions* (eds J.E. L'Abate, J.E. Farrar and D.A. Serritella), Allyn and Bacon, Boston, 242–251.

Farrell, A.D., Danish, S.J. and Howard, C.W. (1992). Risk factors for drug use in urban adolescents: Identification and cross-validation, *American Journal of Community Psychology*, **20**, 263–285.

Farrell, M. (1999). Cannabis dependence and withdrawal, *Addiction*, **94**, 1277–1278.

Farrell, M., and Strang, J. (1990). Confusion between the drug legalization and the drug prescribing debate, *Drug and Alcohol Review*, **9**, 364–368.

Fenichel, O. (1945). *The Psychoanalytic Theory of Neuroses*, Norton, New York.

Fergusson, D.M., Horwood, L.J. and Lynskey, M.T. (1995). The prevalence and risk factors associated with abusive or hazardous alcohol consumption in 16-year-olds, *Addiction*, **90**, 935–946.

Fibiger, H.C. (1996). Centres, circuits and the neurobiology of drug abuse: Comments on White, 1996, *Addiction*, **91**, 954–955.

Fichter, M.M. and Quadflieg, N. (1997). Six-year course of bulimia nervosa, *Eating Disorders*, **22**, 361–384.

Fidler, W., Michell, L., Raab, G. and Charlton, A. (1992). Smoking: a special need? *British Journal of Addiction*, **87**, 1583–1591.

Finney, J.W. and Monahan, S.C. (1996). The cost-effectiveness of treatment for alcoholism: a second approximation, *Journal of Studies on Alcohol*, **57**, 229–243.

Finney, J.W. and Moos, R.H. (1996). The effectiveness of in-patient and out-patient treatment for alcohol abuse: effect sizes, research design issues and explanatory mechanisms, *Addiction*, **91**, 1813–1820.

Finney, J.W., Moos, R.H. and Mewborn, C. (1980). Posttreatment experiences and treatment outcome of alcoholic patients six months and two years after hospitalisation, *Journal of Consulting and Clinical Psychology*, **48**, 17–29.

Finney, J.W., Hahn, A.C. and Moos, R.H. (1996). The effectiveness of in-patient and out-patient treatment for alcohol abuse: the need to focus on mediators and moderators of setting effects, *Addiction*, **91**, 1773–1796.

Finney, J.W., Noyes, C.A., Coutts, A.I. and Moos, R.H. (1998). Evaluating substance abuse treatment process models: 1. Changes on proximal outcome variables during 12-step and cognitive-behavioral treatment, *Journal of Studies on Alcohol*, **59**, 371–380.

Fischer, B. (1995). Sexual addiction revisited, *The Addictions Newsletter*, **2**, 5–27 (cited by Gold and Heffner, 1998).

Fishbein, M. and Ajzen, I. (1975). *Belief, Attitude, Intention, and Behavior: An Introduction to Theory and Research*, Addison-Wesley, Reading, Massachusetts (cited by Sutton, 1989).

Fisher, S. (1991). Government response to juvenile fruit machine gambling in the UK: Where do we go from here? *Journal of Gambling Studies*, **7**, 217–247.

Fisher, S. and Balding, J. (1996). *Underage Participation on the National Lottery*, Office of the National Lottery, London.

Fisher, S. and Griffiths, M. (1995). Current trends in slot machine gambling: research and policy issues, *Journal of Gambling Studies*, **11**, 239–247.

Fleming, J., Watson, C., McDonald, D. and Alexander, K. (1991). Drug use patterns in Northern Territory aboriginal communities 1986–1987, *Drug and Alcohol Review*, **10**, 367–380.

Fleming, J., Mullen, P. E., Sibthorpe, B., Attewell, R. and Bammer, G. (1998). The relationship between childhood sexual abuse and alcohol abuse in women—a case-control study, *Addiction*, **93**, 1787–1798.

Foltin, R.W. and Fischman, M.W. (1991). Methods for the assessment of abuse liability of psychomotor stimulants and anorectic agent in humans, *British Journal of Addiction*, **86**, 1633–1640.

Fombonne, E. (1996). Is bulimia nervosa increasing in frequency? *International Journal of Eating Disorders*, **19**, 287–296.

Foreyt, J. (ed.) (1977). *Behavioural Treatments of Obesity*, Pergamon, Oxford.

Foulkes, E.F. (1987). Social stratification and alcohol use in North Alaska, *Journal of Community Psychology*, **15**, 349–356.

France, C. (1902). The gambling impulsive, *American Journal of Psychology*, **13**, 364–407.

Galanter, M. (1999). *Network Therapy for Alcohol and Drug Abuse*, Guilford, New York (2nd ed.).

Gambling Impact and Behavior Study (1999). *Report to the National Gambling Impact Study Commission*, National Opinion Research Center at the University of Chicago, Gemini Research, The Lewin Group, Christiansen/Cummings Associates.

Gaming Board (1969). *Report of the Gaming Board for Great Britain*, HMSO, London (cited by Dixey, 1996).

Ganguly, K.K., Sharma, H.K. and Krishnamachari, K.A.V.R. (1995). An ethnographic account of opium consumers of Rajasthan (India): socio-medical perspective, *Addiction*, **90**, 9–12.

Gardner, J. (1964). *Spin the Bottle: The Autobiography of an Alcoholic*, Muller, London.

Garfinkel, P.E., Lin, E., Goering, P., Spegg, C., Goldbloom, D.S., Kennedy, S., Kaplan, A.S. and Woodside, D.B. (1996). Purging and Nonpurging forms of bulimia nervosa in a community sample, *International Journal of Eating Disorders*, **20**, 231–238.

Garner, D.M. and Wooley, S.C. (1991). Confronting the failure of behavioral and dietary treatments for obesity, *Clinical Psychology Review*, **11**, 729–780.

Garret, J., Landau, J., Shea, R., Stantion, M.D., Baciewicz, G. and Brinkman-Sull, D. (1998). The ARISE intervention: using family and network links to engage addicted persons in treatment, *Journal of Substance Abuse Treatment*, **15**, 333–343.

Gawin, R.H. (1991). Cocaine addiction: psychology and neurophysiology, *Science*, **251**, 1580–1586.

Gilbert, R.M. (1984). Caffeine consumption, in *The Methylxanthine Beverages and Foods; Chemistry, Consumption and Health Effects* (ed. G.A. Spiller), Allan R. Liss, New York, 185–213 (cited by Griffiths and Woodson, 1988).

Glaser, F. (1973). Some historical aspects of the drug-free therapeutic community, Unpublished paper presented at *Conference on Intervening in Drug Misuse: The Therapeutic Community and Other Self-Help Efforts*, at Saddlebrook, New Jersey.

Glaser, F. (1980). The core shell model and the matching hypothesis, in *Alcoholism Treatment in Transition* (eds G. Edwards and M. Grant), Croom Helm, London.

Glasser, W. (1976). *Positive Addiction*, Harper & Row, New York (cited by Farrar, 1992).

Glatt, M. (1958). The English drink problem: its rise and decline through the ages, *British Journal of Addiction*, **55**, 51–65.

Glautier, S. (1994). Classical conditioning, drug cues and drug addiction, in *Appetite, Neural and Behavioural Bases* (eds C.R. Legg and D. Booth), Oxford University Press, Oxford, 165–192.

Glautier, S. and Spencer, K. (1999). Activation of alcohol-related associative networks by recent alcohol consumption and alcohol-related cues, *Addiction*, **94**, 1033–1042.

Goddard, E. (1990). *Why Children Start Smoking*, HMSO, London.

Goddard, E. (1992). Why children start smoking, *British Journal of Addiction*, **87**, 17–25.

Godfrey, C. (1997). Lost productivity and costs to society, *Addiction*, **92**, S49–S54.

Godfrey, C. and Hardman, G. (1994). *Changing the Social Costs of Alcohol*, Final report to the Alcohol Education and Research Council, Centre for Health Economics, York.

Gold, S.N. and Heffner, C.L. (1998). Sexual addiction: many conceptions, minimal data, *Clinical Psychology Review*, **18**, 367–381.

Golden, J. (1968). What is sexual promiscuity? *Medical Aspects of Human Sexuality*, **October**, 37–53.

Goodman, A. (1993). Diagnosis and treatment of sexual addiction, *Journal of Sex and Marital Therapy*, **19**, 225–251.

Goodman, A. (1998). *Sexual Addiction: An Integrated Approach*, International Universities Press, Connecticut.

Goorney, A. (1968). Treatment of a compulsive horse race gambler by aversion therapy, *British Journal of Psychiatry*, **114**, 329–333.

Gossop, M. (1993). Volatile substances and the law, *Addiction*, **88**, 311–313.

Götestam, K.G., and Agras, W.S. (1995). General population-based epidemiological study of eating disorders in Norway, *International Journal of Eating Disorders*, **18**, 119–126.

Graham, H. (1996). Smoking prevalence among women in the European Community 1950–1990, Social Science and Medicine, **43**, 243–254.

Graham, J. (1988). *Amusement Machines: Dependency and Delinquency*, Home Office Research Study No. 101, HMSO, London.

Gray, J.A. (1972). The psychophysiological basis of introversion–extraversion: a modification of Eysenck's theory, in *The Biological Bases of Individual Behavior* (eds V.D. Nebylitsyn and J.A. Gray), Academic Press, San Diego, California (cited by Cooper *et al.*, 1995).

Greden, J.F. (1981). Caffeinism and caffeine withdrawal, in *Substance Abuse: Clinical Problems and Perspectives* (eds J.H. Lowinson and P. Reiz), Williams & Wilkins, Baltimore (cited by Hughes *et al.*, 1992).

Greenaway, J.R. (1998). The 'improved' public house, 1870–1950: the key to civilized drinking or the primrose path to drunkenness? *Addiction*, **93**, 173–181.

Greeno, C.G., Marcus, M.D. and Wing, R.R. (1995). Diagnosis of binge eating disorder: discrepancies between a questionnaire and clinical interview, *International Journal of Eating Disorders*, **17**, 153–160.

Griffiths, M. (1990). Addiction to fruit machines: a preliminary study among young males, *Journal of Gambling Studies*, **6**, 113–126.

Griffiths, M. (1991). Book review of—Graham, J. (1988). *Amusement Machines: Dependency and Delinquency*, Home Office Research Study No. 101, HMSO, London—*Journal of Gambling Studies*, **7**, 79–86.

Griffiths, M. (1993a). Factors in problem adolescent fruit machine gambling: results of a small postal survey, *Journal of Gambling Studies*, **9**, 31–45.

Griffiths, M. (1993b). Fruit machine addiction in adolescents: a case study, *Journal of Gambling Studies*, **9**, 387–399.

Griffiths, M. (1994). The role of cognitive bias and skill in fruit machine gambling, *British Journal of Psychology*, **85**, 351–369.

Griffiths, M. (1995a). Brief report: towards a risk factor model of fruit machine addiction: a brief note, *Journal of Gambling Studies*, **11**, 343–346.

Griffiths, M. (1995b). Scratch-card gambling: a potential addiction? *Education and Health*, **13**, 17–20.

Griffiths, M. (1995c). The role of subjective mood states in the maintenance of fruit machine gambling behavior, *Journal of Gambling Studies*, **11**, 123–135.

Griffiths, M. (1996). Behavioural addiction: an issue for everybody? *Employee Counselling Today: The Journal of Workplace Learning*, **8**, 18–25.

Griffiths, M. (1997). Exercise addiction: a case study, *Addiction Research*, **5**, 161–168.

Griffiths, M. (1999). Internet addiction: fact or fiction? *The Psychologist: Bulletin of the British Psychological Society*, **12**, 246–250.

Griffiths, P., Gossop, M., Powis, B. and Strang, J. (1994). Transitions in patterns of heroin administration: a study of heroin chasers and heroin injectors, *Addiction*, **89**, 301–310.

Griffiths, P., Gossop, M., Wickenden, S., Dunworth, J., Harris, K. and Lloyd, C. (1997). A transcultural pattern of drug use: qat (khat) in the UK, *British Journal of Psychiatry*, **170**, 281–284.

Griffiths, R.R., Evans, S.N., Heishman, S.J., Preston, K.L., Sannerud, C.A., Wolf, B. and Woodson, P.P. (1990). Low-dose caffeine physical dependence in humans, *Journal of Pharmacology and Experimental Therapeutics*, **255**, 1123–1132.

Griffiths, R.R. and Woodson, P.P. (1988). Caffeine physical dependence and reinforcement in humans and laboratory animals, in *The Psychopharmacology of Addiction* (ed. M. Lader), Oxford University Press, Oxford, 141–156.

Grilo, C.M. and Shiffman, S. (1994). Longitudinal investigation of the abstinence violation effect in binge eaters, *Journal of Consulting and Clinical Psychology*, **62**, 611–619.

Gritz, E.R., Carr, C.R. and Marcus, A.C. (1991). The tobacco withdrawal syndrome in unaided quitters, *British Journal of Addiction*, **86**, 57–69.

Groneman, C. (1994). Nymphomania: the historical construction of female sexuality, *Signs: Journal of Women in Culture and Society*, **19**, 337–367.

Gross, A. (1978). The male role and heterosexual behaviour, *Journal of Social Issues*, **34**, 87–107.

Groth-Marnat, G., Leslie, S. and Renneker, M. (1996). Tobacco control in a traditional Fijian village; indigenous methods of smoking cessation and relapse prevention, *Social Science and Medicine*, **43**, 473–477.

Groves, P. and Farmer, R. (1994). Buddhism and addictions, *Addiction Research*, **2**, 183–194.

Guertin, T.L. (1999). Eating behavior of bulimics, self-identified binge eaters, and non-eating-disordered individuals: What differentiates these populations? *Clinical Psychology Review*, **19**, 1–23.

Gunn, J. (1968). Compulsive gambler, Letter, *British Medical Journal*, **April**, 240.

Gusfield, J. (1962). Status conflicts and the changing ideologies of the American temperance movement, in *Society, Culture and Drinking Patterns* (eds D. Pittman and C. Snyder), Wiley, New York.

Haberman, P. (1969). Drinking and other self-indulgences: complements or counterattractions, *International Journal of the Addictions*, **4**, 157–167.

Habitual Drunkards, Report of a Select Committee (1968, orig. 1872), in *British Parliamentary Papers*, Irish University Press.

Hagaman, B.L. (1980). Food for thought: beer in a social and ritual context in a West African society, *Journal of Drug Issues*, **10**, 203–214.

Hajema, K.J. and Knibbe, R.A. (1998). Changes in social roles as predictors of changes in drinking behaviour, *Addiction*, **93**, 1717–1727.

Hall, W. and Hando, J. (1994). Route of administration and adverse effects of amphetamine use among young adults in Sydney, Australia, *Drug and Alcohol Review*, **13**, 277–284.

Hall, W., Hunger, E. and Spargo, R. (1993). Alcohol-related problems among Aboriginal drinkers in the Kimberley Region of Western Australia, *Addiction*, **88**, 1091–1100.

Hall, W., Solowij, N. and Lemon, J. (1994). *The Health and Psychological Consequences of Cannabis Use*, Australian Government Publishing Service, Canberra.

Hamburger, W. (1951). Emotional aspects of obesity, *Medical Clinics of North America*, **35**, 483–499.

Hammer, T. (1992). Unemployment and use of drug and alcohol among young people: a longitudinal study in the general population, *British Journal of Addiction*, **87**, 1571–1581.

Hammersley, R., Forsyth, A., Morrison, V. and Davies, J.B. (1989). The relationship between crime and opioid use, *British Journal of Addiction*, **84**, 1029–1043.

Hammersley, R., Cassidy, M.T. and Oliver, J. (1995). Drugs associated with drug-related deaths in Edinburgh and Glasgow, November 1990 to October 1992, *Addiction*, **90**, 959–966.

Hardy, K. (1964). An appetitional theory of sexual motivation, *Psychological Review*, **71**, 1–18.

Harrison, L. and Gardiner, E. (1999). Do the rich really die young? Alcohol-related mortality and social class in Great Britain, 1988–94, *Addiction*, **94**, 1871–1880.

Hartmann, A., Herzog, T. and Drinkmann, A. (1992). Psychotherapy of bulimia nervosa: What is effective? A meta-analysis, *Journal of Psychosomatic Research*, **36**, 159–167.

Hartnoll, R.L. (1994). Opiates; prevalence and demographic factors, *Addiction*, **89**, 1377–1384.

Hasin, D.S. (1994). Treatment/self-help for alcohol-related problems: relationship to social pressure and alcohol dependence, *Journal of Studies on Alcohol*, **55**, 660–666.

Hasin, D.S., Muthuen, B., Wisnicki, K.S. and Grant, B. (1994). Validity of the bi-axial dependence concept: a test in the US general population, *Addiction*, **89**, 573–579.

Hattie, J., Sharpley, C. and Rogers, H. (1984). Comparative effectiveness of professional and para-professional helpers, *Psychological Bulletin*, **95**, 534–541.

Hawker, R. and Orford, J. (1998). Predicting alcohol withdrawal severity: support for the role of expectations and anxiety, *Addiction Research*, **6**, 265–287.

Hawkins, J.D., Catalano, R.F. and Miller, J.Y. (1992). Risk and protective factors for alcohol and other drug problems in adolescence and early adulthood: implications for substance abuse prevention, *Psychological Bulletin*, **112**, 64–105.

Hawton, K. (1992). By their own hand, *British Medical Journal*, **304**, 1000.

Hay, P. (1998). The epidemiology of eating disorder behaviors: an Australian community-based survey, *International Journal of Eating Disorders*, **23**, 371–382.

Hay, P. and Fairburn, C.G. (1998). The validity of the DSM-IV scheme for classifying bulimic eating disorders, *International Journal of Eating Disorders*, **23**, 7–15.

Hay, P., Fairburn, C.G. and Doll, H.A. (1996). The classification of bulimic eating disorders: a community-based cluster analysis study, *Psychological Medicine*, **26**, 801–812.

Hayward, P., Wardle, J. and Higgitt, A. (1989). Benzodiazepine research: current findings and practical consequences, *British Journal of Clinical Psychology*, **28**, 307–327.

Heather, N. (1994). Weakness of will: A suitable topic for scientific study? *Addiction Research*, **2**, 135–139.

Heather, N. and Robertson, I. (1981). *Controlled Drinking*, Methuen, London (rev. ed., 1983).

Heatherton, T.F. and Baumeister, R.F. (1991). Binge eating as escape from self-awareness, *Psychological Bulletin*, **110**, 86–108.

Heatherton, T.F., Mahamedi, F., Striepe, M., Field, A.E. and Keel, P. (1997). A 10-year longitudinal study of body weight, dieting, and eating disorder symptoms, *Journal of Abnormal Psychology*, **106**, 117–125.

Hedlund, H. and Lundahl, M. (1984). The economic role of beer in rural Zambia, *Human Organisation*, **32**, 61–65.

Heilizer, F. (1964). Conflict models, alcohol, and drinking patterns, *Journal of Psychology*, **57**, 457–473.

Hemming, J. (1969). *Individual Morality*, Nelson, London.

Herd, D. and Grube, J. (1996). Black identity and drinking in the US: a national study, *Addiction*, **91**, 845–857.

Herman, C. and Polivy, J. (1975). Anxiety, restraint, and eating behavior, *Journal of Abnormal Psychology*, **84**, 666–672.

Herman, C. and Polivy, J. (1980). Restrained eating, in *Obesity* (ed. A. Stunkard), W.V. Saunders, Philadelphia (cited by Stice *et al.*, 1998).

Herman, R. (1976). *Gamblers and Gambling: Motives, Institutions and Controls*, Lexington Books, Lexington, Massachusetts.

Herrnstein, R.J. and Prelec, D. (1992). A theory of addiction, in *Choice over Time* (eds G. Loewenstein and J. Elster), Russel Sage Foundation, New York (cited by Skog, 1994).

Hetherington, M. and MacDiarmid, J.I. (1993). Chocolate addiction: a preliminary study of its description and its relationship to problem eating, *Appetite*, **21**, 233–246.

Hickman, M., Cox, S., Harvey, J., Howes, S., Farrell, M., Frischer, M., Stimson, G., Taylor, C. and Tilling, K. (1999). Estimating the prevalence of problem drug use in inner London: a discussion of three capture–recapture studies, *Addiction*, **94**, 1653–1662.

Hirschi, T. (1969). *Causes of Delinquency*, University of California Press, Berkeley, California.

Hochbaum, G. (1965). Psychosocial aspects of smoking with special reference to cessation, *American Journal of Public Health*, **55**, 692–697 (cited by Reinert, 1968).

Hodge, J.E., McMurran, M. and Hollin, C.R. (1997). *Addicted to Crime?* Wiley, Chichester.

Hodgson, R. and Rachman, S. (1976). The modification of compulsive behaviour, in *Case Studies in Behaviour Therapy* (ed. H. Eysenck), Routledge & Kegan Paul, London.

Hodgson, R., Stockwell, T. and Rankin, H. (1979a). Can alcohol reduce tension? *Behavior Research and Therapy*, **17**, 459–466.

Hodgson, R., Rankin, H. and Stockwell, T. (1979b). Craving and loss of control, in *Alcoholism: New Directions in Behavioral Research and Treatment* (eds P. Nathan, G. Marlatt and T. Loberg), Plenum, New York.

Holmila, M. (1991). *Social control experienced by heavy drinking women*, Paper presented at *Symposium, Alcohol, Family and Significant Others, Helsinki, 4–8 March*.

Hopson, R.E. and Beaird-Spiller, B. (1994). Why AA works: a psychological analysis of the addictive experience and the efficacy of Alcoholics Anonymous, *Alcoholism Treatment Quarterly*, **12**, No. 3.

Horn, D. (1972). Determinants of change, in *The Second World Conference on Smoking and Health* (ed. G. Richardson), Pitman Medical, London.

Horn, J. and Wanberg, K. (1969). Symptom patterns related to excessive use of alcohol, *Quarterly Journal of Studies on Alcohol*, **30**, 35–58.

Howard, C.E. and Porzelius, L. K. (1999). The role of dieting in binge eating disorder: etiology and treatment implications, *Clinical Psychology Review*, **19**, 25–44.

Hraba, J. and Lee, G. (1996). Gender, gambling and problem gambling, *Journal of Gambling Studies*, **12**, 83–101.

Hsu, L.K.G. (1990). Experiential aspects of bulimia nervosa, *Behavior Modification*, **14**, 50–65.

Hughes, J.R., Higgins, S.T., Bickel, W.K., Hunt, W.K., Fenwick, J.W., Gulliver, S.B. and Mireaul, G.C. (1991). Caffeine self-administration, with withdrawal, and adverse effects among coffee drinkers, *Archives of General Psychiatry*, **48**, 611–617.

Hughes, J.R., Olivetto, A.H., Helzer, J.E., Higgins, S.T. and Bickel, W.K. (1992). Should caffeine abuse, dependence, or withdrawal be added to DSM-IV and ICD-10? *American Journal of Psychiatry*, **149**, 33–40.

Hull, J. (1981). A self-awareness model of the causes and effects of alcohol consumption, *Journal of Abnormal Psychology*, **90**, 586–600.

Humphreys, K. and Rappaport, J. (1993). From the Community Mental Health Movement to the war on drugs: a study in the definition of social problems, *American Psychologist*, **48**, 892–901.

Humphreys, K., Finney, J.W. and Moos, R.H. (1994). Applying a stress and coping framework to research on mutual help organizations, *Journal of Community Psychology*, **22**, 312–327.

Humphreys, K., Moos, R.H. and Finney, J.W. (1996). Life domains, Alcoholics Anonymous, and role incumbency in the 3-year course of problem drinking, *Journal of Nervous and Mental Disease*, **184**, 475–481.

Humphreys, K., Moos, R.H. and Cohen, C. (1997). Social and community resources and long-term recovery from treated and untreated alcoholism, *Journal of Studies on Alcohol*, **58**, 221–238.

Hunt, H. (1968). Prospects and possibilities in the development of behavior therapy, in *Ciba Foundation Symposium on the Role of Learning in Psychotherapy* (ed. R. Poster), Churchill, London (cited by Hunt and Matarazzo, 1973).

Hunt, W. and Bespalec, D. (1974). Relapse rates after treatment for heroin addiction, *Journal of Community Psychology*, **2**, 85–87.

Hunt, W. and General, W. (1973). Relapse rates after treatment for alcoholism, *Journal of Community Psychology*, **1**, 66–68.

Hunt, W. and Matarazzo, J. (1973). Three years later: recent developments in the experimental modification of smoking behavior, *Journal of Abnormal Psychology*, **81**, 107–114.

Huon, G.F. (1994). Dieting, binge eating, and some of their correlates among secondary school girls, *International Journal of Eating Disorders*, **15**, 159–164.

Hyman, M. (1979). The Ledermann curve: comments on a symposium, *Journal of Studies on Alcohol*, **40**, 339–347.

Inglis, B. (1976). *The Opium War*, Hodder & Stoughton, London.

Inquiry Into Drunkenness, Report from the Select Committee (1968, orig. 1834), in *British Parliamentary Papers*, Irish University Press.

Institute of Medicine (1990). *Broadening the Base of Treatment for Alcohol Problems*, National Academy Press, Washington, DC.

International Narcotic Education Association (1936). Los Angeles (cited by Edwards, 1968).

Iwawaki, S. and Eysenck, H. (1978). Sexual attitudes among British and Japanese students, *Journal of Psychology*, **98**, 289–298.

Jacobs, D.F. (1988). Evidence for a common dissociative-like reaction among addicts, *Journal of Gambling Behaviour*, **4**, 27–37.

Jacobs, D.F. (1989). Illegal and undocumented: a review of teenage gambling and the plight of children of problem gamblers in America, in *Compulsive Gambling: Theory, Research and Practice* (eds H.J. Shaffer, S.A. Stein, B. Gambino and T.N. Cummings), D.C. Heath, Lexington, Massachusetts, 249–292.

Jaffe, J. (1977). Tobacco use as mental disorder: the rediscovery of a medical problem, in *Research on Smoking Behavior* (eds M. Jarvik, J. Cullen, E. Gritz, T. Vogt and L. West), National Institute on Drug Abuse Research Monograph 17, US Department of Health, Education and Welfare, NIDA, Rockville, Maryland.

Jaffe, J. (1992). Current concepts of addiction, in *Addictive States* (eds C.P. O'Brien and J. Jaffe), Raven Press, New York.

Jahoda, G. and Cramond, J. (1972). *Children and Alcohol: A Developmental Study in Glasgow*, HMSO, London.

James, W. (1891). *The Principles of Psychology* (Vol. 1), Macmillan, London.

James, W. (1976). *Research on Obesity: A Report of the Department of Health and Social Security/Medical Research Council Group*, HMSO, London.

Janis, I. and Mann, L. (1968). A conflict theory approach to attitude change and decision making, in *Psychological Foundations of Attitudes* (eds A. Greenwald, T. Brock and T. Ostrom), Academic Press, New York.

Janis, I. and Mann, L. (1977). *Decision-making: A Psychological Analysis of Conflict, Choice, and Commitment*, Free Press, New York.

Janis, I. and Rodin, J. (1979). Attribution, control, and decision-making: social psychology and health care, in *Health Psychology: a Handbook: Theories, Applications and Challenges of a Psychological Approach to the Health Care System* (eds. G. Stone, F. Cohen and N. Adler), Jossey-Bass, San Francisco.

Janlert, U. and Hammarström, A. (1992). Alcohol consumption among unemployed youths: results from a prospective study, *British Journal of Addiction*, **87**, 703–714.

Jarvik, M.E. and Hatsukami, D.K. (1989). Tobacco dependence, in *Smoking and Human Behavior* (eds T. Ney and A. Gale), Wiley, Chichester.

Jarvinen, M. (1991). The controlled controllers: women, men, and alcohol, Paper presented at *Symposium, Alcohol, Family and Significant Others*, Helsinki, 4–8 March.

Jarvis, M. (1987). Psychology, smoking and smoking policies. Paper presented at the Joint Annual Symposium of the Society for the Study of Addiction and the British Psychological Society, Cardiff, November.

Jarvis, M. (1991). A time for conceptual stocktaking, *British Journal of Addiction*, **86**, 643–647.

Jellinek, E. (1960). *The Disease Concept of Alcoholism*, Hillhouse, New Jersey.

Jessor, R. and Jessor, S. (1975). Adolescent development and the onset of drinking: a longitudinal study, *Journal of Studies on Alcohol*, **36**, 27–51.

Jessor, R. and Jessor, S. (1977). *Problem Behaviour and Psycho-Social Development: A Longitudinal Study of Youth*, Academic Press, New York.

Jessor, R., Jessor, S. and Finney, J. (1973). A social psychology of marijuana use: longitudinal studies of high school and college youth, *Journal of Personality and Social Psychology*, **26**, 1–15.

Jessor, R., Donovan, J.E. and Costa, F.M. (1991). *Beyond Adolescence: Problem Behavior and Young Adult Development*, Cambridge University Press, Cambridge.

Johanson, E.E., Duffy, F.F. and Anthony, J.C. (1996). Associations between drug use and behavioral repertoire in urban youths, *Addiction*, **91**, 523–534.

Johnson, T.P., Freels, S.A., Parsons, J.A. and Vangeest, J.B. (1997). Substance abuse and homelessness: social selection or social adaptation?, *Addiction*, **92**, 437–446.

Jolly, S. and Orford, J. (1983). Religious observance, attitudes towards drinking, and knowledge about drinking, amongst university students, *Alcohol and Alcoholism*, **18**, 271–278.

Jones, E. and Davis, K. (1965). From acts to dispositions: the attribution process in person perception, in *Experimental Social Psychology* (Vol. 2) (ed. L. Berkowitz), Academic Press, New York.

Joseph, M.H., Young, A.M.J. and Gray, J.A. (1996) Are neurochemistry and reinforcement enough—Can the abuse potential of drugs be explained by common actions on a dopamine reward system in the brain? *Human Psychopharmacology Clinical and Experimental*, **11**, S55–S63.

Kafka, M.P. (1997). Hypersexual desire in males: an operational definition and clinical implications for males with paraphilias and paraphilia-related disorders, *Archives of Sexual Behaviour*, **26**, 505–526.

Kahn, M.W., Hunter, E., Heather, N. and Tebbutt, J. (1990). Australian Aborigines and alcohol: a review, *Drug and Alcohol Review*, **10**, 351–366.

Kandel, D. (eds.) (1978). *Longitudinal Research on Drug Use: Empirical Findings and Methodological Issues*, Hemisphere, Washington, DC.

Kanfer, F. (1970). Self-regulation: research, issues and speculations, in *Behavior Modification in Clinical Psychology* (eds C. Neuringer and J.L. Michael), Appleton-Century-Crofts, New York (cited by Miller and Brown, 1991).

Kanfer, F. and Karoly, P. (1972). Self-control: a behavioristic excursion into the lion's den, *Behavior Therapy*, **3**, 389–433.

Kaplan, H.I. and Kaplan, H.S. (1957). The psychosomatic concept of obesity, *Journal of Nervous and Mental Disorder*, **125**, 181–201.

Kaufman, E. and de Leon, G. (1978). The therapeutic community: a treatment approach for drug abusers, in *Treatment Aspects of Drug Dependence* (ed. A. Schecter), CRC Press, West Palm Beach, Florida.

Keller, M. (1972). On the loss-of-control phenomenon in alcoholism, *British Journal of Addiction*, **67**, 153–166.

Kerr, N. (1889). *Inebriety, its Etiology, Pathology, Treatment and Jurisprudence* (2nd ed.), London (cited by Berridge, 1979).

Keutzer, C. (1968). Behaviour modification of smoking: the experimental investigation of diverse techniques, *Behaviour Research and Therapy*, **6**, 137–157.

Kielholz, P. (1973). Addictive behaviour in man, in *Psychic Dependence: Definition, Assessment in Animals and Man, Theoretical and Clinical Implications* (eds L. Goldberg and F. Hoffmeister), Springer-Verlag, Heidelberg.

Kilpatrick, R. (1997). Joy-riding: an addictive behaviour? in *Addicted to Crime?* (eds J.E. Hodge, M. McMurran and C.R. Hollin), Wiley, Chichester.

Kinsey, A., Pomeroy, W. and Martin, C. (1948). *Sexual Behaviour in the Human Male*, Saunders, Philadelphia.

Klass, E. (1978). Psychological effects of immoral actions: the experimental evidence, *Psychological Bulletin*, **85**, 756–771.

Klee, H.H. (1992). A new target for behaviour research—amphetamine mis-use, *British Journal of Addiction*, **87**, 439–446.

Klingemann, H.K.H. (1991). The motivation for change from problem alcohol and heroin use, *British Journal of Addiction*, **86**, 727–744.

Knapp, T.J. and Lech, B.C. (1987). Pathological gambling: A review with recommendations, *Advances in Behavioural Research and Therapy*, **9**, 21–49.

Korkia, P. and Stimson, G.V. (1993). *Anabolic Steroid Use in Great Britain: An Exploratory Investigation*, The Centre for Research on Drugs and Health Behaviour, Imperial College of Medicine, London.

Kornetsky, C. and Porrino, L.J. (1992). Brain mechanisms of drug-induced reinforcement, in *Addictive States* (eds. C.P. O'Brien and J. Jaffe), Raven Press, New York.

Koski-Jännes, A. (1998). Turning points in addiction careers: five case studies, *Journal of Substance Misuse*, **3**, 226–233.

Krafft-Ebbing, R. von (1965). *Psychopathia Sexualis* (English translation by F. Klaf), Stein and Day, New York.

Kranzler, H.R. and Anton, R.F. (1994). Implications of recent neuropsychopharmacologic research for understanding the etiology and development of alcoholism, *Journal of Consulting and Clinical Psychology*, **62**, 1116–1126.

Kronhausen, E. and Kronhausen, P. (1967). *Walter, the English Casanova: A Presentation of His Unique Memoirs 'My Secret Life'*, Polybooks, London.

Kumar, R. and Stolerman, I. (1977). Experimental and clinical aspects of drug dependence, in *Handbook of Psychopharmacology* (Vol. 7) (eds I. Iversen, S. Iversen and S. Snyder), Plenum, New York.

Kunitz, S.J. and Levy, J.E. (1994). *Drinking Careers: A Twenty-five-year Study of Three Navajo Populations*, Yale University Press, Newhaven and London.

Kurland, A. (1978). *Psychiatric Aspects of Opiate Dependence*, CRC Press, West Palm Beach, Florida.

Lacey, J.H. (1993). Self-damaging and addictive behaviour in bulimia nervosa: a catchment area study, *British Journal of Psychiatry*, **163**, 190–194.

Lader, M. (1981). Benzodiazepine dependence, in *The Misuse of Psychotropic Drugs* (eds R. Murray, H. Ghodse, C. Harris, D. Williams and P. Williams), Gaskell, The Royal College of Psychiatrists, London.

Ladouceur, R. (1996). The prevalence of pathological gambling in Canada, *Journal of Gambling Studies*, **12**, 129–142.

Ladouceur, R., Boisvert, J.M., Pepin, M., Lorangere, M. and Sylvain, C. (1994). Social cost of pathological gambling, *Journal of Gambling Studies*, **10**, 399–409.

Lando, H.A. (1991). Toward a comprehensive strategy for reducing the health burden of tobacco, *British Journal of Addiction*, **86**, 649–652.

Langeland, W. and Hartgers, C. (1998). Child sexual and physical abuse and alcoholism: a review, *Journal of Studies on Alcohol*, **59**, 336–348.

Langner, E.J. (1975). The illusion of control, *Journal of Personality and Social Psychology*, **32**, 311–328 (cited by Carroll and Huxley, 1994).

Laschet, U. (1973). Antiandrogen in the treatment of sex offenders: mode of action and therapeutic outcome, in *Contemporary Sexual Behaviour: Critical Issues in the 1970s* (eds J. Zubin and J. Money), Johns Hopkins University Press.

Ledermann, S. (1956). *Alcool, Alcoolisme, Alcoolisation*, Presses Universitaires de France, Paris (cited by Schmidt, 1977).

Legarda, J.J., Babio, R. and Abreu, J.M. (1992). Prevalence estimates of pathological gambling in Seville (Spain), *British Journal of Addiction*, **87**, 767–770.

Legg, C.R. (1994). Appetite—a psychological concept, in, *Appetite, Neural and Behavioural Bases* (eds C.R. Legg and D. Booth), Oxford University Press, Oxford, 1–10.

Legg, C.R. and Booth, D. (eds) (1994). *Appetite, Neural and Behavioural Bases*, Oxford University Press, Oxford.

LeGrand, J. (1995). *The Observer*, 29 October 1995 (cited by Miers, 1996).

Lemert, E. (1951). *Social Pathology*, McGraw-Hill, New York.

Leon, G. (1976). Current directions in the treatment of obesity, *Psychological Bulletin*, **83**, 557–578.

Leon, G. and Roth, L. (1977). Obesity: psychological causes, correlations, and speculations, *Psychological Bulletin*, **84**, 117–139.

Lesieur, H.R. (1984). *The Chase: The Career of the Compulsive Gambler*, Schenkman, Rochester, Vermont.

Lesieur, H.R. (1988). The female pathological gambler, in *Gambling Studies: Proceedings of the 7th International Conference on Gambling and Risk Taking* (ed. W.R. Eadington), University of Nevada, Reno, Nevada (cited by Lesieur and Rosenthal, 1991).

Lesieur, H.R. (1994). Epidemiological surveys of pathological gambling: critique and suggestions for modification, *Journal of Gambling Studies*, **10**, 385–397.

Lesieur, H.R. and Blume, S.B. (1987). The South Oaks Gambling Screen (SOGS). A new instrument for the identification of pathological gamblers, *American Journal of Psychiatry*, **14**, 1184–1188.

Lesieur, H.R. and Rosenthal, R.J. (1991). Pathological gambling: a review of the literature (prepared for the American Psychiatric Association Task Force on DSM-IV Committee on Disorders of Impulse Control Not Elsewhere Classified), *Journal of Gambling Studies*, **7**, 5–39.

Leung, F., Geller, J. and Katzman, M. (1996). Issues and concerns associated with different risk models for eating disorders, *International Journal of Eating Disorders*, **19**, 249–256.

Leventhal, H. and Cleary, P. (1980). The smoking problem: a review of the research and theory in behavioral risk modification, *Psychological Bulletin*, **88**, 370–405.

Leventhal, H., Keeshan, P., Baker, T. and Wetter, D. (1991). Smoking prevention: towards a process approach, *British Journal of Addiction*, **86**, 583–587.

Levin, R.J. (1994). Human male sexuality: appetite and arousal, desire and drive, in *Appetite, Neural and Behavioural Bases* (eds C.R. Legg and D. Booth), Oxford University Press, Oxford, 127–164.

Levine, H. (1978). The discovery of addiction: changing conceptions of habitual drunkenness in America, *Journal of Studies on Alcohol*, **39**, 143–176.

Levine, M.P. and Troiden, R.R. (1988). The myth of sexual compulsivity, *The Journal of Sex Research*, **25**, 347–363 (cited by Gold and Heffner, 1998).

Levine, M.D., Marcus, M.D. and Moulton, P. (1996). Exercise in the treatment of binge eating disorder, *International Journal of Eating Disorders*, **19**, 171–177.

Levitt, E. (1973). Nymphomania, *Sexual Behaviour*, **March**, 13–17.

Lewandowski, L.M., Gebing, T.A., Anthony, J.L. and O'Brien, W.H. (1997). Meta-analysis of cognitive-behavioral treatment studies for bulimia, *Clinical Psychology Review*, **7**, 703–718.

Lewin, K. (1935). *Dynamic Theory of Personality*, McGraw-Hill, New York.

Lewin, L. (1964, orig. 1924). *Phantastica: Narcotic and Stimulating Drugs*, Dutton, New York (cited by Jaffe, 1977).

Lewis, D. and Duncan, C. (1958). Expectation and resistance to extinction of a lever-pulling response as a function of percentage reinforcement and number of acquisition trials, *Journal of Experimental Psychology*, **55**, 121–128 (cited by Cornish, 1978).

Lewis, J. (1971). Promiscuous women, *Sexual Behaviour*, **November**, 75–80.

Ley, P. (1980). The psychology of obesity: its causes, consequences and control, in *Contributions to Medical Psychology* (Vol. 2) (ed. S. Rachman), Pergamon, Oxford.

Ley, P., Bradshaw, P., Kincey, J., Couper-Smartt, H. and Wilson, M. (1974). Psychological variables in the control of obesity, in *Obesity* (eds W. Burland, P. Samuel and J. Yudkin), Churchill Livingstone, London.

Ley, P., Whitworth, M., Skilbeck, C., Woodward, R., Pinsent, R., Pike, L., Clarkson, M. and Clark, P. (1976). Improving doctor patient communications in general practice, *Journal of the Royal College of General Practitoners*, **26**, 720–724.

Lezard, N. (1997). Review of Peter Cook: A Biography by H. Thompson. *Guardian Weekly*, 7th September.

Liepman, M.R. (1993). Using family influence to motivate alcoholics to enter treatment and begin recovery: the Johnson Institute Intervention Approach, in *Marital and Family Therapy in Alcoholism Treatment* (ed. T.J. O'Farrell), Guilford, New York, 54–77.

Lindner, R. (1950). The psychodynamics of gambling, *Annals of the American Academy of Political and Social Science*, **269**, 93.

Lindström, L. (1991). Basic assumptions reconsidered, *British Journal of Addiction*, **86**, 846–848.

Litman, G. (1976). Behavior modification techniques in the treatment of alcoholism: a review and critique, in *Research Advances in Alcohol and Drug Problems* (eds R. Gibbins, Y. Israel, H. Kalant, R. Popham, W. Schmidt and R. Smart), Wiley, New York.

Litman, G., Eiser, J. and Taylor, C. (1979). Dependence, relapse and extinction: a theoretical critique and a behavioral examination, *Journal of Clinical Psychology*, **35**, 192–199.

Liu, S. and Cheng, A.T.A. (1998). Alcohol use disorders among the Yami aborigines in Taiwan, *British Journal of Psychiatry*, **172**, 168–174.

Lloyd, G., Chick, J., Crombie, E. and Anderson, S. (1986). Problem drinkers in medical wards: consumption patterns and disabilities in newly identified male cases, *British Journal of Addiction*, **81**, 780–795.

Long, C.G., Hinton, C. and Gillespie, N.K. (1994). Selective processing of food and body size words: application of the Stroop Test with obese restrained eaters, anorexics, and normals, *International Journal of Eating Disorders*, **15**, 279–283.

Longabaugh, R., Wirtz, P.W., DiClemente, C.C. and Litt, M. (1994). Issues in the development of client-treatment matching hypotheses? *Journal of Studies on Alcohol*, supplement **12**, 46–59.

Longabaugh, R., Wirtz, P.W., Zweben, A. and Stout, R.L. (1998). Network support for drinking, Alcoholics Anonymous and long-term matching effects, *Addiction*, **93**, 1313–1333.

Longmate, N. (1968). *The Water Drinkers: A History of Temperance*, Hamish Hamilton, London.

López-Viets, V.C. and Miller, W.R. (1997). Treatment approaches for pathological gamblers, *Clinical Psychology Review*, **17**, 689–702.

Lorenz, V.C. and Yaffee, R.A. (1984). Pathological gambling: medical, emotional and interpersonal aspects, Paper presented at *Sixth National Conference on Gambling and Risk Taking, Atlantic City, New Jersey, December*.

Lorenz, V.C. and Yaffee, R.A. (1988). Pathological gambling: psychosomatic, emotional and marital difficulties as reported by the spouse, *Journal of Gambling Behaviour*, **4**, 13–26.

Loro, A. and Orleans, C. (1981). Binge eating in obesity: preliminary findings and guidelines for behavioral analysis and treatment, *Addictive Behaviors*, **6**, 155–166.

MacAndrew, C. and Edgerton, R. (1970). *Drunken Comportment: A Social Explanation*, Nelson, London.

Mäkelä, K. (1991). Social and cultural preconditions of Alcoholics Anonymous (AA) and factors associated with the strength of AA, *British Journal of Addiction*, **86**, 1405–1413.

Mäkelä, K. (1996). How to describe the domains of drinking and consequences, *Addiction*, **91**, 1447–1449.

Mäkelä, K., Arminen, I., Bloomfield, K., Eisenbach-Stangl, I., Bergmark, K.H., Kurube, N., Mariolini, N., Olafsdóttir, H., Peterson, J.H., Phillips, M., Rehm, J., Room, R., Rosenqvist, P., Rosovsky, H., Stenius, K., Swiatkiewicz, G., Woronowicz, B., Zielinski, A. (1996). *Alcoholics Anonymous as a Mutual-Help Movement: A Study of Eight Societies*, The University of Wisconsin Press, Madison, Wisconsin.

Maletzky, B. and Klotter, J. (1976). Addiction to diazepam, *International Journal of the Addictions*, **11**, 95–115.

Marcus, S. (1966). *The Other Victorians: A Study of Sexuality and Pornography in Mid-Nineteenth-Century England*, Weidenfeld and Nicolson, London.

Marlatt, G. (1996). Taxonomy of high-risk situations for alcohol relapse: evolution and development of a cognitive-behavioral model, *Addiction*, **91**, S37–S49.

Marlatt, G., Demming, B. and Reid, J. (1973). Loss of control drinking in alcoholics: an experimental analogue, *Journal of Abnormal Psychology*, **81**, 233–241.

Marshall, D. (1971). Sexual behaviour in Mangaia, in *Human Sexual Behaviour: The Range and Diversity of Human Sexual Experience Throughout the World as Seen in Six Representative Cultures* (eds D. Marshall and R. Suggs), Basic Books, New York.

Marshall, D. and Suggs, R. (eds) (1971). *Human Sexual Behaviour: The Range and Diversity of Human Sexual Experience Throughout the World as Seen in Six Representative Cultures*, Basic Books, New York.

Marshall, E.J., Edwards, G. and Taylor, C. (1994). Mortality in men with drinking problems: a 20 year follow-up, *Addiction*, **89**, 1293–1298.

Martin, J.E., Clafas, K.M., Polarek, M., Hofstetter, R.R., Noto, J., Beach, D. and Patten, C.A. (1997). Prospective evaluation of three smoking interventions in 205 recovering alcoholics: one-year results of project SCRAP-Tobacco, *Journal of Consulting and Clinical Psychology*, **65**, 190–194.

Masserman, J. and Yum, K. (1946). An analysis of the influence of alcohol in experimental neurosis in cats, *Psychosomatic Medicine*, **8**, 36–52.

Matarazzo, J. (1973). Some commonalities among the preceding reports of studies on the psychology of smoking, in *Smoking Behavior: Motives and Incentives* (ed. W. Dunn), Wiley, New York.

Matejcek, Z. (1981a). Children in families of alcoholics I: the rearing situation, *Psychologija i Patopsychologia Dietata*, **16**, 303–318 (translated into English for the present author).

Matejcek, Z. (1981b). Children in families of alcoholics II: competency in school and peer group, *Psychologija i Patopsychologia Dietata*, **16**, 537–560 (translated into English for the present author).

Mattson, M.E., Allen, J.P., Longabaugh, R., Nickless, C.J., Connors, G.J. and Kadden, R.M. (1994). A chronological review of empirical studies matching alcoholic clients to treatment, *Journal of Studies on Alcohol*, supplement **12**, 16–29.

Mausner, B. and Platt, E. (1971). *Smoking: A Behavioral Analysis*, Pergamon, New York.

McConaghy, N. (1991). Case studies: a pathological or a compulsive gambler? *Journal of Gambling Studies*, **7**, 55–63.

McConaghy, N., Armstrong, M.S. Blaszczynski, A. and Allcock, C. (1983). Controlled comparison of aversive therapy and imaginal desensitization in compulsive gambling, *British Journal of Psychiatry*, **142**, 366–372.

McConaghy, N., Armstrong, M.S., Blaszczynski, A. and Allcock, C. (1988). Behavior completion versus stimulus control in compulsive gambling, *Behavior Modification*, **12**, 371–384.

McCrady, B.S. (1990). The marital relationship and alcoholism treatment, in *Alcohol and the Family: Research and Clinical Perspectives* (eds R.L. Collins, K.E. Leonard and J.S. Searles), Guilford Press, New York.

McCrady, B.S. (1994). Alcoholics Anonymous and behavior therapy: Can habits be treated as diseases? Can diseases be treated as habits? *Journal of Consulting and Clinical Psychology*, **62**, 1159–1166.

McCrady, B.S., Epstein, E.E. and Hirsch, L. (1996). Issues in the implementation of a randomized clinical trial that includes Alcoholics Anonymous: studying AA-related behaviors during treatment, *Journal of Studies on Alcohol*, **57**, 604–612.

McCusker, C.G. and Gettings, B. (1997). Automaticity of cognitive biases in addictive behaviours: further evidence with gamblers, *British Journal of Clinical Psychology*, **36**, 543–554.

McCusker, C.G., Roberts, G., Douthwaite, J. and Williams, E. (1995a). Teenagers and illicit drug use: expanding the user versus non-user dichotomy, *Journal of Community and Applied Social Psychology*, **5**, 221–242.

McCusker, C.G., McClements, R. and McCartney, U. (1995b). Cognitive bias for addiction-related stimuli, Paper presented at *London Conference of the British Psychological Society, December*.

McDermott, P. (1993). Ecstasy and the rave scene: new drug, new sub-culture, old problems? Executive Summary, the Centre for Research on Drugs and Health Behaviour, 25 May.

McGee, L. and Newcomb, M.D. (1992). General deviance syndrome: expanded hierarchical evaluations at four ages from early adolescence to adulthood, *Journal of Consulting and Clinical Psychology*, **60**, 766–776.

McGregor, G. and Howells, K. (1997). Addiction models of sexual offending, in *Addicted to Crime?* (eds J.E. Hodge, M. McMurran and C.R. Hollin), Wiley, Chichester, 107–138.

McGuire, J. (1997). 'Irrational' shoplifting and models of addiction, in *Addicted to Crime?* (eds J.E. Hodge, M. McMurran and C.R. Hollin), Wiley, Chichester, 207–232.

McKay, J.R., Longabaugh, R., Beattie, M.C., Maisto, S.A. and Noel, N.E. (1993). Does adding conjoint therapy to individually focused alcoholism treatment lead to better family functioning? *Journal of Substance Abuse*, **5**, 45–59.

McKennell, A. and Thomas, R. (1967). *Adults' and Adolescents' Smoking Habits and Attitudes*, Government Social Survey, HMSO, London.

McKirnan, D. (1977). A community approach to the recognition of alcohol abuse: the drinking norms of three Montreal communities, *Canadian Journal of Behavioral Science*, **9**, 108–122.

McKirnan, D. (1978). Community perspectives on deviance: some factors in the definition of alcohol abuse, *American Journal of Community Psychology*, **6**, 219–238.

McLellan, A.T., Woody, G.E., Luborsky, L. and Goehl, L. (1988). Is the counselor an 'active ingredient' in substance abuse rehabilitation? *The Journal of Nervous and Mental Disease*, **176**, 423–430.

McLellan, A.T., Alterman, A.I., Metzger, D.S., Grissom, G.R., Woody, G.E., Luborsky, L. and O'Brien, C.P. (1994). Similarity of outcome predictors across opiate, cocaine, and alcohol treatments: role of treatment services, *Journal of Consulting and Clinical Psychology*, **62**, 1141–1158.

McLellan, A.T., Hagan, T.A., Levine, M., Gould, F., Meyers, K., Bencivengo, M. and Durell, J. (1998). Supplemental social services improve outcomes in public addiction treatment, *Addiction*, **93**, 1489–1499.

McMillen, J. (ed.) (1996). *Gambling Cultures: Studies in History and Interpretation*, Routledge, London.

McMurray, G. (1989). Benzodiazepine use: A comparative study of ex long-term regular sporadic users. Unpublished MSc thesis, University of Exeter.

McNair, D.M., Lorr, M. and Droppleman, L.F. (1971). *Profile of Mood States* (Manual), San Diego Education and Industrial Testing Service, San Diego, California.

McNeill, A.D. (1991). The development of dependence on smoking in children, *British Journal of Addiction*, **86**, 589–592.

McNeill, A. (1992). Why children start smoking: the need for a comprehensive tobacco control Policy, *British Journal of Addiction*, **87**, 24–25.

McPeek, F. (1972). The role of religious bodies in the treatment of inebriety in the United States, in *Alcohol, Science and Society: 29 Lectures with Discussions as Given at the Yale Summer School of Alcohol Studies*, Greenword Press, Westport, Connecticut.

Meichenbaum, D. (1977). *Cognitive-Behaviour Modification: An Integrative Approach*, Plenum, New York.

Mellor, C.S., Farid, N.R. and Craig, D.F. (1988). Female hypersexuality treated with cyproterone acetate, *American Journal of Psychiatry*, **145**, 1037.

Meltzer, H., Gill, B. and Petticrew, M. (1994). *The Prevalence of Psychiatric Morbidity Among Adults Aged 16–61, Living in Private Households, in Great Britain*, OPCS Surveys of Psychiatric Morbidity in Great Britain, HMSO, London.

Meltzer, H., Gill, B., Petticrew, M. and Hinds, K. (1995). *Economic Activity and Social Functioning of Adults with Psychiatric Disorders*, OPCS Surveys of Psychiatric Morbidity in Great Britain, HMSO, London.

Messenger, J. (1971). Sex and repression in an Irish folk community, in *Human Sexual Behaviour: The Range and Diversity of Human Sexual Experience Throughout the World as Seen in Six Representative Cultures* (eds D. Marshall and R. Suggs), Basic Books, New York.

Meyer, A., Friedman, L. and Lazarsfeld, P. (1973). Motivational conflicts engendered by the on-going discussion of cigarette smoking, in *Smoking Behavior: Motives and Incentives* (ed. W. Dunn), Winston, Washington, DC.

Meyer, G. (1992). The gambling market in the Federal Republic of Germany and the help-seeking of pathological gamblers, *Journal of Gambling Studies*, **8**, 11–20.

Meyer, G. and Fabian, T. (1992). Delinquency among pathological gamblers; a causal approach, *Journal of Gambling Studies*, **8**, 61–77.

Miers, D. (1996). The implementation and effects of Great Britain's National Lottery, *Journal of Gambling Studies*, **12**, 343–373.

Mill, J.S. (1974, orig. 1859). *On Liberty*, Penguin Books, London.

Miller, N. (1944). Experimental studies of conflict, in *Personality and the Behavior Disorders* (ed. J. Hunt), Ronald, New York.

Miller, N.S., Gold, M.S. and Millman, R.B. (1989). Cocaine: general characteristics, abuse and addiction, *New York State Journal of Medicine*, **89**, 390–395 (cited by Ditton and Hammersley, 1996).

Miller, P. (1980). Theoretical and practical issues in substance abuse assessment and treatment, in *The Addictive Behaviors: Treatment of Alcoholism, Drug Abuse, Smoking and Obesity* (ed. W.R. Miller), Pergamon, New York.

Miller, W.R. (1990). Spirituality: the silent dimension in addiction research (The 1990 Leonard Ball Oration), *Drug and Alcohol Review*, **9**, 259–266.

Miller, W. R. (1996). What is a relapse? Fifty ways to leave the wagon, *Addiction*, **91**, S15–S27.

Miller, W.R. (1998). Researching the spiritual dimensions of alcohol and other drug problems, *Addiction*, **93**, 979–990.

Miller, W.R. and Brown, J.M. (1991). Self-regulation as a conceptual basis for the prevention and treatment of addictive behaviours, in *Self-control and the Addictive Behaviours* (eds N. Heather, W.R. Miller and J. Greeley), Maxwell Macmillan, Botany, New South Wales, Australia, 3–60.

Miller, W.R. and Cooney, N.L. (1994). Designing studies to investigate client-treatment matching? *Journal of Studies on Alcohol*, supplement **12**, 38–45.

Miller, W.R. and Kurtz, E. (1994). Models of alcoholism used in treatment: contrasting AA and other perspectives with which it is often confused, *Journal of Studies on Alcohol*, **55**, 159–166.

Miller, W.R. and Meyers, R.J. (1998). Engaging the unmotivated in treatment for alcohol problems: a comparison of three intervention strategies. Paper presented at *Eighth International Conference on Treatment of Addictive Behaviors, Santa Fe, New Mexico, January 11–15*.

Miller, W.R. and Rollnick, S. (1991). *Motivational Interviewing: Preparing People for Change*, Guilford Press, New York.

Miller, W.R. and Taylor, C. (1980). Relative effectiveness of bibliotherapy, individual and group self-control training in the treatment of problem drinkers, *Addictive Behaviors*, **5**, 13–24.

Miller, W.R., Brown, J.M., Simpson, T.L., Handmaker, N.S., Bien, T.H., Luckie, L.F., Montgomery, H.A., Hester, R.K. and Tonigan, J.S. (1995). What works? A methodological analysis of the alcohol treatment outcome literature, in *Handbook of Alcoholism Treatment Approaches—Effective Alternatives* (2nd ed.) (eds R.K. Hester and W.R. Miller), Allyn and Bacon, Boston.

Mills, C.K. (1885). A case of nymphomania with hystero-epilepsy and peculiar mental perversions—the results of clitoridectomy and oophorectomy—the patient's history as told by herself, *Philadelphia Medical Times*, **15 April**, 534–540 (cited by Groneman, 1994).

Minihan, M. (1967). *Dostoevsky: His Life and Work by Konstantin Mochulsky*, Princeton University Press, Princeton, New Jersey.

Mitchell, P. (1995). Alcohol policies—in poverty and in wealth, Letter, *Addiction*, **90**, 441.

Moore, S.M. and Ohtsuka, K. (1997). Gambling activities of young Australians: developing a model of behaviour, *Journal of Gambling Studies*, **13**, 207–235.

Moos, R.H., Finney, J.W. and Cronkite, R. (1990). *Alcoholism Treatment: Context, Process and Outcome*, Oxford University Press, New York.

Moosburger, R., Plant, A.J. and Pierce, J.P. (1990). The drug use behaviour of cocaine users, *Drug and Alcohol Review*, **9**, 251–258.

Moran, E. (1970). Gambling as a form of dependence, *British Journal of Addiction*, **64**, 419–428.

Moran, E. (1975). Pathological gambling, in *Contemporary Psychiatry, British Journal of Psychiatry*, **Special Publication No. 9**, Royal College of Psychiatrists, London.

Moran, E. (1987). *Gambling Among Schoolchildren: The Impact of the Fruit Machine*, The National Council on Gambling, London.

Morganstern, K. (1977). Cigarette smoke as a noxious stimulus in self-managed aversion therapy for compulsive eating: technique and case illustration, in *Behavioral Treatments of Obesity* (ed. J. Foreyt), Pergamon, Oxford.

Morse, B. (1963). *The Sexually Promiscuous Female*, Pamar, New York.

Mort, F. (1987, 2nd ed. 1998). *Dangerous Sexualities: Medico-moral Politics in England since 1830*, Routledge & Kegan Paul, London.

Mugford, S. (1991). Controlled drug use among recreational users: sociological perspectives, in: *Self-control and the Addictive Behaviours* (eds N. Heather, W.R. Miller and J. Greeley), Maxwell MacMillan, Botany, New South Wales, Australia, 243–261,.

Mugford, S. and Cohen, P. (1989). *Drug Use, Social Relations and Commodity Consumption*, Report to the National Campaign Against Drug Abuse, Canberra, Australian Capital Territory, Australia (cited by Mugford, 1991).

Murphy, S.M. and Tyrer, P. (1988). The essence of benzodiazepine dependence, in *The Psychopharmacology of Addiction* (ed. M. Lader), Oxford University Press, Oxford, 157–167.

Murphy, S.M. Reineman, C. and Waldorf, B. (1989). An eleven year follow-up of a network of cocaine users, *British Journal of Addiction*, **84**, 427–436.

Musto, D.F. (1991). Opium, cocaine and marijuana in American history, *Scientific American*, July, 40–47.

Myerson, A. (1940). Alcohol: a study of social ambivalence, *Quarterly Journal of Studies on Alcohol*, **1**, 13–20.

Najavits, L.M. and Weiss, R.D. (1994). Variations in therapist effectiveness in the treatment of patients with substance use disorders: an empirical review, *Addiction*, **89**, 679–688.

National Heritage Committee (1993). *Third Report: National Lottery etc Bill*, House of Commons Session 1992–93, HMSO, London (cited by Miers, 1996).

National Housing and Town Planning Council (1988). *The Use of the Fruit Machine*, The National Council on Gambling, London (cited by Griffiths, 1990).

Negrete, J. (1980). The Andean region of South America: indigenous coca chewing in the rural areas and coca paste smoking in the cities, in *Drug Problems in the Sociocultural Context: A Basis for Policies and Programme Planning* (eds G. Edwards and A. Arif), World Health Organisation, Geneva.

Nesbitt, P. (1969). Smoking, physiological arousal, and emotional response, Unpublished doctoral dissertation, Columbia University (cited by Schachter, 1973).

Newcomb, M.D. (1993). Beyond adolescence, problem behavior and young adult development, R. Jessor, J.E. Donovan and F.M. Costa (review), *Contemporary Psychology*, **38**, 895–898.

Newcomb, M.D. (1994). Drug use and intimate relationships among women and men: separating specific from general effects in prospective data using structural equation models, *Journal of Consulting and Clinical Psychology*, **62**, 463–476.

Newman, O. (1972). *Gambling: Hazard and Reward*, Athlone Press. London

News and Notes (1992). Drug hangings, *British Journal of Addiction*, **87**, 1356.

News and Views (1990). *Drug and Alcohol Review*, **9**, 377–378.

Niaura, R., Goldstein, M. and Abrams, D. (1991). A bioinformational systems perspective on tobacco dependence, *British Journal of Addiction*, **86**, 593–597.

Nides, M.A., Rakos, R.F., Gonzales, D., Murray, R.P., Tashkin, D.P. and Bjornson-Benson, W.M. (1995). Predictors of initial smoking cessation and relapse through the first 2 years of the lung health study, *Journal of Consulting and Clinical Psychology*, **63**, 60–69.

O'Brien, C.P., Childress, A.R., McLellan, A.T. and Ehrman, R. (1992). A learning model of addiction, in *Addictive States* (eds C.P. O'Brien and J. Jaffe), Raven Press, New York, 157–178.

O'Connor, E.A., Carbonari, J.P. and DiClemente, C.C. (1996). Gender and smoking cessation: a factor structure comparison of processes of change, *Journal of Consulting and Clinical Psychology*, **64**, 130–138.

O'Connor, J. (1978). *The Young Drinkers: A Cross-National Study of Social and Cultural Influences*, Tavistock, London.

O'Connor, K. (1989). Individual differences and motor systems in smoker motivation, in *Smoking and Human Behavior* (eds T. Ney and A. Gale), Wiley, Chichester.

Oei, T.P.S., Tilley, D. and Gow, K. (1991). Differences in reasons for smoking between younger and older smokers, *Drug and Alcohol Review*, **10**, 323–329.

O'Farrell, T.J., Choquette, K.A. and Cutter, H.S.G. (1998). Couples relapse prevention sessions after behavioral marital therapy for male alcoholics: outcomes during the three years after starting treatment, *Journal of Studies on Alcohol*, **59**, 357–370.

OFLOT (Office of the National Lottery) (1994). *Director General of the National Lottery, Annual Report 1993–94*, HMSO, London (cited by Miers, 1996).

OFLOT (Office of the National Lottery) (1996). *Social Research Programme*, February 1996 (cited by Miers, 1996).

Ogden, J., Veale, D. and Summers, Z. (1997). The development and validation of the exercise dependence questionnaire, *Addiction Research*, **5**, 343–356 (cited by Cox, 1999).

Oliven, J. (1974). *Clinical Sexuality: A Manual for the Physician and the Professions*, Lippincott, Philadelphia.

Orford, J. (1978). Hypersexuality: implications for a theory of dependence, *British Journal of Addiction*, **73**, 299–310.

Orford, J. (1980). Understanding treatment: controlled trials and other strategies, in *Alcoholism Treatment in Transition* (eds G. Edwards and M. Grant), Croom Helm, London.

Orford, J. (1987). The need for a community response to alcohol-related problems, in *Helping the Problem Drinker: New Initiatives in Community Care* (eds T. Stockwell and S. Clement), Croom Helm, London, 4–32.

Orford, J. (1992a). Davidson's dilemma: comment on Davidson's 'Prochaska and DiClemente's Model of change: a case study?' *British Journal of Addiction*, **87**, 832–833.

Orford, J. (1992b). *Community Psychology: Theory and Practice*, Wiley, Chichester.

Orford, J. (1992c). Control, confront or collude: how family and society respond to excessive drinking, *British Journal of Addiction*, **87**, 1513–1525.

Orford, J. (2001). Addiction as excessive appetite, *Addiction*, **96**, 15–33.

Orford, J. and Velleman, R. (1990). Offspring of parents with drinking problems: drinking and drug-taking as young adults, *British Journal of Addiction*, **85**, 779–794.

Orford, J. and Edwards, G. (1977). *Alcoholism: A Comparison of Treatment and Advice, with a Study of the Influence of Marriage*, Oxford University Press, Oxford.

Orford, J., Oppenheimer, E. and Edwards, G. (1976). Abstinence or control: the outcome of excessive drinking two years after consultation, *Behaviour Research and Therapy*, **14**, 409–418.

Orford, J., Somers, M., Daniels, V. and Kirby, B. (1992). Drinking amongst medical patients: levels of risk and models of change, *Addiction*, **87**, 1691–1702.

Orford, J., Morison, V. and Somers, M. (1996). Drinking and gambling: a comparison with implications for theories of addiction, *Drug and Alcohol Review*, **15**, 47–56.

Orford, J., Natera, G., Davies, J., Nava, A., Mora, J., Rigby, K., Bradbury, C., Copello, A. and Velleman, R. (1998a). Stresses and strains for family members living with drinking or drug problems in England and Mexico, *Salud Mental (Mexico)*, **21**, 1–13.

Orford, J., Natera, G., Davies, J., Nava, A., Mora, J., Rigby, K., Bradbury, C., Copello, A. and Velleman, R. (1998b). Tolerate, engage or withdraw: a study of the structure of families coping with alcohol and drug problems in south-west England and Mexico City, *Addiction*, **93**, 1799–1813.

Orford, J., Templeton, L., Copello, A., Velleman, R. and Bradbury, C. (1999a). *Worrying for Drinkers in the Family: An Interview Study with Aboriginal Australians in Urban Areas and Remote Communities in the Northern Territory*, Report for Northern Territory Health, Living with Alcohol Programme.

Orford, J., Dalton, S., Hartney, E., Ferrins-Brown, M., Kerr, C. and Maslin, J. (1999b). How is excessive drinking maintained? Untreated heavy drinkers' experiences of the personal benefits and drawbacks of their drinking, *Addiction Research* (in press).

Otto, S. and Orford, J. (1978). *Not Quite Like Home: Small Hostels for Alcoholics and Others*, Wiley, Chichester.

Ouimette, P.C., Finney, J.W. and Moos, R.H. (1997). Twelve-step and cognitive-behavioral treatment for substance abuse: a comparison of treatment effectiveness, *Journal of Consulting and Clinical Psychology*, **65**, 230–240.

Parker, H., Baker, K. and Newcombe, R. (1988). *Living with Heroin: The Impact of a Drug 'Epidemic' on an English Community*, Open University Press, Milton Keynes.

Parker, H., Aldridge, J. and Measham, F. (1998). *Illegal Leisure. The Normalization of Adolescent Recreational Drug Use*, Routledge, London.

Parrott, A.C. (1995). Stress modulation over the day in cigarette smokers, *Addiction*, **90**, 233–244.

Parrott, A.C. (1998). Nesbitt's paradox resolved? Stress and arousal modulation during cigarette smoking, *Addiction*, **93**, 27–39.

Partanen, J. (1996). Why alcohol and drug research remains a marginal activity—Comment on Room *et al.*, 1996, *Addiction*, **91**, 225–226.

Paxton, R. (1980). The effects of different deposit contracts in maintaining abstinence from cigarette smoking, Unpublished PhD thesis, University of London.

Pearson, G. (1987). *The New Heroin Users*, Basil Blackwell, Oxford.

Pearson, M. (1972). *The Age of Consent: Victorian Prostitution and its Enemies*, David and Charles, Newton Abbot.

Pedersen, W. and Skrondal, A. (1999). Ecstasy and new patterns of drug use: a normal population study, *Addiction*, **94**, 1695–1706.

Peele, S. (1977). Redefining addiction I: making addiction a scientifically and socially useful concept, *International Journal of Health Services*, **7**, 103–123.

Peele, S. and Brodsky, A. (1975). *Love and Addiction*, Taplinger, New York.

Pelc, I., Verbanck, P., LeBon, O., Gavrilovic, M., Lion, K. and Lehert, P. (1997). Efficacy and safety of acamprosate in the treatment of detoxified alcohol-dependent patients, *British Journal of Psychiatry*, **171**, 73–77.

Phillips, G.T., Gossop, M. and Bradley, B. (1986). The influence of psychological factors on the opiate withdrawal syndrome, *British Journal of Psychiatry*, **149**, 235–238.

Pickering, H. and Stimson, G. (1994). Prevalence and demographic factors of stimulant use, *Addiction*, **89**, 1385–1390.

Plant, M.A., Peck, D.F. and Samule, E. (1985). *Alcohol, Drugs and School-leavers*, Tavistock, London.

Polcin, D.L. and Weisner, C. (1999). Factors associated with coercion in entering treatment for alcohol problems, *Drug and Alcohol Dependence*, **54**, 63–68.

Polivy, J. (1976). Perception of calories and regulation of intake in restrained and unrestrained subjects, *Addictive Behaviors*, **1**, 237–243.

Pomerleau, O.F. and Pomerleau, C.S. (1989). A biobehavioral perspective on smoking, in *Smoking and Human Behavior* (eds T. Ney and A. Gale), Wiley, Chichester.

Powell, J. (1995). Conditioned responses to drug-related stimuli: is context crucial? *Addiction*, **90**, 1089–1095.

Power, R., Green, A., Foster, R. and Stimson, G. (1995). A qualitative study of the purchasing and distribution patterns of cocaine and crack users in England and Wales, *Addiction Research*, **2**, 363–380.

Premack, D. (1970). Mechanisms of self-control, in *Learning Mechanisms in Smoking* (ed. W. Hunt), Aldine, Chicago.

Prescott, J. (1990). Kava use in Australia, *Drug and Alcohol Review*, **9**, 325–328.

Primrose, D. and Orford, J. (1997). Coping with behaviour-attitude dissonance: a study amongst heroin addicts in Karachi, *Addiction Research*, **5**, 395–410.

Prochaska, J.O., Velicer, W., Guadagnoli, E., Rossi, J.S. and DiClemente, C.C. (1991). Patterns of change: dynamic typology applied to smoking cessation, *Multivariate Behavioral Research*, **26**, 83–107.

Prochaska, J.O., DiClemente, C.C. and Norcross, J.C. (1992). In search of how people change, *American Psychologist*, **47**, 1102–1114.

Productivity Commission (1999). *Australia's Gambling Industries*, Draft report, Canberra, July.

Project MATCH Research Group (1997a). Matching alcoholism treatments to client heterogeneity: Project MATCH post-treatment drinking outcomes, *Journal of Studies on Alcohol*, **58**, 7–29.

Project MATCH Research Group (1997b). Project MATCH secondary a priori hypotheses, *Addiction*, **92**, 1671–1698.

Purser, R., Johnson, M., Orford, J. and Davis, P. (1999). *Drinking in Second Generation Black and Asian Communities in the English Midlands*, Aquarius, Birmingham.

Rachman, S. and Teasdale, J. (1969). *Aversion Therapy and Behaviour Disorders: An Analysis*, Routledge & Kegan Paul, London.

Radin, S. (1972). The Don Juan, *Sexual Behaviour*, **December**, 4–9.

Rado, S. (1933). The psychoanalysis of pharmacothymia (drug addiction), *Psychoanalytic Quarterly*, **2**, 1–23 (reprinted in Shaffer and Burglass, 1981).

Raistrick, D., Bradshaw, J., Tober, G., Weiner, J., Allison, J. and Healey, C. (1994). Development of the Leeds Dependence Questionnaire (LDQ): A questionnaire to measure alcohol and opiate dependence in the context of a treatment evaluation package, *Addiction*, **89**, 563–572.

Reilly, D., Didcott, P., Swift, W. and Hall, W. (1998). Long-term cannabis use: characteristics of users in an Australian rural area, *Addiction*, **93**, 837–846.

Reinert, R. (1968). The concept of alcoholism as a bad habit, *Bulletin of the Menninger Clinic*, **32**, 35–46.

Reiss, D. (1996). Abnormal eating attitudes and behaviours in two ethnic groups from a female British urban population, *Psychological Medicine*, **26**, 289–299.

Reuter, P. (1994). Identifying new policy trade-offs, *Addiction*, **89**, 806–807.

Richmond, R.L., Kehone, L. and de Almeida Neto, A.C. (1997). Effectiveness of a 24 hour transdermal nicotine patch in conjunction with a cognitive behavioural programme: 1 year outcome, *Addiction*, **92**, 27–31.

Robertson, I. and Heather, N. (1983). *Let's Drink to Your Health: A Self Help Guide to Sensible Drinking*, The British Psychological Society, Leicester.

Robins, L., Davis, D., and Wish, E. (1977). Detecting predictors of rare events: demographic, family and personal deviance as predictors of stages in the progression toward narcotic addiction, in *The Origins and Course of Psychopathology: Methods of Longitudinal Research* (eds S. Strauss, H. Babigian and M. Roff), Plenum, New York.

Robinson, D. (1979). *Talking Out of Alcoholism: The Self-Help Process of Alcoholics Anonymous*, Croom Helm, London.

Robinson, T.E. and Berridge, K.C. (1993). The neural basis of drug craving: an incentive-sensitization theory of addiction, *Brain Research Reviews*, **18**, 247–291.

Rodin, J. (1978). Has the distinction between internal versus external control of feeding outlived its usefulness? in *Recent Advances in Obesity Research, II, Proceedings of the Second International Congress on Obesity, Washington DC, October 1977* (ed. G. Bray), Newman, London.

Roesler, T.A. and Dafler, C.E. (1993). Chemical dissociation in adults sexually victimized as children: alcohol and drug use in adult survivors, *Journal of Substance Abuse Treatment*, **10**, 537–543.

Rogers, P. (1998). Seminar given at the School of Psychology, University of Birmingham, June 23.

Roget's Thesaurus (1998). B. Kirkpatrick (ed.), Penguin Books, Harmondsworth, Middlesex.

Roizen, R., Cahalan, D. and Shanks, P. (1978). Spontaneous remission among untreated problem drinkers, in *Longitudinal Research on Drug Use: Empirical Findings and Methodological Issues* (ed. D. Kandel), Hemisphere, Washington.

Rolleston, H. (1926). Medical aspects of tobacco, *The Lancet*, **i**, 961–965 (cited by Jaffe, 1977).

Romelsjö, A. and Lundberg, M. (1996). The changes in the social class distribution of moderate and high alcohol consumption and of alcohol-related disabilities over time in Stockholm County and in Sweden, *Addiction*, **91**, 1307–1323.

Rook, K. and Hammen, C. (1977). A cognitive perspective on the experience of sexual arousal, *Journal of Social Issues*, **33**, 7–29.

Room, R. (1997). Alcohol, the individual and society: what history teaches us, *Addiction*, **92**, S7–S11.

Room, R. (1998). Thirsting for attention, *Addiction*, **93**, 797–798.

Room, R., Janca, A., Bennett, L.A., Schmidt, L. and Sartorius, N. (1996). WHO cross-cultural applicability research on diagnosis and assessment of substance use disorders: an overview of methods and selected results, *Addiction*, **91**, 199–220.

Room, R., Turner, N.E. and Ialomiteanu, A. (1999). Community effects of the opening of the Niagara Casino, *Addiction*, **94**, 1449–1466.

Root, M.P.P. and Fallon, P. (1989). Treating the victimized bulimic: the functions of binge–purge behavior, *Journal of Interpersonal Violence*, **4**, 90–100.

Ross, J., Darke, S. and Hall, W. (1997). Transitions between routes of benzodiazepine administration among heroin users in Sydney, *Addiction*, **12**, 697–706.

Rossiter, E.M. and Agras, W.S. (1990). An empirical test of the DSM-III-R definition of binge, *International Journal of Eating Disorders*, **9**, 513–518 (cited by Walsh, 1993).

Rossow, I. and Amundsen, A. (1997). Alcohol abuse and mortality: a 40-year prospective study of Norwegian conscripts, *Social Science and Medicine*, **44**, 261–267.

Roth, L. (1978). *I'll Cry Tomorrow*, Chivers, Bath.

Rounsaville, B.J., Bryant, K.J., Babor, T. F., Kranzler, H. and Kadden, R. (1993). Cross system agreement for substance use disorders: DSM-III-R, DSM-IV and ICD-10, *Addiction*, **88**, 337–348.

Royal College of General Practitioners (1986). *Alcohol: A Balanced View*, RCGP, London.

Royal College of Physicians (1987). *A Great and Growing Evil: The Medical Consequences of Alcohol Abuse*, RCPhys, London.

Royal College of Psychiatrists (1979, 2nd ed. 1986). *Alcohol and Alcoholism: The Report of a Special Committee of the College*, Tavistock, London.

Royal Commission on Betting, Lotteries and Gaming (1949–1951). *Final Report*, HMSO, London (cited by Moran, 1987).

Royal Commission on Gambling (1976–1978). *Final Report*, HMSO, London (cited by Moran, 1987).

Rozin, P., Levine, E. and Stoess, C. (1991). Chocolate craving and liking, *Appetite*, **17**, 199–212.

Rubington, E. and Weinberg, M. (1968). *Deviance, the Interactionist Perspective: Text and Readings in the Sociology of Deviance*, Collier-Macmillan, London.

Rush, B. (1943, orig. 1785). An inquiry into the effects of ardent spirits upon the human body and mind with an account of the means of preventing and of the remedies for curing them. (reprinted with an introduction by the editor), *Quarterly Journal of Studies on Alcohol*, **4**, 321–341.

Russell, A. (1932). *For Sinners Only*, Hodder & Stoughton, London.

Russell, G.F.M. (1979). Bulimia nervosa: an ominous variant of anorexia nervosa, *Psychological Medicine*, **9**, 429–448. (cited by Stunkard, 1993).

Russell, M.A.H. (1971). Cigarette smoking: natural history of a dependence disorder, *British Journal of Medical Psychology*, **44**, 1–16.

Russell, M.A.H. (1991). The future of nicotine replacement, *British Journal of Addiction*, **86**, 653–658.

Russell, M.A.H., Peto, J. and Patel, U. (1974). The classification of smoking by factorial structure of motives, *Journal of the Royal Statistical Society*, **137**, 313–346.

Russell, M.A.H., Armstrong, E. and Patel, U. (1976). Temporal contiguity in electric aversion therapy for cigarette smoking, *Behaviour Research and Therapy*, **14**, 103–123.

Russell, M., Henderson, C. and Blume, S. (1985). *Children of Alcoholics: A Review of the Literature*, Children of Alcoholics Foundation, New York.

Sadava, S. (1975). Research approaches to illicit drug use: a critical review, *Genetic Psychology Monographs*, **91**, 3–59.

Sadava, S. (1985). Problem behavior theory and consumption and consequences of alcohol use, *Journal of Studies on Alcohol*, **46**, 392–397.

Sadava, S. and Forsythe, R. (1977). Person–environment interaction and college student drug use: multivariate longitudinal study, *Genetic Psychology Monographs*, **96**, 211–245.

Sadava, S. and Pak, A.W. (1993). Stress-related problem drinking and alcohol problems: a longitudinal study and extension of Marlatt's model, *Canadian Journal of Behavioural Science*, **25**, 446–464.

Sagarin, E. (1969). *Odd Man In: Societies of Deviants in America*, Quadrangle, Chicago.

Salvation Army (1974). *In Darkest England Now: A Salvation Army Survey of Religious and Social Conditions in Britain Eighty Years after William Booth's Blueprint for Salvation*, Hodder & Stoughton, London.

Sanchez-Craig, M., Spivak, K. and Davila, R. (1991). Superior outcome of females over males after brief treatment for the reduction of heavy drinking: replication and report of therapist effects, *British Journal of Addiction*, **86**, 867–876.

Sanchez-Craig, M., Davila, R. and Cooper, G. (1996). A self-help approach for high-risk drinking; effect of an initial assessment, *Journal of Consulting and Clinical Psychology*, **64**, 694–700.

Sanders, D., Peveler, R., Mant, D. and Fowler, G. (1993). Predictors of successful smoking cessation following advice from nurses in general practice, *Addiction*, **88**, 1699–1705.

Sarbin, T. and Nucci, L. (1973). Self-reconstitution processes: a proposal for reorganizing the conduct of confirmed smokers, *Journal of Abnormal Psychology*, **81**, 182–195.

Sargent, M. (1979). *Drinking and Alcoholism in Australia: A Power Relations Theory*, Longman Cheshire, Melbourne.

Sargent, M. (1992). *Women, Drugs and Policy in Sydney, London and Amsterdam*, Avebury, Sydney.

Saunders, W. and Kershaw, P. (1979). Spontaneous remission from alcoholism—a community study, *British Journal of Addiction*, **74**, 251–266.

Saxon, A.J., Wells, E.A. Fleming, C., Jackson, T.R. and Calsyn, D.A. (1996). Pre-treatment characteristics, program philosophy and level of ancillary services as predictors of methadone maintenance treatment outcome, *Addiction*, **91**, 1197–1209.

Sayette, M.A. (1993). An appraisal-disruption model of alcohol's effects on stress responses in social drinkers, *Psychological Bulletin*, **114**, 459–476.

Schachter, S. (1971). *Emotion, Obesity and Crime*, Academic Press, New York.

Schachter, S. (1973). Nesbitt's paradox, in *Smoking Behavior: Motives and Incentives* (ed. W. Dunn), Wiley, New York.

Schachter, S. (1982). Recidivism and self-cure of smoking and obesity, *American Psychologist*, **37**, 436–444.

Schachter, S. and Singer, J. (1962). Cognitive, social and physiological determinants of emotional state, *Psychological Review*, **69**, 379–399.

Schecter, A. (1978). *Treatment Aspects of Drug Dependence*, CRC Press, West Palm Beach, Florida.

Schmidt, W. (1977). Cirrhosis and alcohol consumption: an epidemiological perspective, in *Alcoholism: New Knowledge and New Responses* (eds. G. Edwards and M. Grant), Croom Helm, London.

Schuckit, M.A. (1996). Recent developments in the pharmacotherapy of alcohol dependence, *Journal of Consulting and Clinical Psychology*, **64**, 669–676.

Schuster, C. and Woods, J. (1968). The conditioned reinforcing effects of stimuli associated with morphine reinforcement, *International Journal of the Addictions*, **3**, 223–230 (cited by Kumar and Stolerman, 1977).

Scodel, A. (1964). Inspirational group therapy: a study of Gamblers Anonymous, *American Journal of Psychotherapy*, **18**, 115–125.

Scopinaro, N., Gianetta, E., Adami, G.F., Friedman, D., Traverso, E., Marinari, G.M., Cuneo, S., Vitale, B., Ballari, F., Colummbini, M., Baschieri, G. and Bachi, V. (1996). Bilopancreatic diversion for obesity at eighteen years, *Surgery*, **119**, 261–268.

Shaffer, H.J. (1996). Understanding the means and objects of addiction: technology, the Internet, and gambling, *Journal of Gambling Studies*, **12**, 461–469.

Shaffer, H.J. and Burglass, M. (eds) (1981). *Classic Contributions in the Addictions*, Brunner/Mazel, New York.

Shaffer, H.J., LaBrie, R., Scanlan, K.M. and Cumming, T.N. (1994). Pathological gambling among adolescents: Massachusetts Gambling Screen (MAGS), *Journal of Gambling Studies*, **10**, 339–362.

Shapiro, D.A., Harper, H., Startup, M.J., Reynolds, S., Bird, D. and Suokas, A. (1994). The high watermark of the drug metaphor: a meta-analytic critique of process-outcome research, in *Reassessing Psychotherapy Research* (ed. R.I. Russell), Guilford Press, New York.

Shapiro, H. (1991). Running scared: the use of drugs in sport, *British Journal of Addiction*, **86**, 5–8.

Sharpe, L. and Tarrier, N. (1993). Towards a cognitive-behavioural theory of problem gambling, *British Journal of Psychiatry*, **162**, 407–412.

Shaw, S., Cartwright, A., Spratley, T. and Harwin, J. (1978). *Responding to Drinking Problems*, Croom Helm, London.

Sher, K.J. (1991). *Children of Alcoholics: A Critical Appraisal of Theory and Research*, University of Chicago Press, Chicago.

Shiman, L.L. (1988). *Crusade against Drink in Victorian England*, Macmillan Press, London.

Shisslak, C.M., Crago, M. and Estes, L.S. (1995). The spectrum of eating disturbances, *International Journal of Eating Disorders*, **18**, 209–219.

Sidorov, P. (1995). The social role of alcohol in Russian culture, *Scandinavian Journal of Social Welfare*, **4**, 64–74.

Siegel, S. (1978). Morphine tolerance: is there evidence for a conditioning model? *Science*, **200**, 343–344.

Siegel, S. (1986). Drug anticipation and drug tolerance, Paper presented at: *The Psychopharmacology of Addiction, a Joint Annual Symposium of the Society for the Study of Addiction to Alcohol and Other Drugs and the British Association of Psychopharmacology, London, November*.

Singer, K. (1974). The choice of intoxicant among the Chinese, *British Journal of Addiction*, **69**, 257–268.

Sisson, R.W. and Azrin. N.H. (1993). Community reinforcement training for families: a method to get alcoholics into treatment, in *Marital and Family Therapy in Alcoholism Treatment* (ed. T.J. O'Farrell), Guilford, New York, 34–53.

Skinner, H.A. (1990). Validation of the dependence syndrome: have we crossed the half-life of this concept? in *The Nature of Drug Dependence* (eds G. Edwards and M. Lader), Oxford University Press, Oxford, 41–62.

Skog, O. (1977). On the distribution of alcohol consumption, in *The Ledermann Curve, Report of a Symposium, Alcohol Education Centre, London, January*.

Skog, O. (1994). Rationality, irrationality, and addiction, Unpublished paper prepared for *Addiction Seminar, Collioure, France, September*.

Slade, P.D. (1982). Towards a functional analysis of anorexia nervosa and bulimia nervosa, *British Journal of Clinical Psychology*, **21**, 167–179 (cited by Leung *et al.*, 1996).

Slay, H.A., Hayaki, J., Napolitani, M.A. and Brownell, K.D. (1998). Motivations for running and eating attitudes in obligatory versus nonobligatory runners, *International Journal of Eating Disorders*, **23**, 267–275.

Snow, M.G., Prochaska, J.O. and Rossi, J.S. (1994). Processes of change in Alcoholics Anonymous: maintenance factors in long-term sobriety, *Journal of Studies on Alcohol*, **55**, 362–371.

Sobell, L.C., Sobell, M.B. and Toneatto, T. (1991). Recovery from alcohol problems without treatment, in *Self-control and Addictive Behaviors* (eds N. Heather, W.R. Miller and J. Greeley), Maxwell MacMillan, Botany, New South Wales, Australia, 198–242.

Sobell, L.C., Sobell, M.B., Toneatto, T. and Leo, G.I. (1993). What triggers the resolution of alcohol problems without treatment? *Alcoholism, Clinical and Experimental Research*, **17**, 217–224.

Sobell, L.C., Cunningham, J.A. and Sobell, M.B. (1996). Recovery from alcohol problems with and without treatment: prevalence in two population surveys, *American Journal of Public Heath*, **86**, 966–972.

Society for the Study of Addiction (1999). *Tackling Alcohol Together* (eds D. Raistrick, R. Hodgson and B. Ritson), Free Association Press, London.

Solomon, R. (1980). The opponent–process theory of acquired motivation: the costs of pleasure and the benefits of pain, *American Psychologist*, **35**, 691–712.

Solomon, R. and Corbit, J. (1973). An opponent–process theory of motivation II: cigarette addiction, *Journal of Abnormal Psychology*, **81**, 158–171.

Solomon, R. and Corbit, J. (1974). An opponent–process theory of motivation I: temporal dynamics of affect, *Psychological Review*, **81**, 119–145.

Solowij, N., Hall, W. and Lee, N. (1992). Recreational MDMA use in Sydney. A profile of 'ecstasy' users and their experiences with the drug, *British Journal of Addiction*, **87**, 1161–1172.

Spectrum Children's Trust (1988). *Slot Machine Playing by Children: Results of a Survey in Minehead and Taunton*, SCT, London (cited by Griffiths, 1991).

Spitzer, R.L., Devlin, M., Walsh, B.T., Hasin, D., Wing, R.R., Marcus, M., Stunkard, A.J., Wadden, T.A., Yanovski, S.Z., Agras, W.S., Mitchell, J. and Nonas, C. (1992). Binge eating disorder: a multisite field trial of the diagnostic criteria, *International Journal of Eating Disorders*, **11**, 191–203 (cited by Fairburn and Wilson, 1993).

Spooner, C.J., Flaherty, B.J. and Homel, P.J. (1993). Illicit drug use by young people in Sydney: results of a street intersect survey, *Drug and Alcohol Review*, **12**, 159–168.

Sproston, K., Ehrens, R. and Orford, J. (2000). *Gambling Behaviour in Britain: Results from the British Gambling Prevalence Survey*, National Centre for Social Research, London.

Spurrell, E.B. Wilfley, D.E. Tanofsky, M.B. and Brownell, K.D. (1997). Age of onset for binge eating: Are there different pathways to binge eating? *International Journal of Eating Disorders*, **21**, 55–65.

Squires, P. (1937). Fyodor Dostoevsky: A psychopathographical sketch, *Psychoanalytical Review*, **24**, 365–388.

Staats, G. (1978). An empirical assessment of controls affecting marijuana usage, *British Journal of Addiction*, **73**, 391–398.

Stack, S. and Bankowski, E. (1994). Divorce and drinking: an analysis of Russian data, *Journal of Marriage and the Family*, **56**, 805–812.

Stacy, A.W., Widaman, K.E. and Marlatt, G.A. (1990). Expectancy models of alcohol use, *Journal of Personality and Social Psychology*, **58**, 918–928.

Stanton, W.R., McClelland, M., Elwood, C., Ferry, D. and Silva, P.A. (1996). Prevalence, reliability and bias of adolescents' reports of smoking and quitting, *Addiction*, **91**, 1705–1714.

Stebbins, K.R. (1994). Making a killing south of the border: transnational cigarette companies in Mexico and Guatemala, *Social Science and Medicine*, **38**, 105–115.

Steele, C.M. and Josephs, R.A. (1990). Alcohol myopia: its prized and dangerous effects, *American Psychologist*, **45**, 921–933.

Steffen, V. (1997). Life stories and shared experience, *Social Science and Medicine*, **45**, 99–111.

Stekel, W. (1924). *Peculiarities of Behaviour: Wandering Mania, Dipsomania, Cleptomania, Pyromania and Allied Impulsive Acts* (English publication 1938 trans. J. van Teslaar), Bodley Head, London.

Stephens, R.S. and Roffman, R. (1993). Adult marijuana dependence, in *Addictive Behaviors Across the Lifespan: Prevention, Treatment, and Policy Issues* (eds J.S. Baer, G.A. Marlatt and R.J. McMahon), Sage, Newbury Park, California.

Stephens, R.S., Roffman, R. and Simpson, E.E. (1993). Adult marijuana users seeking treatment, *Journal of Consulting and Clinical Psychology*, **61**, 1100–1104.

Stepney, R. (1996). The concept of addiction: its use and abuse in the media and science, *Human Psychopharmacology*, **11**, S15–S20.

Stewart, J. (1992). Conditioned stimulus control of the expression of sensitization of the behavioral activating effects of opiate and stimulant drugs, in *Learning and Memory: The Behavioral and Biological Substrates* (eds E.A. Gormezano and E.A. Wasserman), Lawrence Erlbaum, New Jersey.

Stewart, J. (1996). Knowledge, affect, habit: an effective parsing of addiction?—Comments on White (1996) *Addiction*, **91**, 955–957.

Stice, E., Killen, J.D., Hayward, C. and Barr Taylor, C. (1998). Age of onset for binge eating and purging during late adolescence: a 4-year survival analysis, *Journal of Abnormal Psychology*, **107**, 671–675.

Stockton, O. (1682). *A Warning to Drunkards Delivered in Several Sermons to a Congregation in Colchester upon the Occasion of a Sad Providence towards a Young Man, Dying in the Act of Drunkenness*, J.R., London (cited by Warner, 1994).

Stockwell, T., Murphy, D. and Hodgson, R. (1983). The severity of alcohol dependence questionnaire: its use, reliability and validity, *British Journal of Addiction*, **78**, 145–155.

Stockwell, T., Lang, E. and Rydon, P. (1993). High risk drinking settings: the association of serving and promotional practices with harmful drinking, *Addiction*, **88**, 1519–1526.

Stolerman, I.P. (1991). Behavioural pharmacology of nicotine: multiple mechanisms, *British Journal of Addiction*, **86**, 533–536.

Strang, J., Griffiths, P. and Gossop, M. (1997). Heroin smoking by 'chasing the dragon': origins and history, *Addiction*, **92**, 673–683.

Strauss, R. (1946). Alcohol and the homeless man, *Quarterly Journal of Studies on Alcohol*, **7**, 360–404 (cited by Johnson *et al.*, 1997).

Stone L. (1979). *The Family, Sex and Marriage in England 1500–1800*, Penguin, Harmondsworth, Middlesex (orig. unabridged ed., Weidenfeld and Nicolson, 1977).

Stuart, R. (1967). Behavioural control of overeating, *Behaviour Research and Therapy*, **5**, 357–365.

Stunkard, A.J. (1959). Eating patterns of obesity, *Psychiatric Quarterly*, **33**, 284–295.

Stunkard, A.J. (1993). A history of binge eating, in *Binge Eating: Nature, Assessment and Treatment* (eds C.G. Fairburn and G.T. Wilson), Guilford, New York, 15–34.

Sulkunen, P. (1997). Ethics of alcohol policy in a saturated society, *Addiction*, **92**, 1117–1122.

Sullivan, P.F., Bulik, C.M. and Kendler, K.S. (1998). The epidemiology and classification of bulimia nervosa, *Psychological Medicine*, **28**, 599–610.

Sutherland, G., Edwards, G., Taylor, C., Phillips, G., Gossop, M. and Brady, R. (1986). The measurement of opiate dependence, *British Journal of Addiction*, **81**, 485–494.

Sutherland, I. and Willner, P. (1998). Patterns of alcohol, cigarette and illicit drug use in English adolescents, *Addiction*, **93**, 1119–1208.

Sutton, S. (1979). Interpreting relapse curves, *Journal of Consulting and Clinical Psychology*, **47**, 96–98.

Sutton, S. (1989). Smoking attitudes and behavior; applications of Fishbein and Ajzen's theory of reasoned action to predicting and understanding smoking decisions, in *Smoking and Human Behavior* (eds. T. Ney and A. Gale), Wiley, Chichester.

Sutton, S. (1992). Is taking up smoking a reasoned action?—Comments on Goddard (1990), *Addiction*, **87**, 21–23.

Sutton, S. (1996). Can 'Stages of Change' Provide Guidance in the Treatment of Addictions? A Critical Examination of Prochaska and DiClemente's Model, in *Psychotherapy, Psychological Treatments and the Addictions* (eds G. Edwards and C. Dare), Cambridge University Press, Cambridge, 189–207.

Swift, W., Copeland, J. and Hall, W. (1996). Characteristics of women with alcohol and other drug problems: findings of an Australian National Survey, *Addiction*, **91**, 1141–1150.

Swinson, R. and Eaves, D. (1978). *Alcoholism and Addiction*, MacDonald & Evans, Plymouth.

Sylvain, C., Ladouceur, R. and Boisvert, J.M. (1997). Cognitive and behavioral treatment of pathological gambling: a controlled study, *Journal of Consulting and Clinical Psychology*, **65**, 727–732.

Sysenko, V.A. (1982). Divorce: dynamics, motives and consequences, *Sotsiologicheskie Issledovaniya*, **9**, 99–104 (translated into English for the present author).

Tanofsky, M.B., Wilfley, D.E., Spurrell, E.B., Welch, R. and Brownell, K.D. (1997). Comparison of men and women in binge eating disorder, *International Journal of Eating Disorders*, **21**, 49–54.

Tate, J.C., Pomerleau, C.S. and Pomerleau, O.F. (1994). Pharmacological and non-pharmacological smoking motives: a replication and extension, *Addiction*, **89**, 321–330.

Taylor, A. (1993). *Women Drug Users: An Ethnography of a Female Injecting Community*, Clarendon Press, Oxford.

Teasdale, J. (1973). Conditioned abstinence in narcotic addicts, *International Journal of the Addictions*, **8**, 273–292.

Telch, C., Pratt, E.M. and Niego, S.H. (1998). Obese women with binge eating disorder define the term binge, *Binge Eating Criteria*, 313–317.

Terenius, L.T. and O'Brien, C.P. (1992). Receptors and endogenous ligands: implications for addiction, in *Addictive States* (eds C.P. O'Brien and J. Jaffe), Raven Press, New York, 123–130.

Terry, P. (1995). Talk given at All Saints Hospital, Birmingham, 11 September.

Thackwray, D.E., Smith, M.C., Bodfish, J.W. and Meyers, A.W. (1993). A comparison of behavioral and cognitive-behavioral interventions for bulimia nervosa, *Journal of Consulting and Clinical Psychology*, **61**, 639–645.

Thomas, C. and Tremlett, G. (1986). *Caitlin: Life with Dylan Thomas*, Holt, New York.

Thomas, E.J. and Ager, R.D. (1993). Unilateral family therapy with the spouses of uncooperative alcohol abusers, in *Marital and Family Therapy in Alcoholism Treatment* (ed. T.J. O'Farrell), Guilford Press, New York, 3–33.

Thompson, H. (1997). *Peter Cook: a Biography*, Hodder and Stoughton, London.

Thorley, A., Oppenheimer, E. and Stimson, G. (1977). Clinic attendance and opiate prescription status of heroin addicts over a six-year period, *British Journal of Psychiatry*, **130**, 565–569.

Thornley. S.J. and Windsor, J.A. (1998). The role of surgery in the management of obesity, *New Zealand Medical Journal*, **111**, 445–448.

Tiebout, H. (1944). Therapeutic mechanisms of Alcoholics Anonymous, *American Journal of Psychiatry*, **100**, 468–473.

Tiffany, S.T. (1990). A cognitive model of drug urges and drug-use behavior: role of automatic and nonautomatic processes, *Psychological Review*, **97**, 147–168.

Tiffany, S.T. and Drobes, D.J. (1991). The development and initial validation of a questionnaire on smoking urges, *British Journal of Addiction*, **86**, 1467–1476.

Tiggemann, M. (1994). Gender differences in the interrelationships between weight dissatisfaction, restraint, and self-esteem, *Sex Roles*, **30**, 319–330.

Toates, F. (1994). Comparing motivational systems—an incentive motivation perspective, in *Appetite, Neural and Behavioural Bases* (eds C.R. Legg and D. Booth), Oxford University Press, Oxford, 305–327.

Tomkins, S. (1968). A modified model of smoking behavior, in *Smoking, Health and Behavior* (eds E. Borgatta and R. Evans), Aldine, Chicago.

Tonigan, J.S., Toscova, R. and Miller, W.R. (1996). Meta-analysis of the literature on Alcoholics Anonymous: sample and study characteristics moderate findings, *Journal of Studies on Alcohol*, **57**, 65–72.

Townsend, J. (1993). Policies to halve smoking deaths, *Addiction*, **88**, 43–52.

Townsend, P. and Davidson, N. (1992). *Inequalities in Health: the Black Report*, Penguin, Harmondsworth.

Trachtenberg, P. (1988). *The Casanova Complex: Compulsive Lovers and Their Women*, Angus & Robertson, North Ryde, Australia.

Trevelyan, G. (1967, orig. 1942). *English Social History: A Survey of Six Centuries, Chaucer to Queen Victoria*, Penguin, Harmondsworth, Middlesex.

Trotter, R.T., Bowen, A.M. and Potter, J.M. (1995). Network models of HIV outreach and prevention programs for drug users, in *Social Networks, Drug Abuse, and HIV Transmission* (eds R.H. Needle, S.G. Genser and R.T. Trotter), National Institute on Drug Abuse, Rockville, Maryland, 144–180.

Tuchfeld, B. (1981). Spontaneous remission in alcoholics: empirical observations and theoretical implications, *Journal of Studies on Alcohol*, **42**, 626–641.

Tucker, J.A., Vuchinich, R.E. and Sobell, M. (1979). Differential discriminative stimulus control of non-alcoholic beverage consumption in alcoholics and in normal drinkers, *Journal of Abnormal Psychology*, **88**, 145–152.

Tucker, J.A., Vuchinich, R.E. and Gladsjo, J.A. (1994). Environmental events surrounding natural recovery from alcohol-related problems, *Journal of Studies of Alcohol*, **55**, 401–411.

Vaillant, G. (1980). The doctor's dilemma, in *Alcoholism Treatment in Transition* (eds. G. Edwards and M. Grant), Croom Helm, London.

Vaillant, G. (1983). *The Natural History of Alcoholism*, Harvard University Press, Cambridge, Massachusetts.

Van Lancker, J. (1977). Smoking and disease, in *Research on Smoking Behavior* (eds. M. Jarvik, J. Cullen, E. Gritz, T. Vogt and L. West), National Institute on Drug Abuse Research Monograph 17, US Department of Health, Education and Welfare, NIDA, Rockville, Maryland.

Vassilas, C.A. and Morgan, H.G. (1997). Suicide in Avon: life stress, alcohol misuse and use of services, *British Journal of Psychiatry*, **170**, 453–455.

Veale, D.M.W. (1987). Exercise dependence, *British Journal of Addiction*, **82**, 735–740.

Velleman. R. and Orford, J. (1999). *Risk and Resilience: Adults who Were the Children of Problem Drinkers*, Harwood, Reading.

Volberg, R.A. (1996). Prevalence studies of problem gambling in the United States, *Journal of Gambling Studies*, **12**, 111–127.

Volberg, R.A. and Steadman, H.J. (1988). Refining prevalence estimates of pathological gambling, *American Journal of Psychiatry*, **145**, 502–505.

Volume, C.I. and Farris, K.B. (1998). Control with anorexiant medications, *Canadian Family Physician*, **44**, 2423–2428.

Vuchinich, R.E., Tucker, J., and Sobell, M. (1979). Alcohol, expectancy, cognitive labelling and mirth, *Journal of Abnormal Psychology*, **88**, 641–651.

Wada, K. and Fukui, S. (1993). Prevalence of volatile solvent inhalation among junior high school students in Japan and background lifestyle of users, *Addiction*, **88**, 89–100.

Wagenaar, W.A. (1988). *Paradoxes of Gambling Behaviour*, Lawrence Erlbaum Associates, London.

Waldorf, D., Reinarman, C. and Murphy, S. (1991). *Cocaine Changes: The Experience of Using and Quitting*, Temple University Press, Philadephia.

Walker, M.B. (1989). Some problems with the concept of 'gambling addiction': Should theories of addiction be generalised to include excessive gambling? *Journal of Gambling Behavior*, **5**, 179–200.

Wallack, L. (1992). Warning: the alcohol industry is not your friend? *British Journal of Addiction*, **87**, 1109–1111.

Waller, S., Thom, B., Harris, S. and Kelly, M. (1998). Perceptions of alcohol-related attendances in accident and emergency departments in England: a national survey, *Alcohol and Alcoholism*, **33**, 354–361.

Walsh, B.T. (1993). Binge eating in bulimia nervosa, in *Binge Eating: Nature, Assessment and Treatment* (eds C.G. Fairburn and G.T. Wilson) Guilford, New York, 37–49.

Walsh, B.T., Hadigan, C.M., Kissileff, H.R. and LaChausee, J.L. (1992). Bulimia nervosa: a syndrome of feast and famine, in *The Biology of Feast and Famine* (eds G.H. Anderson and S.H. Kennedy) Academic Press, New York (cited by Walsh, 1993).

Wanberg, K.W. and Horn, J.L. (1983). Assessment of alcohol use with multidimensional concept and measures, *American Psychologist*, **38**, 1055–1069 (cited by Skinner, 1990).

Warburton, D. (1986). The puzzle of nicotine use, Paper presented at *The Psychopharmacology of Addiction, a Joint Annual Symposium of the Society for the Study of the Addiction to Alcohol and other Drugs and the British Association of Pyschopharmacology, London, November*.

Warburton, D. (1988). The puzzle of nicotine use, in *The Psychopharmacology of Addiction* (ed. M. Lader), Oxford University Press, Oxford.

Wardle, J. (1980). Dietary restraint and binge eating, *Behaviour Analysis and Modification*, **4**, 201–209.

Wardle, J. and Beinart, H. (1981). Binge eating: a theoretical review, *British Journal of Clinical Psychology*, **20**, 97–109.

Wardle, J. and Marsland, L. (1990). Adolescent concerns about weight and eating: a social-developmental perspective, *Journal of Psychosomatic Research*, **34**, 377–391.

Warner, J. (1994). 'Resolv'd to drink no more': addiction as a preindustrial construct, *Journal of Studies on Alcohol*, **55**, 685–691.

Weinsten, D. and Deitch, L. (1974). *The Impact of Legalised Gambling: the Socioeconomic Consequences of Lotteries and Off-Track Betting*, Praeger, New York (cited by Cornish, 1978).

Weisner, C. and Schmidt, L. (1995). The Community Epidemiology Laboratory: studying alcohol problems in community and agency-based populations, *Addiction*, **90**, 329–341.

Welch, S.L., Doll, H.A. and Fairburn, C.G. (1997). Life events and the onset of bulimia nervosa: a controlled study, *Psychological Medicine*, **27**, 515–522.

Wellings, K., Field, J., Johnson, A.M. and Wadsworth, J. (1994). *Sexual Behaviour in Britain: The National Survey of Sexual Attitudes and Lifestyles*, Penguin, Harmondsworth.

Wells, J.E., Bushnell, J.A., Joyce, P.R., Oakley-Browne, M.A. and Hornblow, A.R. (1992). Problems with alcohol, drugs and gambling in Christchurch, New Zealand, in *Alcohol and Drug Dependence and Disorders of Impulse Control* (eds M. Abbot and K. Evans), Alcohol Liquor Advisory Council, Auckland.

West, R. (1991). The focus and conduct of clinical trials, *British Journal of Addiction*, **86**, 663–666.

West, R. (1993). Beneficial effects of nicotine: fact or fiction? *Addiction*, **88**, 589–590.

West, M. and Prinz, R. (1987). Parental alcoholism and childhood psychopathology, *Psychological Bulletin*, **102**, 204–218.

West, P., Sweeting, H. and Ecob, R. (1999). Family and friends' influences on the uptake of regular smoking from mid-adolescent to early adulthood, *Addiction*, **94**, 1397–1412.

Wesson, D. and Smith, D. (1977). *Barbiturates: Their Use, Misuse, and Abuse*, Human Sciences Press, New York.

White, N.M. (1996). Addictive drugs as reinforcers: multiple partial actions on memory systems, *Addiction*, **91**, 921–949.

WHO (World Health Organisation) (1964). *Thirteenth Report*, WHO Expert Committee on Addiction-producing Drugs Technical Report Series No. 273, WHO, Geneva.

Widiger, T.A. and Smith, G.T. (1994). Substance use disorder: abuse, dependence and discontrol, *Addiction*, **89**, 267–282.

Wiers, R.W., Hoogeveen, K.J., Sergeant, J.A. and Gunning, W.B. (1997). High- and low-dose alcohol-related expectancies and the differential associations with drinking in male and female adolescents and young adults, *Addiction*, **92**, 871–888.

Wiesbeck, G.A., Schuckit, M.A., Kalmijn, J.A., Tipp, J.E., Bucholz, K.K. and Smith, T.L. (1996). An evaluation of the history of a marijuana withdrawal syndrome in a large population, *Addiction*, **91**, 1469–1478.

Wijesinghe, B. (1977). Massed electrical aversion treatment of compulsive eating, in *Behavioral Treatments of Obesity* (ed. J Foreyt), Pergamon, Oxford.

Wikler, A. (1973). Dynamics of drug dependence: implications of conditioning theory for research and treatment, *Archives of General Psychiatry*, **28**, 611.

Wild, T.C., Newton-Taylor, B. and Alletto, R. (1998). Perceived coercion among clients entering substance abuse treatment: structural and psychological determinants, *Addictive Behaviors*, **23**, 81–95.

Wilkins, L. (1964). *Social Deviance: Social Policy, Action and Research*, Tavistock, London.

Wilkins, R. (1974). *The Hidden Alcoholic in General Practice*, Elek, London.

Willems, P., Letemendia, F., and Arroyave, F. (1973). A two-year follow-up study comparing short- with long-stay in-patient treatment of alcoholics, *British Journal of Psychiatry*, **122**, 637–648.

Williams, A. (1966). Social drinking, anxiety, and depression, *Journal of Personality and Social Psychology*, **3**, 689–693.

Wills, T.A., McNamara, G., Vaccaro, D. and Hirky, A.E. (1996). Escalated substance use: a longitudinal grouping analysis from early to middle adolescence, *Journal of Abnormal Psychology*, **105**, 166–180.

Wilps, R.F. (1990). Male bulimia nervosa: an autobiographical case study, in *Males with Eating Disorders* (ed. A.E. Andersen), Brunner/Mazel, New York.

Wilsnack, S.C., Vogeltanz, N.D., Klassen, A. and Harris, T.R. (1997). Childhood sexual abuse and women's substance abuse: national survey findings, *Journal of Studies on Alcohol*, **58**, 264–271.

Wilson. G.T. (1993). Binge eating and addictive disorders, in *Binge Eating: Nature, Assessment and Treatment* (eds. C.G. Fairburn and G.T. Wilson), Guilford, New York, 97–119.

Wilson, W.G. (1967). *As Bill Sees It: The AA Way of Life*, AA World Services, New York (cited by Miller and Kurtz, 1994).

Winick, C. (1962). Maturing out of narcotic addiction, *Bulletin of Narcotics*, **14**, 1.

Wise, J. and Wise, S. (1979). *The Overeaters: Eating Styles and Personality*, Human Sciences Press, New York.

Wise, R.A. (1994). A brief history of the anhedonia hypothesis, in: *Appetite, Neural and Behavioural Bases* (eds. C.R. Legg and D. Booth), Oxford University Press, Oxford, 243–263.

Wise, R.A. and Munn, E. (1995). Withdrawal from chronic amphetamine elevates baseline intracranial self-stimulation thresholds, *Psychopharmacology*, **117**, 130–136.

Wiseman, J. (1970). *Stations of the Lost: The Treatment of Skid Row Alcoholics*, Prentice-Hall, Englewood Cliffs, New Jersey.

Wodak, A. (1990). The never-ending story, *Drug and Alcohol Review*, **9**, 346–350.

Wodak, A. (1994). Olympian ideas of pragmatism? *Addiction*, **89**, 803–805.

Wolcott, H. (1974). *The African Beer Gardens of Bulawayo: Integrated Drinking in a Segregated Society*, Rutgers Centre of Alcohol Studies, New Brunswick, New Jersey.

Wormington, J.A., Cockerill, I.M. and Neville, A.M. (1992). Mood alterations with running: the effects of mileage, gender, age and ability, *Journal of Human Movement Studies*, **22**, 1–12.

Wray, I. and Dickerson, M. (1981). Cessation of high frequency gambling and 'withdrawal symptoms', *British Journal of Addiction*, **76**, 401–405.

Wu, Z., Zhang, J., Detels, R., Duan, S., Cheng, H., Li, Z., Dong, L., Huang, S., Jia, M. and Bi, X. (1996). Risk factors for initiations of drug use among young males in southwest China, *Addiction*, **91**, 1675–1685.

Yankofsky, L., Wilson, G.T., Adler, J.L., Hay, W.M. and Vrana, S. (1986). The effect of alcohol on self-evaluation and perception of negative interpersonal feedback, *Journal of Studies on Alcohol*, **47**, 26–33.

Yates, A. (1991). *Compulsive Exercise and Eating Disorders: Toward an Integrated Theory of Activity*, Brunner/Mazel, New York.

Yates, F. (1988). The evaluation of a 'co-operative counselling' alcohol service which uses family and affected others to reach and influence problem drinkers, *British Journal of Addiction*, **83**, 1309–1319.

Young, J. (1971). *The Drugtakers: The Social Meaning of Drug Use*, Paladin, London.

Young, K.S. (1998). *Caught in the Net: How to Recognise the Signs of Internet Addiction and a Winning Strategy for Recovery*, Wiley, New York.

Zinberg, N. (1978). *Drug, Set, and Setting: The Basis for Controlled Intoxicant Use*, Yale University Press, New Haven.

Zinberg, N., Harding, W., and Winkeller, M. (1977). A study of social regulatory mechanisms in controlled illicit drug users, *Journal of Drug Issues*, **7**, 117–133 (reprinted in *Classic Contributions in the Addictions*, eds. M. Shaffer and M. Burglass, Brunner/Mazel, New York, 1981).

Author Index

Subject Index